Morality in Practice

Second Edition

Morality in Practice

Second Edition

Edited by
James P. Sterba
University of Notre Dame

Wadsworth Publishing Company
Belmont, California
A division of Wadsworth, Inc.

Philosophy Editor: Kenneth King
Production: Greg Hubit Bookworks
Designer: Vargas/Williams/Design
Compositor: Kachina Typesetting, Tempe, Arizona
Cover: Lois Stanfield

Printed in the United States of America
1 2 3 4 5 6 7 8 9 10—90 89 88 87 86

ISBN 0-534-08616-0

Library of Congress Cataloging-in-Publication Data

Sterba, James P.
  Morality in practice.

  1. Social ethics.   I. Title.
HM216.M667   1988   170   87-23109
ISBN 0-534-08616-0

To Sonya,
who no longer takes long naps but has contributed
in other ways to make this second edition possible

Contents

Preface

This anthology was born of exasperation. First there were the generous omissions in the available moral problems anthologies—omissions of sufficiently opposing articles on the moral problems covered. Then there were the copy centers that provided the missing articles for student consumption—tardily delivered in one uncollated heap. Then there were the students (only a handful, to be sure) who never seemed to have the $5.82 copying fee the entire month I collected for it in class. The only way out, alas, was to provide a new moral problems anthology that minimized these and other sources of frustration. The first edition of this anthology was the result.

There followed a period of peace and satisfaction—happy students, happy colleagues, happy publisher. . . . But this was not to last. My students here at Notre Dame and at the University of Rochester showed increasing interest in new and different moral problems. Helpful suggestions arrived from colleagues across the country who were using the first edition. The U.S. Supreme Court made a number of decisions that were relevant to practical applications in various sections of the anthology. And so the second edition emerged. It has, to recommend it, the following:

New Features

1. There are new sections on sex equality (containing a full range of feminist and anti-feminist positions), terrorism, strategic defense, and animal rights.
2. A general introduction provides a background discussion of ethical theory as well as a justification for morality.
3. Twelve new articles are incorporated into the other sections of the anthology.

Retained Features

1. The anthology contains radically opposing articles defending alternative solutions to nine mainline moral problems. Every article included has been published before, edited, and tested for class use.
2. Introductions are provided which help to set out the framework for the discussion and criticism of the articles in each section.
3. Brief summaries are provided at the beginning of each article to enable students to test and improve their comprehension.
4. Each section of the anthology concludes with one or more articles discussing specific practical applications.
5. Suggestions for further reading are found at the end of each section.

In putting together this second edition I have again benefitted enormously from the advice and help of many different people. In particular, I would like to thank Ken King of Wadsworth Publishing Co., Greg Hubit of Bookworks, my wife and fellow philosopher Janet Kourany, Robert Phillips of the University of Connecticut, my Notre Dame colleagues Clark Powers and Joseph Mellon, R. G. Frey of Bowling Green University, and Louis Pojman of the University of Mississippi. I would also like to thank the following reviewers: Laurence BonJour, University of Washington; David A. Crocker, Colorado State University; and John Lachs, Vanderbilt University. Work on this anthology was made possible by financial assistance from the University of Notre Dame and the University of Rochester.

Morality in Practice

Second Edition

General Introduction

Most of us like to think of ourselves as just and moral people. To be truly such, however, we need to know something about the demands of justice and how they apply in our own particular circumstances. We should be able to assess, for example, whether our society's economic and legal systems are just—that is, whether the ways income and wealth are distributed in society as well as the methods of enforcing that distribution give people what they deserve. We should also consider whether other societal institutions, such as the military defense system, the educational system, and the foreign aid program, are truly just. Without investigating these systems and coming to an informed opinion, we cannot say with any certainty that we are just and moral persons rather than perpetrators or beneficiaries of injustice.

This anthology has been created to help you acquire some of the knowledge you will need to justify your belief that you are a just and moral person. For this purpose, the anthology contains a wide spectrum of readings on nine important contemporary practical problems:

1. The problem of the distribution of income and wealth—who should control what resources within a society?

2. The problem of distant peoples and future generations—what obligations do we have to distant peoples and future generations?

3. The problem of abortion and euthanasia—do fetuses have a right to life, and what should we do for the dying?

4. The problem of sex equality—should the sexes be treated equally, and what constitutes equal treatment?

5. The problem of compensation for past wrongs—what specifically is owed to people for past wrongs?

6. The problem of animal rights—what should our policy be for the treatment of animals?

7. The problem of punishment and responsibility—who should be punished, and in what should their punishment consist?

8. The problem of terrorism—how should we respond to the political use of violence against innocent people?

9. The problem of nuclear deterrence and strategic defense—are there any limits to military defense?

Before you get into these problems, however, you should know what it means to take a moral approach to these issues and how such an approach is justified.

1

The Essential Features of a Moral Approach to Practical Problems

To begin with, a moral approach to practical problems must be distinguished from various nonmoral approaches. Nonmoral approaches to practical problems include the *legal approach* (what the law requires with respect to this practical problem), the *group- or self-interest approach* (what the group- or self-interest is of the parties affected by this problem), and the *scientific approach* (how this practical problem can best be accounted for or understood). To call these approaches nonmoral, of course, does not imply that they are immoral. All that is implied is that the requirements of these approaches may or may not accord with the requirements of morality.

What, then, essentially characterizes a moral approach to practical problems? I suggest that there are two essential features to such an approach:

1. The approach is prescriptive, that is, it issues in prescriptions, such as "do this" and "don't do that."
2. The approach's prescriptions are acceptable to everyone affected by them.

The first feature distinguishes a moral approach from a scientific approach because a scientific approach is not prescriptive. The second feature distinguishes a moral approach from both a legal approach and a group- or self-interest approach because the prescriptions that accord best with the law or serve the interest of particular groups or individuals may not be acceptable to everyone affected by them.

Here the notion of "acceptable" means "ought to be accepted" or "is reasonable to accept" and not simply "is capable of being accepted." Understood in this way, certain prescriptions may be acceptable even though they are not actually accepted by everyone affected by them. For example, a particular welfare program may be acceptable even though many people oppose it because it involves an increased tax burden. Likewise, cer-

tain prescriptions may be unacceptable even though they have been accepted by everyone affected by them. For example, it may be that most women have been socialized to accept prescriptions requiring them to fill certain social roles even though these prescriptions are unacceptable because they impose second-class status on them.

Alternative Moral Approaches to Practical Problems

Using the two essential features of a moral approach to practical problems, let us consider three principal alternative moral approaches to practical problems: the *Utilitarian Approach,* the *Human Nature Approach,* and the *Social Contract Approach.*[1] The basic principle of the Utilitarian Approach is:

> Do those actions that maximize the net utility or satisfaction of everyone affected by them.

The Utilitarian Approach qualifies as a moral approach because it is prescriptive and because it can be argued that its prescriptions are acceptable to everyone affected by them since they take the utility or satisfaction of all those individuals equally into account.

To illustrate, let's consider how this approach applies to the question of whether nation A should adopt a particular defense policy with respect to nation B when nation A's choice would have the following consequences:

	Nation A's Choice	
	Adopt the policy	*Don't adopt the policy*
Net utility to A	8½ trillion units	4 trillion units
Net utility to B	−2 trillion units	2 trillion units
Total utility	6½ trillion units	6 trillion units

Given that these are all the consequences that are relevant to nation A's choice, the Utilitarian Approach favors adopting the particular defense policy. Note that in this case, the choice favoring the Utilitarian Approach does not conflict with the group-interest of nation A, although it does conflict with the group-interest of nation B.

But are such calculations of utility possible? Admittedly, they are difficult to make. At the same time, such calculations seem to serve as a basis for public discussion. Recently, President Reagan, while addressing a group of black business leaders, asked whether blacks were better off now because of the Great Society programs, and although many disagreed with the answer he gave, no one found his question unanswerable.[2] Thus, faced with the exigencies of measuring utility, the Utilitarian Approach simply counsels that we do our best to determine what maximizes net utility and act on the result.

The second approach to be considered is the Human Nature Approach. Its basic principle is:

Do those actions that would further one's proper development as a human being.

This approach also qualifies as a moral approach because it is prescriptive and because it can be argued that its prescriptions are acceptable to everyone affected by them.

There are, however, different versions of this approach. According to some versions, each person can determine through the use of reason his or her proper development as a human being. Other versions disagree. For example, from a Marxist perspective, many people in capitalist societies are deluded by false consciousness and will be unable to appreciate what fosters their proper development as human beings until their society is transformed economically. Similarly, many religious traditions rely on revelation to guide people in their proper development as human beings. However, although the Human Nature Approach can take these various forms, I want to focus on what is probably its philosophically most interesting form. That form specifies proper development in terms of virtuous activity and understands virtuous activity to preclude intentionally doing evil that good may come of it. In this form, the Human Nature Approach conflicts most radically with the Utilitarian Approach, which requires intentionally doing evil whenever a *greater* good would come of it.

The third approach to be considered is the Social Contract Approach. This approach has its origins in seventeenth and eighteenth century social contract theories, which tended to rely on actual contracts to specify moral requirements. However, actual contracts may or may not have been made, and, even if they were made, they may or may not have been moral or fair. This has led some philosophers to resort to hypothetical contracts to ground moral requirements. A difficulty with this approach is in determining under what conditions a hypothetical contract is fair and moral. Currently, the most favored Social Contract Approach is specified by the following basic principle:

Do those actions that persons behind an imaginary veil of ignorance would unanimously agree should be done.[3]

This imaginary veil extends to most particular facts about oneself—anything that would bias one's choice or stand in the way of a unanimous agreement. Accordingly, the imaginary veil of ignorance would mask one's knowledge of one's social position, talents, sex, race, and religion, but not one's knowledge of such general information as would be contained in political, social, economic, and psychological theories. The Social Contract Approach qualifies as a moral approach because it is prescriptive and because it can be argued that its prescriptions would be acceptable to everyone affected by them since they would be agreed to by everyone affected behind an imaginary veil of ignorance.

To illustrate the approach, let's return to the example of nation A and nation B used earlier. The choice facing nation A was the following:

Nation A's Choice

	Adopt the policy	Don't adopt the policy
Net utility to A	8½ trillion units	4 trillion units
Net utility to B	−2 trillion units	2 trillion units
Total utility	6½ trillion units	6 trillion units

Given that these are all the consequences relevant to nation A's choice, the Social Contract Approach favors rejecting the particular defense policy because persons behind the imaginary veil of ignorance would have to consider that they might turn out to be in nation B, and, in that case, they would not want to be so disadvantaged for the greater benefit of those in nation A. This resolution conflicts with the resolution favored by the Utilitarian Approach and the group-interest of nation A but not with the group-interest of nation B.

Assessing Alternative Moral Approaches

Needless to say, each of these moral approaches has its strengths and weaknesses. The main strength of the Utilitarian Approach is that once the relevant utilities are determined, there is an effective decision-making procedure that can be used to resolve all practical problems. After determining the relevant utilities, all that remains is to total the net utilities and choose the alternative with the highest net utility. The basic weakness of this approach, however, is that it does not give sufficient weight to the distribution of utility among the relevant parties. For example, consider a society equally divided between the Privileged Rich and the Alienated Poor, who face the following alternatives:

Nation A's Choice

	Alternative A	Alternative B
Net utility to Privileged Rich	5½ trillion units	4 trillion units
Net utility to Alienated Poor	1 trillion units	2 trillion units
Total utility	6½ trillion units	6 trillion units

Given that these are all the relevant utilities, the Utilitarian Approach favors Alternative A even though Alternative B provides a higher minimum payoff. And if the utility values for two alternatives were:

Nation A's Choice

	Alternative A	Alternative B
Net utility to Privileged Rich	4 trillion units	5 trillion units
Net utility to Alienated Poor	2 trillion units	1 trillion units
Total utility	6 trillion units	6 trillion units

the Utilitarian Approach would be indifferent between the alternatives, despite the fact that Alternative A again provides a higher minimum payoff. In this way, the Utilitarian Approach fails to take into account the distribution of utility among the relevant parties. All that matters for this approach is maximizing total utility, and the distribution of utility among the affected parties is taken into account only insofar as it contributes toward the attainment of that goal.

By contrast, the main strength of the Human Nature Approach in the form we are considering is that it limits the means that can be chosen in pursuit of good consequences. In particular, it absolutely prohibits intentionally doing evil that good may come of it. However, although some limit on the means available for the pursuit of good consequences seems desirable, the main weakness of this version of the Human Nature Approach is that the limit it imposes is too strong. Indeed, exceptions to this limit would seem to be justified whenever the evil to be done is:

1. Trivial (e.g., stepping on someone's foot to get out of a crowded subway).
2. Easily reparable (e.g., lying to a temporarily depressed friend to keep her from committing suicide).
3. Sufficiently outweighed by the consequences of the action (e.g., shooting one of 200 civilian hostages to prevent in the only way possible the execution of all 200).

Still another weakness of this approach is that it lacks an effective decision-making procedure for resolving practical problems. Beyond imposing limits on the means that can be employed in the pursuit of good consequences, the advocates of this approach have not agreed on criteria for selecting among the available alternatives.

The main strength of the Social Contract Approach is that like the Human Nature Approach, it seeks to limit the means available for the pursuit of good consequences. However, unlike the version of the Human Nature Approach we considered, the Social Contract Approach does not impose an absolute limit on intentionally doing evil that good may come of it. Behind the veil of ignorance, persons would surely agree that if the evil were trivial, easily reparable, or sufficiently outweighed by the consequences, there would be an adequate justification for permitting it. On the other hand, the main weakness of the Social Contract Approach is that although it provides an effective decision-making procedure for resolving some practical problems, such as the problem of how to distribute income and wealth and the problem of distant peoples and future generations, the Social Contract Approach cannot be applied to all problems. For example, it will not work for the problems of animal rights and abortion unless we assume that animals and fetuses should be behind the veil of ignorance.

So far, we have seen that prescriptivity and acceptability of prescriptions by everyone affected by them are the two essential features of a moral approach to practical problems, and we have considered three principal alternative approaches which qualify as moral approaches to these problems. Let's now examine what reasons there are for giving a moral approach to practical problems precedence over any nonmoral approach with which it conflicts.

The Justification for Following a Moral Approach to Practical Problems

To begin with, the ethical egoist, by denying the priority of morality over self-interest, presents the most serious challenge to a moral approach to practical problems. Basically, that challenge takes two forms: Individual Ethical Egoism and Universal Ethical Egoism. The basic principle of Individual Ethical Egoism is:

> Everyone ought to do what is in the overall self-interest of just one particular individual.

The basic principle of Universal Ethical Egoism is:

> Everyone ought to do what is in his or her overall self-interest.

Obviously, the prescriptions deriving from these two forms of egoism would conflict significantly with prescriptions following from a moral approach to practical problems. How then can we show that a moral approach is preferable to an egoist's approach?

Individual Ethical Egoism

In Individual Ethical Egoism, all prescriptions are based on the overall interests of just one particular individual. Let's call that individual Gladys. Because in Individual Ethical Egoism Gladys's interests constitute the sole basis for determining prescriptions, there should be no problem of inconsistent prescriptions, assuming, of course, that Gladys's own particular interests are in harmony. The crucial problem for Individual Ethical Egoism, however, is justifying that only Gladys's interests count in determining prescriptions. Individual Ethical Egoism must provide at least some reason for accepting that view. Otherwise, it would be irrational to accept the theory. But what reason or reasons could serve this function? Clearly, it will not do to cite as a reason some characteristic Gladys shares with other persons because whatever justification such a characteristic would provide for favoring Gladys's interests, it would also provide for favoring the interests of those other persons. Nor will it do to cite as a reason some unique characteristic of Gladys, such as knowing all of Shakespeare's writings by heart, because such a characteristic involves a comparative element, and consequently others with similar characteristics, like knowing some or most of Shakespeare's corpus by heart, would still have some justification, although a proportionally lesser justification, for having their interests favored. But again the proposed characteris-

tic would not serve to justify favoring only
Gladys's interests.

A similar objection could be raised if a
unique relational characteristic were proposed
as a reason for Gladys's special status—like
Gladys's being the wife of Seymour. Because
other persons would have similar but not identical relational characteristics, similar but not
identical reasons would hold for them. Nor
will it do to argue that the reason for Gladys's
special status is not the particular unique traits
that she possesses, but rather the mere fact
that she has unique traits. For the same would
hold true of everyone else. Every individual
has unique traits. If recourse to unique traits is
dropped and Gladys claims that she is special
simply because she is herself and wants to
further her own interests, every other person
could claim the same.[4]

For the Individual Ethical Egoist to argue
that the same or similar reasons do *not* hold for
other peoples with the same or similar characteristics to those of Gladys, she must explain
why they do not hold. It must always be possible to understand how a characteristic serves
as a reason in one case but not in another. If
no explanation can be provided, and in the
case of Individual Ethical Egoism none has
been forthcoming, the proposed characteristic
either serves as a reason in both cases or does
not serve as a reason at all.

Universal Ethical Egoism

Unfortunately, these objections to Individual
Ethical Egoism do not work against Universal
Ethical Egoism because Universal Ethical Egoism does provide a reason why the egoist
should be concerned simply about maximizing
his or her own interests, which is simply that
the egoist is herself and wants to further her
own interests. The Individual Ethical Egoist
could not recognize such a reason without giving up her view, but the Universal Ethical
Egoist is willing and able to universalize her
claim and recognize that everyone has a similar justification for adopting Universal Ethical
Egoism.

Accordingly, the objections that typically
have been raised against Universal Ethical
Egoism are designed to show that the view is
fundamentally inconsistent. For the purpose

of evaluating these objections, let's consider
the case of Gary Gyges, an otherwise normal
human being who, for reasons of personal
gain, has embezzled $300,000 while working
at People's National Bank and is in the process
of escaping to a South Sea island where he will
have the good fortune to live a pleasant life
protected by the local authorities and un-
troubled by any qualms of conscience. Suppose that Hedda Hawkeye, a fellow employee,
knows that Gyges has been embezzling money
from the bank and is about to escape. Suppose, further, that it is in Hawkeye's overall
self-interest to prevent Gyges from escaping
with the embezzled money because she will be
generously rewarded for doing so by being
appointed vice president of the bank. Given
that it is in Gyges's overall self-interest to escape with the embezzled money, it now
appears that we can derive a contradiction
from the following:

1. Gyges ought to escape with the embezzled
   money.
2. Hawkeye ought to prevent Gyges from escaping with the embezzled money.
3. Hawkeye's preventing Gyges from escaping with the embezzled money means she is
   preventing Gyges from doing what he
   ought to do.
4. One ought never to prevent someone from
   doing what he ought to do.
5. Therefore, Hawkeye ought not to prevent
   Gyges from escaping with the embezzled
   money.

Because 2 and 5 are contradictory, Universal
Ethical Egoism appears to be inconsistent.

The soundness of this argument depends,
however, on premise number 4, and defenders of Universal Ethical Egoism believe there
are grounds for rejecting this premise. For if
"preventing an action" means "rendering the
action impossible," it would appear that there
are cases in which a person is justified in preventing someone else from doing what he or
she ought to do. Consider, for example, the
following case. Suppose Irma and Igor are
both actively competing for the same position
at a prestigious law firm. If Irma accepts the
position, she obviously renders it impossible

for Igor to obtain the position. But surely this is *not* what we normally think of as an unacceptable form of prevention. Nor would Hawkeye's prevention of Gyges's escape appear to be unacceptable. Thus, to sustain the argument against Universal Ethical Egoism, one must distinguish between acceptable and unacceptable forms of prevention and then show that the argument succeeds even for forms of prevention that a Universal Ethical Egoist would regard as unacceptable. This requires elucidating the force of "ought" in Universal Ethical Egoism.

To illustrate the sense in which a Universal Ethical Egoist claims that other persons ought to do what is in their overall self-interest, defenders often appeal to an analogy of competitive games. For example, in football a defensive player might think that the opposing team's quarterback ought to pass on third down with five yards to go, while not wanting the quarterback to do so and planning to prevent any such attempt. Or to use Jesse Kalin's example:

> I may see how my chess opponent can put my king in check. This is how he ought to move. But believing that he ought to move his bishop and check my king does not commit me to wanting him to do that, nor to persuading him to do so. What I ought to do is sit there quietly, hoping he does not move as he ought.[5]

The point of these examples is to suggest that a Universal Ethical Egoist may, like a player in a game, judge that others ought to do what is in their overall self-interest while simultaneously attempting to prevent such actions or at least refraining from encouraging them.

The analogy of competitive games also illustrates the sense in which a Universal Ethical Egoist claims that she herself ought to do what is in her overall self-interest. For just as a player's judgment that she ought to make a particular move is followed, other things being equal, by an attempt to perform the appropriate action, so likewise when a Universal Ethical Egoist judges that she ought to do some particular action, other things being equal, an at-

tempt to perform the appropriate action follows. In general, defenders of Universal Ethical Egoism stress that because we have little difficulty understanding the implications of the use of "ought" in competitive games, we should also have little difficulty understanding the analogous use of "ought" by the Universal Ethical Egoist.

To claim, however, that the "oughts" in competitive games are analogous to the "oughts" of Universal Ethical Egoism does not mean there are no differences between them. Most importantly, competitive games are governed by moral constraints such that when everyone plays the game properly, there are acceptable moral limits as to what one can do. For example, in football one cannot poison the opposing quarterback in order to win the game. By contrast, when everyone holds self-interested reasons to be supreme, the only limit to what one can do is the point beyond which one ceases to benefit. But this important difference between "oughts" of Universal Ethical Egoism and the "oughts" found in publicly recognized activities like competitive games does not defeat the appropriateness of the analogy. That the "oughts" found in publicly recognized activities are always limited by various moral constraints (What else would get publicly recognized?) does not preclude their being a suggestive model for the unlimited action-guiding character of the "oughts" of Universal Ethical Egoism.[6]

A Standard for Reasonable Conduct

Although the most promising attempts to show that Universal Ethical Egoism is inconsistent have failed, the challenge the view presents to a moral approach to practical problems can still be turned aside. It can be shown that, while consistent, the egoist acts contrary to reason in rejecting a moral approach to practical problems. To show this, I will draw on and generalize insights we have about holding people morally responsible to arrive at what purports to be a standard for reasonable conduct that succeeds in showing that the egoist acts contrary to reason.

Now is it generally recognized that the reasons people could have acquired can be relevant when assessing their conduct from a moral perspective. In such assessments, people are said to be morally responsible even when they presently lack any moral reasons to act otherwise, provided they are morally responsible for the lack. For example, if political leaders had the capabilities and opportunities to become aware of their society's racist and sexist practices, but, in fact, failed to do so, with the consequence that they presently lack any moral reasons to oppose such practices, we would still hold them morally responsible because their lack of moral reasons is something for which they are morally responsible. Similarly, if people allow themselves to become so engrossed in advancing their own personal and family projects that they ignore the most basic needs of others and as a result come to lack any moral reasons for helping people who are truly in need, we could still hold them morally responsible in this regard.

As these examples indicate, having moral reasons to act otherwise is not necessary for imputing responsibility. Rather, what is necessary for such moral assessments is that people are or were able to acquire the relevant moral reasons. What is not so generally recognized, however, is that the reasons a person could have acquired can also be relevant when judging a person's conduct from a self-interested perspective.

Consider the following example. On the last day a house was being offered for sale, a friend of mine bought what turned out to be a termite-infested dwelling requiring several thousands of dollars in repairs. Apparently, the previous owners did not know about the termites, and my friend, having inspected the house on her own, did not think she needed to have the house inspected professionally. She now admits that she acted unreasonably in purchasing the house, but I think it is plausible to say that her action wasn't unreasonable in terms of any reasons she had when she bought the house because at that time she didn't know or have reason to believe the house had termites. Rather, her action is best seen as unreasonable in terms of the reasons she could have had at the time of purchase—reasons she would have had if only she had arranged to have the house inspected professionally.[7]

What these examples taken together appear to support is the following general standard:

A Standard for Reasonable Conduct

Reasonable conduct accords with a rational weighing of all the relevant reasons that people are or were able to acquire.

Obviously, not all the reasons people are or were able to acquire are *relevant* to an assessment of the reasonableness of their conduct. Some reasons are not important enough to be relevant to such an assessment. Relevant reasons are those that lead one to avoid significant harm to oneself (or others) or secure significant benefit to oneself (or others) at an acceptable cost to oneself (or others). Thus, the Standard for Reasonable Conduct is not concerned with the possibility of maximizing benefit or minimizing harm overall but only with the possibility of avoiding a significant harm or securing a significant benefit at an acceptable cost.[8]

Needless to say, people do not always consider all of the reasons that are relevant for deciding what to do. In fact, they could do so only if they had already acquired all the relevant reasons. Nevertheless, reasonable conduct is ultimately determined by a rational weighing of all the relevant reasons. To fail to accord with a rational weighing of all such reasons is to act contrary to reason.[9]

Although defenders of ethical egoism certainly would not want to deny the relevance of the self-interested reasons people are or were able to acquire to the rational assessment of conduct, they might want to deny that the moral reasons people are or were able to acquire are similarly relevant. But what would be the basis for that denial? It could not be that ethical egoists fail to act on moral reasons. That would no more show the irrelevance of moral reasons to the rational assessment of conduct than the fact that pure altruists fail to act on self-interested reasons would show the irrelevance of self-interested reasons to such an assessment. To argue on such grounds simply begs the question against the opposing view. And most defenders of ethical egoism have at least tried to support the view in a non-question-begging way.

In fact, most defenders of ethical egoism have argued for egoism in its universal form, defending the principle that everyone ought to do what is in his or her overall self-interest. However, defenders of ethical egoism cannot support this principle simply by denying the relevance of moral reasons to a rational assessment of conduct any more than defenders of pure altruism can support their opposing principle that everyone ought to do what is in the overall interests of others by denying the relevance of self-interested reasons to a rational assessment of conduct. Consequently, defenders of ethical egoism have no other alternative but to grant that moral reasons are relevant to the rational assessment of conduct and then try to show that such an assessment would never rationally require us to act on moral reasons.

Unfortunately for the defenders of ethical egoism, a rational assessment of the relevant reasons does not lead to this result. On the contrary, such an assessment shows that we are rationally required to act on moral reasons. To see why this is so, two kinds of cases must be considered: cases where the relevant moral reasons and self-interested reasons conflict and cases where no such conflict exists.

It seems obvious that where there is no conflict and both reasons are conclusive, they should both be acted on. In such contexts, we should do what is favored by both morality and self-interest.

Consider the following example. Suppose that you accept a job marketing a baby formula in underdeveloped countries, where the formula is improperly used, leading to increased infant mortality.[10] Imagine that you could just as well have accepted an equally attractive and rewarding job marketing a similar formula in developed countries where the product was not misused, so that a rational weighing of the relevant self-interested reasons alone would not have favored your accepting one of these jobs over the other.[11] At the same time, there were obvious moral reasons why you should not take the first job—reasons that you presumably are or were able to acquire. Moreover, by assumption in this case, the moral reasons do not clash with the relevant self-interested reasons; they simply make a recommendation where the relevant self-interested reasons are silent. Consequently, a

rational weighing of all the relevant reasons in this case could not but favor acting in accord with the relevant moral reasons.[12]

Needless to say, defenders of ethical egoism have to be disconcerted with this result because it shows that actions that accord with ethical egoism are contrary to reason at least when there are two equally good ways of pursuing one's self-interest, only one of which does not conflict with the basic requirements of morality. Note also that in cases where there are two equally good ways of fulfilling the basic requirements of morality, only one of which does not conflict with a person's overall self-interest, it is not at all disconcerting for defenders of morality to admit that we are rationally required to choose the way that does not conflict with our overall self-interest. Nevertheless, exposing this defect in ethical egoism for cases where moral reasons and self-interested reasons do not conflict would be a small victory for defenders of morality if it were not also possible to show that in cases where such reasons do conflict, moral reasons would have priority over self-interested reasons.

When rationally assessing the relevant reasons in cases of such conflict, it is best to view the conflict not as a conflict between self-interested reasons and moral reasons but rather as a conflict between self-interested reasons and altruistic reasons. Viewed in this way, three solutions are possible. First, one could say that self-interested reasons always have priority over conflicting altruistic reasons. Second, one could say just the opposite—that altruistic reasons always have priority over conflicting self-interested reasons. Third, one could say that some kind of a compromise is rationally required. In this compromise, self-interested reasons would sometimes have priority over altruistic reasons, and altruistic reasons would sometimes have priority over self-interested reasons.

Once the conflict is described in this manner, the third solution is clearly the one that is rationally required because the first and second solutions give exclusive priority to one class of relevant reasons over the other without justifying such an exclusive priority from the standpoint of the Standard for Reasonable Conduct. Only the third solution, which sometimes gives priority to self-interested reasons

and sometimes gives priority to altruistic reasons, provides a non–question begging resolution from the standpoint of the Standard for
Reasonable Conduct.

Consider the following example. Suppose
you are in the waste disposal business and you
decide to dispose of toxic wastes in a way that
is cost-efficient for you but is predicted to significantly harm future generations. Imagine
that there are alternative methods available
for disposing of the waste that are only slightly
less cost-efficient and that will not cause any
significant harm to future generations.[13] In
this case, the Standard for Reasonable Conduct requires that you weigh your self-
interested reasons, which favor the most cost-
efficient method of disposing of the toxic
wastes, against the relevant altruistic reasons,
which favor avoiding significant harm to future generations. If we suppose that the projected loss of benefit to yourself is very slight
and the projected harm to future generations
very great, any acceptable general compromise between the relevant self-interested and
altruistic reasons would have to favor the
altruistic reasons. Hence, as judged by the
Standard for Reasonable Conduct, your
method of waste disposal is contrary to the
relevant reasons.

It is important to see how morality can be
viewed as just such a compromise between
self-interested and altruistic reasons. First, a
certain amount of self-regard is morally required or at least morally acceptable. Where
this is the case, the relevant self-interested reasons have priority over the relevant altruistic
reasons. Second, morality obviously places
limits on the extent to which people should
pursue their own self-interest. Where this is
the case, the relevant altruistic reasons have
priority over the relevant self-interested reasons. In this way, morality can be seen as a
compromise between self-interested and
altruistic reasons, and the "moral reasons"
which constitute that compromise can be seen
as having an absolute priority over the self-
interested or altruistic reasons with which they
conflict.

Of course, exactly how this compromise is
to be worked out is a matter of considerable
debate. The Utilitarian Approach favors one
sort of resolution, the Human Nature Ap-

proach another, and the Social Contract
Approach yet another. However, irrespective
of how this debate is best resolved, it is clear
that some sort of a compromise view or moral
solution is rationally preferable to either ethical egoism or pure altruism from the standpoint of the Standard for Reasonable Conduct.[14]

The Interconnectedness
of Moral Solutions to
Practical Problems

Given this justification for following a moral
approach to practical problems, we are in a
good position to begin examining the nine
practical problems covered in this anthology.
Each section contains readings defending
radically opposing solutions to the problem at
hand, as well as one or more readings discussing specific practical applications. Working
through these readings should give you a
more informed view about the demands
morality places on us with respect to each of
these practical problems.

Even if you do not cover all of these practical problems, you should still come to
appreciate why a solution to any one of them
requires solutions to the others as well. That is
to say, the readings on the distribution of income and wealth (in Section I) may help you to
characterize a morally defensible system for
distributing income and wealth within a society, but you would still not know fully how to
apply such a system in a particular society
without also inquiring how just that society is
with respect to the other problem areas
covered by this anthology.

Or suppose justice requires us to provide
for the basic nutritional needs of distant peoples and future generations as well as for people within our own society. (See the readings
in Section II.) Such a requirement would at
least restrict the use of nonrenewable resources to satisfy the nonbasic or luxury needs
of persons within our society—a use that
might otherwise be permitted by a morally
defensible system for distributing income and
wealth within our society.

Further moral restrictions on the satisfaction of nonbasic or luxury needs could arise from a correct determination of who has a right to life. For example, if fetuses have a right to life, many of us may be morally required to sacrifice the satisfaction of certain nonbasic or luxury needs to bring fetuses to term. If, by contrast, euthanasia can be morally justified, scarce resources that are now used to sustain human life could be freed for other purposes. (See the readings in Section III.)

Justice also may demand that we sacrifice some nonbasic or luxury needs to satisfy the requirements of sex equality and remedy past discrimination and prejudice. For example, at the cost of considerable redistribution, we may be required to provide women with the same opportunities for self-development now open to men. (See the readings in Section IV.) We may also be required to turn away qualified candidates for medical schools and law schools so that other candidates who have suffered past injustices may be compensated by admission to these schools. (See the readings in Section V.)

Moral restrictions on the satisfaction of nonbasic needs and even on the way basic needs are satisfied could arise from a determination of what rights, if any, animals have. For example, if vegetarianism were morally required and recognized as such, the impact on our lives would be far-reaching. (See the readings in Section VI.)

Similarly, the legitimate costs of legal enforcement must ultimately enter into any calculation of who gets to keep what in society. This will require a solution to the problem of punishment and responsibility. (See the readings in Section VII.)

A solution to the problem of punishment and responsibility, in turn, presupposes solutions to the other practical problems discussed in the anthology. Suppose that in a society with a just distribution of income and wealth persons who put forth their best efforts receive a yearly income of at least $10,000. (If you think a just distribution of income would provide some other amount, plug that amount in and make the corresponding adjustments in subsequent figures.) Further suppose that the society in which you and I live has an unjust distribution of income and wealth because, al-though there are enough resources for a just distribution, many persons who put forth their best efforts receive no more than $5,000 per year whereas others receive as much as $500,000. Let's say that your income is $500,000 and mine is only $5,000, even though I have tried every legal way to increase my income. Assume also that any resort to civil disobedience or armed revolution would be ineffectual and too costly for me personally. If I then rob you of $5,000, thus bringing my yearly income up to the just allotment of $10,000, what would a morally defensible system of punishment and responsibility do to me if I were caught? To require a punishment equal in severity to the $5,000 I took simply reinforces an unjust distribution of income and wealth. So it seems that only a fairly light punishment or no punishment at all should be required.[15] This example shows that the application of a morally defensible solution to the problem of punishment and responsibility depends on a solution to the problem of the distribution of income and wealth in a society. To know, therefore, how to apply a morally defensible system of punishment and responsibility in a particular society, you must know to what degree that society incorporates a morally defensible distribution of income and wealth.

Likewise, a solution to the problem of terrorism presupposes solutions both to the problem of the distribution of income and wealth and to the problem of distant peoples and future generations. The moral legitimacy of particular responses to terrorism will depend on a correct determination of the rights of those people on whose behalf terrorism is being employed. (See the readings in Section VIII.)

Finally, as we in the United States are painfully aware at the present time, proposed allocations for distributing income and wealth through social welfare programs can come into conflict with proposed allocations for military defense. Many have argued that when this happens we must sacrifice social welfare programs to meet the requirements of military defense, but many other people have disagreed. Obviously, then, to know exactly how your solutions to the other problem areas treated in this anthology should be applied in a particular society, you also need to know what a morally defensible system of military defense requires for that society. (See the readings in Section IX.)

Put briefly, what is required (or permitted) by a morally defensible solution to the problem of the distribution of income and wealth within a society will depend on what is required (or permitted) by morally defensible solutions to the problems of distant peoples and future generations, abortion and euthanasia, animal rights, sex equality, compensation for past wrongs, punishment and responsibility, terrorism, nuclear deterrence, and strategic defense. Moreover, as we have seen in the cases of the problem of punishment and the problem of terrorism, the dependency can run both ways. This means that any solution you might devise to one of these problems is only provisional until you can determine solutions to the others as well. And even if you are unable at the moment to devise solutions to all of these practical problems (because, for example, the course you are now taking is only considering some of them), you must still acknowledge that in the final analysis your solutions to these practical problems will have to be interconnected.

Note too that acknowledging the interconnectedness of the solutions to these practical problems does not presuppose a commitment to any particular political or moral ideal. For example, whether you tend to be a libertarian, a liberal, a socialist, a communitarian, or anything else, the interconnectedness of the solutions to the practical problems we are discussing still holds true. Individuals who endorse different political and moral ideals will presumably devise different solutions to these practical problems, but the solutions will still be interconnected.

Working through the readings in this anthology will not always be an easy task. Some articles will be clear on the first reading, whereas others will require closer scrutiny. You should also make sure you give each selection a fair hearing, for while some will accord with your current views, others will not. It is important that you evaluate these latter with an open mind, allowing for the possibility that after sufficient reflection you may come to view them as the most morally defensible. Indeed, to approach the selections of this anthology in any other way would surely undermine the grounds you have for thinking you are a just and moral person.

Notes

1. Obviously, other moral approaches to practical problems could be distinguished, but I think the three I will be considering reflect the range of possible approaches that are relevant to the resolution of these problems.

2. In fact, the debate as to whether blacks are better off now because of the programs of the Great Society has taken a more scholarly turn. See Charles Murray, *Losing Ground* (New York: Basic Books, 1984), and Christopher Jencks, "How Poor Are the Poor?" *New York Review of Books*, May 9, 1985.

3. See Section II of this text and my book, *The Demands of Justice* (Notre Dame; University of Notre Dame Press, 1980), especially Chapter 2.

4. For further argument on this point, see Marcus Singer, *Generalization in Ethics* (New York: Alfred A. Knopf, Inc., 1961), Chapter 2, and Alan Gewirth, "The Non-Trivializability of Universalizability," *Australasian Journal of Philosophy* (1969), pp. 123–131.

5. Jesse Kalin, "In Defense of Egoism," in *Morality and Rational Self-interest*, ed. David Gauthier (Englewood Cliffs: Prentice-Hall, Inc., 1970), pp. 73–74.

6. For additional reasons why ethical egoism is a consistent view, see my article, "Ethical Egoism and Beyond," *Canadian Journal of Philosophy* (1979), pp. 91–108.

7. Note that on the last day the house was being offered for sale, it would have been unreasonable for my acquaintance to decide to have the house inspected professionally because the inspection and the sale presumably could not have been completed in the same day.

8. Even utilitarians would find this interpretation of the Standard for Reasonable Conduct acceptable because they would not regard all failures to maximize benefits overall as unreasonable.

9. Of course, for individuals who neither possess nor have possessed the capabilities and opportunities to acquire such reasons for acting, the

question of the reasonableness of their conduct simply doesn't arise. The same is true for those who have lost the capabilities and opportunities to acquire such reasons for acting through no fault of their own.

10. For a discussion of the causal links involved here, see *Marketing and Promotion of Infant Formula in Developing Countries*. Hearing before the Subcommittee on International Economic Policy and Trade of the Committee on Foreign Affairs, U.S. House of Representatives, 1980. See also Fred D. Miller, *Out of the Mouths of Babes* (Bowling Green: Bowling Green State University Press, 1983).

11. Assume that both jobs have the same beneficial effects on the interests of others.

12. I am assuming that acting contrary to reason is an important failing with respect to the requirements of reason and that there are many ways of not acting in (perfect) accord with reason that do not constitute acting contrary to reason.

13. Assume that all of these methods of waste disposal have roughly the same amount of beneficial effects on the interests of others.

14. For further argument, see my article, "Justifying Morality: The Right and the Wrong Ways," (Kurt Baier Festschift) *Syntheses* (1987).

15. For further argument, see my article, "Is There a Rationale for Punishment?" *The American Journal of Jurisprudence* (1984), pp. 29–43.

The Distribution of Income and Wealth

Basic Concepts

The problem of the distribution of income and wealth within a society has traditionally been referred to as the problem of distributive justice. Less frequently, this problem has been taken to include the distribution of other social goods (for example, political freedoms such as freedom of speech and freedom of the press), and at times it has been expanded to embrace distribution on a worldwide scale. The majority of philosophers, however, tend to agree that the distribution of income and wealth within a specific society is at the heart of the problem of distributive justice.

Just as traditionally, a variety of solutions have been proposed to the problem of distributive justice. Before examining some of these solutions, let's observe what they all have in common.

First, even though the solutions may differ as to exactly how much income and wealth people deserve or should rightfully possess, they all purport to tell us what people deserve or what they have a right to possess. For example, some solutions propose that people deserve to have their needs fulfilled, whereas others state that what people deserve or should rightfully possess is what they can produce by their labor.

Second, all solutions to the problem of distributive justice distinguish between justice and charity. *Justice* is what we should do as a matter of obligation or duty, whereas *charity* is what we should do if we want to choose the morally best possible action available to us. Accordingly, the demands of charity go beyond duty. In addition, failure to fulfill the demands of justice is blameworthy, violates someone's rights, and can legitimately be punished. By contrast, failure to fulfill the demands of charity, although not ideal, is not blameworthy, does not violate anyone's rights, and cannot legitimately be punished. Some solutions to the problem of distributive justice give more scope to justice and less to charity, whereas others do just the opposite.

Turning from common ground to disputed territory, solutions offered to the problem of distributive justice have appealed to a number of political ideals. In our times, libertarians have appealed to an ideal of liberty, welfare liberals to an ideal of contractual fairness, socialists to an ideal of equality, and communitarians to an ideal of the common good.

Libertarianism

Libertarians, such as John Hospers (see pp. 24–33), take liberty as the ultimate political ideal and typically define liberty as "the state of being unconstrained by other persons from doing what one wants." This definition limits the scope of liberty in two ways. First, not all constraints, whatever the source, count as a restriction of liberty; the constraints must come from other persons. For example, people who are constrained by natural forces from getting to the top of Mount Everest do not lack liberty in this regard. Second, the constraints must run counter to people's wants. Thus, people who do not want to hear Beethoven's Fifth Symphony do not feel their liberty is restricted when other people forbid its performance, even though the proscription does in fact constrain what they are able to do.

Of course, libertarians may argue that these constraints do restrict a person's liberty because people normally want to be unconstrained by others. But other philosophers have claimed that such constraints point to a serious defect in the libertarian's definition of liberty, which can only be remedied by defining liberty more broadly as "the state of being unconstrained by other persons from doing what one is able to do." If we apply this revised definition to the previous example, we find that people's liberty to hear Beethoven's Fifth Symphony would be restricted even if they did not want to hear it (and even if, perchance, they did not want to be unconstrained by others) because other people would still be constraining them from doing what they are able to do.

Confident that problems of defining liberty can be overcome in some satisfactory manner, libertarians go on to characterize their political ideal as requiring that each person should have the greatest amount of liberty commensurate with the same liberty for all. From this ideal, libertarians claim that a number of more specific requirements, in particular a right to life, a right to freedom of speech, press, and assembly, and a right to property can be derived.

It is important to note that the libertarian's right to life is not a right to receive from others the goods and resources necessary for preserving one's life; it is simply a right not to be killed. So understood, the right to life is not a right to welfare. In fact, there are no welfare rights in the libertarian view. Accordingly, the libertarian's understanding of the right to property is not a right to receive from others the goods and resources necessary for one's welfare, but rather a right to acquire goods and resources either by initial acquisition or by voluntary agreement.

Obviously, by defending rights such as these, libertarians can only support a limited role for government. That role is simply to prevent and punish initial acts of coercion— the only wrongful actions for libertarians.

Libertarians do not deny that it is a good thing for people to have sufficient goods and resources to meet at least their basic nutritional needs, but libertarians do deny that government has a duty to provide for such needs. Some good things, such as the provision of welfare to the needy, are requirements of charity rather than justice, libertarians claim. Accordingly, failure to make such provisions is neither blameworthy nor punishable.

In defense of a libertarian ideal, Robert Nozick (see pp. 34–42) asks us to imagine that we are in a society that has just distributed income according to some ideal pattern, possibly a pattern of equality. We are to further imagine that in such a society Wilt Chamberlain (or Larry Bird, if we wish to update the example) offers to play basketball for us provided that he receives a quarter for every home game ticket that is sold. Suppose we agree to these terms and a million people attend the home games to see Wilt Chamberlain (or Larry Bird) play, thereby securing him an income of $250,000. Since such an income would surely upset the initial pattern of income distribution, whatever that happened to be, Nozick contends that this illustrates how an ideal of liberty upsets the patterns required by other political ideals and hence calls for their rejection.

Nozick's critique, however, seems to apply only to political ideals that require an absolute equality of income. Yet for many political ideals, the inequalities of income generated in Nozick's example would be objectionable only if they deprived people of something to which they had a right, such as equal opportunity. And whether people were so deprived would depend on to what uses the Wilt Chamberlains or Larry Birds of the world put their greater income. However, there is no necessity for those who have legitimately acquired greater income to use it in ways that violate the rights of others.

A basic difficulty with the libertarian's solution to the problem of distributive justice as defended by Hospers and Nozick is the claim that rights to life and property (as the libertarian understands these rights) derive from an ideal of liberty. Why should we think that an ideal of liberty requires a right to life and a right to property that excludes a right to welfare? Surely it would seem that a right to property (as the libertarian understands this right) might well justify a rich person's depriving a poor person of the liberty to acquire the goods and resources necessary for meeting his or her basic nutritional needs. How then could we appeal to an ideal of liberty to justify such a deprivation? Surely we couldn't claim that such a deprivation is justified for the sake of preserving a rich person's freedom to use the goods and resources he or she possesses to meet luxury needs. Or could we?

To deal with this difficulty, some libertarians have resorted to defining liberty in terms of rights, so that a restriction of liberty is a violation of someone's rights, usually a violation of a right to life or a right to property. But this approach gives rise to a difficulty akin to the one it seeks to resolve. How can the libertarian interpret a right to life and a right to property so as to favor a rich person's nonbasic or luxury needs rather than a poor person's basic nutritional needs? Thus, whether rights are defined in terms of liberty or liberty is defined in terms of rights, we can still question how libertarians justify their interpretation of a right to life and a right to property.

Welfare Liberalism

In contrast with libertarians, welfare liberals, such as John Rawls (pp. 43–55), take contractual fairness to be the ultimate political ideal and contend that the fundamental rights and duties in a society are those that people would agree to under fair conditions.

Note that welfare liberals do not say that the fundamental rights and duties in a society are those to which people actually do agree, because these might not be fair at all. For example, people might agree to a certain system of fundamental rights and duties only because they have been forced to do so or because their only alternative is starving to death. Thus, actual agreement is not sufficient, nor is it even necessary, for determining an adequate conception of justice. According to welfare liberals, what is necessary and sufficient is that people would agree to such rights and duties under fair conditions.

But what are fair conditions? According to John Rawls, fair conditions can be expressed by an "original position" in which people are concerned to advance their own interests behind a "veil of ignorance." The effect of the veil of ignorance is to deprive people in the original position of the knowledge they would need to advance their own interests in ways that are morally arbitrary.

Rawls presents the principles of justice he believes would be derived in the original position in two successive formulations. The first formulation is as follows:

I. Special conception of justice
   1. Each person is to have an equal right to the most extensive basic liberty compatible with a similar liberty for others.
   2. Social and economic inequalities are to be arranged so that they are (a) reasonably expected to be to everyone's advantage and (b) attached to positions and offices open to all.
II. General conception of justice
   All social values—liberty and opportunity, income and wealth, and the bases of self-respect—are to be distributed equally un-

less an unequal distribution of any or all of these values is to everyone's advantage.

Later these principles are more accurately formulated as:

I. Special conception of justice
   1. Each person is to have an equal right to the most extensive total system of equal basic liberties compatible with a similar system of liberty for all.
   2. Social and economic inequalities are to be arranged so that they are (a) to the greatest benefit of the least advantaged, consistent with the just savings principle and (b) attached to offices and positions open to all under conditions of fair equality of opportunity.
II. General conception of justice
   All social goods—liberty and opportunity, income and wealth, and the bases of self-respect—are to be distributed equally unless an unequal distribution of any or all of these goods is to the advantage of the least favored.

Under both formulations, the general conception of justice differs from the special conception of justice by allowing trade-offs between liberty and other social goods. According to Rawls, persons in the original position would want the special conception of justice to be applied in place of the general conception of justice whenever social conditions allowed all representative persons to exercise their basic liberties.

Rawls holds that these principles of justice would be chosen in the original position because persons so situated would find it reasonable to follow the conservative dictates of a "maximin strategy" and thereby secure for themselves the highest minimum payoff.

Rawls' defense of a welfare liberal conception of justice has been challenged in a variety of ways. Some critics have endorsed Rawls' contractual approach while disagreeing with Rawls over what principles of justice would be derived thereby. These critics usually attempt to undermine the use of a maximin strategy in the original position.[1] Other critics, however, have found fault with the contractual approach itself. Libertarians, for example, have challenged the moral adequacy of the very ideal of contractual fairness.

This second challenge to the ideal of contractual fairness is potentially the more damaging because, if valid, it would force supporters to embrace some other political ideal. This challenge, however, fails if it can be shown that the libertarian's own ideal of liberty, when correctly interpreted, leads to much the same practical requirements as are usually associated with the welfare liberal's ideal of contractual fairness.[2]

Socialist Justice

Nevertheless, resolving the debate between libertarians and welfare liberals will not provide a morally acceptable conception of justice—at least, not if socialists are correct. Socialists maintain that libertarians and welfare liberals both fail (although to varying degrees) to recognize the ultimate moral significance of an ideal of equality.

More specifically, socialists defend an ideal that calls for equality of need fulfillment. As Kai Nielson contends (pp. 56–66), radical egalitarianism is justified because it produces the conditions for the most extensive satisfaction of the needs of everyone.

At first hearing, this ideal might sound simply crazy to someone brought up in a capitalist society. The obvious problem is how to get persons to put forth their best effort if income will be distributed on the basis of individual need rather than individual contribution.

The socialist answer is to make the work that must be done enjoyable in itself, as much as is possible. As a result, people will want to do the work they are capable of doing because they find it intrinsically rewarding. For a start, socialists might try to convince workers to accept lower salaries for presently existing jobs that are intrinsically rewarding. For example, they might ask top executives to work for $300,000 a year rather than $600,000. Yet socialists ultimately hope to make all jobs intrinsically as rewarding as possible so that, after people are no longer working primarily for external rewards when making their best contributions to society, distribution can proceed on the basis of need.

Socialists propose to implement their ideal of equality by giving workers democratic control over the workplace. They believe that if workers have more to say about how they do their work, they will find their work intrinsically more rewarding. As a consequence, they will be more motivated to work, since their work itself will be meeting their needs. Socialists believe that extending democracy to the workplace will necessarily lead to socialization of the means of production and the end of private property.

However, even with democratic control of the workplace, some jobs, such as collecting garbage or changing bedpans, probably can't be made intrinsically rewarding. Now what socialists propose to do with respect to such jobs is to divide them up in some equitable manner. Some people might, for example, collect garbage one day a week and then work at intrinsically rewarding jobs for the rest of the week. Others would change bedpans or do some other slop job one day a week and then work at an intrinsically rewarding job the other days of the week. By making jobs intrinsically as rewarding as possible, in part through democratic control of the workplace and an equitable assignment of unrewarding tasks, socialists believe people will contribute according to their ability even when distribution proceeds according to need.

Finally, it is important to note that the socialist ideal of equality does not accord with what exists in such countries as the Soviet Union or Albania. Judging the acceptability of the socialist ideal of equality by what takes place in those countries would be as unfair as judging the acceptability of the libertarian ideal of liberty by what takes place in countries like Chile or South Korea, where citizens are arrested and imprisoned without cause. By analogy, it would be like judging the merits of college football by the way Vanderbilt's or Northwestern's teams play rather than by the way Alabama's or Notre Dame's teams play. Actually, a fairer comparison would be to judge the socialist ideal of equality by what takes place in countries like Sweden or Yugoslavia and to judge the libertarian ideal of liberty by what takes place in the United

States. Even these comparisons, however, are not wholly appropriate because none of these countries fully conforms to those ideals.

To justify the ideal of equality, Kai Nielson argues that it is required by liberty or at least by a fair distribution of liberty. By "liberty" Nielson means both "positive liberty to receive certain goods" and "negative liberty not to be interfered with," so his argument from liberty will not have much weight with libertarians, who only value negative liberty. Rather, his argument is directed primarily at welfare liberals, who value both positive and negative liberty as well as a fair distribution of liberty.

Another basic difficulty with Nielson's socialist solution to the problem of distributive justice concerns the proclaimed necessity of abolishing private property and socializing the means of production. It seems perfectly possible to give workers more control over their workplace while at the same time the means of production remain privately owned. Of course, private ownership would have a somewhat different character in a society with democratic control of the workplace, but it need not cease to be private ownership. After all, private ownership would also have a somewhat different character in a society where private holdings, and hence bargaining power, were distributed more equally than is found in most capitalist societies, yet it would not cease to be private ownership. Accordingly, we could imagine a society where the means of production are privately owned but where—because ownership is so widely dispersed throughout the society (e.g., nearly everyone owns 10 shares of major industrial stock and no one more than 20 shares) and because of the degree of democratic control of the workplace—many of the valid criticisms socialists make of existing capitalist societies would no longer apply.

Communitarian Justice

As one might expect, many contemporary defenders of communitarian justice regard their conception of justice as rooted in Aristotelian moral theory. Like Aristotle, communitarians endorse a fundamental contrast between human beings as they are and human beings as

they could be if they realized their essential nature. Ethics is then viewed as a science that enables human beings to understand how they can make the transition from the former state to the latter. This view of ethics requires some account of potency to act and some account of the essence of human beings and the end or telos they seek. Moreover, for human beings to make this transition from potency to act, a particular set of virtues is needed, and people who fail to acquire these virtues cannot realize their true nature and reach their true end.

Given that the communitarian conception of justice is not a widely endorsed ideal today, communitarians have frequently chosen to defend their conception by attacking other conceptions of justice, and, by and large, they have focused their attacks on the welfare liberal conception of justice.

One of the best-known attacks of this sort has been put forth by Michael J. Sandel (pp. 66–70). Sandel claims that a welfare liberal conception of justice is founded on an inadequate conception of the nature of persons, according to which none of the particular wants, interests, or ends that we happen to have at any given time constitute what we are essentially. According to this conception, we are independent of and prior to all such wants, interests, or ends.

Sandel claims that this conception of the nature of persons is inadequate because:

> . . . we cannot regard ourselves as independent in this way without great cost to those loyalties and convictions whose moral force consists partly in the fact that living by them is inseparable from understanding ourselves as the particular persons we are—as members of this family or community or nation or people, as bearers of this history, as sons and daughters of that revolution, as citizens of this republic. Allegiances such as these are more than values I happen to have or aims I "espouse at any given time." They go beyond the obligations I voluntarily incur and the "natural duties" I owe to human beings as such. They allow that to some I owe more than justice requires or even permits, not by reason of agreements I have made but instead in virtue of those more or less enduring

attachments and commitments which taken together partly define the person I am.[3]

Thus, according to Sandel, the conception of the nature of persons required by a welfare liberal conception of justice is inadequate because it fails to take into account the fact that some of our wants, interests, and ends are at least in part constitutive of what we are essentially. Without these desires, interests, and ends, we would not be the same persons we presently happen to be.

Sandel contends that welfare liberals are led to rely on this inadequate conception of persons for reasons that are fundamental to the conception of justice they want to defend. Specifically, welfare liberals want to maintain the priority of justice and more generally the priority of the right over the good. For example, according to Rawls:

> The principles of right and so of justice put limits on which satisfactions have value; they impose restrictions on what are reasonable conceptions of one's good. We can express this by saying that in justice as fairness the concept of right is prior to that of the good.[4]

To support these priorities, Sandel argues that welfare liberals endorse this inadequate conception of the nature of persons. For example, Rawls argues:

> It is not our aims that primarily reveal our nature but rather the principles that we would acknowledge to govern the background conditions under which these aims are to be found and the manner in which they are to be pursued. *For the self is prior to the ends which are affirmed by it;* even a dominant end must be chosen from among numerous possibilities. . . . We should therefore reverse the relation between the right and the good proposed by teleological doctrines and view the right as prior.[5]

What this passage shows, according to Sandel, is that welfare liberals like Rawls believe that the priority of justice and the priority of the right are grounded in the priority of the self to its ends.

At first glance, Sandel's case against welfare liberalism looks particularly strong. After all, Rawls actually does say that "the self is prior to the ends which are affirmed by it" and this claim seems to express just the inadequate conception of the nature of persons that Sandel contends underlies a Welfare Liberal Conception of Justice. Nor is Rawls' claim made specifically about persons in the original position. So Sandel cannot be dismissed for failing to distinguish between the characterization of persons in the original position and the characterization of persons in ordinary life. Nevertheless, Sandel's case against welfare liberalism presupposes that there is no other plausible interpretation that can be given to Rawls' claim than the metaphysical one that Sandel favors. And unfortunately for Sandel's argument, a more plausible interpretation of Rawls' claim does appear to be available. According to this interpretation, to say that persons are prior to their ends means simply that they are morally responsible for their ends, either because they can or could have changed those ends. Of course, the degree to which people can or could have changed their ends is a matter of considerable debate, but what is clear is that it is the degree to which people can or could have changed their ends that determines the degree to which they are morally responsible for those ends.

Nor does this interpretation deny that certain ends may in fact be constitutive of the persons we are, so that if those ends were to change we would become different persons. We can see, therefore, that nothing in this interpretation of Rawls' claim presupposes a self that is metaphysically prior to its ends. Rather, the picture we are given is that of a self that is responsible for its ends insofar as its ends can or could have been revised. Such a self may well be constituted by at least some of its ends, but it is only responsible for those ends to the degree to which they can or could have been revised. So the sense in which a self is prior to its ends is simply moral: insofar as its ends can or could have been revised, a self may be called upon to change them or compensate others for their effects when they turn out to be morally objectionable. Clearly, this interpretation of Rawls' claim avoids any commitment to the inadequate conception of the nature of persons which Sandel contends underlies a welfare liberal conception of justice. Of course, this does not show that a communitarian conception of justice might not in the end be the most morally defensible. It only shows that this particular communitarian attack on a welfare liberal conception of justice is not successful.

Practical Applications

The application of the ideals of libertarianism, welfare liberalism, socialism or communitarianism to a particular society obviously has basic and far-reaching effects. These ideals have implications for constitutional structure, the control of industry, taxing policy, social welfare programs, and property law, and much more. The next two readings in this section are from important United States Supreme Court decisions to which our four political ideals can be usefully related.

The U.S. Supreme Court, of course, does not view itself as directly applying one or the other of these political ideals to the laws of the land. Rather the Court views itself as deciding whether particular laws accord with the provisions of the United States Constitution. However, most people, including Supreme Court Justices, do not clearly separate their views about what are the practical applications of the political ideal they take to be the most morally defensible from their views about what sort of laws accord with the U.S. Constitution. Hence, it is frequently possible to see how commitment to a political ideal is decisive in judicial decision-making.

Beyond coming to appreciate how political ideals and their presumed applications function in judicial decision-making, it is important that you examine U.S. Supreme Court decisions to determine to what degree the laws of your society accord with the political ideal you take to be the most morally defensible. For you to have good reasons to believe that you are a just and moral person, you need to assess to what degree the laws and institutions of your society are just—in this case, to what degree

they accord with the requirements of distributive justice. Examining the two U.S. Supreme Court decisions included in this anthology should serve this purpose well.

In the first decision (Wyman v. James), the majority of the Court decided that the rights of welfare recipients are limited in various ways, and in particular that recipients are not protected against mandatory visits by caseworkers. Such a decision would surely seem justified if one believed, as libertarians do, that the provision of welfare is, at best, only a requirement of charity. Welfare liberals, socialists, and communitarians, however, would have difficulty accepting this decision, as did the dissenting justices of the Court.

In the second decision (San Antonio School District v. Rodriguez), the majority of the Court determined that education is not a right afforded strict protection by the U.S. Constitution, as long as no one is being deprived of an education. Again, this decision seems to agree with the way libertarians would understand the practical applications of their ideal of liberty; welfare liberals, socialists, and communitarians would probably find themselves persuaded by the arguments of the dissenting justices.

It is important to notice that you can also work backward from your considered judgments about these Supreme Court cases to the political ideal you should favor. Frequently, only by considering the practical applications of alternative political ideals can we clarify our views about which ideal is the most morally defensible.

In the final reading in this section, Peter Marin (see pp. 80–82) paints a vivid picture of the homeless in America and asks the relevant question, "What does a society owe its members in trouble, and how is that debt to be paid?" Surely, at least one of our four political ideals must have an adequate answer.

Notice, too, that any fully adequate solution to the problem of distributive justice within a society presupposes a solution to the other moral problems presented in this anthology. In particular, the problem of distant peoples and future generations, which is discussed in the following section, seems to be clearly connected with the problem of distributive justice.

We cannot know for sure what resources particular persons within a society should receive unless we also know what obligations persons within that society have to distant peoples and future generations.

Notes

1. See, for example, my article, "Distributive Justice," *American Journal of Jurisprudence* (1977), pp. 55–79, and John C. Harsanyi, *Essays on Ethics,* *Social Behavior, and Scientific Explanation* (Boston: D. Reidel Publishing Co., 1976), pp. 37–85.

2. For an argument of this sort, see my article, "A Libertarian Justification for a Welfare State," *Social Theory and Practice* (1985), pp. 285–306.

3. Michael J. Sandel, *Liberalism and the Limits of Justice* (Cambridge: Cambridge University Press, 1982), p. 179.

4. John Rawls, *A Theory of Justice* (Cambridge: Harvard University Press, 1971), p. 31.

5. Ibid, p. 560.

The Libertarian Manifesto

John Hospers

John Hospers explores various ways of understanding the basic libertarian thesis that every person is the owner of his or her own life. According to Hospers, such ownership entails rights to life, liberty, and property. Since these rights are violated by an initial use of force, the proper role of government is said to be limited to the retaliatory use of force against those who have initiated its use. All other possible roles for government, such as protecting individuals against themselves or requiring people to help one another, are regarded as illegitimate by the libertarian.

The political philosophy that is called libertarianism (from the Latin *libertas*, liberty) is the doctrine that every person is the owner of his own life, and that no one is the owner of anyone else's life: and that consequently every human being has the right to act in accordance with his own choices, unless those actions infringe on the equal liberty of other human beings to act in accordance with their choices.

There are several other ways of stating the same libertarian thesis:

1. *No one is anyone else's master, and no one is anyone else's slave.* Since I am the one to decide how my life is to be conducted just as you decide about yours, I have no right (even if I had the power) to make you my slave and be your master, nor have you the right to become the master by enslaving me. Slavery is *forced* servitude, and since no one owns the life of anyone else, no one has the right to enslave another. Political theories past and present have traditionally been concerned with who should be the master (usually the king, the dictator, or government bureaucracy) and who should be the slaves, and what the extent of the slavery should be. Libertarianism holds that no one has the right to use force to enslave the life of another, or any portion or aspect of that life.

From "What Libertarianism Is," in *The Libertarian Alternative* edited by Tibor Machan (1974). Reprinted by permission of the author, the editor, and Nelson-Hall Inc.

2. *Other men's lives are not yours to dispose of.* I enjoy seeing operas; but operas are expensive to produce. Opera-lovers often say, "The state (or the city, etc.) should subsidize opera, so that we can all see it. Also it would be for people's betterment, cultural benefit, etc." But what they are advocating is nothing more or less than legalized plunder. They can't pay for the productions themselves, and yet they want to see opera, which involves a large number of people and their labor; so what they are saying in effect is, "Get the money through legalized force. Take a little bit more out of every worker's paycheck every week to pay for the operas we want to see." But I have no right to take by force from the workers' pockets to pay for what I want.

Perhaps it would be better if he *did* go to see opera—then I should try to convince him to go voluntarily. But to take the money from him forcibly, because in my opinion it would be good for *him*, is still seizure of his earnings, which is plunder.

Besides, if I have the right to force him to help pay for my pet projects, hasn't he equally the right to force me to help pay for his? Perhaps he in turn wants the government to subsidize rock-and-roll, or his new car, or a house in the country? If I have the right to milk him, why hasn't he the right to milk me? If I can be a moral cannibal, why can't he too?

We should beware of the inventors of utopias. They would remake the world according to their vision—with the lives and fruits of the labor of *other* human beings. Is it someone's utopian vision that others should build pyramids to beautify the landscape? Very well, then other men should provide the labor; and if he is in a position of political power, and he can't get men to do it voluntarily, then he must *compel* them to "cooperate"—i.e. he must enslave them.

A hundred men might gain great pleasure from beating up or killing just one insignificant human being; but other men's lives are not theirs to dispose of. "In order to achieve the worthy goals of the next five-year-plan, we must forcibly collectivize the peasants . . ."; but other men's lives are not theirs to dispose of. Do you want to occupy, rent-free, the mansion that another man has worked for twenty years to buy? But other men's lives are not yours to dispose of. Do you want operas so badly that everyone is forced to work harder to pay for their subsidization through taxes? But other men's lives are not yours to dispose of. Do you want to have free medical care at the expense of other people, whether they wish to provide it or not? But this would require them to work longer for you whether they want to or not, and other men's lives are not yours to dispose of. . . .

3. *No human being should be a nonvoluntary mortgage on the life of another.* I cannot claim your life, your work, or the products of your effort as mine. The fruit of one man's labor should not be fair game for every freeloader who comes along and demands it as his own. The orchard that has been carefully grown, nurtured, and harvested by its owner should not be ripe for the plucking for any bypasser who has a yen for the ripe fruit. The wealth that some men have produced should not be fair game for looting by government, to be used for whatever purposes its representatives determine, no matter what their motives in so doing may be. The theft of your money by a robber is not justified by the fact that he used it to help his injured mother.

It will already be evident that libertarian doctrine is embedded in a view of the rights of

man. Each human being has the right to live his life as he chooses, compatibly with the equal right of all other human beings to live their lives as they choose.

All man's rights are implicit in the above statement. Each man has the right to life: any attempt by others to take it away from him, or even to injure him, violates this right, through the use of coercion against him. Each man has the right to liberty: to conduct his life in accordance with the alternatives open to him without coercive action by others. And every man has the right to property: to work to sustain his life (and the lives of whichever others he chooses to sustain, such as his family) and to retain the fruits of his labor.

People often defend the rights of life and liberty but denigrate property rights, and yet the right to property is as basic as the other two: indeed, without property rights no other rights are possible. Depriving you of property is depriving you of the means by which you live. . . .

I have no right to decide how *you* should spend your time or your money. I can make that decision for myself, but not for you, my neighbor. I may deplore your choice of lifestyle, and I may talk with you about it provided you are willing to listen to me. But I have no right to use force to change it. Nor have I the right to decide how you should spend the money you have earned. I may appeal to you to give it to the Red Cross, and you may prefer to go to prize-fights. But that is your decision, and however much I may chafe about it I do not have the right to interfere forcibly with it, for example by robbing you in order to use the money in accordance with *my* choices. (If I have the right to rob you, have you also the right to rob me?)

When I claim a right, I carve out a niche, as it were, in my life, saying in effect, "This activity I must be able to perform without interference from others. For you and everyone else, this is off limits." And so I put up a "no trespassing" sign, which marks off the area of my right. Each individual's right is his "no trespassing" sign in relation to me and others. I may not encroach upon his domain any more than he upon mine, without my consent. Every right entails a duty, true—but the duty is only that of *forbearance*—that is, of *refraining* from violating the other person's right. If you have a right to life, I have no right to take your life; if you have a right to the products of your labor (property), I have no right to take it from you without your consent. The nonviolation of these rights will not guarantee you protection against natural catastrophes such as floods and earthquakes, but it will protect you against the aggressive activities *of other men.* And rights, after all, have to do with one's relations to other human beings, not with one's relations to physical nature.

Nor were these rights created by government; governments—some governments, obviously not all—*recognize* and *protect* the rights that individuals already have. Governments regularly forbid homicide and theft; and, at a more advanced stage, protect individuals against such things as libel and breach of contract. . . .

The *right to property* is the most misunderstood and unappreciated of human rights, and it is one most constantly violated by governments. "Property" of course does not mean only real estate; it includes anything you can call your own—your clothing, your car, your jewelry, your books and papers.

The right of property is not the right to just *take* it from others, for this would interfere with *their* property rights. It is rather the right to work for it, to obtain non-coercively, the money or services which you can present in voluntary exchange.

The right to property is consistently underplayed by intellectuals today, sometimes even frowned upon, as if we should feel guilty for upholding such a right in view of all the poverty in the world. But the right to property is absolutely basic. It is your hedge against the future. It is your assurance that what you have worked to earn will still be there and be yours, when you wish or need to use it, especially when you are too old to work any longer.

Government has always been the chief enemy of the right to property. The officials of government, wishing to increase their power, and finding an increase of wealth an effective way to bring this about seize some or all of what a person has earned—and since government has a monopoly of physical force within the geographical area of the nation, it has the power (but not the right) to do this. When this happens, of course, every citizen of that country is insecure: he knows that no matter how hard he works the government can swoop down on him at any time and confiscate his earnings and possessions. A person sees his life savings wiped out in a moment when the tax-collectors descend to deprive him of the fruits of his work; or, an industry which has been fifty years in the making and cost millions of dollars and millions of hours of time and planning, is nationalized overnight. Or the government, via inflation, cheapens the currency, so that hard-won dollars aren't worth anything any more. The effect of such actions, of course, is that people lose hope and incentive: if no matter how hard they work the government agents can take it all away, why bother to work at all, for more than today's needs? Depriving people of property is *depriving them of the means by which they live*—the freedom of the individual citizen to do what he wishes with his own life and to plan for the future. Indeed only if property rights are respected is there any point to planning for the future and working to achieve one's goals. *Property rights are what makes long-range planning possible*—the kind of planning which is a distinctively human endeavor, as opposed to the day-by-day activity of the lion who hunts, who depends on the supply of game tomorrow but has no real insurance against starvation in a day or a week. Without the right to property, the right to life itself amounts to little: how can you sustain your life if you cannot plan ahead? and how can you plan ahead if the fruits of your labor can at any moment be confiscated by government? . . .

Indeed, the right to property may well be considered second only to the right to life. Even the freedom of speech is limited by considerations of property. If a person visiting in your home behaves in a way undesired by you, you have every right to evict him; he can scream or agitate elsewhere if he wishes, but not in your home without your consent. Does a person have a right to shout obscenities in a cathedral? No, for the owners of the cathedral (presumably the Church) have not allowed others on their property for that purpose; one may go there to worship or to visit, but not just for any purpose one wishes. Their property right is prior to your or my wish to scream or expectorate or write graffiti on their building.

Or, to take the stock example, does a person have a right to shout "Fire!" falsely in a crowded theater? No, for the theater owner has permitted others to enter and use his property only for a specific purpose, that of seeing a film or watching a stage show. If a person heckles or otherwise disturbs other members of the audience, he can be thrown out. (In fact, he can be removed for any reason the owner chooses, provided his admission money is returned.) And if he shouts "Fire!" when there is no fire, he may be endangering other lives by causing a panic or a stampede. The right to free speech doesn't give one the right to say anything anywhere; it is circumscribed by property rights.

Again, some people seem to assume that the right to free speech (including written speech) means that they can go to a newspaper publisher and demand that he print in his newspaper some propaganda or policy statement for their political party (or other group). But of course they have no right to the use of his newspaper. Ownership of the newspaper is the product of his labor, and he has a right to put into his newspaper whatever he wants, for whatever reason. If he excludes material which many readers would like to have in, perhaps they can find it in another newspaper or persuade him to print it himself (if there are enough of them, they will usually do just that). Perhaps they can even cause his newspaper to fail. But as long as he owns it, he has the right to put in it what he wishes; what would a property right be if he could not do this? They have no right to place their material in his newspaper without his consent—not for free, nor even for a fee. Perhaps other newspapers will include it, or perhaps they can start their own newspaper (in which case they have a right to put in it what they like). If not, an option open to them would be to mimeograph and distribute some handbills.

In exactly the same way, no one has a right to "free television time" unless the owner of the television station consents to give it; it is his station, he has the property rights over it, and it is for him to decide how to dispose of his time. He may not decide wisely, but it is his right to decide as he wishes. If he makes enough unwise decisions, and courts enough unpopularity with the viewing public or the sponsors, he may have to go out of business; but as he is free to make his own decisions, so is he free to face their consequences. (If the government owns the television station, then government officials will make the decisions, and there is no guarantee of *their* superior wisdom. The difference is that when "the government" owns the station, you are forced to help pay for its upkeep through your taxes, whether the bureaucrat in charge decides to give you television time or not.)

"But why have *individual* property rights? Why not have lands and houses owned by everybody together?" Yes, this involves no violation of individual rights, as long as everybody consents to this arrangement and no one is forced to join it. The parties to it may enjoy the communal living enough (at least for a time) to overcome certain inevitable problems: that some will work and some not, that some will achieve more in an hour than others can do in a day, and still they will all get the same income. The few who do the most will in the end consider themselves "workhorses" who do the work of two or three or twelve, while the others will be "freeloaders" on the efforts of these few. But as long as they can get out of the arrangement if they no longer like it, no violation of rights is involved. They got in voluntarily, and they can get out voluntarily; no one has used force.

"But why not say that everybody owns everything? That we *all* own everything there is?"

To some this may have a pleasant ring—but let us try to analyze what it means. If everybody owns everything, then everyone has an equal right to go everywhere, do what he pleases, take what he likes, destroy if he wishes, grow crops or burn them, trample them under, and so on. Consider what it would be like in practice. Suppose you have saved money to buy a house for yourself and your family. Now suppose that the principle, "everybody owns everything," becomes adopted. Well then, why shouldn't every itinerant hippie just come in and take over, sleeping in your beds and eating in your kitchen and not bothering to replace the food supply or clean up the mess? After all, it belongs to all of us, doesn't it? So we have just as much right to it as you, the buyer, have. What happens if we *all* want to sleep in the bedroom and there's not room for all of us? Is it the strongest who wins?

What would be the result? Since no one would be responsible for anything, the property would soon be destroyed, the food used up, the facilities nonfunctional. Beginning as a house that *one* family could use, it would end up as a house that *no one* could use. And if the principle continued to be adopted, no one would build houses any more—or anything else. What for? They would only be occupied and used by others, without remuneration.

Suppose two men are cast ashore on an island, and they agree that each will cultivate half of it. The first man is industrious and grows crops and builds a shelter, making the most of the situation with which he is confronted. The second man, perhaps thinking that the warm days will last forever, lies in the sun, picks coconuts while they last, and does a minimum of work to sustain himself. At the time of harvest, the second man has nothing to harvest, nor does he assist the first man in his labors. But later when there is a dearth of food on the island, the second man comes to the first man and demands half of the harvest as his right. But of course he has no right to the product of the first man's labors. The first man may freely choose to give part of his harvest to the second out of charity rather than see him starve; but that is just what it is—charity, not the second man's right.

How can any of man's rights be violated? Ultimately, only by the use of force. I can make suggestions to you, I can reason with you, entreat you (if you are willing to listen), but I cannot *force* you without violating your rights; only by forcing you do I cut the cord between your free decisions and your actions. Voluntary relations between individuals involve no deprivation of rights, but murder, assault, and rape do, because in doing these things I make you the unwilling victim of my actions. A man's beating his wife involves no violation of rights if she *wanted* to be beaten. *Force is behavior that requires the unwilling involvement of other persons.*

Thus the use of force need not involve the use of physical violence. If I trespass on your property or dump garbage on it, I am violating your property rights, as indeed I am when

I steal your watch; although this is not force in the sense of violence, it *is* a case of your being an unwilling victim of my action. Similarly, if you shout at me so that I cannot be heard when I try to speak, or blow a siren in my ear, or start a factory next door which pollutes my land, you are again violating my rights (to free speech, to property); I am, again, an unwilling victim of your actions. Similarly, if you steal a manuscript of mine and publish it as your own, you are confiscating a piece of my property and thus violating my right to keep what is the product of my labor. Of course, if I give you the manuscript with permission to sign your name to it and keep the proceeds, no violation of rights is involved—any more than if I give you permission to dump garbage on my yard.

According to libertarianism, the role of government should be limited to the retaliatory use of force against those who have initiated its use. It should not enter into any other areas, such as religion, social organization, and economics.

Government

Government is the most dangerous institution known to man. Throughout history it has violated the rights of men more than any individual or group of individuals could do: it has killed people, enslaved them, sent them to forced labor and concentration camps, and regularly robbed and pillaged them of the fruits of their expended labor. Unlike individual criminals, government has the power to arrest and try; unlike individual criminals, it can surround and encompass a person totally, dominating every aspect of one's life, so that one has no recourse from it but to leave the country (and in totalitarian nations even that is prohibited). Government throughout history has a much sorrier record than any individual, even that of a ruthless mass murderer. The signs we see on bumper stickers are chillingly accurate: "Beware: the Government Is Armed and Dangerous."

The only proper role of government, according to libertarians, is that of the protector of the citizen against aggression by other individuals. The government, of course, should never initiate aggression; its proper role is as the embodiment of the *retaliatory* use of force against anyone who initiates its use.

If each individual had constantly to defend himself against possible aggressors, he would have to spend a considerable portion of his life in target practice, karate exercises, and other means of self-defenses, and even so he would probably be helpless against groups of individuals who might try to kill, maim, or rob him. He would have little time for cultivating those qualities which are essential to civilized life, nor would improvements in science, medicine, and the arts be likely to occur. The function of government is to take this responsibility off his shoulders: the government undertakes to defend him against aggressors and to punish them if they attack him. When the government is effective in doing this, it enables the citizen to go about his business unmolested and without constant fear for his life. To do this, of course, government must have physical power—the police, to protect the citizen from aggression within its borders, and the armed forces, to protect him from aggressors outside. Beyond that, the government should not intrude upon his life, either to run his business, or adjust his daily activities, or prescribe his personal moral code.

Government, then, undertakes to be the individual's protector; but historically governments have gone far beyond this function. Since they already have the physical power, they have not hesitated to use it for purposes far beyond that which was entrusted to them in the first place. Undertaking initially to protect its citizens against aggression, it has often itself become an aggressor—a far greater aggressor, indeed, than the criminals against whom it was supposed to protect its citizens. Governments have done what no private citizen can do: arrest and imprison individuals without a trial and send them to slave labor camps. Government must have power in order to be effective—and yet the very means by which alone it can be effective make it vulnerable to the abuse of power, leading to managing the lives of individuals and even inflicting terror upon them.

What then should be the function of gov-ernment? In a word, the *protection of human rights.*

1. *The right to life:* libertarians support all such legislation as will protect human beings against the use of force by others, for example, laws against killing, attempting killing, maiming, beating, and all kinds of physical violence.
2. *The right to liberty:* there should be no laws compromising in any way freedom of speech, of the press, and peaceable assembly. There should be no censorship of ideas, books, films, or of anything else by government.
3. *The right to property:* libertarians support legislation that protects the property rights of individuals against confiscation, nationalization, eminent domain, robbery, trespass, fraud and misrepresentation, patent and copyright, libel and slander.

Someone has violently assaulted you. Should he be legally liable? Of course. He has violated one of your rights. He has knowingly injured you and since he has initiated aggression against you he should be made to expiate.

Someone has negligently left his bicycle on the sidewalk where you trip over it in the dark and injure yourself. He didn't do it intentionally; he didn't mean you any harm. Should he be legally liable? Of course; he has, however unwittingly, injured you, and since the injury is caused by him and you are the victim, he should pay.

Someone across the street is unemployed. Should you be taxed extra to pay for his expenses? Not at all. You have not injured him, you are not responsible for the fact that he is unemployed (unless you are a senator or bureaucrat who agitated for further curtailing of business, which legislation passed, with the result that your neighbor was laid off by the curtailed business). You may voluntarily wish to help him out, or better still, try to get him a job to put him on his feet again; but since you have initiated no aggressive act against him, and neither purposely nor accidentally injured him in any way, you should not be legally penalized for the fact of his unemployment.

(Actually, it is just such penalties that increase unemployment.)

One man, A, works hard for years and finally earns a high salary as a professional man. A second man, B, prefers not to work at all, and to spend wastefully what money he has (through inheritance), so that after a year or two he has nothing left. At the end of this time he has a long siege of illness and lots of medical bills to pay. He demands that the bills be paid by the government—that is, by the taxpayers of the land, including Mr. A.

But of course B has no such right. He chose to lead his life in a certain way—that was his voluntary decision. One consequence of that choice is that he must depend on charity in case of later need. Mr. A chose not to live that way. (And if everyone lived like Mr. B, on whom would he depend in case of later need?) Each has a right to live in the way he pleases, but each must live with the consequences of his own decision (which, as always, fall primarily on himself). He cannot, in time of need, claim A's beneficence as his right.

If a house-guest of yours starts to carve his initials in your walls and break up your furniture, you have a right to evict him, and call the police if he makes trouble. If someone starts to destroy the machinery in a factory, the factory-owner is also entitled to evict him and call the police. In both cases, persons other than the owner are permitted on the property only under certain conditions, at the pleasure of the owner. If those conditions are violated, the owner is entitled to use force to set things straight. The case is exactly the same on a college or university campus: if a campus demonstrator starts breaking windows, occupying the president's office, and setting fire to a dean, the college authorities are certainly within their rights to evict him forcibly; one is permitted on the college grounds only under specific conditions, set by the administration: study, peaceful student activity, even political activity if those in charge choose to permit it. If they do not choose to permit peaceful political activity on campus, they may be unwise, since a campus is after all a place where all sides of every issue should get discussed, and the college that doesn't permit this may soon lose its reputation and its students. All the same, the college official who does not permit it is quite within his rights; the students do not own the campus, nor do the hired trouble-makers imported from elsewhere. In the case of a privately owned college, the owners, or whoever they have delegated to administer it, have the right to make the decisions as to who shall be permitted on the campus and under what conditions. In the case of a state university or college, the ownership problem is more complex: one could say that the "government" owns the campus or that "the people" do since they are the taxpayers who support it; but in either case, the university administration has the delegated task of keeping order, and until they are removed by the state administration or the taxpayers, it is theirs to decide who shall be permitted on campus, and what non-academic activities will be permitted to their students on the premises.

Property rights can be violated by physical trespass, of course, or by anyone entering on your property for any reason without your consent. (If you *do* consent to having your neighbor dump garbage on your yard, there is no violation of your rights.) But the physical trespass of a person is only a special case of violation of property rights. Property rights can be violated by sound-waves, in the form of a loud noise, or the sounds of your neighbor's hi-fi set while you are trying to sleep. Such violations of property rights are of course the subject of action in the courts.

But there is another violation of property rights that has not thus far been honored by the courts; this has to do with the effects of *pollution* of the atmosphere.

> *From the beginnings of modern air pollution, the courts made a conscious decision not to protect, for example, the orchards of farmers from the smoke of nearby factories or locomotives. They said, in effect, to the farmers: yes, your private property is being invaded by this smoke, but we hold that "public policy" is more important than private property, and public policy holds factories and locomotives to be good things. These goods were allowed to override the defense of property rights—with our consequent headlong rush into pollution disaster. The remedy is both "radical" and crystal clear, and it has nothing to do with multi-billion dollar palliative programs at the ex-*

pense of the taxpayers which do not even meet the real issue. The remedy is simply to enjoin anyone from injecting pollutants into the air, and thereby invading the rights of persons and property. Period. The argument that such an injunction prohibition would add to the costs of industrial production is as reprehensible as the pre-Civil War argument that the abolition of slavery would add to the costs of growing cotton, and therefore should not take place. For this means that the polluters are able to impose the high costs of pollution upon those whose property rights they are allowed to invade with impunity.[1]

What about automobiles, the chief polluters of the air? One can hardly sue every automobile owner. But one can sue the manufacturers of automobiles who do not install anti-smog devices on the cars which they distribute—and later (though this is more difficult), owners of individual automobiles if they discard the equipment or do not keep it functional.

The violation of rights does not apply only to air-pollution. If someone with a factory upstream on a river pollutes the river, anyone living downstream from him, finding his water polluted, should be able to sue the owner of the factory. In this way the price of adding the anti-pollutant devices will be the owner's responsibility, and will probably be added to the cost of the products which the factory produces and thus spread around among all consumers, rather than the entire cost being borne by the users of the river in the form of polluted water, with the consequent impossibility of fishing, swimming, and so on. In each case, pollution would be stopped at the source rather than having its ill effects spread around to numerous members of the population.

What about property which you do not work to earn, but which you *inherit* from someone else? Do you have a right to that? You have no right to it until someone decides to give it to you. Consider the man who willed it to you; it was his, he had the right to use and dispose of it as *he* saw fit; and if he decided to give it to you, this is a windfall for you, but it was only the exercise of *his* right. Had the property been seized by the government at the

man's death, or distributed among numerous other people designated by the government, it *would* have been a violation of his rights: for he, who worked to earn and sustain it, would not have been able to dispose of it according to his own judgment. If he doesn't have the right to determine who shall have it, who does?

What about the property status of your intellectual activity, such as inventions you may devise and books you write? These, of course, are your property also; they are the products of your mind; you worked at them, you created them. Prior to that, they did not exist. If you worked five years to write a book, and someone stole it and published it as his own, receiving royalties from its sales, he would have stolen your property just as surely as if he had robbed your home. The same is true if someone used and sold without your permission an invention which was the product of your labor and ingenuity.

The role of government with respect to this issue, at least most governments of the Western world, is a proper one: government protects the products of your labor from the moment they materialize. Copyright law protects your writings from piracy. In the United States, one's writings are protected for a period of twenty-seven years, and another twenty-seven if one applies for renewal of the copyright. In most other countries, they are protected for a period of fifty years after the author's death, permitting both himself and his surviving heirs to reap the fruits of his labor. After that they enter the "public domain"— that is, anyone may reprint them without your or your heirs' permission. Patent law protects your inventions for a limited period, which varies according to the type of invention. In no case are you forced to avail yourself of this protection; you need not apply for patent or copyright coverage if you do not wish to do so. But the protection of your intellectual property is there, in case you wish to use it.

What about the property status of the airwaves? Here the government's position is far more questionable. The government now claims ownership of the airwaves, leasing them to individuals and corporations. The government renews leases or refuses them depending on whether the programs satisfy authorities in the Federal Communications Commission. The official position is that "we all own the airwaves": but since only one party can broadcast on a certain frequency at a certain time without causing chaos, it is simply a fact of reality that "everyone" cannot use it. In fact the government decides who shall use the airwaves and one courts its displeasure only at the price of a revoked license. One can write without government approval, but one cannot use the airwaves without the approval of government.

What policy should have been observed with regard to the airwaves? Much the same as the policy that was followed in the case of the Homestead Act, when the lands of the American West were opening up for settlement. There was a policy of "first come, first served," with the government parcelling out a certain acreage for each individual who wanted to claim the land as his own. There was no charge for the land, but if a man had not used it and built a dwelling during the first two-year period, it was assumed that he was not homesteading and the land was given to the next man in line. The airwaves too could have been given out on a "first come, first served" basis. The first man who used a given frequency would be its owner, and the government would protect him in the use of it against trespassers. If others wanted to use the same frequency, they would have to buy it from the first man, if he was willing to sell, or try to buy another, just as one now does with the land.

Laws may be classified into three types: (1) laws protecting individuals against themselves, such as laws against fornication and other sexual behavior, alcohol, and drugs; (2) laws protecting individuals against aggressions by other individuals, such as laws against murder, robbery, and fraud; (3) laws requiring people to help one another; for example, all laws which rob Peter to pay Paul, such as welfare.

Libertarians reject the first class of laws totally. Behavior which harms no one else is strictly the individual's own affair. Thus, there should be no laws against becoming intoxicated, since whether or not to become intoxicated is the individual's own decision: but there should be laws against driving while intoxicated, since the drunken driver is a threat to every other motorist on the highway (drunken driving falls into type 2). Similarly, there should be no laws against drugs (except the prohibition of sale of drugs to minors) as long as the taking of these drugs poses no threat to anyone else. Drug addiction is a psychological problem to which no present solution exists. Most of the social harm caused by addicts, other than to themselves, is the result of thefts which they perform in order to continue their habit—and then the *legal* crime is the theft, not the addiction. The actual cost of heroin is about ten cents a shot; if it were legalized, the enormous traffic in illegal sale and purchase of it would stop, as well as the accompanying proselytization to get new addicts (to make more money for the pusher) and the thefts performed by addicts who often require eighty dollars a day just to keep up the habit. Addiction would not stop, but the crimes would: it is estimated that 75 percent of the burglaries in New York City today are performed by addicts, and all these crimes could be wiped out at one stroke through the legalization of drugs. (Only when the taking of drugs could be shown to constitute a threat to *others*, should it be prohibited by law. It is only laws protecting people against *themselves* that libertarians oppose.)

Laws should be limited to the second class only: aggression by individuals against other individuals. These are laws whose function is to protect human beings against encroachment by others; and this, as we have seen, is (according to libertarianism) the sole function of government.

Libertarians also reject the third class of laws totally: no one should be forced by law to help others, not even to tell them the time of day if requested, and certainly not to give them a portion of one's weekly paycheck. Governments, in the guise of humanitarianism, have given to some by taking from others (charging a "handling fee" in the process, which, because of the government's waste and inefficiency, sometimes is several hundred percent). And in so doing they have decreased incentive, violated the rights of individuals and lowered the standard of living of almost everyone.

All such laws constitute what libertarians call *moral cannibalism*. A cannibal in the physical sense is a person who lives off the flesh of other human beings. A *moral* cannibal is one who believes he has a right to live off the "spirit" of other human beings—who believes that he has a moral claim on the productive capacity, time, and effort expended by others.

It has become fashionable to claim virtually everything that one needs or desires as one's *right*. Thus, many people claim that they have a right to a job, the right to free medical care, to free food and clothing, to a decent home, and so on. Now if one asks, apart from any specific context, whether it would be desirable if everyone had these things, one might well say yes. But there is a gimmick attached to each of them: *At whose expense?* Jobs, medical care, education, and so on, don't grow on trees. These are goods and services *produced only by men*. Who then is to provide them, and under what conditions?

If you have a right to a job, who is to supply it? Must an employer supply it even if he doesn't want to hire you? What if you are unemployable, or incurably lazy? (If you say "the government must supply it," does that mean that a job must be created for you which no employer needs done, and that you must be kept in it regardless of how much or little you work?) If the employer is forced to supply it at his expense even if he doesn't need you, then isn't *he* being enslaved to that extent? What ever happened to *his* right to conduct his life and his affairs in accordance with his choices?

If you have a right to free medical care, then, since medical care doesn't exist in nature as wild apples do, some people will have to supply it to you for free: that is, they will have to spend their time and money and energy taking care of you whether they want to or not. What ever happened to *their* right to conduct their lives as they see fit? Or do you have a right to violate theirs? Can there be a right to violate rights?

All those who demand this or that as a "free service" are consciously or unconsciously evading the fact that there is in reality no such thing as free services. All man-made goods and services are the result of human expenditure of time and effort. There is no such thing as "something for nothing" in this world. If you demand something free, you are demanding that other men give their time and effort to you without compensation. If they voluntarily choose to do this, there is no problem; but if you demand that they be *forced* to do it, you are interfering with their right not to do it if they so choose. "Swimming in this pool ought to be free!" says the indignant passerby. What he means is that others should build a pool, others should provide the material, and still others should run it and keep it in functioning order, so that *he* can use it without fee. But what right has he to the expenditure of *their* time and effort? To expect something "for free" is to expect it *to be paid for by others* whether they choose to or not.

Many questions, particularly about economic matters, will be generated by the libertarian account of human rights and the role of government. Should government have no role in assisting the needy, in providing social security, in legislating minimum wages, in fixing prices and putting a ceiling on rents, in curbing monopolies, in erecting tariffs, in guaranteeing jobs, in managing the money supply? To these and all similar questions the libertarian answers with an unequivocal no.

"But then you'd let people go hungry!" comes the rejoinder. This, the libertarian insists, is precisely what would not happen; with the restrictions removed, the economy would flourish as never before. With the controls taken off business, existing enterprises would expand and new ones would spring into existence satisfying more and more consumer needs; millions more people would be gainfully employed instead of subsisting on welfare, and all kinds of research and production, released from the stranglehold of government, would proliferate, fulfilling man's needs and desires as never before. It has always been so whenever government has permitted men to be free traders on a free market. But *why* this is so, and how the free market is the best solution to all problems relating to the material aspect of man's life, is another and far longer story.

Note

1. Murray Rothbard, "The Great Ecology Issue," *The Individualist*, 2, no. 2 (Feb. 1970), p. 5.

Liberty and Patterns

Robert Nozick

Robert Nozick endorses a libertarian ideal of a just society whose requirements can best be captured by the slogan "from each as he chooses, to each as he is chosen." For Nozick, the holdings of persons in society are just if and only if those persons are "entitled" to them by certain principles that specify how those holdings came about. There is a principle of original appropriation and a principle of exchange and, for situations in which such principles have been violated, a principle of rectification. In Nozick's view, what distinguishes his "entitlement principles" from other principles of justice is that the entitlement principles are-"historical process principles" rather than "end-state principles"; that is, they specify justice in terms of how holdings came about rather than in terms of how holdings are distributed. By specifying justice in this way, Nozick believes, his entitlement principles avoid the continual interference with people's lives required by end-state conceptions of justice.

The Entitlement Theory

The subject of justice in holdings consists of three major topics. The first is the *original acquisition of holdings,* the appropriation of unheld things. This includes the issues of how unheld things may come to be held, the process, or processes, by which unheld things may come to be held, the things that may come to be held by these processes, the extent of what comes to be held by a particular process, and so on. We shall refer to the complicated truth about this topic, which we shall not formulate here, as the principle of justice in acquisition. The second topic concerns the *transfer of holdings* from one person to another. By what processes may a person transfer holdings to another? How may a person acquire a holding from another who holds it? Under this topic come general descriptions of voluntary exchange, and gift and (on the other hand) fraud, as well as reference to particular conventional details fixed upon in a given society. The complicated truth about this subject (with placeholders for conventional details) we shall

call the principle of justice in transfer. (And we shall suppose it also includes principles governing how a person may divest himself of a holding, passing it into an unheld state.)

If the world were wholly just, the following inductive definition would exhaustively cover the subject of justice in holdings.

1. A person who acquires a holding in accordance with the principle of justice in acquisition is entitled to that holding.

2. A person who acquires a holding in accordance with the principle of justice in transfer, from someone else entitled to the holding, is entitled to the holding.

3. No one is entitled to a holding except by (repeated) applications of 1 and 2.

The complete principle of distributive justice would say simply that a distribution is just if everyone is entitled to the holdings they possess under the distribution.

A distribution is just if it arises from another just distribution by legitimate means. The legitimate means of moving from one distribution to another are specified by the principle of justice in transfer. The legitimate first "moves" are specified by the principle of justice in acquisition.[1] Whatever arises from a just situation by just steps is itself just. The means of change specified by the principle of justice in transfer preserve justice. As correct rules of inference are truth-preserving, and any conclusion deduced via repeated application of such rules from only true premises is itself true, so the means of transition from one situation to another specified by the principle of justice in transfer are justice-preserving, and any situation actually arising from repeated transitions in accordance with the principle from a just situation is itself just. The parallel between justice-preserving transformations and truth-preserving transformations illuminates where it fails as well as where it holds. That a conclusion could have been deduced by truth-preserving means from premises that are true suffices to show its truth. That from a just situation a situation *could* have arisen via justice-preserving means does *not* suffice to show its justice. The fact that a thief's victims voluntarily *could* have presented him with gifts does not entitle the thief to his ill-gotten gains. Justice in holdings is historical; it depends upon what actually has happened. We shall return to this point later.

Not all actual situations are generated in accordance with the two principles of justice in holdings: the principle of justice in acquisition and the principle of justice in transfer. Some people steal from others, or defraud them, or enslave them, seizing their product and preventing them from living as they choose, or forcibly exclude others from competing in exchanges. None of these are permissible modes of transition from one situation to another. And some persons acquire holdings by means not sanctioned by the principle of justice in acquisition. The existence of past injustice (previous violations of the first two principles of justice in holdings) raises the third major topic under justice in holdings: the rectification of injustice in holdings. If past injustice has shaped present holdings in various ways, some identifiable and some not, what now, if anything, ought to be done to rectify these injustices? What obligations do the performers of injustice have toward those whose position is worse than it would have been had the injustice not been done? Or, than it would have been had compensation been paid promptly? How, if at all, do things change if the beneficiaries and those made worse off are not the direct parties in the act of injustice, but, for example, their descendants? Is an injustice done to someone whose holding was itself based upon an unrectified injustice? How far back must one go in wiping clean the historical slate of injustices? What may victims of injustice permissibly do in order to rectify the injustices being done to them, including the many injustices done by persons acting through their government? I do not know of a thorough or theoretically sophisticated treatment of such issues. Idealizing greatly, let us suppose theoretical investigation will produce a principle of rectification. This principle uses historical information about previous situations and injustices done in them (as defined by the first two principles of justice and rights against interference), and information about the actual course of events that flowed from these injustices, until the present, and it yields a description (or descriptions) of holdings in the society. The principle of rectification presumably will make use of its best estimate of subjunctive information about what would have occurred (or a probability distribution over what might have occurred, using the expected value) if the injustice had not taken place. If the actual description of holdings turns out not to be one of the descriptions yielded by the principle, then one of the descriptions yielded must be realized.[2]

The general outlines of the theory of justice in holdings are that the holdings of a person are just if he is entitled to them by the principles of justice in acquisition and transfer, or by the principle of rectification of injustice (as specified by the first two principles). If each person's holdings are just, then the total set (distribution) of holdings is just. To turn these general outlines into a specific theory we would have to specify the details of each of the three principles of justice in holdings: the principle of acquisition of holdings, the principle of transfer of holdings, and the principle of rectification of violations of the first two principles. I shall not attempt that task here.

Historical Principles and End-Result Principles

The general outlines of the entitlement theory illuminate the nature and defects of other conceptions of distributive justice. The entitlement theory of justice in distribution is *historical;* whether a distribution is just depends upon how it came about. In contrast, *current time-slice principles* of justice hold that the justice of a distribution is determined by how things are distributed (who has what) as judged by some *structural* principle(s) of just distribution. A utilitarian who judges between any two distributions by seeing which has the greater sum of utility and, if the sums tie, applies some fixed equality criterion to choose the more equal distribution, would hold a current time-slice principle of justice. As would someone who had a fixed schedule of trade-offs between the sum of happiness and equality. According to a current time-slice principle, all that needs to be looked at, in judging the justice of a distribution, is who ends up with what; in comparing any two distributions one need look only at the matrix presenting the distributions. No further information need be fed into a principle of justice. It is a consequence of such principles of justice that any two structurally identical distributions are equally just. (Two distributions are structurally identical if they present the same profile, but perhaps have different persons occupying the particular slots. My having ten and your having five, and my having five and your having ten are structurally identical distributions.) Welfare economics is the theory of current time-slice principles of justice. The subject is conceived as operating on matrices representing only current information about distribution. This, as well as some of the usual conditions (for example, the choice of distribution is invariant under relabeling of columns), guarantees that welfare economics will be a current time-slice theory, with all of its inadequacies.

Most persons do not accept current time-slice principles as constituting the whole story about distributive shares. They think it relevant in assessing the justice of a situation to consider not only the distribution it embodies, but also how that distribution came about. If some persons are in prison for murder or war crimes, we do not say that to assess the justice of the distribution in the society we must look only at what this person has, and that person has, and that person has, . . . at the current time. We think it relevant to ask whether someone did something so that he *deserved* to be punished, deserved to have a lower share. Most will agree to the relevance of further information with regard to punishments and penalties. Consider also desired things. One traditional socialist view is that workers are entitled to the product and full fruits of their labor; they have earned it; a distribution is unjust if it does not give the workers what they are entitled to. Such entitlements are based upon some past history. No socialist holding this view would find it comforting to be told that because the actual distribution *A* happens to coincide structurally with the one he desires *D, A* therefore is no less just than *D;* it differs only in that the "parasitic" owners of capital receive under *A* what the workers are entitled to under *D,* and the workers receive under *A* what the owners are entitled to under *D,* namely very little. This socialist rightly, in my view, holds onto the notions of earning, producing, entitlement, desert, and so forth, and he rejects current time-slice principles that look only to the structure of the resulting set of holdings. (The set of holdings resulting from what? Isn't it implausible that how holdings are produced and come to exist has no effect at all on who should hold what?) His mistake lies in his view of what entitlements arise out of what sorts of productive processes.

We construe the position we discuss too narrowly by speaking of *current* time-slice principles. Nothing is changed if structural principles operate upon a time sequence of current time-slice profiles and, for example, give someone more now to counterbalance the less he has had earlier. A utilitarian or an egalitarian or any mixture of the two over time will inherit the difficulties of his more myopic comrades. He is not helped by the fact that *some* of the information others consider relevant in assessing a distribution is reflected, unrecoverably, in past matrices. Henceforth, we shall refer to such unhistorical principles of distributive justice, including the current time-slice principles, as *end-result principles* or *end-state principles.*

In contrast to end-result principles of justice, *historical principles* of justice hold that past circumstances or actions of people can create differential entitlements or differential deserts to things. An injustice can be worked by moving from one distribution to another structurally identical one, for the second, in profile the same, may violate people's entitlements or deserts; it may not fit the actual history.

Patterning

The entitlement principles of justice in holdings that we have sketched are historical principles of justice. To better understand their precise character, we shall distinguish them from another subclass of the historical principles. Consider, as an example, the principle of distribution according to moral merit. This principle requires that total distributive shares vary directly with moral merit; no person should have a greater share than anyone whose moral merit is greater. (If moral merit could be not merely ordered but measured on an interval or ratio scale, stronger principles could be formulated.) Or consider the principle that results by substituting "usefulness to society" for "moral merit" in the previous principle. Or instead of "distribute according to moral merit," or "distribute according to usefulness to society," we might consider "distribute according to the weighted sum of moral merit, usefulness to society, and need," with the weights of the different dimensions equal. Let us call a principle of distribution patterned if it specifies that a distribution is to vary along with some natural dimensions, weighted sum of natural dimensions, or lexicographic ordering of natural dimensions. And let us say a distribution is patterned if it accords with some patterned principle. (I speak of natural dimensions, admittedly without a general criterion for them, because for any set of holdings some artificial dimensions can be gimmicked up to vary along with the distribution of the set.) The principle of distribution in accordance with moral merit is a patterned historical principle, which specifies a patterned distribution. "Distribute according to I.Q." is a patterned principle that looks to information not contained in distributional matrices. It is not historical, however, in that it does not look to any past actions creating differential entitlements to evaluate a distribution; it requires only distributional matrices whose columns are labeled by I.Q.

scores. The distribution in a society, however, may be composed of such simple patterned distributions, without itself being simply patterned. Different sectors may operate different patterns, or some combination of patterns may operate in different proportions across a society. A distribution composed in this manner, from a small number of patterned distributions, we also shall term "patterned." And we extend the use of "pattern" to include the overall designs put forth by combinations of end-state principles.

Almost every suggested principle of distributive justice is patterned: to each according to his moral merit, or needs, or marginal product, or how hard he tries, or the weighted sum of the foregoing, and so on. The principle of entitlement we have sketched is *not* patterned.[3] There is no one natural dimension or weighted sum or combination of a small number of natural dimensions that yields the distributions generated in accordance with the principle of entitlement. The set of holdings that results when some persons receive their marginal products, others win at gambling, others receive a share of their mate's income, others receive gifts from foundations, others receive interest on loans, others receive gifts from admirers, others receive returns on investment, others make for themselves much of what they have, others find things, and so on, will not be patterned. Heavy strands of patterns will run through it; significant portions of the variance in holdings will be accounted for by pattern-variables. If most people most of the time choose to transfer some of their entitlements to others only in exchange for something from them, then a large part of what many people hold will vary with what they held that others wanted. More details are provided by the theory of marginal productivity. But gifts to relatives, charitable donations, bequests to children, and the like, are not best conceived, in the first instance, in this manner. Ignoring the strands of pattern, let us suppose for the moment that a distribution actually arrived at by the operation of the principle of entitlement is random with respect to any pattern. Though the resulting set of holdings will be unpatterned, it will not be incomprehensible, for it can be seen as arising from the operation of a small number of principles. These principles specify how an initial distribution may arise (the principle of acquisition of holdings) and how distributions may be transformed into others (the principle of transfer of holdings). The process whereby the set of holdings is generated will be intelligible, though the set of holdings itself that results from this process will be unpatterned.

The writings of F. A. Hayek focus less than is usually done upon what patterning distributive justice requires. Hayek argues that we cannot know enough about each person's situation to distribute to each according to his moral merit (but would justice demand we do so if we did have this knowledge?); and he goes on to say, "our objection is against all attempts to impress upon society a deliberately chosen pattern of distribution, whether it be an order of equality or of inequality."[4] However, Hayek concludes that in a free society there will be distribution in accordance with value rather than moral merit; that is, in accordance with the perceived value of a person's actions and services to others. Despite his rejection of a patterned conception of distributive justice, Hayek himself suggests a pattern he thinks justifiable: distribution in accordance with the perceived benefits given to others, leaving room for the complaint that a free society does not realize exactly this pattern. Stating this patterned strand of a free capitalist society more precisely, we get "To each according to how much he benefits others who have the resources for benefiting those who benefit them." This will seem arbitrary unless some acceptable initial set of holdings is specified, or unless it is held that the operation of the system over time washes out any significant effects from the initial set of holdings. As an example of the latter, if almost anyone would have bought a car from Henry Ford, the supposition that it was an arbitrary matter who held the money then (and so bought) would not place Henry Ford's earnings under a cloud. In any event, *his* coming to hold it is not arbitrary. Distribution according to benefits to others *is* a major patterned strand in a free capitalist society, as Hayek correctly points out, but it is only a strand and does not constitute the whole pattern of a system of entitlements (namely, inheritance, gifts for arbitrary reasons, charity, and so on) or a standard that one should insist society fit. Will people tolerate for long a system yielding distributions that

they believe are unpatterned?[5] No doubt people will not long accept a distribution they believe is *unjust*. People want their society to be and to look just. But must the look of justice reside in a resulting pattern rather than in the underlying generating principles? We are in no position to conclude that the inhabitants of a society embodying an entitlement conception of justice in holdings will find it unacceptable. Still, it must be granted that were people's reasons for transferring some of their holdings to others always irrational or arbitrary, we would find this disturbing. (Suppose people always determined what holdings they would transfer, and to whom, by using a random device.) We feel more comfortable upholding the justice of an entitlement system if most of the transfers under it are done for reasons. This does not mean necessarily that all deserve what holdings they receive. It means only that there is a purpose or point to someone's transferring a holding to one person rather than to another; that usually we can see what the transferrer thinks he's gaining, what cause he thinks he's serving, what goals he thinks he's helping to achieve, and so forth. Since in a capitalist society people often transfer holdings to others in accordance with how much they perceive these others benefiting them, the fabric constituted by the individual transactions and transfers is largely reasonable and intelligible.[6] (Gifts to loved ones, bequests to children, charity to the needy also are nonarbitrary components of the fabric.) In stressing the large strand of distribution in accordance with benefit to others, Hayek shows the point of many transfers, and so shows that the system of transfer of entitlements is not just spinning its gears aimlessly. The system of entitlements is defensible when constituted by the individual aims of individual transactions. No overarching aim is needed, no distributional pattern is required.

To think that the task of a theory of distributive justice is to fill in the blank in "to each according to his _____" is to be predisposed to search for a pattern; and the separate treatment of "from each according to his _____" treats production and distribution as two separate and independent issues. On an entitlement view these are *not* two separate questions. Whoever makes something, having bought or contracted for all other held resources used in the process (transferring some of his holdings for these cooperating factors), is entitled to it. The situation is *not* one of something's getting made, and there being an open question of who is to get it. Things come into the world already attached to people having entitlements over them. From the point of view of the historical entitlement conception of justice in holdings, those who start afresh to complete "to each according to his _____" treat objects as if they appeared from nowhere, out of nothing. A complete theory of justice might cover this limit case as well; perhaps here is a use for the usual conceptions of distributive justice.[7]

So entrenched are maxims of the usual form that perhaps we should present the entitlement conception as a competitor. Ignoring acquisition and rectification, we might say:

> From each according to what he chooses to do, to each according to what he makes for himself (perhaps with the contracted aid of others) and what others choose to do for him and choose to give him of what they've been given previously (under this maxim) and haven't yet expended or transferred.

This, the discerning reader will have noticed, has its defects as a slogan. So as a summary and great simplification (and not as a maxim with any independent meaning) we have:

> *From each as they choose, to each as they are chosen.*

How Liberty Upsets Patterns

It is not clear how those holding alternative conceptions of distributive justice can reject the entitlement conception of justice in holdings. For suppose a distribution favored by one of these nonentitlement conceptions is realized. Let us suppose it is your favorite one and let us call this distribution D_1; perhaps everyone has an equal share, perhaps shares vary in accordance with some dimension you

treasure. Now suppose that Wilt Chamberlain is greatly in demand by basketball teams, being a great gate attraction. (Also suppose contracts run only for a year, with players being free agents.) He signs the following sort of contract with a team: In each home game, twenty-five cents from the price of each ticket of admission goes to him. (We ignore the question of whether he is "gouging" the owners, letting them look out for themselves.) The season starts, and people cheerfully attend his team's games; they buy their tickets, each time dropping a separate twenty-five cents of their admission price into a special box with Chamberlain's name on it. They are excited about seeing him play; it is worth the total admission price to them. Let us suppose that in one season one million persons attend his home games, and Wilt Chamberlain winds up with $250,000, a much larger sum than the average income and larger even than anyone else has. Is he entitled to this income? Is this new distribution D_2, unjust? If so, why? There is *no* question about whether each of the people was entitled to the control over the resources they held in D_1, because that was the distribution (your favorite) that (for the purposes of argument) we assumed was acceptable. Each of these persons *chose* to give twenty-five cents of their money to Chamberlain. They could have spent it on going to the movies, or on candy bars, or on copies of *Dissent* magazine, or of *Monthly Review*. But they all, at least one million of them, converged on giving it to Wilt Chamberlain in exchange for watching him play basketball. If D_1 was a just distribution, and people voluntarily moved from it to D_2 transferring parts of their shares they were given under D_1 (what was it for if not to do something with?), isn't D_2 also just? If people were entitled to dispose of the resources to which they were entitled (under D_1), didn't this include their being entitled to give it to, or exchange it with, Wilt Chamberlain? Can anyone else complain on grounds of justice? Each other person already has his legitimate share under D_1. Under D_1, there is nothing that anyone has that anyone else has a claim of justice against. After someone transfers something to Wilt Chamberlain, third parties *still* have their legitimate shares; *their* shares are not changed. By what process could such a transfer among two persons give rise to a legitimate claim of distributive justice on a portion of what was transferred, by a third party who had no claim of justice on any holding of the others *before* the transfer?[8] To cut off objections irrelevant here, we might imagine the exchanges occurring in a socialist society, after hours: After playing whatever basketball he does in his daily work, or doing whatever other daily work he does, Wilt Chamberlain decides to put in *overtime* to earn additional money. (First his work quota is set; he works time over that.) Or imagine it is a skilled juggler people like to see, who puts on shows after hours.

Why might someone work overtime in a society in which it is assumed their needs are satisfied? Perhaps because they care about things other than needs. I like to write in books that I read, and to have easy access to books for browsing at odd hours. It would be very pleasant and convenient to have the resources of Widener Library in my back yard. No society, I assume, will provide such resources close to each person who would like them as part of his regular allotment (under D_1). Thus, persons either must do without some extra things that they want, or be allowed to do something extra to get some of these things. On what basis could the inequalities that would eventuate be forbidden? Notice also that small factories would spring up in a socialist society, unless forbidden. I melt down some of my personal possessions (under D_1) and build a machine out of the material. I offer you, and others, a philosophy lecture once a week in exchange for your cranking the handle on my machine, whose products I exchange for yet other things, and so on. (The raw materials used by the machine are given to me by others who possess them under D_1, in exchange for hearing lectures.) Each person might participate to gain things over and above their allotment under D_1. Some persons even might want to leave their job in socialist industry and work full time in this private sector. [In any case] I wish merely to note how private property even in means of production would occur in a socialist society that did not forbid people to use as they wished some of the resources they are given under the socialist distribution D_1.[9] The social-

ist society would have to forbid capitalist acts between consenting adults.

The general point illustrated by the Wilt Chamberlain example and the example of the entrepreneur in a socialist society is that no end-state principle or distributional patterned principle of justice can be continuously realized without continuous interference with people's lives. Any favored pattern would be transformed into one unfavored by the principle, by people choosing to act in various ways; for example, by people exchanging goods and services with other people, or giving things to other people, things the transferrers are entitled to under the favored distributional pattern. To maintain a pattern one must either continually interfere to stop people from transferring resources as they wish to, or continually (or periodically) interfere to take from some persons resources that others for some reason chose to transfer to them. (But if some time limit is to be set on how long people may keep resources others voluntarily transfer to them, why let them keep these resources for *any* period of time? Why not have immediate confiscation?) It might be objected that all persons voluntarily will choose to refrain from actions which would upset the pattern. This presupposes unrealistically (1) that all will most want to maintain the pattern (are those who don't, to be "reeducated" or forced to undergo "self-criticism"?), (2) that each can gather enough information about his own actions and the ongoing activities of others to discover which of his actions will upset the pattern, and (3) that diverse and far-flung persons can coordinate their actions to dovetail into the pattern. Compare the manner in which the market is neutral among persons' desires, as it reflects and transmits widely scattered information via prices, and coordinates persons' activities.

It puts things perhaps a bit too strongly to say that every patterned (or end-state) principle is liable to be thwarted by the voluntary actions of the individual parties transferring some of their shares they receive under the principle. For perhaps some *very* weak patterns are not so thwarted.[10] Any distributional pattern with any egalitarian component is overturnable by the voluntary actions of individual persons over time; as is every patterned condition with sufficient content so as actually to have been proposed as presenting the central core of distributive justice. Still, given the possibility that some weak conditions or patterns may not be unstable in this way, it would be better to formulate an explicit description of the kind of interesting and contentful patterns under discussion, and to prove a theorem about their instability. Since the weaker the patterning, the more likely it is that the entitlement system itself satisfies it, a plausible conjecture is that any patterning either is unstable or is satisfied by the entitlement system. . . .

Notes

---

1. Applications of the principle of justice in acquisition may also occur as part of the move from one distribution to another. You may find an unheld thing now and appropriate it. Acquisitions also are to be understood as included when, to simplify, I speak only of transitions by transfers.

2. If the principle of rectification of violations of the first two principles yields more than one description of holdings, then some choice must be made as to which of these is to be realized. Perhaps the sort of considerations about distributive justice and equality that I argue against play a legitimate role in *this* subsidiary choice. Similarly, there may be room for such considerations in deciding which otherwise arbitrary features a statute will embody, when such features are unavoidable because other considerations do not specify a precise line; yet a line must be drawn.

3. One might try to squeeze a patterned conception of distributive justice into the framework of the entitlement conception, by formulating a gimmicky obligatory "principle of transfer" that would lead to the pattern. For example, the principle that if one has more than the mean income one must transfer everything one holds above the mean to persons below the mean so as to bring them up to (but not over) the mean. We can formulate a criterion for a "principle of transfer" to rule out such obligatory transfers, or we can say that no correct principle of transfer, no principle of transfer in a free society will be

like this. The former is probably the better course, though the latter also is true.

Alternatively, one might think to make the entitlement conception instantiate a pattern, by using matrix entries that express the relative strength of a person's entitlements as measured by some real-valued function. But even if the limitation to natural dimensions failed to exclude this function, the resulting edifice would *not* capture our system of entitlements to *particular* things.

4. F. A. Hayek, *The Constitution of Liberty* (Chicago: University of Chicago Press, 1960), p. 87.

5. This question does not imply that they will tolerate any and every patterned distribution. In discussing Hayek's views, Irving Kristol has recently speculated that people will not long tolerate a system that yields distributions patterned in accordance with value rather than merit. ("'When Virtue Loses All Her Loveliness'—Some Reflections on Capitalism and 'The Free Society,'" *The Public Interest,* Fall 1970, pp. 3–15.) Kristol, following some remarks of Hayek, equates the merit system with justice. Since some case can be made for the external standard of distribution in accordance with benefit to others, we ask about a weaker (and therefore more plausible) hypothesis.

6. We certainly benefit because great economic incentives operate to get others to spend much time and energy to figure out how to serve us by providing things we will want to pay for. It is not mere paradox mongering to wonder whether capitalism should be criticized for most rewarding, and hence encouraging, not individualists like Thoreau who go about their own lives, but people who are occupied with serving others and winning them as customers. But to defend capitalism one need not think businessmen are the finest human types. (I do not mean to join here the general maligning of businessmen, either.) Those who think the finest should acquire the most can try to convince their fellows to transfer resources in accordance with *that* principle.

7. Varying situations continuously from that limit situation to our own would force us to make explicit the underlying rationale of entitlements and to consider whether entitlement considerations lexicographically precede the considerations of the usual theories of distributive

justice, so that the *slightest* strand of entitlement outweighs the considerations of the usual theories of distributive justice.

8. Might not a transfer have instrumental effects on a third party, changing his feasible options? (But what if the two parties to the transfer independently had used their holdings in this fashion?) I discuss this question below, but note here that this question concedes the point for distributions of ultimate intrinsic noninstrumental goods (pure utility experiences, so to speak) that are transferable. It also might be objected that the transfer might make a third party more envious because it worsens his position relative to someone else. I find it incomprehensible how this can be thought to involve a claim of justice. . . .

Here and elsewhere in this chapter, a theory which incorporates elements of pure procedural justice might find what I say acceptable, *if* kept in its proper place; that is, if background institutions exist to ensure the satisfaction of certain conditions on distributive shares. But if these institutions are not themselves the sum or invisible-hand result of people's voluntary (nonaggressive) actions, the constraints they impose require justification. At no point does *our* argument assume any background institutions more extensive than those of the minimal nightwatchman state, a state limited to protecting persons against murder, assault, theft, fraud, and so forth.

9. See the selection from John Henry MacKay's novel, *The Anarchists,* reprinted in Leonard Krimmerman and Lewis Perry, eds., *Patterns of Anarchy* (New York: Doubleday Anchor Books, 1966), in which an individualist anarchist presses upon a communist anarchist the following question: "Would you, in the system of society which you call 'free Communism' prevent individuals from exchanging their labor among themselves by means of their own medium of exchange? And further: Would you prevent them from occupying land for the purpose of personal use?" The novel continues: "[the] question was not to be escaped. If he answered 'Yes!' he admitted that society had the right of control over the individual and threw overboard the autonomy of the individual which he had always zealously defended; if, on the other hand, he answered 'No!' he admitted the right of private property which he had just denied so emphatically. . . . Then he answered, 'In Anarchy any number of men must have the right of forming a voluntary association, and so realizing their ideas in practice. Nor can I understand how anyone could justly be driven from the land and house which he uses and occupies . . . every serious man must declare himself: for Socialism, and thereby for force and against liberty, or for Anarchism, and thereby for liberty and against force.' " In contrast, we find Noam Chomsky writing, "Any consistent anarchist must oppose private ownership of the means of production," "the consistent anarchist then . . . will be a socialist . . . of a particular sort." Introduction to Daniel Guerin, *Anarchism: From Theory to Practice* (New York: Monthly Review Press, 1970), pages xiii, xv.

10. Is the patterned principle stable that requires merely that a distribution be Pareto-optimal? One person might give another a gift or bequest that the second could exchange with a third to their mutual benefit. Before the second makes this exchange there is not Pareto-optimality. Is a stable pattern presented by a principle choosing that among the Pareto-optimal positions that satisfies some further condition *C*? It may seem that there cannot be a counterexample, for won't any voluntary exchange made away from a situation show that the first situation wasn't Pareto-optimal? (Ignore the implausibility of this last claim for the case of bequests.) But principles are to be satisfied over time, during which new possibilities arise. A distribution that at one time satisfies the criterion of Pareto-optimality might not do so when some new possibilities arise (Wilt Chamberlain grows up and starts playing basketball); and though people's activities will tend to move then to a new Pareto-optimal position, *this* new one need not satisfy the contentful condition *C*. Continual interference will be needed to insure the continual satisfaction of *C*. (The theoretical possibility of a pattern's being maintained by some invisible-hand process that brings it back to an equilibrium that fits the pattern when deviations occur should be investigated.

A Social Contract Perspective

John Rawls

John Rawls believes that principles of justice are those on which free and rational persons would agree if they were in an original position of equality. This original position is characterized as a hypothetical position in which persons are behind an imaginary veil of ignorance with respect to most particular facts about themselves. Rawls claims that persons in his original position would choose principles requiring equal political liberty and opportunity and the highest possible economic minimum because they would be committed to the maximin rule, which requires maximizing the minimum payoff.

My aim is to present a conception of justice which generalizes and carries to a higher level of abstraction the familiar theory of the social contract as found, say, in Locke, Rousseau, and Kant.[1] In order to do this we are not to think of the original contract as one to enter a particular society or to set up a particular form of government. Rather, the guiding idea is that the principles of justice for the basic structure of society are the object of the original agreement. They are the principles that free and rational persons concerned to further their own interests would accept in an initial position of equality as defining the fundamental terms of their association. These principles are to regulate all further agreements; they specify the kinds of social cooperation that can be entered into and the forms of government that can be established. This way of regarding the principles of justice I shall call justice as fairness.

Thus we are to imagine that those who engage in social cooperation choose together, in one joint act, the principles which are to assign basic rights and duties and to determine the division of social benefits. Men are to decide in advance how they are to regulate their claims against one another and what is to be the foundation charter of their society. Just as each person must decide by rational reflection what constitutes his good—that is, the system of ends which it is rational for him to pursue so a group of persons must decide once and for all what is to count among them as just and unjust. The choice which rational men would make in this hypothetical situation of equal liberty, assuming for the present that this choice problem has a solution, determines the principles of justice.

In justice as fairness the original position of equality corresponds to the state of nature in the traditional theory of the social contract. This original position is not, of course, thought of as an actual historical state of affairs, much less as a primitive condition of culture. It is understood as a purely hypothetical situation characterized so as to lead to a certain conception of justice.[2] Among the essential features of this situation is that no one knows his place in society, his class position or social status, nor does any one know his fortune in the distribution of natural assets and abilities, his intelligence, strength, and the like. I shall even assume that the parties do not know their conceptions of the good or their special psychological propensities. The principles of justice are chosen behind a veil of ignorance. This ensures that no one is advantaged or disadvantaged in the choice of principles by the outcome of natural chance or the contingency of social circumstances. Since all are similarly situated and no one is able to design principles to favor his particular condition, the principles of justice are the result of a fair agreement or bargain. For given the circumstances of the original position, the sym-

Abridged from *A Theory of Justice* (1971), pp. 11–22, 60–65, 150–156, 302–303. Excerpted by permission of the publishers from *A Theory of Justice* by John Rawls. Cambridge, Mass.: Harvard University Press. Copyright © 1971 by the President and Fellows of Harvard College.

metry of everyone's relations to each other, this initial situation is fair between individuals as moral persons; that is, as rational beings with their own ends and capable, I shall assume, of a sense of justice. The original position is, one might say, the appropriate initial status quo, and thus the fundamental agreements reached in it are fair. This explains the propriety of the name "justice as fairness"; it conveys the idea that the principles of justice are agreed to in an initial situation that is fair. The name does not mean that the concepts of justice and fairness are the same, any more than the phrase "poetry as metaphor" means that the concepts of poetry and metaphor are the same.

Justice as fairness begins, as I have said, with one of the most general of all choices which persons might make together, namely, with the choice of the first principles of a conception of justice which is to regulate all subsequent criticism and reform of institutions. Then, having chosen a conception of justice, we can suppose that they are to choose a constitution and a legislature to enact laws, and so on, all in accordance with the principles of justice initially agreed upon. Our social situation is just if it is such that by this sequence of hypothetical agreements we would have contracted into the general system of rules which defines it. Moreover, assuming that the original position does determine a set of principles (that is, that a particular conception of justice would be chosen), it will then be true that whenever social institutions satisfy these principles those engaged in them can say to one another that they are cooperating on terms to which they would agree if they were free and equal persons whose relations with respect to one another were fair. They could all view their arrangements as meeting the stipulations which they would acknowledge in an initial situation that embodies widely accepted and reasonable constraints on the choice of principles. The general recognition of this fact would provide the basis for a public acceptance of the corresponding principles of justice. No society can, of course, be a scheme of cooperation which men enter voluntarily in a literal sense; each person finds himself placed at birth in some particular position in some particular society, and the nature of this position materially affects his life prospects. Yet a society satisfying the principles of justice as fairness comes as close as a society can to being a voluntary scheme, for it meets the principles which free and equal persons would assent to under circumstances that are fair. In this sense its members are autonomous and the obligations they recognize self-imposed.

One feature of justice as fairness is to think of the parties in the initial situation as rational and mutually disinterested. This does not mean that the parties are egoists; that is, individuals with only certain kinds of interests, say in wealth, prestige, and domination. But they are conceived as not taking an interest in one another's interests. They are to presume that even their spiritual aims may be opposed, in the way that the aims of those of different religions may be opposed. Moreover, the concept of rationality must be interpreted as far as possible in the narrow sense, standard in economic theory, of taking the most effective means to given ends. I shall modify this concept to some extent . . ., but one must try to avoid introducing into it any controversial ethical elements. The initial situation must be characterized by stipulations that are widely accepted.

In working out the conception of justice as fairness one main task clearly is to determine which principles of justice would be chosen in the original position. To do this we must describe this situation in some detail and formulate with care the problem of choice which it presents. It may be observed, however, that once the principles of justice are thought of as arising from an original agreement in a situation of equality, it is an open question whether the principle of utility would be acknowledged. Offhand it hardly seems likely that persons who view themselves as equals, entitled to press their claims upon one another, would agree to a principle which may require lesser life prospects for some simply for the sake of a greater sum of advantages enjoyed by others. Since each desires to protect his interests, his capacity to advance his conception of the good, no one has a reason to acquiesce in an enduring loss for himself in order to bring about a greater net balance of satisfaction. In the absence of strong and lasting benevolent impulses, a rational man would not accept a basic structure merely because it maximized the algebraic sum of advantages irrespective of its permanent effects on his own basic rights and interests. Thus it seems that the principle of utility is incompatible with the conception of social cooperation among equals for mutual advantage. It appears to be inconsistent with the idea of reciprocity implicit in the notion of a well-ordered society. Or, at any rate, so I shall argue.

I shall maintain instead that the persons in the initial situation would choose two rather different principles: the first requires equality in the assignment of basic rights and duties, while the second holds that social and economic inequalities; for example, inequalities of wealth and authority; are just only if they result in compensating benefits for everyone, and in particular for the least advantaged members of society. These principles rule out justifying institutions on the grounds that the hardships of some are offset by a greater good in the aggregate. It may be expedient but it is not just that some should have less in order that others may prosper. But there is no injustice in the greater benefits earned by a few provided that the situation of persons not so fortunate is thereby improved. The intuitive idea is that since everyone's well-being depends upon a scheme of cooperation without which no one could have a satisfactory life, the division of advantages should be such as to draw forth the willing cooperation of everyone taking part in it, including those less well situated. Yet this can be expected only if reasonable terms are proposed. The two principles mentioned seem to be a fair agreement on the basis of which those better endowed, or more fortunate in their social position, neither of which we can be said to deserve, could expect the willing cooperation of others when some workable scheme is a necessary condition of the welfare of all.[3] Once we decide to look for a conception of justice that nullifies the accidents of natural endowment and the contingencies of social circumstance as counters in quest for political and economic advantage, we are led to these principles. They express the result of leaving aside those aspects of the social world that seem arbitrary from a moral point of view.

The problem of the choice of principles, however, is extremely difficult. I do not expect the answer I shall suggest to be convincing to everyone. It is, therefore, worth noting from the outset that justice as fairness, like other contract views, consists of two parts: (1) an interpretation of the initial situation and of the problem of choice posed there, and (2) a set of principles which, it is argued, would be agreed to. One may accept the first part of the theory (or some variant thereof), but not the other, and conversely. The concept of the initial contractual situation may seem reasonable although the particular principles proposed are rejected. To be sure, I want to maintain that the most appropriate conception of this situation does lead to principles of justice contrary to utilitarianism and perfectionism, and therefore that the contract doctrine provides an alternative to these views. Still, one may dispute this contention even though one grants that the contractarian method is a useful way of studying ethical theories and of setting forth their underlying assumptions.

Justice as fairness is an example of what I have called a contract theory. Now there may be an objection to the term "contract" and related expressions, but I think it will serve reasonably well. Many words have misleading connotations which at first are likely to confuse. The terms "utility" and "utilitarianism" are surely no exception. They too have unfortunate suggestions which hostile critics have been willing to exploit; yet they are clear enough for those prepared to study utilitarian doctrine. The same should be true of the term "contract" applied to moral theories. As I have mentioned, to understand it one has to keep in mind that it implies a certain level of abstraction. In particular, the content of the relevant agreement is not to enter a given society or to adopt a given form of government, but to accept certain moral principles. Moreover, the undertakings referred to are purely hypothetical: a contract view holds that certain principles would be accepted in a well-defined initial situation.

The merit of the contract terminology is that it conveys the idea that principles of justice may be conceived as principles that would be chosen by rational persons, and that in this way conceptions of justice may be explained and justified. The theory of justice is a part, perhaps the most significant part, of the theory of rational choice. Furthermore, principles of justice deal with conflicting claims upon the advantages won by social cooperation; they apply to the relations among several persons or groups. The word "contract" suggests this plurality as well as the condition that the appropriate division of advantages must be in accordance with principles acceptable to all parties. The condition of publicity for principles of justice is also connoted by the contract phraseology. Thus, if these principles are the outcome of an agreement, citizens have a knowledge of the principles that others follow. It is characteristic of contract theories to stress the public nature of political principles. Finally there is the long tradition of the contract doctrine. Expressing the tie with this line of thought helps to define ideas and accords with natural piety. There are then several advantages in the use of the term "contract." With due precautions taken, it should not be misleading.

A final remark. Justice as fairness is not a complete contract theory. For it is clear that the contractarian idea can be extended to the choice of more or less an entire ethical system; that is, to a system including principles for all the virtues and not only for justice. Now for the most part I shall consider only principles of justice and others closely related to them; I make no attempt to discuss the virtues in a systematic way. Obviously if justice as fairness succeeds reasonably well, a next step would be to study the more general view suggested by the name "rightness as fairness." But even this wider theory fails to embrace all moral relationships, since it would seem to include only our relations with other persons and to leave out of account how we are to conduct ourselves toward animals and the rest of nature. I do not contend that the contract notion offers a way to approach these questions, which are certainly of the first importance; and I shall have to put them aside. We must recognize the limited scope of justice as fairness and of the general type of view that it exemplifies. How far its conclusions must be revised once these other matters are understood cannot be decided in advance.

The Original Position and Justification

I have said that the original position is the appropriate initial status quo which insures

that the fundamental agreements reached in it are fair. This fact yields the name "justice as fairness." It is clear, then, that I want to say that one conception of justice is more reasonable than another, or justifiable with respect to it, if rational persons in the initial situation would choose its principles over those of the other for the role of justice. Conceptions of justice are to be ranked by their acceptability to persons so circumstanced. Understood in this way the question of justification is settled by working out a problem of deliberation: we have to ascertain which principles it would be rational to adopt given the contractual situation. This connects the theory of justice with the theory of rational choice.

If this view of the problem of justification is to succeed, we must, of course, describe in some detail the nature of this choice problem. A problem of rational decision has a definite answer only if we know the beliefs and interests of the parties, their relations with respect to one another, the alternatives between which they are to choose, the procedure whereby they make up their minds, and so on. As the circumstances are presented in different ways, correspondingly different principles are accepted. The concept of the original position, as I shall refer to it, is that of the most philosophically favored interpretation of this initial choice situation for the purposes of a theory of justice.

But how are we to decide what is the most favored interpretation? I assume, for one thing, that there is a broad measure of agreement that principles of justice should be chosen under certain conditions. To justify a particular description of the initial situation one shows that it incorporates these commonly shared presumptions. One argues from widely accepted but weak premises to more specific conclusions. Each of the presumptions should by itself be natural and plausible; some of them may seem innocuous or even trivial. The aim of the contract approach is to establish that taken together they impose significant bounds on acceptable principles of justice. The ideal outcome would be that these conditions determine a unique set of principles; but I shall be satisfied if they suffice to rank the main traditional conceptions of social justice.

One should not be misled, then, by the

somewhat unusual conditions which characterize the original position. The idea here is simply to make vivid to ourselves the restrictions that it seems reasonable to impose on arguments for principles of justice, and therefore on these principles themselves. Thus it seems reasonable and generally acceptable that no one should be advantaged or disadvantaged by natural fortune or social circumstances in the choice of principles. It also seems widely agreed that it should be impossible to tailor principles to the circumstances of one's own case. We should ensure further that particular inclinations and aspirations, and persons' conceptions of their good, do not affect the principles adopted. The aim is to rule out those principles that it would be rational to propose for acceptance, however little the chance of success, only if one knew certain things that are irrelevant from the standpoint of justice. For example, if a man knew that he was wealthy, he might find it rational to advance the principle that various taxes for welfare measures be counted unjust; if he knew that he was poor, he would most likely propose the contrary principle. To represent the desired restrictions one imagines a situation in which everyone is deprived of this sort of information. One excludes the knowledge of those contingencies which sets men at odds and allows them to be guided by their prejudices. In this manner the veil of ignorance is arrived at in a natural way. This concept should cause no difficulty if we keep in mind the constraints on arguments that it is meant to express. At any time we can enter the original position, so to speak, simply by following a certain procedure; namely, by arguing for principles of justice in accordance with these restrictions.

It seems reasonable to suppose that the parties in the original position are equal. That is, all have the same rights in the procedure for choosing principles; each can make proposals, submit reasons for their acceptance, and so on. Obviously the purpose of these conditions is to represent equality between human beings as moral persons, as creatures having a conception of their good and capable of a sense of justice. The basis of equality is taken to be similarity in these two respects. Systems of ends are not ranked in value; and each man

is presumed to have the requisite ability to understand and to act upon whatever principles are adopted. Together with the veil of ignorance, these conditions define the principles of justice as those which rational persons concerned to advance their interests would consent to as equals when none are known to be advantaged or disadvantaged by social and natural contingencies.

There is, however, another side to justifying a particular description of the original position. This is to see if the principles which would be chosen match our considered convictions of justice or extend them in an acceptable way. We can note whether applying these principles would lead us to make the same judgments about the basic structure of society which we now make intuitively and in which we have the greatest confidence; or whether, in cases where our present judgments are in doubt and given with hesitation, these principles offer a resolution which we can affirm on reflection. There are questions which we feel sure must be answered in a certain way. For example, we are confident that religious intolerance and racial discrimination are unjust. We think that we have examined these things with care and have reached what we believe is an impartial judgment not likely to be distorted by an excessive attention to our own interests. These convictions are provisional fixed points which we presume any conception of justice must fit. But we have much less assurance as to what is the correct distribution of wealth and authority. Here we may be looking for a way to remove our doubts. We can check an interpretation of the initial situation, then, by the capacity of its principles to accommodate our firmest convictions and to provide guidance where guidance is needed.

In searching for the most favored description of this situation we work from both ends. We begin by describing it so that it represents generally shared and preferably weak conditions. We then see if these conditions are strong enough to yield a significant set of principles. If not, we look for further premises equally reasonable. But if so, and these principles match our considered convictions of justice, then so far well and good. But presumably there will be discrepancies. In this case we have a choice. We can either modify the account of the initial situation or we can revise our existing judgments, for even the judgments we take provisionally as fixed points are liable to revision. By going back and forth, sometimes altering the conditions of the contractual circumstances, at others withdrawing our judgments and conforming them to principle, I assume that eventually we shall find a description of the initial situation that both expresses reasonable conditions and yields principles which match our considered judgments duly pruned and adjusted. This state of affairs I refer to as reflective equilibrium.[4] It is an equilibrium because at last our principles and judgments coincide; and it is reflective since we know to what principles our judgments conform and the premises of their derivation. At the moment everything is in order. But this equilibrium is not necessarily stable. It is liable to be upset by further examination of the conditions which should be imposed on the contractual situation and by particular cases which may lead us to revise our judgments. Yet for the time being we have done what we can to render coherent and to justify our convictions of social justice. We have reached a conception of the original position.

I shall not, of course, actually work through this process. Still, we may think of the interpretation of the original position that I shall present as the result of such a hypothetical course of reflection. It represents the attempt to accommodate within one scheme both reasonable philosophical conditions on principles as well as our considered judgments of justice. In arriving at the favored interpretation of the initial situation there is no point at which an appeal is made to self-evidence in the traditional sense either of general conceptions or particular convictions. I do not claim for the principles of justice proposed that they are necessary truths or derivable from such truths. A conception of justice cannot be deduced from self-evident premises or conditions on principles; instead, its justification is a matter of the mutual support of many considerations, of everything fitting together into one coherent view.

A final comment. We shall want to say that certain principles of justice are justified because they would be agreed to in an initial situation of equality. I have emphasized that this original position is purely hypothetical. It is natural to ask why, if this agreement is never actually entered into, we should take any interest in these principles, moral or otherwise. The answer is that the conditions embodied in the description of the original position are ones that we do in fact accept. Or if we do not, then perhaps we can be persuaded to do so by philosophical reflection. Each aspect of the contractual situation can be given supporting grounds. Thus what we shall do is to collect together into one conception a number of conditions on principles that we are ready upon due consideration to recognize as reasonable. These constraints express what we are prepared to regard as limits on fair terms of social cooperation. One way to look at the idea of the original position, therefore, is to see it as an expository device which sums up the meaning of these conditions and helps us to extract their consequences. On the other hand, this conception is also an intuitive notion that suggests its own elaboration, so that led on by it we are drawn to define more clearly the standpoint from which we can best interpret moral relationships. We need a conception that enables us to envision our objective from afar: the intuitive notion of the original position is to do this for us. . . .

Two Principles of Justice

I shall now state in a provisional form the two principles of justice that I believe would be chosen in the original position. In this section I wish to make only the most general comments, and therefore the first formulation of these principles is tentative. As we go on I shall run through several formulations and approximate step by step the final statement to be given much later. I believe that doing this allows the exposition to proceed in a natural way.

The first statement of the two principles reads as follows:

First: each person is to have an equal right to the most extensive basic liberty compatible with a similar liberty for others.

Second: social and economic inequalities are to be arranged so that they are both (a) reasonably expected to be to everyone's advantage, and (b) attached to positions and offices open to all.

There are two ambiguous phrases in the second principle, namely "everyone's advantage" and "open to all." Determining their sense more exactly will lead to a second formulation of the principle. . . .

By way of general comment, these principles primarily apply, as I have said, to the basic structure of society. They are to govern the assignment of rights and duties and to regulate the distribution of social and economic advantages. As their formulation suggests, these principles presuppose that the social structure can be divided into two more or less distinct parts, the first principle applying to the one, the second to the other. They distinguish between those aspects of the social system that define and secure the equal liberties of citizenship and those that specify and establish social and economic inequalities. The basic liberties of citizens are, roughly speaking, political liberty (the right to vote and to be eligible for public office) together with freedom of speech and assembly; liberty of conscience and freedom of thought; freedom of the person along with the right to hold personal property; and freedom from arbitrary arrest and seizure as defined by the concept of the rule of law. These liberties are all required to be equal by the first principle, since citizens of a just society are to have the same basic rights.

The second principle applies, in the first approximation, to the distribution of income and wealth and to the design of organizations that make use of differences in authority and responsibility, or chains of command. While the distribution of wealth and income need not be equal, it must be to everyone's advantage, and at the same time, positions of authority and offices of command must be accessible to all. One applies the second principle by holding positions open, and then, subject to

this constraint, arranges social and economic inequalities so that everyone benefits.

These principles are to be arranged in a serial order with the first principle prior to the second. This ordering means that a departure from the institutions of equal liberty required by the first principle cannot be justified by, or compensated for, by greater social and economic advantages. The distribution of wealth and income, and the hierarchies of authority, must be consistent with both the liberties of equal citizenship and equality of opportunity.

It is clear that these principles are rather specific in their content, and their acceptance rests on certain assumptions that I must eventually try to explain and justify. A theory of justice depends upon a theory of society in ways that will become evident as we proceed. For the present, it should be observed that the two principles (and this holds for all formulations) are a special case of a more general conception of justice that can be expressed as follows:

All social values—liberty and opportunity, income and wealth, and the bases of self-respect—are to be distributed equally unless an unequal distribution of any, or all, of these values is to everyone's advantage.

Injustice, then, is simply inequalities that are not to the benefit of all. Of course, this conception is extremely vague and requires interpretation.

As a first step, suppose that the basic structure of society distributes certain primary goods, that is, things that every rational man is presumed to want. These goods normally have a use whatever a person's rational plan of life. For simplicity, assume that the chief primary goods at the disposition of society are rights and liberties, powers and opportunities, income and wealth. (Later on . . . the primary good of self-respect has a central place.) These are the social primary goods. Other primary goods such as health and vigor, intelligence and imagination, are natural goods; although their possession is influenced by the basic structure, they are not so directly under its control. Imagine, then, a hypothetical initial arrangement in which all the social primary goods are equally distributed: everyone has similar rights and duties, and income and wealth are evenly shared. This state of affairs provides a benchmark for judging improvements. If certain inequalities of wealth and organizational powers would make everyone better off than in this hypothetical starting situation, then they accord with the general conception.

Now it is possible, at least theoretically, that by giving up some of their fundamental liberties men are sufficiently compensated by the resulting social and economic gains. The general conception of justice imposes no restrictions on what sort of inequalities are permissible; it only requires that everyone's position be improved. We need not suppose anything so drastic as consenting to a condition of slavery. Imagine instead that men forgo certain political rights when the economic returns are significant and their capacity to influence the course of policy by the exercise of these rights would be marginal in any case. It is this kind of exchange which the two principles as stated rule out; being arranged in serial order they do not permit exchanges between basic liberties and economic and social gains. The serial ordering of principles expresses an underlying preference among primary social goods. When this preference is rational so likewise is the choice of these principles in this order.

In developing justice as fairness I shall, for the most part, leave aside the general conception of justice and examine instead the special case of the two principles in serial order. The advantage of this procedure is that from the first the matter of priorities is recognized and an effort made to find principles to deal with it. One is led to attend throughout to the conditions under which the acknowledgment of the absolute weight of liberty with respect to social and economic advantages, as defined by the lexical order of the two principles, would be reasonable. Offhand, this ranking appears extreme and too special a case to be of much interest; but there is more justification for it than would appear at first sight. Or at any rate, so I shall maintain. . . . Furthermore, the distinction between fundamental rights and liberties and economic and social benefits marks a difference among primary social

goods that one should try to exploit. It suggests an important division in the social system. Of course, the distinctions drawn and the ordering proposed are bound to be at best only approximations. There are surely circumstances in which they fail. But it is essential to depict clearly the main lines of a reasonable conception of justice; and under many conditions, anyway, the two principles in serial order may serve well enough. When necessary we can fall back on the more general conception.

The fact that the two principles apply to institutions has certain consequences. Several points illustrate this. First of all, the rights and liberties referred to by these principles are those that are defined by the public rules of the basic structure. Whether men are free is determined by the rights and duties established by the major institutions of society. Liberty is a certain pattern of social forms. The first principle simply requires that certain sorts of rules, those defining basic liberties, apply to everyone equally and that they allow the most extensive liberty compatible with a like liberty for all. The only reason for circumscribing the rights defining liberty and making men's freedom less extensive than it might otherwise be is that these equal rights as institutionally defined would interfere with one another.

Another thing to bear in mind is that when principles mention persons, or require that everyone gain from an inequality, the reference is to representative persons holding the various social positions, or offices, or whatever, established by the basic structure. Thus in applying the second principle I assume that it is possible to assign an expectation of well-being to representative individuals holding these positions. This expectation indicates their life prospects as viewed from their social station. In general, the expectations of representative persons depend upon the distribution of rights and duties throughout the basic structure. When this changes, expectations change. I assume, then, that expectations are connected: by raising the prospects of the representative man in one position we presumably increase or decrease the prospects of representative men in other positions. Since it applies to institutional forms, the second principle (or rather the first part of it) refers to the expectations of representative individuals. As I shall discuss below, neither principle applies to distributions of particular goods to particular individuals who may be identified by their proper names. The situation where someone is considering how to allocate certain commodities to needy persons who are known to him is not within the scope of the principles. They are meant to regulate basic institutional arrangements. We must not assume that there is much similarity from the standpoint of justice between an administrative allotment of goods to specific persons and the appropriate design of society. Our common sense intuitions for the former may be a poor guide to the latter.

Now the second principle insists that each person benefit from permissible inequalities in the basic structure. This means that it must be reasonable for each relevant representative man defined by this structure, when he views it as a going concern, to prefer his prospects with the inequality, to his prospects without it. One is not allowed to justify differences in income or organizational powers on the ground that the disadvantages of those in one position are outweighed by the greater advantages of those in another. Much less can infringements of liberty be counterbalanced in this way. Applied to the basic structure, the principle of utility would have us maximize the sum of expectations of representative men (weighted by the number of persons they represent, on the classical view); and this would permit us to compensate for the losses of some by the gains of others. Instead, the two principles require that everyone benefit from economic and social inequalities.

The Reasoning Leading to the Two Principles of Justice

It will be recalled that the general conception of justice as fairness requires that all primary social goods be distributed equally unless an unequal distribution would be to everyone's advantage. No restrictions are placed on exchanges of these goods and therefore a lesser liberty can be compensated for by greater social and economic benefits. Now looking at the situation from the standpoint of one person selected arbitrarily, there is no way for him to win special advantages for himself. Nor, on the other hand, are there grounds for his acquiescing in special disadvantages. Since it is not reasonable for him to expect more than an equal share in the division of social goods, and since it is not rational for him to agree to less, the sensible thing for him to do is to acknowledge as the first principle of justice one requiring an equal distribution. Indeed, this principle is so obvious that we would expect it to occur to anyone immediately.

Thus, the parties start with a principle establishing equal liberty for all, including equality of opportunity, as well as an equal distribution of income and wealth. But there is no reason why this acknowledgment should be final. If there are inequalities in the basic structure that work to make everyone better off in comparison with the benchmark of initial equality, why not permit them? The immediate gain which a greater equality might allow can be regarded as intelligently invested in view of its future return. If, for example, these inequalities set up various incentives which succeed in eliciting more productive efforts, a person in the original position may look upon them as necessary to cover the costs of training and to encourage effective performance. One might think that ideally individuals should want to serve one another. But since the parties are assumed not to take an interest in one another's interests, their acceptance of these inequalities is only the acceptance of the relations in which men stand in the circumstances of justice. They have no grounds for complaining of one another's motives. A person in the original position would, therefore, concede the justice of these inequalities. Indeed, it would be shortsighted of him not to do so. He would hesitate to agree to these regularities only if he would be dejected by the bare knowledge or perception that others were better situated; and I have assumed that the parties decide as if they are not moved by envy. In order to make the principle regulating inequalities determinate, one looks at the system from the standpoint of the least advantaged representative man. Inequalities are permissible when they maximize, or at least all contribute to, the long-term expectations of the least fortunate group in society.

Now this general conception imposes no constraints on what sorts of inequalities are allowed, whereas the special conception, by putting the two principles in serial order (with the necessary adjustments in meaning), forbids exchanges between basic liberties and economic and social benefits. I shall not try to justify this ordering here. . . . But roughly, the idea underlying this ordering is that if the parties assume that their basic liberties can be effectively exercised, they will not exchange a lesser liberty for an improvement in economic well-being. It is only when social conditions do not allow the effective establishment of these rights that one can concede their limitation; and these restrictions can be granted only to the extent that they are necessary to prepare the way for a free society. The denial of equal liberty can be defended only if it is necessary to raise the level of civilization so that in due course these freedoms can be enjoyed. Thus in adopting a serial order we are in effect making a special assumption in the original position, namely, that the parties know that the conditions of their society, whatever they are, admit the effective realization of the equal liberties. The serial ordering of the two principles of justice eventually comes to be reasonable if the general conception is consistently followed. This lexical ranking is the long-run tendency of the general view. For the most part I shall assume that the requisite circumstances for the serial order obtain.

It seems clear from these remarks that the two principles are at least a plausible conception of justice. The question, though, is how one is to argue for them more systematically. Now there are several things to do. One can work out their consequences for institutions and note their implications for fundamental social policy. In this way they are tested by a comparison with our considered judgments of justice. . . . But one can also try to find arguments in their favor that are decisive from the standpoint of the original position. In order to see how this might be done, it is useful as a heuristic device to think of the two principles as the maximin solution to the problem of social justice. There is an analogy between the two principles and the maximin rule for choice under uncertainty.[5] This is evident from the fact that the two principles are those a person would choose for the design of a society in which his enemy is to assign him his place. The maximin rule tells us to rank alternatives by their worst possible outcomes: we are to adopt the alternative the worst outcome of which is superior to the worst outcomes of the others. The persons in the original position do not, of course, assume that their initial place in society is decided by a malevolent opponent. As I note below, they should not reason from false premises. The veil of ignorance does not violate this idea, since an absence of information is not misinformation. But that the two principles of justice would be chosen if the parties were forced to protect themselves against such a contingency explains the sense in which this conception is the maximin solution. And this analogy suggests that if the original position has been described so that it is rational for the parties to adopt the conservative attitude expressed by this rule, a conclusive argument can indeed be constructed for these principles. Clearly the maximin rule is not, in general, a suitable guide for choices under uncertainty. But it is attractive in situations marked by certain special features. My aim, then, is to show that a good case can be made for the two principles based on the fact that the original position manifests these features to the fullest possible degree, carrying them to the limit, so to speak.

Consider the gain-and-loss table below. It represents the gains and losses for a situation which is not a game of strategy. There is no one playing against the person making the decision; instead he is faced with several possible circumstances which may or may not obtain. Which circumstances happen to exist does not depend upon what the person choosing decides or whether he announces his moves in advance. The numbers in the table are monetary values (in hundreds of dollars) in comparison with some initial situation. The gain (g) depends upon the individual's decision (d) and the circumstances (c). Thus $g = f(d,c)$. Assuming that there are three possible decisions and three possible circumstances, we might have this gain-and-loss table.

Decisions	Circumstances		
	c_1	c_2	c_3
d_1	−7	8	12
d_2	−8	7	14
d_3	5	6	8

The maximin rule requires that we make the third decision. For in this case the worst that can happen is that one gains five hundred dollars, which is better than the worst for the other actions. If we adopt one of these we may lose either eight or seven hundred dollars. Thus, the choice of d_3 maximizes f(d,c) for that value of c which for a given d, minimizes f. The term "maximin" means the *maximum minimorum;* and the rule directs our attention to the worst that can happen under any proposed course of action, and to decide in the light of that.

Now there appear to be three chief features of situations that give plausibility to this unusual rule.[6] First, since the rule takes no account of the likelihoods of the possible circumstances, there must be some reason for sharply discounting estimates of these probabilities. Offhand, the most natural rule of choice would seem to be to compute the expectation of monetary gain for each decision and then to adopt the course of action with the highest prospect. (This expectation is defined as follows: let us suppose that g_{ij} represent the numbers in the gain-and-loss table, where i is the row index and j is the column index; and let p_i, j = 1, 2, 3, be the likelihoods of the circumstances, with $\Sigma p_j = 1$. Then the expectation for the ith decision is equal to $\Sigma p_i g_{ij}$.) Thus it must be, for example, that the situation is one in which a knowledge of likelihoods is impossible, or at best extremely insecure. In this case it is unreasonable not to be skeptical of probabilistic calculations unless there is no other way out, particularly if the decision is a fundamental one that needs to be justified to others.

The second feature that suggests the maximin rule is the following: the person choosing has a conception of the good such that he cares very little, if anything, for what he might gain above the minimum stipend that he can, in fact, be sure of by following the maximin rule.

It is not worthwhile for him to take a chance for the sake of a further advantage, especially when it may turn out that he loses much that is important to him. This last provision brings in the third feature; namely, that the rejected alternatives have outcomes that one can hardly accept. The situation involves grave risks. Of course these features work most effectively in combination. The paradigm situation for following the maximin rule is when all three features are realized to the highest degree. This rule does not, then, generally apply, nor of course is it self-evident. Rather, it is a maxim, a rule of thumb, that comes into its own in special circumstances. Its application depends upon the qualitative structure of the possible gains and losses in relation to one's conception of the good, all this against a background in which it is reasonable to discount conjectural estimates of likelihoods.

It should be noted, as the comments on the gain-and-loss table say, that the entries in the table represent monetary values and not utilities. This difference is significant since for one thing computing expectations on the basis of such objective values is not the same thing as computing expected utility and may lead to different results. The essential point, though, is that in justice as fairness the parties do not know their conception of the good and cannot estimate their utility in the ordinary sense. In any case, we want to go behind de facto preferences generated by given conditions. Therefore expectations are based upon an index of primary goods and the parties make their choice accordingly. The entries in the example are in terms of money and not utility to indicate this aspect of the contract doctrine.

Now, as I have suggested, the original position has been defined so that it is a situation in which the maximin rule applies. In order to see this, let us review briefly the nature of this situation with these three special features in mind. To begin with, the veil of ignorance excludes all but the vaguest knowledge of likelihoods. The parties have no basis for determining the probable nature of their society, or their place in it. Thus they have strong reasons for being wary of probability calculations if any other course is open to them. They must also take into account the fact that their choice of principles should seem reasonable to others, in particular their descendants, whose rights will be deeply affected by it. There are further grounds for discounting that I shall mention as we go along. For the present it suffices to note that these considerations are strengthened by the fact that the parties know very little about the gain-and-loss table. Not only are they unable to conjecture the likelihoods of the various possible circumstances, they cannot say much about what the possible circumstances are, much less enumerate them and foresee the outcome of each alternative available. Those deciding are much more in the dark than the illustration by a numerical table suggests. It is for this reason that I have spoken of an analogy with the maximin rule.

Several kinds of arguments for the two principles of justice illustrate the second feature. Thus, if we can maintain that these principles provide a workable theory of social justice, and that they are compatible with reasonable demands of efficiency, then this conception guarantees a satisfactory minimum. There may be, on reflection, little reason for trying to do better. Thus much of the argument . . . is to show, by their application to the main questions of social justice, that the two principles are a satisfactory conception. These details have a philosophical purpose. Moreover, this line of thought is practically decisive if we can establish the priority of liberty, the lexical ordering of the two principles. For this priority implies that the persons in the original position have no desire to try for greater gains at the expense of the equal liberties. The minimum assured by the two principles in lexical order is not one that the parties wish to jeopardize for the sake of greater economic and social advantages. . . .

Finally, the third feature holds if we can assume that other conceptions of justice may lead to institutions that the parties would find intolerable. For example, it has sometimes been held that under some conditions the utility principle (in either form) justifies, if not slavery or serfdom, at any rate serious infractions of liberty for the sake of greater social benefits. We need not consider here the truth of this claim, or the likelihood that the requisite conditions obtain. For the moment, this contention is only to illustrate the way in which conceptions of justice may allow for outcomes which the parties may not be able to accept. And having the ready alternative of the two principles of justice which secure a satisfactory minimum, it seems unwise, if not irrational, for them to take a chance that these outcomes are not realized.

So much, then, for a brief sketch of the features of situations in which the maximin rule comes into its own and of the way in which the arguments for the two principles of justice can be subsumed under them. . . .

The Final Formulation of the Principles of Justice

. . . I now wish to give the final statement of the two principles of justice for institutions. For the sake of completeness, I shall give a full statement including earlier formulations.

First Principle
Each person is to have an equal right to the most extensive total system of equal basic liberties compatible with a similar system of liberty for all.

Second Principle
Social and economic inequalities are to be arranged so that they are both:
(a) to the greatest benefit of the least advantaged, consistent with the just savings principle, and
(b) attached to offices and positions open to all under conditions of fair equality of opportunity.

First Priority Rule (The Priority of Liberty)
The principles of justice are to be ranked in lexical order and therefore liberty can be restricted only for the sake of liberty. There are two cases:
(a) a less extensive liberty must strengthen the total system of liberty shared by all;
(b) a less than equal liberty must be acceptable to those with the lesser liberty.

Second Priority Rule (The Priority of Justice over Efficiency and Welfare)
The second principle of justice is lexically prior to the principle of efficiency and to that of maximizing the sum of advantages; and fair opportunity is prior to the difference principle. There are two cases:

(a) an inequality of opportunity must enhance the opportunities of those with the lesser opportunity;
(b) an excessive rate of saving must on balance mitigate the burden of those bearing this hardship.

General Conception
All social primary goods—liberty and opportunity, income and wealth, and the bases of self-respect—are to be distributed equally unless an unequal distribution of any or all of these goods is to the advantage of the least favored.

By way of comment, these principles and priority rules are no doubt incomplete. Other modifications will surely have to be made, but I shall not further complicate the statement of the principles. It suffices to observe that when we come to nonideal theory, we do not fall back straightway upon the general conception of justice. The lexical ordering of the two principles, and the valuations that this ordering implies, suggest priority rules which seem to be reasonable enough in many cases. By various examples I have tried to illustrate how these rules can be used and to indicate their plausibility. Thus the ranking of the principles of justice in ideal theory reflects back and guides the application of these principles to nonideal situations. It identifies which limitations need to be dealt with first. The drawback of the general conception of justice is that it lacks the definite structure of the two principles in serial order. In more extreme and tangled instances of nonideal theory there may be no alternative to it. At some point the priority of rules for nonideal cases will fail; and indeed, we may be able to find no satisfactory answer at all. But we must try to postpone the day of reckoning as long as possible, and try to arrange society so that it never comes. . . .

Notes

1. As the text suggests, I shall regard Locke's *Second Treatise of Government,* Rousseau's *The Social Contract,* and Kant's ethical works beginning with *The Foundations of the Metaphysics of Morals* as definitive of the contract tradition. For all of its greatness, Hobbes's *Leviathan* raises special problems. A general historical survey is provided by J. W. Gough, *The Social Contract,* 2nd ed. (Oxford, The Clarendon Press, 1957), and Otto Gierke, *Natural Law and the Theory of Society,* trans. with an introduction by Ernest Barker (Cambridge, The University Press, 1934). A presentation of the contract view as primarily an ethical theory is to be found in G. R. Grice, *The Grounds of Moral Judgment* (Cambridge: The University Press, 1967).

2. Kant is clear that the original agreement is hypothetical. See *The Metaphysics of Morals,* pt. I *(Rechtslehre),* especially §§ 47, 52; and pt. II of the essay "Concerning the Common Saying: This May Be True in Theory but It Does Not Apply in Practice," in *Kant's Political Writings,* ed. Hans Reiss and trans. by H. B. Nisbet (Cambridge, The University Press, 1970), pp. 73–87. See Georges Vlachos, *La Pensée politique de Kant* (Paris, Presses Universitaires de France, 1962), pp. 326–335; and J. G. Murphy, *Kant: The Philosophy of Right* (London, Macmillan, 1970), pp. 109–112, 133–136, for a further discussion.

3. For the formulation of this intuitive idea I am indebted to Allan Gibbard.

4. The process of mutual adjustment of principles and considered judgments is not peculiar to moral philosophy. See Nelson Goodman, *Fact, Fiction, and Forecast* (Cambridge, Mass., Harvard University Press, 1955), pp. 65–68, for parallel remarks concerning the justification of the principles of deductive and inductive inference.

5. An accessible discussion of this and other rules of choice under uncertainty can be found in W. J. Baumol, *Economic Theory and Operations Analysis,* 2nd ed. (Englewood Cliffs, N.J., Prentice-Hall, 1965), ch. 24. Baumol gives a geometric interpretation of these rules, including the diagram used . . . to illustrate the difference principle. See pp. 558–562. See also R. D. Luce and Howard Raiffa, *Games and Decisions* (New York, John Wiley and Sons, Inc., 1957, ch. XIII, for a fuller account.

6. Here I borrow from William Fellner, *Probability and Profit* (Homewood, Ill., Richard D. Irwin, 1965), pp. 140–142, where these features are noted.

Radical Egalitarianism

Kai Nielson

The fundamental requirement of radical egalitarianism is equality of basic condition for everyone. Kai Nielson justifies this requirement on the grounds that it produces the conditions for the most extensive satisfaction of needs for everyone. He also contends that radical egalitarianism is required by the moral point of view and would lead to two specific principles of justice. Lastly, Nielson defends radical egalitarianism on the grounds that it is required by liberty or at least a fair distribution of liberty.

I

I have talked of equality as a right and of equality as a goal. And I have taken, as the principal thing, to be able to state what goal we are seeking when we say equality is a goal. When we are in a position actually to achieve that goal, then that same equality becomes a right. The goal we are seeking is an equality of basic condition for everyone. Let me say a bit what this is: everyone, as far as possible, should have equal life prospects, short of genetic engineering and the like and the rooting out any form of the family and the undermining of our basic freedoms. There should, where this is possible, be an equality of access to equal resources over each person's life as a whole, though this should be qualified by people's varying needs. Where psychiatrists are in short supply only people who are in need of psychiatric help should have equal access to such help. This equal access to resources should be such that it stands as a barrier to their being the sort of differences between people that allow some to be in a position to control and to exploit others; such equal access to resources should also stand as a barrier to one adult person having power over other adult persons that does not rest on the revokable consent on the part of the persons over whom he comes to have power. Where, be-

Abridged from *Equality and Liberty* (1985), pp. 283–292, 302–306, 309. Reprinted by permission of Rowman & Allanheld, Publishers. Notes renumbered.

cause of some remaining scarcity in a society of considerable productive abundance, we cannot reasonably distribute resources equally, we should first, where considerations of desert are not at issue, distribute according to stringency of need, second according to the strength of unmanipulated preferences and third, and finally, by lottery. We should, in trying to attain equality of condition, aim at a condition of autonomy (the fuller and the more rational the better) for everyone and at a condition where everyone alike, to the fullest extent possible, has his or her needs and wants satisfied. The limitations on the satisfaction of people's wants should be only where that satisfaction is incompatible with everyone getting the same treatment. Where we have conflicting wants, such as where two persons want to marry the same person, the fair thing to do will vary with the circumstances. In the marriage case, freedom of choice is obviously the fair thing. But generally, what should be aimed at is having everyone have their wants satisfied as far as possible. To achieve equality of condition would be, as well, to achieve a condition where the necessary burdens of the society are equally shared, where to do so is reasonable, and where each person has an equal voice in deciding what these burdens shall be. Moreover, everyone, as much as possible, should be in a position—and should be equally in that position—to control his own life. The goals of egalitarianism are to achieve such equalities.

Minimally, classlessness is something we should all aim at if we are egalitarians. It is necessary for the stable achievement of equalities of the type discussed in the previous paragraph. Beyond that, we should also aim at a statusless society, though not at an undifferentiated society or a society which does not recognize merit. . . . It is only in such a classless, statusless society that the ideals of equality (the conception of equality as a very general goal to be achieved) can be realized. In aiming for a statusless society, we are aiming for a society which, while remaining a society of material abundance, is a society in which there are to be no extensive differences in life prospects between people because some have far greater income, power, authority or prestige than others. This is the *via negativia* of the egalitarian way. The *via postiva* is to produce social conditions, where there is generally material abundance, where well-being and satisfaction are not only maximized (the utilitarian thing) but, as well, a society where this condition, as far as it is achievable, is sought equally for all (the egalitarian thing). This is the underlying conception of the egalitarian commitment to equality of condition.

II

Robert Nozick asks "How do we decide how much equality is enough?"[1] In the preceding section we gestured in the direction of an answer. I should now like to be somewhat more explicit. Too much equality, as we have been at pains to point out, would be to treat everyone identically, completely ignoring their differing needs. Various forms of "barracks equality" approximating that would also be too much. Too little equality would be to limit equality of condition, as did the old egalitarianism, to achieving equal legal and political rights, equal civil liberties, to equality of opportunity and to a redistribution of gross disparities in wealth sufficient to keep social peace, the rationale for the latter being that such gross inequalities if allowed to stand would threaten social stability. This Hobbesist stance indicates that the old egalitarianism proceeds in a very pragmatic manner. Against the old egalitarianism I would argue that we must at least aim at an equality of whole life prospects, where that is not read simply as the right to compete for scarce positions of advantage, but where there

is to be brought into being the kind of equality of condition that would provide everyone equally, as far as possible, with the resources and the social conditions to satisfy their needs as fully as possible compatible with everyone else doing likewise. (Note that between people these needs will be partly the same but will still often be importantly different as well.) Ideally, as a kind of ideal limit for a society of wondrous abundance, a radical egalitarianism would go beyond that to a similar thing for wants. We should, that is, provide all people equally, as far as possible, with the resources and social conditions to satisfy their wants, as fully as possible compatible with everyone else doing likewise. (I recognize that there is a slide between wants and needs. As the wealth of a society increases and its structure changes, things that started out as wants tend to become needs, e.g. someone in the Falkland Islands might merely reasonably want an auto while someone in Los Angeles might not only want it but need it as well. But this does not collapse the distinction between wants and needs. There are things in any society people need, if they are to survive at all in anything like a commodious condition, whether they want them or not, e.g., they need food, shelter, security, companionship and the like. An egalitarian starts with basic needs, or at least with what are taken in the cultural environment in which a given person lives to be basic needs, and moves out to other needs and finally to wants as the productive power of the society increases.)

I qualified my above formulations with "as far as possible" and with "as fully as possible compatible with everyone else doing likewise." These are essential qualifications. Where, as in societies that we know, there are scarcities, even rather minimal scarcities, not everyone can have the resources or at least all the resources necessary to have their needs satisfied. Here we must first ensure that, again as far as possible, their basic needs are all satisfied and then we move on to other needs and finally to wants. But sometimes, to understate it, even in very affluent societies, everyone's needs cannot be met, or at least they cannot be equally met. In such circumstances we have to make some hard choices. I am thinking of a situation where there are not enough dialysis machines to go around so that everyone who needs one can have one. What then should we do? The thing to aim at, to try as far as possible to approximate, if only as a heuristic ideal, is the full and equal meeting of needs and wants of everyone. It is when we have that much equality that we have enough equality. But, of course, "ought implies can," and where we can't achieve it we can't achieve it. But where we reasonably can, we ought to do it. It is something that fairness requires.

The "reasonably can" is also an essential modification: we need situations of sufficient abundance so that we do not, in going for such an equality of condition, simply spread the misery around or spread very Spartan conditions around. Before we can rightly aim for the equality of condition I mentioned, we must first have the productive capacity and resource conditions to support the institutional means that would make possible the equal satisfaction of basic needs and the equal satisfaction of other needs and wants as well.

Such achievements will often not be possible; perhaps they will never be fully possible, for, no doubt, the physically handicapped will always be with us. Consider, for example, situations where our scarcities are such that we cannot, without causing considerable misery, create the institutions and mechanisms that would work to satisfy all needs, even all basic needs. Suppose we have the technology in place to develop all sorts of complicated life-sustaining machines all of which would predictably provide people with a quality of life that they, viewing the matter clearly, would rationally choose if they were simply choosing for themselves. But suppose, if we put such technologies in place, we will then not have the wherewithal to provide basic health care in outlying regions in the country or adequate educational services in such places. We should not, under those circumstances, put those technologies in place. But we should also recognize that where it becomes possible to put these technologies in place without sacrificing other more pressing needs, we should do so. The underlying egalitarian rationale is evident enough: produce the conditions for the most extensive satisfaction of needs for everyone. Where A's need and B's need are equally important (equally stringent) but cannot both be satisfied, satisfy A's need rather than B's if the satisfaction of A's need would be more fecund

for the satisfaction of the needs of others than B's, or less undermining of the satisfaction of the needs of others than B's. (I do not mean to say that that is our only criterion of choice but it is the criterion most relevant for us here.) We should seek the satisfaction of the greatest compossible set of needs where the conditions for compossibility are (a) that everyone's needs be considered, (b) that everyone's needs be *equally* considered and where two sets of needs cannot both be satisfied, the more stringent set of needs shall first be satisfied. (Do not say we have no working criteria for what they are. If you need food to keep you from starvation or debilitating malnutrition and I need a vacation to relax after a spate of hard work, your need is plainly more stringent than mine. There would, of course, be all sorts of disputable cases, but there are also a host of perfectly determinate cases indicating that we have working criteria.) The underlying rationale is to seek compossible sets of needs so that we approach as far as possible as great a satisfaction of needs as possible for everyone.

This might, it could be said, produce a situation in which very few people got those things that they needed the most, or at least wanted the most. Remember Nozick with his need for the resources of Widner Library in an annex to his house. People, some might argue, with expensive tastes and extravagant needs, say a need for really good wine, would never, with a stress on such compossibilia, get things they are really keen about.[2] Is that the kind of world we would reflectively want? Well, *if* their not getting them is the price we have to pay for everyone having their basic needs met, then it is a price we ought to pay. I am very fond of very good wines as well as fresh ripe mangos, but if the price of my having them is that people starve or suffer malnutrition in the Sahel, or indeed anywhere else, then plainly fairness, if not just plain human decency, requires that I forego them.

In talking about how much equality is enough, I have so far talked of the benefits that equality is meant to provide. But egalitarians also speak of an equal sharing of the necessary burdens of the society as well. Fairness requires a sharing of the burdens, and for a radical egalitarian this comes to an equal sharing of the burdens where people are equally capable of sharing them. Translated into the concrete this does *not* mean that a child or an old man or a pregnant woman are to be required to work in the mines or that they be required to collect garbage, but it would involve something like requiring every able bodied person, say from nineteen to twenty, to take his or her turn at a fair portion of the necessary unpleasant jobs in the world. In that way we all, where we are able to do it, would share equally in these burdens—in doing the things that none of us want to do but that we, if we are at all reasonable, recognize the necessity of having done. (There are all kinds of variations and complications concerning this—what do we do with the youthful wonder at the violin? But, that notwithstanding, the general idea is clear enough.) And, where we think this is reasonably feasible, it squares with our considered judgments about fairness.

I have given you, in effect appealing to my considered judgments but considered judgments I do not think are at all eccentric, a picture of what I would take to be enough equality, too little equality and not enough equality. But how can we know that my proportions are right? I do not think we can avoid or should indeed try to avoid an appeal to considered judgments here. But working with them there are some arguments we can appeal to to get them in wide reflective equilibrium. Suppose we go back to the formal principle of justice, namely that we must treat like cases alike. Because it does not tell us *what* are like cases, we cannot derive substantive criteria from it. But it may, indirectly, be of some help here. We all, if we are not utterly zany, want a life in which our needs are satisfied and in which we can live as we wish and do what we want to do. Though we differ in many ways, in our abilities, capacities for pleasure, determination to keep on with a job, we do not differ about wanting our needs satisfied or being able to live as we wish. Thus, *ceterus paribus*, where questions of desert, entitlement and the like do not enter, it is only fair that all of us should have our needs equally considered and that we should, again *ceterus paribus*, all be able to do as we wish in a way that is compatible with others doing likewise. From the for-

mal principle of justice and a few key facts about us, we can get to the claim that *ceterus paribus* we should go for this much equality. But this is the core content of a radical egalitarianism.

However, how do we know that *ceterus is paribus* here? What about our entitlements and deserts? Suppose I have built my house with my own hands, from materials I have purchased and on land that I have purchased and that I have lived in it for years and have carefully cared for it. The house is mine and I am entitled to keep it even if by dividing the house into two apartments greater and more equal satisfaction of need would obtain for everyone. Justice requires that such an entitlement be respected here. (Again, there is an implicit *ceterus paribus* clause. In extreme situations, say after a war with housing in extremely short supply, that entitlement could be rightly overridden.)

There is a response on the egalitarian's part similar to a response utilitarianism made to criticisms of a similar logical type made of utilitarians by pluralistic deontologists. One of the things that people in fact need, or at least reflectively firmly want, is to have such entitlements respected. Where they are routinely overridden to satisfy other needs or wants, we would *not* in fact have a society in which the needs of everyone are being maximally met. To the reply, but what if more needs for everyone were met by ignoring or overriding such entitlements, the radical egalitarian should respond that that is, given the way we are, a thoroughly hypothetical situation and that theories of morality cannot be expected to give guidance for all logically possible worlds but only for worlds which are reasonably like what our actual world is or plausibly could come to be. Setting this argument aside for the moment, even if it did turn out that the need satisfaction linked with having other things—things that involved the overriding of those entitlements—was sufficient to make it the case that more need satisfaction all around for *everyone* would be achieved by overriding those entitlements, then, for reasonable people who clearly saw that, these entitlements would not have the weight presently given to them. They either would not have the importance presently attached to them or the need for the additional living space would be so great that their being overridden would seem, everything considered, the lesser of two evils (as in the example of the postwar housing situation).

There are without doubt genuine entitlements and a theory of justice must take them seriously, but they are not absolute. If the need is great enough we can see the merit in overriding them, just as in law as well as morality the right of eminent domain is recognized. Finally, while I have talked of entitlements here, parallel arguments will go through for desert.

III

I want now to relate this articulation of what equality comes to to my radically egalitarian principles of justice. My articulation of justice is a certain spelling out of the slogan proclaimed by Marx "From each according to his ability, to each according to his needs." The egalitarian conception of society argues for the desirability of bringing into existence a world, once the springs of social wealth flow-freely, in which everyone's needs are as fully satisfied as possible and in which everyone gives according to his ability. Which means, among other things, that everyone, according to his ability, shares the burdens of society. There is an equal giving and equal responsibility here according to ability. It is here, with respect to giving according to ability and with respect to receiving according to need, that a complex equality of result, i.e., equality of condition, is being advocated by the radical egalitarian. What it comes to is this: each of us, where each is to count for one and none to count for more than one, is to give according to ability and receive according to need.

My radical egalitarian principles of justice read as follows:

(1) Each person is to have an equal right to the most extensive total system of equal basic liberties and opportunities (including equal opportunities for meaningful work, for self-determination and political and economic participation) compatible with a similar treatment of all. (This principle gives expression to a commitment to attain and/or sustain equal moral autonomy and equal self-respect.)

(2) After provisions are made for common social (community) values, for capital overhead to preserve the society's productive capacity, allowances made for differing unmanipulated needs and preferences, and due weight is given to the just entitlements of individuals, the income and wealth (the common stock of means) is to be so divided that each person will have a right to an equal share. The necessary burdens requisite to enhance human well-being are also to be equally shared, subject, of course, to limitations by differing abilities and differing situations. (Here I refer to different natural environments and the like and not to class position and the like.)

Here we are talking about equality as a right rather than about equality as a goal as has previously been the subject matter of equality in this chapter. These principles of egalitarianism spell out rights people have and duties they have under *conditions of very considerable productive abundance*. We have a right to certain basic liberties and opportunities and we have, subject to certain limitations spelled out in the second principle, a right to an equal share of the income and wealth in the world. We also have a duty, again subject to the qualifications mentioned in the principle, to do our equal share in shouldering the burdens necessary to protect us from ills and to enhance our well-being.

What is the relation between these rights and the ideal of equality of condition discussed earlier? That is a goal for which we can struggle now to bring about conditions which will some day make its achievement possible, while these rights only become rights when the goal is actually achievable. We have no such rights in slave, feudal or capitalist societies or such duties in those societies. In that important way they are not natural rights for they depend on certain social conditions and certain social structures (socialist ones) to be realizable. What we can say is that it is always desirable that socio-economic conditions come into being which would make it possible to achieve the goal of equality of condition so that these rights and duties I speak of could obtain. But that is a far cry from saying we have such rights and duties now.

It is a corollary of this, if these radical egalitarian principles of justice are correct, that capitalist societies (even capitalist welfare state societies such as Sweden) and statist societies such as the Soviet Union or the People's Republic of China cannot be just societies or at least they must be societies, structured as they are, which are defective in justice. (This is not to say that some of these societies are not juster than others. Sweden is juster than South Africa, Canada than the United States and Cuba and Nicaragua than Honduras and Guatemala.) But none of these statist or capitalist societies can satisfy these radical egalitarian principles of justice, for equal liberty, equal opportunity, equal wealth or equal sharing of burdens are not at all possible in societies having their social structure. So we do not have such rights now but we can take it as a goal that we bring such a society into being with a commitment to an equality of condition in which we would have these rights and duties. Here we require first the massive development of productive power.

The connection between equality as a goal and equality as a right spelled out in these principles of justice is this. The equality of condition appealed to in equality as a goal would, if it were actually to obtain, have to contain the rights and duties enunciated in those principles. There could be no equal life prospects between all people or anything approximating an equal satisfaction of needs if there were not in place something like the system of equal basic liberties referred to in the first principle. Furthermore, without the rough equality of wealth referred to in the second principle, there would be disparities in power and self-direction in society which would render impossible an equality of life prospects or the social conditions required for an equal satisfaction of needs. And plainly, without a roughly equal sharing of burdens, there cannot be a situation where everyone has equal life prospects or has the chance equally to satisfy his needs. The principles of radical

egalitarian justice are implicated in its conception of an ideally adequate equality of condition.

IV

The principles of radical egalitarian justice I have articulated are meant to apply globally and not just to particular societies. But it is certainly fair to say that not a few would worry that such principles of radical egalitarian justice, if applied globally, would force the people in wealthier sections of the world to a kind of financial hari-kari. There are millions of desperately impoverished people. Indeed millions are starving or malnourished and things are not getting any better. People in the affluent societies cannot but worry about whether they face a bottomless pit. Many believe that meeting, even in the most minimal way, the needs of the impoverished is going to put an incredible burden on people—people of all classes—in the affluent societies. Indeed it will, if acted on non-evasively, bring about their impoverishment, and this is just too much to ask. Radical egalitarianism is forgetting Rawls' admonitions about "the strains of commitment"—the recognition that in any rational account of what is required of us, we must at least give a minimal healthy self-interest its due. We must construct our moral philosophy for human beings and not for saints. Human nature is less fixed than conservatives are wont to assume, but it is not so elastic that we can reasonably expect people to impoverish themselves to make the massive transfers between North and South—the industrialized world and the Third World—required to begin to approach a situation where even Rawls' principles would be in place on a global level, to say nothing of my radical egalitarian principles of justice.[3]

The first thing to say in response to this is that my radical egalitarian principles are meant actually to guide practice, to directly determine what we are to do, only in a world of extensive abundance where, as Marx put it, the springs of social wealth flow freely. If such a world cannot be attained with the undermining of capitalism and the full putting into place, stabilizing, and developing of socialist relations of production, then such radical egalitarian principles can only remain as heuristic ideals against which to measure the distance of our travel in the direction of what would be a perfectly just society.

Aside from a small capitalist class, along with those elites most directly and profitably beholden to it (together a group constituting not more than 5 percent of the world's population), there would, in taking my radical egalitarian principles as heuristic guides, be no impoverishment of people in the affluent societies, if we moved in a radically more egalitarian way to start to achieve a global fairness. There would be massive transfers of wealth between North and South, but this could be done in stages so that, for the people in the affluent societies (capitalist elites apart), there need be no undermining of the quality of their lives. Even what were once capitalist elites would not be impoverished or reduced to some kind of bleak life though they would, the incidental Spartan types aside, find their life styles altered. But their health and general well being, including their opportunities to do significant and innovative work, would, if anything, be enhanced. And while some of the sources of their enjoyment would be a thing of the past, there would still be a considerable range of enjoyments available to them sufficient to afford anyone a rich life that could be lived with verve and zest.

A fraction of what the United States spends on defense spending would take care of immediate problems of starvation and malnutrition for most of the world. For longer range problems such as bringing conditions of life in the Third World more in line with conditions of life in Sweden and Switzerland, what is necessary is the dismantling of the capitalist system and the creation of a socio-economic system with an underlying rationale directing it toward producing for needs—everyone's needs. With this altered productive mode, the irrationalities and waste of capitalist production would be cut. There would be no more built-in obsolescence, no more merely cosmetic changes in consumer durables, no more fashion roulette, no more useless products and the like. Moreover, the enormous expen-

ditures that go into the war industry would be a thing of the past. There would be great transfers from North to South, but it would be from the North's capitalist fat and not from things people in the North really need. (There would, in other words, be no self-pauperization of people in the capitalist world.) . . .

V

It has been repeatedly argued that equality undermines liberty. Some would say that a society in which principles like my radical egalitarian principles were adopted, or even the liberal egalitarian principles of Rawls or Dworkin were adopted, would not be a free society. My arguments have been just the reverse. I have argued that it is only in an egalitarian society that full and extensive liberty is possible.

Perhaps the egalitarian and the anti-egalitarian are arguing at cross purposes? What we need to recognize, it has been argued, is that we have two kinds of rights both of which are important to freedom but to rather different freedoms and which are freedoms which not infrequently conflict.[4] We have rights to *fair terms of cooperation* but we also have rights to *non-interference*. If a right of either kind is overridden our freedom is diminished. The reason why it might be thought that the egalitarian and the anti-egalitarian may be arguing at cross purposes is that the egalitarian is pointing to the fact that rights to fair terms of cooperation and their associated liberties require equality while the anti-egalitarian is pointing to the fact that rights to non-interference and their associated liberties conflict with equality. They focus on different liberties.

What I have said above may not be crystal clear, so let me explain. People have a right to fair terms of cooperation. In political terms this comes to the equal right of all to effective participation in government and, in more broadly social terms, and for a society of economic wealth, it means people having a right to a roughly equal distribution of the benefits and burdens of the basic social arrangements that affect their lives and for them to stand in such relations to each other such that no one has the power to dominate the life of another. By contrast, rights to non-interference come to the equal right of all to be left alone by the government and more broadly to live in a society in which people have a right peacefully to pursue their interests without interference.

The conflict between equality and liberty comes down to, very essentially, the conflicts we get in modern societies between rights to fair terms of cooperation and rights to non-interference. As Joseph Schumpeter saw and J. S. Mill before him, one could have a thoroughly democratic society (at least in conventional terms) in which rights to non-interference might still be extensively violated. A central anti-egalitarian claim is that we cannot have an egalitarian society in which the very precious liberties that go with the rights to non-interference would not be violated.

Socialism and egalitarianism plainly protect rights to fair terms of cooperation. Without the social (collective) ownership and control of the means of production, involving with this, in the initial stages of socialism at least, a workers' state, economic power will be concentrated in the hands of a few who will in turn, as a result, dominate effective participation in government. Some right-wing libertarians blind themselves to that reality, but it is about as evident as can be. Only an utter turning away from the facts of social life could lead to any doubts about this at all. But then this means that in a workers' state, if some people have capitalistic impulses, that they would have their rights peacefully to pursue their own interests interfered with. They might wish to invest, retain and bequeath in economic domains. In a workers' state these capitalist acts in many circumstances would have to be forbidden, but that would be a violation of an individual's right to non-interference and the fact, if it was a fact, that we by democratic vote, even with vast majorities, had made such capitalist acts illegal would still not make any difference because individuals' rights to non-interference would still be violated.

We are indeed driven, by egalitarian impulses, of a perfectly understandable sort, to accept interference with laissez-faire capitalism to protect non-subordination and non-domination of people by protecting the egalitarian right to fair terms of cooperation and the enhanced liberty that that brings. Still, as things stand, this leads inevitably to violations of the right to non-interference and this brings with it a diminution of liberty. There will be people with capitalist impulses and they will be interfered with. It is no good denying, it will be said, that egalitarianism and particularly socialism will not lead to interference with very precious individual liberties, namely with our right peacefully to pursue our interests without interference.[5]

The proper response to this, as should be apparent from what I have argued throughout, is that to live in any society at all, capitalist, socialist or whatever, is to live in a world in which there will be some restriction or other on our rights peacefully to pursue our interests without interference. I can't lecture in Albanian or even in French in a standard philosophy class at the University of Calgary, I can't jog naked on most beaches, borrow a book from your library without your permission, fish in your trout pond without your permission, take your dog for a walk without your say so and the like. At least some of these things have been thought to be things which I might peacefully pursue in my own interests. Stopping me from doing them is plainly interfering with my peaceful pursuit of my own interests. And indeed it is an infringement on liberty, an interference with my doing what I may want to do.

However, for at least many of these activities, and particularly the ones having to do with property, even right-wing libertarians think that such interference is perfectly justified. But, justified or not, they still plainly constitute a restriction on our individual freedom. However, what we must also recognize is that there will always be some such restrictions on freedom in any society whatsoever, just in virtue of the fact that a normless society, without the restrictions that having norms imply, is a contradiction in terms.[6] Many restrictions are hardly felt as restrictions, as in the attitudes of many people toward seat-belt legislation, but they are, all the same, plainly restrictions on our liberty. It is just that they are thought to be unproblematically justified.

To the question would a socialism with a radical egalitarianism restrict some liberties, including some liberties rooted in rights to noninterference, the answer is that it indeed would; but so would laissez-faire capitalism, aristocratic conceptions of justice, liberal conceptions or any social formations at all, with their associated conceptions of justice. The relevant question is which of these restrictions are justified.

The restrictions on liberty proferred by radical egalitarianism and socialism, I have argued, are justified for they, of the various alternatives, give us both the most extensive and the most abundant system of liberty possible in modern conditions with their thorough protection of the right to fair terms of cooperation. Radical egalitarianism will also, and this is central for us, protect our civil liberties and these liberties are, of course, our most basic liberties. These are the liberties which are the most vital for us to protect. What it will not do is to protect our unrestricted liberties to invest, retain and bequeath in the economic realm and it will not protect our unrestricted freedom to buy and sell. There is, however, no good reason to think that these restrictions are restrictions of anything like a basic liberty. Moreover, we are justified in restricting our freedom to buy and sell if such restrictions strengthen, rather than weaken, our total system of liberty. This is in this way justified, for only by such market restrictions can the rights of the vast majority of people to effective participation in government and an equal role in the control of their social lives be protected. I say this because if we let the market run free in this way, power will pass into the hands of a few who will control the lives of the many and determine the fundamental design of the society. The actual liberties that are curtailed in a radically egalitarian social order are inessential liberties whose restriction in contemporary circumstances enhances human well-being and indeed makes for a firmer entrenchment of basic liberties and for their greater extension globally. That is to say, we here restrict some liberty in order to attain more liberty and a more equally distributed pattern of liberty. More people will be able to do what they want and have a greater control over their own lives than in a capitalist world order with its at least implicit inegalitarian commitments.

However, some might say I still have not faced the most central objection to radical egalitarianism, namely its statism. (I would prefer to say its putative statism.) The picture is this. The egalitarian state must be in the redistribution business. It has to make, or make sure there is made, an equal relative contribution to the welfare of every citizen. But this in effect means that the socialist state or, for that matter, the welfare state, will be deeply interventionist in our personal lives. It will be in the business, as one right-winger emotively put it, of cutting one person down to size in order to bring about that person's equality with another person who was in a previously disadvantageous position.[7] That is said to be morally objectionable and it would indeed be deeply morally objectionable in many circumstances. But it isn't in the circumstances in which the radical egalitarian presses for redistribution. (I am not speaking of what might be mere equalizing upwards.) The circumstances are these: Capitalist A gets his productive property confiscated so that he could no longer dominate and control the lives of proletarians B, C, D, E, F, and G. But what is wrong with it where this "cutting down to size"—in reality the confiscation of productive property or the taxation of the capitalist—involves no violation of A's civil liberties or the harming of his actual well-being (health, ability to work, to cultivate the arts, to have fruitful personal relations, to live in comfort and the like) and where B, C, D, E, F, and G will have their freedom and their well-being thoroughly enhanced if such confiscation or taxation occurs? Far from being morally objectionable, it is precisely the sort of state of affairs that people ought to favor. It certainly protects more liberties and more significant liberties than it undermines.

There is another familiar anti-egalitarian argument designed to establish the liberty-undermining qualities of egalitarianism. It is an argument we have touched upon in discussing meritocracy. It turns on the fact that in any society there will be both talents and handicaps. Where they exist, what do we want to do about maintaining equal distribution? Egalitarians, radical or otherwise, certainly do not want to penalize people for talent. That being so, then surely people should be allowed to retain the benefits of superior talent. But this in some circumstances will lead to significant inequalities in resources and in the meeting of needs. To sustain equality there will have to be an ongoing redistribution in the direction of the less talented and less fortunate. But this redistribution from the more to the less talented does plainly penalize the talented for their talent. That, it will be said, is something which is both unfair and an undermining of liberty.

The following, it has been argued, makes the above evident enough.[8] If people have talents they will tend to want to use them. And if they use them they are very likely to come out ahead. Must not egalitarians say they ought not to be able to come out ahead no matter how well they use their talents and no matter how considerable these talents are? But that is intolerably restrictive and unfair.

The answer to the above anti-egalitarian argument is implicit in a number of things I have already said. But here let me confront this familiar argument directly. Part of the answer comes out in probing some of the ambiguities of "coming out ahead." Note, incidentally, that (1) not all reflective, morally sensitive people will be so concerned with that, and (2) that being very concerned with that is a mentality that capitalism inculcates. Be that as it may, to turn to the ambiguities, note that some take "coming out ahead" principally to mean "being paid well for the use of those talents" where "being paid well" is being paid sufficiently well so that it creates inequalities sufficient to disturb the preferred egalitarian patterns. (Without that, being paid well would give one no relative advantage.) But, as we have seen, "coming out ahead" need not take that form at all. Talents can be recognized and acknowledged in many ways. First, in just the respect and admiration of a fine employment of talents that would naturally come from people seeing them so displayed where these people were not twisted by envy; second, by having, because of these talents, interesting and secure work that their talents fit them for and they merit in virtue of those talents. Moreover, having more money is not going to matter much—for familiar marginal utility reasons—

where what in capitalist societies would be called the welfare floors are already very high, this being made feasible by the great productive wealth of the society. Recall that in such a society of abundance everyone will be well off and secure. In such a society people are not going to be very concerned about being a little better off than someone else. The talented are in no way, in such a situation, robbed to help the untalented and handicapped or penalized for their talents. They are only prevented from amassing wealth (most particularly productive wealth), which would enable them to dominate the untalented and the handicapped and to control the social life of the world of which they are both a part. . . .

I think that the moral authority for abstract egalitarianism, for the belief that the interests of everyone matters and matters equally, comes from its being the case that it is *required by the moral point of view*.[9] What I am predicting is that a person who has a good understanding of what morality is, has a good knowledge of the facts, is not ideologically mystified, takes an impartial point of view, and has an attitude of impartial caring, would, if not conceptually confused, come to accept the abstract egalitarian thesis. I see no way of arguing someone into such an egalitarianism who does not in this general way have a love of humankind.[10] A hard-hearted Hobbesist is not reachable here. But given that a person has that love of humankind—that impartial and impersonal caring—together with the other qualities mentioned above, then, I predict, that that person would be an egalitarian at least to the extent of accepting the abstract egalitarian thesis. What I am claiming is that if these conditions were to obtain (if they ceased to be just counterfactuals), then there would be a consensus among moral agents about accepting the abstract egalitarian thesis. . . .

Notes

1. See the debate between Robert Nozick, Daniel Bell and James Tobin, "If Inequality Is Inevitable What Can Be Done About It?" *The New York Times*, January 3, 1982, p. E5. The exchange between Bell and Nozick reveals the differences

between the old egalitarianism and right wing libertarianism. It is not only that the right and left clash but sometimes right clashes with right.

2. Amartya Sen, "Equality of What?" *The Tanner Lectures on Human Values,* vol. 1 (1980), ed. Sterling M. McMurrin (Cambridge, England: Cambridge University Press, 1980), pp. 198–220.

3. Henry Shue, "The Burdens of Justice," *The Journal of Philosophy* 80, no. 10 (October 1983): 600–601; 606–8.

4. Richard W. Miller, "Marx and Morality," in *Marxism,* eds. J. R. Pennock and J. W. Chapman, Nomos 26 (New York: New York University Press, 1983), pp. 9–11.

5. Ibid., p. 10.

6. This has been argued from both the liberal center and the left. Ralf Dahrendorf, *Essays in the Theory of Society* (Stanford, Cal.: Stanford University Press, 1968), pp. 151–78; and G. A. Cohen, "Capitalism, Freedom and the Proletariat" in *The Idea of Freedom: Essays in Honour of Isaiah Berlin,* ed. Alan Ryan (Oxford: Oxford University Press, 1979).

7. The graphic language should be duly noted. Jan Narveson, "On Dworkinian Equality," *Social Philosophy and Policy* 1, no. 1 (autumn 1983): 4.

8. Ibid., p. 1–24.

9. Some will argue that there is no such thing as a moral point of view. My differences with him about the question of whether the amoralist can be argued into morality not withstanding, I think Kurt Baier, in a series of articles written subsequent to his *The Moral Point of View,* has clearly shown that there is something reasonably determinate that can, without ethnocentrism, be called "the moral point of view."

10. Richard Norman has impressively argued that this is an essential background assumption of the moral point of view. Richard Norman, "Critical Notice of Rodger Beehler's *Moral Life,*" *Canadian Journal of Philosophy* 11, no. 1 (March 1981): 157–83.

Morality and the Liberal Ideal

Michael J. Sandel

Michael J. Sandel believes that recent political philosophy has offered both a utilitarian and a rights-based defense of liberalism. The utilitarian defense, which sees liberalism as maximizing the sum of utility, has even been criticized by other liberals for failing to take seriously the distinction between persons. The rights-based defense, which sees liberalism as guaranteeing each person certain rights, has been criticized for giving the self priority over its ends. According to communitarians, we cannot even conceive of ourselves as distinct from our ends.

Liberals often take pride in defending what they oppose—pornography, for example, or unpopular views. They say the state should not impose on its citizens a preferred way of life, but should leave them as free as possible to choose their own values and ends, consistent with a similar liberty for others. This commitment to freedom of choice requires liberals constantly to distinguish between permission and praise, between allowing a prac-

From "Morality and the Liberal Ideal," *New Republic* (May 7, 1984), pp. 15–17. Reprinted by permission of *New Republic.*

tice and endorsing it. It is one thing to allow pornography, they argue, something else to affirm it.

Conservatives sometimes exploit this distinction by ignoring it. They charge that those who would allow abortions favor abortion, that opponents of school prayer, oppose prayer, that those who defend the rights of Communists sympathize with their cause. And in a pattern of argument familiar in our politics, liberals reply by invoking higher principles; it is not that they dislike pornography less, but rather that they value toleration, or freedom of choice, or fair procedures more.

But in contemporary debate, the liberal rejoinder seems increasingly fragile, its moral basis increasingly unclear. Why should toleration and freedom of choice prevail when other important values are also at stake? Too often the answer implies some version of moral relativism, the idea that it is wrong to "legislate morality" because all morality is merely subjective. "Who is to say what is literature and what is filth? That is a value judgment, and whose values should decide?"

Relativism usually appears less as a claim than as a question. "Who is to judge?" But it is a question that can also be asked of the values that liberals defend. Toleration and freedom and fairness are values too, and they can hardly be defended by the claim that no values can be defended. So it is a mistake to affirm liberal values by arguing that all values are merely subjective. The relativist defense of liberalism is no defense at all.

What, then, can be the moral basis of the higher principles the liberal invokes? Recent political philosophy has offered two main alternatives—one utilitarian, the other Kantian. The utilitarian view, following John Stuart Mill, defends liberal principles in the name of maximizing the general welfare. The state should not impose on its citizens a preferred way of life, even for their own good, because doing so will reduce the sum of human happiness, at least in the long run; better that people choose for themselves, even if, on occasion, they get it wrong. "The only freedom which deserves the name," writes Mill in *On Liberty*, "is that of pursuing our own good in our own way so long as we do not attempt to deprive others of theirs, or impede their efforts to obtain it." He adds that his argument does not depend on any notion of abstract right, only on the principle of the greatest good for the greatest number. "I regard utility as the ultimate appeal on all ethical questions; but it must be utility in the largest sense, grounded on the permanent interests of man as a progressive being."

Many objections have been raised against utilitarianism as a general doctrine of moral philosophy. Some have questioned the concept of utility, and the assumption that all human goods are in principle commensurable. Others have objected that by reducing all values to preferences and desires, utilitarians are unable to admit qualitative distinctions of worth, unable to distinguish noble desires from base ones. But most recent debate has focused on whether utilitarianism offers a convincing basis for liberal principles, including respect for individual rights.

In one respect, utilitarianism would seem well suited to liberal purposes. Seeking to maximize overall happiness does not require judging people's values, only aggregating them. And the willingness to aggregate preferences without judging them suggests a tolerant spirit, even a democratic one. When people go to the polls we count their votes, whatever they are.

But the utilitarian calculus is not always as liberal as it first appears. If enough cheering Romans pack the Coliseum to watch the lion devour the Christian, the collective pleasure of the Romans will surely outweigh the pain of the Christian, intense though it be. Or if a big majority abhors a small religion and wants it banned, the balance of preferences will favor suppression, not toleration. Utilitarians sometimes defend individual rights on the grounds that respecting them now will serve utility in the long run. But this calculation is precarious and contingent. It hardly secures the liberal promise not to impose on some the values of others. As the majority will is an inadequate instrument of liberal politics—by itself it fails to secure individual rights—so the utilitarian philosophy is an inadequate foundation for liberal principles.

The case against utilitarianism was made most powerfully by Immanuel Kant. He argued that empirical principles, such as utility, were unfit to serve as basis for the moral law. A wholly instrumental defense of freedom and rights not only leaves rights vulnerable, but fails to respect the inherent dignity of persons. The utilitarian calculus treats people as means to the happiness of others, not as ends in themselves, worthy of respect.

Contemporary liberals extend Kant's argument with the claim that utilitarianism fails to take seriously the distinction between persons. In seeking above all to maximize the general welfare, the utilitarian treats society as a whole as if it were a single person, it conflates our many, diverse desires into a single system of desires. It is indifferent to the distribution of satisfactions among persons, except insofar as this may affect the overall sum. But this fails to respect our plurality and distinctness. It uses some as means to the happiness of all, and so fails to respect each as an end in himself.

In the view of modern day Kantians, certain rights are so fundamental that even the general welfare cannot override them. As John Rawls writes in his important work, *A Theory of Justice,* "Each person possesses an inviolability founded on justice that even the welfare of society as a whole cannot override. . . . The rights secured by justice are not subject to political bargaining or to the calculus of social interests."

So Kantian liberals need an account of rights that does not depend on utilitarian considerations. More than this, they need an account that does not depend on any particular conception of the good, that does not presuppose the superiority of one way of life over others. Only a justification neutral about ends could preserve the liberal resolve not to favor any particular ends, or to impose on its citizens a preferred way of life. But what sort of justification could this be? How is it possible to affirm certain liberties and rights as fundamental without embracing some vision of the good life, without endorsing some ends over others? It would seem we are back to the relativist predicament—to affirm liberal principles without embracing any particular ends.

The solution proposed by Kantian liberals is to draw a distinction between the "right" and the "good"—between a framework of basic rights and liberties, and the conceptions of the good that people may choose to pursue within the framework. It is one thing for the state to support a fair framework, they argue, something else to affirm some particular ends. For example, it is one thing to defend the right to free speech so that people may be free to form their own opinions and choose their own ends, but something else to support it on the grounds that a life of political discussion is inherently worthier than a life unconcerned with public affairs, or on the grounds that free speech will increase the general welfare. Only the first defense is available in the Kantian view, resting as it does on the ideal of a neutral framework.

Now, the commitment to a framework neutral with respect to ends can be seen as a kind of value—in this sense the Kantian liberal is no relativist—but its value consists precisely in its refusal to affirm a preferred way of life or conception of the good. For Kantian liberals, then, the right is prior to the good, and in two senses. First, individual rights cannot be sacrificed for the sake of the general good; and second, the principles of justice that specify these rights cannot be premised on any particular vision of the good life. What justifies the rights is not that they maximize the general welfare or otherwise promote the good, but rather that they comprise a fair framework within which individuals and groups can choose their own values and ends, consistent with a similar liberty for others.

Of course, proponents of the rights-based ethic notoriously disagree about what rights are fundamental, and about what political arrangements the ideal of the neutral framework requires. Egalitarian liberals support the welfare state, and favor a scheme of civil liberties together with certain social and economic rights—rights to welfare, education, health care, and so on. Libertarian liberals defend the market economy, and claim that redistributive policies violate peoples' rights; they favor a scheme of civil liberties combined with a strict regime of private property rights. But whether egalitarian or libertarian, rights-based liberalism begins with the claim that we are separate, individual persons, each with our own aims, interests, and conceptions of the good; it seeks a framework of rights that will enable us to realize our capacity as free moral agents, consistent with a similar liberty for others.

Within academic philosophy, the last decade or so has seen the ascendance of the rights-based ethic over the utilitarian one, due in large part to the influence of Rawls's *A Theory of Justice.* The legal philosopher H. I. A. Hart recently described the shift from "the old faith that some form of utilitarianism must capture the essence of political morality" to the new faith that "the truth must lie with a doctrine of basic human rights, protecting specific basic liberties and interests of individuals. . . . Whereas not so long ago great energy and much ingenuity of many philosophers were devoted to making some form of utilitarianism work, latterly such energies and ingenuity have been devoted to the articulation of theories of basic rights."

But in philosophy as in life, the new faith becomes the old orthodoxy before long. Even as it has come to prevail over it: utilitarian rival, the rights-based ethic has recently faced a growing challenge from a different direction, from a view that gives fuller expression to the claims of citizenship and community than the liberal vision allows. The communitarian critics, unlike modern liberals, make the case for a politics of the common good. Recalling the arguments of Hegel against Kant, they question the liberal claim for the priority of the right over the good, and the picture of the freely choosing individual it embodies. Following Aristotle, they argue that we cannot justify political arrangements without reference to common purposes and ends, and that we cannot conceive of ourselves without reference to our role as citizens, as participants in a common life.

This debate reflects two contrasting pictures of the self. The rights-based ethic, and the conception of the person it embodies, were shaped in large part in the encounter with utilitarianism. Where utilitarians conflate our many desires into a single system of desire, Kantians insist on the separateness of persons. Where the utilitarian self is simply defined as the sum of its desires, the Kantian-self is a choosing self, independent of the desires and ends it may have at any moment. As Rawls writes, "The self is prior to the ends which are affirmed by it, even a dominant end must be chosen from among numerous possibilities."

The priority of the self over its ends means I am never defined by my aims and attachments, but always capable of standing back to survey and assess and possibly to revise them. This is what it means to be a free and independent self, capable of choice. And this is the vision of the self that finds expression in the ideal of the state as a neutral framework. On the rights-based ethic, it is precisely because we are essentially separate, independent selves that we need a neutral framework, a framework of rights that refuses to choose among competing purposes and ends. If the self is prior to its ends, then the right must be prior to the good.

Communitarian critics of rights-based liberalism say we cannot conceive ourselves as independent in this way, as bearers of selves wholly detached from our aims and attachments. They say that certain of our roles are partly constitutive of the persons we are—as citizens of a country, or members of a movement, or partisans of a cause. But if we are partly defined by the communities we inhabit, then we must also be implicated in the purposes and ends characteristic of those communities. As Alasdair MacIntyre writes in his book, *After Virtue*, "What is good for me has to be the good for one who inhabits these roles." Open-ended though it be, the story of my life is always embedded in the story of those communities from which I derive my identity—whether family or city, tribe or nation, party or cause. In the communitarian view, these stories make a moral difference, not only a psychological one. They situate us in the world and give our lives their moral particularity.

What is at stake for politics in the debate between unencumbered selves and situated ones? What are the practical differences between a politics of rights and a politics of the common good? On some issues, the two theories may produce different arguments for similar policies. For example, the civil rights movement of the 1960s might be justified by liberals in the name of human dignity and respect for persons, and by communitarians in the name of recognizing the full membership of fellow citizens wrongly excluded from the common life of the nation. And where liberals might support public education in hopes of equipping students to become autonomous individuals, capable of choosing their own ends and pursuing them effectively, communitarians might support public education in hopes of equipping students to become good citizens, capable of contributing meaningfully to public deliberations and pursuits.

On other issues, the two ethics might lead to different policies. Communitarians would be more likely than liberals to allow a town to ban pornographic book stores, on the grounds that pornography offends its way of life and the values that sustain it. But a politics of civic virtue does not always part company with liberalism in favor of conservative policies. For example, communitarians would be more willing than some rights-oriented liberals to see states enact laws regulating plant closings, to protect their communities from the disruptive effects of capital mobility and sudden industrial change. More generally, where the liberal regards the expansion of individual rights and entitlements as unqualified moral and political progress, the communitarian is troubled by the tendency of liberal programs to displace politics from smaller forms of association to more comprehensive ones. Where libertarian liberals defend the private economy and egalitarian liberals defend the welfare state, communitarians worry about the concentration of power in both the corporate economy and the bureaucratic state, and the erosion of those intermediate forms of community that have at times sustained a more vital public life.

Liberals often argue that a politics of the common good, drawing as it must on particular loyalties, obligations, and traditions, opens the way to prejudice and intolerance. The modern nation-state is not the Athenian polis, they point out; the scale and diversity of modern life have rendered the Aristotelian political ethic nostalgic at best and dangerous at worst. Any attempt to govern by a vision of the good is likely to lead to a slippery slope of totalitarian temptations.

Communitarians reply, rightly in my view, that intolerance flourishes most where forms of life are dislocated, roots unsettled, traditions undone. In our day, the totalitarian impulse has sprung less from the convictions of confidently situated selves than from the confusions of atomized, dislocated, frustrated selves, at sea in a world where common meanings have lost their force. As Hannah Arendt has written, "What makes mass society so difficult to bear is not the number of people involved, or at least not primarily, but the fact that the world between them has lost its power to gather them together, to relate and to separate them." Insofar as our public life has withered, our sense of common involvement diminished, we lie vulnerable to the mass politics of totalitarian solutions. So responds the party of the common good to the party of rights. If the party of the common good is right, our most pressing moral and political project is to revitalize those civic republican possibilities implicit in our tradition but fading in our time.

Wyman, Commissioner of New York Department of Social Services v. James

Supreme Court of the United States

The issue before the Supreme Court of the United States was whether the Fourth Amendment prohibition of unreasonable searches applies to visits by welfare caseworkers to recipients of Aid to Families with Dependent Children. The majority of the Court held that the Fourth Amendment does not apply in this case because the visitation is not forced or compelled, and even if it were, the visitation serves the state's overriding interest in the welfare of dependent children. Dissenting Justices Douglas and Marshall argued that the Fourth Amendment prohibition does apply because the visitation is forced and compelled (although not normally by a threat of a criminal penalty) and because there are other ways of protecting the state's interest in this case. Justices Douglas and Marshall also argued that the decision of the majority is inconsistent with the Supreme Court's rulings with respect to the allocation of benefits in other cases.

Mr. Justice Blackmun delivered the opinion of the Court.

This appeal presents the issue whether a beneficiary of the program for Aid to Families with Dependent Children (AFDC) may refuse a home visit by the caseworker without risking the termination of benefits.

The New York State and City social services commissioners appeal from a judgment and decree of a divided three-judge District Court. . . .

The District Court majority held that a mother receiving AFDC relief may refuse, without forfeiting her right to that relief, the periodic home visit which the cited New York statutes and regulations prescribe as a condition for the continuance of assistance under the program. The beneficiary's thesis, and that of the District Court majority, is that home visitation is a search and, when not consented to or when not supported by a warrant based on probable cause, violates the beneficiary's Fourth and Fourteenth Amendment rights. . . .

Plaintiff Barbara James is the mother of a son, Maurice, who was born in May 1967. They reside in New York City. Mrs. James first applied for AFDC assistance shortly before Maurice's birth. A caseworker made a visit to her apartment at that time without objection. The assistance was authorized.

Two years later, on May 8, 1969, a caseworker wrote Mrs. James that she would visit her home on May 14. Upon receipt of this advice, Mrs. James telephoned the worker that, although she was willing to supply information "reasonable and relevant" to her need for public assistance, any discussion was not to take place at her home. The worker told Mrs. James that she was required by law to visit in her home and that refusal to permit the visit would result in the termination of assistance. Permission was still denied. . . .

A notice of termination issued on June 2.

Thereupon, without seeking a hearing at the state level, Mrs. James, individually and on behalf of Maurice, and purporting to act on behalf of all other persons similarly situated, instituted the present civil rights suit. . . .

When a case involves a home and some type of official intrusion into that home, as this case appears to do, an immediate and natural reaction is one of concern about Fourth Amendment rights and the protection which that Amendment is intended to afford. Its emphasis indeed is upon one of the most precious aspects of personal security in the home: "The right of the people to be secure in their persons, houses, papers, and effects. . . ." This Court has characterized that right as "basic to a free society. . . ." And over the years the Court consistently has been most protective of the privacy of the dwelling. . . .

This natural and quite proper protective attitude, however, is not a factor in this case, for the seemingly obvious and simple reason that we are not concerned here with any search by the New York social service agency in the Fourth Amendment meaning of that term. It is true that the governing statute and regulations appear to make mandatory the initial home visit and the subsequent periodic "contacts" (which may include home visits) for the inception and continuance of aid. It is also true that the caseworker's posture in the home visit is perhaps, in a sense, both rehabilitative and investigative. But this latter aspect, we think, is given too broad a character and far more emphasis than it deserves if it is equated with a search in the traditional criminal law context. We note, too, that the visitation in itself is not forced or compelled, and that the beneficiary's denial of permission is not a criminal act. If consent to the visitation is withheld, no visitation takes place. The aid then never begins or merely ceases, as the case may be. There is no entry of the home and there is no search.

If however, we were to assume that a caseworker's home visit, before or subsequent to the beneficiary's initial qualification for benefits, somehow (perhaps because the average beneficiary might feel she is in no position to refuse consent to the visit), and despite its interview nature, does possess some of the characteristics of a search in the traditional sense, we nevertheless conclude that does not fall within the Fourth Amendment's proscription. This is because it does not descend to the level of unreasonableness. It is unreasonableness which is the Fourth Amendment's standard.

There are a number of factors that compel

us to conclude that the home visit proposed for Mrs. James is not unreasonable.

The public's interest in this particular segment of the area of assistance to the unfortunate is protection and aid for the dependent child whose family requires such aid for that child. . . . The dependent child's needs are paramount, and only with hesitancy would we relegate those needs, in the scale of comparative values, to a position secondary to what the mother claims as her rights.

The agency, with tax funds provided from federal as well as from state sources, is fulfilling a public trust. The State, working through its qualified welfare agency, has appropriate and paramount interest and concern in seeing and assuring that the intended and proper objects of that tax-produced assistance are the ones who benefit from the aid it dispenses. . . .

One who dispenses purely private charity naturally has an interest in and expects to know how his charitable funds are utilized and put to work. The public, when it is the provider, rightly expects the same. . . .

We therefore conclude that the home visitation as structured by the New York statutes and regulations is a reasonable administrative tool; that it serves a valid and proper administrative purpose for the dispensation of the AFDC program; that it is not an unwarranted invasion of personal privacy; and that it violates no right guaranteed by the Fourth Amendment.

Reversed and remanded with directions to enter a judgment of dismissal.

It is so ordered. . . .

Mr. Justice Douglas, dissenting. . . .

In 1969 roughly 127 billion dollars were spent by the federal, state, and local governments on "social welfare." To farmers alone almost four billion dollars were paid, in part for not growing certain crops. . . .

Yet almost every beneficiary whether rich or poor, rural or urban, has a "house"—one of the places protected by the Fourth Amendment against "unreasonable searches and seizures." The question in this case is whether receipt of largesse from the government makes the *home* of the beneficiary subject to access by an inspector of the agency of oversight, even though the beneficiary objects to the intrusion and even though the Fourth

Amendment's procedure for access to one's *house* or *home* is not followed. The penalty here is not, of course, invasion of the privacy of Barbara James, only her loss of federal or state largesse. That, however, is merely rephrasing the problem. Whatever the semantics, the central question is whether the government by force of its largesse has the power to "buy up" rights guaranteed by the Constitution. But for the assertion of her constitutional right, Barbara James in this case would have received the welfare benefit. . . .

The applicable principle, as stated in *Camara* as "justified by history and by current experience" is that "except in certain carefully defined classes of cases, a search of private property without proper consent is 'unreasonable' unless it has been authorized by a valid search warrant."

In *See* we [decided] that the "businessman, like the occupant of a residence, has a constitutional right to go about his business free from unreasonable official entries upon his private commercial property." There is not the slightest hint in *See* that the Government could condition a business license on the "consent" of the licensee to the administrative searches we held violated the Fourth Amendment. It is a strange jurisprudence indeed which safeguards the businessman at his place of work from warrantless searches but will not do the same for a mother in her *home*.

Is a search of her home without a warrant made "reasonable" merely because she is dependent on government largesse?

Judge Skelly Wright has stated the problem succinctly:

"Welfare has long been considered the equivalent of charity and its recipients have been subjected to all kinds of dehumanizing experiences in the government's effort to police its welfare payments. In fact, over half a billion dollars are expended annually for administration and policing in connection with the Aid to Families with Dependent Children program. Why such large sums are necessary for administration and policing has never been adequately explained. No such sums are spent policing the government subsidies granted to farmers, airlines, steamship companies, and junk mail dealers, to name but a few. The truth is that in this subsidy area society has simply adopted a double standard, one for aid to business and the farmer and a different one for welfare." Poverty, Minorities, and Respect for Law, 1970 Duke L. J. 425, 437–438.

If the welfare recipient was not Barbara James but a prominent, affluent cotton or wheat farmer receiving benefit payments for not growing crops, would not the approach be different? Welfare in aid of dependent children, like social security and unemployment benefits, has an aura of suspicion. There doubtless are frauds in every sector of public welfare whether the recipient be a Barbara James or someone who is prominent or influential. But constitutional rights—here the privacy of the *home*—are obviously not dependent on the poverty or on the affluence of the beneficiary. It is the precincts of the *home* that the Fourth Amendment protects; and their privacy is as important to the lowly as to the mighty.

I would sustain the judgment of the three-judge court in the present case.

Mr. Justice Marshall, whom Mr. Justice Brennan joins, dissenting.

. . . The record plainly shows . . . that Mrs. James offered to furnish any information that the appellants desired and to be interviewed at any place other than her home. Appellants rejected her offers and terminated her benefits solely on the ground that she refused to permit a home visit. In addition, appellants make no contention that any sort of probable cause exists to suspect appellee of welfare fraud or child abuse.

Simply stated, the issue in this case is whether a state welfare agency can require all recipients of AFDC benefits to submit to warrantless "visitations" of their homes. In answering that question, the majority dodges between constitutional issues to reach a result clearly inconsistent with the decisions of this Court. We are told that there is no such search involved in this case; that even if there were a

search, it would not be unreasonable; and that even if this were an unreasonable search, a welfare recipient waives her right to object by accepting benefits. I emphatically disagree with all three conclusions. . . .

. . . In an era of rapidly burgeoning governmental activities and their concomitant inspectors, caseworkers, and researchers, a restriction of the Fourth Amendment to "the traditional criminal law context" tramples the ancient concept that a man's home is his castle. Only last Term, we reaffirmed that this concept has lost none of its vitality. . . .

. . . [I]t is argued that the home visit is justified to protect dependent children from "abuse" and "exploitation." These are heinous crimes, but they are not confined to indigent households. Would the majority sanction, in the absence of probable cause, compulsory visits to all American homes for the purpose of discovering child abuse? Or is this Court prepared to hold as a matter of constitutional law that a mother, merely because she is poor, is substantially more likely to injure or exploit her children? Such a categorical approach to an entire class of citizens would be dangerously at odds with the tenets of our democracy. . . .

Although the Court does not agree with my conclusion that the home visit is an unreasonable search, its opinion suggests that even if the visit were unreasonable, appellee has somehow waived her right to object. Surely the majority cannot believe that valid Fourth Amendment consent can be given under the threat of the loss of one's sole means of support. . . .

In deciding that the homes of AFDC recipients are not entitled to protection from warrantless searches by welfare caseworkers, the Court declines to follow prior case law and employs a rationale that, if applied to the claims of all citizens, would threaten the validity of the Fourth Amendment. . . . Perhaps the majority has explained why a commercial warehouse deserves more protection than does this poor woman's home. I am not convinced; and, therefore, I must respectfully dissent.

San Antonio Independent School District v. Rodriguez

Supreme Court of the United States

The issue before the Supreme Court of the United States was whether the Texas School System, by making the availability of funds to school districts a function of the taxable wealth in those districts, violates the Fourteenth Amendment requirement that all citizens receive the "equal protection of the laws." The majority of the Court held that since education is not a right afforded strict protection by the Federal Constitution and since the absolute deprivation of education is not at stake, the Texas School System does not violate the Fourteenth Amendment. Dissenting Justices Marshall and Douglas held that since a right to education (although not implicitly or explicitly guaranteed by the Federal Constitution) is a fundamental right from the perspective of the Fourteenth Amendment and since the Texas School System does provide significantly unequal funding to different school districts, the School System does violate the Fourteenth Amendment, even though no one has been absolutely deprived of an education.

Mr. Justice Powell delivered the opinion of the Court.

This suit attacking the Texas system of financing public education was initiated by Mexican-American parents whose children attend the elementary and secondary schools in the Edgewood Independent School District, an urban school district in San Antonio, Texas. They brought a class action on behalf of schoolchildren throughout the State who are members of minority groups or who are poor and reside in school districts having a low property tax base. Named as defendants were the State Board of Education, the Commissioner of Education, the State Attorney General, and the Bexar County (San Antonio) Board of Trustees. The complaint was filed in the summer of 1968 and a three-judge court was impaneled in January 1969. In December 1971 the panel rendered its judgment in a *per curiam* opinion holding the Texas school finance system unconstitutional under the Equal Protection Clause of the Fourteenth Amendment. The State appealed, and we noted probable jurisdiction to consider the far-reaching constitutional questions presented. . . . For the reasons stated in this opinion, we reverse the decision of the Distinct Court. . . .

The school district in which appellees reside, the Edgewood Independent School District, has been compared throughout this litigation with the Alamo Heights Independent School District. This comparison between the least and most affluent districts in the San Antonio area serves to illustrate the manner in which the dual system of finance operates and to indicate the extent to which substantial disparities exist despite the State's impressive progress in recent years. Edgewood is one of seven public school districts in the metropolitan area. Approximately 22,000 students are enrolled in its 25 elementary and secondary schools. The district is situated in the core-city sector of San Antonio in a residential neighborhood that has little commercial or industrial property. The residents are predominantly of Mexican-American descent: approximately 90% of the student population is Mexican-American and over 6% is Negro. The average assessed property value per pupil is $5,960—the lowest in the metropolitan area—and the median family income ($4,686) is also the lowest. At an equalized tax rate of $1.05 per $100 of assessed property—the highest in the metropolitan area—the district contributed $26 to the education of each child for the 1967–1968 school year above its Local Fund Assignment for the Minimum Foundation Program. The Foundation Program contributed $222 per pupil for a state-local total of $248. Federal funds added another $108 for a total of $356 per pupil.

Alamo Heights is the most affluent school district in San Antonio. Its six schools, housing approximately 5,000 students, are situated in a residential community quite unlike the Edgewood District. The school population is predominantly "Anglo," having only 18% Mexican-Americans and less than 1% Negroes. The assessed property value per pupil exceeds $49,000, and the median family income is $8,001. In 1967–1968 the local tax rate of $.85 per $100 of valuation yielded $333 per pupil over and above its contribution to the Foundation Program. Coupled with the $225 provided from that Program, the district was able to supply $558 per student. Supplemented by a $36 per-pupil grant from federal sources, Alamo Heights spent $594 per pupil. . . .

. . . [T]hese disparities, largely attributable to differences in the amounts of money collected through local property taxation . . . led the District Court to conclude that Texas' dual system of public school financing violated the Equal Protection Clause. The District Court held that the Texas system discriminates on the basis of wealth in the manner in which education is provided for its people. . . . Finding that *wealth* is a *"suspect"* classification and that *education* is a *"fundamental"* interest, the District Court held that the Texas system could be sustained only if the State could show that it was premised upon some compelling state interest. On this issue the court concluded that "[n]ot only are defendants unable to demonstrate compelling state interests . . . they fail even to establish a reasonable basis for these classifications." . . .

Texas virtually concedes that its historically rooted dual system of financing education could not withstand the strict judicial scrutiny that this Court has found appropriate in reviewing legislative judgments that interfere with fundamental constitutional rights or that involve suspect classifications. If, as previous decisions have indicated, strict scrutiny means that the State's system is not entitled to the usual presumption of validity, that the State rather than the complainants must carry a "heavy burden of justification," that the State must demonstrate that its educational system has been structured with "precision," and is "tailored" narrowly to serve legitimate objectives and that it has selected the "less drastic means" for effectuating its objectives, the Texas financing system and its counterpart in virtually every other State will not pass muster. The State defends the system's rationality with vigor and disputes the District Court's finding that it lacks a "reasonable basis."

This, then, establishes the framework for our analysis. We must decide, first, whether the Texas system of financing public education operates to the disadvantage of some suspect class or impinges upon a fundamental right explicitly or implicitly protected by the Constitution, thereby requiring strict judicial scrutiny. If so, the judgment of the District Court should be affirmed. If not, the Texas scheme must still be examined to determine whether it rationally furthers some legitimate, articulated state purpose and therefore does not constitute an invidious discrimination in violation of the Equal Protection Clause of the Fourteenth Amendment.

The District Court's opinion does not reflect the novelty and complexity of the constitutional questions posed by appellees' challenge to Texas' system of school financing. In concluding that strict judicial scrutiny was required, that court relied on decisions dealing with the rights of indigents to equal treatment in the criminal trial and appellate processes, and on cases disapproving wealth restrictions on the right to vote. Those cases, the District Court concluded, established wealth as a suspect classification. Finding that the local property tax system discriminated on the basis of wealth, it regarded those precedents as controlling. It then reasoned, based on decisions of this Court affirming the undeniable importance of education, that there is a fundamental right to education and that, absent some compelling state justification, the Texas system could not stand.

We are unable to agree that this case, which in significant aspects is *sui generis,* may be so neatly fitted into the conventional mosaic of constitutional analysis under the Equal Protection Clause. Indeed, for the several reasons that follow, we find neither the suspect-classification nor the fundamental interest analysis persuasive.

The wealth discrimination discovered by the District Court in this case, and by several other courts that have recently struck down school-financing laws in other States, is quite unlike any of the forms of wealth discrimination heretofore reviewed by this Court. Rather than focusing on the unique features of the alleged discrimination, the courts in these cases have virtually assumed their findings of a suspect classification through a simplistic process of analysis: since, under the traditional systems of financing public schools, some poorer people receive less expensive educations than other more affluent people, these systems discriminate on the basis of wealth. This approach largely ignores the hard threshold questions, including whether it makes a difference for purposes of consideration under the Constitution that the class of disadvantaged "poor" cannot be identified or defined in customary equal protection terms, and whether the relative—rather than absolute—nature of the asserted deprivation is of significant consequence. Before a State's laws and the justifications for the classifications they create are subjected to strict judicial scrutiny, we think these threshold considerations must be analyzed more closely than they were in the court below. . . .

. . . The individuals, or groups of individuals, who constituted the class discriminated against in our prior cases shared two distinguishing characteristics: because of their impecunity they were completely unable to pay for some desired benefit, and as a consequence, they sustained an absolute deprivation of a meaningful opportunity to enjoy that benefit. . . .

. . . [N]either appellees nor the District Court addressed the fact that, unlike the foregoing cases, lack of personal resources has not occasioned an absolute deprivation of the desired benefit. The argument here is not that the children in districts having relatively low assessable property values are receiving no public education; rather, it is that they are receiving a poorer quality education than that available to children in districts having more assessable wealth. Apart from the unsettled and disputed question whether the quality of education may be determined by the amount of money expended for it, a sufficient answer to appellees' argument is that, at least where wealth is involved, the Equal Protection Clause does not require absolute equality or precisely equal advantages. . . .

. . . [I]n recognition of the fact that this Court has never heretofore held that wealth discrimination alone provides an adequate basis for invoking strict scrutiny, appellees have not relied solely on this contention. They also assert that the State's system impermissibly interferes with the exercise of a "fundamental" right and that accordingly the prior decisions of this Court require the application of the strict standard of judicial review. . . . It is this question—whether education is a fundamental right, in the sense that it is among the rights and liberties protected by the Constitution—which has so consumed the attention of courts and commentators in recent years.

In *Brown v. Board of Education,* . . . a unanimous Court recognized that "education is perhaps the most important function of state and local governments." What was said there in the context of racial discrimination has lost none of its vitality with the passage of time. . . .

> ". . . In these days, it is doubtful that any child may reasonably be expected to succeed in life if he is denied the opportunity of an education. Such an opportunity, where the state has undertaken to provide it, is a right which must be made available to all on equal terms."

. . . But the importance of a service performed by the State does not determine whether it must be regarded as fundamental for purposes of examination under the Equal Protection Clause. . . .

. . . It is not the province of this Court to create substantive constitutional rights in the name of guaranteeing equal protection of the laws. Thus, the key to discovering whether education is "fundamental" is not to be found in comparisons of the relative societal significance of education as opposed to subsistence or housing. Nor is it to be found by weighing whether education is as important as the right to travel. Rather, the answer lies in assessing whether there is a right to education explicitly or implicitly guaranteed by the Constitution. . . .

Education, of course, is not among the rights afforded explicit protection under our Federal Constitution. Nor do we find any basis for saying it is implicitly so protected. . . . It is appellees' contention, however, that education is distinguishable from other services and benefits provided by the State because it bears a peculiarly close relationship to other rights and liberties accorded protection under the Constitution. Specifically, they insist that education is itself a fundamental personal right because it is essential to the effective exercise of First Amendment freedoms and to intelligent utilization of the right to vote. In asserting a nexus between speech and education, appellees urge that the right to speak is meaningless unless the speaker is capable of articulating his thoughts intelligently and persuasively. The "marketplace of ideas" is an empty forum for those lacking basic communicative tools. Likewise, they argue that the corollary right to receive information becomes little more than a hollow privilege when the recipient has not been taught to read, assimilate, and utilize available knowledge.

A similar line of reasoning is pursued with respect to the right to vote. Exercise of the franchise, it is contended, cannot be divorced from the educational foundation of the voter. The electoral process, if reality is to conform to the democratic ideal, depends on an informed electorate: a voter cannot cast his ballot intelligently unless his reading skills and thought processes have been adequately developed.

We need not dispute any of these propositions. The Court has long afforded zealous protection against unjustifiable governmental interference with the individual's rights to speak and to vote. Yet we have never presumed to possess either the ability or the authority to guarantee to the citizenry the

most *effective* speech or the most *informed* electoral choice. That these may be desirable goals of a system of freedom of expression and of a representative form of government is not to be doubted. These are indeed goals to be pursued by a people whose thoughts and beliefs are freed from governmental interference. But they are not values to be implemented by judicial intrusion into otherwise legitimate state activities.

. . . Whatever merit appellees' argument might have if a State's financing system occasioned an absolute denial of educational opportunities to any of its children, that argument provides no basis for finding an interference with fundamental rights where only relative differences in spending levels are involved and where—as is true in the present case—no charge fairly could be made that the system fails to provide each child with an opportunity to acquire the basic minimal skills necessary for the enjoyment of the rights of speech and of full participation in the political process.

. . . [T]he logical limitations on appellees' nexus theory are difficult to perceive. How, for instance, is education to be distinguished from the significant personal interests in the basics of decent food and shelter? Empirical examination might well buttress an assumption that the ill-fed, ill-clothed, and ill-housed are among the most ineffective participants in the political process, and that they derive the least enjoyment from the benefits of the First Amendment. . . .

We have carefully considered each of the arguments supportive of the District Court's finding that education is a fundamental right or liberty and have found those arguments unpersuasive. . . .

Mr. Justice Marshall, with whom Mr. Justice Douglas concurs, dissenting.

The Court today decides, in effect, that a State may constitutionally vary the quality of education which it offers its children in accordance with the amount of taxable wealth located in the school districts within which they reside. The majority's decision represents an abrupt departure from the mainstream of recent state and federal court decisions concerning the unconstitutionality of state educational financing schemes dependent upon taxable local wealth. More unfortunately, though, the majority's holding can only be seen as a retreat from our historic commitment to equality of educational opportunity and as unsupportable acquiescence in a system which deprives children in their earliest years of the chance to reach their full potential as citizens. The Court does this despite the absence of any substantial justification for a scheme which arbitrarily channels education resources in accordance with the fortuity of the amount of taxable wealth within each district.

In my judgment, the right of every American to an equal start in life, so far as the provision of a state service as important as education is concerned, is far too vital to permit state discrimination on grounds as tenuous as those presented by this record. Nor can I accept the notion that it is sufficient to remit these appellees to the vagaries of the political process which, contrary to the majority's suggestion, has proved singularly unsuited to the task of providing a remedy for this discrimination. I, for one, am unsatisfied with the hope of an ultimate "political" solution sometime in the indefinite future while, in the meantime, countless children unjustifiably receive inferior educations that "may affect their hearts and minds in a way unlikely ever to be undone." *Brown v. Board of Education,* 347 U.S. 483, 494 (1954). I must therefore respectfully dissent. . . .

. . . [T]his Court has never suggested that because some "adequate" level of benefits is provided to all, discrimination in the provision of services is therefore constitutionally excusable. The Equal Protection Clause is not addressed to the minimal sufficiency but rather to the unjustifiable inequalities of state action. It mandates nothing less than that "all persons similarly circumstanced shall be treated alike."
. . .

Even if the Equal Protection Clause encompassed some theory of constitutional adequacy, discrimination in the provision of educational opportunity would certainly seem to be a poor candidate for its application. Neither the majority nor appellants inform us how judicially manageable standards are to be derived for determining how much education is "enough" to excuse constitutional discrimination. One would think that the majority would

heed its own fervent affirmation of judicial self-restraint before undertaking the complex task of determining at large what level of education is constitutionally sufficient. . . .

In my view, then, it is inequality—not some notion of gross inadequacy—of educational opportunity that raises a question of denial of equal protection of the laws.

. . . A principled reading of what this Court has done reveals that it has applied a spectrum of standards in reviewing discrimination allegedly violative of the Equal Protection Clause. This spectrum clearly comprehends variations in the degree of care with which the Court will scrutinize particular classifications, depending, I believe, on the constitutional and societal importance of the interest adversely affected and the recognized invidiousness of the basis upon which the particular classification is drawn. . . .

I therefore cannot accept the majority's labored efforts to demonstrate that fundamental interests, which call for strict scrutiny of the challenged classification, encompass only established rights which we are somehow bound to recognize from the text of the Constitution itself. To be sure, some interests which the Court has deemed to be fundamental for purposes of equal protection analysis are themselves constitutionally protected rights. Thus, discrimination against the guaranteed right of freedom of speech has called for strict judicial scrutiny. . . . But it will not do to suggest that the "answer" to whether an interest is fundamental for purposes of equal protection analysis is *always* determined by whether that interest "is a right . . . explicitly or implicitly guaranteed by the Constitution."
. . .

I would like to know where the Constitution guarantees the right to procreate . . . or the right to vote in state elections, . . . or the right to an appeal from a criminal conviction. . . . These are instances in which, due to the importance of the interests at stake, the Court has displayed a strong concern with the existence of discriminatory state treatment. But the Court has never said or indicated that these are interests which independently enjoy full-blown constitutional protection. . . .

While ultimately disputing little of this, the majority seeks refuge in the fact that the Court has "never presumed to possess either the ability or the authority to guarantee to the citizenry the most *effective* speech or the most *informed* electoral choice." This serves only to blur what is in fact at stake. With due respect, the issue is neither provision of the most *effective* speech nor of the most *informed* vote. Appellees do not seek the best education Texas might provide. They do seek, however, an end to state discrimination resulting from the unequal distribution of taxable district property wealth that directly impairs the ability of some districts to provide the same educational opportunity that other districts can provide with the same or even substantially less tax effort. The issue is, in other words, one of discrimination that affects the quality of the education which Texas has chosen to provide its children; and, the precise question here is what importance should attach to education for purposes of equal protection analysis of that discrimination.

. . . This Court has frequently recognized that discrimination on the basis of wealth may create a classification of a suspect character and thereby call for exacting judicial scrutiny. The majority, however, considers any wealth classification in this case to lack certain essential characteristics which it contends are common to the instances of wealth discrimination that this Court has heretofore recognized. We are told that in every prior case involving a wealth classification, the members of the disadvantaged class have "shared two distinguishing characteristics: because of their impecunity they were completely unable to pay for some desired benefit, and as a consequence, they sustained an absolute deprivation of a meaningful opportunity to enjoy that benefit." . . . I cannot agree. The Court's distinctions . . . are not in fact consistent with the decisions in *Harper v. Virginia Bd. of Elections*, . . . or *Griffin v. Illinois*, . . . or *Douglas v. California*. . . .

In *Harper*, the Court struck down as violative of the Equal Protection Clause an annual Virginia poll tax of $1.50, payment of which by persons over the age of 21 was a prerequisite to voting in Virginia elections. . . . [T]he Court struck down the poll tax *in toto;* it did not order merely that those too poor to pay the tax be exempted; complete impecunity clearly was not determinative of the limits of

the disadvantaged class, nor was it essential to make an equal protection claim.

Similarly, *Griffin* and *Douglas* refute the majority's contention that we have in the past required an absolute deprivation before subjecting wealth classifications to strict scrutiny. The Court characterizes *Griffin* as a case concerned simply with the denial of a transcript or an adequate substitute therefore, and *Douglas* as involving the denial of counsel. But in both cases the question was in fact whether "a State that [grants] *appellate review* can do so in a way that discriminates against some convicted defendants on account of their poverty" (emphasis added). In that regard, the Court concluded that inability to purchase a transcript denies "the poor an adequate *appellate review* accorded to all who have money enough to pay the costs in advance," (emphasis added), and that "the type of an *appeal* a person is afforded . . . hinges upon whether or not he can pay for the assistance of counsel," *Douglas v. California*, . . . (emphasis added). The right of appeal itself was not absolutely denied to those too poor to pay; but because of the cost of a transcript and of counsel, the appeal was a substantially less meaningful right for the poor than for the rich. It was on these terms that the Court found a denial of equal protection, and those terms clearly encompassed degrees of discrimination on the basis of wealth which do not amount to outright denial of the affected right or interest. . . .

Nor can we ignore the extent to which, in contrast to our prior decisions, the State is responsible for the wealth discrimination in this instance. *Griffin, Douglas, Williams, Tate*, and our other prior cases have dealt with discrimination on the basis of indigency which was attributable to the operation of the private sector. But we have no such simple *de facto* wealth discrimination here. The means for financing public education in Texas are selected and specified by the State. It is the State that has created local school districts, and tied educational funding to the local property tax and thereby to local district wealth. At the same time, governmentally imposed land use controls have undoubtedly encouraged and rigidified natural trends in the allocation of particular areas for residential or commercial use, and thus determined each district's amount of taxable property wealth. In short, this case, in contrast to the Court's previous wealth discrimination decisions, can only be seen as "unusual in the extent to which governmental action *is* the cause of the wealth classifications."

In the final analysis, then, the invidious characteristics of the group wealth classification present in this case merely serve to emphasize the need for careful judicial scrutiny of the State's justifications for the resulting interdistrict discrimination in the educational opportunity afforded to the schoolchildren of Texas. . . .

The Court seeks solace for its action today in the possibility of legislative reform. The Court's suggestions of legislative redress and experimentation will doubtless be of great comfort to the schoolchildren of Texas' disadvantaged districts, but considering the vested interests of wealthy school districts in the preservation of the status quo, they are worth little more. The possibility of legislative action is, in all events, no answer to this Court's duty under the Constitution to eliminate unjustified state discrimination. . . .

I would therefore affirm the judgment of the District Court.

Homelessness

Peter Marin

Homelessness, in itself, is nothing more than a condition visited upon men and women (and, increasingly, children) as the final stage of a variety of problems about which the word *homelessness* tells us almost nothing. Or, to put it another way, it is a catch basin into which pour all of the people disenfranchised or marginalized or scared off by processes beyond their control, those that lie close to the heart of American life. Here are the groups packed into the single category of "the homeless":

- Veterans, mainly from the war in Vietnam. In many American cities, vets make up close to 50 percent of all homeless males.
- The mentally ill. In some parts of the country, roughly a quarter of the homeless would, a couple of decades ago, have been institutionalized.
- The physically disabled or chronically ill, who do not receive any benefits or whose benefits do not enable them to afford permanent shelter.

- The elderly on fixed incomes whose funds are no longer sufficient for their needs.
- Men, women, and whole families pauperized by the loss of a job. Some 28 percent of the homeless population is composed of families with children, and 15 percent are single women.
- Single parents, usually women, without the resources or skills to establish new lives.
- Runaway children, many of whom have been abused.
- Alcoholics and those in trouble with drugs (whose troubles often begin with one of the other conditions listed here).
- Traditional tramps, hobos and transients, who have taken to the road or the streets for a variety of reasons and who prefer to be there.

You can quickly learn two things about the homeless from this list. First, you can learn that many of the homeless, before they were homeless, were people more or less like ourselves: members of the working or middle class. And you can learn that the world of the homeless has its roots in various policies, events and ways of life for which some of us are responsible and from which some of us actually prosper.

We decide, as a people, to go to war, we ask our children to kill and to die, and the result, years later, is grown men homeless on the street.

We change, with the best intentions, the laws pertaining to the mentally ill and then, without intention, neglect to provide them with services; and the result, in our streets, drives some of us crazy with rage.

We cut taxes and prune budgets, we modernize industry and shift the balance of trade, and the result of all these actions and errors can be read, sleeping form by sleeping form, on our city streets.

The liberals cannot blame the conservatives. The conservatives cannot blame the liberals. Homelessness is the sum total of our dreams, policies, intentions, errors, omissions, cruelties, kindnesses, all of it recorded, in flesh, in the life of the streets.

The homeless can be roughly divided into two groups: those who have had homelessness forced upon them and want nothing more than to escape it; and those who have at least in part chosen it for themselves, and now accept it, or in some cases embrace it.

I understand how dangerous it is to introduce the idea of choice into a discussion of homelessness. It can all too easily be used to justify indifference or brutality toward the homeless, or to argue that they are only getting what they "deserve." And yet it seems to me that it is only by taking choice into account, in all of the intricacies of its various forms and expressions, that one can really understand certain kinds of homelessness.

The fact is, many of the homeless are not only hapless victims but voluntary exiles, "domestic refugees," people who have turned not against life itself but against us, our life, American life. Look for a moment at the vets. The price of returning to America was to forget what they had seen or learned in Vietnam, to "put it behind them." But some could not do that, and the stress of trying showed up as alcoholism, broken marriages, drug addiction, crime. And it showed up too as life on the street, which was for some vets a desperate choice made in the name of life—the best they could manage.

We must learn to accept that there may indeed be people, and not only vets, who have seen so much of our world, or seen it so clear-ly, that to live in it becomes impossible. Here, for example, is the story of Alice, a homeless middle-aged woman in Los Angeles, where there are perhaps 50,000 homeless people, a 50 percent increased over the previous year. It was set down last year by one of my students at the University of California at Santa Barbara, where I taught for a semester. I had encouraged them to go find the homeless and listen to their stories. And so, one day, when this student saw Alice foraging in a dumpster outside a McDonald's, he stopped and talked to her:

"She told me she had led a pretty normal life as she grew up and eventually went to college. From there she went on to Chicago to teach school. She was single and lived in a small apartment.

"One night, after she got off the train after school, a man began to follow her to her apartment building. When she got to her door she saw a knife and the man hovering behind her. She had no choice but to let him in. The man raped her.

"After that, things got steadily worse. She had a nervous breakdown. She went to a mental institution for three months, and when she went back to her apartment she found her belongings gone. The landlord had sold them to cover the rent.

"She had no place to go and no job because the school had terminated her employment. She slipped into depression. She lived with friends until she could muster enough money for a ticket to Los Angeles. She said she no longer wanted to burden her friends, and that if she had to live outside, at least Los Angeles was warmer than Chicago.

"It is as if she began back then to take on the mentality of a street person. She resolved herself to homelessness. She's been out West since 1980, without a home or job. She seems happy, with her best friend being her cat. But the scars of memories still haunt her, and she is running from them, or should I say, him."

This is, in essence, the same story one hears over and over again on the street. You begin with an ordinary life; then an event occurs—traumatic, catastrophic; smaller events follow, each one deepening the original wound; finally, homelessness becomes inevitable, or begins to seem inevitable to the person involved—the only way out of an intolerable situation.

Every government program, almost every private project, is geared as much to the needs of those giving help as it is to the needs of the homeless.

Santa Barbara is as good an example as any. There are three main shelters in the city—all of them private. Between them they provide fewer than 100 beds a night for the homeless. Two of three shelters are religious in nature: the Rescue Mission and the Salvation Army. In the mission, as in most places in the country, there are elaborate and stringent rules. Beds go first to those who have not been there for two months, and you can stay for only two nights in any two-month period. No shelter is given to those who are not sober.

Even if you go to the mission only for a meal, you are required to listen to sermons and participate in prayer, and you are regularly proselytized. There are obligatory, regimented showers. You go to bed precisely at 10: lights out, no reading, no talking. After the lights go out you will find 15 men in a room with double-decker bunks. As the night progresses the room grows stuffier and hotter. Men toss, turn, cough and moan. In the morning you are awakened precisely at 5:45. Then breakfast. At 7:30 you are back on the street.

The town's newest shelter was opened almost a year ago by a consortium of local churches. Families and those who are employed have first call on the beds—a policy that excludes the congenitally homeless. Alcohol is not simply forbidden in the shelter; those with a history of alcoholism must sign a "contract" pledging to remain sober and chemical-free. Finally, in a paroxysm of therapeutic bullying, the shelter has added a new wrinkle: If you stay more than two days you are required to fill out and then discuss with a social worker a complex form listing what you perceive as your personal failings, goals and strategies—all of this for men and women who simply want a place to lie down out of the rain.

We are moved either to "redeem" the homeless or to punish them. Perhaps there is nothing consciously hostile about it. Perhaps it is simply that as the machinery of bureaucracy cranks itself up to deal with these problems, attitudes assert themselves automatically. But whatever the case, the fact remains that almost every one of our strategies for helping the homeless is simply an attempt to rearrange the world cosmetically, in terms of how it looks and smells to us. Compassion is little more than the passion for control.

The central question emerging from all this is, What does a society owe to its members in trouble, and how is that debt to be paid? It is a question that must be answered in two parts: first, in relation to the men and women who have been marginalized against their will, and then, in a slightly different way, in relation to those who have chosen (or accept or even prize) their marginality.

Suggestions for Further Reading

Anthologies

Arthur, John, and Shaw, William. *Justice and Economic Distribution.* Englewood Cliffs: Prentice-Hall, 1978.

Held, Virginia. *Property, Profits and Economic Justice.* Belmont: Wadsworth Publishing Co., 1980.

Sterba, James P. *Justice: Alternative Political Perspectives.* Belmont: Wadsworth Publishing Co., 1980.

Basic Concepts

Plato. *The Republic.* Translated by Francis Cornford. New York: Oxford University Press, 1945.

Aristotle. *Nicomachean Ethics.* Translated by Martin Ostwald. Indianapolis: Bobbs-Merrill, 1962.

Pieper, Joseph. *Justice.* London: Faber and Faber, 1957.

Libertarianism

Hospers, John. *Libertarianism*. Los Angeles: Nash Publishing, 1971.

Nozick, Robert. *Anarchy, State and Utopia*. New York: Basic Books, 1974.

Rothbard, Murray N. *For a New Liberty*. London: Collier Macmillan, 1973.

Welfare Liberalism

Mill, John Stuart. *On Liberty*. Indianapolis: Bobbs-Merrill Co., 1956.

Ackerman, Bruce A. *Social Justice in The Liberal State*. New Haven: Yale University Press, 1980.

Rawls, John. *A Theory of Justice*. Cambridge: Harvard University Press, 1971.

Sterba, James P. *The Demands of Justice*. Notre Dame: University of Notre Dame Press, 1980.

Singer, Peter. *Practical Ethics*. Cambridge: Cambridge University Press, 1979.

Socialism

Marx, Karl. *Critique of the Gotha Program*. Edited by C. P. Dutt. New York: International Publishers, 1966.

Fisk, Milton. *Ethics and Society: A Marxist Interpretation of Value*. New York: New York University Press, 1980.

Harrington, Michael. *Socialism*. New York: Bantam Books, 1970.

Heilbroner, Robert L. *Marxism For and Against*. New York: W. W. Norton & Co., 1980.

Communitarianism

Finnis, John, *Natural Law and Natural Rights* Oxford: Clarendon Press, 1980.

MacIntyre, Alasdair, *After Virtue*, Notre Dame: University of Notre Dame Press, 1981.

Oldenquist, Andrew, *The Nonsuicidal Society*. Bloomington: University of Indiana Press, 1986.

Walzer, Michael, *The Spheres of Justice*, New York: Basic Books, 1983.

Practical Applications

Brown, Peter G., and others, eds. *Income Support*. Totowa: Rowman and Littlefield, 1981.

Friedman, David. *The Machinery of Freedom*. New York: Harper and Row, 1973.

Lynd, Straughton, and Alperovitz, Gar. *Strategy and Program*. Boston: Beacon Press, 1973.

Distant Peoples and Future Generations

Basic Concepts

The moral problem of distant peoples and future generations has only recently begun to be discussed by professional philosophers. There are many reasons for this neglect, not all of them complimentary to the philosophical profession. Suffice it to say that once it became widely recognized that modern technology could significantly benefit or harm distant peoples and future generations, philosophers could no longer ignore the importance of this moral problem.

Nevertheless, because the problem has only recently been addressed by philosophers, a generally acceptable way of even setting out the problem has yet to be developed. Unlike the problem of the distribution of income and wealth (see Section I), there is almost no common conceptual framework shared by all solutions to the problem of distant peoples and future generations. Some philosophers have even attempted to "solve" the problem, or at least part of it, by arguing that talk about "the rights of future generations" is conceptually incoherent and thus analogous to talk about "square circles." Accordingly, the key question that must be answered first is: Can we meaningfully speak of distant peoples and future generations as having rights against us or of our having obligations to them?

This question is much easier to answer with respect to distant peoples than to future generations. Few philosophers have thought that the mere fact that people are at a distance from us precludes our having any obligations to them or their having any rights against us. Some philosophers, however, have argued that our ignorance of the specific membership of the class of distant peoples does rule out these moral relationships. Yet this cannot be right, given that in other contexts we recognize obligations to indeterminate classes of people, such as a police officer's obligation to help people in distress or the obligation of food processors not to harm those who consume their products.

What does, however, seem to be a necessary requirement before distant peoples can be said to have rights against us is that we are capable of acting across the distance that separates us. (This is simply a version of the widely accepted philosophical principle that "ought implies can.") As long as this condition is met—as it typically is for people living in most technologically advanced societies—there seems to be no conceptual obstacle to claiming that distant peoples have rights against us or that we have obligations to them. Of course, showing that it is conceptually possible does not yet prove that these rights and obligations actually exist. Such proof requires a substantial moral argument.

By contrast, answering the above question with respect to future generations is much more difficult and has been the subject of considerable debate among contemporary philosophers.

One issue concerns the question whether it is logically coherent to speak of future generations as having rights now. Of course, no one who finds talk about rights to be generally meaningful should question whether we can coherently claim that future generations *will* have rights at some point in the future (specifically, when they come into existence and are no longer *future* generations). But what is questioned, since it is of considerable practical significance, is whether we can coherently claim that future generations have rights *now* when they don't yet exist.

Some philosophers, such as Richard T. De George, have argued that such claims are logically incoherent (pp. 108–115). According to De George, rights logically require the existence of rights-holders, and obligations logically require the existence of obligation-recipients. There are, however, at least two difficulties with this view.

The first difficulty has to do with the presuppositions said to underlie all talk about rights on the one hand and obligations on the other. The two are treated as if they were similar when they are not. The existence of rights-holders is held to be logically presupposed in any talk about rights, whereas in talk about obligations it is not the existence of obligation-holders but of obligation-*recipients* that is said to be logically presupposed. So it seems perfectly possible to grant that rights-talk presupposes the existence of rights-holders and obligation-talk that of obligation-holders, but then deny that obligation-talk also logically presupposes the existence of obligation-recipients. Instead, one might reasonably hold that what obligation-talk presupposes in this regard is only that there either exists or *will exist* obligation-recipients whose interests can be affected by the obligation-holders.

The second difficulty with this view is that even if it were correct about the existence presuppositions we make when talking about rights and obligations, retaining such usage would still be objectionable because it tends to beg important normative questions. For example, since this usage renders rights-talk and obligation-talk inapplicable to future generations, it tends to favor a negative answer to the question of whether we are morally required to begin *now* to provide for the welfare of future generations. On this account, it would be preferable to adopt alternative ways of talking about rights and obligations that are morally more neutral and allow the normative and conceptual questions to be addressed more independently.

Still another issue relevant to whether we can meaningfully speak of future generations as having rights against us or our having obligations to them concerns the referent of the term *future generations*. Most philosophers seem to agree that the class of future generations is not "the class of all persons who simply could come into existence." But there is some disagreement concerning whether we should refer to the class of future generations as "the class of persons who will definitely come into existence, assuming that there are such" or as "the class of persons we can reasonably expect to come into existence." The first approach is more "metaphysical," specifying the class of future generations in terms of what will exist; the second approach is more "epistemological," specifying the class of future generations in terms of our knowledge. Fortunately, there does not appear to be any practical moral significance to the choice of either approach.

A final issue that is relevant to whether we can meaningfully speak of future generations as having rights against us and our having obligations to them concerns whether in a given case the actions of the existing generations that affect future generations can actually benefit or harm those generations. Some philosophers would surely hold that only in cases where future generations can benefit from or be harmed by our actions can there be a question of future generations having rights against us or our having obligations to them.

Of course, no one doubts that some of our actions that affect future generations actually do benefit or harm them. For example, consider an artist who creates a great work of art that will survive for the enjoyment of future generations. Surely such a person will benefit future generations. Just as surely, future generations will be harmed by the careless manner in which many governments and private corporations today dispose of nuclear wastes and other toxic substances.

But suppose some of our actions affect future generations by affecting the membership of the class of future generations. That is, suppose our actions cause different people to be born than otherwise would have been born had we acted differently. For example, imagine that a woman is deciding whether or not to get pregnant. Because of the medication she is taking, she will give birth to a defective child if she gets pregnant now. However, if she stops taking her medication and waits three months before getting pregnant, she will almost certainly have a normal child. If the woman decides not to wait and gives birth to a defective child, has she harmed that child? If the mother had waited three months, the child she would then have given birth to would certainly have been a different child. So it does not seem that she has harmed the child to which she did give birth, provided the child's life is worth living. Some people, however, would surely think the mother was wrong not to wait and give birth to a normal child. But how can such a judgment be supported?

At the level of social choice we can also imagine a similar situation arising. Consider a developing country choosing between a laissez-faire population policy and one that restricts population growth. If the restrictive policy is followed, capital accumulation will produce general prosperity within one or two generations. If the laissez-faire policy is followed, low wages and high unemployment will continue indefinitely. Since the choice of either of these will, over time, produce different populations, those born subsequently under the laissez-faire policy could hardly claim they were harmed by the choice of that policy because they wouldn't have been born if the restricted policies had been adopted. Still, some people would surely want to claim that it was wrong for the country to pursue a laissez-faire policy. But how could such a claim be supported if no one in subsequent generations is harmed by the choice of that policy?

Contemporary philosophers have sought to deal with the question of whether we can wrong future generations without harming them in three ways. The first is simply to recommend that we "bite the bullet" and claim that "if no one is harmed, no wrong is done." This approach is not very satisfactory, however, because it flies in the face of our strong intuitions about the examples cited previously. The second approach is to claim that regardless of whether one is harmed, we still have an obligation to produce as much happiness or utility as we possibly can. Applied to our examples, this utilitarian approach would probably require the delayed pregnancy. However, it would not call for the restricted population policy because one of the generally recognized problems with this second approach is that it is said to require massive population increases that maximize happiness or utility overall, with little regard for the quality of life. The third approach adopted by contemporary philosophers is to claim that even though we don't have an obligation to produce as much happiness or utility as we possibly can, we do have an obligation to ensure that persons are only brought into existence if they are likely to have lives that are well worth living. Applied to our examples, this obligation would require both the delayed pregnancy and the restricted population policy. Some proponents of this approach, like Sterba (pp. 115–127), claim that we also have an obligation to bring into existence persons whose lives are well worth living; this, however, is not the general view.

Of these three approaches, the last seems to be the most promising. But exactly how to work out the details of this approach (e.g., what constitutes a life well worth living?) is still the subject of considerable debate among contemporary philosophers.

Alternative Views

Fortunately, all of these issues do not have to be resolved fully before we can profitably examine some of the practical solutions that have been proposed to the problem of distant peoples and future generations. In fact, some of the issues we've discussed lead us directly to particular solutions for this moral problem.

Not surprisingly, most of the solutions that have been proposed are analogous to the solutions we discussed with regard to the problem of the distribution of income and wealth within a society (see Section I).

As before, there is a libertarian solution. According to this view, distant peoples and future generations have no right to receive aid from persons living in today's affluent societies, but only a right not to be harmed by them. As before, these requirements are said to be derived from a political ideal of liberty. And, as before, we can question whether such an ideal actually supports these requirements.

Both Garrett Hardin and De George endorse a "no aid" view in their selections. However, neither Hardin nor De George supports his view on libertarian grounds. Without denying that there is a general obligation to help those in need, Hardin argues that helping those who live in absolute poverty in today's world would not do any good, and for *that reason* is not required. Hardin justifies this view on empirical grounds, claiming that the giving of aid would be ineffective and even counterproductive for controlling population growth. By contrast, De George supports a "no aid" view for future generations (but not for distant peoples, who he thinks do have a right to receive aid) on purely conceptual grounds, claiming that future generations cannot logically have rights against us nor we obligations to them.

We have already noted some of the difficulties with the view De George defends. Peter Singer and Sterba both challenge the empirical grounds on which Hardin's view rests. Singer claims that Hardin's view accepts the certain evil of unrelieved poverty in today's Third

World countries, like Bangladesh and Somalia, in order to avoid the future possibility of still greater poverty in Third World countries together with deteriorating conditions in First and Second World countries. Singer argues, however, that with a serious commitment to aid from First World countries, there is a "fair chance" that Third World countries will bring their population growth under control, thus avoiding the greater evil Hardin fears. Given the likelihood of this result, Singer argues that we have no moral justification for embracing, as Hardin does, the certain evil of unrelieved poverty in today's Third World countries by denying them aid. Sterba too objects to Hardin's willingness to sacrifice existing generations for the sake of a "better future" for subsequent generations. He argues that even if Hardin were right that providing aid would reduce the "maximal sustainable yield" of the planet's resources, we still ought to provide that aid. He claims this is so even if the population level of future generations, once a rational population policy is in effect, would have to be smaller than would otherwise have been possible.

The positive solution to the problem of distant peoples and future generations defended by both Singer and Sterba can be characterized as a welfare liberal or a communitarian solution. Singer at some point would want to defend his "pro aid" view on utilitarian grounds, but in his selection (pp. 97–107), he tries to base his view on premises of a more general appeal. The fundamental premise he relies on is this: If we can prevent something bad without sacrificing anything of comparable significance, we ought to do it. Singer notes that libertarians, like Robert Nozick, would at least initially have difficulty accepting this premise. Nozick would surely claim that the requirement this premise imposes is at best only one of charity rather than justice, so that failing to abide by it is neither blameworthy nor punishable. Sterba, too, although he is primarily concerned with defending a "pro aid" view on the basis of a right to life and a right to fair treatment interpreted as positive rights, is sensitive to the possibility that libertarians might be able to escape from the conclusion of his argument. Consequently, he tries to show that the same conclusion follows when a right to life is interpreted as a negative right, as libertarians tend to do. But while Sterba may have secured his view against objections by libertarians, socialists would certainly not be satisfied with his defense.

A socialist solution to the problem of distant peoples and future generations would place considerable stress on the responsibility of First World countries for the situation in Third World countries. Socialists claim that much of the poverty and unemployment found in Third World countries is the result of the disruptive and exploitative influence of First World countries. For example, it is claimed that arms supplied by First World countries enable repressive regimes in Third World countries to remain in power when they would otherwise be overthrown. Under these repressive regimes, small groups of landowners and capitalists are allowed to exploit the resources in Third World countries for export markets in First World countries. As a result, the majority of people in Third World countries are forced off the land that their forebears have farmed for generations and are required to compete for the few, frequently low-paying jobs that have been created to serve the export markets.

Nevertheless, even if socialists are right about the responsibility of First World countries for Third World poverty, it is still a further question whether the socialization of the means of production and the abolition of private property are the only viable moral responses to this situation. It certainly seems possible that some form of restricted private property system that provides for the meeting of everyone's basic needs, justified either on welfare liberal grounds or on libertarian grounds, would serve as well.

By contrast, for communitarians the key question with respect to the problem of distant peoples and future generations is whether the requirements of community are compatible with meeting the basic needs of distant peoples and future generations. Thus, communitarians need to be convinced that when the bounds of community are drawn correctly, distant peoples and future generations would in fact be included.

Practical Applications

There does not seem to be as much of a gap between the "alternative views" and the "practical applications" with respect to the problem of distant peoples and future generations as there is in the problem of the distribution of wealth and income. This is because most of the discussions of the alternative views have already taken up the question of practical application (e.g., Singer suggests as a practical application a 10 percent tithe on income in First World countries). The merit of Gus Speth's article, however, is that it focuses squarely on the question of practical application (pp. 127–131). After reviewing the world situation, Speth sketches a practical program involving conservation, sustainable growth, and equity. Because his program obviously involves substantial aid to Third World countries, you should not endorse such a program unless you believe that arguments such as those presented by Singer and Sterba effectively counter arguments such as those presented by Hardin and De George.

Nevertheless, whatever solution to the problem of distant peoples and future generations you favor, you will still not know how goods and resources should ultimately be distributed in society unless you have a solution to the problem of abortion and euthanasia. For if abortion is morally justified, perhaps we should be funding abortions so that every woman, rich or poor, can have an abortion if she wants one. And if euthanasia is morally justified, perhaps we should be reallocating resources that are now being used for the purpose of sustaining life. Appropriately, the next section of this book takes up the problem of abortion and euthanasia.

Lifeboat Ethics: The Case against Helping the Poor

Garrett Hardin

Garrett Hardin argues that our first obligation is to ourselves and our posterity. For that reason, he contends, it would be foolish for rich nations to share their surplus with poor nations, whether through a World Food Bank, the exporting of technology, or unrestricted immigration. In view of the growing populations and improvident behavior of poor nations, such sharing would do no good—it would only overload the environment and lead to demands for still greater assistance in the future.

Environmentalists use the metaphor of the earth as a "spaceship" in trying to persuade countries, industries and people to stop wasting and polluting our natural resources. Since we all share life on this planet, they argue, no single person or institution has the right to destroy, waste, or use more than a fair share of its resources.

From "The Case Against Helping the Poor," *Psychology Today* (1974) pp. 38–43, 123–126. Reprinted with permission from *Psychology Today* magazine. Copyright © 1974 American Psychological Association.

But does everyone on earth have an equal right to an equal share of its resources? The spaceship metaphor can be dangerous when used by misguided idealists to justify suicidal policies for sharing our resources through uncontrolled immigration and foreign aid. In their enthusiastic but unrealistic generosity, they confuse the ethics of a spaceship with those of a lifeboat.

A true spaceship would have to be under the control of a captain, since no ship could possibly survive if its course were determined by committee. Spaceship Earth certainly has no captain; the United Nations is merely a toothless tiger, with little power to enforce any policy upon its bickering members.

If we divide the world crudely into rich nations and poor nations, two thirds of them are desperately poor, and only one third comparatively rich, with the United States the wealthiest of all. Metaphorically each rich nation can be seen as a lifeboat full of comparatively rich people. In the ocean outside each lifeboat swim the poor of the world, who would like to get in, or at least to share some of the wealth. What should the lifeboat passengers do?

First, we must recognize the limited capacity of any lifeboat. For example, a nation's land has a limited capacity to support a population and as the current energy crisis has shown us, in some ways we have already exceeded the carrying capacity of our land.

Adrift in a Moral Sea

So here we sit, say fifty people in our lifeboat. To be generous, let us assume it has room for ten more, making a total capacity of sixty. Suppose the fifty of us in the lifeboat see 100 others swimming in the water outside, begging for admission to our boat or for handouts. We have several options: we may be tempted to try to live by the Christian ideal of being "our brother's keeper," or by the Marxist ideal of "to each according to his needs." Since the needs of all in the water are the same, and since they can all be seen as "our brothers," we could take them all into our boat, making a total of 150 in a boat designed for sixty. The boat swamps, everyone drowns. Complete justice, complete catastrophe.

Since the boat has an unused excess capacity of ten more passengers, we could admit just ten more to it. But which ten do we let in? How do we choose? Do we pick the best ten, the neediest ten, "first come, first served"? And what do we say to the ninety we exclude? If we do let an extra ten into our lifeboat, we will have lost our "safety factor," an engineering principle of critical importance. For example,

if we don't leave room for excess capacity as a safety factor in our country's agriculture, a new plant disease or a bad change in the weather could have disastrous consequences.

Suppose we decide to preserve our small safety factor and admit no more to the lifeboat. Our survival is then possible, although we shall have to be constantly on guard against boarding parties.

While this last solution clearly offers the only means of our survival, it is morally abhorrent to many people. Some say they feel guilty about their good luck. My reply is simple: "Get out and yield your place to others." This may solve the problem of the guilt-ridden person's conscience, but it does not change the ethics of the lifeboat. The needy person to whom the guilt-ridden person yields his place will not himself feel guilty about his good luck. If he did, he would not climb aboard. The net result of conscience-stricken people giving up their unjustly held seats is the elimination of that sort of conscience from the lifeboat.

This is the basic metaphor within which we must work out our solutions. Let us now enrich the image, step by step, with substantive additions from the real world, a world that must solve real and pressing problems of overpopulation and hunger.

The harsh ethics of the lifeboat become even harsher when we consider the reproductive differences between the rich nations and the poor nations. The people inside the lifeboats are doubling in numbers every eighty-seven years; those swimming around outside are doubling, on the average, every thirty-five years, more than twice as fast as the rich. And since the world's resources are dwindling, the difference in prosperity between the rich and the poor can only increase.

As of 1973, the U.S. had a population of 210 million people, who were increasing by 0.8 percent per year. Outside our lifeboat, let us imagine another 210 million people, (say the combined populations of Colombia, Ecuador, Venezuela, Morocco, Pakistan, Thailand, and the Philippines) who are increasing at a rate of 3.3 percent per year. Put differently, the doubling time for this aggregate population is twenty-one years, compared to eighty-seven years for the U.S.

Multiplying the Rich and the Poor

Now suppose the U.S. agreed to pool its resources with those seven countries, with everyone receiving an equal share. Initially the ratio of Americans to non-Americans in this model would be one-to-one. But consider what the ratio would be after eighty-seven years, by which time the Americans would have doubled to a population of 420 million. By then, doubling every twenty-one years, the other group would have swollen to 354 billion. Each American would have to share the available resources with more than eight people.

But, one could argue, this discussion assumes that current population trends will continue, and they may not. Quite so. Most likely the rate of population increase will decline much faster in the U.S. than it will in the other countries, and there does not seem to be much we can do about it. In sharing with "each according to his needs," we must recognize that needs are determined by population size, which is determined by the rate of reproduction, which at present is regarded as a sovereign right of every nation, poor or not. This being so, the philanthropic load created by the sharing ethic of the spaceship can only increase.

The Tragedy of the Commons

The fundamental error of spaceship ethics, and the sharing it requires, is that it leads to what I call "the tragedy of the commons." Under a system of private property, the men who own property recognize their responsibility to care for it, for if they don't they will eventually suffer. A farmer, for instance, will allow no more cattle in a pasture than its carrying capacity justifies. If he overloads it, erosion sets in, weeds take over, and he loses the use of the pasture.

If a pasture becomes a commons open to

all, the right of each to use it may not be matched by a corresponding responsibility to protect it. Asking everyone to use it with discretion will hardly do, for the considerate herdsman who refrains from overloading the commons suffers more than a selfish one who says his needs are greater. If everyone would restrain himself, all would be well; but it takes only one less than everyone to ruin a system of voluntary restraint. In a crowded world of less than perfect human beings, mutual ruin is inevitable if there are no controls. This is the tragedy of the commons.

One of the major tasks of education today should be the creation of such an acute awareness of the dangers of the commons that people will recognize its many varieties. For example, the air and water have become polluted because they are treated as commons. Further growth in the population or per-capita conversion of natural resources into pollutants will only make the problem worse. The same holds true for the fish of the oceans. Fishing fleets have nearly disappeared in many parts of the world, technological improvements in the art of fishing are hastening the day of complete ruin. Only the replacement of the system of the commons with a responsible system of control will save the land, air, water and oceanic fisheries.

The World Food Bank

In recent years there has been a push to create a new commons called a World Food Bank, an international depository of food reserves to which nations would contribute according to their abilities and from which they would draw according to their needs. This humanitarian proposal has received support from many liberal international groups, and from such prominent citizens as Margaret Mead, U.N. Secretary General Kurt Waldheim, and Senators Edward Kennedy and George McGovern.

A world food bank appeals powerfully to our humanitarian impulses. But before we rush ahead with such a plan, let us recognize where the greatest political push comes from, lest we be disillusioned later. Our experience with the "Food for Peace program," or Public Law 480, gives us the answer. This program moved billions of dollars worth of U.S. surplus grain to food-short, population-long countries during the past two decades. But when P.L. 480 first became law, a headline in the business magazine *Forbes* revealed the real power behind it: "Feeding the World's Hungry Millions: How It Will Mean Billions for U.S. Business."

And indeed it did. In the years 1960 to 1970, U.S. taxpayers spent a total of $7.9 billion on the Food for Peace program. Between 1948 and 1970, they also paid an additional $50 billion for other economic-aid programs, some of which went for food and food-producing machinery and technology. Though all U.S. taxpayers were forced to contribute to the cost of P.L. 480, certain special interest groups gained handsomely under the program. Farmers did not have to contribute the grain; the Government, or rather the taxpayers, bought it from them at full market prices. The increased demand raised prices of farm products generally. The manufacturers of farm machinery, fertilizers and pesticides benefited by the farmers' extra efforts to grow more food. Grain elevators profited from storing the surplus until it could be shipped. Railroads made money hauling it to ports, and shipping lines profited from carrying it overseas. The implementation of P.L. 480 required the creation of a vast Government bureaucracy, which then acquired its own vested interest in continuing the program regardless of its merits.

Extracting Dollars

Those who proposed and defended the Food for Peace program in public rarely mentioned its importance to any of these special interests. The public emphasis was always on its humanitarian effects. The combination of silent selfish interests and highly vocal humanitarian apologists made a powerful and successful lobby for extracting money from taxpayers. We can expect the same lobby to push now for the creation of a World Food Bank.

However great the potential benefit to selfish interests, it should not be a decisive argument against a truly humanitarian program. We must ask if such a program would actually do more good than harm, not only momentarily but also in the long run. Those who propose the food bank usually refer to a current "emergency" or "crisis" in terms of world food supply. But what is an emergency? Although they may be infrequent and sudden, everyone knows that emergencies will occur from time to time. A well-run family, company, organization or country prepares for the likelihood of accidents and emergencies. It expects them, it budgets for them, it saves for them.

Learning the Hard Way

What happens if some organizations or countries budget for accidents and others do not? If each country is solely responsible for its own well-being, poorly managed ones will suffer. But they can learn from experience. They may mend their ways, and learn to budget for infrequent but certain emergencies. For example, the weather varies from year to year, and periodic crop failures are certain. A wise and competent government saves out of the production of the good years in anticipation of bad years to come. Joseph taught this policy to Pharaoh in Egypt more than 2,000 years ago. Yet the great majority of the governments in the world today do not follow such a policy. They lack either the wisdom or the competence, or both. Should those nations that do manage to put something aside be forced to come to the rescue each time an emergency occurs among the poor nations?

"But it isn't their fault!" some kindhearted liberals argue. "How can we blame the poor people who are caught in an emergency? Why must they suffer for the sins of their governments?" The concept of blame is simply not relevant here. The real question is, what are the operational consequences of establishing a world food bank? If it is open to every country every time a need develops, slovenly rulers will not be motivated to take Joseph's advice. Someone will always come to their aid. Some countries will deposit food in the world food bank, and others will withdraw it. There will be almost no overlap. As a result of such solutions to food shortage emergencies, the poor countries will not learn to mend their ways, and will suffer progressively greater emergencies as their populations grow.

Population Control the Crude Way

On the average, poor countries undergo a 2.5 percent increase in population each year; rich countries, about 0.8 percent. Only rich countries have anything in the way of food reserves set aside, and even they do not have as much as they should. Poor countries have none. If poor countries received no food from the outside, the rate of their population growth would be periodically checked by crop failures and famines. But if they can always draw on a world food bank in time of need, their population can continue to grow unchecked, and so will their "need" for aid. In the short run, a world food bank may diminish that need, but in the long run it actually increases the need without limit.

Without some system of worldwide food sharing, the proportion of people in the rich and poor nations might eventually stabilize. The overpopulated poor countries would decrease in numbers, while the rich countries that had room for more people would increase. But with a well-meaning system of sharing, such as a world food bank, the growth differential between the rich and the poor countries will not only persist, it will increase. Because of the higher rate of population growth in the poor countries of the world, 88 percent of today's children are born poor, and only 12 percent rich. Year by year the ratio becomes worse, as the fast-reproducing poor outnumber the slow-reproducing rich.

A world food bank is thus a commons in disguise. People will have more motivation to draw from it than to add to any common store. The less provident and less able will multiply at the expense of the abler and more provident, bringing eventual ruin upon all who share in the commons. Besides, any system of "sharing" that amounts to foreign aid from the rich nations to the poor nations will carry the taint of charity, which will contribute little to the world peace so devoutly desired by those who support the idea of a world food bank.

As past U.S. foreign-aid programs have amply and depressingly demonstrated, international charity frequently inspires mistrust and antagonism rather than gratitude on the part of the recipient nation.

Chinese Fish and Miracle Rice

The modern approach to foreign aid stresses the export of technology and advice, rather than money and food. As an ancient Chinese proverb goes: "Give a man a fish and he will eat for a day; teach him how to fish and he will eat for the rest of his days." Acting on this advice, the Rockefeller and Ford Foundations have financed a number of programs for improving agriculture in the hungry nations. Known as the "Green Revolution," these programs have led to the development of "miracle rice" and "miracle wheat," new strains that offer bigger harvests and greater resistance to crop damage. Norman Borlaug, the Nobel Prize winning agronomist who, supported by the Rockefeller Foundation, developed "miracle wheat," is one of the most prominent advocates of a world food bank.

Whether or not the Green Revolution can increase food production as much as its champions claim is a debatable but possibly irrelevant point. Those who support this well-intended humanitarian effort should first consider some of the fundamentals of human ecology. Ironically, one man who did was the late Alan Gregg, a vice president of the Rockefeller Foundation. Two decades ago he expressed strong doubts about the wisdom of such attempts to increase food production. He likened the growth and spread of humanity over the surface of the earth to the spread of cancer in the human body, remarking that "cancerous growths demand food; but, as far as I know, they have never been cured by getting it."

Overloading the Environment

Every human born constitutes a draft on all aspects of the environment: food, air, water, forests, beaches, wildlife, scenery and solitude. Food can, perhaps, be significantly increased to meet a growing demand. But what about clean beaches, unspoiled forests, and solitude? If we satisfy a growing population's need for food, we necessarily decrease its per capita supply of the other resources needed by men.

India, for example, now has a population of 600 million, which increases by 15 million each year. This population already puts a huge load on a relatively impoverished environment. The country's forests are now only a small fraction of what they were three centuries ago, and floods and erosion continually destroy the insufficient farmland that remains. Every one of the 15 million new lives added to India's population puts an additional burden on the environment, and increases the economic and social costs of crowding. However humanitarian our intent, every Indian life saved through medical or nutritional assistance from abroad diminishes the quality of life for those who remain, and for subsequent generations. If rich countries make it possible, through foreign aid, for 600 million Indians to swell to 1.2 billion in a mere twenty-eight years, as their current growth rate threatens, will future generations of Indians thank us for hastening the destruction of their environment? Will our good intentions be sufficient excuse for the consequences of our actions?

My final example of a commons in action is one for which the public has the least desire for rational discussion—immigration. Anyone who publicly questions the wisdom of current U.S. immigration policy is promptly charged with bigotry, prejudice, ethnocentrism, chauvinism, isolationism or selfishness. Rather than encounter such accusations, one would rather talk about other matters, leaving immigration policy to wallow in the crosscurrents of special

interests that take no account of the good of the whole, or the interests of posterity.

Perhaps we still feel guilty about things we said in the past. Two generations ago the popular press frequently referred to Dagos, Wops, Polacks, Chinks and Krauts, in articles about how America was being "overrun" by foreigners of supposedly inferior genetic stock. But because the implied inferiority of foreigners was used then as justification for keeping them out, people now assume that restrictive policies could only be based on such misguided notions. There are other grounds.

A Nation of Immigrants

Just consider the numbers involved. Our Government acknowledges a net inflow of 400,000 immigrants a year. While we have no hard data on the extent of illegal entries, educated guesses put the figure at about 600,000 a year. Since the natural increase (excess of births over deaths) of the resident population now runs about 1.7 million per year, the yearly gain from immigration amounts to at least 19 percent of the total annual increase, and may be as much as 37 percent if we include the estimate for illegal immigrants. Considering the growing use of birth-control devices, the potential effect of educational campaigns by such organizations as Planned Parenthood Federation of America and Zero Population Growth, and the influence of inflation and the housing shortage, the fertility rate of American women may decline so much that immigration could account for all the yearly increase in population. Should we not at least ask if that is what we want?

For the sake of those who worry about whether the "quality" of the average immigrant compares favorably with the quality of the average resident, let us assume that immigrants and nativeborn citizens are of exactly equal quality, however one defines that term. We will focus here only on quantity; and since our conclusions will depend on nothing else, all charges of bigotry and chauvinism become irrelevant.

Immigration vs. Food Supply

World food banks *move food to the people*, hastening the exhaustion of the environment of the poor countries. Unrestricted immigration, on the other hand, *moves people to the food*, thus speeding up the destruction of the environment of the rich countries. We can easily understand why poor people should want to make this latter transfer, but why should rich hosts encourage it?

As in the case of foreign-aid programs, immigration receives support from selfish interests and humanitarian impulses. The primary selfish interest in unimpeded immigration is the desire of employers for cheap labor, particularly in industries and trades that offer degrading work. In the past, one wave of foreigners after another was brought into the U.S. to work at wretched jobs for wretched wages. In recent years the Cubans, Puerto Ricans and Mexicans have had this dubious honor. The interests of the employers of cheap labor mesh well with the guilty silence of the country's liberal intelligentsia. White Anglo-Saxon Protestants are particularly reluctant to call for a closing of the doors to immigration for fear of being called bigots.

But not all countries have such reluctant leadership. Most educated Hawaiians, for example, are keenly aware of the limits of their environment, particularly in terms of population growth. There is only so much room on the islands, and the islanders know it. To Hawaiians, immigrants from the other forty-nine states present as great a threat as those from other nations. At a recent meeting of Hawaiian government officials in Honolulu, I had the ironic delight of hearing a speaker, who like most of his audience was of Japanese ancestry, ask how the country might practically and constitutionally close its doors to further immigration. One member of the audience countered: "How can we shut the doors now? We have many friends and relatives in Japan that we'd like to bring here some day so that they can enjoy Hawaii too." The Japanese-American speaker smiled sympathetically and answered: "Yes, but we have

children now, and someday we'll have grandchildren too. We can bring more people here from Japan only by giving away some of the land that we hope to pass on to our grandchildren some day. What right do we have to do that?"

At this point, I can hear U.S. liberals asking: "How can you justify slamming the door once you're inside? You say that immigrants should be kept out. But aren't we all immigrants, or the descendants of immigrants? If we insist on staying, must we not admit all others?" Our craving for intellectual order leads us to seek and prefer symmetrical rules and morals: a single rule for me and everybody else; the same rule yesterday, today, and tomorrow. Justice, we feel, should not change with time and place.

We Americans of non-Indian ancestry can look upon ourselves as the descendants of thieves who are guilty morally, if not legally, of stealing this land from its Indian owners. Should we then give back the land to the now living American descendants of those Indians? However morally or logically sound this proposal may be, I, for one, am unwilling to live by it and I know no one else who is. Besides, the logical consequence would be absurd. Suppose that, intoxicated with a sense of pure justice, we should decide to turn our land over to the Indians. Since all our wealth has also been derived from the land, wouldn't we be morally obliged to give that back to the Indians too?

Pure Justice vs. Reality

Clearly, the concept of pure justice produces an infinite regression to absurdity. Centuries ago, wise men invented statutes of limitations to justify the rejection of such pure justice, in the interest of preventing continual disorder. The law zealously defends property rights, but only relatively recent property rights. Drawing a line after an arbitrary time has elapsed may be unjust, but the alternatives are worse.

We are all the descendants of thieves, and the world's resources are inequitably distributed. But we must begin the journey to tomorrow from the point where we are today. We cannot remake the past. We cannot safely divide the wealth equitably among all peoples so long as people reproduce at different rates. To do so would guarantee that our grandchildren, and everyone else's grandchildren, would have only a ruined world to inhabit.

To be generous with one's own possessions is quite different from being generous with those of posterity. We should call this point to the attention of those who, from a commendable love of justice and equality, would institute a system of the commons, either in the form of a world food bank, or of unrestricted immigration. We must convince them if we wish to save at least some parts of the world from environmental ruin.

Without a true world government to control reproduction and the use of available resources, the sharing ethic of the spaceship is impossible. For the foreseeable future, our survival demands that we govern our actions by the ethics of a lifeboat, harsh though they may be. Posterity will be satisfied with nothing less.

The Famine Relief Argument

Peter Singer

Peter Singer argues that people in rich countries, by allowing those in poor countries to suffer and die, are actually engaged in reckless homicide. This is because people in rich countries could prevent the deaths of the poor without sacrificing anything of comparable significance. Singer considers a number of objections to his argument and finds them all wanting. Against Hardin's objection that aiding the poor now will lead to disaster in the future, Singer argues that if the right sort of aid is given conditionally, a future disaster of the sort Hardin envisions can be avoided.

Some Facts

Consider these facts: by the most cautious estimates, 400 million people lack the calories, protein, vitamins and minerals needed for a normally healthy life. Millions are constantly hungry; others suffer from deficiency diseases and from infections they would be able to resist on a better diet. Children are worst affected. According to one estimate, 15 million children under five die every year from the combined effects of malnutrition and infection. In some areas, half the children born can be expected to die before their fifth birthday.

From *Practical Ethics* (1979), pp. 158–181. Reprinted by permission of Cambridge University Press.

Nor is lack of food the only hardship of the poor. To give a broader picture, Robert McNamara, President of the World Bank, has suggested the term 'absolute poverty.' The poverty we are familiar with in industrialized nations is relative poverty—meaning that some citizens are poor, relative to the wealth enjoyed by their neighbours. People living in relative poverty in Australia might be quite comfortably off by comparison with old-age pensioners in Britain, and British old-age pensioners are not poor in comparison with the poverty that exists in Mali or Ethiopia. Absolute poverty, on the other hand, is poverty by any standard. In McNamara's words:

Poverty at the absolute level . . . is life at the very margin of existence.

The absolute poor are severely deprived human beings struggling to survive in a set of squalid and degraded circumstances almost beyond the power of our sophisticated imaginations and privileged circumstances to conceive.

Compared to those fortunate enough to live in developed countries individuals in the poorest nations have

An infant mortality rate eight times higher

A life expectancy one-third lower

An adult literacy rate 60% less

A nutritional level, for one out of every two in the population, below acceptable standards; and for millions of infants, less protein than is sufficient to permit optimum development of the brain.

And McNamara has summed up absolute poverty as:

a condition of life so characterized by malnutrition, illiteracy, disease, squalid surroundings, high infant mortality and low life expectancy as to be beneath any reasonable definition of human decency.

Absolute poverty is, as McNamara has said, responsible for the loss of countless lives, especially among infants and young children. When absolute poverty does not cause death it still causes misery of a kind not often seen in the affluent nations. Malnutrition in young children stunts both physical and mental development. It has been estimated that the health, growth and learning capacity of nearly half the young children in developing countries are affected by malnutrition. Millions of people on poor diets suffer from deficiency diseases, like goitre, or blindness caused by a lack of vitamin A. The food value of what the poor eat is further reduced by parasites such as hookworm and ringworm, which are endemic in conditions of poor sanitation and health education.

Death and disease apart, absolute poverty remains a miserable condition of life, with inadequate food, shelter, clothing, sanitation, health services and education. According to World Bank estimates which define absolute poverty in terms of income levels insufficient to provide adequate nutrition, something like 800 million people—almost 40% of the people of developing countries—live in absolute poverty. Absolute poverty is probably the principal cause of human misery today.

This is the background situation, the situation that prevails on our planet all the time. It does not make headlines. People died from malnutrition and related diseases yesterday, and more will die tomorrow. The occasional droughts, cyclones, earthquakes and floods that take the lives of tens of thousands in one place and at one time are more newsworthy. They add greatly to the total amount of human suffering; but it is wrong to assume that when there are no major calamities reported, all is well.

The problem is not that the world cannot produce enough to feed and shelter its people. People in the poor countries consume, on average, 400 lbs of grain a year, while North Americans average more than 2000 lbs. The difference is caused by the fact that in the rich countries we feed most of our grain to animals, converting it into meat, milk and eggs. Because this is an inefficient process, wasting up to 95% of the food value of the animal feed, people in rich countries are responsible for the consumption of far more food than those in poor countries who eat few animal products. If we stopped feeding animals on grains, soybeans and fishmeal the amount of food saved would—if distributed to those who need it—be more than enough to end hunger throughout the world.

These facts about animal food do not mean that we can easily solve the world food problem by cutting down on animal products, but they show that the problem is essentially one of distribution rather than production. The world does produce enough food. Moreover the poorer nations themselves could produce far more if they made more use of improved agricultural techniques.

So why are people hungry? Poor people cannot afford to buy grain grown by American farmers. Poor farmers cannot afford to buy improved seeds, or fertilizers, or the machinery needed for drilling wells and pumping water. Only by transferring some of the wealth of the developed nations to the poor of the underdeveloped nations can the situation be changed.

That this wealth exists is clear. Against the picture of absolute poverty that McNamara has painted, one might pose a picture of 'absolute affluence'. Those who are absolutely affluent are not necessarily affluent by comparison with their neighbours, but they are affluent by any reasonable definition of human needs. This means that they have more income than they need to provide themselves adequately with all the basic necessities of life. After buying food, shelter, clothing, necessary health services and education, the absolutely affluent are still able to spend money on luxuries. The absolutely affluent choose their food for the pleasures of the palate, not to stop hunger; they buy new clothes to look fashionable, not to keep warm; they move house to be in a better neighbourhood or have a play room for the children, not to keep out the rain; and after all this there is still money to spend on books and records, colour television, and overseas holidays.

At this stage I am making no ethical judgments about absolute affluence, merely pointing out that it exists. Its defining characteristic is a significant amount of income above the level necessary to provide for the basic human needs of oneself and one's dependents. By this standard Western Europe, North America, Japan, Australia, New Zealand and the oil-rich Middle Eastern states are all absolutely affluent, and so are many, if not all, of their citizens. The USSR and Eastern Europe might also be included on this list. To quote McNamara once more:

> The average citizen of a developed country enjoys wealth beyond the wildest dreams of the one billion people in countries with per capita incomes under $200 . . .

These, therefore, are the countries—and individuals—who have wealth which they could, without threatening their own basic welfare, transfer to the absolutely poor.

At present, very little is being transferred. Members of the Organization of Petroleum Exporting Countries lead the way, giving an average of 2.1% of their Gross National Product. Apart from them, only Sweden, The Netherlands and Norway have reached the modest UN target of 0.7% of GNP. Britain gives 0.38% of its GNP in official development assistance and a small additional amount in unofficial aid from voluntary organizations. The total comes to less than £1 per month per person, and compares with 5.5% of GNP spent on alcohol, and 3% on tobacco. Other, even wealthier nations, give still less: Germany gives 0.27%, the United States 0.22% and Japan 0.21%

The Moral Equivalent of Murder?

If these are the facts, we cannot avoid concluding that by not giving more than we do, people in rich countries are allowing those in poor countries to suffer from absolute poverty, with consequent malnutrition, ill health and death. This is not a conclusion which applies only to governments. It applies to each absolutely affluent individual, for each of us has the opportunity to do something about the situation; for instance, to give our time or money to voluntary organizations like Oxfam, War on Want, Freedom From Hunger, and so on. If, then, allowing someone to die is not intrinsically different from killing someone, it would seem that we are all murderers.

Is this verdict too harsh? Many will reject it as self-evidently absurd. They would sooner take it as showing that allowing to die cannot be equivalent to killing than as showing that living in an affluent style without contributing to Oxfam is ethically equivalent to going over to India and shooting a few peasants. And no doubt, put as bluntly as that, the verdict *is* too harsh.

There are several significant differences between spending money on luxuries instead of using it to save lives, and deliberately shooting people.

First, the motivation will normally be different. Those who deliberately shoot others go out of their way to kill; they presumably want their victims dead, from malice, sadism, or some equally unpleasant motive. A person who buys a colour television set presumably wants to watch television in colour—not in itself a terrible thing. At worst, spending money on luxuries instead of giving it away indicates selfishness and indifference to the sufferings of others, characteristics which may be understandable but are not comparable with actual malice or similar motives.

Second, it is not difficult for most of us to act in accordance with a rule against killing people: it is, on the other hand, very difficult to obey a rule which commands us to save all the lives we can. To live a comfortable, or even luxurious life it is not necessary to kill anyone; but it is necessary to allow some to die whom we might have saved, for the money that we need to live comfortably could have been given away. Thus the duty to avoid killing is much easier to discharge completely than the duty to save. Saving every life we could would mean cutting our standard of living down to the bare essentials needed to keep us alive.* To discharge this duty completely would require a degree of moral heroism utterly different from what is required by mere avoidance of killing.

A third difference is the greater certainty of the outcome of shooting when compared with not giving aid. If I point a loaded gun at someone and pull the trigger, it is virtually certain that the person will be injured, if not killed; whereas the money that I could give might be spent on a project than turns out to be unsuccessful and helps no one.

Fourth, when people are shot there are identifiable individuals who have been harmed. We can point to them and to their grieving families. When I buy my colour television, I cannot know who my money would have saved if I had given it away. In a time of famine I may see dead bodies and grieving families on my new television, and I

*Strictly, we would need to cut down to the minimum level compatible with earning the income which, after providing for our needs, left us most to give away. Thus if my present position earns me, say, £10,000 a year, but requires me to spend £1,000 a year on dressing respectably and maintaining a car, I cannot save more people by giving away the car and clothes if that will mean taking a job which, although it does not involve me in these expenses, earns me only £5,000.

might not doubt that my money would have saved some of them; even then it is impossible to point to a body and say that had I not bought the set, that person would have survived.

Fifth, it might be said that the plight of the hungry is not my doing, and so I cannot be held responsible for it. The starving would have been starving if I had never existed. If I kill, however, I am responsible for my victims' deaths, for those people would not have died if I had not killed them. . . .

Do the five differences not only explain, but also justify, our attitudes? Let us consider them one by one:

1. Take the lack of an identifiable victim first. Suppose that I am a travelling salesman, selling tinned food, and I learn that a batch of tins contains a contaminant, the known effect of which when consumed is to double the risk that the consumer will died from stomach cancer. Suppose I continue to sell the tins. My decision may have no identifiable victims. Some of those who eat the food will die from cancer. The proportion of consumers dying in this way will be twice that of the community at large, but which among the consumers died because they ate what I sold, and which would have contracted the disease anyway? It is impossible to tell; but surely this impossibility makes my decision no less reprehensible than it would have been had the contaminant had more readily detectable, though equally fatal, effects.

2. The lack of certainty that by giving money I could save a life does reduce the wrongness of not giving, by comparison with deliberate killing; but it is insufficient to show that not giving is acceptable conduct. The motorist who speeds through pedestrian crossings, heedless of anyone who might be on them, is not a murderer. She may never actually hit a pedestrian; yet what she does is very wrong indeed.

3. The notion of responsibility for acts rather than omissions is more puzzling. On the one hand we feel ourselves to be under a greater obligation to help those whose misfortunes we have caused. (It is for this rea-

son that advocates of overseas aid often argue that Western nations have created the poverty of Third World nations, through forms of economic exploitation which go back to the colonial system.) On the other hand any consequentialist would insist that we are responsible for all the consequences of our actions, and if a consequence of my spending money on a luxury item is that someone dies, I am responsible for that death. It is true that the person would have died even if I had never existed, but what is the relevance of that? The fact is that I do exist, and the consequentialist will say that our responsibilities derive from the world as it is, not as it might have been.

One way of making sense of the nonconsequentialist view of responsibility is by basing it on a theory of rights of the kind proposed by John Locke or, more recently, Robert Nozick. If everyone has a right to life, and this right is a right *against* others who might threaten my life, but not a right *to* assistance from others when my life is in danger, then we can understand the feeling that we are responsible for acting to kill but not for omitting to save. The former violates the rights of others, the latter does not.

Should we accept such a theory of rights? If we build up our theory of rights by imagining, as Locke and Nozick do, individuals living independently from each other in a 'state of nature', it may seem natural to adopt a conception of rights in which as long as each leaves the other alone, no rights are violated. I might, on this view, quite properly have maintained my independent existence if I had wished to do so. So if I do not make you any worse off than you would have been if I had had nothing at all to do with you, how can I have violated your rights? But why start from such an unhistorical, abstract and ultimately inexplicable idea as an independent individual? We now know that our ancestors were social beings long before they were human beings, and could not have developed the abilities and capacities of human beings if they had not been social beings first. In any case we are

not, now, isolated individuals. If we consider people living together in a community, it is less easy to assume that rights must be restricted to rights against interference. We might, instead, adopt the view that taking rights to life seriously is incompatible with standing by and watching people die when one could easily save them.

4. What of the difference in motivation? That a person does not positively wish for the death of another lessens the severity of the blame she deserves; but not by as much as our present attitudes to giving aid suggest. The behaviour of the speeding motorist is again comparable, for such motorists usually have no desire at all to kill anyone. They merely enjoy speeding and are indifferent to the consequences. Despite their lack of malice, those who kill with cars deserve not only blame but also severe punishment.

5. Finally, the fact that to avoid killing people is normally not difficult, whereas to save all one possibly could save is heroic, must make an important difference to our attitude to failure to do what the respective principles demand. Not to kill is a minimum standard of acceptable conduct we can require of everyone; to save all one possibly could is not something that can realistically be required, especially not in societies accustomed to giving as little as ours do. Given the generally accepted standards, people who give, say, £100 a year to Oxfam are more aptly praised for above average generosity than blamed for giving less than they might. The appropriateness of praise and blame is, however, a separate issue from the rightness or wrongness of actions. The former evaluates the agent: the latter evaluates the action. Perhaps people who give £100 really ought to give at least £1,000, but to blame them for not giving more could be counterproductive. It might make them feel that what is required is too demanding, and if one is going to be blamed anyway, one might as well not give anything at all.

(That an ethic which put saving all one possibly can on the same footing as not killing would be an ethic for saints or heroes should not lead us to assume that the alternative must be an ethic which makes it obligatory not to kill, but puts us under no obligation to save anyone. There are positions in between these extremes, as we shall soon see.)

To summarize our discussion of the five differences which normally exist between killing and allowing to die, in the context of absolute poverty and overseas aid. The lack of an identifiable victim is of no moral significance, though it may play an important role in explaining our attitudes. The idea that we are directly responsible for those we kill, but not for those we do not help, depends on a questionable notion of responsibility, and may need to be based on a controversial theory of rights. Differences in certainty and motivation are ethically significant, and show that not aiding the poor is not to be condemned as murdering them; it could, however, be on a par with killing someone as a result of reckless driving, which is serious enough. Finally the difficulty of completely discharging the duty of saving all one possibly can makes it inappropriate to blame those who fall short of this target as we blame those who kill; but this does not show that the act itself is less serious. Nor does it indicate anything about those who, far from saving all they possibly can, make no effort to save anyone.

These conclusions suggest a new approach. Instead of attempting to deal with the contrast between affluence and poverty by comparing not saving with deliberate killing, let us consider afresh whether we have an obligation to assist those whose lives are in danger, and if so, how this obligation applies to the present world situation.

The Obligation to Assist

The argument for an obligation to assist.

The path from the library at my university to the Humanities lecture theatre passes a shallow ornamental pond. Suppose that on my way to give a lecture I notice that a small child has fallen in and is in danger of drowning. Would anyone deny that I ought to wade in and pull the child out? This will mean getting my clothes muddy, and either cancelling my lecture or delaying it until I can find something dry to change into; but compared with the avoidable death of a child this is insignificant.

A plausible principle that would support the judgment that I ought to pull the child out is this: if it is in our power to prevent something very bad happening, without thereby sacrificing anything of comparable moral significance, we ought to do it. This principle seems uncontroversial. It will obviously win the assent of consequentialists; but nonconsequentialists should accept it too, because the injunction to prevent what is bad applies only when nothing comparably significant is at stake. Thus the principle cannot lead to the kinds of actions of which non-consequentialists strongly disapprove—serious violations of individual rights, injustice, broken promises, and so on. If a non-consequentialist regards any of these as comparable in moral significance to the bad thing that is to be prevented, he will automatically regard the principle as not applying in those cases in which the bad thing can only be prevented by violating rights, doing injustice, breaking promises, or whatever else is at stake. Most non-consequentialists hold that we ought to prevent what is bad and promote what is good. Their dispute with consequentialists lies in their insistence that this is not the sole ultimate ethical principle: that it is *an* ethical principle is not denied by any plausible ethical theory.

Nevertheless the uncontroversial appearance of the principle that we ought to prevent what is bad when we can do so without sacrificing anything of comparable moral significance is deceptive. If it were taken seriously and acted upon, our lives and our world would be fundamentally changed. For the principle applies, not just to rare situations in which one can save a child from a pond, but to the everyday situation in which we can assist those living in absolute poverty. In saying this I assume that absolute poverty, with its hunger and malnutrition, lack of shelter, illiteracy, disease, high infant mortality and low life expectancy, is a bad thing. And I assume that it is within the power of the affluent to reduce absolute poverty, without sacrificing anything of comparable moral significance. If these two assumptions and the principle we have been discussing are correct, we have an obligation to help those in absolute poverty which is no less strong than our obligation to rescue a drowning child from a pond. Not to help would be wrong, whether or not it is intrinsically equivalent to killing. Helping is not, as conventionally thought, a charitable act which it is praiseworthy to do, but not wrong to omit; it is something that everyone ought to do.

This is the argument for an obligation to assist. Set out more formally, it would look like this.

First premise:	If we can prevent something bad without sacrificing anything of comparable significance, we ought to do it.
Second premise:	Absolute poverty is bad.
Third premise:	There is some absolute poverty we can prevent without sacrificing anything of comparable moral significance.
Conclusion:	We ought to prevent some absolute poverty.

The first premise is the substantive moral premise on which the argument rests, and I have tried to show that it can be accepted by people who hold a variety of ethical positions.

The second premise is unlikely to be challenged. Absolute poverty is, as McNamara put it, 'beneath any reasonable definition of human decency' and it would be hard to find a plausible ethical view which did not regard it as a bad thing.

The third premise is more controversial, even though it is cautiously framed. It claims only that some absolute poverty can be prevented without the sacrifice of anything of comparable moral significance. It thus avoids the objection that any aid I can give is just 'drops in the ocean' for the point is not whether my personal contribution will make any noticeable impression on world poverty as a whole (of course it won't) but whether it will prevent some poverty. This is all the argument needs to sustain its conclusion, since the second premise says that any absolute poverty is bad, and not merely the total amount of absolute poverty. If without sacrificing anything of comparable moral significance we can provide just one family with the means to raise itself out of absolute poverty, the third premise is vindicated.

I have left the notion of moral significance unexamined in order to show that the argument does not depend on any specific values or ethical principles. I think the third premise is true for most people living in industrialized nations, on any defensible view of what is morally significant. Our affluence means that we have income we can dispose of without giving up the basic necessities of life, and we can use this income to reduce absolute poverty. Just how much we will think ourselves obliged to give up will depend on what we consider to be of comparable moral significance to the poverty we could prevent: colour television, stylish clothes, expensive dinners, a sophisticated stereo system, overseas holidays, a (second?) car, a larger house, private schools for our children.... For a utilitarian, none of these is likely to be of comparable significance to the reduction of absolute poverty; and those who are not utilitarians surely must, if they subscribe to the principle of universalizability, accept that at least *some* of these things are of far less moral significance than the absolute poverty that could be prevented by the money they cost. So the third premise seems to be true on any plausible ethical view—although the precise amount of absolute poverty that can be prevented before anything of moral significance is sacrificed will vary according to the ethical view one accepts. . . .

Objections to the Argument

Property rights. Do people have a right to private property, a right which contradicts the view that they are under an obligation to give some of their wealth away to those in absolute poverty? According to some theories of rights (for instance, Robert Nozick's) provided one has acquired one's property without the use of unjust means like force and fraud, one may be entitled to enormous wealth while others starve. This individualistic conception of rights is in contrast to other views, like the early Christian doctrine to be found in the works of Thomas Aquinas, which holds that since property exists for the satisfaction of human needs, 'whatever a man has in super-abundance is owed, of natural right, to the poor for their sustenance'. A socialist would also, of course, see wealth as belonging to the community rather than the individual, while utilitarians, whether socialist or not, would be prepared to override property rights to prevent great evils.

Does the argument for an obligation to assist others therefore presuppose one of these other theories of property rights, and not an individualistic theory like Nozick's? Not necessarily. A theory of property rights can insist on our *right* to retain wealth without pronouncing on whether the rich *ought* to give to the poor. Nozick, for example, rejects the use of compulsory means like taxation to redistribute income, but suggests that we can achieve the ends we deem morally desirable by voluntary means. So Nozick would reject the claim that rich people have an 'obligation' to give to the poor, in so far as this implies that the poor have a right to our aid, but might accept that giving is something we ought to do and failing to give, though within one's rights, is wrong— for rights is not all there is to ethics.

The argument for an obligation to assist can survive, with only minor modifications, even if we accept an individualistic theory of property rights. In any case, however, I do not think we should accept such a theory. It leaves too much to chance to be an acceptable ethical view. For instance, those whose forefathers happened to inhabit some sandy wastes around the Persian Gulf are now fabulously wealthy, because oil lay under those sands; while those whose forefathers settled on better land south of the Sahara live in absolute poverty, because of drought and bad harvests. Can this distribution be acceptable from an impartial point of view? If we imagine ourselves about to begin life as a citizen of either

Kuwait or Chad—but we do not know which— would we accept the principle that citizens of Kuwait are under no obligation to assist people living in Chad?

Population and the ethics of triage. Perhaps the most serious objection to the argument that we have an obligation to assist is that since the major cause of absolute poverty is over-population, helping those now in poverty will only ensure that yet more people are born to live in poverty in the future.

In its most extreme form, this objection is taken to show that we should adopt a policy of 'triage'. The term comes from medical policies adopted in wartime. With too few doctors to cope with all the casualties, the wounded were divided into three categories: those who would probably survive without medical assistance, those who might survive if they received assistance, but otherwise probably would not, and those who even with medical assistance probably would not survive. Only those in the middle category were given medical assistance. The idea, of course, was to use limited medical resources as effectively as possible. For those in the first category, medical treatment was not strictly necessary; for those in the third category, it was likely to be useless. It has been suggested that we should apply the same policies to countries, according to their prospects of becoming self-sustaining. We would not aid countries which even without our help will soon be able to feed their populations. We would not aid countries which, even with our help, will not be able to limit their population to a level they can feed. We would aid those countries where our help might make the difference between success and failure in bringing food and population into balance.

Advocates of this theory are understandably reluctant to give a complete list of the countries they would place into the 'hopeless' category; but Bangladesh is often cited as an example. Adopting the policy of triage would, then, mean cutting off assistance to Bangladesh and allowing famine, disease and natural disasters to reduce the population of that country (now around 80 million) to the level at which it can provide adequately for all.

In support of this view Garrett Hardin has offered a metaphor: we in the rich nations are like the occupants of a crowded lifeboat adrift in a sea full of drowning people. If we try to save the drowning by bringing them aboard our boat will be overloaded and we shall all drown. Since it is better that some survive than none, we should leave the others to drown. In the world today, according to Hardin, 'lifeboat ethics' apply. The rich should leave the poor to starve, for otherwise the poor will drag the rich down with them.

Against this view, some writers have argued that over-population is a myth. The world produces ample food to feed its population, and could, according to some estimates, feed ten times as many. People are hungry not because there are too many but because of inequitable land distribution, the manipulation of Third World economies by the developed nations, wastage of food in the West, and so on.

Putting aside the controversial issue of the extent to which food production might one day be increased, it is true, as we have already seen, that the world now produces enough to feed its inhabitants—the amount lost by being fed to animals itself being enough to meet existing grain shortages. Nevertheless population growth cannot be ignored. Bangladesh could, with land reform and using better techniques, feed its present population of 80 million; but by the year 2000, according to World Bank estimates, its population will be 146 million. The enormous effort that will have to go into feeding an extra 66 million people, all added to the population within a quarter of a century, means that Bangladesh must develop at full speed to stay where she is. Other low income countries are in similar situations. By the end of the century, Ethiopia's population is expected to rise from 29 to 54 million; Somalia's from 3 to 7 million, India's from 620 to 958 million, Zaire's from 25 to 47 million. What will happen then? Population cannot grow indefinitely. It will be checked by a decline in birth rates or a rise in death rates. Those who advocate triage are proposing that we allow the population growth of some countries to be checked by a rise in death rates—that is, by increased malnutrition, and related diseases; by widespread famines; by increased infant mortality; and by epidemics of infectious diseases.

The consequences of triage on this scale are so horrible that we are inclined to reject it without further argument. How could we sit by our television sets, watching millions starve while we do nothing? Would not that be the end of all notions of human equality and respect for human life? Don't people have a right to our assistance, irrespective of the consequences?

Anyone whose initial reaction to triage was not one of repugnance would be an unpleasant sort of person. Yet initial reactions based on strong feelings are not always reliable guides. Advocates of triage are rightly concerned with the long-term consequences of our actions. They say that helping the poor and starving now merely ensures more poor and starving in the future. When our capacity to help is finally unable to cope—as one day it must be—the suffering will be greater than it would be if we stopped helping now. If this is correct, there is nothing we can do to prevent absolute starvation and poverty, in the long run, and so we have no obligation to assist. Nor does it seem reasonable to hold that under these circumstances people have a right to our assistance. If we do accept such a right, irrespective of the consequences, we are saying that, in Hardin's metaphor, we would continue to haul the drowning into our lifeboat until the boat sank and we all drowned.

If triage is to be rejected it must be tackled on its own ground, within the framework of consequentialist ethics. Here it is vulnerable. Any consequentialist ethics must take probability of outcome into account. A course of action that will certainly produce some benefit is to be preferred to an alternative course that may lead to a slightly larger benefit, but is equally likely to result in no benefit at all. Only if the greater magnitude of the uncertain benefit outweighs its uncertainty should we choose it. Better one certain unit of benefit than a 10% chance of 5 units; but better a 50% chance of 3 units than a single certain unit. The same principle applies when we are trying to avoid evils.

The policy of triage involves a certain, very great evil: population control by famine and disease. Tens of millions would die slowly. Hundreds of millions would continue to live in absolute poverty, at the very margin of existence. Against this prospect, advocates of the policy place a possible evil which is greater still: the same process of famine and disease, taking place in, say, fifty years time, when the world's population may be three times its present level, and the number who will die from famine, or struggle on in absolute poverty, will be that much greater. The question is: how probable is this forecast that continued assistance now will lead to greater disasters in the future?

Forecasts of population growth are notoriously fallible, and theories about the factors which affect it remain speculative. One theory, at least as plausible as any other, is that countries pass through a 'demographic transition' as their standard of living rises. When people are very poor and have no access to modern medicine their fertility is high, but population is kept in check by high death rates. The introduction of sanitation, modern medical techniques and other improvements reduces the death rate, but initially has little effect on the birth rate. Then population grows rapidly. Most poor countries are now in this phase. If standards of living continue to rise, however, couples begin to realize that to have the same number of children surviving to maturity as in the past, they do not need to give birth to as many children as their parents did. The need for children to provide economic support in old age diminishes. Improved education and the emancipation and employment of women also reduce the birthrate, and so population growth begins to level off. Most rich nations have reached this stage, and their populations are growing only very slowly.

If this theory is right, there is an alternative to the disasters accepted as inevitable by supporters of triage. We can assist poor countries to raise the living standards of the poorest members of their population. We can encourage the governments of these countries to enact land reform measures, improve education, and liberate women from a purely childbearing role. We can also help other countries to make contraception and sterilization widely available. There is a fair chance that these measures will hasten the onset of the demographic transition and bring population growth down to a manageable level. Success cannot be guaranteed; but the evidence that improved economic security and education re-

duce population growth is strong enough to make triage ethically unacceptable. We cannot allow millions to die from starvation and disease when there is a reasonable probability that population can be brought under control without such horrors.

Population growth is therefore not a reason against giving overseas aid, although it should make us think about the kind of aid to give. Instead of food handouts, it may be better to give aid that hastens the demographic transition. This may mean agricultural assistance for the rural poor, or assistance with education, or the provision of contraceptive services. Whatever kind of aid proves most effective in specific circumstances, the obligation to assist is not reduced.

One awkward question remains. What should we do about a poor and already overpopulated country which, for religious or nationalistic reasons, restricts the use of contraceptives and refuses to slow its population growth? Should we nevertheless offer development assistance? Or should we make our offer conditional on effective steps being taken to reduce the birthrate? To the latter course, some would object that putting conditions on aid is an attempt to impose our own ideas on independent sovereign nations. So it is—but is this imposition unjustifiable? If the argument for an obligation to assist is sound, we have an obligation to reduce absolute poverty: but we have no obligation to make sacrifices that, to the best of our knowledge, have no prospect of reducing poverty in the long run. Hence we have no obligation to assist countries whose governments have policies which will make our aid ineffective. This could be very harsh on poor citizens of these countries—for they may have no say in the government's policies—but we will help more people in the long run by using our resources where they are most effective. (The same principles may apply, incidentally, to countries that refuse to take other steps that could make assistance effective—like refusing to reform systems of land holding that impose intolerable burdens on poor tenant farmers.) . . .

Too high a standard? The final objection to the argument for an obligation to assist is that it sets a standard so high that none but a saint could attain it. How many people can we really expect to give away everything not comparable in moral significance to the poverty their donation could relieve? For most of us, with commonsense views about what is of moral significance, this would mean a life of real austerity. Might it not be counter-productive to demand so much? Might not people say: 'As I can't do what is morally required anyway, I won't bother to give at all.' If, however, we were to set a more realistic standard, people might make a genuine effort to reach it. Thus setting a lower standard might actually result in more aid being given.

It is important to get the status of this objection clear. Its accuracy as a prediction of human behaviour is quite compatible with the argument that we are obliged to give to the point at which by giving more we sacrifice something of comparable moral significance. What would follow from the objection is that public advocacy of this standard of giving is undesirable. It would mean that in order to do the maximum to reduce absolute poverty, we should advocate a standard lower than the amount we think people really ought to give. Of course we ourselves—those of us who accept the original argument, with its higher standard—would know that we ought to do more than we publicly propose people ought to do, and we might actually give more than we urge others to give. There is no inconsistency here, since in both our private and our public behaviour we are trying to do what will most reduce absolute poverty.

For a consequentialist, this apparent conflict between public and private morality is always a possibility, and not in itself an indication that the underlying principle is wrong. The consequences of a principle are one thing, the consequences of publicly advocating it another.

Is it true that the standard set by our argument is so high as to be counterproductive? There is not much evidence to go by, but discussions of the argument, with students and others have led me to think it might be. On the other hand the conventionally accepted standard—a few coins in a collection tin when one is waved under your nose—is obviously far too low. What level should we advocate? Any figure will be arbitrary, but there may be something to be said for a round percentage of one's income like, say, 10%—more than a token donation, yet not so high as to be beyond all but saints. (This figure has the additional advantage of being reminiscent of the ancient tithe, or tenth, which was traditionally given to the church, whose responsibilities included care of the poor in one's local community. Perhaps the idea can be revived and applied to the global community.) Some families, of course, will find 10% a considerable strain on their finances. Others may be able to give more without difficulty. No figure should be advocated as a rigid minimum or maximum; but it seems safe to advocate that those earning average or above average incomes in affluent societies, unless they have an unusually large number of dependents or other special needs, ought to give a tenth of their income to reducing absolute poverty. By any reasonable ethical standards this is the minimum we ought to do, and we do wrong if we do less.

Do We Owe The Future Anything?

Richard T. De George

Richard T. De George argues that, because future generations do not exist, they do not have any rights nor do we have any correlative obligations to them. Still, De George thinks we do have an obligation to promote the continuance of the human race—but an obligation based on considerations of value rather than of rights. At the same time, he denies that we have any obligation to produce a continuously increasing standard of living.

The desire to avoid pollution—however defined—involves concern for the duration and quality of human life. Problems dealing with the quality of human life inevitably involve value judgments. And value judgments are notorious candidates for debate and disagreement. Yet in discussions on pollution the desirability of the continuance of the human race is generally taken for granted; most people feel that a continuous rise in the standard of living would be a good thing; and many express a feeling of obligation towards future generations. How well founded are these judgments? The purpose of this paper is to examine the validity and some of the implications of three statements of principles which have a direct bearing on this question and so on the debate concerning pollution and its control. The three principles are the following:

1. Only existing entities have rights.
2. Continuance of the human race is good.
3. Continuous increase in man's standard of living is good.

I

The argument in favor of the principle that only existing entities have rights is straightforward and simple: Non-existent entities by defi-

From "Do We Owe the Future Anything?" in *Law and the Ecological Challenge* (1978), pp. 180–190. Reprinted by permission of William S. Hein & Co., Inc.

nition do not exist. What does not exist cannot be the subject or bearer of anything. Hence it cannot be the subject or bearer of rights.

Just as non-existent entities have no rights, so it makes no sense to speak about anyone's correlative duty towards non-existent entities. Towards that which does not exist we can have no legal or moral obligation, since there is no subject or term which can be the object of that obligation. Now it is clear that unconceived possible future human beings do not exist, though we can think, e.g., of the class of human beings which will exist two hundred years from now. It follows that since this class does not (yet) exist, we cannot have any obligations to it, nor to any of its possible members. It is a presently empty class.

More generally, then, presently existing human beings have no obligation to any future-and-not-yet existing set or class of human beings. We owe them nothing and they have no legitimate claim on us for the simple reason that they do not exist. No one can legitimately defend their interests or represent their case in court or law or government, because they are not, and so have no interests or rights.

It follows from this that a great deal of contemporary talk about obligations to the future, where this means to some distant future portion of mankind, is simply confused. In dealing with questions of pollution and clean air—as well as with similar issues such as the use of irreplaceable resources—there can be no legitimate question of the **rights** of unconceived future human beings or of any supposedly correlative **obligation** of present-day human beings to them.

Some people may find this to be counter-intuitive. That it is not so may perhaps become clearer if we consider what I take to be the feelings of many—if not most people with respect to the past.

Consider the general attitude towards the ancient Greeks and Romans. Did they owe us anything? Did they have any duties or obligations to us? It is clear there are no sanctions we can impose on them and no way we can enforce any obligations we may claim they had towards us. But surely even to raise the question of their obligation to us is odd. We may rejoice in what has been saved of the past and handed down to us, and we may regret that some of Plato's dialogues have been lost or that the Library at Alexandria was burned, or that Rome was sacked. But though we may regret such events and though we may judge that they were in some sense ills for mankind or the result of immoral actions, they were not immoral because of any obligation past generations had to us.

The situation is little changed if we come up to more recent—though not too recent—times. The American Founding Fathers had no obligation to us. They could scarcely have envisaged our times or have been expected to calculate the effects of their actions on us. Or consider the unrestrained slaughter of American buffalo for sport. Such action may have been immoral and a waste of a natural resource; but if it was immoral it was not because present-day Americans have any right to have inherited more buffalo than we did.

Since it is not possible to impose sanctions on past generations it makes no sense to speak of legal obligations or even of moral obligations of those generations to us. At best, as some minority groups have been arguing, we might claim that present-day beneficiaries of past injustices are obliged to make restitution to the present descendents of those who in the past suffered injustice. This is a plausible claim, and might serve as a model in the future for some portion of mankind claiming that it has a legal or moral claim against another portion for exploitation or oppression by their forefathers. Whatever the obligation to make restoration for past injustices, however, the injustice was an injustice not primarily against present generations but against those past generations whose rights were violated or whose property or lives were unjustly taken, or who were otherwise oppressed or exploited.

The situation is basically similar today vis-a-vis future generations. Our primary obligation with respect to the control of pollution or to the use of resources is to presently existing human beings rather than to possible future human beings. The best way to protect the interests of future generations—if we choose to use this language—may be to conserve the environment for ourselves. But my present point is that in dealing with questions of public policy or legislation, the primary values to be considered are those of presently existing people, and not the projected or supposed values of future generations. To argue or act as if we could know the wants or needs of generations hundreds or more years hence is to deceive ourselves, perhaps so as to have an excuse to ignore present-day wants and needs. Hence questions about the amount and kind of pollution to be tolerated, the resources to be rationed or preserved, should not be decided in terms of far distant future needs or requirements but in terms of present and near-future needs and requirements.

It is correct that for the first time in the history of mankind presently living human beings have it within their power to annihilate mankind or to use up irreplaceable resources. But these new capacities do not change the status of our responsibilities or obligations, despite the fact that they are increased. If we do annihilate mankind, it will be no injustice to those who never were and never will be. If we were foolishly to use up vital, irreplaceable resources or disrupt the ecosystem, the reason it would be wrong or bad, unjust or immoral—and so the reason why it might now be something requiring legislation to prevent—is not its effects on those who do not yet exist, but its effects on those who do.

The thrust of the principle we are considering is that present generations or individuals must be considered primary in any calculation of value with respect to either pollution control or the distribution and use of the limited resources of the earth. The rights of presently existing people carry with them the obligation to respect their rights, e.g., to enjoy at least minimal levels of food, shelter, and the like. No one and no generation is required to sacrifice itself for imaginary, non-existent generations of the future. What does have to be considered is the future of presently existing persons—infants as well as adults.

We undoubtedly feel closer to our as yet unconceived descendents—those one removed from the present generation of children—than we do to many people living in places far distant from us, with different customs and values; and if we were to choose between raising the standard of living of these to us foreign people and preserving our wealth to be shared by our descendents, we might well opt for the latter. To do so is to aggregate to ourselves the right to conserve present resources for those to whom we choose to pass them on at the expense of those presently existing who do not share them. Since, however, presently existing people have rights to the goods of the earth, there seems to be a **prima facie** obligation to attempt to raise the level of living and comfort of presently existing people, wherever they may be, rather than ignoring them and worrying only about our own future heirs. Underfed and impoverished areas of the world may require greater attention and impose greater obligations than non-existent future generations.

Insofar as modern technology is world-significant, so too are some aspects of pollution. Mercury poured into streams finds its way into the ocean and into fish caught in international waters and shipped around the world; fall-out from nuclear blasts circles the globe. If present-day legislative principles in the United States are sufficient to handle the problems posed by pollution in our own country, it is certainly not the case that there are effective means of controlling the problem internationally. The cost of pollution control prevents poorer countries from simultaneously developing their technology in order to raise their living standards and spend the money and resources necessary to curb pollution. It is in cases such as these that it becomes especially important to be conscious of the principle discussed here which emphasizes the overbearing rights of existing persons as opposed to the putative rights of nonexistent persons. . . .

Although there is no full fledged obligation to provide, e.g., clean air, for countless future generations, we will have an obligation to provide something for at least those future persons or generations for whom or for which we are rather closely responsible. Generations overlap considerably; but any group in the position to influence and change things, though it cannot be expected to be responsible for generations hundreds, much less thousands of years hence, can be expected to take into account those persons who will be alive within the next fifty or a hundred years. A large number of these people already exist; and if future generations are produced—as barring some global catastrophe they will be—they **will** have rights and these rights must be considered at least as potential rights. The amount of consideration should be proportional to the probability that they will exist, and should be considered especially by those responsible for bringing them into the world.

Furthermore, if starting from the premise that nonexistent entities can have no rights it follows that presently existing persons have no correlative obligations towards them, and so no such obligations to unborn generations, this does not mean that people may not want to consider future possible generations from some point of view other than one of such obligation and take them into account in other ways and for other reasons.

Obviously men are concerned about their own futures and those of their presently existing children and of the presently acknowledged right of their children to have children; it is a claim which must be weighed. Though we cannot assume that the children of present-day children will have exactly the same desires and values as we, there is good reason to believe they will be sufficiently similar to us so that they will need fresh air, that they will not be able to tolerate excessive amounts of mercury or DDT in their food, and that they will probably share a good many of our desires. To speak of the **right** of non-existing future persons to have children in their turn is to treat them as actual. It amounts to saying that if conditions remain more or less the same and if the presently possible entities become actual, then, when they do, they will have the rights we presently attribute to actually existing persons. Our present interest in their happiness, however, is already an actual interest which must be considered and it might impel—

though not strictly require—us to leave as many options open to those who will come after us as possible, consistent with taking care of our own needs and wants.

Since most people living now would consider it possible to be living twenty years hence, the conditions of life which the next as yet unborn generation will face is a condition of life which we who presently exist will also face. So with respect to at least one, two, three or perhaps four generations hence, or for roughly fifty to a hundred years hence, it can plausibly be argued that we plan not only for unborn generations but also for ourselves. Our concern for them is equally concern for ourselves. And we do have rights. If this is the case, we can legitimately think and plan and act for the future on the basis of our own concerns, which include **our** hopes and desires for our real or anticipated offspring. But we should be clear about what we are arguing, and not confuse our rights and desires with the supposed rights of non-existent entities.

II

The second principle was: Continuance of the human race is good.

What does this mean and what does it imply?

Can we give any sense to the question: how long should the human race survive? We know that some species have had their span of years on earth and have given way to other species. To ask how long the dinosaur should have survived would be an odd question; for to say that it should have survived for a shorter or longer time than it did would be to speak as if the laws of nature should have been different, or as if the dinosaur's continued existence was a good which it could have done something to prolong beyond the time that it did. It is precisely in this sense—that the survival of the human species is a good in itself and that we should do what we can to keep it going—that we say that the human race should continue to survive. To utter this is to make a value judgment and to express our feelings about the race, despite the fact that we as individuals will

die. Some people speak blithely about its being better for the human species to continue for another thousand years than for another five hundred; or for 500,000 rather than 100,000, and so on. But the content which we can give to such statements—other than expressing the judgment that human life is a good in itself, at least under certain circumstances—seems minimal. For we cannot imagine what human life would be like in the far distant future, nor what we can or should do to help make it the case that one of those figures rather than the other is the one that actually becomes the case.

If tomorrow some sort of radiation from the sun were to render all human beings sterile, we could anticipate the demise of the human race as more and more of the present population died off. We could anticipate the difficulties of those who were the relatively last to die. And we could take some solace in the fact that the radiation would have been an act of God and not the result of the acts of men. The demise of the human race would in this case be similar to the extinction of the dinosaur. If a similar occurence was the result of the acts of men, though the result would be the same, it would make more sense in the latter case than in the former to say that man should have continued longer as a species. Just as we consider murder and suicide wrong, so we consider wrong the fouling of the air or water to such an extent that it kills others or ourselves or the whole human race.

Thus, though no injustice is done to those who will never exist because of our actions, and though we do not violate any of their rights—since they have none—we can in some sense say that with the extinction of the human race there would be less value in the world than if it had continued to exist. If we have an obligation to attempt to create and preserve as much value in the world as possible, then we have an obligation to continue the human race, where this does not necessarily mean an obligation to procreate as many people as possible but to achieve as much value as possible, taking into consideration the quality of life of those who will be alive. The basis for the obligation comes not from a consideration of rights, but from a consideration of value.

Such a calculation, obviously, is something which each generation can perform only with respect to the time it is alive and able to act. It can help assure that when it dies those who are still living are in such a condition as to preserve human life and to pass it on at as high a qualitative level as possible. And if that happened consistently each year, each decade, each century, then until there was some act of God presumably man would continue indefinitely—which is a thought we may take some pleasure in contemplating, despite the fact that beyond a rather small number of years we will not be affected by whether the race continues or not.

Thus far, then, though we do not have any obligation **to** non-existent entities, we can legitimately anticipate the future needs and requirements of ourselves and of those who will probably come soon after us; furthermore, since we can make out the case that it would be good for the human race to continue, we have the obligation to do what we can to forestall its demise. This leads us to the third principle.

III

The last of the three principles I proposed at the start of this paper was: Continuous increase in man's standard of living is good. It is a principle which a large number of people seem to subscribe to, one underlying much of our industrial and technological growth and a good deal of the concern for a constantly expanding GNP. As a principle, however, it is both ambiguous and dubious.

There are at least four basic interpretations which can be given to the principle: 1) it can be taken to refer to advancement up the economic ladder by people on an individual basis; 2) it might be understood as a statement about the hopes and aims of each generation for the succeeding generation; 3) it might mean that the standard of living of at least some men should continue to rise, pushing forward the heights to which men can rise; and 4) it can be interpreted to mean that all men in a given society, or throughout the world, should be brought up to a certain constantly rising level of life.

The differences in interpretation are ex-

tremely important and both stem from and give rise to different sets of value judgments concerning production, distribution, development of resources, and expenditure of resources on pollution control.

1) The individualistic interpretation puts its emphasis on an individual's ability through work, savings, ingenuity, or other means to advance himself economically. The Horatio Alger ideal, the rise from poverty to wealth, is the model. Increasing one's standard of living became the goal of workers as expressed in the labor union movements, and its results are clearly visible in the high standard of living enjoyed by many large segments of the population in the United States and other industrialized countries. Together with this rise has come the pollution from automobiles and factories and the birth of a small counterculture which has called into question the necessity, the wisdom, and the value of a constantly rising standard of living.

The hope of a better life expresses an undeniable value when one's life is barely tolerable. It makes less sense as one's needs are more and more taken care of and the principle becomes dubious once one has achieved a certain standard of living somewhere considerably well above the minimal necessary for survival. There is a point of diminishing returns beyond which the price one has to pay in terms of energy, time, money, and resources expended does not produce correspondingly significant benefits. And if enough people reach that state, then the society's energy and efforts become counter-productive. The result we are seeing is that the attempt to achieve a constantly higher standard of living has resulted in a lower quality of life for all, partially through pollution. This fact, admittedly, is little comfort to those who have not yet arrived at a tolerable level of life and for whom the aspiration to raise their standard of living is a real good; the present point, however, is that at least beyond a certain level the principle cannot be achieved and if acted on may serve to produce more harm than good. (The related problem of inequity in a society will be considered further under the fourth interpretation.)

2) The interpretation of the principle which expresses the hope of parents that their chil-

dren will have a better life than they suffers the same fate as the preceding interpretation. Where the level of life is already good, the desire that their children's be even better may well be questionable for the reasons we have already seen. Children, of course, have no right to be better off than their parents, although those who are badly off might well wish those they love to enjoy more of the goods of life than they themselves have.

If some generation is to enjoy a higher standard of living than others, however, it is not necessary that it always be some future generation. The desire that some future generation of human beings should be better off than present generations may be the desire of some members of present generations. But it is nothing owed to future generations. Some parents sacrifice themselves and deny themselves for the benefit of their children; some carefully save their wealth only to have their children squander it. In some cases such self-sacrifice is noble and evokes our praise; in others, it is foolish. But any such case of self-sacrifice is above the demands of duty, as is obvious when we see children attempting to demand such sacrifice from their parents as if it were their right. Nor does any parent or group have the right through legislation to demand such sacrifice from others for his own or for other people's children.

3) The view that at least some men should live at constantly higher levels so as to push mankind constantly forward seems hardly defensible for a number of reasons. The first is that it is difficult to describe what a constantly higher standard of living could mean for only a few since their lives are so closely connected to other men and to the energy, pollution, and population problems they all face. Secondly, standard of living is not the same as quality of life. Simple increase in the standard of living, if measured by the goods one has, simply does not make much sense beyond a certain point. For one's needs beyond that point are artificial, and it is not at all clear that satisfying them makes one happier or more comfortable or any of the other things that an increase in the standard of living is supposed to do, and for which reasons it is desired as a good. Thirdly, it can well be argued that it is unlikely that the constantly higher standard advocated

for the few—if sense can be made of it—will help do anything but increase the difference between the level of life of the haves and the have-nots. If taken to mean not that a few men in an advanced industrial society should push mankind forward but that the advanced industrial societies should continue to advance at the expense of the non-industrial societies, then this seems to go clearly against the rights of the latter, and so not be a worthy end at all.

4) The fourth interpretation is the most plausible and has the most vocal defenders today. It maintains that all men in a given society (and ideally throughout the world) should be brought up to a certain constantly rising minimal level of life—at least constantly rising for the foreseeable future, given the wide distance between the level of life of the haves and the have-nots. This is the impetus behind minimum income legislation on the American domestic scene. Globally, it affects the relations between have and have-not countries, between the industrially developed and the underdeveloped countries, and is one of the bases for advocating foreign aid programs of various sorts.

The right of all men to a minimal standard of living is one that I would argue in favor of. But my present concern is to note that the right to a constantly rising minimum is contingent upon the ability of the earth and of society to provide it. If world resources are able to adequately sustain only a limited number of people, and if more than that number are born, the distribution of goods cannot extend sufficiently far; and those societies which contributed most to the overpopulation of their land and of the earth in general may well have to bear the brunt of the evil consequences.

A continuously rising standard of living therefore is never a right, not always a good, and most often simply one good to be measured against other goods and available resources.

IV

What then, if anything, do we owe future generations? We do not owe them a better life than we enjoy, nor do we owe them resources which we need for ourselves.

When dealing with renewable resources a sound principle might be that, other things being equal, they should not be used up at a faster rate than that at which they can be replaced. But when they are needed at a greater rate than that at which they can be replaced, rationing is insufficient and they raise a problem similar to that raised by non-renewable resources. One can argue that the latter should be used up sufficiently slowly so that there are always reserves; but this may mean using less and less each year or decade, despite increasing demand. An alternative is simply to use what we need, attempting to keep our needs rational, and to face crucially diminished supplies when we are forced to face them, hoping in the meantime that some substitutes will be discovered or developed.

Frequently problems of this type have been approached from a utilitarian point of view, and such an approach is instructive. Let each man count for one, the argument goes, whether he be a present man or a future man. The happiness of each is on a par as far as importance and intrinsic goodness are concerned. But increasing the sum of total happiness is better than its opposite. If by increased growth or unlimited use now of limited resources we increase our happiness by a small amount, but doom those who come after us to struggling along without some important natural resources; and if by conserving our natural resources now our happiness or at least that part which is made up of comfort is somewhat less than it could be, but the happiness of many millions or billions who come after us is greater than it would otherwise be, then the moral thing to do is to conserve our resources now and share them with future generations.

This argument presupposes first that there will be the future generations it hypothesizes, that these future generations will want pretty much the same things that we do in order to be happy, that they will not overuse the goods of the earth, and that they will not be able to find any suitable substitutes. If we saved only to have them squander, then no more good might be achieved than if we had spent liberally and they had proportionally less; or if they find, e.g., alternate energy sources, then our

penury resulted in less good than there might have been.

In earlier times the ploy of this kind of argument was to trade on the happiness of countless generations in the future as a result of some sacrifice of our happiness now. But there are now a sufficient number of doubts about there being future generations, about their not finding alternative resources, and about our present sacrifices leading to their happiness (since there might be so many of them anyway) as to render the argument less convincing than it might formerly have been.

In any calculus of pleasure or good there is no necessity for future generations to enjoy a higher standard of living at the expense of present generations. If there will be a peak in the standard somewhere along the line, followed by a decline, it might just as well be the present generation which enjoys the peak through the utilization of resources, which, since limited, will be used up sooner or later. There is no greater good served by future generations being the peak since obviously when it comes to their turn, if it is improper for us to enjoy more than our successors, and if this is the proper way to feel, they should feel so also.

Both because of these considerations and because of the large number of unknowables concerning the future, short range considerations are surer and more pertinent than long range considerations. The threshold of pollution has been recently crossed so that it is now obvious that something must be done; legislation consequently is being passed. The amount and kind of pollution to be tolerated, the resources to be rationed or preserved should not be decided in terms of far distant needs or requirements but in terms of present and near-future needs and requirement.

Production involves wastes which have now reached the pollution stage. Its control is costly. The cost must be borne either by the producer (who will pass it on to the consumer) or by society at large through the taxes required, e.g., to purify water. The principle that whoever causes the pollution must pay for cleaning it up, or that no production should be allowed without the mechanism provided to prevent pollution, will make some kinds of production unprofitable. In this case, if such production is considered necessary or desirable, it will have to be subsidized. If society cannot pay for total cleanup it might have to settle for less than it would like; or it might have to give up some of its production or some of the goods to which it had become accustomed; or it might have to forego some of the products it might otherwise produce. Such choices should not be made a priori or by the fiat of government, but by the members of society at large or by as many of them interested and aware and informed enough to help in the decision making process.

There are presently available the means nationally for allocating resources and for controlling use and production through automatic market and natural mechanisms as well as through legislation. Where legislation poses the greatest difficulty is not on the national level but on the international level. For technology has brought us into one closely interdependent world faster than the social and legal mechanisms for solving the world-wide problems of resources, population, and pollution have been able to develop.

The problems posed by the ecological challenge are many and complex. But in dealing with them it should be clear that we owe nothing **to** those who do not yet and may never exist; that nonetheless we do have an obligation to promote the continuance of the human race, and so have an obligation **for** those whom we produce; that though at least minimum standards of living for all are desirable, if some generation is to enjoy the peak it need not be other generations; and that the choice of how to use our resources and continue or control our pollution depends on the price all those concerned wish to pay and the values we wish to espouse and promote.

The Welfare Rights of Distant Peoples and Future Generations

James P. Sterba

This article argues that welfare rights of distant peoples and future generations are justified on the basis of a right to life and a right to fair treatment. It contends that whether a right to life is interpreted as a negative right (as libertarians tend to do) or as a positive right (as welfare liberals tend to do), it is possible to show that this right justifies welfare rights, amply providing for the basic needs of distant peoples and future generations. This article discusses what is required for meeting a person's basic needs and explains how these requirements can vary from society to society and from time to time.

In order to formulate social policies to deal with issues like population control, world hunger and energy consumption, we clearly need solutions to many difficult and perplexing problems. Not the least of these problems is the determination of the moral side-constraints we should observe by virtue of our

From "The Welfare Rights of Distant Peoples and Future Generations: Moral Side-Constraints on Social Policy," *Social Theory and Practice* (1981), pp. 99–119. Reprinted by permission of *Social Theory and Practice*.

relationship to persons who are separated from us in space (distant peoples) and time (future generations). In this paper I wish, firstly, to show how these side-constraints, which I shall call "the welfare rights of distant peoples and future generations," can be grounded on fundamental moral requirements to which many of us are already committed and, secondly, to determine some of the practical requirements of these side-constraints for the issues of population control and world hunger.

The Welfare Rights
of Distant Peoples

It used to be argued that the welfare rights of distant peoples would eventually be met as a byproduct of the continued economic growth of the technologically developed societies of the world. It was believed that the transfer of investment and technology to the less developed societies of the world would eventually, if not make everyone well off, at least satisfy everyone's basic needs. Now we are not so sure. Presently more and more evidence points to the conclusion that without some substantial sacrifice on the part of the technologically developed societies of the world, many of the less developed societies will never be able to provide their members with even the basic necessities for survival. For example, according to a study prepared by the World Bank in 1979, depending on the growth of world trade, between 470 and 710 million people will be living in conditions of absolute poverty as the 21st century dawns, unless, that is, the technologically developed societies of the world adopt some plausible policy of redistribution.[1] Even those, like Herman Kahn, who argue that an almost utopian world situation will obtain in the distant future, still would have to admit that unless some plausible policy of redistribution is adopted, malnutrition and starvation will continue in the less developed societies for many years to come.[2] Thus, a recognition of the welfare rights of distant peoples would appear to have significant consequences for developed and underdeveloped societies alike.

Of course, there are various senses in which distant peoples can be said to have welfare rights and various moral grounds on which those rights can be justified. First of all, the welfare rights of distant peoples can be understood to be either negative rights or positive rights.[3] A negative right is a right not to be interfered with in some specific manner. For example, a right to liberty is usually understood to be a negative right; it guarantees each person the right not to have her liberty interfered with provided that she does not unjustifiably interfere with the liberty of any

other person. On the other hand, a positive right is a right to receive some specific goods or services. Typical positive rights are the right to have a loan repaid and the right to receive one's just earnings. Secondly, the welfare rights of distant peoples can be understood to be either *in personam* rights or *in rem* rights. *In personam* rights are rights that hold against some specific namable person or persons while *in rem* rights hold against everyone who is in a position to abide by the rights in question. A right to liberty is usually understood to be an *in rem* right while the right to have a loan repaid or the right to receive one's just earnings are typical *in personam* rights. Finally, the rights of distant peoples can be understood to be either legal rights, that is, rights that *are enforced* by coercive sanctions, or moral rights, that is, rights that *ought to be enforced* either simply by noncoercive sanctions (for example, verbal condemnations) or by both coercive and noncoercive sanctions. Accordingly, what distinguishes the moral rights of distant peoples from the requirements of supererogation (the nonfulfillment of which is never blameworthy) is that the former but not the latter can be justifiably enforced either by noncoercive or by coercive and noncoercive sanctions. Since we will be primarily concerned with the moral rights of distant peoples to a certain minimum of welfare, hereafter "right(s)" should be understood as short for "moral right(s)."

Of the various moral grounds for justifying the welfare rights of distant peoples, quite possibly the most evident are those which appeal either to a right to life or a right to fair treatment.[4] Indeed, whether a person's right to life is interpreted as a negative right (as libertarians tend to do)[5] or as a positive right (as welfare liberals tend to do)[6], it is possible to show that the right justifies welfare rights that would amply provide for a person's basic needs. Alternatively, it is possible to justify those same welfare rights on the basis of a person's positive right to fair treatment.

Thus suppose that a person's right to life is a positive right. So understood the person's right to life would most plausibly be interpreted as a right to receive those goods and resources that are necessary for satisfying her basic needs. For a person's basic needs are those which must be satisfied in order not to seriously endanger her health or sanity. Thus receiving the goods and resources that are necessary for satisfying her basic needs would preserve a person's life in the fullest sense. And if a person's positive right to life is to be universal in the sense that it is possessed by every person (as the right to life is generally understood to be) then it must be an *in rem* right. This is because an *in rem* right, unlike an *in personam* right, does not require for its possession the assumption by other persons of any special roles or contractual obligations. Interpreted as a positive *in rem* right, therefore, a person's right to life would clearly justify the welfare rights of distant peoples to have their basic needs satisfied.

Suppose, on the other hand, that a person's right to life is a negative right. Here again, if the right is to be universal in the sense that it is possessed by all persons then it must also be an *in rem* right. So understood the right would require that everyone who is in a position to do so not interfere in certain ways with a person's attempts to meet her basic needs.

But what sort of noninterference would this right to life justify? If one's basic needs have not been met, would a person's right to life require that others not interfere with her taking the goods she needs from the surplus possessions of those who already have satisfied their own basic needs? As it is standardly interpreted, a person's negative right to life would not require such noninterference. Instead, a person's negative right to life is usually understood to be limited in such circumstances by the property rights of those who have more than enough to satisfy their own basic needs.[7] Moreover, those who claim property rights to such surplus goods and resources are usually in a position to effectively prohibit those in need from taking what they require. For surely most underdeveloped nations of the world would be able to sponsor expeditions to the American Midwest or the Australian Plains for the purpose of collecting the grain necessary to satisfy the basic needs of their citizens if they were not effectively prohibited from doing so at almost every stage of the enterprise.

But are persons with such surplus goods and resources normally justified in so prohibiting others from satisfying their basic needs? Admittedly, such persons may have contributed greatly to the value of the surplus goods and resources they possess, but why should that give them power over the life and death of those less fortunate? While their contribution may well justify favoring their nonbasic needs over the nonbasic needs of others, how could it justify favoring their nonbasic needs over the basic needs of others? After all, a person's negative right to life, being an *in rem* right, does not depend on the assumption by other persons of any special roles or contractual obligations. By contrast, property rights that are *in personam* rights require the assumption by other persons of the relevant roles and contractual obligations which constitute a particular system of acquisition and exchange, such as the role of a neighbor and the obligations of a merchant. Consequently, with respect to such property rights, it would seem that a person could not justifiably be kept from acquiring the goods and resources necessary to satisfy her basic needs by the property rights of others to surplus possessions, unless the person herself had voluntarily agreed to be so constrained by those property rights. But obviously few people would voluntarily agree to have such constraints placed upon their ability to acquire the goods and resources necessary to satisfy their basic needs. For most people their right to acquire the goods and resources necessary to satisfy their basic needs would have priority over any other person's property rights to surplus possessions, or alternatively, they would conceive of property rights such that no one could have property rights to any surplus possessions which were required to satisfy their own basic needs.

Even if some property rights could arise, as *in rem* rights by a Lockean process of mixing one's labor with previously unowned goods and resources, there would still be a need for some sort of a restriction on such appropriations. For if these *in rem* property rights are to be *moral rights* then it must be reasonable for every affected party to accept such rights, since the requirements of morality cannot be contrary to reason. Accordingly, in order to give rise to *in rem* property rights, the appropriation of previously unowned goods and resources cannot justifiably limit anyone's ability to acquire the goods and resources necessary to satisfy her basic needs, unless it would be reasonable for the person to voluntarily agree to be so constrained. But obviously it would not be reasonable for many people, particularly those whose basic needs are not being met, to voluntarily agree to be so constrained by property rights. This means that whether property rights are *in personam* rights and arise by the assumption of the relevant roles and contractual obligations or are *in rem* rights and arise by a Lockean process of mixing one's labor with previously unowned goods and resources, such rights would rarely limit a negative right to life, interpreted as an *in rem* right to noninterference with one's attempts to acquire the goods and resources necessary to satisfy one's basic needs. So interpreted, a negative right to life would clearly justify the welfare rights of distant peoples.

If we turn to a consideration of a person's right to fair treatment, a similar justification of the welfare rights of distant peoples emerges. To determine the requirements of fair treatment, suppose we employ a decision procedure analogous to the one John Rawls developed in *A Theory of Justice*.[8] Suppose, that is to say, that in deciding upon the requirements of fair treatment, we were to discount the knowledge of which particular interests happen to be our own. Since we obviously know what our particular interests are, we would just not be taking that knowledge into account when selecting the requirements for fair treatment. Rather, in selecting these requirements, we would be reasoning from our knowledge of all the particular interests of everyone who would be affected by our decision but not from our knowledge of which particular interests happen to be our own. In employing this decision procedure, therefore, we (like judges who discount prejudicial information in order to reach fair decisions) would be able to give a fair hearing to everyone's particular interests. Assuming further that we are well-informed of the particular interests that would be affected by our decision and are fully capable of rationally deliberating with respect to that information, then our deliberations would culminate in a unanimous decision. This is because each of us would be deliberating in a rationally correct manner with respect to the same information and would be using a decision procedure leading to a uniform evaluation of the alternatives. Consequently,

each of us would favor the same requirements for fair treatment.

But what requirements would we select by using this decision procedure? Since by employing this decision procedure we would not be using our knowledge of which particular interests happen to be our own, we would be quite concerned about the pattern according to which goods and resources would be distributed throughout the world. By using this decision procedure, we would reason as though our particular interests might be those of persons with the largest share of goods and resources as well as those of persons with the smallest share of goods and resources. Consequently, we would neither exclusively favor the interests of persons with the largest share of goods by endorsing an unlimited right to accumulate goods and resources nor exclusively favor the interests of persons with the smallest share of goods and resources by endorsing the highest possible minimum for those who are least advantaged. Rather we would compromise by endorsing a right to accumulate goods and resources that was limited by the guarantee of a minimum sufficient to provide each person with the goods and resources necessary to satisfy his or her basic needs.[9] It seems clear, therefore, that a right to fair treatment as captured by this Rawlsian decision procedure would also justify the welfare rights of distant peoples.

What the preceding arguments have shown is that the welfare rights of distant peoples can be firmly grounded either in each person's right to life or each person's right to fair treatment. As a result, it would be impossible for one to deny that distant peoples have welfare rights without also denying that each person has a right to life and a right to fair treatment, unless, that is, one drastically reinterprets the significance of a right to life and a right to fair treatment.[10]

The Welfare Rights of Future Generations

At first glance, the welfare rights of future generations appear to be just as firmly grounded as the welfare rights of distant peoples. For assuming that there will be future generations, then, they, like generations presently existing, will have their basic needs that must be satisfied. And just as we are now able to make provision for the basic needs of distant peoples, so likewise we are now able to make provision for the basic needs of future generations (for example, through capital investment and the conservation of resources). Consequently, it would seem that there are equally good grounds for taking into account the basic needs of future generations as there are for taking into account the basic needs of distant peoples.

But there is a problem. How can we claim that future generations *now* have rights that we make provision for their basic needs when they don't presently exist? How is it possible for persons who don't yet exist to have rights against those who do? For example, suppose we continue to use up the earth's resources at present or even greater rates, and, as a result, it turns out that the most pessimistic forecasts for the 22nd century are realized.[11] This means that future generations will face widespread famine, depleted resources, insufficient new technology to handle the crisis, and a drastic decline in the quality of life for nearly everyone. If this were to happen, could persons living in the 22nd century legitimately claim that we in the 20th century violated their rights by not restraining our consumption of the world's resources? Surely it would be odd to say that we violated their rights over one hundred years before they existed. But what exactly is the oddness?

Is it that future generations generally have no way of claiming their rights against existing generations? While this does make the recognition and enforcement of rights much more difficult (future generations would need strong advocates in the existing generations), it does not make it impossible for there to be such rights. After all, it is quite obvious that the recognition and enforcement of the rights of distant peoples is a difficult task as well.

Or is it that we don't believe that rights can legitimately exercise their influence over long durations of time? But if we can foresee and control at least some of the effects our actions will have on the ability of future generations to

satisfy their basic needs then why should we not be responsible for those same effects? And if we are responsible for them then why should not future generations have a right that we take them into account?

Perhaps what troubles us is that future generations don't exist when their rights are said to demand action. But how else could persons have a right to benefit from the effects our actions will have in the distant future if they did not exist just when those effects would be felt? Those who exist contemporaneously with us could not legitimately make the same demand upon us, for they will not be around to experience those effects. Only future generations could have a right that the effects our actions will have in the distant future contribute to satisfying their basic needs. Nor need we assume that in order for persons to have rights, they must exist when their rights demand action. Thus, to say that future generations have rights against existing generations we can simply mean that there are enforceable requirements upon existing generations that would benefit or prevent harm to future generations.[12]

Yet most likely what really bothers us is that we cannot know for sure what effects our actions will have on future generations. For example, we may at some cost to ourselves conserve resources that will be of little value to future generations who have developed different technologies. Or, because we regard them as useless, we may destroy or deplete resources that future generations will find to be essential to their well-being. However, we should not allow such possibilities to blind us to the necessity for a social policy in this regard. After all, whatever we do will have its effect on future generations. The best approach, therefore, is to use the knowledge that we presently have and assume that future generations will also require those basic resources we now find to be valuable. If it turns out that future generations will require different resources to meet their basic needs from those we were led to expect, then at least we will not be blamable for acting on the basis of the knowledge we had.[13]

As in the case of the welfare rights of distant peoples, we can justify the welfare rights of future generations by appealing either to a right to life or to a right to fair treatment.

Justifying the welfare rights of future generations on the basis of a right to life presents no new problems. As we have seen, a right to life applied to distant peoples is a positive *in rem* right of existing persons to receive the goods and resources necessary to satisfy their basic needs or a negative *in rem* right of existing persons to noninterference with their attempts to acquire the goods and resources necessary to satisfy their basic needs. Accordingly, assuming that by "future generations" we mean "those whom we can reasonably expect to come into existence," then a right to life applied to future generations would be a right of persons whom we can definitely expect to exist to receive the goods and resources necessary to satisfy their basic needs or to noninterference with their attempts to acquire the goods and resources necessary to satisfy their basic needs. Understood in this way, a right to life of future generations would justify the welfare rights of future generations for much the same reasons that a right to life of distant peoples justifies the welfare rights of distant peoples. For future generations clearly have not voluntarily agreed nor would it be reasonable for them to voluntarily agree to have their ability to receive or acquire the goods and resources necessary to satisfy their basic needs limited by the property rights of existing generations to surplus possessions. Thus a right to life of future generations, interpreted either as a positive *in rem* right or a negative *in rem* right, would clearly justify the welfare rights of future generations to have their basic needs satisfied.

To determine the requirements of fair treatment for future generations, suppose we adapt the decision procedure used before to determine the requirements of fair treatment for distant peoples. That procedure required that in reaching decisions we discount our knowledge of which particular interests happen to be our own. Yet discounting such knowledge would not be sufficient to guarantee a fair result for future generations unless we also discounted the knowledge that we are contemporaries. For otherwise, even without using our knowledge of which particular interests happen to be our own, we could unfairly favor existing generations over future generations. Employing this now modified decision procedure, we would find it rational to endorse a right to accumulate goods and resources that was limited so as to provide each generation with a minimum of goods and resources necessary to satisfy the basic needs of the persons belonging to that generation. In this way, a right to fair treatment, as captured by this decision procedure, would justify the welfare rights of future generations.

Future Generations and Population Control

The welfare rights of future generations are also closely connected with the population policy of existing generations. For example, under a population policy that places restrictions on the size of families and requires genetic screening, some persons will not be brought into existence who otherwise would have come into existence. Thus, the membership of future generations will surely be affected by whatever population policy existing generations adopt. Given that the size and genetic health of future generations will obviously affect their ability to provide for their basic needs, the welfare rights of future generations would require existing generations to adopt a population policy that takes these factors into account.

But what population policy should existing generations adopt? There are two policies that many philosophers have found attractive.[14] Each policy represents a version of utilitarianism and each has its own difficulties. One policy requires population to increase or decrease so as to produce the largest total net utility possible. The other policy requires population to increase or decrease so as to produce the highest average net utility possible. The main difficulty with the policy of total utility is that it would justify any increase in population—even if, as a result, the lives of most people were not very happy—so long as some increase in total utility were produced. On the other hand, the main difficulty with the policy of average utility is that it would not allow persons to be brought into existence—even if they would be quite happy—unless the utility of their lives were equal or greater than the average. Clearly what is needed is a policy that avoids both of these difficulties.

Peter Singer has recently proposed a population policy designed to do just that—a policy designed to restrict the increase of population more than the policy of total utility but less than the policy of average utility.[15] Singer's policy justifies increasing a population of M members to a population of $M + N$ members only if M of the $M + N$ members would have at least as much utility as the population of M members had initially.

At first it might seem that Singer's population policy provides the desired compromise. For his policy does not require increases in population to meet or surpass the average utility of the original population. Nor does his policy seem to justify every increase in population that increases total utility but only those increases that do not provide less utility to members equal in number to the original population. But the success of Singer's compromise is only apparent. As Derek Parfit has shown, Singer's policy shares with the policy of total utility the same tendency to increase population in the face of continually declining average utility.[16]

For consider a population with just two members: Abe and Edna. Imagine that Abe and Edna were deliberating whether to have a child and they calculated that if they had a child

1. the utility of the child's life would be somewhat lower than the average utility of their own lives.
2. the child would have no net effect on the total utility of their own lives taken together.

Applied to these circumstances, Singer's population policy would clearly justify bringing the child into existence. But suppose, further, that after the birth of Clyde, their first child, Abe and Edna were deliberating whether to have a second child and they calculated that if they had a second child

1. the utility of the child's life would be somewhat lower than the utility of Clyde's life.
2. the child would have no net effect on the total utility of their own lives and Clyde's taken together.

Given these circumstances, Singer's policy would again justify bringing this second child into existence. And if analogous circumstances obtained on each of the next ten occasions that Abe and Edna consider the question of whether to bring additional children into existence, Singer's population policy would continue to justify adding new children irrespective of the general decline in average utility resulting from each new addition to Abe and Edna's family. Thus Singer's population policy has the same undesirable result as the policy of total utility. It avoids the severe restriction on population increase of the policy of average utility but fails to restrict existing generations from bringing into existence persons who would not be able to enjoy even a certain minimum of well-being.

Fortunately a policy with the desired restrictions can be grounded on the welfare rights of future generations. As we have seen, the welfare rights of future generations require existing generations to make provision for the basic needs of future generations. As a result, existing generations would have to evaluate their ability to provide both for their own basic needs and for the basic needs of future generations. Since existing generations by bringing persons into existence would be determining the membership of future generations, they would have to evaluate whether they are able to provide for that membership. Existing generations should not have to sacrifice the satisfaction of their basic needs for the sake of future generations, although they would be required to sacrifice some of their nonbasic needs on this account. Thus, if existing generations believe that were population to increase beyond a certain point, they would lack sufficient resources to make the necessary provision for each person's basic needs, then it would be incumbent upon them to restrict the membership of future generations so as not to exceed their ability to provide for each person's basic needs. For if the rights of future generations were respected, the membership of future generations would never increase beyond the ability of existing generations to make the necessary provision for the basic needs of future generations.

But this is to indicate only the "negative half" of the population policy that is grounded on the welfare rights of future generations, that is, the obligation to limit the size of future generations so as not to exceed the ability of existing generations to provide for the basic needs of future generations. The "positive half" of that population policy, which I have defended elsewhere,[17] is the obligation of existing generations, once their basic needs have been met, to bring into existence additional persons whose basic needs could also be met.

Thus, not only are the welfare rights of future generations clearly justified on the basis of each person's right to life and each person's right to fair treatment, but also these welfare rights in turn justify a population policy that provides an alternative to the policies of average and total utility.

Welfare Rights and Basic Needs

It has been argued that the welfare rights of distant peoples and future generations can be justified on the basis of a right to life and a right to fair treatment. Since these welfare rights are understood to be rights to receive or to acquire those goods and resources necessary for satisfying the basic needs of distant peoples and future generations, it is important to get a better understanding of what is necessary for the satisfaction of a person's basic needs in order to more fully appreciate the implications of these welfare rights.

Now a person's basic needs are those which must be satisfied in order not to seriously endanger the person's health and sanity. Thus, the needs a person has for food, shelter, medical care, protection, companionship and self-development are at least in part needs of this sort. Naturally, societies vary in their ability to satisfy a person's basic needs, but the needs themselves would not seem to be similarly subject to variation unless there were a corresponding variation in what constitutes health and sanity in different societies. Consequently, even though the criterion of need would not be an acceptable standard for distributing all social goods because, among other things, of the difficulty of determining both what a person's nonbasic needs are and how

they should be arranged according to priority, the criterion does appear to be an acceptable standard for determining the minimum of goods and resources each person has a right to receive or acquire.

Actually, specifying a minimum of this sort seems to be the goal of the poverty index used in the United States since 1964.[18] This poverty index is based on the U.S. Department of Agriculture's Economy Food Plan (for an adequate diet) and on evidence showing that low income families spend about one-third of their income on food. The index is then adjusted from time to time to take into account changing prices. However, in order to accord with the goal of satisfying basic needs, the poverty index would have to be further adjusted to take into account 1) that the Economy Food Plan was developed for "temporary or emergency use" and is inadequate for a permanent diet and 2) that, according to recent evidence, low income families spend one-fourth rather than one-third of their income on food.[19]

Of course, one might think that a minimum should be specified in terms of a standard of living that is purely conventional and varies over time and between societies. Benn and Peters, following this approach, have suggested specifying a minimum in terms of the income received by the most numerous group in a society.[20] For example, in the United States today the greatest number of household units falls within the $15,000 to $24,999 bracket (in 1979 dollars).[21] Specifying a minimum in this way, however, leads to certain difficulties. Thus, suppose that the most numerous group of household units in society with the wealth of the United States fell within a $500–$999 income bracket (in 1979 dollars). Certainly, it would not thereby follow that a guarantee of $1,000 per household unit would constitute an acceptable minimum for such a society. Or suppose that the income of the most numerous group of household units in such a society fell within the $95,000–$100,000 income bracket (in 1979 dollars). Certainly, a minimum of $100,000 per household unit would not thereby be required. Moreover, there seem to be similar difficulties with any attempt to specify an acceptable minimum in a purely conventional manner.

Nevertheless, it still seems that an acceptable minimum should vary over time and between societies at least to some degree. For example, it could be argued that today a car is almost a necessity in the typical North American household, which was not true fifty years ago nor is it true today in most other areas of the world. Happily, a basic needs approach to specifying an acceptable minimum can account for such variation without introducing any variation into the definition of the basic needs themselves. Instead, variation enters into the cost of satisfying these needs at different times and in different societies.[22] For in the same society at different times and in different societies at the same time, the normal costs of satisfying a person's basic needs can and do vary considerably. These variations are due in large part to the different ways in which the most readily available means for satisfying people's basic needs are produced. For example, in more affluent societies, the most readily available means for satisfying a person's basic needs are usually processed so as to satisfy nonbasic needs at the same time that they satisfy basic needs. This processing is carried out to make the means more attractive to persons in higher income brackets who can easily afford the extra cost. As a result, the most readily available means for satisfying people's basic needs are much more costly in more affluent societies than they are in less affluent societies. This occurs most obviously with respect to the most readily available means for satisfying people's basic needs for food, shelter and transportation, but it also occurs with respect to the most readily available means for satisfying people's basic needs for companionship, self-esteem and self-development. For a person cannot normally satisfy even these latter needs in more affluent societies without participating in at least some relatively costly educational and social development practices. Accordingly, there will be considerable variation in the normal costs of satisfying a person's basic needs as a society becomes more affluent over time, and considerable variation at the same time in societies at different levels of affluence. Consequently, a basic needs approach to specifying an acceptable minimum would guarantee each person the goods and resources necessary to meet the

normal costs of satisfying his basic needs in the society in which he lives.

Welfare Rights and World Hunger

We have seen that the welfare rights of distant peoples and future generations guarantee each person a minimum of goods and resources necessary to meet the normal costs of satisfying her basic needs in the society in which she lives. Let us now determine some of the practical implications of these welfare rights for the issue of world hunger.

At present there is probably a sufficient worldwide supply of goods and resources to meet the normal costs of satisfying the basic nutritional needs of all existing persons in the societies in which they live. According to the former U.S. Secretary of Agriculture, Bob Bergland,

> For the past 20 years, if the available world food supply had been evenly divided and distributed, each person would have received more than the minimum number of calories.

> In fact, the 4 billion people who inhabited the world in 1978 had available about one-fifth more food per person to eat than the world's 2.7 billion had 25 years ago.[23]

Other authorities have made similar assessments of the available world food supply.[24] In fact, it has been projected that if all arable land were optimally utilized a population of between 38 and 48 billion people could be supported.[25]

Needless to say, the adoption of a policy of meeting the basic nutritional needs of all existing persons would necessitate significant changes, especially in developed societies. For example, the large percentage of the U.S. population whose food consumption clearly exceeds even an adequately adjusted poverty index would have to substantially alter their eating habits. In particular, they would have to reduce their consumption of beef and pork so as to make more grain available for direct human consumption. (Presently the amount of grain fed American livestock is as much as all the people of China and India eat in a year.) Thus, at least the satisfaction of some of the nonbasic needs of the more advantaged in developed societies would have to be foregone so that the basic nutritional needs of all existing persons in developing and underdeveloped societies could be met.

Such changes, however, may still have little effect on the relative costs of satisfying people's basic needs in different societies. For even after the basic nutritional needs of all existing persons have been met, the normal costs of satisfying basic needs would still tend to be greater in developed societies than in developing and underdeveloped societies. This is because the most readily available means for satisfying basic needs in developed societies would still tend to be more processed to satisfy nonbasic needs along with basic needs. Nevertheless, once the basic nutritional needs of future generations are also taken into account, then the satisfaction of the nonbasic needs of the more advantaged in developed societies would have to be further restricted in order to preserve the fertility of cropland and other food-related natural resources for the use of future generations.[26] And once basic needs other than nutritional needs are taken into account as well, still further restrictions would be required. For example, it has been estimated that presently a North American uses fifty times more resources than an Indian. This means that in terms of resource consumption the North American continent's population is the equivalent of 12.5 billion Indians.[27] Obviously, this would have to be radically altered if the basic needs of distant peoples and future generations are to be met. Thus, eventually the practice of utilizing more and more efficient means of satisfying people's basic needs in developed societies would appear to have the effect of equalizing the normal costs of meeting people's basic needs across societies.[28]

Although the general character of the changes required to meet the basic nutritional needs of distant peoples and future generations seems clear enough, there is still the problem of deciding between alternative strategies for carrying out these changes. Since each of these strategies would impose somewhat different burdens on developed societies and different burdens on different groups within those societies, the fundamental problem is to decide exactly whose nonbasic needs should be sacrificed in order to meet the basic needs of distant peoples and future generations. While there is no easy solution to this problem, alternative strategies for meeting the basic needs of distant peoples and future generations could be fairly evaluated by means of the Rawlsian decision procedure that was used before to justify the welfare rights of distant peoples and future generations. In using this procedure, we would be deciding which particular strategy for meeting the basic needs of distant peoples and future generations would be preferred by persons who discounted the knowledge of the society to which they belonged. Thus, the particular strategies that would be selected by this decision procedure should adequately take into account the competing interests within and between existing generations and future generations.

While the requirements, with respect to world hunger, that the welfare rights of distant peoples and future generations place upon those in developed affluent societies are obviously quite severe, they are not unconditional. For those in developing and underdeveloped societies are under a corresponding obligation to do what they can to meet their own basic nutritional needs, for example, by bringing all arable land under optimal cultivation and by controlling population growth. However, we should not be unreasonable in judging what particular developing and underdeveloped societies have managed to accomplish in this regard. For in the final analysis, such societies should be judged on the basis of what they have managed to accomplish, *given the options available to them.* For example, developing and underdeveloped societies today do not have the option, which Western European societies had during most of the last two centuries, of exporting their excess population to sparsely populated and resource rich continents. In this and other respects, developing and underdeveloped societies today lack many of the options Western

European societies were able to utilize in the course of their economic and social development. Consequently, in judging what developing and underdeveloped societies have managed to accomplish we must take into account the options that they actually have available to them in their particular circumstances. In practice, this will mean, for example, that it is not reasonable to expect such societies to reduce their population growth as fast as would ideally be desirable. Nevertheless, at some point, it should be reasonable to expect that all existing persons accept the population policy proposed earlier, according to which the membership of future generations would never be allowed to increase beyond the ability of existing generations to make the necessary provision for the basic needs of future generations. In the meantime, it may be necessary in order to meet the basic needs of at least a temporarily growing world population to utilize renewable resources beyond what would secure their maximal sustainable yield. (Presently, certain renewable resources, such as fishing resources, are being so utilized for far less justifiable ends.) This, of course, would have the effect of reducing the size of succeeding generations that, according to the proposed population policy, could justifiably be brought into existence. But while such an effect obviously is not ideally desirable, it surely seems morally preferable to allowing existing persons to starve to death in order to increase the size of succeeding generations that could justifiably be brought into existence.[29]

In conclusion, what has been shown is 1) that the welfare rights of distant peoples and future generations, understood as the right of distant peoples and future generations to receive or acquire the goods and resources that are necessary to meet the normal costs of satisfying their basic needs in the society in which they live, can be justified on the basis of a right to life and a right to fair treatment, and 2) that these welfare rights can be used to justify certain requirements for the issues of population control and world hunger. Thus, given the fundamental nature of the moral foundation for these welfare rights, it would be virtually impossible for many of us to consistently reject these welfare rights with their practical requirements for social policies unless we were to reject in its entirety the moral point of view.[30]

Notes

1. *The Preliminary Report of the Presidential Commission on World Hunger*, December 1979. Section II, Chapter 3.

2. Herman Kahn, William Brown and Leon Martel, *The Next 200 Years* (New York: William Morrow, 1976), Chapter 2.

3. A distinction that is similar to the distinction between positive and negative rights is the distinction between recipient and action rights. Recipient rights, like positive rights, are rights to receive some specific goods or services. However, action rights are a bit more circumscribed than negative rights. Action rights are rights to act in some specific manner, whereas negative rights include both rights of noninterference with actions (and, hence, imply action rights) and rights of noninterference with things or states of affairs (such as a right to one's good name).

Having previously used the distinction between recipient and action rights (*The Demands of Justice* [Notre Dame: University of Notre Dame Press, 1980, Chapter 6]), in a defense of welfare rights, I now hope to show, in response to critics, particularly Jan Narveson, that the distinction between positive and negative rights can serve as well in the fuller defense of welfare rights which I am presenting in this paper.

4. For other possibilities, see Onora Nell, "Lifeboat Earth," *Philosophy and Public Affairs*, 4 (Spring 1975): 273–92; Peter Singer, "Famine, Affluence and Morality," *Philosophy and Public Affairs*, 1 (1972): 229–43.

5. See, for example, Robert Nozick, *State Anarchy and Utopia* (New York: Basic Books, 1974), p. 179n.

6. See, for example, Ronald Dworkin, "Liberalism," in *Public and Private Morality*, edited by Stuart Hampshire (Cambridge: Cambridge University Press, 1978), pp. 112–43.

7. This is why a negative right to life is usually understood to impose lesser moral requirements than a positive right to life.

8. John Rawls, *A Theory of Justice* (Cambridge:

Harvard University Press, 1971). This Rawlsian decision procedure is only designed to secure a fair consideration of everyone's interests. It does not guarantee that *all* will be better off from following the moral requirements that emerge from using the procedure. Thus, some individuals may be required to make significant sacrifices, particularly during the transition to a more favored distribution of goods and resources. On this point, see *The Demands of Justice*, Chapter 4.

9. For further argument, see "Distributive Justice," *American Journal of Jurisprudence*, 55 (1977):55–79 and *The Demands of Justice*, Chapter 2.

10. Notice that even if one interprets a right to life as simply a right not to be killed unjustly, it could still be plausibly argued that a person's right to life would normally be violated when all other legitimate opportunities for preserving his life have been exhausted if he were then *prevented* by others from taking from their surplus goods and resources what he needs to preserve his life.

11. Donella H. Meadows, Dennis L. Meadows, Jorgen Randers and William W. Behrens III, *The Limits to Growth*, second edition (New York: New American Library, 1974), Chapters 3 and 4.

12. Indeed, right claims need not presuppose that there are any rightholders either in the present or in the future, as in the case of a right not to be born and a right to be born. On this point, see my paper "Abortion, Distant Peoples and Future Generations," *The Journal of Philosophy*, 77 (1980): 424–40 and *The Demands of Justice*, Chapter 6.

13. For a somewhat opposing view, see M. P. Golding, "Obligations to Future Generations," *The Monist*, 56 (1972): 85–99.

14. See Henry Sidgwick, *The Methods of Ethics*. 7th edition. (London: Macmillan, 1907), pp. 414–16; Jan Narveson, "Moral Problems of Population," *The Monist*, 57 (1973): 62–86.

15. Peter Singer, "A Utilitarian Population Principle," in *Ethics and Population*, edited by Michael Bayles (Cambridge: Schenkman, 1976), pp. 81–99.

16. Derek Parfit, "On Doing the Best for Our Children," in *Ethics and Population*, edited by Michael Bayles, pp. 100–15.

17. See "Abortion, Distant Peoples and Future Generations," and *The Demands of Justice*, Chapter 6. A version of this is included in Section III.

18. See *Old Age Insurance* submitted to the Joint Economic Committee of the Congress of the United States in December, 1967, p. 186, and *Statistical Abstracts of the United States for 1979*, p. 434.

19. See Sar Levitan, *Programs in Aid of the Poor* (Baltimore: Johns Hopkins University Press, 1976), pp. 2–4; David Gordon, "Trends in Poverty" in *Problems in Political Economy: An Urban Perspective*, edited by David Gordon, (Lexington, Mass.: C. Heath, 1971), pp. 297–8; Arthur Simon, *Bread for the World* (New York: Paulist Press, 1975), Chapter 8.

20. S. Benn and R. S. Peters, *The Principles of Political Thought* (New York: The Free Press, 1959), p. 167.

21. *Statistical Abstracts*, p. 434.

22. See Bernard Gendron, *Technology and the Human Condition* (New York: St. Martin's Press, 1977), pp. 222–7.

23. Bob Bergland, "Attacking the Problem of World Hunger," *The National Forum* (1979), vol. 69, No. 2, p. 4.

24. Diana Manning, *Society and Food* (Sevenoaks, Ky.: Butterworths, 1977), p. 12; Arthur Simon, *Bread for the World*, p. 14.

25. Roger Revelle, "Food and Population," *Scientific American*, 231 (September, 1974), p. 168.

26. Lester Brown, "Population, Cropland and Food Prices," *The National Forum* (1979), Vol. 69, No. 2, pp. 11–16.

27. Janet Besecker and Phil Elder, "Lifeboat Ethics: A Reply to Hardin," in *Readings in Ecology, Energy and Human Society: Contemporary Perspectives*, edited by William R. Burch, Jr. (New York: Harper and Row, 1977), p. 229.

28. There definitely are numerous possibilities for utilizing more and more efficient means of satisfying people's basic needs in developed societies. For example, the American food industry manufactured for the U.S. Agriculture Department CSM, a product made of corn, soy and dried milk, which supplied all the necessary nutrients and 70 percent of minimum calorie intake for children. Poverty children throughout the world, but not in the United States, received half a million pounds of this product from us in

1967—at a cost of two cents per day per child. See Nick Kotz, *Let Them Eat Promises* (Englewood Cliffs, N.J.: Prentice-Hall, Inc., 1969), p. 125.

29. The rejected option seems to be the one preferred by Garrett Hardin. See his "Lifeboat Ethics: the Case Against Helping the Poor," in this anthology, pp. 90–97.

30. Earlier versions of this paper were presented to a Conference on World Hunger held in Denver, Colorado, to the Economics Department of the University of Nebraska and to the University Seminar on Human Rights, Columbia University. I wish to thank all of those who commented on various versions of the paper, in particular, Robert Audi, Dolores Martin, Arthur Danto, Brian Barry, Jan Narveson, Paul Martin, Mark Rollins, D. Greenberg and the referees for this journal. I also want to thank the University of Notre Dame for a summer grant which enabled me to complete the penultimate draft of this paper.

Perspectives from the *Global 2000 Report*

Gus Speth

According to Gus Speth, the *Global 2000 Report* echoes a persistent warning sounded by many others in recent years: "Our international efforts to stem the spread of human poverty, hunger, and misery are not achieving their goals; the staggering growth of human population, coupled with ever-increasing human demands, are beginning to cause permanent damage to the planet's resource base." Speth argues that we must respond to this warning by getting serious about the conservation of resources and by pursuing a policy of sustainable economic development that is fair to the interests of the poor.

Throughout the past decade, a wide variety of disturbing studies and reports have been issued by the United Nations, the Worldwatch Institute, the World Bank, the International Union for the Conservation of Nature and Natural Resources, and other organizations. These reports have sounded a persistent warning: our international efforts to stem the spread of human poverty, hunger and misery are not achieving their goals; the staggering growth of human population, coupled with ever-increasing human demands, are beginning to cause permanent damage to the planet's resource base.

The most recent such warning—and the one with which I am most familiar—was issued in July of 1980 by the Council of Environmen-

From "Resources and Security: Perspectives from the *Global 2000 Report*," *World Future Society Bulletin* (1981), pp. 1–4. Reprinted by permission of *World Future Society Bulletin*.

tal Quality and the U.S. State Department. Called *Global 2000 Report to the President*, it is the result of a three-year effort by more than a dozen agencies of the U.S. Government to make long-term projections across the range of population, resource and environmental concerns. Given the obvious limitations of such projections, the *Global 2000 Report* can best be seen as a reconnaissance of the future. And the results of that reconnaissance are disturbing.

I feel very strongly that the *Global 2000 Reports'* findings confront the United States and other nations with one of the most difficult challenges facing our planet during the next two decades—rivaling the global arms race in importance.

The Report's projections point to continued rapid population growth, with world population increasing from 4.5 billion today to more than 6 billion by 2000. More people will be added to the world's population each day in the year 2000 than were born today—about 100 million a year as compared with 75 million in 1980. Most of these additional people will live in the poorest countries, which will contain about four-fifths of the human race by the end of the century.

Unless other factors intervene, this planetary majority will see themselves growing worse off compared with those living in affluent nations. The income gap between rich and poor nations will widen, and the per capita gross national product of the less-developed countries will remain at generally low levels. In some areas—especially in parts of Latin America and East Asia—income per capita is expected to rise substantially. But gross national product in the great populous nations of South Asia—India, Bangladesh and Pakistan—will be less than $200 per capita (in 1975 dollars) by 2000. Today, some 800 million people live in conditions of absolute poverty, their lives dominated by hunger, ill health, and the absence of hope. By 2000, if current policies remain unchanged, their number could grow by 50 percent.

While the Report projects a 90 percent increase in overall world food production in the 30 years from 1970 to 2000, a global per capita increase of less than 15 percent is projected even for the countries that are already comparatively well-fed. In South Asia, the Middle East, and the poorer countries of Africa, per capita food consumption will increase marginally at best, and in some areas may actually decline below present inadequate levels. Real prices of food are expected to double during the same 30-year period.

The pressures of population and growing human needs and expectations will place increasing strains on the Earth's natural systems and resources. The spread of desert-like conditions due to human activities now claims an area about the size of Maine each year. Croplands are lost to production as soils deteriorate because of erosion, compaction, and waterlogging and salinization, and as rural land is converted to other uses.

The increases in world food production projected by the Report are based on improvements in crop yields per acre continuing at the same rate as the record-breaking increases of the post-World War II period.

These improvements depended heavily on energy-intensive technologies like fertilizer, pesticides, fuel for tractors and power for irrigation. But the Report's projections show no relief from the world's tight energy situation. World oil production is expected to level off by the 1990s. And for the one-quarter of humanity who depend on wood for fuel, the outlook is bleak. Projected needs for wood will exceed available supplies by about 25 percent before the turn of the century.

The conversion of forested land to agricultural use and the demand for fuelwood and forest products are projected to continue to deplete the world's forests. The Report estimates that these forests are now disappearing at rates as high as 18 to 20 million hectares—an area half the size of California—each year. As much as 40 percent of the remaining forests in poor countries may be gone by 2000. Most of the loss will occur in tropical and subtropical areas.

The loss of tropical forests, along with the impact of pollution and other pressures on habitats, could cause massive destruction of the planet's genetic resource base. Between 500,000 and two million plant and animal species—15 to 20 percent of all species on Earth—could become extinct by the year 2000. One-half to two-thirds of the extinctions will result from the clearing or deterioration of tropical forests. This would be a massive loss of potentially valuable sources of food, pharmaceutical chemicals, building materials, fuel sources and other irreplaceable resources.

Deforestation and other factors will worsen severe regional water shortages and contribute to the deterioration of water quality. Population growth alone will cause demands for water to at least double from 1971 levels in nearly half of the world.

Industrial growth is likely to worsen air quality. Air pollution in some cities in less-developed countries is already far above levels considered safe by the World Health Organization. Increased burning of fossil fuels, especially coal, may contribute to acid rain damage to lakes, plantlife, and the exteriors of buildings. It also contributes to the increasing concentration of carbon dioxide in the Earth's atmosphere, which could possibly lead to climatic changes with highly disruptive effects on world agriculture. Depletion of the stratospheric ozone layer, attributed partly to chlorofluorocarbon emissions from aerosol cans and refrigeration equipment, could also have an adverse effect of food crops and human health.

Disturbing as these findings are, it is important to stress that the *Global 2000 Report's* conclusions represent not predictions of what will occur, but projections of what could occur if we do not respond. If there was any doubt before, there should be little doubt now—the nations of the world, industrialized and less developed alike, must act urgently and in concert to alter these dangerous trends before the projections of the *Global 2000 Report* become realities.

The warnings, then, are clear. Will we heed them, and will we heed them in time? For if our response is delayed, the costs could be great.

On these matters, I am cautiously optimistic. I like to think that the human race is *not* self-destructive—that it *is* paying, or can be made to pay, attention—that as people throughout the world come to realize the full dimensions of the challenge before us, we will take the actions needed to meet it.

Our efforts to secure the future must begin with a new appreciation for, and then an application of, three fundamental concepts. They are *conservation, sustainable development,* and *equity.* I am convinced that each of them is essential to the development of the kind of long-term global resource strategy we need to deal with the problems I have been discussing.

Conservation

The first thing we must do is to get serious about the conservation of resources—renewable and nonrenewable alike. We can no longer take for granted the renewability of renewable resources. The natural systems—the air and water, the forests, the land—that yield food, shelter and the other necessities of life are susceptible to disruption, contamination and destruction.

Indeed, one of the most troubling of the findings of the *Global 2000 Report* is the effect that rapid population growth and poverty are already having on the productivity of renewable natural resource systems. In some areas, particularly in the less developed countries, the ability of biological systems to support human populations is already being seriously damaged by efforts of present populations to meet desperate immediate needs, such as the needs for grazing land, firewood and building materials.

And these stresses, while most acute in the developing countries, are not confined to them. In recent years, the United States has been losing annually about 3 million acres of rural land—a third of it prime agricultural land—due to the spread of housing developments, highways, shopping malls and the like. We are also losing annually the rough equivalent—in terms of production capability—of another 3 million acres due to soil degradation—erosion and salinization. Other serious resource threats in the United States include those posed by toxic chemicals and other pollutants to groundwater supplies, which provide drinking water for half of the American public, and directly affect both commercial and sport fishing.

Achieving the necessary restraint in the use of renewable resources will require new ways of thinking by the peoples and governments of the world. It will require the widespread adoption of a "Conserver Society" ethic—an approach to resources and environment that, while attuned to the needs of each society, recognizes not only the importance of resources and environment to our own sustenance, well-being and security, but also our obligation to pass this vital legacy along to future generations. Perhaps the most arrogant attitude of which the human spirit is capable is the notion that the riches of the Earth are ours to plunder or carelessly destroy . . . that the needs and the lives of those who will follow us on this tiny and fragile planet are of no concern to us. "Future generations," someone once said "What have they done for us?"

Fortunately, we are beginning to see signs that people in the United States and in other nations *are* becoming aware of the limits to our resources and the importance of conserving them. Energy problems, for example, are pointing the way to a future in which conservation is the password. As energy supplies go down and prices go up, we are learning that conserving—getting more and more out of each barrel of oil or ton of coal—is the cheapest and safest approach. Learning to conserve non-renewable resources like oil and coal is the first step toward building a Conserver Society that values, nurtures, and protects all of its resources. Such a society appreciates economy in design and avoidance of waste. It realizes the limits to low-cost resources and to the environment's carrying capacity. It insists that market prices reflect all costs, social as well as private, so that consumers are fully aware in the most direct way of the real costs of consumption.

The Conserver Society prizes recycling over pollution, durability over obsolescence, quality over quantity, diversity over uniformity. It knows that beauty—whether natural or man-made—is too precious to be destroyed and that the Earth's wild creatures demand our conserving restraint not simply for utilitarian reasons but because, as part of the community of life that has evolved here with us, they too call this place home.

In this, the United States must take the lead. We cannot expect the rest of the world to adopt a Conserver Society ethic if we ourselves do not set a strong, successful example.

Sustainable Development

But the Conserver Society ethic, by itself, is not enough. It is unrealistic to expect people living at the margin of existence—people fighting desperately for their own survival—to think about the long-term survival of the planet. When people need to burn wood to keep from freezing, they will cut down trees.

We must find a way to break the cycle of poverty, population growth and environmental deterioration. We must find ways to improve the social and economic conditions of the poor nations and poor people of the world—their incomes, their access to productive land, their educational and employ-

ment opportunities. It is only through sustainable economic development that real progress can be made in alleviating hunger and poverty and in erasing the conditions that contribute so dangerously to the destruction of our planet's carrying capacity.

One of the most important lessons of the *Global 2000 Report* is that the conflict between development and environmental protection is, in significant part, a myth. Only a concerted attack on the roots of extreme poverty—one that provides people with the opportunity to earn a decent livelihood in a nondestructive manner—will enable us to protect the world's natural systems. It is also clear that development and economic reforms will have no lasting success unless they are suffused with concern for ecological stability and wise management of resources. The key concept here, of course, is *sustainable* development. Economic development, if it is to be successful over the long term, must proceed in a way that enhances the natural resource base of all the developing nations, instead of exploiting those resources for short-term economic or political gain.

Unfortunately, the realities of the current North-South dialogue between the developed and the developing nations suggest that achieving steady, sustainable development will be a difficult process—one that will require great patience and understanding on all sides. For our part here in the United States, we must resist the strong temptation to turn inward—to tune out the rest of the world's problems and to focus exclusively on our own economic difficulties. We must remember that, relatively speaking, we Americans luxuriate in the Earth's abundance, while other nations can barely feed and clothe their people. Unless we act, this disparity between rich and poor will tend to grow, increasing the possibilities for anger and resentment from those on the short end of the wealth equation—the great majority of mankind. One does not have to be particularly farsighted to see that the trends discussed in *Global 2000* heighten the chances for global instability—for exploitation of fears, resentments and frustrations; for incitement to violence; for conflicts based on resources.

The *Global 2000 Report* itself discusses some

of the destabilizing prospects that may be in store for us if we do not act decisively:

"The world will be more vulnerable both to natural disaster and to disruptions from human causes . . . Most nations are likely to be still more dependent on foreign sources of energy in 2000 than they are today. Food production will be more vulnerable to disruptions of fossil fuel energy supplies and to weather fluctuations as cultivation expands to more marginal areas. The loss of diverse germ plasm in local strains and wild progenitors of food crops, together with the increase of monoculture, could lead to greater risks of massive crop failures. Larger numbers of people will be vulnerable to higher food prices or even famine when adverse weather occurs. The world will be more vulnerable to the disruptive effects of war. The tensions that could lead to war will have multiplied. The potential for conflict over fresh water alone is underscored by the fact that out of 200 of the world's major river basins, 148 are shared by two countries and 52 are shared by three to ten countries."

The 1980 Report of the Brandt Commission on International Development Issues is eloquent in its plea for action: "War is often thought of in terms of military conflict, or even annihilation. But there is a growing awareness that an equal danger might be chaos—as a result of mass hunger, economic disaster, environmental catastrophes, and terrorism, so we should not think only of reducing the traditional threats to peace, but also of the need for change from chaos to order."

Equity

The late Barbara Ward, eminent British scholar, argued that the nations of the world can learn a valuable lesson from the experience of 19th-Century England, where the industrial revolution produced an appalling disparity in the distribution of wealth. It was a time when property owners and industrial managers reaped enormous profits while the laborers and mechanics—and their children—worked themselves into early graves.

Today, Ward observes: "The skew in world income is as great. The already developed peoples—North America, Europe, the Soviet Union, Japan—are the latter-day dukes, commanding over 70 percent of the planet's wealth for less than a quarter of the population. And in all too many developing countries the economic growth of the last two decades has been almost entirely appropriated by the wealthiest ten percent of the people. The comparisons in health, length of life, diet, literacy all work out on the old Victorian patterns of unbelievable injustice."

Ward recommends—and I heartily agree—that the developed nations of today follow the lead of men like Disraeli, who recognized the need to narrow the gap between rich and poor in 19th-Century England and to create a new social order which allowed every citizen a share of the nation's wealth. Without perceptive leaders like Disraeli and other men of conscience who saw the need for reform, Ward argues that the growing pressure for equality and social justice would have torn British society apart. The result would have been similar to that in other nations where far-thinking leadership and compassion were lacking: "social convulsion, violent revolution and an impetus to merciless worldwide war and conquest."

The situation we face in the world today is all too similar. While the humanitarian reasons for acting generously to alleviate global poverty and injustice are compelling enough in themselves, we must also recognize the extent to which global poverty and resource problems can contribute to regional and worldwide political instability—an instability that can threaten the security of nations throughout the world.

Thus, along with conservation and sustainable development, the development of global resource strategy will require a much greater emphasis on *equity*—on a fair sharing of the means to development and the products of growth—not only among nations, but within nations as well.

Suggestions for Further Reading

Anthologies

Aiken, William, and LaFollette, Hugh. *World Hunger and Moral Obligation*. Englewood Cliffs: Prentice-Hall, 1977.

Brown, Peter, and Shue, Henry. *Boundaries*. Totowa: Rowman and Littlefield, 1981.

Lucas, George R. Jr., and Ogletree, Thomas W. *Lifeboat Ethics*. New York: Harper and Row, 1976.

Partridge, Ernest. *Responsibilities to Future Generations*. Buffalo: Prometheus, 1981.

Sikora, R. I., and Barry, Brian. *Obligation to Future Generations*. Philadelphia: Temple University Press, 1978.

Basic Concepts

Parfet, Derek, *Reasons and Persons* Oxford: Oxford University Press, 1985.

Alternative Views

Amur, Samir. *Unequal Development*. New York: Monthly Review Press, 1976.

Bauer, P. T. *Equality, the Third World and Economic Delusion*. Cambridge: Harvard University Press, 1981.

Bayles, Michael D. *Morality and Population Policy*. Birmingham: University of Alabama Press, 1980.

Beitz, Charles R. *Political Theory and International Relations*. Princeton: Princeton University Press, 1979.

Commoner, Barry. *The Closing Circle*. New York: Bantam Books, 1971.

Hardin, Garrett, *Promethean Ethics*. Seattle: University of Washington Press, 1980.

Shue, Henry. *Basic Rights*. Princeton: Princeton University Press, 1980.

Practical Applications

Kahn, Herman; Brown, William; and Martel, Leon. *The Next 200 Years*. New York: William Morrow and Co., 1976.

Schumacher E. F. *Small Is Beautiful*. New York: Harper and Row, 1973.

Lappé, Frances Moore, *World Hunger: Twelve Myths*, New York: Grove Press, 1986.

Abortion and Euthanasia

Basic Concepts

The problem of abortion and euthanasia has been as thoroughly discussed as any contemporary moral problem. As a result, the conceptual issues have been fairly well laid out, and there have been some interesting attempts to bridge the troublesome normative and practical disagreements that remain.

First of all, almost everyone agrees that the fundamental issue with respect to justifying abortion is the moral status of the fetus, although considerable disagreement exists as to what that status is.[1] Conservatives on the abortion question, like John Noonan (pp. 149–159), contend that from conception the fetus has full moral status and hence a serious right to life. Liberals on the abortion question, like Mary Anne Warren (pp. 159–169), hold that, at least until birth, the fetus has almost no moral status whatsoever and lacks a serious right to life.[2] Moderates on the abortion question adopt some position in between these two views. And still others, like Judith Jarvis Thomson (pp. 140–148), Jane English (pp. 170–176), and James P. Sterba (pp. 177–184) adopt for the sake of argument either the conservative or the liberal view on the moral status of the fetus and then try to show that such a view does not lead to the consequences its supporters assume.[3]

Second, almost everyone agrees that the position one takes on the moral status of the fetus has a bearing on whether one considers either the distinction between killing and letting die or the doctrine of double effect as relevant to the abortion question. For example, conservatives are quite interested in whether the killing and letting die distinction can be used to show that it is permissible to let the fetus die in certain contexts, even when it would be impermissible to kill it. However, liberals find the use of this distinction in such contexts to be completely unnecessary. Because liberals hold that the fetus has almost no moral status, they do not object to either killing it or letting it die. Similarly, although conservatives are quite interested in whether the doctrine of double effect can be used to permit the death of the fetus as a foreseen but unintended consequence of some legitimate course of action, liberals find no use for the doctrine of double effect in such contexts.

Third, almost everyone agrees that either the killing and letting die distinction or the doctrine of double effect could prove useful in cases of euthanasia. Agreement is possible because most of the subjects of euthanasia are human beings who, in everyone's view, have full moral status and hence a serious right to life. Accordingly, despite the disagreement as to where it is useful to apply the killing and letting die distinction and the doctrine of double effect, everyone agrees that both of these conceptual tools deserve further examination.

The distinction between killing and letting die has its advocates and its critics. Advocates maintain that, other things being equal, killing is morally worse than letting die, with the consequence that letting die is justified in cases where killing is not. The critics of this distinction maintain that, other things being equal, killing is not morally worse than letting die, with the consequence that killing is morally justified whenever letting die is. Both advocates and critics agree that other things would not be equal if the killing were justified or deserved while the letting die unwanted and undeserved. They tend to disagree, however, over whether other things would be equal if the killing were in response to a patient's request to die while the letting die involved a prolonged and excruciatingly painful death, or if the killing resulted in the death of just a few individuals while the letting die resulted in the death of many people.

Yet whatever view one adopts as to when other things are equal, it is hard to defend the moral preferability of letting die over killing when both are taken to be intentional acts. As James Rachels so graphically illustrates (pp. 184–194), it seems impossible to judge the act of A, who intentionally lets Z die while standing ready to finish Z off if that proves necessary, as being morally preferable to the act of B, who with similar motive and intention kills Y. But it is far from clear whether advocates of the killing and letting die distinction are claiming that the distinction holds when the killing and the letting die are both intentional acts because it is unlikely in such cases that the letting die would be morally justified when the killing is not. Rather, as Bonnie Steinbock argues (pp. 194–199, advocates of the distinction seem to have in mind a contrast between *intentional* killing and *unintentional* letting die, or, more fully stated, a contrast between intentional killing and unintentional letting die when the latter is the foreseen consequence of an otherwise legitimate course of action.

Steinbock maintains that there are at least two types of cases in which letting die, distinguished in this way from killing, seems justified. In the first, a doctor ceases treatment at the patient's request, foreseeing that the patient will die or die sooner than otherwise, yet not intending that result. In the second, a doctor's intention is to avoid employing treatment that is extremely painful and has little hope of benefiting the patient, even though she foresees that this may hasten the patient's death. In addition, conservatives have argued that letting die, distinguished in this way from killing, can be justified in cases of ectopic pregnancy and cancer of the uterus because in such cases the fetus's death is the foreseen but unintended consequence of medical treatment that is necessary to preserve the basic well-being of the pregnant woman.

When the killing and letting die distinction is interpreted in this way, it has much in common with the doctrine of double effect. This doctrine places four restrictions on the permissibility of acting when some of the consequences of one's action are evil. These restrictions are as follows:

1. The act is good in itself or at least indifferent
2. Only the good consequences of the act are intended
3. The good consequences are not the effect of the evil
4. The good consequences are commensurate with the evil consequences

The basic idea of the killing and letting die distinction, as we have interpreted it, is expressed by restrictions 2 and 3.

When conservatives apply the doctrine of double effect to a case in which a pregnant woman has cancer of the uterus, the doctrine is said to justify an abortion because:

1. The act of removing the cancerous uterus is good in itself
2. Only the removal of the cancerous uterus is intended
3. The removal of the cancerous uterus is not a consequence of the abortion
4. Preserving the life of the mother by removing the cancerous uterus is commensurate with the death of the fetus

The doctrine is also said to justify unintentionally letting a person die, or "passive euthanasia," at least in the two types of cases described by Steinbock.

In recent moral philosophy, the main objection to the doctrine of double effect has been to question the necessity of its restrictions. Consider the following example. Imagine that a fat person who is leading a party of spelunkers gets herself stuck in the mouth of a cave in which flood waters are rising. The trapped party of spelunkers just happens to have a stick of dynamite with which they can blast the fat person out of the mouth of the cave; either they use the dynamite or they all drown, the fat person with them. It appears that the doctrine of double effect would *not* permit the use of the dynamite in this case because the evil consequences of the act are intended as a means to securing the good consequences in violation of restrictions 2 and 3. Yet it is plausible to argue in such a case that using the dynamite would be justified on the grounds that (a) the evil to be avoided, i.e., the evil of failing to save the party of spelunkers except for the fat person, is considerably greater than the evil resulting from the means employed, i.e., the evil of intentionally causing the death of the fat person and/or that (b) the greater part of evil resulting from the means employed, i.e., the death of the fat person, would still occur regardless of whether those means were actually employed.

Some people might want to defend the doctrine of double effect against this line of criticism by maintaining that the spelunkers need not intend the death of the fat person, but only that "she be blown into little pieces" or that "the mouth of the cave be suitably enlarged." But how is the use of dynamite expected to produce these results except by way of killing the fat person? Thus, the death of the fat person is part of the means employed by the spelunkers to secure their release from the cave, and thus would be impermissible according to the doctrine of double effect. If, however, we think that bringing about the death of the fat person could be morally justified in this case, because, for example, (a) and/or (b) obtain, we are left with a serious objection to the necessity of the restrictions imposed by the doctrine of double effect for acting morally. And, as we shall see when considering the problem of nuclear deterrence and strategic defense, still other objections can be raised regarding the sufficiency of these restrictions.

Given these objections to the doctrine of double effect, Philippa Foot has suggested that we might more profitably deal with the moral questions at issue by distinguishing between negative and positive duties. *Negative duties* are said to be duties to refrain from doing certain sorts of actions. Typically, these are duties to avoid actions that inflict harm or injury on others. Thus, the duties not to kill or assault others are negative duties. By contrast, *positive duties* are duties to do certain actions, usually those that aid or benefit others. The duties to repay a debt and help others in need are positive duties. This distinction is used to resolve practical disputes by claiming that negative duties have priority over positive duties; accordingly, when negative and positive duties conflict, negative duties always take precedence over positive duties.

Applying this distinction, Foot claims that a doctor is justified in performing an abortion when nothing can be done to save the lives of both child and mother, but the life of the mother can be saved by killing the child. Obviously, this case is quite similar to the example of the fat person stuck in the mouth of the cave. But it is not clear how the distinction between positive and negative duties can help us in either situation. Since both the doctor and the group of spelunkers trapped by the fat person have a negative duty not to kill that takes precedence over any positive duty to help either themselves or others, it would seem that neither aborting the fetus nor blowing up the fat person could be justified on the basis of this distinction. Thus, the distinction between negative and positive duties no more justifies evil consequences in such cases than does the doctrine of double effect. Accordingly, if we want to provide such a justification, we need to find some morally acceptable way of going beyond both of these requirements.

Alternative Views

As we mentioned earlier, conservatives hold that the fetus has full moral status and hence a serious right to life. As a consequence, conservatives oppose abortion in a wide range of cases. Hoping to undercut this antiabortion stance, Judith Jarvis Thomson adopts, for the sake of argument, the conservative position on the moral status of the fetus (pp. 140–148). She then tries to show that abortion is still justified in a wide range of cases. Thomson asks us to imagine that we are kidnapped and connected to an unconscious violinist who now shares the use of our kidneys. The situation is such that if we detach ourselves from the violinist before nine months transpire, the violinist will die. Thomson thinks it obvious that we have no obligation to share our kidneys with the violinist in such a case, and hence that, in analogous cases, abortion can be justified. Thomson's view has provoked so much discussion that the authors of each of the next four selections all feel compelled to consider her view in the course of developing their own positions.

In his selection, John Noonan objects to Thomson's use of fantasized examples (pp. 149–159). In place of Thomson's example of an unconscious violinist, Noonan offers a more realistic example found in the law. It is a case in which a family is found to be liable for the frostbite suffered by a dinner guest whom they refused to allow to stay overnight in their home, although it was very cold outside and the guest showed signs of being sick. But although Noonan is surely correct in pointing out the need for realistic examples, there still is an important difference between allowing a person to stay overnight in one's home and allowing a fetus to remain and develop in one's body for approximately nine months.

Mary Anne Warren also objects to Thomson's violinist example, but on grounds quite different from Noonan's (pp. 159–169). She claims that the example at most justifies abortion in cases of rape and hence will not provide the desired support for abortion on demand. Thomson, however, did provide additional examples and arguments in an attempt to show that abortion is justified in cases other than rape. Jane English has also argued that Thomson's case against abortion can be extended to a wider range of examples (pp. 170–176).

James P. Sterba challenges not so much the fantasized examples Thomson employs as the arguments she provides along with those examples (pp. 177–184). One of these arguments is based on a distinction between what a person can demand as a right and what is required by moral decency. This argument concludes that abortion rarely, if ever, violates anyone's rights. Another argument is based on a restricted interpretation of a right to life. This argument concludes that abortion typically does not violate the fetus's right not to be killed or let die unjustly. Sterba contends that neither of these arguments can be used consistently to support abortion on demand by those who endorse the welfare rights of distant peoples.

Thomson might concede that those who endorse the welfare rights of distant peoples cannot avail themselves of her arguments. But she would then most likely argue that libertarians, and political conservatives generally, who do not endorse welfare rights for distant peoples, could make use of her arguments. Sterba, of course, would deny that this is possible because he believes that libertarians, and political conservatives generally, are also required to accept the welfare rights of distant peoples and thus to reject Thomson's arguments for abortion.

Convinced that Thomson's or anyone else's attempt to argue for abortion will prove unsuccessful if the fetus is assumed to have full moral status, Noonan wants to retain and support that assumption. His approach, however, is quite different from that usually adopted by conservatives.

Conservatives typically employ what are called "slippery slope arguments" to show that any attempt to draw a line—whether at implantation, or at quickening, or at viability, or

at birth—for the purpose of separating those who do not have full moral status from those who do, fails to be nonarbitrary because of the continuity in the development of the fetus. Conservatives then contend that conception is the only point at which the line can be drawn nonarbitrarily.

By contrast, Noonan proposes to examine various models and methods employed in the debate on abortion, distinguishing those that do not work from those that do. We have already noted Noonan's objection to fantasized examples. In addition, he objects to any attempt to make exceptions for abortion when the fetus is known to be seriously defective or the result of a rape, arguing that exceptions in such cases would "eat up the rule." Surprisingly, Noonan also objects to the use of special metaphors such as direct and indirect, and in particular rejects the application of the doctrine of double effect to cases of ectopic pregnancy and the removal of a cancerous uterus containing a fetus. In such cases, Noonan claims, the doctor "necessarily intends to perform the abortion, he necessarily intends to kill." What legitimates abortion in such cases, claims Noonan, is not the doctrine of double effect, but rather the principle that whenever the fetus is a danger to the life of the mother, abortion is permissible on grounds of self-defense. But if the mother is justified on grounds of self-defense in aborting the fetus, surely some representative of the fetus would also be justified in defending the fetus against an abortion, given that in Noonan's view the fetus has a serious right to life. Consequently, Noonan has not provided us with a moral solution to such cases. At the same time, it is difficult to see how anyone could ignore the central plea of Noonan's article that we see what otherwise might be overlooked and respond to the full range of human experience.

Like Noonan, Warren wants to build a consensus on the abortion question. To achieve this, she proposes a set of criteria for being a person with full moral status that she thinks proabortionists and antiabortionists alike could accept. The criteria are (1) consciousness; (2) developed reasoning; (3) self-motivated activity; (4) a capacity to communicate; and (5) the presence of self-concepts and self-awareness. But although most people would certainly agree that these criteria are met in paradigm cases, conservatives would still reject them as necessary requirements for being a person. As Jane English (pp. 170–176) argues, the concept of a person is not sharp or decisive enough to bear the weight of a solution to the abortion controversy.

English, however, agrees with Thomson that even if we endorse the conservative view that the fetus is a full-fledged person, there are still cases where abortion would be justified to prevent serious harm or death to the pregnant woman. Similarly, she contends that even if we endorse the liberal view that the fetus is not a person, there are still cases, at least in the late months of pregnancy, where abortion would not be justified, because of the fetus's resemblance to a person.

Applying the same strategy as English, Sterba contends that a still stronger case can be made against the liberal view on abortion. He assumes for the sake of argument that the fetus has almost no moral status whatsoever and then tries to show that abortion would still not be justified in a wide range of cases. In particular, he argues that, even if the fetus is not a person, those who accept:

1. The welfare rights of future generations *and*

2. An obligation not to bring into existence persons who would lack a reasonable opportunity to lead a good life

are required also to accept:

3. An obligation to bring into existence persons who would have a reasonable opportunity to lead a good life;

and (3) severely limits the legitimate use of abortion. According to Sterba, (3) follows from the acceptance of (1) and (2) because any reason we can give for accepting (2) consistent with (1) will suggest an analogous reason for supporting (3). The type of view Sterba defends has been called the "symmetry view" since it argues for a symmetry between the obligation not to procreate and an obligation to procreate or, as Sterba puts it, a right not to be born and a right to be born.

Derek Parfit has challenged the symmetry view. In effect, Parfit suggests an interpretation of our duty not to harm others and our duty to benefit others such that, under this interpretation, those who accept (1) and (2) need not accept (3). According to Parfit's interpretation:

A. Our duty not to harm others is a duty not to do *x* if doing *x* is bad or worse for people who ever exist *and*

B. Our duty to benefit others is a duty to do *x* if not doing *x* is bad or worse for people who ever exist

Assuming that we construe welfare rights of future generations as simply what follows from (A) and (B), Sterba's argument for the symmetry view would surely fail because (3) is not required by Parfit's interpretation of our duty to benefit others. For although, on Parfit's view, coming into existence can be a benefit, it is not the sort of benefit that is required by our duty to benefit others because—other things being equal—failing to provide that benefit is not bad or worse for anyone who ever exists.

The principal difficulty with Parfit's challenge to the symmetry view is his restricted interpretation of our duty to benefit others. How can we accept a duty to do *x* when not doing *x* would be bad or worse for people who ever exist without also accepting a duty to do *x* when doing *x* would be good or better for people who ever exist? Parfit himself admits that it is hard to accept that:

C. We ought not to increase the sum of suffering without also accepting that

D. We ought to increase the net sum of happiness

For similar reasons, it seems hard to accept Parfit's interpretation of our duty to benefit others without also accepting a still broader interpretation of this duty that would justify (3).[4]

Those who find both the conservative and liberal views on abortion unattractive might be inclined toward the moderate view. This view attempts to draw a line—typically at implantation, or at quickening, or at viability—for the purpose of separating those who do not have full moral status from those who do. The United States Supreme Court in *Wade* v *Roe* (1973) has frequently been understood as supporting a moderate view on abortion. In this decision, the Court by a majority of 7 to 2 decided that the constitutional right to privacy, protected by the due process clause of the Fourteenth Amendment to the Constitution, entails that (1) no law may restrict the right of a woman to be aborted by a physician during the first three months (trimester) of her pregnancy; (2) during the second trimester abortion may be regulated by law only to the extent that the regulation is reasonably related to the preservation and protection of maternal health; and (3) when the fetus becomes viable (not before the beginning of the third trimester) a law may prohibit abortion, but only subject to an exception permitting abortion whenever necessary to protect the woman's life or health (including any aspects of her physical or mental health). But regardless of whether the Court's decision was intended to support the moderate view on abortion, some have argued that in the absence of reasonable constraints, the Court's decision has led to abortion on demand.

Although most of the contemporary discussion of abortion has focused on the moral status of the fetus, most of the discussion of euthanasia has focused on the killing and letting die distinction and the doctrine of double effect. As we noted before, advocates of the killing and letting die distinction and the doctrine of double effect tend to justify only passive euthanasia (i.e., letting a person die as a foreseen but unintended consequence of an otherwise legitimate course of action). In contrast, critics of the killing and letting die distinction and the doctrine of double effect tend also to justify active euthanasia (i.e., intentional killing) on the basis of its consequences. Rachels (pp. 184–194) cites the case of a person suffering from cancer of the throat who has three options: (1) with continued treatment she will have a few more days of pain and then die; (2) if treatment is stopped but nothing else is done, it will be a few more hours; or (3) with a lethal injection she will die at once. In such a case, Rachels thinks, the third option—active euthanasia—is justified on the grounds that the person would be better off dying immediately.

But euthanasia is not only passive or active, it is also voluntary or involuntary. Voluntary euthanasia has the (informed) consent of the person involved. Involuntary euthanasia lacks such consent, usually but not always because the person involved is incapable of providing it. This means that at least four different types of euthanasia are possible: voluntary passive euthanasia, involuntary passive euthanasia, voluntary active euthanasia, and involuntary active euthanasia. Of the four types, voluntary passive euthanasia seems easiest to justify, involuntary active euthanasia the most difficult. But voluntary euthanasia, both passive and active, would seem more justifiable if it could be shown that there were a fundamental moral right to be assisted in bringing about one's own death if one so desired. Even if such a right could be supported, however, it would presumably only have force when one could reasonably be judged to be better off dead.

Practical Applications

It is not at all difficult to see how the various proposed solutions to the problem of abortion and euthanasia could be applied in contemporary societies. For example, in Akron v. Akron Center for Reproductive Life (pp. 200–205), the majority of the U.S. Supreme Court, in attempting to take a moderate position, ruled that a number of the constraints the city of Akron had imposed on obtaining an abortion were unreasonable. However, in a dissenting opinion, Justice Sandra Day O'Connor took a more conservative position and argued that the framework used in Roe vs. Wade and subsequent decisions was faulty because, among other things, thanks to improved technology, the point of fetal viability on which the court had relied in determining when abortion was permissible had been moved back. Similarly, in the Karen Quinlan opinion (pp. 206–213), the Supreme Court of New Jersey presupposed the moral legitimacy of passive euthanasia and affirmed that Karen Quinlan's *legal* right to privacy permitted passive euthanasia in her case.[5] Accordingly, if you think that different solutions to the problem of abortion and euthanasia are more morally defensible, you should favor other laws and judicial decisions.

But even as you begin to formulate the laws and social institutions, with their demands on social goods and resources, that are needed to enforce what you take to be the most morally defensible solution to the problem of abortion and euthanasia, you will still need to take into account the demands on social goods and resources that derive from solutions to other practical moral problems—such as the problem of discrimination and prejudice, which is taken up in the next section.

Notes

1. The term "fetus" is understood to refer to any human organism from conception to birth.

2. Note that liberals on the abortion question need not be welfare liberals, although many of them are. Likewise, conservatives on the abortion question need not be libertarians or political conservatives.

3. Henceforth liberals, conservatives, and moderates on the abortion question are simply referred to as liberals, conservatives, and moderates.

4. For further discussion, see James P. Sterba, "Explaining Asymmetry: A Problem for Parfit," *Philosophy and Public Affairs* (1987), pp. 188–192.

5. The respirator was turned off, and Karen Quinlan survived for a lengthy period of time in a comatose condition before finally expiring.

A Defense of Abortion

Judith Jarvis Thomson

Judith Jarvis Thomson begins by assuming, for the sake of argument, that the fetus is a person. Using a series of examples, she then argues that even granting this assumption, a woman has a right to abortion in cases involving rape, in cases where the woman's life is endangered, and in cases in which the woman had taken reasonable precautions to avoid becoming pregnant. In these cases, Thomson claims, the fetus's assumed right not to be killed unjustly would not be violated by abortion. Thomson further distinguishes between cases in which it would be a good thing for a woman to forego an abortion and cases in which a woman has an obligation to do so.

Most opposition to abortion relies on the premise that the fetus is a human being, a person, from the moment of conception. The premise is argued for, but, as I think, not well. Take, for example, the most common argument. We are asked to notice that the develop-

Abridged from Judith Jarvis Thomson, "A Defense of Abortion," *Philosophy & Public Affairs* 1, no. 1 (Fall 1971). Copyright © 1971 by Princeton University Press. Excerpts, pp. 47–62, 65–66, reprinted by permission of Princeton University Press.

ment of a human being from conception through birth into childhood is continuous; then it is said that to draw a line, to choose a point in this development and say "before this point the thing is not a person, after this point it is a person" is to make an arbitrary choice, a choice for which in the nature of things no good reason can be given. It is concluded that the fetus is, or anyway we had better say it is, a person from the moment of conception. But this conclusion does not follow. Similar things might be said about the development of an acorn into an oak tree, and it does not follow that acorns are oak trees or that we had better say they are. Arguments of this form are sometimes called "slippery slope arguments"—the phrase is perhaps self-explanatory—and it is dismaying that opponents of abortion rely on them so heavily and uncritically.

I am inclined to agree, however, that the prospects for "drawing a line" in the development of the fetus look dim. I am inclined to think also that we shall probably have to agree that the fetus has already become a human person well before birth. Indeed, it comes as a surprise when one first learns how early in its life it begins to acquire human characteristics. By the tenth week, for example, it already has a face, arms and legs, fingers and toes; it has internal organs, and brain activity is detectable.[1] On the other hand, I think that the premise is false, that the fetus is not a person from the moment of conception. A newly fertilized ovum, a newly implanted clump of cells, is no more a person than an acorn is an oak tree. But I shall not discuss any of this. For it seems to me to be of great interest to ask what happens if, for the sake of argument, we allow the premise. How, precisely, are we supposed to get from there to the conclusion that abortion is morally impermissible? Opponents of abortion commonly spend most of their time establishing that the fetus is a person, and hardly any time explaining the step from there to the impermissibility of abortion. Perhaps they think the step too simple and obvious to require much comment. Or perhaps instead they are simply being economical in argument. Many of those who defend abortion rely on the premise that the fetus is not a person, but only a bit of tissue that will become a person at birth; and why pay out more arguments than you have to? Whatever the explanation, I suggest that the step they take is neither easy nor obvious, that it calls for closer examination than it is commonly given, and that when we do give it this closer examination we shall feel inclined to reject it.

I propose, then, that we grant that the fetus is a person from the moment of conception. How does the argument go from here? Something like this, I take it. Every person has a right to life. So the fetus has a right to life. No doubt the mother has a right to decide what shall happen in and to her body; everyone would grant that. But surely a person's right to life is stronger and more stringent than the mother's right to decide what happens in and to her body, and so outweighs it. So the fetus may not be killed; an abortion may not be performed.

It sounds plausible. But now let me ask you to imagine this. You wake up in the morning and find yourself back to back in bed with an unconscious violinist. A famous unconscious violinist. He has been found to have a fatal kidney ailment, and the Society of Music Lovers has canvassed all the available medical records and found that you alone have the right blood type to help. They have therefore kidnapped you, and last night the violinist's circulatory system was plugged into yours, so that your kidneys can be used to extract poisons from his blood as well as your own. The director of the hospital now tells you, "Look, we're sorry the Society of Music Lovers did this to you—we would never have permitted it if we had known. But still, they did it, and the violinist now is plugged into you. To unplug you would be to kill him. But never mind, it's only for nine months. By then he will have recovered from his ailment, and can safely be unplugged from you." Is it morally incumbent on you to accede to this situation? No doubt it would be very nice of you if you did, a great kindness. But do you *have* to accede to it? What if it were not nine months, but nine years? Or longer still? What if the director of the hospital says, "Tough luck, I agree, but you've now got to stay in bed, with the violinist plugged into you, for the rest of your life. Because remember this. All persons have a right to life, and violinists are persons. Granted you have a right to decide what happens in and to your body, but a person's right to life outweighs your right to decide what happens in and to your body. So you cannot ever be unplugged from him." I imagine you would regard this as outrageous, which suggests that something really is wrong with that plausible-sounding argument I mentioned a moment ago.

In this case, of course, you were kidnapped; you didn't volunteer for the operation that plugged the violinist into your kidneys. Can those who oppose abortion on the ground I mentioned make an exception for a pregnancy due to rape? Certainly. They can say that persons have a right to life only if they didn't come into existence because of rape; or they can say that all persons have a right to life, but that some have less of a right to life than others, in particular, that those who came into existence because of rape have less. But these statements have a rather unpleasant sound. Surely the question of whether you have a right to life at all, or how much of it you have, shouldn't turn on the question of whether or not you are the product of a rape. And in fact the people who oppose abortion on the ground I mentioned do not make this distinction, and hence do not make an exception in case of rape.

Nor do they make an exception for a case in which the mother has to spend the nine months of her pregnancy in bed. They would agree that would be a great pity, and hard on the mother; but all the same, all persons have a right to life, the fetus is a person, and so on. I suspect, in fact, that they would not make an exception for a case in which, miraculously enough, the pregnancy went on for nine years, or even the rest of the mother's life.

Some won't even make an exception for a case in which continuation of the pregnancy is likely to shorten the mother's life; they regard abortion as impermissible even to save the mother's life. Such cases are nowadays very rare, and many opponents of abortion do not accept this extreme view. All the same, it is a good place to begin: a number of points of interest come out in respect to it.

1. Let us call the view that abortion is impermissible even to save the mother's life "the extreme view." I want to suggest first that it does not issue from the argument I mentioned earlier without the addition of some fairly powerful premises. Suppose a woman has become pregnant, and now learns that she has a cardiac condition such that she will die if she carries the baby to term. What may be done for her? The fetus, being a person, has a right to life, but as the mother is a person too, so has she a right to life. Presumably they have an equal right to life. How is it supposed to come out that an abortion may not be performed? If mother and child have an equal right to life,

shouldn't we perhaps flip a coin? Or should we add to the mother's right to life her right to decide what happens in and to her body, which everybody seems to be ready to grant— the sum of her rights now outweighing the fetus' right to life?

The most familiar argument here is the following. We are told that performing the abortion would be directly killing[2] the child, whereas doing nothing would not be killing the mother, but only letting her die. Moreover, in killing the child, one would be killing an innocent person, for the child has committed no crime, and is not aiming at his mother's death. And then there are a variety of ways in which this might be continued. (1) But as directly killing an innocent person is always and absolutely impermissible, an abortion may not be performed. Or, (2) as directly killing an innocent person is murder, and murder is always and absolutely impermissible, an abortion may not be performed.[3] Or, (3) as one's duty to refrain from directly killing an innocent person is more stringent than one's duty to keep a person from dying, an abortion may not be performed. Or, (4) if one's only options are directly killing an innocent person or letting a person die, one must prefer letting the person die, and thus an abortion may not be performed.[4]

Some people seem to have thought that these are not further premises which must be added if the conclusion is to be reached, but that they follow from the very fact than an innocent person has a right to life.[5] But this seems to me to be a mistake, and perhaps the simplest way to show this is to bring out that while we must certainly grant that innocent persons have a right to life, the theses in (1) through (4) are all false. Take (2), for example. If directly killing an innocent person is murder, and thus is impermissible, then the mother's directly killing the innocent person inside her is murder, and thus is impermissible. But it cannot seriously be thought to be murder if the mother performs an abortion on herself to save her life. It cannot seriously be said that she *must* refrain, that she *must* sit passively by and wait for her death. Let us look again at the case of you and the violinist. There you are, in bed with the violinist, and the director of the hospital says to you, "It's all most distressing, and I deeply sympathize, but you see this is putting an additional strain on your kidneys, and you'll be dead within the month. But you *have* to stay where you are all the same. Because unplugging you would be directly killing an innocent violinist, and that's murder, and that's impermissible." If anything in the world is true, it is that you do not commit murder, you do not do what is impermissible, if you reach around to your back and unplug yourself from that violinist to save your life.

The main focus of attention in writings on abortion has been on what a third party may or may not do in answer to a request from a woman for an abortion. This is in a way understandable. Things being as they are, there isn't much a woman can safely do to abort herself. So the question asked is what a third party may do, and what the mother may do, if it is mentioned at all, is deduced, almost as an afterthought, from what is concluded that the third parties may do. But it seems to me that to treat the matter in this way is to refuse to grant to the mother that very status of person which is so firmly insisted on for the fetus. For we cannot simply read off what a person may do from what a third party may do. Suppose you find yourself trapped in a tiny house with a growing child. I mean a very tiny house, and a rapidly growing child—you are already up against the wall of the house and in a few minutes you'll be crushed to death. The child on the other hand won't be crushed to death; if nothing is done to stop him from growing he'll be hurt, but in the end he'll simply burst open the house and walk out a free man. Now I could well understand it if a bystander were to say, "There's nothing we can do for you. We cannot choose between your life and his, we cannot be the ones to decide who is to live, we cannot intervene." But it cannot be concluded that you too can do nothing, that you cannot attack it to save your life. However innocent the child may be, you do not have to wait passively while it crushes you to death. Perhaps a pregnant woman is vaguely felt to have the status of a house, to which we don't allow the right of self-defense. But if the woman houses the child, it should be remembered that she is a person who houses it.

I should perhaps stop to say explicitly that I am not claiming that people have a right to do anything whatever to save their lives. I think, rather, that there are drastic limits to the right of self-defense. If someone threatens you with death unless you torture someone else to death, I think you have not the right, even to save your life, to do so. But the case under consideration here is very different. In our case there are only two people involved, one whose life is threatened, and one who threatens it. Both are innocent: the one who is threatened is not threatened because of any fault, the one who threatens does not threaten because of any fault. For this reason we may feel that we bystanders cannot intervene. But the person threatened can.

In sum, a woman surely can defend her life against the threat to it posed by the unborn child, even if doing so involves its death. And this shows not merely that the theses in (1) through (4) are false; it shows also that the extreme view of abortion is false, and so we need not canvass any other possible ways of arriving at it from the argument I mentioned at the outset.

2. The extreme view could of course be weakened to say that while abortion is permissible to save the mother's life, it may not be performed by a third party, but only by the mother herself. But this cannot be right either. For what we have to keep in mind is that the mother and the unborn child are not like two tenants in a small house which has, by an unfortunate mistake, been rented to both: the mother *owns* the house. The fact that she does adds to the offensiveness of deducing that the mother can do nothing from the supposition that third parties can do nothing. But it does more than this: it casts a bright light on the supposition that third parties can do nothing. Certainly it lets us see that a third party who says "I cannot choose between you" is fooling himself if he thinks this is impartiality. If Jones has found and fastened on a certain coat, which he needs to keep him from freezing, but which Smith also needs to keep him from freezing, then it is not impartiality that says "I cannot choose between you" when Smith owns the coat. Women have said again and again "This body is *my* body!" and they have reason to feel angry, reason to feel that it has been like shouting into the wind. Smith, after all, is

hardly likely to bless us if we say to him, "Of course it's your coat, anybody would grant that it is. But no one may choose between you and Jones who is to have it. . . ."

3. Where the mother's life is not at stake, the argument I mentioned at the outset seems to have a much stronger pull. "Everyone has a right to life, so the unborn person has a right to life." And isn't the child's right to life weightier than anything other than the mother's own right to life, which she might put forward as ground for an abortion?

This argument treats the right to life as if it were unproblematic. It is not, and this seems to me to be precisely the source of the mistake.

For we should now, at long last, ask what it comes to, to have a right to life. In some views having a right to life includes having a right to be given at least the bare minimum one needs for continued life. But suppose that what in fact *is* the bare minimum a man needs for continued life is something he has no right at all to be given? If I am sick unto death, and the only thing that will save my life is the touch of Henry Fonda's cool hand on my fevered brow, then all the same, I have no right to be given the touch of Henry Fonda's cool hand on my fevered brow. It would be frightfully nice of him to fly in from the West Coast to provide it. It would be less nice, though no doubt well meant, if my friends flew out to the West Coast and carried Henry Fonda back with them. But I have no right at all against anybody that he should do this for me. Or again, to return to the story I told earlier, the fact that for continued life that violinist needs the continued use of your kidneys does not establish that he has a right to be given the continued use of your kidneys. He certainly has no right against you that *you* should give him continued use of your kidneys. For nobody has any right to use your kidneys unless you give him such a right; and nobody has the right against you that you shall give him this right—if you do allow him to go on using your kidneys, this is a kindness on your part, and not something he can claim from you as his due. Nor has he any right against anybody else that *they* should give him continued use of your kidneys. Certainly he had no right against the Society of Music Lovers that they should plug him into you in the first place. And if you now start to unplug yourself, having learned that you will other-

wise have to spend nine years in bed with him, there is nobody in the world who must try to prevent you, in order to see to it that he is given something he has a right to be given.

Some people are rather stricter about the right to life. In their view, it does not include the right to be given anything, but amounts to, and only to, the right not to be killed by anybody. But here a related difficulty arises. If everybody is to refrain from killing that violinist, then everybody must refrain from doing a great many different sorts of things. Everybody must refrain from slitting his throat, everybody must refrain from shooting him— and everybody must refrain from unplugging you from him. But does he have a right against everybody that they shall refrain from unplugging you from him? To refrain from doing this is to allow him to continue to use your kidneys. It could be argued that he has a right against us that *we* should allow him to continue to use your kidneys. That is, while he had no right against us that we should give him the use of your kidneys, it might be argued that he anyway has a right against us that we shall not now intervene and deprive him of the use of your kidneys. I shall come back to third-party interventions later. But certainly the violinist has no right against you that *you* shall allow him to continue to use your kidneys. As I said, if you do allow him to use them, it is a kindness on your part, and not something you owe him.

The difficulty I point to here is not peculiar to the right to life. It reappears in connection with all the other natural rights; and it is something which an adequate account of rights must deal with. For present purposes it is enough just to draw attention to it. But I would stress that I am not arguing that people do not have a right to life—quite to the contrary, it seems to me that the primary control we must place on the acceptability of an account of rights is that it should turn out in that account to be a truth that all persons have a right to life. I am arguing only that having a right to life does not guarantee having either a right to be given the use of or a right to be allowed continued use of another person's body—even if one needs it for life itself. So the right to life will not serve the opponents of abortion in the very simple and clear way in which they seem to have thought it would.

4. There is another way to bring out the difficulty. In the most ordinary sort of case, to deprive someone of what he has a right to is to treat him unjustly. Suppose a boy and his small brother are jointly given a box of chocolates for Christmas. If the older boy takes the box and refuses to give his brother any of the chocolates, he is unjust to him, for the brother has been given a right to half of them. But suppose that, having learned that otherwise it means nine years in bed with that violinist, you unplug yourself from him. You surely are not being unjust to him, for you gave him no right to use your kidneys, and no one else can have given him any such right. But we have to notice that in unplugging yourself, you are killing him; and violinists, like everybody else, have a right to life, and thus in the view we were considering just now, the right not to be killed.

So here you do what he supposedly has a right you shall not do, but you do not act unjustly to him in doing it.

The emendation which may be made at this point is this: the right to life consists not in the right not to be killed, but rather in the right not to be killed unjustly. This runs a risk of circularity, but never mind: it would enable us to square the fact that the violinist has a right to life with the fact that you do not act unjustly toward him in unplugging yourself, thereby killing him. For if you do not kill him unjustly, you do not violate his right to life, and so it is no wonder you do him no injustice.

But if this emendation is accepted, the gap in the argument against abortion stares us plainly in the face: it is by no means enough to show that the fetus is a person, and to remind us that all persons have a right to life—we need to be shown also that killing the fetus violates its right to life, i.e., that abortion is unjust killing. And is it?

I suppose we may take it as a datum that in a case of pregnancy due to rape the mother has not given the unborn person a right to the use of her body for food and shelter. Indeed, in what pregnancy could it be supposed that the mother has given the unborn person such a right? It is not as if there were unborn persons drifting about the world, to whom a woman who wants a child says "I invite you in."

But it might be argued that there are other ways one can have acquired a right to the use of another person's body than by having been invited to use it by that person. Suppose a woman voluntarily indulges in intercourse, knowing of the chance it will issue in pregnancy, and then she does become pregnant; is she not in part responsible for the presence, in fact the very existence, of the unborn person inside her? No doubt she did not invite it in. But doesn't her partial responsibility for its being there itself give it a right to the use of her body? If so, then her aborting it would be more like the boy's taking away the chocolates, and less like your unplugging yourself from the violinist—doing so would be depriving it of what it does have a right to, and thus would be doing it an injustice.

And then, too, it might be asked whether or not she can kill it even to save her own life: If she voluntarily called it into existence, how can she now kill it, even in self-defense?

The first thing to be said about this is that it is something new. Opponents of abortion have been so concerned to make out the independence of the fetus, in order to establish that it has a right to life, just as its mother does, that they have tended to overlook the possible support they might gain from making out that the fetus is *dependent* on the mother, in order to establish that she has a special kind of responsibility for it, a responsibility that gives it rights against her which are not possessed by any independent person—such as an ailing violinist who is a stranger to her.

On the other hand, this argument would give the unborn person a right to its mother's body only if her pregnancy resulted from a voluntary act, undertaken in full knowledge of the chance a pregnancy might result from it. It would leave out entirely the unborn person whose existence is due to rape. Pending the availability of some further argument, then, we would be left with the conclusion that unborn persons whose existence is due to rape have no right to the use of their mothers' bodies, and thus that aborting them is not depriving them of anything they have a right to and hence is not unjust killing.

And we should also notice that it is not at all plain that this argument really does go even as far as it purports to. For there are cases and cases, and the details make a difference. If the room is stuffy, and I therefore open a window to air it, and a burgular climbs in, it would be absurd to say, "Ah, now he can stay, she's given him a right to the use of her house—for she is partially responsible for his presence there, having voluntarily done what enabled him to get in, in full knowledge that there are such things as burglars, and that burglars burgle." It would be still more absurd to say this if I had had bars installed outside my windows, precisely to prevent burglars from getting in, and a burglar got in only because of a defect in the bars. It remains equally absurd if we imagine it is not a burglar who climbs in, but an innocent person who blunders or falls in. Again, suppose it were like this: people-seeds drift about in the air like pollen, and if you open your windows, one may drift in and take root in your carpets or upholstery. You don't want children, so you fix up your windows with fine mesh screens, the very best you can buy. As can happen, however, and on very, very rare occasions does happen, one of the screens is defective; and a seed drifts in and takes root. Does the person-plant who now develops have a right to the use of your house? Surely not—despite the fact that you voluntarily opened your windows, you knowingly kept carpets and upholstered furniture, and you knew that screens were sometimes defective. Someone may argue that you are responsible for its rooting, that it does have a right to your house, because after all you *could* have lived out your life with bare floors and furniture, or with sealed windows and doors. But this won't do—for by the same token anyone can avoid a pregnancy due to rape by having a hysterectomy, or anyway by never leaving home without a (reliable!) army.

It seems to me that the argument we are looking at can establish at most that there are *some* cases in which the unborn person has a right to the use of its mother's body, and therefore *some* cases in which abortion is unjust killing. There is room for much discussion and argument as to precisely which, if any. But I think we should sidestep this issue and leave it open, for at any rate the argument certainly does not establish that all abortion is unjust killing.

5. There is room for yet another argument here, however. We surely must all grant that there may be cases in which it would be morally indecent to detach a person from your body at the cost of his life. Suppose you learn that what the violinist needs is not nine years of your life, but only one hour: all you need do to save his life is to spend one hour in that bed with him. Suppose also that letting him use your kidneys for that one hour would not affect your health in the slightest. Admittedly you were kidnapped. Admittedly you did not give anyone permission to plug him into you. Nevertheless it seems to me plain you *ought* to allow him to use your kidneys for that hour—it would be indecent to refuse.

Again, suppose pregnancy lasted only an hour, and constituted no threat to life or health. And suppose that a woman becomes pregnant as a result of rape. Admittedly she did not voluntarily do anything to bring about the existence of a child. Admittedly she did nothing at all which would give the unborn person a right to the use of her body. All the same it might well be said, as in the newly emended violinist story, that she *ought* to allow it to remain for that hour—that it would be indecent in her to refuse.

Now some people are inclined to use the term "right" in such a way that it follows from the fact that you ought to allow a person to use your body for the hour he needs, that he has a right to use your body for the hour he needs, even though he has not been given that right by any person or act. They may say that it follows also that if you refuse, you act unjustly toward him. This use of the term is perhaps so common that it cannot be called wrong; nevertheless it seems to me to be an unfortunate loosening of what we would do better to keep a tight rein on. Suppose that box of chocolates I mentioned earlier had not been given to both boys jointly, but was given only to the older boy. There he sits, stolidly eating his way through the box, his small brother watching enviously. Here we are likely to say "You ought not to be so mean. You ought to give your brother some of those chocolates." My own view is that it just does not follow from the truth of this that the brother has any right to any of the chocolates. If the boy refuses to give his brother any, he is greedy, stingy, callous— but not unjust. I suppose that the people I have in mind will say it does follow that the brother has a right to some of the chocolates, and thus that the boy does act unjustly if he refuses to give his brother any. But the effect of saying this is to obscure what we should keep distinct, namely the difference between the boy's refusal in this case and the boy's refusal in the earlier case, in which the box was given to both boys jointly, and in which the small brother thus had what was from any point of view clear title to half.

A further objection to so using the term "right" that from the fact that A ought to do a thing for B, it follows that B has a right against A that A do it for him, is that it is going to make the question of whether or not a man has a right to a thing turn on how easy it is to provide him with it; and this seems not merely unfortunate, but morally unacceptable. Take the case of Henry Fonda again. I said earlier that I had no right to the touch of his cool hand on my fevered brow, even though I needed it to save my life. I said it would be frightfully nice of him to fly in from the West Coast to provide me with it, but that I had no right against him that he should do so. But suppose he isn't on the West Coast. Suppose he has only to walk across the room, place a hand briefly on my brow—and lo, my life is saved. Then surely he ought to do it, it would be indecent to refuse. Is it to be said "Ah, well, it follows that in this case she has a right to the touch of his hand on her brow, and so it would be an injustice in him to refuse"? So that I have a right to it when it is easy for him to provide it, though no right when it's hard? It's rather a shocking idea that anyone's rights should fade away and disappear as it gets harder and harder to accord them to him.

So my own view is that even though you ought to let the violinist use your kidneys for the one hour he needs, we should not conclude that he has a right to do so—we should say that if you refuse, you are, like the boy who owns all the chocolates and will give none away, self-centered and callous, indecent in fact, but not unjust. And similarly, that even supposing a case in which a woman pregnant due to rape ought to allow the unborn person to use her body for the hour he needs, we should not conclude that he has a right to do so; we should conclude that she is self-centered, callous, indecent, but not unjust, if she refuses. The complaints are no less grave; they are just different. However, there is no need to insist on this point. If anyone does wish to deduce "he has a right" from "you ought," then all the same he must surely grant that there are cases in which it is not morally required of you that you allow that violinist to use your kidneys, and in which he does not have a right to use them, and in which you do not do him injustice if you refuse. And so also for mother and unborn child. Except in such cases as the unborn person has a right to demand it—and we were leaving open the possibility that there may be such cases—nobody is morally *required* to make large sacrifices, of health, of all other interests and concerns, of all other duties and commitments, for nine years, or even for nine months, in order to keep another person alive. . . .

8. My argument will be found unsatisfactory on two counts by many of those who want to regard abortion as morally permissible. First, while I do argue that abortion is not impermissible, I do not argue that it is always permissible. I am inclined to think it a merit of my account precisely that it does *not* give a general yes or a general no. It allows for and supports our sense that, for example, a sick and desperately frightened fourteen-year-old schoolgirl, pregnant due to rape, may *of course* choose abortion, and that any law which rules this out is an insane law. And it also allows for and supports our sense that in other cases resort to abortion is even positively indecent. It would be indecent in the woman to request an abortion, and indecent in a doctor to perform it, if she is in her seventh month, and wants the abortion just to avoid the nuisance of postponing a trip abroad. The very fact that the arguments I have been drawing attention to treat all cases of abortion, or even all cases of abortion in which the mother's life is not at stake, as morally on a par ought to have made them suspect at the outset.

Secondly, while I am arguing for the permissibility of abortion in some cases, I am not arguing for the right to secure the death of the unborn child. It is easy to confuse these two things in that up to a certain point in the life of the fetus it is not able to survive outside the mother's body; hence removing it from her body guarantees its death. But they are importantly different. I have argued that you are not morally required to spend nine months in bed, sustaining the life of that violinist; but to say this is by no means to say that if, when you unplug yourself, there is a miracle and he survives, you then have a right to turn round and slit his throat. You may detach yourself even if this costs him his life; you have no right to be guaranteed his death, by some other means, if unplugging yourself does not kill him. There are some people who will feel dissatisfied by this feature of my argument. A woman may be utterly devastated by the thought of a child, a bit of herself, put out for adoption and never seen or heard of again. She may therefore want not merely that the child be detached from her, but more, that it die. Some opponents of abortion are inclined to regard this as beneath contempt—thereby showing insensitivity to what is surely a powerful source of despair. All the same, I agree that the desire for the child's death is not one which anybody may gratify, should it turn out to be possible to detach the child alive.

At this place, however, it should be remembered that we have only been pretending throughout that the fetus is a human being from the moment of conception. A very early abortion is surely not the killing of a person, and so is not dealt with by anything I have said here.

Notes

1. Daniel Callahan, *Abortion: Law, Choice and Morality* (New York, 1970), p. 373. This book gives a fascinating survey of the available information on abortion. The Jewish tradition is surveyed in David M. Feldman, *Birth Control in Jewish Law* (New York, 1968), Part 5, the Catholic tradition in John T. Noonan, Jr., "An Almost

Absolute Value in History," in *The Morality of Abortion,* ed. John T. Noonan, Jr. (Cambridge, Mass., 1970).

2. The term "direct" in the arguments I refer to is a technical one. Roughly, what is meant by "direct killing" is either killing as an end in itself, or killing as a means to some end, for example, the end of saving someone else's life. See note 5, below, for an example of its use.

3. Cf. *Encyclical Letter of Pope Pius XI on Christian Marriage,* St. Paul Editions (Boston, n.d.), p. 32: "however much we may pity the mother whose health and even life is gravely imperiled in the performance of the duty allotted to her by nature, nevertheless what could ever be a sufficient reason for excusing in any way the direct murder of the innocent? This is precisely what we are dealing with here." Noonan (*The Morality of Abortion,* p. 43) reads this as follows: "What cause can ever avail to excuse in any way the direct killing of the innocent? For it is a question of that."

4. The thesis in (4) is in an interesting way weaker than those in (1), (2), and (3): they rule out abortion even in cases in which both mother *and* child will die if the abortion is not performed. By contrast, one who held the view expressed in (4) could consistently say that one needn't prefer letting two persons die to killing one.

5. Cf. the following passage from Pius XII, *Address to the Italian Catholic Society of Midwives:* "The baby in the maternal breast has the right to life immediately from God.—Hence there is no man, no human authority, no science, no medical, eugenic, social, economic or moral 'indication' which can establish or grant a valid juridical ground for a direct deliberate disposition of an innocent human life, that is a disposition which looks to its destruction either as an end or as a means to another end perhaps in itself not illicit.—The baby, still not born, is a man in the same degree and for the same reason as the mother" (quoted in Noonan, *The Morality of Abortion,* p. 45).

How to Argue About Abortion

John Noonan

John Noonan examines various models and methods used in the debate on abortion, distinguishing those that do not work from those that do. According to Noonan, those that do not work involve (1) fantasized examples, such as Thomson's unconscious violinist; (2) hard cases that are resolved in ways that ignore the child's interests; and (3) spatial metaphors, such as "direct" and "indirect," which obscure the moral distinctions involved. Those that do work are (1) balancing values in a nonquantitative manner; (2) seeing what might be otherwise overlooked; and (3) responding to the full range of human experience.

At the heart of the debate about abortion is the relation of person to person in social contexts. Analogies, metaphors, and methods of debate which do not focus on persons and which do not attend to the central contexts are mischievous. Their use arises from a failure to appreciate the distinctive character of moral argument—its requirement that values be organically related and balanced, its dependence on personal vision, and its rootedness in social experience. I propose here to examine various models and methods used in the debate on abortion distinguishing those such as fantasized situations, hard cases, and linear metaphors, all of which do not work, from the balancing, seeing, and appeal to human experience which I believe to be essential. I shall move from models and metaphors which take the rule against abortion as the expression of a single value to the consideration of ways of argument intended to suggest the variety of values which have converged in the formulation of the rule. The values embodied in the rule are various because abortion is an aspect of the relation of person to person, and persons are larger than single values; and abortion is an act in a social context which cannot be reduced to a single value. I write as a critic of abortion, with no doubt a sharper eye for the weaknesses of its friends than of its foes,

From "Responding to Persons: Methods of Moral Argument in Debate over Abortion," *Theology Digest* (1973), pp. 291–307. Reprinted by permission of *Theology Digest.*

but my chief aim is to suggest what arguments count.

Artificial Cases

One way of reaching the nub of a moral issue is to construct a hypothetical situation endowed with precisely the characteristics you believe are crucial in the real issue you are seeking to resolve. Isolated from the clutter of detail in the real situation, these characteristics point to the proper solution. The risk is that the features you believe crucial you will enlarge to the point of creating a caricature. The pedagogy of your illustration will be blunted by the uneasiness caused by the lack of correspondence between the fantasized situation and the real situation to be judged. Such is the case with recent efforts by philosopher Judith Jarvis Thomson to construct arguments justifying abortion.

Suppose, says Thomson, a violinist whose continued existence depends on acquiring new kidneys. Without the violinist's knowledge—he remains innocent—a healthy person is kidnapped and connected to him so that the violinist now shares the use of healthy kidneys. May the victim of the kidnapping break the connection and thereby kill the violinist? Thomson intuits that the normal judgment will be Yes. The healthy person should not be imposed upon by a lifelong physical connection with the violinist. This construct, Thomson contends, bears upon abortion by establishing that being human does not carry with it a right to life which must be respected by another at the cost of serious inconvenience.

This ingenious attempt to make up a parallel to pregnancy imagines a kidnapping; a serious operation performed on the victim of the kidnapping; and a continuing interference with many of the activities of the victim. It supposes that violinist and victim were unrelated. It supposed nothing by which the victim's initial aversion to his yoke-mate might be mitigated or compensated. It supposes no degree of voluntariness. The similitude to pregnancy is grotesque. It is difficult to think of another age or society in which a caricature of this sort could be seriously put forward as a paradigm illustrating the moral choice to be made by a mother.

While Thomson focuses on this fantasy, she ignores a real case from which American tort law has generalized. On a January night in Minnesota, a cattle buyer, Orlando Depue, asked a family of farmers, the Flateaus, with whom he had dined, if he could remain overnight at their house. The Flateaus refused and, although Depue was sick and had fainted, put him out of the house into the cold night. Imposing liability on the Flateaus for Depue's loss of his frostbitten fingers the court said, "In the case at bar defendants were under no contract obligation to minister to plaintiff in his distress; but humanity demanded they do so, if they understood and appreciated his condition . . . The law as well as humanity required that he not be exposed in his helpless condition to the merciless elements." Depue was a guest for supper although not a guest after supper. The American Law Institute, generalizing, has said that it makes no difference whether the helpless person is a guest or a trespasser. He has the privilege of staying. His host has the duty not to injure him or put him into an environment where he becomes nonviable. The obligation arises when one person "understands and appreciates" the condition of the other. Although the analogy is not exact, the case seems closer to the mother's situation than the case imagined by Thomson; and the emotional response of the Minnesota judges seems to be a truer reflection of what humanity requires. . . .

Hard Cases and Exceptions

In the presentation of permissive abortion to the American public, major emphasis has been put on situations of great pathos—the child deformed by thalidomide, the child affected by rubella, the child known to suffer from Tay-Sachs disease or Downs syndrome, the raped adolescent, the exhausted mother of small children. These situations are not imagined, and the cases described are not analogies to those where abortion might be sought; they are themselves cases to which abortion is a solution. Who could deny the poignancy of their appeal?

Hard cases make bad law, runs the venerable legal adage, but it seems to be worse law if the distress experienced in situations such as these is not taken into account. If persons are to be given preeminence over abstract principle, should not exceptions for these cases be made in the most rigid rule against abortion? Does not the human experience of such exceptions point to a more sweeping conclusion—the necessity of abandoning any uniform prohibition of abortion, so that all the elements of a particular situation may be weighted by the woman in question and her doctor?

So far, fault can scarcely be found with this method of argumentation, this appeal to common experience. But the cases are oversimplified if focus is directed solely on the parents of a physically defective child or on the mother in the cases of rape or psychic exhaustion. The situations are very hard for the parents or the mother; they are still harder for the fetus who is threatened with death. If the fetus is a person as the opponents of abortion contend, its destruction is not the sparing of suffering by the sacrifice of a principle but by the sacrifice of a life. Emotion is a proper element in moral response, but to the extent that the emotion generated by these cases obscures the claims of the fetus, this kind of argumentation fosters erroneous judgment.

In three of the cases—the child deformed by drugs, disease, or genetic defect—the neglect of the child's point of view seems stained by hypocrisy. Abortion is here justified as putting the child out of the misery of living a less than normal life. The child is not consulted as to the choice. Experience, which teaches that even the most seriously incapacitated prefer living to dying, is ignored. The feelings of the parents are the actual consideration, and these feelings are treated with greater tenderness than the fetal desire to live. The common unwillingness to say frankly that the abortion is sought for the parents' benefit is testimony, unwillingly given, to the intuition that such self-preference by the parents is difficult for society or for the parents themselves to accept.

The other kind of hard case does not mask preference for the parent by a pretense of concern for the fetus. The simplest situation is that of a pregnancy due to rape—in presentations to some legislatures it was usual to add a racist fillip by supposing a white woman and a black rapist—but this gratuitous pandering to bias is not essential. The fetus, unwanted in the most unequivocal way, is analogized to an invader of the mother's body—is it even appropriate to call her a mother when she did nothing to assume the special fiduciary cares of motherhood? If she is prevented from having an abortion, she is being compelled for nine months to be reminded of a traumatic assault. Do not her feelings override the right to life of her unwanted tenant?

Rape arouses fear and a desire for revenge, and reference to rape evokes emotion. The emotion has been enough for the state to take the life of the rapist. Horror of the crime is easily extended to horror of the product, so that the fetal life becomes forfeit too. If horror is overcome, adoption appears to be a more humane solution than abortion. If the rape case is not being used as a stalking horse by proponents of abortion—if there is a desire to deal with it in itself—the solution is to assure the destruction of the sperm in the one to three days elapsing between insemination and impregnation.

Generally, however, the rape case is presented as a way of suggesting a general principle, a principle which could be formulated as follows: Every unintended pregnancy may be interrupted if its continuation will cause emotional distress to the mother. Pregnancies due to bad planning or bad luck are analogized to pregnancies due to rape; they are all involuntary. Indeed many pregnancies can without great difficulty be assimilated to the hard case, for how often do persons undertake an act of sexual intercourse consciously intending that a child be the fruit of that act? Many pregnancies are unspecified by a particular intent, are unplanned, are in this sense involuntary. Many pregnancies become open to termination if only the baby consciously sought has immunity.

This result is unacceptable to those who believe that the fetus is human. It is acceptable to those who do not believe the fetus is human, but to reach it they do not need the argument based on the hard case. The result would follow immediately from the mother's dominion over a portion of her body. Opponents of abortion who out of consideration for the emotional distress caused by rape will grant the rape exception must see that the exception can be generalized to destroy the rule. If, on other grounds they believe the rule good, they must deny the exception which eats it up.

Direct and Indirect

From the paradigmatic arguments, I turn to metaphors and especially those which, based on some spatial image, are misleading. I shall begin with "direct" and "indirect" and their cousins, "affirmative" and "negative." In the abortion argument "direct" and "indirect," "affirmative" and "negative" occur more frequently in these kinds of questions: If one denies that a fetus may be killed directly, but admits that indirect abortion is permissible, is he guilty of inconsistency? If one maintains that there is a negative duty not to kill fetuses, does he thereby commit himself to an affirmative obligation of assuring safe delivery of every fetus? If one agrees that there is no affirmative duty to actualize as many spermatic, ovoid, embryonic, or fetal potentialities as possible, does one thereby concede that it is generally permissible to take steps to destroy fertilized ova? The argumentative implications of these questions can be best unravelled by looking at the force of the metaphors invoked.

"Direct" and "indirect" appeal to our experience of linedrawing and of travel. You reach a place on a piece of paper by drawing a straight or crooked line—the line is direct or indirect. You go to a place without detours or you go in a roundabout fashion—your route is direct or indirect. In each instance, whether your path is direct or indirect your destination is the same. The root experience is that you can reach the same spot in ways distinguished by their immediacy and the amount of ground covered. "Indirectly" says you proceed more circuitously and cover more ground. It does not, however, say anything of the reason why you go circuitously. You may go indirectly because you want to cover more ground or because you want to disguise your destination.

The ambiguity in the reason for indirectness—an ambiguity present in the primary usage of the term—carries over when "indirect" is applied metaphorically to human intentions. There may be a reason for doing something indirectly—you want to achieve another objective besides the indirect action. You may also act indirectly to conceal from another or from yourself what is your true destination. Because of this ambiguity in the reason for indirection, "indirect" is apt to cause confusion when applied in moral analysis.

Defenders of an absolute prohibition of abortion have excepted the removal of a fertilized ovum in an ectopic pregnancy and the removal of a cancerous uterus containing an embryo. They have characterized the abortion involved as "indirect." They have meant that the surgeon's attention is focused on correcting a pathological condition dangerous to the mother and he only performs the operation because there is no alternative way of correcting it. But the physician has to intend to achieve not only the improvement of the mother but the performance of action by which the fertilized ovum becomes nonviable. He necessarily intends to perform an abortion, he necessarily intends to kill. To say that he acts indirectly is to conceal what is being done. It is a confusing and improper use of the metaphor.

A clearer presentation of the cases of the cancerous uterus and the ectopic pregnancy would acknowledge them to be true exceptions to the absolute inviolability of the fetus. Why are they not exceptions which would eat up the rule? It depends on what the rule is considered to be. The principle that can be discerned in them is, whenever the embryo is a danger to the life of the mother, an abortion is permissible. At the level of reason nothing more can be asked of the mother. The exceptions do eat up any rule of preferring the fetus to the mother—any rule of fetus first. They do not destroy the rule that the life of the fetus has precedence over other interests of the mother. The exceptions of the ectopic pregnancy and the cancerous uterus are special cases of the general exception to the rule against killing, which permits one to kill in self-defense. Characterization of this kind of killing as "indirect" does not aid analysis.

It is a basic intuition that one is not responsible for all the consequences of one's acts. By living at all one excludes others from the air one breathes, the food one eats. One cannot foresee all the results which will flow from any given action. It is imperative for moral discourse to be able to distinguish between injury foreseeably inflicted on another, and the harm which one may unknowingly bring about. "Direct" and "indirect" are sometimes used to distinguish the foreseen consequence from the unconsidered or unknown consequence. This usage does not justify terming abortion to save a mother's life "indirect." In the case of terminating the ectopic pregnancy, the cancerous uterus, the life-threatening fetus generally, one considers precisely the consequence, the taking of the fetal life.

Just as one intuits that one is not responsible for all the consequences, so one intuits that one is not called to right all wrongs. No one is bound to the impossible. There is, therefore, an intuitive difference between the duty to refrain from doing harm to anyone and the duty to help everyone in distress. The duty to refrain is possible of fulfillment if it refers only to conscious infliction of harm. The duty to help is impossible if one is going to develop as a human being, getting educated, earning a living, marrying, raising a family, and so forth. The needs of other human beings are subordinated or postponed by everyone to the fulfillment of many of one's own needs, and rightly so. The distinction between affirmative and negative duties, another linear metaphor, rests on this universal experience. The terms do have a basis in moral life. Their usefulness in moral analysis, however, is not great. The crucial distinction is not between negative and affirmative, but between limited and unlimited duty.

It is possible to state the duty not to kill the fetus as the duty to care for the fetus. Opponents of abortion, however, do not commit thereby themselves to the position that all fertilized ova must be born. A pregnant woman may, for example, take the chance of killing the baby by going for a walk or a drive instead of staying safely in bed. She is not responsible for all the consequences of her acts. She is not called to help the fetus in every possible way. The negative duty or the convertible affirmative duty excludes acts which have a high probability of death for the fetus, but not those with a low probability of death. Similarly, one has a duty not to kill one's older children, and a duty to care for them, but no duty to keep them free from all risk of harm. No inconsistency exists in not equating a limited negative duty with an unlimited affirmative duty; no inconsistency exists in rejecting high risk acts and approving low risks acts.

Linedrawing

The prime linear metaphor is, of course, linedrawing. It is late in the history of moral thought for anyone to suppose that an effective moral retort is, "Yes, but where do you draw the line?" or to make the inference that, because any drawing of a line requires a decision, all linedrawing is arbitrary. One variant or another of these old ploys is, however, frequently used in the present controversy. From living cell to dying corpse a continuum exists. Proponents of abortion are said to be committed to murder, to euthanasia, or, at a minimum, to infanticide. Opponents are alleged to be bound to condemn contraception—after all, spermatazoa are living human cells. Even if contraception is admitted and infanticide re-

jected, the range of choice is still large enough for the line drawn to be challenged—is it to be at nidation, at formation of the embryo, at quickening, at viability, at birth? Whoever adopts one point is asked why he does not move forward or backward by one stage of development. The difficulty of presenting apodictic reasons for preferring one position is made to serve as proof that the choice may be made as best suits the convenience of an individual or the state.

The metaphor of linedrawing distracts attention from the nature of the moral decision. The metaphor suggests an empty room composed of indistinguishable grey blocks. In whatever way the room is divided, there are grey blocks on either side of the line. Or if the metaphor is taken more mathematically, it suggests a series of points, which, wherever bisected, are fungible with each other. What is obscured in the spatial or mathematical model is the variety of values whose comparison enters into any moral decision. The model appeals chiefly to those novices in moral reasoning who believe that moral judgment is a matter of pursuing a principle to its logical limit. Single-mindedly looking at a single value, they ask, if this is good, why not more of it? In practice, however, no one can be so single-hearted. Insistence of this kind of logical consistency becomes the preserve of fanatics or of controversialists eager to convict their adversaries of inconsistency. If more than one good is sought by a human being, he must bring the goods he seeks into relationship with each other; he must limit one to maintain another; he must mix them.

The process of choosing multiple goods occurs in many particular contexts—in eating, in studying, in painting. No one supposes that those who take the first course must forego dessert, that the election of English means History shall not be studied, that the use of blue excludes red. Linear models for understanding choice in these matters are readily perceived as inappropriate. The commitment to values, the cutting off of values, and the mixing of values accompany each other.

Is, however, the choice of the stage of development which should not be destroyed by abortion a choice requiring the mixing of multiple goods? Is not the linear model appropriate when picking a point on the continuum of life? Are not the moral choices which require commitment and mixing made only after the selection of the stage at which a being becomes a person? To these related questions the answers must all be negative. To recognize a person is a moral decision; it depends on objective data but it also depends on the perceptions and inclinations and ends of the decision makers; it cannot be made without commitment and without consideration of alternative values. Who is a person? This is not a question asked abstractly, in the air, with no purpose in mind. To disguise the personal involvement in the response to personhood is to misconceive the issue of abortion from the start.

Those who identify the rational with the geometrical, the algebraic, the logical may insist that, if the fundamental recognition of personhood depends upon the person who asks, then the arbitrariness of any position on abortion is conceded. If values must be mixed even in identifying the human, who can object to another's mixture? The issue becomes like decisions in eating, studying, and painting, a matter of discretion. A narrow rationalism of this kind uses "taste" as the ultimate epithet for the non-rational. It does not acknowledge that each art has its own rules. It claims for itself alone the honorable term "reason."

As this sort of monopoly has become unacceptable in general philosophy, so it is unnecessary to accept it here. Taste, that is perceptiveness, is basic; and if it cannot be disputed, it can be improved by experience. Enology, painting, or moral reasoning all require basic aptitude, afford wide ranges of options, have limits beyond which a choice can be counterproductive, and are better done by the experienced than by amateurs. Some persons may lack almost any capacity for undertaking one or another of them. Although all men are moral beings, not all are proficient at moral judgment, so that morality is not a democratic business. Selecting multiple goods, those who are capable of the art perceive, test, mix and judge. The process has little in common with linedrawing. In the case of abortion, it is the contention of its opponents that in such a process the right response to the data is that the fetus is a human being.

Balancing

The process of decisionmaking just described is better caught by the term "balancing." In contrast to linedrawing, balancing is a metaphor helpful in understanding moral judgment. Biologically understood, balancing is the fundamental metaphor for moral reasoning. A biological system is in balance when its parts are in the equilibrium necessary for it to live. To achieve such equilibrium, some parts—the heart, for example—must be preserved at all costs; others may be sacrificed to maintain the whole. Balance in the biological sense does not demand an egalitarian concern for every part, but an ordering and subordination which permit the whole to function. So in moral reasoning the reasoner balances values.

The mistaken common reading of this metaphor is to treat it as equivalent to weighing, so that balancing is understood as an act of quantitative comparison analogous to that performed by an assayer or a butcher. This view tacitly supposes that values are weights which are tangible and commensurate. One puts so many units on one pan of the scales and matches them with so many units on the other to reach a "balanced" judgment. To give a personal example, Daniel Callahan has questioned my position that the value of innocent life cannot be sacrificed to achieve the other values which abortion might secure. The "force of the rule," he writes, "is absolutist, displaying no 'balance' at all." He takes balancing in the sense of weighing and wonders how one value can be so heavy.

That justice often consists in the fair distribution or exchange of goods as in the familiar Aristotelian examples has no doubt worked to confirm a quantitative approach. Scales as the symbol of justice seem to suggest the antiquity of the quantitative meaning of balance. But the original sense of the scales was otherwise. In Egypt where the symbol was first used, a feather, the Egyptian hieroglyphic for truth, turned the balance. As put by David Daube in his illuminating analysis of the ancient symbolism, "The slightest turning of the scales—'but in the estimation of a hair'—will decide the issue, and the choice is between salvation and annihilation." Not a matching of weights, but a response to reality was what justice was seen to require, and what was at stake was not a slight overweighing in one direction or the other, but salvation. Moral choice, generally, has this character of a hair separating good from evil.

A fortiori then, in moral judgment, where more values are in play than in any system of strict law or commutative justice, balancing is a misleading metaphor if it suggests a matching of weights. It is an indispensable metaphor if it stands for the equilibrium of a living organism making the choices necessary for its preservation. A single value cannot be pursued to the point of excluding all other values. This is the caricature of moral argument I have already touched on in connection with the metaphor of linedrawing. But some values are more vital than others, as the heart is more vital to the body than the hand. A balanced moral judgment requires a sense of the limits, interrelations, and priority of values. It is the position of those generally opposed to abortion that a judgment preferring interests less than human life to human life is unbalanced, that a judgment denying a mother's fiduciary responsibility to her child is unbalanced, that a judgment making killing a principal part of the profession of a physician is unbalanced, that a judgment permitting agencies of the state to procure and pay for the destruction of the offspring of the poor or underprivileged is unbalanced. They contend that such judgments expand the right limits of a mother's responsibility for herself, destroy the fiduciary relation which is a central paradigm for the social bond, fail to relate to the physician's service to life and the state's care for its citizens. At stake in the acceptance of abortion is not a single value, life, against which the suffering of the mother or parents may be balanced. The values to be considered are the child's life, the mother's faithfulness to her dependent, the physician's commitment to preserving life; and in the United States today abortion cannot be discussed without awareness that if law does not prohibit it, the state will fund it, so that the value of the state's abstention from the taking of life is also at issue. The judgment which accepts abortion, it is contended, is unbalanced in subordinating these values to the personal autonomy of the mother and the social interest in population control.

Seeing

The metaphor of balancing points to the process of combining values. But we do not combine values like watercolors. We respond to values situated in subjects. "Balancing" is an inadequate metaphor for moral thinking in leaving out of account the central moral transaction—the response of human beings to other human beings. In making moral judgments we respond to those human beings whom we see.

The metaphor of sight is a way of emphasizing the need for perception, whether by eyes or ears or touch, of those we take as subjects to whom we respond. Seeing in any case is more than the registration of a surface. It is a penetration yielding some sense of the other's structure, so that the experiencing of another is never merely visual or auditory or tactile. We see the features and comprehend the humanity at the same time. Look at the fetus, say the anti-abortionists, and you will see humanity. How long, they ask, can a man turn his head and pretend that he just doesn't see?

An accusation of blindness, however, does not seem to advance moral argument. A claim to see where others do not see is a usual claim of charlatans. "Illumination" or "enlightenment" appear to transcend experience and make moral disputation impossible. "Visionary" is often properly a term of disparagement. Is not an appeal to sight the end of rational debate?

In morals, as in epistemology, there is nonetheless no substitute for perception. Are animals within the range of beings with a right to life, and babies not, as Michael Tooley has recently suggested? Should trees be persons, as Christopher Stone has recently maintained? Questions of this kind are fundamentally frivolous for they point to the possibility of moral argument while attempting to deny the foundation of moral argument, our ability to recognize human persons. If a person could in no way perceive another person to be like himself, he would be incapable of moral response. If a person cannot perceive a cat or a tree as different from himself, he cuts off the possibility of argument. Debate should not end with pointing, but it must begin there.

Is there a contradiction in the opponents of abortion appealing to perception when fetuses are normally invisible? Should one not hold that until beings are seen they have not entered the ranks of society? Falling below the threshold of sight, do not fetuses fall below the threshold of humanity? If the central moral transaction is response to the other person, are not fetuses peculiarly weak subjects to elicit our response? These questions pinpoint the principal task of the defenders of the fetus—to make the fetus visible. The task is different only in degree from that assumed by defenders of other persons who have been or are "overlooked." For centuries, color acted as a psychological block to perception, and the blindness induced by color provided a sturdy basis for discrimination. Minorities of various kinds exist today who are "invisible" and therefore unlikely to be "heard" in the democratic process. Persons literally out of sight of society in prisons and mental institutions are often not "recognized" as fellow humans by the world with which they have "lost touch." In each of these instances those who seek to vindicate the rights of the unseen must begin by calling attention to their existence. "Look" is the exhortation they address to the callous and the negligent.

Perception of fetuses is possible with not substantially greater effort than that required to pierce the physical or psychological barriers to recognizing other human beings. The main difficulty is everyone's reluctance to accept the extra burdens of care imposed by an expansion of the numbers in whom humanity is recognized. It is generally more convenient to have to consider only one's kin, one's peers, one's country, one's race. Seeing requires personal attention and personal response. The emotion generated by identification with a human form is necessary to overcome the inertia which is protected by a vision restricted to a convenient group. If one is willing to undertake the risk that more will be required in one's action, fetuses may be seen in multiple ways—circumstantially, by the observation of a pregnant woman; photographically, by pictures of life in the womb; scientifically, in accounts written by investigators of prenatal life and child psychologists; visually, by observing a blood transfusion or an abortion while the fetus is alive or by examination of a fetal corpse after death. The proponent of abortion is invited to consider the organism kicking the mother, swimming peacefully in amniotic fluid, responding to the prick of an instrument, being extracted from the womb, sleeping in death. Is the kicker or swimmer similar to him or to her? Is the response to pain like his or hers? Will his or her own face look much different in death?

Response

Response to the fetus begins with grasp of the data which yield the fetus' structure. That structure is not merely anatomical form; it is dynamic—we apprehend the fetus' origin and end. It is this apprehension which makes response to the nameless fetus different from the conscious analogizing that goes on when we name a cat. Seeing, we are linked to the being in the womb by more than an inventory of shared physical characteristics and by more than a number of made-up psychological characteristics. The weakness of the being as potential recalls our own potential state, the helplessness of the being evokes the human condition of contingency. We meet another human subject.

Seeing is impossible apart from experience, but experience is the most imprecise of terms. What kind of experience counts, and whose? There are experiences which only women and usually only those within the ages of 14 to 46 who are fertile can have: conceiving a child, carrying a child, having an abortion, being denied an abortion, giving birth. There are experiences only a fetus can have: being carried, being aborted, being born. There is the experience of obstetricians who regularly deliver children and occasionally abort them; there is the differently-textured experience of the professional abortionist. There is the experience of nurses who prepare the mother for abortion, care for her after the abortion, and dispose of the aborted fetus. There is the experience of physicians, social workers, and ministers, who advise a woman to have an abortion or not to have one. There is the experience of those who enforce a law against abortion, and those who stealthily or openly, for profit or for conscience's sake, defy it. There is the experience of those who have sexual intercourse knowing that abortion is or is not a remedy if an accidental pregnancy should result. There is the experience of society at large of a pattern of uncontrolled abortion or of its regulation.

Some arguments are unduly exclusivist in the experience they will admit. Those who suggest that abortion is peculiarly a matter for women disqualify men because the unique experience of pregnancy is beyond their achievement. Yet such champions of abortion do not regularly disqualify sterile women whose experience of pregnancy must be as vicarious as a man's. Tertullian taught that only those who have known motherhood themselves have a right to speak from experience on the choices presented by abortion. Yet even Tertullian did not go so far as to say that only mothers who had both given birth and had had abortions were qualified to speak. Efforts of this sort to restrict those who are competent rest on a confusion between the relevant and the personal. You do not have to be a judge to know that bribery is evil or a slave to know that slavery is wrong. Vicarious experience, in this as in other moral matters, is a proper basis for judgment.

Vicarious experience appears strained to the outer limit when one is asked to consider the experience of the fetus. No one remembers being born, no one knows what it is like to die. Empathy may, however, supply for memory, as it does in other instances when we refer to the experience of infants who cannot speak or to the experience of death by those who

cannot speak again. The experience of the fetus is no more beyond our knowledge than the experience of the baby and the experience of dying.

Participation in an abortion is another sort of experience relevant to moral judgment. Generals are not thought of as the best judges of the morality of war, nor is their experience thought to be unaffected by their profession, but they should be heard, when the permissibility of war is urged. Obstetricians are in an analogous position, their testimony subject to a discount. The testimony of professional abortionists is also relevant, although subject to an even greater discount. Nurses are normally more disinterested witnesses. They speak as ones who have empathized with the female patient, disposed of the fetal remains, and, like the Red Cross in wartime, have known what the action meant by seeing the immediate consequences.

The experience of individuals becomes a datum of argument through autobiography and testimony, inference and empathy. The experience of a society has to be captured by the effort of sociologists and novelists, historians and lawyers, psychologists and moralists; and it is strongly affected by the prism of the medium used. Typically the proponents of abortion have put emphasis on quantitative evidence—for example, on the number of abortions performed in the United States or in the world at large. The assumption underlying this appeal to experience is that what is done by a great many persons cannot be bad, is indeed normal. This assumption, often employed when sexual behavior is studied, is rarely favored when racial discrimination or war are considered. It is a species of natural law, identifying the usual with the natural. The experience appealed to counts as argument only for those who accept this identification and consider the usual the good.

Psychological evidence has been called upon by the opponents of abortion. Trauma and guilt have been found associated with the election of abortion. The inference is made that abortion is the cause of this unhappiness. As in many arguments based on social consequences, however, the difficulty is to isolate the cause. Do persons undergoing abortion have character pre-dispositions which would in any event manifest themselves in psychic disturbance? Do they react as they do because of social conditioning which could be changed to encourage a positive attitude to abortion? Is the act of abortion at the root of their problems or the way in which the process is carried out? None of these questions is settled; the evidence is most likely to be convincing to those already inclined to believe that abortion is an evil.

Another kind of experience is that embedded in law. In Roman law where children generally had little status independent of their parents, the fetus was "a portion of the mother or her viscera." This view persisted in nineteenth century American tort law, Justice Holmes in a leading case describing the fetus as "a part of the body of the mother." In recent years, however, the tort cases have asked, in Justice Bok's phrase, if the fetus is a person; and many courts have replied affirmatively. The change, a striking revolution in torts law, came from the courts incorporating into their thought new biological data on the fetus as a living organism. Evidence on how the fetus is now perceived is also provided by another kind of case where abortion itself is not involved—the interpretation in wills and trusts of gifts to "children" or "issue." In these cases a basic question is, "What is the common understanding of people when they speak of children?" The answer, given repeatedly by American courts, is that "the average testator" speaking of children means to include a being who has been conceived but not born. Free from the distorting pressures of the conflict over abortion, this evidence of the common understanding suggests that social experience has found the fetus to be within the family of man.

The most powerful expression of common experience is that given by art and literature. Birth has almost everywhere been celebrated in painting. The Nativity has been a symbol of gladness not only because of its sacral significance, but because of its human meaning— "joy that a man is born into the world." Abortion, in contrast, has rarely been the subject of art. Unlike other forms of death, abortion has not been seen by painters as a release, a sacrifice, or a victory. Characteristically it has stood for sterility, futility, and absurdity. Consider,

for example, Orozco's mural, "Gods of the Modern World" in the Baker Library at Dartmouth College. Academia is savagely satirized by portraying professors as impotent attendants in an operating room in which truth is stillborn. Bottled fetuses in the foreground attest the professors' habitual failure. The entire force of the criticism of academic achievement comes from the painter's knowledge that everyone will recognize abortion as a grave defeat and the bottling of dead fetuses as a travesty of healthy birth. Whoever sees such a painting sees how mankind has commonly experienced abortion.

In contemporary American literature, John Updike's *Couples* comments directly upon abortion, using it at a crucial turn as both event and symbol. Piet Hanema, married to Angela, has promiscuously pursued other married women, among them Foxy Whitman, who is now pregnant by him. They have this exchange:

> All I know is what I honestly want. I want this damn thing to stop growing inside me.
>   Don't cry.
>   Nature is so stupid. It has all my maternal glands working, do you know what that means, Piet? You know what the great thing about being pregnant I found out was? It's something I just couldn't have imagined. You're never alone. When you have a baby inside you you are not alone. It's a person.

To procure the abortion it becomes necessary for Piet to surrender his own wife Angela to Freddy who has access to the abortionist. Embarked upon his course Piet does not stop at this act which destroys his own marriage irretrievably. Foxy's feelings at the time of the abortion are then described through Piet:

> Not until days later, after Foxy had survived the forty-eight hours alone in the house with Toby and the test of Ken's return from Chicago, did Piet learn, not from Freddy but from her as told by Freddy, that at the moment of anesthesia she had panicked; she had tried to strike the Negress pressing the sweet, sweet

mask to her face and through the first waves of ether had continued to cry that she should go home, that she was supposed to have this baby, that the child's father was coming to smash the door down with a hammer and would stop them.

Updike's only comment as an author is given as Piet then goes to Foxy's house: "Death, once invited in, leaves his muddy bootprints everywhere." The elements of the experience of abortion are here: the hatred of the depersonalized burden growing, willy-nilly, in the womb; the sense of a baby, a person, one's own child; the desperate desire to be rid of the burden extinguishing all other considerations; the ineffectual hope of delivery the moment before the child's death. A mask covers the human face of the mother. Symbolically the abortion seals a course of infidelity. Conclusively it becomes death personified. . . .

On the Moral and Legal Status of Abortion

Mary Anne Warren

Mary Anne Warren argues that if the fetus is assumed to be a person, there are a wide range of cases in which abortion cannot be defended. To provide such a defense, Warren sets out five criteria for being a person she feels should be acceptable to antiabortionists and proabortionists alike. Appealing to these criteria, she contends that fetuses, even when their potentiality is taken into account, do not sufficiently resemble persons to have a significant right to life.

In a "Postscript" to her article, she defends her view against the objection that it would justify infanticide. Although by her criteria newborn infants would not have a significant right to life, she claims that infanticide would still not be permissible, so long as there are people willing to care and provide for the well-being of such infants.

We will be concerned with both the moral status of abortion, which for our purposes we may define as the act which a woman performs in voluntarily terminating, or allowing another person to terminate, her pregnancy, and the legal status which is appropriate for this act. I will argue that, while it is not possible to produce a satisfactory defense of a woman's right to obtain an abortion without showing that a fetus is not a human being, in the morally relevant sense of that term, we ought not to conclude that the difficulties involved in determining whether or not a fetus is human

make it impossible to produce any satisfactory solution to the problem of the moral status of abortion. For it is possible to show that, on the basis of intuitions which we may expect even the opponents of abortion to share, a fetus is not a person, and hence not the sort of entity to which it is proper to ascribe full moral rights.

Of course, while some philosophers would deny the possibility of any such proof,[1] others will deny that there is any need for it, since the moral permissibility of abortion appears to them to be too obvious to require proof. But the inadequacy of this attitude should be evident from the fact that both the friends and the foes of abortion consider their position to be morally self-evident. Because proabortionists have never adequately come to grips with the conceptual issues surrounding abortion, most if not all, of the arguments which they advance in opposition to laws restricting access to abortion fail to refute or even weaken the traditional antiabortion argument, i.e., that a fetus is a human being, and therefore abortion is murder.

These arguments are typically of one of two sorts. Either they point to the terrible side effects of the restrictive laws, e.g., the deaths due to illegal abortions, and the fact that it is poor women who suffer the most as a result of these laws, or else they state that to deny a woman access to abortion is to deprive her of her right to control her own body. Unfortunately, however, the fact that restricting access to abortion has tragic side effects does not, in itself, show that the restrictions are unjustified, since murder is wrong regardless of the consequences of prohibiting it; and the appeal to the right to control one's body, which is generally construed as a property right, is at best a rather feeble argument for the permissibility of abortion. Mere ownership does not give me the right to kill innocent people whom I find on my property, and indeed I am apt to be held responsible if such people injure themselves while on my property. It is equally unclear that I have any moral right to expel an innocent person from my property when I know that doing so will result in his death.

Furthermore, it is probably inappropriate to describe a woman's body as her property, since it seems natural to hold that a person is something distinct from her property, but not from her body. Even those who would object to the identification of a person with his body, or with the conjunction of his body and his mind, must admit that it would be very odd to describe, say, breaking a leg, as damaging one's property, and much more appropriate to describe it as injuring one*self*. Thus it is probably a mistake to argue that the right to obtain an abortion is in any way derived from the right to own and regulate property.

But however we wish to construe the right to abortion, we cannot hope to convince those who consider abortion a form of murder of the existence of any such right unless we are able to produce a clear and convincing refutation of the traditional antiabortion argument, and this has not, to my knowledge, been done. With respect to the two most vital issues which that argument involves, i.e., the humanity of

the fetus and its implication for the moral status of abortion, confusion has prevailed on both sides of the dispute.

Thus, both proabortionists and antiabortionists have tended to abstract the question of whether abortion is wrong to that of whether it is wrong to destroy a fetus, just as though the rights of another person were not necessarily involved. This mistaken abstraction has led to the almost universal assumption that if a fetus is a human being, with a right to life, then it follows immediately that abortion is wrong (except perhaps when necessary to save the woman's life), and that it ought to be prohibited. It has also been generally assumed that unless the question about the status of the fetus is answered, the moral status of abortion cannot possibly be determined. . . . John Noonan is correct in saying that "the fundamental question in the long history of abortion is, How do you determine the humanity of a being?"[2] He summarizes his own antiabortion argument, which is a version of the official position of the Catholic Church, as follows:

> . . . it is wrong to kill humans, however poor, weak, defenseless, and lacking in opportunity to develop their potential they may be. It is therefore morally wrong to kill Biafrans. Similarly, it is morally wrong to kill embryos.[3]

Noonan bases his claim that fetuses are human upon what he calls the theologians' criterion of humanity: that whoever is conceived of human beings is human. But although he argues at length for the appropriateness of this criterion, he never questions the assumption that if a fetus is human then abortion is wrong for exactly the same reason that murder is wrong.

Judith Thomson is, in fact, the only writer I am aware of who has seriously questioned this assumption; she has argued that, even if we grant the antiabortionist his claim that a fetus is a human being, with the same right to life as any other human being, we can still demonstrate that, in at least some and perhaps most cases, a woman is under no moral obligation to complete an unwanted pregnancy.[4] Her argument is worth examining, since if it holds up it may enable us to establish the moral permissibility of abortion without becoming involved in problems about what entitles an entity to be considered human, and accorded full moral rights. To be able to do this would be a great gain in the power and simplicity of the proabortion position, since, although I will argue that these problems can be solved at least as decisively as can any other moral problem, we should certainly be pleased to be able to avoid having to solve them as part of the justification of abortion.

On the other hand, even if Thomson's argument does not hold up, her insight, i.e., that it requires *argument* to show that if fetuses are human then abortion is properly classified as murder, is an extremely valuable one. The assumption she attacks is particularly invidious, for it amounts to the decision that it is appropriate, in deciding the moral status of abortion, to leave the rights of the pregnant woman out of consideration entirely, except possibly when her life is threatened. Obviously, this will not do; determining what moral rights, if any, a fetus possesses is only the first step in determining the moral status of abortion. Step two, which is at least equally essential, is finding a just solution to the conflict between whatever rights the fetus may have, and the rights of the woman who is unwillingly pregnant. While the historical error has been to pay far too little attention to the second step, Ms. Thomson's suggestion is that if we look at the second step first we may find that a woman has a right to obtain an abortion *regardless* of what rights the fetus has.

Our own inquiry will also have two stages. In Section I, we will consider whether or not it is possible to establish that abortion is morally permissible even on the assumption that a fetus is an entity with a full-fledged right to life. I will argue that in fact this cannot be established, at least not with the conclusiveness which is essential to our hopes of convincing those who are skeptical about the morality of abortion, and that we therefore cannot avoid dealing with the question of whether or not a fetus really does have the same right to life as a (more fully developed) human being.

In Section II, I will propose an answer to this question, namely, that a fetus cannot be considered a member of the moral community, the set of beings with full and equal moral rights, for the simple reason that it is not a person, and that it is personhood, and not genetic humanity, i.e., humanity as defined by Noonan, which is the basis for membership in this community. I will argue that a fetus, whatever its stage of development, satisfies none of the basic criteria of personhood, and is not even enough *like* a person to be accorded even some of the same rights on the basis of this resemblance. Nor, as we will see, is a fetus's *potential* personhood a threat to the morality of abortion, since, whatever the rights of potential people may be, they are invariably overridden in any conflict with the moral rights of actual people.

I

We turn now to Professor Thomson's case for the claim that even if a fetus has full moral rights, abortion is still morally permissible, at least sometimes, and for some reasons other than to save the woman's life. Her argument is based upon a clever, but I think faulty, analogy. She asks us to picture ourselves waking up one day, in bed with a famous violinist. Imagine that you have been kidnapped, and your bloodstream hooked up to that of the violinist, who happens to have an ailment which will certainly kill him unless he is permitted to share your kidneys for a period of nine months. No one else can save him, since you alone have the right type of blood. He will be unconscious all that time, and you will have to stay in bed with him, but after the nine months are over he may be unplugged, completely cured, that is provided that you have cooperated.

Now then, she continues, what are your obligations in this situation? The antiabortionist, if he is consistent, will have to say that you are obligated to stay in bed with the violinist: for all people have a right to life, and violinists are people, and therefore it would be murder for you to disconnect yourself from him and let him die. But this is outrageous, and so there must be something wrong with the same argument when it is applied to abortion. It would certainly be commendable of you to agree to save the violinist, but it is absurd to suggest that your refusal to do so would be murder. His right to life does not obligate you to do whatever is required to keep him alive; nor does it justify anyone else in forcing you to do so. A law which required you to stay in bed with the violinist would clearly be an unjust law, since it is no proper function of the law to force unwilling people to make huge sacrifices for the sake of other people toward whom they have no such prior obligation.

Thomson concludes that, if this analogy is an apt one, then we can grant the anti-abortionist his claim that a fetus is a human being, and still hold that it is at least sometimes the case that a pregnant woman has the right to refuse to be a Good Samaritan towards the fetus, i.e., to obtain an abortion. For there is a great gap between the claim that x has a right to life, and the claim that y is obligated to do whatever is necessary to keep x alive, let alone that he ought to be forced to do so. It is y's duty to keep x alive only if he has somehow contracted a *special* obligation to do so; and a woman who is unwillingly pregnant, e.g., who was raped, has done nothing which obligates her to make the enormous sacrifice which is necessary to preserve the conceptus.

This argument is initially quite plausible, and in the extreme case of pregnancy due to rape is probably conclusive. Difficulties arise, however, when we try to specify more exactly the range of cases in which abortion is clearly justifiable even on the assumption that the fetus is human. Professor Thomson considers it a virtue of her argument that it does not enable us to conclude that abortion is *always* permissible. It would, she says, be "indecent" for a woman in her seventh month to obtain an abortion just to avoid having to postpone a trip to Europe. On the other hand, her argument enables us to see that "a sick and desperately frightened schoolgirl pregnant due to rape may *of course* choose abortion, and that any law which rules this out is an insane law" (p. 65). So far, so good; but what are we to say about the woman who becomes pregnant not through rape but as a result of her own carelessness, or because of contraceptive failure, or who gets pregnant intentionally and then changes her mind about wanting a child? With respect to such cases, the violinist analogy is of much less use to the defender of the woman's right to obtain an abortion.

Indeed, the choice of a pregnancy due to rape, as an example of a case in which abortion is permissible even if a fetus is considered a human being, is extremely significant; for it is only in the case of pregnancy due to rape that the woman's situation is adequately analogous to the violinist case for our intuitions about the latter to transfer convincingly. The crucial difference between a pregnancy due to rape and the *normal* case of an unwanted pregnancy is that in the normal case we cannot claim that the woman is in no way responsible for her predicament; she could have remained chaste, or taken her pills more faithfully, or abstained on dangerous days, and so on. If, on the other hand, you are kidnapped by strangers, and hooked up to a strange violinist, then you are free of any shred of responsibility for the situation, on the basis of which it could be argued that you are obligated to keep the violinist alive. Only when her pregnancy is due to rape is a woman clearly just as nonresponsible.[5]

Consequently, there is room for the anti-abortionist to argue that in the normal case of unwanted pregnancy a woman has, by her own actions, assumed responsibility for the fetus. For if x behaves in a way which he could have avoided, and which he knows involves, let us say, a 1 percent chance of bringing into existence a human being, with a right to life, and does so knowing that if this should happen then that human being will perish unless x does certain things to keep him alive, then it is by no means clear that when it does happen x is free of any obligation to what he knew in advance would be required to keep that human being alive.

The plausibility of such an argument is enough to show that the Thomson analogy can provide a clear and persuasive defense of a woman's right to obtain an abortion only with respect to those cases in which the woman is in no way responsible for her pregnancy, e.g., where it is due to rape. In all other cases, we would almost certainly conclude that it was necessary to look carefully at the particular circumstances in order to determine the extent of the woman's responsibility, and hence the extent of her obligation. This is an extremely unsatisfactory outcome, from the viewpoint of the opponents of restrictive abortion laws, most of whom are convinced that a woman has a right to obtain an abortion regardless of how and why she got pregnant.

Of course a supporter of the violinist analogy might point out that it is absurd to suggest that forgetting her pill one day might be sufficient to obligate a woman to complete an unwanted pregnancy. And indeed it *is* absurd to suggest this. As we will see, the moral right to obtain an abortion is not in the least dependent upon the extent to which the woman is responsible for her pregnancy. But unfortunately, once we allow the assumption that a fetus has full moral rights, we cannot avoid taking this absurd suggestion seriously. Perhaps we can make this point more clear by altering the violinist story just enough to make it more analogous to a normal unwanted pregnancy and less to a pregnancy due to rape, and then seeing whether it is still obvious that you are not obligated to stay in bed with the fellow.

Suppose, then, that violinists are peculiarly prone to the sort of illness the only cure for which is the use of someone else's bloodstream for nine months, and that because of this there has been formed a society of music lovers who agree that whenever a violinist is stricken they will draw lots and the loser will, by some means, be made the one and only person capable of saving him. Now then, would you be obligated to cooperate in curing the violinist if you had voluntarily joined this society, knowing the possible consequences, and then your name had been drawn and you had been kidnapped? Admittedly, you did not promise ahead of time that you would, but you did deliberately place yourself in a position in which it might happen that a human life would be lost if you did not. Surely this is at least a prima facie reason for supposing that you have an obligation to stay in bed with the violinist. Suppose that you had gotten your name drawn deliberately; surely *that* would be quite a strong reason for thinking that you had such an obligation.

It might be suggested that there is one important disanalogy between the modified violinist case and the case of an unwanted pregnancy, which makes the woman's responsibility significantly less, namely, the fact that the fetus *comes into existence* as the result of the woman's actions. This fact might give her a right to refuse to keep it alive, whereas she would not have had this right had it existed previously, independently, and then as a result of her actions become dependent upon her for its survival.

My own intuition, however, is that x has no more right to bring into existence, either deliberately or as a foreseeable result of actions he could have avoided, a being with full moral rights (y), and then refuse to do what he knew beforehand would be required to keep that being alive, than he has to enter into an agreement with an existing person, whereby he may be called upon to save that person's life, and then refuse to do so when so called upon. Thus, x's responsibility for y's existence does not seem to lessen his obligation to keep y alive, if he is also responsible for y's being in a situation in which only he can save him.

Whether or not this intuition is entirely correct, it brings us back once again to the conclusion that once we allow the assumption that a fetus has full moral rights it becomes an extremely complex and difficult question whether and when abortion is justifiable. Thus the Thomson analogy cannot help us produce a clear and persuasive proof of the moral permissibility of abortion. Nor will the opponents of the restrictive laws thank us for anything less; for their conviction (for the most part) is that abortion is obviously *not* a morally serious and extremely unfortunate, even though sometimes justified act, comparable to killing in self-defense or to letting the violinist die, but rather is closer to being a morally neutral act, like cutting one's hair.

The basis of this conviction, I believe, is the realization that a fetus is not a person, and thus does not have a full-fledged right to life. Perhaps the reason why this claim has been so inadequately defended is that it seems self-evident to those who accept it. And so it is, insofar as it follows from what I take to be perfectly obvious claims about the nature of personhood, and about the proper grounds for ascribing moral rights, claims which ought, indeed, to be obvious to both the friends and foes of abortion. Nevertheless, it is worth examining these claims, and showing how they demonstrate the moral innocuousness of abortion, since this apparently has not been adequately done before.

II

The question which we must answer in order to produce a satisfactory solution to the problem of the moral status of abortion is this: How are we to define the moral community, the set of beings with full and equal moral rights, such that we can decide whether a human fetus is a member of this community or not? What sort of entity, exactly, has the inalienable rights to life, liberty, and the pursuit of happiness? Jefferson attributed these rights to all *men,* and it may or may not be fair to suggest that he intended to attribute them *only* to men. Perhaps he ought to have attributed them to all human beings. If so, then we arrive, first, at Noonan's problem of defining what makes a being human, and, second, at the equally vital question which Noonan does not consider, namely, What reason is there for identifying the moral community with the set of all human beings, in whatever way we have chosen to define that term?

1. On the Definition of 'Human'

One reason why this vital second question is so frequently overlooked in the debate over the moral status of abortion is that the term 'human' has two distinct, but not often distinguished, senses. This fact results in a slide of meaning, which serves to conceal the fallaciousness of the traditional argument that since (1) it is wrong to kill innocent human beings, and (2) fetuses are innocent human beings, then (3) it is wrong to kill fetuses. For if 'human' is used in the same sense in both (1) and (2) then, whichever of the two senses is meant, one of these premises is question-begging. And if it is used in two different senses then of course the conclusion doesn't follow.

Thus, (1) is a self-evident moral truth,[6] and avoids begging the question about abortion, only if 'human being' is used to mean something like "a full-fledged member of the moral community." (It may or may not also be meant to refer exclusively to members of the species *Homo sapiens.*) *We may call this the moral* sense of

'human'. It is not to be confused with what we will call the *genetic* sense, i.e., the sense in which *any* member of the species is a human being, and no member of any other species could be. If (1) is acceptable only if the moral sense is intended, (2) is non-question-begging only if what is intended is the genetic sense.

In "Deciding Who is Human," Noonan argues for the classification of fetuses with human beings by pointing to the presence of the full genetic code, and the potential capacity for rational thought (p. 135). It is clear that what he needs to show, for his version of the traditional argument to be valid, is that fetuses are human in the moral sense, the sense in which it is analytically true that all human beings have full moral rights. But, in the absence of any argument showing that whatever is genetically human is also morally human, and he gives none, nothing more than genetic humanity can be demonstrated by the presence of the human genetic code. And, as we will see, the *potential* capacity for rational thought can at most show that an entity has the potential for *becoming* human in the moral sense.

2. Defining the Moral Community

Can it be established that genetic humanity is sufficient for moral humanity? I think that there are very good reasons for not defining the moral community in this way. I would like to suggest an alternative way of defining the moral community, which I will argue for only to the extent of explaining why it is, or should be, self-evident. The suggestion is simply that the moral community consists of all and only *people,* rather than all and only human beings;[7] and probably the best way of demonstrating its self-evidence is by considering the concept of personhood, to see what sorts of entity are and are not persons, and what the decision that a being is or is not a person implies about its moral rights.

What characteristics entitle an entity to be considered a person? This is obviously not the place to attempt a complete analysis of the concept of personhood, but we do not need such a fully adequate analysis just to determine whether and why a fetus is or isn't a person. All we need is a rough and approximate list of the most basic criteria of personhood, and some idea of which, or how many, of these an entity must satisfy in order to properly be considered a person.

In searching for such criteria, it is useful to look beyond the set of people with whom we are acquainted, and ask how we would decide whether a totally alien being was a person or not. (For we have no right to assume that genetic humanity is necessary for personhood.) Imagine a space traveler who lands on an unknown planet and encounters a race of beings utterly unlike any he has ever seen or heard of. It he wants to be sure of behaving morally toward these beings, he has to somehow decide whether they are people, and hence have full moral rights, or whether they are the sort of thing which he need not feel guilty about treating as, for example, a source of food.

How should he go about making this decision? If he has some anthropological background, he might look for such things as religion, art, and the manufacturing of tools, weapons, or shelters, since these factors have been used to distinguish our human from our prehuman ancestors, in what seems to be closer to the moral than the genetic sense of 'human'. And no doubt he would be right to consider the presence of such factors as good evidence that the alien beings were people, and morally human. It would, however, be overly anthropocentric of him to take the absence of these things as adequate evidence that they were not, since we can imagine people who have progressed beyond, or evolved without ever developing, these cultural characteristics.

I suggest that the traits which are most central to the concept of personhood, or humanity in the moral sense, are, very roughly, the following:

1. consciousness (of objects and events external and/or internal to the being), and in particular the capacity to feel pain;
2. reasoning (the *developed* capacity to solve new and relatively complex problems);
3. self-motivated activity (activity which is relatively independent of either genetic or direct external control);
4. the capacity to communicate, by whatever means, messages of an indefinite variety of types, that is, not just with an indefinite number of possible contents, but on indefinitely many possible topics;
5. the presence of self-concepts, and self-awareness, either individual or racial, or both.

Admittedly, there are apt to be a great many problems involved in formulating precise definitions of these criteria, let alone in developing universally valid behavioral criteria for deciding when they apply. But I will assume that both we and our explorer know approximately what (1)–(5) mean, and that he is also able to determine whether or not they apply. How, then, should he use his findings to decide whether or not the alien beings are people? We needn't suppose that an entity must have *all* of these attributes to be properly considered a person; (1) and (2) alone may well be sufficient for personhood, and quite probably (1)–(3) are sufficient. Neither do we need to insist that any one of these criteria is *necessary* for personhood, although once again (1) and (2) look like fairly good candidates for necessary conditions, as does (3), if 'activity' is construed so as to include the activity of reasoning.

All we need to claim, to demonstrate that a fetus is not a person, is that any being which satisfies *none* of (1)–(5) is certainly not a person. I consider this claim to be so obvious that I think anyone who denied it, and claimed that a being which satisfied none of (1)–(5) was a person all the same, would thereby demonstrate that he had no notion at all of what a person is—perhaps because he had confused the concept of a person with that of genetic humanity. If the opponents of abortion were to deny the appropriateness of these five criteria, I do not know what further arguments would convince them. We would probably have to admit that our conceptual schemes were indeed irreconcilably different, and that our dispute could not be settled objectively.

I do not expect this to happen, however, since I think that the concept of a person is one which is very nearly universal (to people), and that it is common to both proabortionists and antiabortionists, even though neither group has fully realized the relevance of this concept to the resolution of their dispute. Furthermore, I think that on reflection even the antiabortionists ought to agree not only that (1)–(5) are central to the concept of personhood, but also that it is a part of this concept that all and only people have full moral rights. The concept of a person is in part a moral concept; once we have admitted that *x* is a person we have recognized, even if we have not agreed to respect, *x*'s right to be treated as a member of the moral community. It is true that the claim that *x* is a *human being* is more commonly voiced as part of an appeal to treat *x* decently than is the claim that *x* is a person, but this is either because 'human being' is here used in the sense which implies personhood, or because the genetic and moral senses of 'human' have been confused.

Now if (1)–(5) are indeed the primary criteria of personhood, then it is clear that genetic humanity is neither necessary nor sufficient for establishing that an entity is a person. Some human beings are not people, and there may well be people who are not human beings. A man or woman whose consciousness has been permanently obliterated but who remains alive is a human being which is no longer a person; defective human beings, with no appreciable mental capacity, are not and presumably never will be people; and a fetus is a human being which is not yet a person, and which therefore cannot coherently be said to have full moral rights. Citizens of the next century should be prepared to recognize highly advanced, self-aware robots or computers, should such be developed, and intelligent inhabitants of other worlds, should such be found, as people in the fullest sense, and to respect their moral rights. But to ascribe full moral rights to an entity which is not a person is as absurd as to ascribe moral obligations and responsibilities to such an entity.

3. Fetal Development and the Right to Life

Two problems arise in the application of these suggestions for the definition of the moral community to the determination of the precise moral status of a human fetus. Given that the paradigm example of a person is a normal adult human being, then (1) How like this paradigm, in particular how far advanced since conception, does a human being need to be before it begins to have a right to life by virtue, not of being fully a person as of yet, but of being *like* a person? and (2) To what extent, if any, does the fact that a fetus has the *potential* for becoming a person endow it with some of the same rights? Each of these questions requires some comment.

In answering the first question, we need not attempt a detailed consideration of the moral rights of organisms which are not developed enough, aware enough, intelligent enough, etc., to be considered people, but which resemble people in some respects. It does seem reasonable to suggest that the more like a person, in the relevant respects, a being is, the stronger is the case for regarding it as having a right to life, and indeed the stronger its right to life is. Thus we ought to take seriously the suggestion that, insofar as "the human individual develops biologically in a continuous fashion . . . the rights of a human person might develop in the same way."[8] But we must keep in mind that the attributes which are relevant in determining whether or not an entity is enough like a person to be regarded as having some of the same moral rights are no different from those which are relevant to determining whether or not it is fully a person—i.e., are no different from (1)–(5)—and that being genetically human, or having recognizably human facial and other physical features, or detectable brain activity, or the capacity to survive outside the uterus, are simply not among these relevant attributes.

Thus it is clear that even though a seven- or eight-month fetus has features which make it apt to arouse in us almost the same powerful protective instinct as is commonly aroused by a small infant, nevertheless it is not significantly more personlike than is a very small embryo. It is *somewhat* more personlike; it can apparently feel and respond to pain, and it may even have a rudimentary form of consciousness, insofar as its brain is quite active. Nevertheless, it seems safe to say that it is not fully conscious, in the way that an infant of a few months is, and that it cannot reason, or communicate messages of indefinitely many sorts, does not engage in self-motivated activity, and has no self-awareness. Thus, in the *relevant* respects, a fetus, even a fully developed one, is considerably less personlike than is the average mature mammal, indeed the average fish. And I think that a rational person must conclude that if the right to life of a fetus is to be based upon its resemblance to a person, then it cannot be said to have any more right to life than, let us say, a newborn guppy (which also seems to be capable of feeling pain), and that a right of that magnitude could never override a woman's right to obtain an abortion, at any stage of her pregnancy.

There may, of course, be other arguments in favor of placing legal limits upon the stage of pregnancy in which an abortion may be performed. Given the relative safety of the new techniques of artificially inducing labor during the third trimester, the danger to the woman's life or health is no longer such an argument. Neither is the fact that people tend to respond to the thought of abortion in the later stages of pregnancy with emotional repulsion, since mere emotional responses cannot take the place of moral reasoning in determining what ought to be permitted. Nor, finally, is the frequently heard argument that legalizing abortion, especially late in the pregnancy, may erode the level of respect for human life, leading, perhaps, to an increase in unjustified euthanasia and other crimes. For this threat, if it is a threat, can be better met by educating people to the kinds of moral distinctions which we are making here than by limiting access to abortion (which limitation may, in its disregard for the rights of women, be just as damaging to the level of respect for human rights).

Thus, since the fact that even a fully developed fetus is not personlike enough to have any significant right to life on the basis of its personlikeness shows that no legal restrictions upon the stage of pregnancy in which an abortion may be performed can be justified on the grounds that we should protect the rights of the older fetus; and since there is no other apparent justification for such restrictions, we may conclude that they are entirely un-

justified. Whether or not it would be *indecent* (whatever that means) for a woman in her seventh month to obtain an abortion just to avoid having to postpone a trip to Europe, it would not, in itself, be *immoral,* and therefore it ought to be permitted.

4. Potential Personhood and the Right to Life

We have seen that a fetus does not resemble a person in any way which can support the claim that it has even some of the same rights. But what about its *potential*, the fact that if nurtured and allowed to develop naturally it will very probably become a person? Doesn't that alone give it at least some right to life? It is hard to deny that the fact that an entity is a potential person is a strong prima facie reason for not destroying it; but we need not conclude from this that a potential person has a right to life, by virtue of that potential. It may be that our feeling that it is better, other things being equal, not to destroy a potential person is better explained by the fact that potential people are still (felt to be) an invaluable resource, not to be lightly squandered. Surely, if every speck of dust were a potential person, we would be much less apt to conclude that every potential person has a right to become actual.

Still, we do not need to insist that a potential person has no right to life whatever. There may well be something immoral, and not just imprudent, about wantonly destroying potential people, when doing so isn't necessary to protect anyone's rights. But even if a potential person does have some prima facie right to life, such a right could not possibly outweigh the right of a woman to obtain an abortion, since the rights of any actual person invariably outweigh those of any potential person, whenever the two conflict. Since this may not be immediately obvious in the case of a human fetus, let us look at another case.

Suppose that our space explorer falls into the hands of an alien culture, whose scientists decide to create a few hundred thousand or more human beings, by breaking his body into its component cells, and using these to create fully developed human beings, with, of course, his genetic code. We may imagine that each of these newly created men will have all of the original man's abilities, skills, knowledge, and so on, and also have an individual self-concept, in short that each of them will be a bona fide (though hardly unique) person. Imagine that the whole project will take only seconds, and that its chances of success are extremely high, and that our explorer knows all of this, and also knows that these people will be treated fairly. I maintain that in such a situation he would have every right to escape if he could, and thus to deprive all of these potential people of their potential lives; for his right to life outweighs all of theirs together, in spite of the fact that they are all genetically human, all innocent, and all have a very high probability of becoming people very soon, if only he refrains from acting.

Indeed, I think he would have a right to escape even if it were not his life which the alien scientists planned to take, but only a year of his freedom, or, indeed, only a day. Nor would he be obligated to stay if he had gotten captured (thus bringing all these people-potentials into existence) because of his own carelessness, or even if he had done so deliberately, knowing the consequences. Regardless of how he got captured, he is not morally obligated to remain in captivity for *any* period of time for the sake of permitting any number of potential people to come into actuality, so great is the margin by which one actual person's right to liberty outweighs whatever right to life even a hundred thousand potential people have. And it seems reasonable to conclude that the rights of a woman will outweigh by a similar margin whatever right to life a fetus may have by virtue of its potential personhood.

Thus, neither a fetus's resemblance to a person, nor its potential for becoming a person provides any basis whatever for the claim that it has any significant right to life. Consequently, a woman's right to protect her health, happiness, freedom, and even her life,[9] by terminating an unwanted pregnancy, will always override whatever right to life it may be appropriate to ascribe to a fetus, even a fully developed one. And thus, in the absence of any overwhelming social need for every

possible child, the laws which restrict the right to obtain an abortion, or limit the period of pregnancy during which an abortion may be performed, are a wholly unjustified violation of a woman's most basic moral and constitutional rights.[10] . . .

Postscript on Infanticide

Since the publication of this article, many people have written to point out that my argument appears to justify not only abortion, but infanticide as well. For a new-born infant is not significantly more person-like than an advanced fetus, and consequently it would seem that if the destruction of the latter is permissible so too must be that of the former. Inasmuch as most people, regardless of how they feel about the morality of abortion, consider infanticide a form of murder, this might appear to represent a serious flaw in my argument.

Now, if I am right in holding that it is only people who have a full-fledged right to life, and who can be murdered, and if the criteria of personhood are as I have described them, then it obviously follows that killing a new-born infant isn't murder. It does *not* follow, however, that infanticide is permissible, for two reasons. In the first place, it would be wrong, at least in this country and in this period of history, and other things being equal, to kill a new-born infant, because even if its parents do not want it and would not suffer from its destruction, there are other people who would like to have it, and would, in all probability, be deprived of a great deal of pleasure by its destruction. Thus, infanticide is wrong for reasons analogous to those which make it wrong to wantonly destroy natural resources, or great works of art.

Secondly, most people, at least in this country, value infants and would much prefer that they be preserved, even if foster parents are not immediately available. Most of us would rather be taxed to support orphanages than allow unwanted infants to be destroyed. So long as there are people who want an infant preserved, and who are willing and able to provide the means of caring for it, under reasonably humane conditions, it is, *ceteris parabis*, wrong to destroy it.

But, it might be replied, if this argument shows that infanticide is wrong, at least at this time and in this country, doesn't it also show that abortion is wrong? After all, many people value fetuses, are disturbed by their destruction, and would much prefer that they be preserved, even at some cost to themselves. Furthermore, as a potential source of pleasure to some foster family, a fetus is just as valuable as an infant. There is, however, a crucial difference between the two cases: so long as the fetus is unborn, its preservation, contrary to the wishes of the pregnant woman, violates her rights to freedom, happiness, and self-determination. Her rights override the rights of those who would like the fetus preserved, just as if someone's life or limb is threatened by a wild animal, his right to protect himself by destroying the animal overrides the rights of those who would prefer that the animal not be harmed.

The minute the infant is born, however, its preservation no longer violates any of its mother's rights, even if she wants it destroyed, because she is free to put it up for adoption. Consequently, while the moment of birth does not mark any sharp discontinuity in the degree to which an infant possesses the right to life, it does mark the end of its mother's right to determine its fate. Indeed, if abortion could be performed without killing the fetus, she would never possess the right to have the fetus destroyed, for the same reasons that she has no right to have an infant destroyed.

On the other hand, it follows from my argument that when an unwanted or defective infant is born into a society which cannot afford and/or is not willing to care for it, then its destruction is permissible. This conclusion will, no doubt, strike many people as heartless and immoral; but remember that the very existence of people who feel this way, and who are willing and able to provide care for unwanted infants, is reason enough to conclude that they should be preserved.

Notes

1. For example, Roger Wertheimer, who in "Understanding the Abortion Argument" (*Philosophy and Public Affairs*, 1, No. 1 [Fall, 1971], 67–95), argues that the problem of the moral status of abortion is insoluble, in that the dispute over the status of the fetus is not a question of fact at all, but only a question of how one responds to the facts.

2. John Noonan, "Abortion and the Catholic Church: A Summary History," *Natural Law Forum*, 12 (1967), 125.

3. John Noonan, "Deciding Who Is Human," *Natural Law Forum*, 13 (1968), 134.

4. "A Defense of Abortion."

5. We may safely ignore the fact that she might have avoided getting raped, e.g., by carrying a gun, since by similar means you might likewise have avoided getting kidnapped, and in neither case does the victim's failure to take all possible precautions against a highly unlikely event (as opposed to reasonable precautions against a rather likely event) mean that he is morally responsible for what happens.

6. Of course, the principle that it is (always) wrong to kill innocent human beings is in need of many other modifications, e.g., that it may be permissible to do so to save a greater number of other innocent human beings, but we may safely ignore these complications here.

7. From here on, we will use 'human' to mean genetically human, since the moral sense seems closely connected to, and perhaps derived from, the assumption that genetic humanity is sufficient for membership in the moral community.

8. Thomas L. Hayes, "A Biological View," *Commonweal*, 85 (March 17, 1967), 677–78; quoted by Daniel Callahan, in *Abortion, Law, Choice, and Morality* (London: Macmillan & Co., 1970).

9. That is, insofar as the death rate, for the woman, is higher for childbirth than for early abortion.

10. My thanks to the following people, who were kind enough to read and criticize an earlier version of this paper: Herbert Gold, Gene Glass, Anne Lauterbach, Judith Thomson, Mary Mothersill, and Timothy Binkley.

Abortion and the Concept of a Person

Jane English

According to Jane English, our concept of a person is not sharp or decisive enough to bear the weight of a solution to the abortion controversy. However, she argues that even if the fetus is a full-fledged person, there are still cases in which abortion would be justified to prevent harm or death to the pregnant woman. Similarly, English argues that even if the fetus is not a person, there are still cases, at least in the late months of pregnancy, in which abortion would not be justified because of the fetus's resemblance to a person.

The abortion debate rages on. Yet the two most popular positions seem to be clearly mistaken. Conservatives maintain that a human life begins at conception and that therefore abortion must be wrong because it is murder. But not all killings of humans are murders. Most notably, self defense may justify even the killing of an innocent person.

Liberals, on the other hand, are just as mistaken in their argument that since a fetus does not become a person until birth, a woman may do whatever she pleases in and to her own body. First, you cannot do as you please with your own body if it affects other people adversely.[1] Second, if a fetus is not a person, that does not imply that you can do to it anything you wish. Animals, for example, are not persons, yet to kill or torture them for no reason at all is wrong.

At the center of the storm has been the issue of just when it is between ovulation and adulthood that a person appears on the scene. Conservatives draw the line at conception, liberals at birth. In this paper I first examine our concept of a person and conclude that no single criterion can capture the concept of a person and no sharp line can be drawn. Next I argue that if a fetus is a person, abortion is still justifiable in many cases; and if a fetus is not a person, killing it is still wrong in many cases. To a large extent, these two solutions are in agreement. I conclude that our concept of a person cannot and need not bear the weight

From the *Canadian Journal of Philosophy* 5, no. 2 (October 1975), pp. 233–243. Reprinted with permission of the publisher.

that the abortion controversy has thrust upon it.

I

The several factions in the abortion argument have drawn battle lines around various proposed criteria for determining what is and what is not a person. For example, Mary Anne Warren[2] lists five features (capacities for reasoning, self-awareness, complex communication, etc.) as her criteria for personhood and argues for the permissibility of abortion because a fetus falls outside this concept. Baruch Brody[3] uses brain waves. Michael Tooley[4] picks having-a-concept-of-self as his criterion and concludes that infanticide and abortion are justifiable, while the killing of adult animals is not. On the other side, Paul Ramsey[5] claims a certain gene structure is the defining characteristic. John Noonan[6] prefers conceived-of-humans and presents counterexamples to various other candidate criteria. For instance, he argues against viability as the criterion because the newborn and infirm would then be non-persons, since they cannot live without the aid of others. He rejects any criterion that calls upon the sorts of sentiments a being can evoke in adults on the grounds that this would allow us to exclude other races as non-persons if we could just view them sufficiently unsentimentally.

These approaches are typical: foes of abortion propose sufficient conditions for personhood which fetuses satisfy, while friends of abortion counter with necessary conditions for personhood which fetuses lack. But these both presuppose that the concept of a person can be captured in a strait jacket of necessary and/or sufficient conditions.[7] Rather, "person" is a cluster of features, of which rationality, having a self concept and being conceived of humans are only part.

What is typical of persons? Within our concept of a person we include, first, certain biological factors: descended from humans, having a certain genetic makeup, having a head, hands, arms, eyes, capable of locomotion, breathing, eating, sleeping. There are psychological factors: sentience, perception, having a concept of self and of one's own interests and desires, the ability to use tools, the ability to use language or symbol systems, the ability to joke, to be angry, to doubt. There are rationality factors: the ability to reason and draw conclusions, the ability to generalize and to learn from past experience, the ability to sacrifice present interests for greater gains in the future. There are social factors: the ability to work in groups and respond to peer pressures, the ability to recognize and consider as valuable the interests of others, seeing oneself as one among "other minds," the ability to sympathize, encourage, love, the ability to evoke from others the responses of sympathy, encouragement, love, the ability to work with others for mutual advantage. Then there are legal factors: being subject to the law and protected by it, having the ability to sue and enter contracts, being counted in the census, having a name and citizenship, the ability to own property, inherit, and so forth.

Now the point is not that this list is incomplete, or that you can find counterinstances to each of its points. People typically exhibit rationality, for instance, but someone who was irrational would not thereby fail to qualify as a person. On the other hand, something could exhibit the majority of these features and still fail to be a person, as an advanced robot might. There is no single core of necessary and sufficient features which we can draw upon with the assurance that they constitute what really makes a person; there are only features that are more or less typical.

This is not to say that no necessary or suf-ficient conditions can be given. Being alive is a necessary condition for being a person, and being a U.S. Senator is sufficient. But rather than falling inside a sufficient condition or outside a necessary one, a fetus lies in the penumbra region where our concept of a person is not so simple. For this reason I think a conclusive answer to the question whether a fetus is a person is unattainable.

Here we might note a family of simple fallacies that proceed by stating a necessary condition for personhood and showing that a fetus has that characteristic. This is a form of the fallacy of affirming the consequent. For example, some have mistakenly reasoned from the premise that a fetus is human (after all, it is a human fetus rather than, say, a canine fetus), to the conclusion that it is *a* human. Adding an equivocation on "being," we get the fallacious argument that since a fetus is something both living and human, it is a human being.

Nonetheless, it does seem clear that a fetus has very few of the above family of characteristics, whereas a newborn baby exhibits a much larger proportion of them—and a two-year-old has even more. Note that one traditional anti-abortion argument has centered on pointing out the many ways in which a fetus resembles a baby. They emphasize its development ("It already has ten fingers. . . .") without mentioning its dissimilarities to adults (it still has gills and a tail). They also try to evoke the sort of sympathy on our part that we only feel toward other persons ("Never to laugh . . . or feel the sunshine?"). This all seems to be a relevant way to argue, since its purpose is to persuade us that a fetus satisfies so many of the important features on the list that it ought to be treated as a person. Also note that a fetus near the time of birth satisfies many more of these factors than a fetus in the early months of development. This could provide reason for making distinctions among the different stages of pregnancy, as the U.S. Supreme Court has done.[8]

Historically, the time at which a person has been said to come into existence has varied widely. Muslims date personhood from fourteen days after conception. Some medievals followed Aristotle in placing ensoulment at forty days after conception for a male fetus and eighty days for a female fetus.[9] In European common law since the Seventeenth Century, abortion was considered the killing of a person only after quickening, the time when a pregnant woman first feels the fetus move on its own. Nor is this variety of opinions surprising. Biologically, a human being develops gradually. We shouldn't expect there to be any specific time or sharp dividing point when a person appears on the scene.

For these reasons I believe our concept of a person is not sharp or decisive enough to bear the weight of a solution to the abortion controversy. To use it to solve that problem is to clarify *obscurum per obscurius*.

II

Next let us consider what follows if a fetus is a person after all. Judith Jarvis Thomson's landmark article, "A Defense of Abortion,"[10] correctly points out that some additional argumentation is needed at this point in the conservative argument to bridge the gap between the premise that a fetus is an innocent person and the conclusion that killing it is always wrong. To arrive at this conclusion, we would need the additional premise that killing an innocent person is always wrong. But killing an innocent person is sometimes permissible, most notably in self defense. Some examples may help draw out our intuitions or ordinary judgments about self defense.

Suppose a mad scientist, for instance, hypnotized innocent people to jump out of the bushes and attack innocent passers-by with knives. If you are so attacked, we agree you have a right to kill the attacker in self defense, if killing him is the only way to protect your life or to save yourself from serious injury. It does not seem to matter here that the attacker is not malicious but himself an innocent pawn, for your killing of him is not done in a spirit of retribution but only in self defense.

How severe an injury may you inflict in self defense? In part this depends upon the severity of the injury to be avoided: you may not shoot someone merely to avoid having your clothes torn. This might lead one to the mis-

taken conclusion that the defense may only equal the threatened injury in severity; that to avoid death you may kill, but to avoid a black eye you may only inflict a black eye or the equivalent. Rather, our laws and customs seem to say that you may create an injury somewhat, but not enormously, greater than the injury to be avoided. To fend off an attack whose outcome would be as serious as rape, a severe beating or the loss of a finger, you may shoot; to avoid having your clothes torn, you may blacken an eye.

Aside from this, the injury you may inflict should only be the minimum necessary to deter or incapacitate the attacker. Even if you know he intends to kill you, you are not justified in shooting him if you could equally well save yourself by the simple expedient of running away. Self defense is for the purpose of avoiding harms rather than equalizing harms.

Some cases of pregnancy present a parallel situation. Though the fetus is itself innocent, it may pose a threat to the pregnant woman's well-being, life prospects or health, mental or physical. If the pregnancy presents a slight threat to her interests, it seems self defense cannot justify abortion. But if the threat is on a par with a serious beating or the loss of a finger, she may kill the fetus that poses such a threat, even if it is an innocent person. If a lesser harm to the fetus could have the same defensive effect, killing it would not be justified. It is unfortunate that the only way to free the woman from the pregnancy entails the death of the fetus (except in very late stages of pregnancy). Thus a self defense model supports Thomson's point that the woman has a right only to be freed from the fetus, not a right to demand its death.[11]

The self defense model is most helpful when we take the pregnant woman's point of view. In the pre-Thomson literature, abortion is often framed as a question for a third party: do you, a doctor, have a right to choose between the life of the woman and that of the fetus? Some have claimed that if you were a passer-by who witnessed a struggle between the innocent hypnotized attacker and his equally innocent victim, you would have no reason to kill either in defense of the other. They have concluded that the self defense model implies that a woman may attempt to abort herself, but that a doctor should not assist her. I think the position of the third party is somewhat more complex. We do feel some inclination to intervene on behalf of the victim rather than the attacker, other things equal. But if both parties are innocent, other factors come into consideration. You would rush to the aid of your husband whether he was attacker or attackee. If a hypnotized famous violinist were attacking a skid row bum, we would try to save the individual who is of more value to society. These considerations would tend to support abortion in some cases.

But suppose you are a frail senior citizen who wishes to avoid being knifed by one of these innocent hypnotics, so you have hired a bodyguard to accompany you. If you are attacked, it is clear we believe that the bodyguard, acting as your agent, has a right to kill the attacker to save you from a serious beating. Your rights of self defense are transferred to your agent. I suggest that we should similarly view the doctor as the pregnant woman's agent in carrying out a defense she is physically incapable of accomplishing herself.

Thanks to modern technology, the cases are rare in which pregnancy poses as clear a threat to a woman's bodily health as an attacker brandishing a switchblade. How does self defense fare when more subtle, complex and long-range harms are involved?

To consider a somewhat fanciful example, suppose you are a highly trained surgeon when you are kidnapped by the hypnotic attacker. He says he does not intend to harm you but to take you back to the mad scientist who, it turns out, plans to hypnotize you to have a permanent mental block against all your knowledge of medicine. This would automatically destroy your career which would in turn have a serious adverse impact on your family, your personal relationships and your happiness. It seems to me that if the only way you can avoid this outcome is to shoot the innocent attacker, you are justified in so doing. You are defending yourself from a drastic injury to your life prospects. I think it is no exaggeration to claim that unwanted pregnancies (most obviously among teenagers) often have such adverse life-long consequences as the surgeon's loss of livelihood.

Several parallels arise between various views on abortion and the self defense model. Let's suppose further that these hypnotized attackers only operate at night, so that it is well known that they can be avoided completely by the considerable inconvenience of never leaving your house after dark. One view is that since you could stay home at night, therefore if you go out and are selected by one of these hypnotized people, you have no right to defend yourself. This parallels the view that abstinence is the only acceptable way to avoid pregnancy. Others might hold that you ought to take along some defense such as Mace which will deter the hypnotized person without killing him, but that if this defense fails, you are obliged to submit to the resulting injury, no matter how severe it is. This parallels the view that contraception is all right but abortion is always wrong, even in cases of contraceptive failure.

A third view is that you may kill the hypnotized person only if he will actually kill you, but not if he will only injure you. This is like the position that abortion is permissible only if it is required to save a woman's life. Finally we have the view that it is all right to kill the attacker, even if only to avoid a very slight inconvenience to yourself and even if you knowingly walked down the very street where all these incidents have been taking place without taking along any Mace or protective escort. If we assume that a fetus is a person, this is the analogue of the view that abortion is always justifiable, "on demand."

The self defense model allows us to see an important difference that exists between abortion and infanticide, even if a fetus is a person from conception. Many have argued that the only way to justify abortion without justifying infanticide would be to find some characteristic of personhood that is acquired at birth. Michael Tooley, for one, claims infanticide is justifiable because the really significant characteristics of person are acquired some time after birth. But all such approaches look to characteristics of the developing human and ignore the relation between the fetus and the woman. What if, after birth, the presence of an infant or the need to support it posed a grave threat to the woman's sanity or life prospects? She could escape this threat by the simple expedient of running away. So a solution that does not entail the death of the infant is available. Before birth, such solutions are not available because of the biological dependence of the fetus on the woman. Birth is the crucial point not because of any characteristics the fetus gains, but because after birth the woman can defend herself by a means less drastic than killing the infant. Hence self defense can be used to justify abortion without necessarily thereby justifying infanticide.

III

On the other hand, supposing a fetus is not after all a person, would abortion always be morally permissible? Some opponents of abortion seem worried that if a fetus is not a full-fledged person, then we are justified in treating it in any way at all. However, this does not follow. Non-persons do get some consideration in our moral code, though of course they do not have the same rights as persons have (and in general they do not have moral responsibilities), and though their interests may be overridden by the interests of persons. Still, we cannot just treat them in any way at all.

Treatment of animals is a case in point. It is wrong to torture dogs for fun or to kill wild birds for no reason at all. It is wrong Period, even though dogs and birds do not have the same rights persons do. However, few people think it is wrong to use dogs as experimental animals, causing them considerable suffering in some cases, provided that the resulting research will probably bring discoveries of great benefit to people. And most of us think it all right to kill birds for food or to protect our crops. People's rights are different from the consideration we give to animals, then, for it is wrong to experiment on people, even if others might later benefit a great deal as a result of their suffering. You might volunteer to be a subject, but this would be supererogatory; you certainly have a right to refuse to be a medical guinea pig.

But how do we decide what you may or may not do to non-persons? This is a difficult problem, one for which I believe no adequate

account exists. You do not want to say, for instance, that torturing dogs is all right whenever the sum of its effects on people is good—when it doesn't warp the sensibilities of the torturer so much that he mistreats people. If that were the case, it would be all right to torture dogs if you did it in private, or if the torturer lived on a desert island or died soon afterward, so that his actions had no effect on people. This is an inadequate account, because whatever moral consideration animals get, it has to be indefeasible, too. It will have to be a general proscription of certain actions, not merely a weighing of the impact on people on a case-by-case basis.

Rather, we need to distinguish two levels on which consequences of actions can be taken into account in moral reasoning. The traditional objections to Utilitarianism focus on the fact that it operates solely on the first level, taking all the consequences into account in particular cases only. Thus Utilitarianism is open to "desert island" and "lifeboat" counterexamples because these cases are rigged to make the consequences of actions severely limited.

Rawls' theory could be described as a teleological sort of theory, but with teleology operating on a higher level.[12] In choosing the principles to regulate society from the original position, his hypothetical choosers make their decision on the basis of the total consequences of various systems. Furthermore, they are constrained to choose a general set of rules which people can readily learn and apply. An ethical theory must operate by generating a set of sympathies and attitudes toward others which reinforces the functioning of that set of moral principles. Our prohibition against killing people operates by means of certain moral sentiments including sympathy, compassion and guilt. But if these attitudes are to form a coherent set, they carry us further: we tend to perform supererogatory actions, and we tend to feel similar compassion toward person-like non-persons.

It is crucial that psychological facts play a role here. Our psychological constitution makes it the case that for our ethical theory to work, it must prohibit certain treatment of non-persons which are significantly person-like. If our moral rules allowed people to treat some person-like non-persons in ways we do not want people to be treated, this would undermine the system of sympathies and attitudes that makes the ethical system work. For this reason, we would choose in the original position to make mistreatment of some sorts of animals wrong in general (not just wrong in the cases with public impact), even though animals are not themselves parties in the original position. Thus it makes sense that it is those animals whose appearance and behavior are most like those of people that get the most consideration in our moral scheme.

It is because of "coherence of attitudes," I think, that the similarity of a fetus to a baby is very significant. A fetus one week before birth is so much like a newborn baby in our psychological space that we cannot allow any cavalier treatment of the former while expecting full sympathy and nurturative support for the latter. Thus, I think that anti-abortion forces are indeed giving their strongest arguments when they point to the similarities between a fetus and a baby, and when they try to evoke our emotional attachment to and sympathy for the fetus. An early horror story from New York about nurses who were expected to alternate between caring for six-week premature infants and disposing of viable 24-week aborted fetuses is just that—a horror story. These beings are so much alike that no one can be asked to draw a distinction and treat them so very differently.

Remember, however, that in the early weeks after conception, a fetus is very much unlike a person. It is hard to develop these feelings for a set of genes which doesn't yet have a head, hands, beating heart, response to touch or the ability to move by itself. Thus it seems to me that the alleged "slippery slope" between conception and birth is not so very slippery. In the early stages of pregnancy, abortion can hardly be compared to murder for psychological reasons, but in the latest stages it is psychologically akin to murder.

Another source of similarity is the bodily continuity between fetus and adult. Bodies play a surprisingly central role in our attitudes toward persons. One has only to think of the philosophical literature on how far physical identity suffices for personal identity or Wittgenstein's remark that the best picture of the human soul is the human body. Even after death, when all agree the body is no longer a person, we still observe elaborate customs of respect for the human body; like people who torture dogs, necrophiliacs are not to be trusted with people.[13] So it is appropriate that we show respect to a fetus as the body continuous with the body of a person. This is a degree of resemblance to persons that animals cannot rival.

Michael Tooley also utilizes a parallel with animals. He claims that it is always permissible to drown newborn kittens and draws conclusions about infanticide.[14] But it is only permissible to drown kittens when their survival would cause some hardship. Perhaps it would be a burden to feed and house six more cats or to find other homes for them. The alternative of letting them starve produces even more suffering than the drowning. Since the kittens get their rights second-hand, so to speak, via the need for coherence in our attitudes, their interests are often overridden by the interests of fullfledged persons. But if their survival would be no inconvenience to people at all, then it is wrong to drown them, contra Tooley.

Tooley's conclusions about abortion are wrong for the same reason. Even if a fetus is not a person, abortion is not always permissible, because of the resemblance of a fetus to a person. I agree with Thomson that it would be wrong for a woman who is seven months pregnant to have an abortion just to avoid having to postpone a trip to Europe. In the early months of pregnancy when the fetus hardly resembles a baby at all, then, abortion is permissible whenever it is in the interests of the pregnant woman or her family. The reasons would only need to outweigh the pain and inconvenience of the abortion itself. In the middle months, when the fetus comes to resemble a person, abortion would be justifiable only when the continuation of the pregnancy or the birth of the child would cause harms— physical, psychological, economic or social—to the woman. In the late months of pregnancy, even on our current assumption that a fetus is not a person, abortion seems to be wrong except to save a woman from significant injury or death.

The Supreme Court has recognized similar gradations in the alleged slippery slope stretching between conception and birth. To this point, the present paper has been a discussion of the moral status of abortion only, not its legal status. In view of the great physical, financial and sometimes psychological costs of abortion, perhaps the legal arrangement most compatible with the proposed moral solution would be the absence of restrictions, that is, so-called abortion "on demand."

So I conclude, first, that application of our concept of a person will not suffice to settle the abortion issue. After all, the biological development of a human being is gradual. Second, whether a fetus is a person or not, abortion is justifiable early in pregnancy to avoid modest harms and seldom justifiable late in pregnancy except to avoid significant injury or death.[15]

Notes

1. We also have paternalistic laws which keep us from harming our own bodies even when no one else is affected. Ironically, antiabortion laws were originally designed to protect pregnant women from a dangerous but tempting procedure.

2. Mary Anne Warren, "On the Moral and Legal Status of Abortion," *Monist* 57 (1973), p. 55.

3. Baruch Brody, "Fetal Humanity and the Theory of Essentialism," in Robert Baker and Frederick Elliston, eds., *Philosophy and Sex* (Buffalo, N.Y., 1975).

4. Michael Tooley, "Abortion and Infanticide," *Philosophy and Public Affairs* 2 (1971).

5. Paul Ramsey, "The Morality of Abortion," in James Rachels, ed., *Moral Problems* (New York, 1971).

6. John Noonan, "Abortion and the Catholic Church: A Summary History," *Natural Law Forum* 12 (1967), pp. 125–131.

7. Wittgenstein has argued against the possibility of so capturing the concept of a game. *Philosophical Investigations* (New York, 1958), §66–71.

8. Not because the fetus is partly a person and so has some of the rights of persons, but rather because of the rights of person-like non-persons. This I discuss in part III below.

9. Aristotle himself was concerned, however, with the different question of when the soul takes form. For historical data, see Jimmye Kimmey, "How the Abortion Laws Happened," *Ms.* I (April, 1973), pp. 48ff, and John Noonan, *loc. cit.*

10. J. J. Thomson, "A Defense of Abortion," *Philosophy and Public Affairs* 1 (1971).

11. *Ibid.*, p. 52.

12. John Rawls, *A Theory of Justice* (Cambridge, Mass., 1971), §3–4.

13. On the other hand, if they can be trusted with people, then our moral customs are mistaken. It all depends on the facts of psychology.

14. *Op. cit.*, pp. 40, 60–61.

15. I am deeply indebted to Larry Crocker and Arthur Kuflik for their constructive comments.

Abortion, Distant Peoples, and Future Generations

James P. Sterba

This article argues that, with or without the assumption that the fetus is a person, liberals on the abortion issue who are also committed to the welfare rights of distant peoples and future generations cannot consistently endorse abortion on demand. For if we assume, on the one hand, that the fetus is a person, then a distinction between what a person can demand as a right and what is required by moral decency cannot be used to justify abortion on demand by liberals who support the welfare rights of distant peoples. The same holds true for a restricted interpretation of a right to life. If we assume, on the other hand, that the fetus is not a person and hold that we have an obligation not to bring into existence persons who would lack a reasonable opportunity to lead a good life, liberals who support the welfare rights of future generations would in consistency be committed to endorsing an obligation to bring into existence persons who would have a reasonable opportunity to lead a good life. According to this article this obligation would severely limit the use of both abortion and contraception.

Those who favor a liberal view on abortion and thus tend to support abortion on demand are just as likely to support the rights of distant peoples to basic economic assistance and the rights of future generations to a fair share of the world's resources.[1] Yet, as I shall argue, many of the arguments offered in support of abortion on demand by those who favor a liberal view on abortion are actually inconsistent with a workable defense of these other social goals. If I am right, many of those who favor a liberal view on abortion (whom I shall henceforth refer to as "liberals") will have to make an unwelcome choice: either moderate their support for abortion or moderate their commitment to the rights of distant peoples and future generations. I shall argue that the most promising way for liberals to make this choice is to moderate their support for abortion. . . .

The Welfare Rights of Distant Peoples

Of the various moral grounds for justifying the welfare rights of distant peoples, quite

From "Abortion, Distant Peoples, and Future Generations," *The Journal of Philosophy* (1980), pp. 424–440. Reprinted by permission of *The Journal of Philosophy*.

possibly the most evident are those which appeal either to a right to life or a right to fair treatment.[2] Indeed, whether one interprets a person's right to life as a negative right (as libertarians tend to do) or as a positive right (as welfare liberals tend to do), it is possible to show that the right justifies welfare rights that would amply provide for a person's basic needs.[3] Alternatively, it is possible to justify those same welfare rights on the basis of a person's positive right to fair treatment. In what follows, however, I do not propose to work out these moral justifications for the welfare rights of distant peoples.[4] Rather I wish to show that if one affirms welfare rights of distant peoples, as liberals tend to do, then there are certain arguments for abortion that one in consistency should reject. These arguments for abortion all begin with the assumption that the fetus is a person and then attempt to show that abortion can still be justified in many cases.

Distant Peoples and Abortion

One such argument is based on a distinction between what a person can demand as a right and what is required by moral decency. Abortion, it is said, may offend against the requirements of moral decency, but it rarely, if ever, violates anyone's rights. Judith Jarvis Thomson[5] illustrates this view as follows:

. . . even supposing a case in which a woman pregnant due to rape ought to allow the unborn person to use her body for the hour he needs, we should not conclude that he has a right to do so; we should conclude that she is self-centered, callous, indecent, but not unjust if she refuses (132–133).

In Thomson's example, the sacrifice the pregnant woman would have to make to save the innocent fetus-person's life is certainly quite minimal.[6] Yet Thomson and other defenders of abortion contend that this minimal sacrifice is simply a requirement of moral decency and that neither justice nor the rights of the fetus-person requires the woman to contribute the use of her womb even for one hour! But if such a minimal life-sustaining sacrifice is required neither by justice nor by the rights of the fetus-person, then how could one maintain that distant peoples have a right to have their basic needs satisfied? Obviously to satisfy the basic needs of distant peoples would require a considerable sacrifice from many people in the technologically developed nations of the world. Taken individually, such sacrifices would be far greater than the sacrifice of Thomson's pregnant woman. Consequently, if the sacrifice of Thomson's pregnant woman is merely a requirement of moral decency, then the far greater sacrifices necessary to meet the basic needs of distant peoples, if required at all, could only be requirements of moral decency. Thus liberals who want to support the welfare rights of distant peoples would in consistency have to reject this first argument for abortion.

Another argument for abortion that is also inconsistent with the welfare rights of distant peoples grants that the fetus-person has a right to life and then attempts to show that her right to life often does not entitle her to the means of survival. Thomson again illustrates this view:

If I am sick unto death, and the only thing that will save my life is the touch of Henry Fonda's cool hand on my fevered brow, then all the same, I have no right to be given the touch of Henry Fonda's cool hand on my fevered brow. It would be frightfully nice of him to fly in from the West Coast to provide it. It would be less nice, though no doubt well meant, if my friends flew out to the West Coast and carried Henry Fonda back with them. But I have no right at all against anybody that he should do this for me (129–130).

According to Thomson, what a person's right to life explicitly entitles her to is not the right to receive or acquire the means of survival, but only the right not to be killed or let die unjustly.

To understand what this right not to be killed or let die unjustly amounts to, consider the following example:

Tom, Dick, and Gertrude are adrift on a lifeboat. Dick managed to bring aboard provisions that are just sufficient for his own survival. Gertrude managed to do the same. But Tom brought no provisions at all. So Gertrude, who is by far the strongest, is faced with a choice. She can either kill Dick to provide Tom with the provisions he needs or she can refrain from killing Dick, thus letting Tom die.

Now, as Thomson understands the right not to be killed or let die unjustly, Gertrude's killing Dick would be unjust, but her letting Tom die would not be unjust because Dick has a greater right to his life and provisions than either Tom or Gertrude.[7] Thus killing or letting die unjustly always involves depriving a person of something to which she has a greater right—typically either her functioning body or property the person has which she needs to maintain her life. Consequently, a person's right to life would entitle her to her functioning body and whatever property she has which she needs to maintain her life.

Yet Thomson's view allows that some persons may not have property rights to goods that are necessary to meet their own basic needs whereas others may have property rights to more than enough goods to meet their own basic needs. It follows that if persons with property rights to surplus goods choose not to share their surplus with anyone else, then, according to Thomson's account, they would still not be violating anyone's right to life. For although, by their decision not to share, they would be killing or letting die those who lack the means of survival, they would not be doing so unjustly, because they would not be depriving anyone of her property.

Unfortunately, Thomson never explains how some persons could justifiably acquire property rights to surplus goods that would restrict others from acquiring or receiving the goods necessary to satisfy their basic needs. And Thomson's argument for abortion crucially depends on the justification of just such restrictive property rights. For otherwise the fetus-person's right to life would presumably entail a right to receive the means of survival.

It is also unclear how such restrictive property rights would be compatible with each person's rights to fair treatment. Apparently, one would have to reinterpret the right to fair treatment so that it had nothing to do with receiving the necessary means of survival. A difficult task indeed.

But most importantly, accepting this defense of abortion with its unsupported assumption of restrictive property rights would undermine the justification for the welfare rights of distant peoples. For the same sort of rights that would restrict the fetus-person from receiving what she needs for survival would also restrict distant people from receiving or acquiring what they need for survival. Thus liberals who support the welfare rights of distant peoples would have an additional reason to reject this argument for abortion.[8]

Nor would it do for liberals who support the welfare rights of distant peoples to concede that a fetus-person's right to life supports a right to receive or acquire what she needs for survival but then maintain that such a right is normally overridden by a pregnant woman's right to her body. For that would mean that bringing to term an unwanted fetus-person normally requires a pregnant woman to sacrifice her basic needs to some degree, and at least when society has provided adequate supporting institutions, this would not seem to be the case. Consequently, liberals who support the welfare rights of distant peoples would generally have the same grounds for enforcing a fetus-person's right to receive or acquire what he needs for survival as they have

for enforcing the welfare rights of distant peoples.

Of course, many liberals cannot but be unhappy with the rejection of the two arguments for abortion which we have considered. For although they would not want to give up their support for the welfare rights of distant peoples, they are still inclined to support abortion on demand.

Searching for an acceptable resolution of this conflict, liberals might claim that what is wrong with the preceding arguments for abortion is that they both make the generous assumption that the fetus is a person. Once that assumption is dropped, liberals might claim, arguments for abortion on demand can be constructed which are perfectly consistent with the welfare rights of distant peoples. Although this line of argument initially seems quite promising, on closer examination it turns out that even accepting arguments for abortion on demand that do not assume that the fetus is a person raises a problem of consistency for the liberal. This is most clearly brought out in connection with the liberal's support for the welfare rights of future generations.

The Welfare Rights of Future Generations

At first glance the welfare rights of future generations appear to be on a par with the welfare rights of distant peoples. For, assuming that there will be future generations, then, they, like generations presently existing, will have their basic needs that must be satisfied. And, just as we are now able to take action to provide for the basic needs of distant peoples, so likewise we are now able to take action to provide for the basic needs of future generations (e.g., through capital investment and the conservation of resources). Thus, it should be possible to justify welfare rights for future generations by appealing either to a right to life or a right to fair treatment, but here again, as in the case of the welfare rights of distant peoples, I shall simply assume that such justifications can be worked out.

The welfare rights of future generations are also closely connected with the population policy of existing generations. For example, under a population policy that places restrictions on the size of families and requires genetic screening, some persons will not be brought into existence who otherwise would come into existence under a less restrictive population policy. Thus, the membership of future generations will surely be affected by whatever population policy existing generations adopt. Given that the size and genetic health of future generations will obviously affect their ability to provide for their basic needs, the welfare rights of future generations would require existing generations to adopt a population policy that takes these factors into account. . . .

Fortunately, a policy with the desired restrictions can be grounded on the welfare rights of future generations. Given that the welfare rights of future generations require existing generations to make provision for the basic needs of future generations, existing generations would have to evaluate their ability to provide both for their own basic needs and for the basic needs of future generations. Since existing generations by bringing persons into existence would be determining the membership of future generations, they would have to evaluate whether they are able to provide for that membership. And if existing generations discover that, were population to increase beyond a certain point, they would lack sufficient resources to make the necessary provision for each person's basic needs, then it would be incumbent upon them to restrict the membership of future generations so as not to exceed their ability to provide for each person's basic needs. Thus, if the rights of future generations are respected, the membership of future generations would never increase beyond the ability of existing generations to make the necessary provision for the basic needs of future generations. . . .

Future Generations and Abortion

Now the population policy that the welfare rights of future generations justify suggests an argument for abortion that liberals would be inclined to accept. The argument assumes that the fetus is not a person and then attempts to show that aborting the fetus is either justified

or required if the fetus will develop into a person who lacks a reasonable opportunity to lead a good life. Most versions of the argument even go so far as to maintain that the person who would otherwise be brought into existence in these unfavorable circumstances has in fact a right not to be born, i.e., a right to be aborted. Joel Feinberg puts the argument as follows:

> . . . if, before the child has been born, we know that the conditions for the fulfillment of his most basic interests have already been destroyed, and we permit him nevertheless to be born, we become a party to the violation of his rights.

> In such circumstances, therefore, a proxy for the fetus might plausibly claim on its behalf, *a right not to be born*. That right is based on his future rather than his present interests (he has no actual present interests); but of course it is not contingent on his birth because he has it before birth, from the very moment that satisfaction of his most basic future interests is rendered impossible ("Is There a Right to Be Born?" 354).

The argument is obviously analogous to arguments for euthanasia. For, as in arguments for euthanasia, it is the nonfulfillment of a person's basic interests which is said to provide the legitimate basis for the person's right to have her life terminated.

However, in order for this argument to function as part of a defense for abortion on demand, it is necessary to show that no similar justification can be given for a right to be born. And it is here that the assumption that the fetus is not a person becomes important. For if the fetus were a person and if, moreover, this fetus-person had a reasonable opportunity to lead a good life, then, it could be argued, this fetus-person would have a right to be born. Thus, proceeding from the assumption that the fetus is not a person, various arguments have been offered to show that a similar justification cannot be given for a right to be born.[9]

One such argument bases the asymmetry on a failure of reference in the case of the fetus that would develop into a person with a reasonable opportunity for a good life. The argument can be summarized as follows:

> If I bring into existence a person who lacks a reasonable opportunity to lead a good life, there will be a person who can reproach me that I did not prevent his leading an unfortunate existence. But if I do not bring into existence a person who would have a reasonable opportunity to lead a good life, there will be no person who can reproach me for preventing his leading a fortunate existence. Hence, only the person who lacks a reasonable opportunity to lead a good life can claim a right not to be born.

But notice that, if I do not bring into existence a person who would lack a reasonable opportunity to lead a good life, there will be no person who can thank me for preventing her leading an unfortunate existence. And, if I do bring into existence a person who had a reasonable opportunity to lead a good life, there will be a person who can thank me for not preventing her leading a fortunate existence. Thus, whatever failure of reference there is, it occurs in both cases, and therefore, cannot be the basis for any asymmetry between them.[10]

A second argument designed to establish the asymmetry between the two cases begins with the assumption that a person's life cannot be compared with her nonexistence unless the person already exists. This means that, if one allows a fetus to develop into a person who has a reasonable opportunity to lead a good life, one does not make that person better off than if she never existed. And it also means that if one allows a fetus to develop into a person who lacks a reasonable opportunity to lead a good life one does not make that person worse off than if she never existed. But what then justifies a right not to be born in the latter case? According to the argument, it is simply the fact that unless the fetus is aborted a person will come into existence who lacks a reasonable opportunity to lead a good life. But if this fact justifies a right not to be born, why, in the former case, would not the fact that unless the fetus is aborted a person will come into existence who has a reasonable opportunity to

lead a good life suffice to justify a right to be born? Clearly, no reason has been given to distinguish the cases.

Furthermore, consider the grounds for aborting a fetus that would develop into a person who lacks a reasonable opportunity to lead a good life. It is not simply that the person is sure to experience some unhappiness in her life because in every person's life there is some unhappiness. Rather it is because the amount of expected unhappiness in this person's life would render her life not worth living. This implies that the justification for aborting in this case is based on a comparison of the value of the person's life with the value of her nonexistence. For how else can we say that the fact that a fetus would develop into a person who lacks a reasonable opportunity to lead a good life justifies our preventing the person's very existence? Consequently, this argument depends upon a denial of the very assumption with which it began, namely that the person's life cannot be compared with his nonexistence unless that person already exists.

Nevertheless, it might still be argued that an analogous justification cannot be given for a right to be born on the grounds that there is a difference in strength between one's duty to prevent a fetus from developing into a person who lacks a reasonable opportunity to lead a good life and one's duty not to prevent a fetus from developing into a person who has a reasonable opportunity to lead a good life. For example, it might be argued that the former duty is a relatively strong duty to prevent harm, whereas the latter duty is a relatively weak duty to promote well-being, and that only the relatively strong duty justifies a correlative right—in this case, a right not to be born. But, even granting that our duty to prevent harm is stronger than our duty to promote well-being, in the case at issue we are dealing not just with a duty to promote well-being but with a duty to promote *basic* well-being. And, as liberals who are committed to the welfare rights of future generations would be the first to admit, our duty to prevent basic harm and our duty to promote basic well-being are not that distinct from a moral point of view. From which it follows that, if our duty to prevent basic harm justifies a right not to be born in the one case, then our duty to promote basic well-being would justify a right to be born in the other.

Nor will it do to reject the notion of a right to be born on the grounds that if the fetus is not a person then the bearer of such a right, especially when we violate that right by performing an abortion, would *seem* to be a potential or possible person. For the same would hold true of the right not to be born which is endorsed by liberals such as Feinberg and Narveson: the bearer of such a right, especially when we respect that right by performing an abortion, would also *seem* to be a potential or possible person. In fact, however, neither notion necessarily entails any metaphysical commitment to possible persons who "are" whether they exist or not. For to say that a person into whom a particular fetus would develop has a right not to be born is to say that there is an enforceable requirement upon certain persons the violation of which would fundamentally harm the person who would thereby come into existence. Similarly, to say that a person into whom a particular fetus would develop has a right to be born is to say that there is an enforceable requirement upon certain persons the respecting of which would fundamentally benefit the person who would thereby come into existence. So understood, neither the notion of a right to be born nor that of a right not to be born entails any metaphysical commitment to possible persons as bearers of rights.

Of course, recognizing a right to be born may require considerable personal sacrifice, and some people may want to reject any morality that requires such sacrifice. This option, however, is not open to liberals who are committed to the welfare rights of future generations. For such liberals are already committed to making whatever personal sacrifice is necessary to provide for the basic needs of future generations. Consequently, liberals committed to the welfare rights of future generations cannot consistently reject a prohibition of abortion in cases involving a right to be born simply on the grounds that it would require considerable personal sacrifice.

But there is an even more basic inconsistency in being committed both to the welfare rights of future generations and to abortion on demand. For, as we have seen, commit-ment to the welfare rights of future generations requires the acceptance of a population policy according to which existing generations must ensure that the membership of future generations does not exceed the ability of existing generations to provide for the basic needs of future generations. Thus for liberals who assume that the fetus is not a person, this population policy would have the same implications as the argument we considered which justifies abortion in certain cases on the basis of a person's right not to be born. For if existing generations violate this population policy by bringing into existence persons whose basic needs they cannot fulfill, they would also thereby be violating the right not to be born of those same persons, since such persons would not have a reasonable opportunity to lead a good life. But, as we have also seen, accepting this argument which justifies abortion in certain cases on the basis of a person's right not to be born commits one to accepting also a parallel argument for prohibiting abortion in certain other cases on the basis of a person's right to be born. Consequently, commitment to the population policy demanded by the welfare rights of future generations will likewise commit liberals to accepting this parallel argument for prohibiting abortion in certain cases. Therefore, even assuming that the fetus is not a person, liberals cannot consistently uphold the welfare rights of future generations while endorsing abortion on demand.

There remains the further question of whether liberals who are committed to the welfare rights of distant peoples and future generations can make a moral distinction between contraception and abortion—assuming, that is, that the fetus is not a person. In support of such a distinction, it might be argued that, in cases where abortion is at issue, we can roughly identify the particular person into whom a fetus would develop and ask whether that person would be fundamentally benefited or fundamentally harmed by being brought into existence, whereas we cannot do anything comparable in cases where contraception is at issue. Yet, though this difference does exist, it does not suffice for morally distinguishing abortion from contraception. For notice that if persons do not practice contraception when conditions are known to be suitable for bringing persons into existence who would have a reasonable opportunity to lead a good life, then there will normally come into existence persons who have thereby benefited. Similarly, if persons do not practice contraception when conditions are known to be unsuitable for bringing persons into existence who would have a reasonable opportunity to lead a good life (e.g., when persons who would be brought into existence would very likely have seriously debilitating and ultimately fatal genetic defects), then there will normally come into existence persons who have thereby been harmed. On grounds such as these, therefore, we could certainly defend a "right not to be conceived" and a "right to be conceived" which are analogous to our previously defended "right not to be born" and "right to be born." Hence, it would follow that liberals who are committed to the welfare rights of distant peoples and future generations can no more consistently support "contraception on demand" than they can consistently support abortion on demand.

Needless to say, considerably more sacrifice would normally be required of existing generations in order to fulfill a person's right to be born or right to be conceived than would be required to fulfill a person's right not to be born or right not to be conceived. For example, fulfilling a person's right to be born may ultimately require caring for the needs of a child for many years whereas fulfilling a person's right not to be born may require only an early abortion. Therefore, because of the greater sacrifice that would normally be required to fulfill a person's right to be born, that right might often be overridden in particular circumstances by the rights of existing persons to have their own basic needs satisfied. The existing persons whose welfare would have priority over a person's right to be born are not only those who would be directly involved in bringing the person into existence but also those distant persons whose welfare rights would otherwise be neglected if goods and resources were diverted to bringing additional persons into existence. This would, of course, place severe restrictions on any population increase in technologically developed nations so long as persons in technologically underdeveloped nations still fail to have their

basic needs satisfied. But for persons committed to the welfare rights of distant peoples as well as to the welfare rights of future generations, no other policy would be acceptable.

Obviously these results cannot but be embarrassing for many liberals. For what has been shown is that, with or without the assumption that the fetus is a person, liberals who are committed to the welfare rights of distant peoples and future generations cannot consistently endorse abortion on demand. Thus, assuming that the welfare rights of distant peoples and future generations can be firmly grounded on a right to life and a right to fair treatment, the only morally acceptable way for liberals to avoid this inconsistency is to moderate their support for abortion on demand.

Notes

1. It is not difficult to find philosophers who not only favor a liberal view on abortion and thus tend to support abortion on demand, but also favor these other social goals as well. See Jan Narveson, "Moral Problems of Population," *Monist*, LVII, 1 (January 1973): 62–86, and "Aesthetics, Charity, Utility and Distributive Justice," *ibid.*, LVI, 4 (October 1972): 527–551; Joel Feinberg, "Is There a Right to Be Born?" in James Rachels, ed., *Understanding Moral Philosophy* (Encino, Calif.: Dickenson, 1976), pp. 346–357, and "The Rights of Animals and Future Generations," in William Blackstone, *Philosophy and Environmental Crisis* (Athens: Univ. of Georgia Press, 1972), pp. 41–68; Michael Tooley, "Abortion and Infanticide," *Philosophy & Public Affairs*, II, 1 (Fall 1972): 37–65, and "Michael Tooley Replies," *ibid.*, II, 4 (Summer 1973): 419–432; Mary Anne Warren, "Do Potential People Have Moral Rights?", *Canadian Journal of Philosophy*, VII, 2 (June 1977): 275–289.

2. For other possibilities, see Onora Nell, "Lifeboat Earth," *Philosophy & Public Affairs*, IV, 3 (Spring 1975): 273–292; Peter Singer, "Famine, Affluence and Morality," *ibid.*, I, 3 (Spring 1972): 229–243.

3. A person's basic needs are those which must be satisfied if the person's health and sanity are not to be seriously endangered.

4. For an attempt to work out these justifications, see this anthology, page 115.

5. See pages 140–148.

6. Hereafter the term 'fetus-person' will be used to indicate the assumption that the fetus is a person. The term 'fetus' is also understood to refer to any human organism from conception to birth.

7. See her "Killing, Letting Die, and the Trolley Problem," *Monist*, LIX, 2 (April 1976): 204–217.

8. Notice that my critique of Thomson's arguments for abortion on demand differs from critiques that attempt to find an *internal* defect in Thomson's arguments. [For example, see Richard Werner's "Abortion: the Moral Status of the Unborn." *Social Theory and Practice*, III, 2

(Fall 1974): 210–216.] My approach has been to show that Thomson's arguments are *externally* defective in that a liberal who is committed to the welfare rights of distant peoples cannot consistently accept those arguments. Thus, Jan Narveson's telling objections to Werner's internalist critique of Thomson's arguments [see his "Semantics, Future Generations and the Abortion Problem," *ibid.*, III, 4 (Fall 1975): 464–466] happily do not apply to my own critique.

9. See Narveson, "Utilitarianism and New Generations," *Mind*, LXXVI, 301 (January 1967): 62–72, and "Moral Problems of Population," *op. cit.*

10. For a similar argument, see Timothy Sprigge "Professor Narveson's Utilitarianism," *Inquiry*, XI, 3 (Autumn 1968: 332–346), p. 338.

Euthanasia, Killing, and Letting Die

James Rachels

James Rachels criticizes a recent policy statement of the American Medical Association on the grounds that it endorses the doctrine that there is an important moral difference between active and passive euthanasia. Rachels denies that there is any moral difference between the two. He argues that once we judge a patient would be better off dead, it should not matter much whether that patient is killed or let die. He points out that both killing and letting die can be intentional and deliberate and can proceed from the same motives; further, that when killing and letting die are similar in these and other relevant respects, our moral assessment of these acts is also similar. Rachels concludes by considering a number of counterarguments to his view and finds them all wanting. In particular, Rachels rejects the idea that the killing and letting die distinction can be supported on the grounds that our duty to refrain from harming people is much stronger than our duty to help people in need. Rather, he contends that when conditions are similar our duty to refrain from harming people and our duty to help people in need have a similar moral force.

Dr F. J. Ingelfinger, former editor of the *The New England Journal of Medicine,* observes that

This is the heyday of the ethicist in medicine. He delineates the rights of patients, of experimental subjects, of fetuses, of mothers, of animals, and even of doctors.

From *Ethical Issues Relating to Life and Death*, edited by John Ladd. Copyright © 1979 Oxford University Press, Inc. Reprinted by permission.

(And what a far cry it is from the days when medical "ethics" consisted of condemning economic improprieties such as fee splitting and advertising!) With impeccable logic—once certain basic assumptions are granted—and with graceful prose, the ethicist develops his arguments. . . . Yet his precepts are essentially the products of armchair exercise and remain abstract and idealistic until they have been tested in the laboratory of experience.[1]

One problem with such armchair exercises, he complains, is that in spite of the impeccable logic and the graceful prose, the result is often an absolutist ethic which is unsatisfactory when applied to particular cases, and which is therefore of little use to the practicing physician. Unlike some absolutist philosophers, "the practitioner appears to prefer the principles of individualism. As there are few atheists in fox holes, there tend to be few absolutists at the bedside."[2]

I must concede at the outset that this chapter is another exercise in "armchair ethics" in the sense that I am not a physician but a philosopher. Yet I am no absolutist; and my purpose is to examine a doctrine that *is* held in an absolute form by many doctors. The doctrine is that there is an important moral difference between active and passive euthanasia, such that even though the latter is sometimes permissible, the former is always forbidden. This is an absolute which doctors hold "at the bedside" as well as in the seminar room, and the "principles of individualism" make little headway against it. But I will argue that this is an irrational dogma, and that there is no sound moral basis for it.

I will not argue, simply, that active euthanasia is all right. Rather, I will be concerned with the *relation* between active euthanasia and passive euthanasia: I will argue that there is no moral difference between them. By this I mean that there is no reason to prefer one over the other as a matter of principle—the fact that one case of euthanasia is active, while another is passive, is not *itself* a reason to think one morally better than the other. If you already think that passive euthanasia is all right, and you are convinced by my arguments, then you may conclude that active euthanasia must be all right, too. On the other hand, if you believe that active euthanasia is immoral, you may want to conclude that passive euthanasia must be immoral, too. Although I prefer the former alternative, I will not argue for it here. I will only argue that the two forms of euthanasia are morally equivalent—either both are acceptable or both are unacceptable.

I am aware that this will at first seem incredible to many readers, but I hope that this impression will be dispelled as the discussion proceeds. The discussion will be guided by two methodological considerations, both of which are touched on in the editorial quoted above. The first has to do with my "basic assumptions." My arguments are intended to appeal to all reasonable people, and not merely to those who already share my philosophical preconceptions. Therefore, I will try not to rely on any assumptions that cannot be accepted by any reasonable person. None of my arguments will depend on morally eccentric premises. Second, Dr. Ingelfinger is surely correct when he says that we must be as concerned with the realities of medical practice as with the more abstract issues of moral theory. As he notes, the philosopher's precepts "remain abstract and idealistic until they are tested in the laboratory of experience." Part of my argument will be precisely that, when "tested in the laboratory of experience," the doctrine in question has terrible results. I believe that if this doctrine were to be recognized as irrational, and rejected by the medical profession, the benefit to both doctors and patients would be enormous. In this sense, my paper is not intended as an "armchair exercise" at all.

The American Medical Association Policy Statement

"Active euthanasia," as the term is used, means taking some positive action designed to kill the patient; for example, giving him a lethal injection of potassium chloride. "Passive euthanasia," on the other hand, means simply refraining from doing anything to keep the patient alive. In passive euthanasia we withhold medication or other life-sustaining therapy, or we refuse to perform surgery, etc., and let the patient die "naturally" of whatever ills already afflict him.

Many doctors and theologians prefer to use the term "euthanasia" only in connection with active euthanasia, and they use other words to refer to what I am calling "passive euthanasia"—for example, instead of "passive euthanasia" they may speak of "the right to death with dignity." One reason for this choice of terms is the emotional impact of the words:

it *sounds* so much better to defend "death with dignity" than to advocate "euthanasia" of any sort. And of course if one believes that there is a great moral difference between active and passive euthanasia—as most doctors and religious writers do—then one may prefer a terminology which puts as much psychological distance as possible between them. However, I do not want to become involved in a pointless dispute about terminology, because nothing of substance depends on which label is used. I will stay with the terms "active euthanasia" and "passive euthanasia" because they are the most convenient; but if the reader prefers a different terminology he may substitute his own throughout, and my arguments will be unaffected.

The belief that there is an important moral difference between active and passive euthanasia obviously has important consequences for medical practice. It makes a difference to what doctors are willing to do. Consider, for example, the following familiar situation. A patient who is dying from incurable cancer of the throat is in terrible pain that we can no longer satisfactorily alleviate. He is certain to die within a few days, but he decides that he does not want to go on living for those days since the pain is unbearable. So he asks the doctor to end his life now; and his family joins in the request. One way that the doctor might comply with this request is simply by killing the patient with a lethal injection. Most doctors would not do that, not only because of the possible legal consequences, but because they think such a course would be immoral. And this is understandable: the idea of killing someone goes against very deep moral feelings; and besides, as we are often reminded, it is the special business of doctors to save and protect life, not to destroy it. Yet, even so, the physician may sympathize with the dying patient's request and feel that it is entirely reasonable for him to prefer death now rather than after a few more days of agony. The doctrine that we are considering tells the doctor what to do: it says that although he may not administer the lethal injection—that would be "active euthanasia," which is forbidden—he *may* withhold treatment and let the patient die sooner than he otherwise would.

It is no wonder that this simple idea is so widely accepted, for it seems to give the doctor a way out of his dilemma without having to kill the patient, and without having to prolong the patient's agony. The idea is not a new one. What *is* new is that the idea is now being incorporated into official documents of medical ethics. What was once unofficially done is now becoming official policy. The idea is expressed, for example, in a 1973 policy statement of the American Medical Association, which says (in its entirety):

> The intentional termination of the life of one human being by another—mercy killing—is contrary to that for which the medical profession stands and is contrary to the policy of the American Medical Association.
>
> The cessation of the employment of extraordinary means to prolong the life of the body when there is irrefutable evidence that biological death is imminent is the decision of the patient and/or his immediate family. The advice and judgment of the physician should be freely available to the patient and/or his immediate family.[3]

This is a cautiously worded statement, and it is not clear *exactly* what is being affirmed. I take it, however, that at least these three propositions are intended:

1. Killing patients is absolutely forbidden; however, it is sometimes permissible to allow patients to die.
2. It is permissible to allow a patient to die if
   a. there is irrefutable evidence that he will die soon anyway;
   b. "extraordinary" measures would be required to keep him alive; and
   c. the patient and/or his immediate family requests it.
3. Doctors should make their own advice and judgments available to the patient and/or his immediate family when the latter are deciding whether to request that the patient be allowed to die.

The first proposition expresses the doctrine which is the main subject of this paper. As for the third, it seems obvious enough, provided that 1 and 2 are accepted, so I shall say nothing further about it.

I do want to say a few things about 2. Physicians often allow patients to die; however, they do *not* always keep to the guidelines set out in 2. For example, a doctor may leave instructions that if a hopeless, comatose patient suffers cardiac arrest, nothing be done to start his heart beating again. "No-coding" is the name given to this practice, and the consent of the patient and/or his immediate family is not commonly sought. This is thought to be a medical decision (in reality, of course, it is a moral one) which is the doctor's affair. To take a different sort of example, when a Down's infant (a mongoloid) is born with an intestinal blockage, the doctor and parents may agree that there will be no operation to remove the blockage, so that the baby will die.[4] (If the same infant were born without the obstruction, it certainly would not be killed. This is a clear application of the idea that "letting die" is all right even though killing is forbidden.) But in such cases it is clear that the baby is *not* going to die soon anyway. If the surgery were performed, the baby would proceed to a "normal" infancy—normal, that is, for a mongoloid. Moreover, the treatment required to save the baby—abdominal surgery—can hardly be called "extraordinary" by today's medical standards.

Therefore, all three conditions which the AMA statement places on the decision to let die are commonly violated. It is beyond the scope of this paper to determine whether doctors are right to violate those conditions. But I firmly believe that the second requirement—2b—is not acceptable. Only a little reflection is needed to show that the distinction between ordinary and extraordinary means is not important. Even a very conservative, religiously-oriented writer such as Paul Ramsey stresses this. Ramsey gives these examples:

> Suppose that a diabetic patient long accustomed to self-administration of insulin falls victim to terminal cancer, or suppose that a terminal cancer patient suddenly develops diabetes. Is he in the first case obliged to continue, and in the second case obliged to begin, insulin treatment and die painfully of cancer, or in either or both cases may the patient choose rather to pass into diabetic coma and an earlier death? . . . Or an old man slowly deteriorating who from simply being inactive and recumbent gets pneumonia: are we to use antibiotics in a likely successful attack upon this disease which from time immemorial has been called "the old man's friend"?[5]

I agree with Ramsey, and with many other writers, that in such cases treatment may be withheld even though it is not "extraordinary" by any reasonable standard. Contrary to what is implied by the AMA statement, the distinction between heroic and nonheroic means of treatment can *not* be used to determine when treatment is or is not mandatory.

Killing and Letting Die

I return now to the distinction between active and passive euthanasia. Of course, not every doctor believes that this distinction is morally important. Over twenty years ago Dr. D. C. S. Cameron of the American Cancer Society said that "Actually the difference between euthanasia [i.e., killing] and letting the patient die by omitting life-sustaining treatment is a moral quibble."[6] I argue that Cameron was right.

The initial thought can be expressed quite simply. In any case in which euthanasia seems desirable, it is because we think that the patient would literally be better off dead—or at least, no worse off dead—than continuing the kind of life available to him. (Without this assumption, even *passive* euthanasia would be unthinkable.) But, as far as the main question of ending the patient's life is concerned, it does not matter whether the euthanasia is active or passive: *in either case,* he ends up dead sooner than he otherwise would. And if the results are the same, why should it matter so much which method is used?

Moreover, we need to remember that, in cases such as that of the terminal cancer-patient, the justification for allowing him to die, rather than prolonging his life for a few more hopeless days, is that he is in horrible pain. But if we simply withhold treatment, it may take him *longer* to die, and so he will suffer *more* than he would if we were to administer the lethal injection. This fact provides strong reason for thinking that, once we have made the initial decision not to prolong his agony, active euthanasia is actually preferable to passive euthanasia rather than the reverse. It also shows a kind of incoherence in the conventional view: to say that passive euthanasia is preferable is to endorse the option which leads to more suffering rather than less, and is contrary to the humanitarian impulse which prompts the decision not to prolong his life in the first place.

But many people are convinced that there is an important moral difference between active and passive euthanasia because they think that, in passive euthanasia, the doctor does not really *do* anything. No action whatever is taken; the doctor simply does nothing, and the patient dies of whatever ills already afflict him. In active euthanasia, however, we *do something* to bring about the patient's death. We kill him. Thus, the difference between active and passive euthanasia is thought to be the difference between doing something to bring about someone's death, and not doing anything to bring about anyone's death. And of course if we conceive the matter in *this* way, passive euthanasia seems preferable. Ramsey, who denounces the view I am defending as "extremist" and who regards the active/passive distinction as one of the "flexibly wise categories of traditional medical ethics," takes just this view of the matter. He says that the choice between active and passive euthanasia "is not a choice between directly and indirectly willing and doing something. *It is rather the important choice between doing something and doing nothing,* or (better said) ceasing to do something that was begun in order to do something that is better because now more fitting."[7]

This is a very misleading way of thinking, for it ignores the fact that in passive euthanasia the doctor *does* do one thing which is very important: namely, he lets the patient die. We may overlook this obvious fact—or at least, we may put it out of our minds—if we concentrate only on a very restricted way of describing what happens: "The doctor does not administer medication or any other therapy; he does not instruct the nurses to administer any such medication; he does not perform any surgery"; and so on. And of course this description of what happens is correct, as far as it goes—these are all things that the doctor does not do. But the point is that the doctor *does* let the patient die when he could save him, and this must be included in the description, too.

There is another reason why we might fall into this error. We might confuse *not saving* someone with *letting him die*. Suppose a patient is dying, and Dr. X could prolong his life. But he decides not to do so and the patient dies. Now it is true of everyone on earth that he did not save the patient. Dr. X did not save him, and neither did you, and neither did I. So we might be tempted to think that all of us are in the same moral position, reasoning that since neither you nor I are responsible for the patient's death, neither is Dr. X. None of us did anything. This, however, is a mistake, for even though it is true that none of us saved the patient, it is *not* true that we all let him die. In order to let someone die, one must be *in a position* to save him. You and I were not in a position to save the patient, so we did not let him die. Dr. X, on the other hand, was in a position to save him, and did let him die. Thus the doctor is in a special moral position which not just everyone is in.

Here we must remember some elementary points, which are so obvious that they would not be worth mentioning except for the fact that overlooking them is a source of so much confusion in this area. The act of letting someone die may be intentional and deliberate, just as the act of killing someone may be intentional and deliberate. Moreover, the doctor is *responsible* for his decision to let the patient die, just as he would be responsible for giving the patient a lethal injection. The decision to let a patient die is subject to moral appraisal in the same way that a decision to kill is subject to moral appraisal: it may be assessed as wise or unwise, compassionate or sadistic, right or wrong. If a doctor deliberately let a patient die who was suffering from a routinely curable illness, then he would be to blame for what he did, just as he would be to blame if he had needlessly killed the patient. It would be no defense at all for him to insist that, *really,* he didn't "do anything" but just stand there. We would all know that he did do something very serious indeed, for he let the patient die.

These considerations show how misleading it is to characterize the difference between active and passive euthanasia as a difference between doing something (killing), for which the doctor may be morally culpable; and doing nothing (just standing there while the patient dies), for which the doctor is not culpable. The real difference between them is, rather, the difference between *killing* and letting die, both of which are actions for which a doctor, or anyone else, will be morally responsible.

Now we can formulate our problem more precisely. If there is an important moral difference between active and passive euthanasia, it must be because *killing someone is morally worse than letting someone die.* But is it? Is killing, in itself, worse than letting die? In order to investigate this issue, we may consider two cases which are exactly alike except that one involves killing where the other involves letting someone die. Then we can ask whether this difference makes any difference to our moral assessments. It is important that the cases be *exactly* alike except for this one difference, since otherwise we cannot be confident that it is *this* difference which accounts for any variation in our assessments.

1. Smith stands to gain a large inheritance if anything should happen to his six-year-old cousin. One evening while the child is taking his bath, Smith sneaks into the bathroom and drowns the child, and then arranges things so that it will look like an accident.

2. Jones also stands to gain if anything should happen to his six-year-old cousin. Like Smith, Jones sneaks in planning to drown the child in his bath. However, just as he enters the bathroom Jones sees the child slip, hit his head, and fall face down in the water. Jones is delighted; he stands by, ready to push the child's head back under if it is necessary, but it is not necessary. With only a little thrashing about, the child drowns all by himself, "accidentally," as Jones watches and does nothing.

Now Smith killed the child, while Jones "merely" let the child die. That is the only difference between them. Did either man behave better, from a moral point of view? Is there a moral difference between them? *If the difference between killing and letting die were itself a morally important matter, then we should say that Jones's behavior was less reprehensible than Smith's.* But do we actually want to say that? I think not, for several reasons. In the first place, both men acted from the same motive, personal gain, and both had exactly the same end in view when they acted. We may infer from Smith's conduct that he is a bad man, although we may withdraw or modify that judgment if we learn certain further facts about him; for example, that he is mentally deranged. But would we not also infer the very same thing about Jones from his conduct? And would not the same further considerations also be relevant to any modification of that judgment? Moreover, suppose Jones pleaded in his defense, "After all, I didn't kill the child. I only stood there and let him die." Again, if letting die were in itself less bad than killing, this defense should have some weight. But—morally, at least—it does not. Such a "defense" can only be regarded as a grotesque perversion of moral reasoning.

Thus, it seems that when we are careful not to smuggle in any further differences which prejudice the issue, the mere difference between killing and letting die does not itself make any difference to the morality of actions concerning life and death.[8]

Now it may be pointed out, quite properly, that the cases of euthanasia with which doctors are concerned are not like this at all. They do not involve personal gain or the destruction of normal, healthy children. Doctors are concerned only with cases in which the patient's life is of no further use to him, or in which the patient's life has become or soon will become a positive burden. However, the point is the same in those cases: the difference between killing or letting die does not, *in itself*, make a difference, from the point of view of morality. If a doctor lets a patient die, for humane reasons, he is in the same moral position as if he had given the patient a lethal injection for humane reasons. If his decision was wrong—if, for example, the patient's illness was in fact curable—then the decision would be equally regrettable no matter which method was used to carry it out. And if the doctor's decision was the right one, then the method he used is not itself important.

The AMA statement isolates the crucial

issue very well: "the intentional termination of the life of one human being by another." But then the statement goes on to deny that the cessation of treatment *is* the intentional termination of a life. This is where the mistake comes in, for what is the cessation of treatment, in those circumstances, if it is not "the intentional termination of the life of one human being by another"? Of course it is exactly that; if it were not, there would be no point to it.

Counter-Arguments

Our argument has now brought us to this point: we cannot draw any moral distinction between active and passive euthanasia on the grounds that one involves killing while the other only involves letting someone die, because that is a difference that does not make a difference, from a moral point of view. Some people will find this hard to accept. One reason, I think, is that they fail to distinguish the question of whether killing is, in itself, worse than letting die, from the very different question of whether most actual cases of killing are more reprehensible than most actual cases of letting die. Most actual cases of killing are clearly terrible—think of the murders reported in the newspapers—and we hear of such cases almost every day. On the other hand, we hardly ever hear of a case of letting die, except for the actions of doctors who are motivated by humanitarian reasons. So we learn to think of killing in a much worse light than letting die; and we conclude, invalidly, that there must be something about killing which makes it *in itself* worse than letting die. But this does not follow for it is not the bare difference between killing and letting die that makes the difference in these cases. Rather, it is the other factors—the murderer's motive of personal gain, for example, contrasted with the doctor's humanitarian motivation, or the fact that the murderer kills a healthy person while the doctor lets die a terminal patient racked with disease—that account for our different reactions to the different cases.

There are, however, some substantial arguments that may be advanced to oppose my conclusion. Here are two of them:

The first counter-argument focuses specifically on the concept of *being the cause of someone's death*. If we kill someone, then we are the cause of his death. But if we merely let someone die, we are not the cause; rather, he dies of whatever condition he already has. The doctor who gives the cancer patient a lethal injection will have caused his patient's death, and will have this on his conscience; whereas if he merely ceases treatment, the cancer and not the doctor is the cause of death. This is supposed to make a moral difference. This argument has been advanced many times. Ramsey, for example, urges us to remember that "In omission no human agent causes the patient's death, directly or indirectly."[9] And, writing in the *Villanova Law Review* for 1968, Dr. J. Russell Elkinton said that what makes the active/passive distinction important is that in passive euthanasia, "the patient does not die from the act [e.g. the act of turning off the respirator] but from the underlying disease or injury."[10]

This argument will not do, for two reasons. First, just as there is a distinction to be drawn between being and not being the cause of someone's death, there is also a distinction to be drawn between letting someone die and not letting anyone die. It is certainly desirable, in general, not to be the cause of anyone's death; but it is also desirable, in general, not to let anyone die when we can save them. (Doctors act on this precept every day.) Therefore, we cannot draw any special conclusion about the relative desirability of passive euthanasia just on these grounds. Second, the reason why we think it is bad to be the cause of someone's death is that we think that death is a great evil—and so it is. However, if we have decided that euthanasia, even passive euthanasia, is desirable in a given case, then we have decided that in *this* instance death is no greater an evil than the patient's continued existence. And if this is true, then the usual reason for not wanting to be the cause of someone's death simply does not apply. To put the point just a bit differently: There is nothing wrong with being the cause of someone's death if his death is, all things considered, a good thing. And if his death is *not* a good thing, then *no* form of euthanasia, active or passive, is justified. So once again we see that the two kinds of euthanasia stand or fall together.

The second counter-argument appeals to a

favorite idea of philosophers, namely that our duty not to harm people is generally more stringent than our duty to help them. The law affirms this when it forbids us to kill people, or steal their goods, but does not require us in general to save people's lives or give them charity. And this is said to be not merely a point about the law, but about morality as well. We do not have a strict moral duty to help some poor man in Ethiopa—although it might be kind and generous of us if we did—but we *do* have a strict moral duty to refrain from doing anything to harm him. Killing someone is a violation of our duty not to harm, whereas letting someone die is merely a failure to give help. Therefore, the former is a more serious breach of morality than the latter; and so, contrary to what was said above, there is a morally significant difference between killing and letting die.

This argument has a certain superficial plausibility, but it cannot be used to show that there is a morally important difference between active and passive euthanasia. For one thing, it only seems that our duty to help people is less stringent than our duty not to harm them when we concentrate on certain sorts of cases: cases in which the people we could help are very far away, and are strangers to us; or cases in which it would be very difficult for us to help them, or in which helping would require a substantial sacrifice on our part. Many people feel that, in *these* types of cases, it may be kind and generous of us to give help, but we are not morally required to do so. Thus it is felt that when we give money for famine relief we are being especially big-hearted, and we deserve special praise—even if it would be immodest of us to seek such praise—because we are doing more than, strictly speaking, we are required to do.[11]

However, if we think of cases in which it would be very easy for us to help someone who is close at hand and in which no great personal sacrifice is required, things look very different. Think again of the child drowning in the bathtub: *of course* a man standing next to the tub would have a strict moral duty to help the child. Here the alleged asymmetry between the duty to help and the duty not to do harm vanishes. Since most of the cases of euthanasia with which we are concerned are of this latter type—the patient is close at hand, it is well

within the professional skills of the physician to keep him alive—the alleged asymmetry has little relevance.

It should also be remembered, in considering this argument, that the duty of doctors toward their patients *is* precisely to help them; that is what doctors are supposed to do. Therefore, even if there were a general asymmetry between the duty to help and the duty not to harm—which I deny—it would not apply in the special case of the relation between doctors and their patients. Finally, it is not clear that killing such a patient *is* harming him, even though in other cases it certainly is a great harm to someone to kill him, for as I said before, we are going under the assumption that the patient would be no worse off dead than he is now; if this is so, then killing him is not harming him. For the same reason we should not classify letting such a patient die as failing to help him. Therefore, even if we grant that our duty to help people is less stringent than our duty not to harm them, nothing follows about our duties with respect to killing and letting die in the special case of euthanasia.

Practical Consequences

This is enough, I think, to show that the doctrine underlying the AMA statement is false. There is no general moral difference between active and passive euthanasia; if one is permissible, so is the other. Now if this were merely an intellectuual mistake, having no significant consequences for medical practice, the whole matter would not be very important. But the opposite is true: the doctrine has terrible consequences for, as I have already mentioned—and as doctors know very well—the process of being "allowed to die" can be relatively slow and painful, while being given a lethal injection is relatively quick and painless. Dr. Anthony Shaw describes what happens when the decision has been made not to perform the surgery necessary to "save" a mongoloid infant:

When surgery is denied [the doctor] must try to keep the infant from suffering while natural forces sap the baby's life away. As a surgeon whose natural inclination is to use the scalpel to fight off death, standing by and watching a salvageable baby die is the most emotionally exhausting experience I know. It is easy at a conference, in a theoretical discussion, to decide that such infants should be allowed to die. It is altogether different to stand by in the nursery and watch as dehydration and infection wither a tiny being over hours and days. This is a terrible ordeal for me and the hospital staff—much more so than for the parents who never set foot in the nursery.[12]

Why must the hospital staff "stand by in the nursery and watch as dehydration and infection wither a tiny being over hours and days"? Why must they merely "try" to reduce the infant's suffering? The doctrine which says that the baby may be allowed to dehydrate and wither, but not be given an injection which would end its life without suffering, is not only irrational but cruel.

The same goes for the case of the man with cancer of the throat. Here there are three options: with continued treatment, he will have a few more days of pain, and then die; if treatment is stopped, but nothing else is done, it will be a few more hours; and with a lethal injection, he will die at once. Those who oppose euthanasia in all its forms say that we must take the first option, and keep the patient alive for as long as possible. This view is so patently inhumane that few defend it; nevertheless, it does have a certain kind of integrity. It is at least consistent. The third option is the one I think best. But the *middle* position—that, although the patient need not suffer for days before dying, he must nevertheless suffer for a few more hours—is a "moderate" view which incorporates the worst, and not the best, features of both extremes.

Let me mention one other practice that we would be well rid of if we stopped thinking that the distinction between active and passive euthanasia is important. About one in six hundred babies born in the United States is mongoloid. Most of these babies are otherwise healthy—that is, with only the usual pediatric care, they will proceed to a "normal" infancy. Some, however, are born with other con-

genital defects such as intestinal obstructions which require surgery if the baby is to live. As I have already mentioned, sometimes the surgery is withheld and the baby dies. But when there is no defect requiring surgery, the baby lives on.[13] Now surgery to remove an intestinal obstruction is not difficult; the reason why it is not performed in such cases is, clearly, that the child is mongoloid and the parents and doctor judge that because of *this* it is better for the child to die.

But notice that this situation is absurd, no matter what view one takes of the lives and potentials of such babies. If you think that the life of such an infant is worth preserving, then what does it matter if it needs a simple operation? Or, if you think it better that such a baby not live on, then what difference does it make if its intestinal tract is *not* blocked? In either case, the matter of life or death is being decided on irrelevant grounds. It is the mongolism, and not the intestine, that is the issue. The matter should be decided, if at all, on *that* basis, and not be allowed to depend on the essentially irrelevant question of whether the intestinal tract is blocked.

What makes this situation possible, of course, is the idea that when there is an intestinal obstruction we can "let the baby die," but when there is no such defect there is nothing we can do, for we must not "kill" it. The fact that this idea leads to such results as deciding life or death on irrelevant grounds is another good reason why it should be rejected.

Doctors may think that all of this is only of academic interest, the sort of thing which philosophers may worry about but which has no practical bearing on their own work. After all, doctors must be concerned about the legal consequences of what they do, and active euthanasia is clearly forbidden by the law. They are right to be concerned about this. There have not been many prosecutions of doctors in the United States for active euthanasia, but there have been some. Prosecutions for passive euthanasia, on the other hand, are virtually nonexistent, even though there are laws under which charges could be brought, and even though this practice is much more widespread. Passive euthanasia, unlike active euthanasia, is by and large tolerated by the law. The law may sometimes compel a doctor to take action which he might not otherwise take to keep a patient alive,[14] but of course this is very different from bringing criminal charges against him after the patient is dead.

Even so, doctors should be concerned with the fact that the law and public opinion are forcing upon them an indefensible moral position, which has a considerable effect on their practices. Of course, most doctors are not now in the position of being coerced in this matter, for they do not regard themselves as merely going along with what the law requires. Rather, in statements such as the AMA statement that I quoted, they are endorsing the doctrine as a central point of medical ethics. In that statement, active euthanasia is condemned not merely as illegal but as "contrary to that for which the medical profession stands," while passive euthanasia is approved. However, if my arguments have been sound, there really is no intrinsic moral difference between them (although there may be morally important differences in their consequences, varying from case to case); so while doctors may have to discriminate between them to satisfy the law, they should not do any *more* than that. In particular, they should not give the distinction any added authority and weight by writing it into official statements of medical ethics.

Notes

1. F. J. Ingelfinger, "Bedside Ethics for the Hopeless Case," *The New England Journal of Medicine* 289 (25 October 1973), p. 914.

2. Ibid.

3. This statement was approved by the House of Delegates of the AMA on December 4, 1973. It is worth noting that some state medical societies have advised *patients* to take a similar attitude toward the termination of their lives. In 1973 the Connecticut State Medical Society approved a "background statement" to be signed by terminal patients which includes this sentence: "I value life and the dignity of life, so that I am not asking that my life be directly taken, but that my life not be unreasonably prolonged or the dignity of life be destroyed." Other state medical societies have followed suit.

4. A discussion of this type of case can be found in Anthony Shaw, " 'Doctor, Do We Have a Choice?' " *The New York Times Magazine*, 30 January 1972, pp. 44–54. Also see Shaw's "Dilemmas of 'Informed Consent' in Children," *The New England Journal of Medicine* 289 (25 October 1973), pp. 885–90.

5. Paul Ramsey, *The Patient as Person* (New Haven, Conn.: Yale University Press, 1970), pp. 115–16.

6. D. C. S. Cameron, *The Truth About Cancer* (Englewood Cliffs, N.J.: Prentice-Hall, 1956), p. 116.

7. Ramsey, *The Patient as Person*, p. 151.

8. Judith Jarvis Thomson has argued that this line of reasoning is unsound. Consider, she says, this argument which is parallel to the one involving Smith and Jones:

Alfrieda knows that if she cuts off Alfred's head he will die, and wanting him to die, cuts it off; Bertha knows that if she punches Bert in the nose he will die—Bert is in peculiar physical condition—and, wanting him to die, punches him in the nose. But what Bertha does is surely every bit as bad as what Alfrieda does. So cutting off a man's head isn't worse than punching a man in the nose. ["*Killing, Letting Die, and the Trolley Problem*," The Monist 59 (1976), p. 204.]

She concludes that, since this absurd argument doesn't prove anything, the Smith/Jones argument doesn't prove anything either.

However, I think that the Alfrieda/Bertha argument is not absurd, as strange as it is. A little analysis shows that it is a sound argument and that its conclusion is true. We need to notice first that the reason why it is wrong to chop someone's head off is, obviously, that this causes death. The act is objectionable because of its consequences. Thus, a different act with the same consequences may be equally objectionable. In Thomson's example, punching Bert in the nose has the same consequences as chopping off Alfred's head; and, indeed, the two actions are equally bad.

Now the Alfrieda/Bertha argument presupposes a distinction between the act of chopping off someone's head, and the results of this act, the victim's death. (It is stipulated that, except for the fact that Alfrieda chops off someone's head, while Bertha punches someone in the nose, the two acts are "in all other respects alike." The "*other*" respects include the act's consequence, the victim's death.) This is not a distinction we would normally think to make, since we cannot in fact cut off someone's head without killing him. Yet in thought the distinction can be drawn.

The question raised in the argument, then, is whether, *considered apart from their consequences,* head-chopping is worse than nose-punching. And the answer to *this* strange question is No, just as the argument says it should be.

The conclusion of the argument should be construed like this: The bare fact that one act is an act of head-chopping, while another act is an act of nose-punching, is not a reason for judging the former to be worse than the latter. At the same time—and this is perfectly compatible with the argument—the fact that one act causes death, while another does not, *is* a reason for judging the former to be worse. The parallel construal of my conclusion is: The bare fact that one act is an act of killing, while another act is an act of letting die, is not a reason for judging the former to be worse than the latter. At the same time—and this is perfectly compatible with my argument—the fact that an act (of killing, for example) prevents suffering, while another act (of letting die, for example) does not, *is* a reason for preferring one over the other. So once we see exactly how the Alfrieda/Bertha argument *is* parallel to the Smith/Jones argument, we find that Thomson's argument is, surprisingly, quite all right.

9. Ramsey, *The Patient as Person,* p. 151.

10. J. Russell Elkinton, "The Dying Patient, the Doctor, and the Law," *Villanova Law Review* 13 (Summer 1968), p. 743.

11. For the purposes of this essay we do not need to consider whether this way of thinking about "charity" is justified. There are, however, strong arguments that it is morally indefensible: see Peter Singer. "Famine, Affluence, and Morality," *Philosophy and Public Affairs* 1 (Spring 1972), pp. 229–43. Also see James Rachels, "Killing and Letting People Die of Starvation," forthcoming in *Philosophy,* for a discussion of the killing/letting die distinction in the context of world hunger, as well as further arguments that the distinction is morally unimportant.

12. Shaw, " 'Doctor, Do We Have a Choice?' " p. 54.

13. See the articles by Shaw cited in note 4.

14. For example, in February 1974 a Superior Court judge in Maine ordered a doctor to proceed with an operation to repair a hole in the esophagus of a baby with multiple deformities. Otherwise the operation would not have been performed. The baby died anyway a few days later. "Deformed Baby Dies Amid Controversy," *The Miami Herald,* 25 February 1974, p. 4-B.

The Intentional Termination of Life

Bonnie Steinbock

Bonnie Steinbock defends the policy statement of the American Medical Association on euthanasia against James Rachels's critique. She argues that the statement does not rest on the belief that there is a moral difference between active and passive euthanasia. Rather, she contends that the statement rejects both active and passive euthanasia but permits "the cessation of the employment of extraordinary means," which she claims is not the same as passive euthanasia. She points out that doctors can cease to employ extraordinary means to respect the wishes of the patient or because continued treatment is painful and has little chance of success, without intending to let the patient die. She allows, however, that in some cases, ceasing to employ extraordinary means does amount to intending to let the patient die and also that in other cases, killing may even be morally preferable to letting die.

Reprinted with permission from *Ethics in Science and Medicine,* pp. 59–64, Bonnie Steinbock, "The Intentional Termination of Life." Copyright 1979, Pergamon Press, Ltd.

According to James Rachels[1] a common mistake in medical ethics is the belief that there is a moral difference between active and passive euthanasia. This is a mistake, [he] argues, because the rationale underlying the distinction between active and passive euthanasia is the idea that there is a significant moral difference between intentionally killing and letting die. . . . Whether the belief that there is a significant moral difference (between intentionally killing and intentionally letting die) is mistaken is not my concern here. For it is far from clear that this distinction *is* the basis of the doctrine of the American Medical Association which Rachels attacks. And if the killing/letting die distinction is not the basis of the AMA doctrine, then arguments showing that the distinction has no moral force do not, in themselves, reveal in the doctrine's adherents either "confused thinking" or "a moral point of view unrelated to the interests of individuals". Indeed, as we examine the AMA doctrine, I think it will become clear that it appeals to and makes use of a number of overlapping distinctions, which may have moral significance in particular cases, such as the distinction between intending and foreseeing, or between ordinary and extraordinary care. Let us then turn to the statement, from the House of Delegates of the American Medical Association, which Rachels cites:

The intentional termination of the life of one human being by another—mercy-killing—is contrary to that for which the medical profession stands and is contrary to the policy of the American Medical Association.

The cessation of the employment of extraordinary means to prolong the life of the body when there is irrefutable evidence that biological death is imminent is the decision of the patient and/or his immediate family. The advice and judgment of the physician should be freely available to the patient and/or his immediate family.[2]

Rachels attacks this statement because he believes that it contains a moral distinction between active and passive euthanasia. . . .

I intend to show that the AMA statement does not imply support of the active/passive euthanasia distinction. In forbidding the intentional termination of life, the statement rejects both active and passive euthanasia. It does allow for ". . . the cessation of the employment of extraordinary means . . ." to prolong life. The mistake Rachels makes is in identifying the cessation of life-prolonging treatment with passive euthanasia, or intentionally letting die. If it were right to equate the two, then the AMA statement would be self-contradictory, for it would begin by condemning, and end by allowing, the intentional termination of life. But if the cessation of life-prolonging treatment is not always or necessarily passive euthanasia, then there is no confusion and no contradiction.

Why does Rachels think that the cessation of life-prolonging treatment is the intentional termination of life? He says:

The AMA policy statement isolates the crucial issue very well: the crucial issue is "the intentional termination of the life of one human being by another". But after identifying this issue, and forbidding "mercy-killing", the statement goes on to deny that the cessation of treatment is the intentional termination of a life. This is where the mistake comes in, for what is the cessation of treatment, in these circumstances, if it is not "the intentional termination of the life of one human being of another"? Of course it is exactly that, and if it were not, there would be no point to it.[3]

However, there *can* be a point (to the cessation of life-prolonging treatment) other than an endeavor to bring about the patient's death, and so the blanket identification of cessation of treatment with the intentional termination of a life is inaccurate. There are at least two situations in which the termination of life-prolonging treatment cannot be identified with the intentional termination of the life of one human being by another.

The first situation concerns the patient's right to refuse treatment. Rachels gives the example of a patient dying of an incurable disease, accompanied by unrelievable pain, who wants to end the treatment which cannot cure him but can only prolong his miserable existence. Why, they ask, may a doctor accede to the patient's request to stop treatment, but not provide a patient in a similar situation with a lethal dose? The answer lies in the patient's right to refuse treatment. In general, a competent adult has the right to refuse treatment, even where such treatment is necessary to prolong life. Indeed, the right to refuse treatment has been upheld even when the patient's reason for refusing treatment is generally agreed to be inadequate.[4] This right can be overridden (if, for example, the patient has dependent children) but, in general, no one may legally compel you to undergo treatment to which you have not consented. "Historically, surgical intrusion has always been considered a technical battery upon the person and one to be excused or justified by consent of the patient or justified by necessity created by the circumstances of the moment. . . ."[5]

At this point, it might be objected that if one has the right to refuse life-prolonging treatment, then consistency demands that one have the right to decide to end his life, and to obtain help in doing so. The idea is that the right to refuse treatment somehow implies a right to voluntary euthanasia, and we need to see why someone might think this. The right to refuse treatment has been considered by legal writers as an example of the right to privacy or, better, the right to bodily self-determination. You have the right to decide what happens to your own body, and the right to refuse treatment is an instance of that more general right. But if you have the right to determine what happens to your body, then should you not have the right to choose to end your life, and even a right to get help in doing so?

However, it is important to see that the right to refuse treatment is not the same as, nor does it entail, a right to voluntary euthanasia, even if both can be derived from the right to bodily self-determination. The right to refuse treatment is not itself a "right to die"; that one may choose to exercise this right even at the risk of death, or even *in order to die,* is irrelevant. The purpose of the right to refuse medical treatment is not to give persons a right to decide whether to live or die, but to protect them from the unwanted interferences of others. Perhaps we ought to interpret the right to

bodily self-determination more broadly so as to include a right to die: but this would be a substantial extension of our present understanding of the right to bodily self-determination, and not a consequence of it. Should we recognize a right to voluntary euthanasia, we would have to agree that people have the right not merely to be left alone, but also the right to be killed. I leave to one side that substantive moral issue. My claim is simply that there can be a reason for terminating life-prolonging treatment other than "to bring about the patient's death".

The second case in which termination of treatment cannot be identified with intentional termination of life is where continued treatment has little chance of improving the patient's condition and brings greater discomfort than relief.

The question here is what treatment is appropriate to the particular case. A cancer specialist describes it in this way:

> My general rule is to administer therapy as long as a patient responds well and has the potential for a reasonably good quality of life. But when all feasible therapies have been administered and a patient shows signs of rapid deterioration, the continuation of therapy can cause more discomfort than the cancer. From that time I recommend surgery, radiotherapy, or chemotherapy only as a means of relieving pain. But if a patient's condition should once again stabilize after the withdrawal of active therapy and if it should appear that he could still gain some good time, I would immediately reinstitute active therapy. The decision to cease anticancer treatment is never irrevocable, and often the desire to live will push a patient to try for another remission, or even a few more days of life.[6]

The decision here to cease anticancer treatment cannot be construed as a decision that the patient die, or as the intentional termination of life. It is a decision to provide the most appropriate treatment for that patient at that time. Rachels suggests that the point of the cessation of treatment is the intentional termination of life. But here the point of discontinuing treatment is not to bring about the patient's death but to avoid treatment that will cause more discomfort than the cancer and has little hope of benefiting the patient. Treatment that meets this description is often called "extraordinary".[7] The concept is flexible, and what might be considered "extraordinary" in one situation might be ordinary in another. The use of a respirator to sustain a patient through a severe bout with a respiratory disease would be considered ordinary; its use to sustain the life of a severely brain damaged person in an irreversible coma would be considered extraordinary.

Contrasted with extraordinary treatment is ordinary treatment, the care a doctor would normally be expected to provide. Failure to provide ordinary care constitutes neglect, and can even be construed as the intentional infliction of harm, where there is a legal obligation to provide care. The importance of the ordinary/extraordinary care distinction lies partly in its connection to the doctor's intention. The withholding of extraordinary care should be seen as a decision not to inflict painful treatment on a patient without reasonable hope of success. The withholding of ordinary care, by contrast, must be seen as neglect. Thus, one doctor says, "We have to draw a distinction between ordinary and extraordinary means. We never withdraw what's needed to make a baby comfortable, we would never withdraw the care a parent would provide. We never kill a baby. . . . But we may decide certain heroic intervention is not worthwhile."[8]

We should keep in mind the ordinary/extraordinary care distinction when considering an example given by Rachels to show the irrationality of the active/passive distinction with regard to infanticide. The example is this: a child is born with Down's syndrome and also has an intestinal obstruction which requires corrective surgery. If the surgery is not performed, the infant will starve to death, since it cannot take food orally. This may take days or even weeks, as dehydration and infection set in. Commenting on this situation, Rachels says:

I can understand why some people are opposed to all euthanasia, and insist that such infants must be allowed to live. I think I can also understand why other people favor destroying these babies quickly and painlessly. But why should anyone favor letting "dehydration and infection wither a tiny being over hours and days"? The doctrine that says that a baby may be allowed to dehydrate and wither, but may not be given an injection that would end its life without suffering, seems so patently cruel as to require no further refutation.[9]

Such a doctrine perhaps does not need further refutation; but this is not the AMA doctrine. For the AMA statement criticized by Rachels allows only for the cessation of extraordinary means to prolong life when death is imminent. Neither of these conditions is satisfied in this example. Death is not imminent in this situation, any more than it would be if a normal child had an attack of appendicitis. Neither the corrective surgery to remove the intestinal obstruction, nor the intravenous feeding required to keep the infant alive until such surgery is performed, can be regarded as extraordinary means, for neither is particularly expensive, nor does either place an overwhelming burden on the patient or others. (The continued existence of the child might be thought to place an overwhelming burden on its parents, but that has nothing to do with the characterization of the means to prolong its life as extraordinary. If it had, then *feeding* a severely defective child who required a great deal of care could be regarded as extraordinary.) The chances of success if the operation is undertaken are quite good, though there is always a risk in operating on infants. Though the Down's syndrome will not be alleviated, the child will proceed to an otherwise normal infancy.

It cannot be argued that the treatment is withheld for the infant's sake, unless one is prepared to argue that all mentally retarded babies are better off dead. This is particularly implausible in the case of Down's syndrome babies who generally do not suffer and are capable of giving and receiving love, of learning and playing, to varying degrees.

In a film on this subject entitled, "Who Should Survive?", a doctor defended a decision not to operate, saying that since the parents did not consent to the operation, the doctors' hands were tied. As we have seen, surgical intrusion requires consent, and in the case of infants, consent would normally come from the parents. But, as their legal guardians, parents are required to provide medical care for their children, and failure to do so can constitute criminal neglect or even homicide. In general, courts have been understandably reluctant to recognize a parental right to terminate life-prolonging treatment.[10] Although prosecution is unlikely, physicians who comply with invalid instructions from the parents and permit the infant's death could be liable for aiding and abetting, failure to report child neglect, or even homicide. So it is not true that, in this situation, doctors are legally bound to do as the parents wish.

To sum up, I think that Rachels is right to regard the decision not to operate in the Down's syndrome example as the intentional termination of life. But there is no reason to believe that either the law or the AMA would regard it otherwise. Certainly the decision to withhold treatment is not justified by the AMA statement. That such infants have been allowed to die cannot be denied; but this, I think, is the result of doctors misunderstanding the law and the AMA position.

Withholding treatment in this case is the intentional termination of life because the infant is deliberately allowed to die; that is the point of not operating. But there are other cases in which that is not the point. If the point is to avoid inflicting painful treatment on a patient with little or no reasonable hope of success, this is not the intentional termination of life. The permissibility of such withholding of treatment, then, would have no implications for the permissibility of euthanasia, active or passive.

The decision whether or not to operate, or to institute vigorous treatment, is particularly agonizing in the case of children born with spina bifida, an opening in the base of the spine usually accompanied by hydrocephalus and mental retardation. If left unoperated, these children usually die of meningitis or kidney failure within the first few years of life. Even if they survive, all affected children face a lifetime of illness, operations and varying degrees of disability. The policy used to be to save as many as possible, but the trend now is toward selective treatment, based on the physician's estimate of the chances of success. If operating is not likely to improve significantly the child's condition, parents and doctors may agree not to operate. This is not the intentional termination of life, for again the purpose is not the termination of the child's life but the avoidance of painful and pointless treatment. Thus, the fact that withholding treatment is justified does not imply that killing the child would be equally justified.

Throughout the discussion, I have claimed that intentionally ceasing life-prolonging treatment is not the intentional termination of life unless the doctor has, as his or her purpose in stopping treatment, the patient's death.

It may be objected that I have incorrectly characterized the conditions for the intentional termination of life. Perhaps it is enough that the doctor intentionally ceases treatment, foreseeing that the patient will die; perhaps the reason for ceasing treatment is irrelevant to its characterization as the intentional termination of life. I find this suggestion implausible, but am willing to consider arguments for it. Rachels has provided no such arguments: indeed, he apparently shares my view about the intentional termination of life. For when he claims that the cessation of life-prolonging treatment *is* the intentional termination of life, his reason for making the claim is that "if it were not, there would be no point to it". Rachels believes that the point of ceasing treatment, "in these cases", is to bring about the patient's death. If that were not the point, he suggests, why would the doctor cease treatment? I have shown, however, that there can be a point to ceasing treatment which is not the death of the patient. In showing this, I have refuted Rachels' reason for identifying the cessation of life-prolonging treatment with the intentional termination of life, and thus his argument against the AMA doctrine.

Here someone might say: Even if the withholding of treatment is not the intentional termination of life, does that make a difference, morally speaking? If life-prolonging treatment may be withheld, for the sake of the child, may not an easy death be provided, for the sake of the child, as well? The unoperated child with spina bifida may take months or even years to die. Distressed by the spectacle of children "lying around waiting to die", one doctor has written, "It is time that society and medicine stopped perpetuating the fiction that withholding treatment is ethically different from terminating a life. It is time that society began to discuss mechanisms by which we can alleviate the pain and suffering for those individuals whom we cannot help."[11]

I do not deny that there may be cases in which death is in the best interests of the patient. In such cases, a quick and painless death may be the best thing. However, I do not think that, once active or vigorous treatment is stopped, a quick death is always preferable to a lingering one. We must be cautious about attributing to defective children *our* distress at seeing them linger. Waiting for them to die may be tough on parents, doctors and nurses—it isn't necessarily tough on the child. The decision not to operate need not mean a decision to neglect, and it may be possible to make the remaining months of the child's life comfortable, pleasant and filled with love. If this alternative is possible, surely it is more decent and humane than killing the child. In such a situation, withholding treatment, foreseeing the child's death, is not ethically equivalent to killing the child, and we cannot move from the permissibility of the former to that of the latter. I am worried that there will be a tendency to do precisely that if active euthanasia is regarded as morally equivalent to the withholding of life-prolonging treatment.

Conclusion

The AMA statement does not make the distinction Rachels wishes to attack, i.e. that between active and passive euthanasia. Instead, the statement draws a distinction between the intentional termination of life, on the one hand, and the cessation of the employment of extraordinary means to prolong life, on the other. Nothing said by Rachels shows that this distinction is confused. It may be that doctors

have misinterpreted the AMA statement, and that this had led, for example, to decisions to allow defective infants slowly to starve to death. I quite agree with Rachels that the decisions to which they allude were cruel and made on irrelevant grounds. Certainly it is worth pointing out that allowing someone to die can be the intentional termination of life, and that it can be just as bad as, or worse than, killing someone. However, the withholding of life-prolonging treatment is not necessarily the intentional termination of life, so that if it is permissible to withhold life-prolonging treatment, it does not follow that, other things being equal, it is permissible to kill. Furthermore, most of the time, other things are not equal. In many of the cases in which it would be right to cease treatment, I do not think that it would also be right to kill.

Notes

1. James Rachels. Active and passive euthanasia. *New Engl. J. Med.*, **292**, 78–80, 1975.

2. Rachels, p. 78.

3. Rachels, p. 79–80.

4. For example, *In re Yetter*, 62 Pa. D. & C. 2d 619, C.P., Northampton County Ct., 1974.

5. David W. Meyers, Legal aspects of voluntary euthanasia, *Dilemmas of Euthanasia* (Edited by John Behnke and Sissela Bok), p. 56. Anchor Books, New York, 1975.

6. Ernest H. Rosenbaum, Md., *Living with Cancer*, p. 27. Praeger, New York, 1975.

7. Cf. Tristam Engelhardt, Jr., Ethical issues in aiding the death of young children, *Beneficent Euthanasia* (Edited by Marvin Kohl), Prometheus Books, Buffalo, N.Y. 1975.

8. B. D. Colen, *Karen Ann Quinlan: Living and Dying in the Age of Eternal Life*, p. 115. Nash, 1976.

9. Rachels, p. 79.

10. Cf. Norman L. Cantor, Law and the termination of an incompetent patient's life-preserving care. *Dilemmas of Euthanasia. op. cit.*, pp. 69–105.

11. John Freeman, Is there a right to die—quickly?, *J. Pediat.* **80**. p. 905.

Akron v. Akron Center for Reproductive Life

Supreme Court of the United States

The issue before the Supreme Court was whether a number of constraints on obtaining an abortion imposed by the City of Akron were unreasonable. These constraints required (1) that all abortions performed after the first trimester of pregnancy be performed in a hospital; (2) the notification of consent by parents before abortions could be performed on unmarried minors; (3) that the attending physician make certain specified statements to the patient "to insure that the consent for an abortion is truly informed consent;" (4) a 24-hour waiting period between the time the woman signs a consent form and the time the abortion is performed; and (5) that fetal remains be "disposed of in a humane and sanitary manner." The majority of the Supreme Court ruled that these constraints were not reasonable. In dissent, Justice O'Connor, joined by Justices White and Rehnquist, argued that these constraints were reasonable and, moreover, that the framework used in Roe v. Wade and subsequent decisions was faulty because, among other things, improved medical technology has moved back the point of fetal viability on which the court had relied in determining when abortion was permissible.

Justice Powell delivered the opinion of the Court.

In this litigation we must decide the constitutionality of several provisions of an ordinance enacted by the city of Akron, Ohio, to regulate the performance of abortions. . . .

These cases come to us a decade after we held in *Roe* v. *Wade* . . . that the right of privacy, grounded in the concept of personal liberty guaranteed by the Constitution, encompasses a woman's right to decide whether to terminate her pregnancy. Legislative responses to the Court's decision have required us on several occasions, and again today, to define the limits of a State's authority to regulate the performance of abortions. And arguments continue to be made, in these cases as well, that we erred in interpreting the Constitution. Nonetheless, the doctrine of *stare decisis*, while perhaps never entirely persuasive on a constitutional question, is a doctrine that demands respect in a society governed by the rule of law.[1] We respect it today, and reaffirm *Roe* v. *Wade*. . . .

In *Roe* v. *Wade*, the Court held that the "right of privacy, . . . founded in the Fourteenth Amendment's concept of personal liberty and restrictions upon state action, . . . is broad enough to encompass a woman's decision whether or not to terminate her pregnancy." . . . Although the Constitution does not specifically identify this right, the history of this Court's constitutional adjudication leaves no doubt that "the full scope of the liberty guaranteed by the Due Process Clause cannot be found in or limited by the precise terms of the specific guarantees elsewhere provided in the Constitution." . . . Central among these protected liberties is an individual's "freedom of personal choice in matters of marriage and family life." . . . The decision in *Roe* was based firmly on this long-recognized and essential element of personal liberty.

The Court also has recognized, because abortion is a medical procedure, that the full vindication of the woman's fundamental right necessarily requires that her physician be given "the room he needs to make his best medical judgment." . . . The physician's exercise of this medical judgment encompasses both assisting the woman in the decisionmaking process and implementing her decision should she choose abortion. . . .

At the same time, the Court in *Roe* acknowledged that the woman's fundamental right "is not unqualified and must be considered against important state interests in abortion." . . . But restrictive state regulation of the right to choose abortion, as with other fundamental rights subject to searching judicial examination, must be supported by a compelling state interest. . . . We have recognized two such interests that may justify state regulation of abortions.

First, a State has an "important and legitimate interest in protecting the potentiality of human life." . . . Although this interest exists "throughout the course of the woman's pregnancy," . . . it becomes compelling only at viability, the point at which the fetus "has the capability of meaningful life outside the mother's womb." . . . At viability this interest in protecting the potential life of the unborn child is so important that the State may proscribe abortions altogether, "except when it is necessary to preserve the life or health of the mother." . . .

Second, because a State has a legitimate concern with the health of women who undergo abortions, "a State may properly assert important interests in safeguarding health [and] in maintaining medical standards." . . . We held in *Roe*, however, that this health interest does not become compelling until "approximately the end of the first trimester of pregnancy. . . . Until that time, a pregnant woman must be permitted, in consultation with her physician, to decide to have an abortion and to effectuate that decision "free of interference by the State." . . .

. . . We noted, for example, that States could establish requirements relating "to the facility in which the procedure is to be performed, that is, whether it must be in a hospital or may be a clinic or some other place of less-than-hospital status." . . . We recognized the State's legitimate health interests in establishing, for second-trimester abortions, "standards for licensing all facilities where abortions may be performed." . . . We found, however, that "the State must show more than [was shown in *Doe*] in order to prove that only the full resources of a licensed hospital, rather than those of some other appropriately licensed institution, satisfy these health interests." . . .

There can be no doubt that [the city of Akron's] second-trimester hospitalization requirement places a significant obstacle in the path of women seeking an abortion. A primary burden created by the requirement is additional cost to the woman. . . . [A] second-trimester hospitalization requirement may force women to travel to find available facilities, resulting in both financial expense and additional health risk. It therefore is apparent that a second-trimester hospitalization requirement may significantly limit a woman's ability to obtain an abortion. . . . Since [*Roe*], however, the safety of second-trimester abortions has increased dramatically. The principal reason is that the D&E procedure is now widely and successfully used for second-trimester abortions. . . .

These developments, and the professional commentary supporting them, constitute impressive evidence that—at least during the early weeks of the second trimester—D&E abortions may be performed as safely in an outpatient clinic as in a full-service hospital. We conclude, therefore, that "present medical knowledge" . . . convincingly undercuts Akron's justification for requiring that *all* second-trimester abortions be performed in a hospital. . . .

The Akron ordinance provides that no abortion shall be performed except "with the informed written consent of the pregnant woman, . . . given freely and without coercion." . . . Furthermore, "in order to insure that the consent for an abortion is truly informed consent," the woman must be orally informed by her attending physician" of the status of her pregnancy, the development of her fetus, the date of possible viability, the physical and emotional complications that may result from an abortion, and the availability of agencies to provide her with assistance and information with respect to birth control, adoption, and childbirth. . . . In addition, the attending physician must inform her "of the particular risks associated with her own pregnancy and the abortion technique to be employed . . . [and] other information which in his own medical judgment is relevant to her decision as to whether to have an abortion or carry her pregnancy to term." . . .

Viewing the city's regulations in this light, we believe that [they attempt] to extend the State's interest in ensuring "informed consent" beyond permissible limits. First, it is fair to say that much of the information required is designed not to inform the woman's consent but rather to persuade her to withhold it altogether. Subsection (3) requires the physician to inform his patient that "the unborn child is a human life from the moment of conception," a requirement inconsistent with the Court's holding in *Roe* v. *Wade* that a State may not adopt one theory of when life begins to justify its regulation of abortions. . . . Moreover, much of the detailed description of "the anatomical and physiological characteristics of the particular unborn child" required by subsection (3) would involve at best speculation by the physician. And subsection (5), that begins with the dubious statement that "abortion is a major surgical procedure" and proceeds to describe numerous possible physical and psychological complications of abortion,[2] is a "parade of horribles" intended to suggest that abortion is a particularly dangerous procedure. . . .

The Akron ordinance prohibits a physician from performing an abortion until 24 hours after the pregnant woman signs a consent form. . . . The District Court upheld this provision on the ground that it furthered Akron's interest in ensuring "that a woman's abortion decision is made after careful consideration of all the facts applicable to her particular situation." . . . The Court of Appeals reversed, finding that the inflexible waiting period had "no medical basis, and that careful consideration of the abortion decision by the woman "is beyond the state's power to require." . . . We affirm the Court of Appeals' judgment. . . .

We affirm the judgment of the Court of Appeals invalidating those sections of Akron's "Regulations of Abortions" ordinance that deal with parental consent, informed consent, a 24-hour waiting period, and the disposal of fetal remains. The remaining portion of the judgment, sustaining Akron's requirement that all second-trimester abortions be performed in a hospital, is reversed.

It is so ordered.

Justice O'Connor, with whom Justice White and Justice Rehnquist join, dissenting.

In *Roe* v. *Wade*, 410 U. S. 113 (1973), the Court held that the "right of privacy . . . founded in the Fourteenth Amendment's concept of personal liberty and restrictions upon state action . . . is broad enough to encompass a woman's decision whether or not to terminate her pregnancy." . . . The parties in these cases have not asked the Court to re-examine the validity of that holding and the court below did not address it. Accordingly, the Court does not re-examine its previous holding. Nonetheless, it is apparent from the Court's opinion that neither sound constitutional theory nor our need to decide cases based on the application of neutral principles can accommodate an analytical framework that varies according to the "stages" of pregnancy, where those stages, and their concomitant standards of review, differ according to the level of medical technology available when a particular challenge to state regulation occurs. The Court's analysis of the Akron regulations is inconsistent both with the methods of analysis employed in previous cases dealing with abortion, and with the Court's approach to fundamental rights in other areas. . . .

The trimester or "three-stage" approach adopted by the Court in *Roe*, and, in a modified form, employed by the Court to analyze the regulations in these cases, cannot be supported as a legitimate or useful framework for accommodating the woman's right and the State's interests. The decision of the Court today graphically illustrates why the trimester approach is a completely unworkable method of accommodating the conflicting personal rights and compelling state interests that are involved in the abortion context.

As the Court indicates today, the State's compelling interest in maternal health changes as medical technology changes, and any health regulation must not "depart from accepted medical practice." . . . In applying this standard, the Court holds that "the safety of second-trimester abortions has increased dramatically" since 1973, when *Roe* was decided.

. . . Although a regulation such as one requiring that all second trimester abortions be performed in hospitals "had strong support" in 1973 "as a reasonable health regulation," . . . this regulation can no longer stand because, according to the Court's diligent research into medical and scientific literature, the dilation and evacuation (D&E) procedure, used in 1973 only for first-trimester abortions, "is now widely and successfully used for second-trimester abortions.". . . Further, the medical literature relied on by the Court indicates that the D&E procedure may be performed in an appropriate nonhospital setting for "at least . . . the early weeks of the second trimester. . . ." The Court then chooses the period of 16 weeks of gestation as that point at which D&E procedures may be performed safely in a nonhospital setting, and thereby invalidates the Akron hospitalization regulation.

It is not difficult to see that despite the Court's purported adherence to the trimester approach adopted in *Roe,* the lines drawn in that decision have now been "blurred" because of what the Court accepts as technological advancement in the safety of abortion procedure. The State may no longer rely on a "bright line" that separates permissible from impermissible regulation, and it is no longer free to consider the second trimester as a unit and weigh the risks posed by all abortion procedures throughout that trimester. Rather, the State must continuously and conscientiously study contemporary medical and scientific literature in order to determine whether the effect of a particular regulation is to "depart from accepted medical practice" insofar as particular procedures and particular periods within the trimester are concerned. Assuming that legislative bodies are able to engage in this exacting task,[3] it is difficult to believe that our Constitution *requires* that they do it as a prelude to protecting the health of their citizens. It is even more difficult to believe that this Court, without the resources available to those bodies entrusted with making legislative choices, believes itself competent to make these inquiries and to revise these standards every time the American College of Obstetricians and Gynecologists (ACOG) or similar group revises its views about what is and what is not appropriate medical procedure in this area. Indeed, the ACOG Standards on which

the Court relies were changed in 1982 after trial in the present cases. Before ACOG changed its Standards in 1982, it recommended that all mid-trimester abortions be performed in a hospital. . . . As today's decision indicates, medical technology is changing, and this change will necessitate our continued functioning as the Nation's "*ex officio* medical board with powers to approve or disapprove medical and operative practices and standards throughout the United States." . . .

Just as improvements in medical technology inevitably will move *forward* the point at which the State may regulate for reasons of maternal health, different technological improvements will move *backward* the point of viability at which the state may proscribe abortions except when necessary to preserve the life and health of the mother. . . .

The *Roe* framework, then, is clearly on a collision course with itself. As the medical risks of various abortion procedures decrease, the point at which the State may regulate for reasons of maternal health is moved further forward to actual childbirth. As medical science becomes better able to provide for the separate existence of the fetus, the point of viability is moved further back toward conception. . . .

The Court adheres to the *Roe* framework because the doctrine of *stare decisis* "demands respect in a society governed by the rule of law." . . . Although respect for *stare decisis* cannot be challenged, "this Court's considered practice [is] not to apply *stare decisis* as rigidly in constitutional as in nonconstitutional cases." . . . Although we must be mindful of the "desirability of continuity of decision in constitutional questions . . . when convinced of former error, this Court has never felt constrained to follow precedent. In constitutional questions, where correction depends upon amendment and not upon legislative action this Court throughout its history has freely exercised its power to reexamine the basis of its constitutional decisions." . . .

Even assuming that there is a fundamental right to terminate pregnancy in some situations, there is no justification in law or logic for the trimester framework adopted in *Roe* and employed by the Court today on the basis of *stare decisis*. For the reasons stated above, that framework is clearly an unworkable means of balancing the fundamental right and the compelling state interests that are indisputably implicated.

. . . In *Roe*, the Court held that although the State had an important and legitimate interest in protecting potential life, that interest could not become compelling until the point at which the fetus was viable. The difficulty with this analysis is clear: *potential* life is no less potential in the first weeks of pregnancy than it is at viability or afterward. At any stage in pregnancy, there is the *potential* for human life. Although the Court refused to "resolve the difficult question of when life begins," . . . the Court chose the point of viability—when the fetus is *capable* of life independent of its mother—to permit the complete proscription of abortion. The choice of viability as the point at which the state interest in *potential* life becomes compelling is no less arbitrary than choosing any point before viability or any point afterward. Accordingly, I believe that the State's interest in protecting potential human life exists throughout the pregnancy. . . .

We must always be mindful that "[t]he Constitution does not compel a state to fine tune its statutes so as to encourage or facilitate abortions. To the contrary, state action 'encouraging childbirth except in the most urgent circumstances' is 'rationally related to the legitimate governmental objective of protecting potential life.' . . ."

Section 1870.03 of the Akron ordinance requires that second-trimester abortions be performed in hospitals. The Court holds that this requirement imposes a "significant obstacle" in the form of increased costs and decreased availability of abortions. . . .

For the reasons stated above, I find no justification for the trimester approach used by the Court to analyze this restriction. I would apply the "unduly burdensome" test and find that the hospitalization requirement does not impose an undue burden on that decision. . . .

Section 1870.07 of the Akron ordinance requires a 24-hour waiting period between the signing of a consent form and the actual performance of the abortion, except in cases of emergency. . . . The Court accepts the arguments made by Akron Center that the waiting period increases the costs of obtaining an abortion by requiring the pregnant woman to make two trips to the clinic, and increases the risks of abortion through delay and scheduling difficulties. . . .

. . . [This] decision also has grave consequences for the fetus, whose life the State has a compelling interest to protect and preserve. "[N]o other [medical] procedure involves the purposeful termination of a potential life." . . . The waiting period is surely a small cost to impose to ensure that the woman's decision is well considered in light of its certain and irreparable consequences on fetal life, and the possible effects on her own. . . .

Finally, . . . the Akron ordinance requires that "[a]ny physician who shall perform or induce an abortion upon a pregnant woman shall insure that the remains of the unborn child are disposed of in a humane and sanitary manner." The Court finds this provision void for vagueness. I disagree. . . .

. . . [T]he city of Akron has informed this Court that the intent of the "humane" portion of its statute, as distinguished from the "sanitary" portion, is merely to ensure that fetuses will not be " 'dump[ed] . . . on garbage piles.' " . . . In light of the fact that the city of Akron indicates no intent to require that physicians provide "decent burials" for fetuses, and that "humane" is no more vague than the term "sanitary," the vagueness of which Akron Center does not question, I cannot conclude that the statute is void for vagueness. . . .

For the reasons set forth above, I dissent from the judgment of the Court in these cases.

Notes

1. There are especially compelling reasons for adhering to *stare decisis* in applying the principles of *Roe* v. *Wade*. That case was considered with

special care. It was first argued during the 1971 Term, and reargued—with extensive briefing—the following Term. The decision was joined by The Chief Justice and six other Justices. Since *Roe* was decided in January 1973, the Court repeatedly and consistently has accepted and applied the basic principle that a woman has a fundamental right to make the highly personal choice whether or not to terminate her pregnancy. . . .

Today, however, the dissenting opinion rejects the basic premise of *Roe* and its progeny. The dissent stops short of arguing flatly that *Roe* should be overruled. Rather, it adopts reasoning that, for all practical purposes, would accomplish precisely that result. The dissent states that "[e]ven assuming that there is a fundamental right to terminate pregnancy in some situations," the State's compelling interests in maternal health and potential human life are present *throughout* pregnancy." (emphasis in original). The existence of these compelling interests turns out to be largely unnecessary, however, for the dissent does not think that even one of the numerous abortion regulations at issue imposes a sufficient burden on the "limited fundamental right, to require heightened scrutiny. Indeed, the dissent asserts that, regardless of cost, "[a] health regulation, such as the hospitalization requirement, simply does not rise to the level of 'official interference' with the abortion decision." (quoting *Harris* v. *McRae, supra*, at 328 (White, J., concurring)). The dissent therefore would hold that a requirement that all abortions be performed in an acute-care, general hospital does

not impose an unacceptable burden on the abortion decision. It requires no great familiarity with the cost and limited availability of such hospitals to appreciate that the effect of the dissent's view would be to drive the performance of many abortions back underground free of effective regulation and often without the attendance of a physician.

In sum, it appears that the dissent would uphold virtually any abortion regulation under a rational-basis test. It also appears that even where heightened scrutiny is deemed appropriate, the dissent would uphold virtually any abortion-inhibiting regulation because of the State's interest in preserving potential human life. ([e.g.,] arguing that a 24-hour waiting period is justified in part because the abortion decision "has grave consequences for the fetus"). This analysis is wholly incompatible with the existence of the fundamental right recognized in *Roe* v. *Wade*.

2. Section 1870.06(B)(5) requires the physician to state "[t]hat abortion is a major surgical procedure which can result in serious complications, including hemorrhage, perforated uterus, infection, menstrual disturbances, sterility and miscarriage and prematurity in subsequent pregnancies; and that abortion may leave essentially unaffected or may worsen any existing psychological problems she may have, and can result in severe emotional disturbances."

3. Irrespective of the difficulty of the task, legislatures, with their superior factfinding capabilities, are certainly better able to make the necessary judgments than are courts.

The Karen Quinlan Opinion

Supreme Court of New Jersey

After being examined by a number of physicians, Karen Quinlan was found to be in a "chronic, persistent vegetative state," although not "brain dead" by the ordinary medical standard. It was judged that no form of treatment could restore her to cognitive or sapient life. At the time, she was being sustained by a respirator. Her father, Joseph Quinlan, asked to be appointed her legal guardian with the expressed purpose of discontinuing the use of the respirator. A lower court refused this request. The Supreme Court of New Jersey, however, granted the request on the condition that (1) attending physicians of Joseph Quinlan's choice conclude that there was no reasonable possibility of Karen's ever being restored to cognitive, sapient life and that the use of the respirator should be discontinued; and on the further condition that (2) the "Ethics Committee" of the institution where Karen was hospitalized concur in the physicians' judgment.

The Factual Base

On the night of April 15, 1975, for reasons still unclear, Karen Quinlan ceased breathing for at least two 15 minute periods. She received some ineffectual mouth-to-mouth resuscitation from friends. She was taken by ambulance to Newton Memorial Hospital. There she had a temperature of 100 degrees, her pupils were unreactive and she was unresponsive even to deep pain. The history at the time of her admission to that hospital was essentially incomplete and uninformative. . . .

Dr. Morse and other expert physicians who examined her characterized Karen as being in a "chronic persistent vegetative state." Dr. Fred Plum, one of such expert witnesses, defined this as a "subject who remains with the capacity to maintain the vegetative parts of neurological function but who no longer has any cognitive function."

From "In the Matter of Karen Quinlan, An Alleged Incompetent," Supreme Court of New Jersey 355A 2d 647.

Dr. Morse, as well as the several other medical and neurological experts who testified in this case, believed with certainty that Karen Quinlan is not "brain dead." They identified the Ad Hoc Committee of Harvard Medical School report (*infra*) as the ordinary medical standard for determining brain death, and all of them were satisfied that Karen met none of the criteria specified in that report and was therefore not "brain dead" within its contemplation.

In this respect it was indicated by Dr. Plum that the brain works in essentially two ways, the vegetative and the sapient. He testified

We have an internal vegetative regulation which controls body temperature which controls breathing, which controls to a considerable degree blood pressure, which controls to some degree heart rate, which controls chewing, swallowing and which controls sleeping and waking. We have a more highly developed brain which is uniquely human which controls our relation to the outside world, our capacity to talk, to see, to feel, to sing, to think. Brain death necessarily must mean the death of both of these functions of the brain, vegetative and the sapient. Therefore, the presence of any function which is regulated or governed or controlled by the deeper parts of the brain which in laymen's terms might be considered purely vegetative would mean that the brain is not biologically dead.

Because Karen's neurological condition affects her respiratory ability (the respiratory system being a brain stem function) she requires a respirator to assist her breathing. From the time of her admission to Saint Clare's Hospital Karen has been assisted by an MA-1 respirator, a sophisticated machine which delivers a given volume of air at a certain rate and periodically provides a "sigh" volume, a relatively large measured volume of air designed to purge the lungs of excretions. Attempts to "wean" her from the respirator were unsuccessful and have been abandoned.

The experts believe that Karen cannot now survive without the assistance of the respirator; that exactly how long she would live without it is unknown; that the strong likelihood is that death would follow soon after its removal, and that removal would also risk further brain damage and would curtail the assistance the respirator presently provides in warding off infection.

It seemed to be the consensus not only of the treating physicians but also of the several qualified experts who testified in the case, that removal from the respirator would not conform to medical practices, standards and traditions.

The further medical consensus was that Karen in addition to being comatose is in a chronic and persistent "vegetative" state, having no awareness of anything or anyone around her and existing at a primitive reflex level. Although she does have some brain stem function (ineffective for respiration) and has other reactions one normally associates with being alive, such as moving, reacting to light, sound and noxious stimuli, blinking her eyes, and the like, the quality of her feeling impulses is unknown. She grimaces, makes stereotyped cries and sounds and has chewing motions. Her blood pressure is normal.

Karen remains in the intensive care unit at Saint Clare's Hospital, receiving 24-hour care by a team of four nurses characterized, as was the medical attention, as "excellent." She is nourished by feeding by way of a nasal-gastro tube and is routinely examined for infection, which under these circumstances is a serious life threat. The result is that her condition is considered remarkable under the unhappy circumstances involved.

Karen is described as emaciated, having suffered a weight loss of at least 40 pounds, and undergoing a continuing deteriorative process. Her posture is described as fetal-like and grotesque; there is extreme flexion-rigidity of the arms, legs and related muscles and her joints are severely rigid and deformed.

From all of this evidence, and including the whole testimonial record, several basic findings in the physical area are mandated. Severe brain and associated damage, albeit of uncertain etiology, has left Karen in a chronic and persistent vegetative state. No form of treatment which can cure or improve that condition is known or available. As nearly as may be determined, considering the guarded area of remote uncertainties characteristic of most medical science predictions, she can *never* be restored to cognitive or sapient life. Even with regard to the vegetative level and improvement therein (if such it may be called) the prognosis is extremely poor and the extent unknown if it should in fact occur.

She is debilitated and moribund and although fairly stable at the time of argument before us (no new information having been filed in the meanwhile in expansion of the record), no physician risked the opinion that she could live more than a year and indeed she may die much earlier. Excellent medical and nursing care so far has been able to ward off the constant threat of infection, to which she is peculiarly susceptible because of the respirator, the tracheal tube and other incidents of care in her vulnerable condition. Her life accordingly is sustained by the respirator and tubal feeding, and removal from the respirator would cause her death soon, although the time cannot be stated with more precision.

The determination of the fact and time of death in past years of medical science was keyed to the action of the heart and blood circulation, in turn dependent upon pulmonary activity, and hence cessation of these functions spelled out the reality of death.

Developments in medical technology have obfuscated the use of the traditional definition of death. Efforts have been made to define irreversible coma as a new criterion for death, such as by the 1968 report of the Ad Hoc Committee of the Harvard Medical School (the Committee comprising ten physicians, an historian, a lawyer and a theologian), which asserted that:

From ancient times down to the recent past it was clear that, when the respiration and heart stopped, the brain would die in a few minutes; so the obvious criterion of no heart beat as synonymous with death was sufficiently accurate. In those times the heart was considered to be the central organ of the body; it is not surprising that its failure marked the onset of death. This is no longer valid when modern resuscitative and supportive measures are used. These improved activities can now restore "life" as judged by the ancient standards of persistent respiration and continuing heart beat. This can be the case even when there is not the remotest possibility of an individual recovering consciousness following massive brain damage.

The Ad Hoc standards, carefully delineated, included absence of response to pain or other stimuli, pupilary reflexes, corneal, pharyngeal and other reflexes, blood pressure, spontaneous respiration, as well as "flat" or isoelectric electroencephalograms and the like, with all tests repeated "at least 24 hours later with no change." In such circumstances, where all of such criteria have been met as showing "brain death," the Committee recommends with regard to the respirator:

The patient's condition can be determined only by a physician. When the patient is hopelessly damaged as defined above, the family and all colleagues who have participated in major decisions concerning the patient, and all nurses involved, should be so informed. Death is to be declared and then *the respirator turned off. The decision to do this and the responsibility for it are to be taken by the physician-in-charge, in consultation with one or more physicians who have been directly involved in the case. It is unsound and undesirable to force the family to make the decision.* . . . (emphasis in original).

But, as indicated, it was the consensus of medical testimony in the instant case that Karen, for all her disability, met none of these criteria, nor indeed any comparable criteria extant in the medical world and representing, as does the Ad Hoc Committee report, according to the testimony in this case, prevailing and accepted medical standards.

We have adverted to the "brain death" concept and Karen's disassociation with any of its criteria, to emphasize the basis of the medical decision made by Dr. Morse. When plaintiff and his family, finally reconciled to the certainty of Karen's impending death, requested the withdrawal of life support mechanisms, he demurred. His refusal was based upon his conception of medical standards, practice and ethics described in the medical testimony, such as in the evidence given by another neurologist, Dr. Sidney Diamond, a witness for the State. Dr. Diamond asserted that no physician would have failed to provide respirator support at the outset, and none would interrupt its life-saving course thereafter, except in the case of cerebral death. In the latter case, he thought the respirator would in effect be disconnected from one already dead, entitling the physician under medical standards and, he thought, legal concepts, to terminate the supportive measures. We note Dr. Diamond's distinction of major surgical or transfusion procedures in a terminal case not involving cerebral death, such as here:

The subject has lost human qualities. It would be incredible, and I think unlikely, that any physician would respond to a sudden hemorrhage, massive hemorrhage, or a loss of all her defensive blood cells, by giving her large quantities of blood. I think that major surgical procedures would be out of the question even if they were known to be essential for continued physical existence.

This distinction is adverted to also in the testimony of Dr. Julius Korein, a neurologist called by plaintiff. Dr. Korein described a medical practice concept of "judicious neglect" under which the physician will say:

Don't treat this patient anymore, it does not serve either the patient, the family, or society in any meaningful way to continue treatment with this patient.

Dr. Korein also told of the unwritten and unspoken standard of medical practice implied in the foreboding initials DNR (do not resuscitate), as applied to the extraordinary terminal case:

Cancer, metastatic cancer, involving the lungs, the liver, the brain, multiple involvements, the physician may or may not write: Do not resuscitate. [I]t could be said to the nurse: if this man stops breathing don't resuscitate him. No physician that I know personally is going to try and resuscitate a man riddled with cancer and in agony and he stops breathing. They are not going to put him on a respirator. I think that would be the height of misuse of technology.

While the thread of logic in such distinctions may be elusive to the non-medical lay mind, in relation to the supposed imperative to sustain life at all costs, they nevertheless relate to medical decisions, such as the decision of Dr. Morse in the present case. We agree with the trial court that that decision was in accord with Dr. Morse's conception of medical standards and practice.

We turn to that branch of the factual case pertaining to the application for guardianship, as distinguished from the nature of the authorization sought by the applicant. The character and general suitability of Joseph Quinlan as guardian for his daughter, in ordinary circumstances, could not be doubted. The record bespeaks the high degree of familial love which pervaded the home of Joseph Quinlan and reached out fully to embrace Karen, although she was living elsewhere at the time of her collapse. The proofs showed him to be deeply religious, imbued with a morality so sensitive that months of tortured indecision preceded his belated conclusion (despite earlier moral judgments reached by the other family members, but unexpressed to him in order not to influence him) to seek the termination of life-supportive measures sustaining Karen. A communicant of the Roman Catholic Church, as were other family members, he first sought solace in private prayer looking with confidence, as he says, to the Creator, first for the recovery of Karen and then, if that were not possible, for guidance with respect to the awesome decision confronting him.

To confirm the moral rightness of the decision he was about to make he consulted with his parish priest and later with the Catholic chaplain of Saint Clare's Hospital. He would not, he testified, have sought termination if that act were to be morally wrong or in conflict with the tenets of the religion he so profoundly respects. He was disabused of doubt, however, when the position of the Roman Catholic Church was made known to him as it reflected in the record in this case. While it is not usual for matters of religious dogma or concepts to enter a civil litigation (except as they may bear upon constitutional rights, or sometimes, familial matters) they were rightly admitted in evidence here. The judge was bound to measure the character and motivations in all respects of Joseph Quinlan as prospective guardian; and insofar as these religious matters bore upon them, they were properly scrutinized and considered by the court.

Thus germane, we note the position of that Church as illuminated by the record before us. We have no reason to believe that it would be at all discordant with the whole of Judeo-Christian tradition, considering its central respect and reverence for the sanctity of human life. It was in this sense of relevance that we admitted as *amicus curiae* the New Jersey Catholic Conference, essentially the spokesman for the various Catholic bishops of New Jersey, organized to give witness to spiritual values in public affairs in the statewide community. The position statement of Bishop Lawrence B. Casey, reproduced in the *amicus* brief, projects these views:

(a) The verification of the fact of death in a particular case cannot be deduced from any religious or moral principle and, under this aspect, does not fall within the competence of the church;—that dependence must be had upon traditional and medical standards, and by these standards Karen Ann Quinlan is assumed to be alive.

(b) The request of plaintiff for authority to terminate a medical procedure characterized as "an extraordinary means of treatment" would not involve euthanasia. This upon the reasoning expressed by Pope Pius XII in his *allocutio* (address) to anesthesiologists on November 24, 1957, when he dealt with the question:

Does the anesthesiologist have the right, or is he bound, in all cases of deep unconsciousness, even in those that are completely hopeless in the opinion of the competent doctor, to use modern artificial respiration apparatus, even against the will of the family?

His answer made the following points:

1. In ordinary cases the doctor has the right to act in this manner, but is not bound to do so unless this is the only way of fulfilling another certain moral duty.

2. The doctor, however, has no right independent of the patient. He can act only if the patient explicitly or implicitly, directly or indirectly, gives him the permission.

3. The treatment as described in the question constitutes extraordinary means of preserving life and so there is no obligation to use them nor to give the doctor permission to use them.

4. The rights and the duties of the family depend on the presumed will of the unconscious patient if he or she is of legal age, and the family, too, is bound to use only ordinary means.

5. This case is not to be considered euthanasia in any way; that would never be licit. The interruption of attempts at resuscitation, even when it causes the arrest of circulation, is not more than an indirect cause of the cessation of life, and we must apply in this case the principle of double effect.

So it was that the Bishop Casey statement validated the decision of Joseph Quinlan:

Competent medical testimony has established that Karen Ann Quinlan has no reasonable hope of recovery from her comatose state by the use of any available medical procedures. The continuance of mechanical (cardiorespiratory) supportive measures to sustain continuance of her body functions and her life constitute extraordinary means of treatment. Therefore, the decision of Joseph Quinlan to request the discontinuance of this treatment is, according to the teachings of the Catholic Church, a morally correct decision. . . .

It is from this factual base that the Court confronts and responds to three basic issues:

1. Was the trial court correct in denying the specific relief requested by plaintiff, *i.e.*, authorization for termination of the life-supporting apparatus, on the case presented to him? Our determination on that question is in the affirmative.

2. Was the court correct in withholding letters of guardianship from the plaintiff and appointing in his stead a stranger? On that issue our determination is in the negative.

3. Should this Court, in the light of the foregoing conclusions, grant declaratory relief to the plaintiff? On that question our Court's determination is in the affirmative.

This brings us to a consideration of the constitutional and legal issues underlying the foregoing determinations.

Constitutional and Legal Issues

The claimed interests of the State in this case are essentially the preservation and sanctity of human life and defense to the right of the physician to administer medical treatment according to his best judgment. In this case the doctors say that removing Karen from the respirator will conflict with their professional judgment. The plaintiff answers that Karen's present treatment serves only a maintenance function; that the respirator cannot cure or improve her condition but at best can only prolong her inevitable slow deterioration and death; and that the interests of the patient, as seen by her surrogate, the guardian, must be evaluated by the court as predominant, even in the face of an option *contra* by the present attending physicians. Plaintiff's distinction is significant. The nature of Karen's care and the realistic chances of her recovery are quite unlike those of the patients discussed in many of the cases where treatments were ordered. In many of those cases the medical procedure required (usually a transfusion) constituted a minimal bodily invasion and the chances of recovery and return to functioning life were very good. We think that the State's interest *contra* weakens and the individual's right to privacy grows as the degree of bodily invasion increases and the prognosis dims. Ultimately there comes a point at which the individual's rights overcome the State interest. It is for that reason that we believe Karen's choice, if she were competent to make it, would be vindicated by the law. Her prognosis is extremely poor,—she will never resume cognitive life. And the bodily invasion is very great,—she requires 24-hour intensive nursing care, antibiotics, and the assistance of a respirator, a catheter and feeding tube.

Our affirmance of Karen's independent right of choice, however, would ordinarily be based upon her competency to assert it. The sad truth, however, is that she is grossly incompetent and we cannot discern her supposed choice based on the testimony of her previous conversations with friends, where such testimony is without sufficient probative weight. Nevertheless we have concluded that Karen's right of privacy may be asserted on her behalf by her guardian under the peculiar circumstances here present.

If a putative decision by Karen to permit this noncognitive, vegetative existence to terminate by natural forces is regarded as a valuable incident of her right of privacy, as we believe it to be, then it should not be discarded solely on the basis that her condition prevents her conscious exercise of the choice. The only practical way to prevent destruction of the right is to permit the guardian and family of Karen to render their best judgment, subject to the qualifications hereinafter stated, as to whether she would exercise it in these circumstances. If their conclusion is in the affirmative this decision should be accepted by a society the overwhelming majority of whose members would, we think, in similar circumstances, exercise such a choice in the same way for themselves or for those closest to them. It is for this reason that we determine that Karen's right of privacy may be asserted in her behalf, in this respect, by her guardian and family under the particular circumstances presented by this record. . . .

Having concluded that there is a right of privacy that might permit termination of treatment in the circumstances of this case, we turn to consider the relationship of the exercise of that right to the criminal law. We are aware that such termination of treatment would accelerate Karen's death. The County Prosecutor and the Attorney General stoutly maintain that there would be criminal liability for such acceleration. Under the statutes of this State, the unlawful killing of another human being is criminal homicide. We conclude that there would be no criminal homicide in the circumstances of this case. We believe, first, that the ensuing death would not be homicide but rather expiration from existing natural causes. Secondly, even if it were to be regarded as homicide, it would not be unlawful. . . .

Declaratory Relief

We thus arrive at the formulation of the declaratory relief which we have concluded is appropriate to this case. Some time has passed since Karen's physical and mental condition was described to the Court. At that time her continuing deterioration was plainly projected. Since the record has not been expanded we assume that she is now even more fragile and nearer to death than she was then. Since her present treating physicians may give reconsideration to her present posture in the light of this opinion, and since we are transferring to the plaintiff as guardian the choice of the attending physician and therefor other physicians may be in charge of the case who may take a different view from that of the present attending physicians, we herewith declare the following affirmative relief on behalf of the plaintiff. Upon the concurrence of the guardian and family of Karen, should the responsible attending physicians conclude that there is no reasonable possibility of Karen's ever emerging from her present comatose condition to a cognitive, sapient state and that the life-support apparatus now being administered to Karen should be discontinued, they shall consult with the hospital "Ethics Committee" or like body of the institution in which Karen is then hospitalized. If that consultative body agrees that there is no reasonable possibility of Karen's ever emerging from her present comatose condition to a cognitive, sapient state, the present life-support system may be withdrawn and said action shall be without any civil or criminal liability therefor on the part of any participant, whether guardian, physician, hospital or others. We herewith specifically so hold.

Conclusion

We therefore remand this record to the trial court to implement (without further testimonial hearing) the following decisions:

1. To discharge, with the thanks of the Court for his service, the present guardian of the person of Karen Quinlan, Thomas R. Curtin, Esquire, a member of the Bar and an officer of the court.
2. To appoint Joseph Quinlan as guardian of the person of Karen Quinlan with full power to make decisions with regard to the identity of her treating physicians.

We repeat for the sake of emphasis and clarity that upon the concurrence of the guardian and family of Karen, should the responsible attending physicians conclude that there is no reasonable possibility of Karen's ever emerging from her present comatose condition to a cognitive, sapient state and that the life-support apparatus now being administered to Karen should be discontinued, they shall consult with the hospital "Ethics Committee" or like body of the institution in which Karen is then hospitalized. If that consultative body agrees that there is no reasonable possibility of Karen's ever emerging from her present comatose condition to a cognitive, sapient state, the present life-support system may be withdrawn and said action shall be without any civil or criminal liability therefor, on the part of any participant, whether guardian, physician, hospital or others.

By the above ruling we do not intend to be understood as implying that a proceeding for judicial declaratory relief is necessarily required for the implementation of comparable decisions in the field of medical practice.

Modified and remanded.

Suggestions for Further Reading

Anthologies

Cohen, Marshall, and others. *The Rights and Wrongs of Abortion*. Princeton: Princeton University Press, 1974.

Feinberg, Joel. *The Problem of Abortion*. Belmont: Wadsworth Publishing Co., 1973.

Kohl, Marvin. *Beneficent Euthanasia*. Buffalo: Prometheus, 1975.

Ladd, John. *Ethical Issues Relating to Life and Death*. New York: Oxford University Press, 1979.

Munson, Ronald. *Interventions and Reflections*. Belmont: Wadsworth Publishing Co., 1979.

Noonan, John. *The Morality of Abortion*. Cambridge: Harvard University Press, 1970.

Basic Concepts

Devine, Philip. *The Ethics of Homicide*. Ithaca: Cornell University Press, 1978.

Glover, Jonathan. *Causing Death and Saving Lives*. New York: Penguin Books, 1977.

Steinbock, Bonnie, editor. *Killing and Letting Die*. Englewood Cliffs: Prentice-Hall, 1980.

Alternative Views

Callahan, Daniel. *Abortion: Law, Choice and Morality*. New York: Macmillan, 1970.

Grisez, Germain. *Abortion*. New York: Corpus, 1970.

Grisez, Germain, and Boyle, Joseph. *Life and Death with Liberty and Justice*. Notre Dame: University of Notre Dame Press, 1979.

Kluge, Eike-Henner. *The Practice of Death*. New Haven: Yale University Press, 1975.

Luker, Kristin. *Abortion and the Politics of Motherhood*. Berkeley: University of California Press, 1984.

Nicholson, Susan. *Abortion and The Roman Catholic Church*. Knoxville: Religious Ethics, 1978.

Ramsey, Paul. *The Patient as Person*. New Haven: Yale University Press, 1970.

Summer, L. W. *Abortion and Moral Theory*. Princeton: Princeton University Press, 1981.

Practical Applications

Denes, Magda. *In Necessity and Sorrow: Life and Death in an Abortion Hospital*. New York: Penguin Books, 1977.

Manier, Edward, and others, eds. *Abortion: New Directions for Policy Studies*. Notre Dame: University of Notre Dame Press, 1977.

Law Reform Commission of Canada. *Euthanasia, Aiding Suicide and Cessation of Treatment*. Working Paper 28, 1982.

Sex
Equality

Basic Concepts

The problem of sex equality concerns the question of whether the sexes should be treated equally, and, if so, what constitutes equal treatment. This question was at the heart of the decade-long public debate on the Equal Rights Amendment to the Constitution (the ERA), which began in March of 1972, when the Senate passed the amendment with a vote of 84 to 8, and ended in June of 1982, when the extended deadline for the ERA expired—three states short of the 38 required for ratification.

The complete text of the ERA was as follows:

1. Equality of rights under the law shall not be denied or abridged by the United States or by any state on account of sex.
2. The Congress shall have the power to enforce by appropriate legislation the provisions of this article.
3. This amendment shall take effect two years after the date of ratification.

Public support for the ERA over this period, judging from opinion polls, hovered between 55 and 60 percent, but in key states anti-ERA forces were able to mount sufficient resistance to prevent its passage. In the end, Alabama, Arizona, Arkansas, Florida, Georgia, Illinois, Louisiana, Mississippi, Missouri, Nevada, North Carolina, Oklahoma, Utah, and Virginia failed to ratify the amendment.

Anti-ERA forces were able to block ratification because they successfully shifted the debate from equal rights to the substantive changes the ERA might bring about. This strategy was effective because support for the amendment generally came from individuals sympathetic to the notion of "equal rights" but not necessarily committed to substantive changes in women's roles.[1] For example, in one national survey, 67 percent of the people who claimed to have heard or read about the ERA favored it, 25 percent were opposed to it, and 8 percent had no opinion. Many people in the sample, however, had quite traditional views about women's roles. Two thirds of respondents thought that preschool children would suffer if their mothers worked, 62 percent thought married women should not hold jobs when jobs were scarce and their husbands could support them, and 55 percent thought it more important for a woman to advance her husband's career than to have one of her own.

But what substantive changes would the ERA have brought about if it had been ratified in 1982? The surprising answer is not many, at least in the short run.[2] In 1970, when the ERA first reached the floor of Congress, a significant number of laws and official practices denied women "equality of rights under the law." For example, in 1970, eight states treated all property that a couple bought with their earnings during marriage as "community property," and these states normally gave the husband managerial control over such property. By 1976, most of these laws had been voluntarily changed or struck down by the Supreme Court's interpretation of the equal protection clause of the Fourteenth Amendment. Of course, supporters of the ERA did attempt to argue for the amendment on the grounds that it would bring about equal pay for equal work. Lobbyists for the ERA in state capitols wore buttons that said "59¢" to remind legislators that women who worked full time outside the home still typically earned only 59 cents for every dollar men earned—a ratio that has changed little since the federal government first began publishing such statistics in the 1950s. But the passage of the ERA would have had little immediate impact on that inequality. The ERA would have kept the federal or state governments from legally denying or abridging "equality of rights under the law." However, to help workers, the ERA would have had to do more than just make the law gender blind. It would have had to forbid wage discrimination by *private* organizations and individuals. And this it did not do.

Moreover, the ERA would have had few of the effects its opponents predicted. For example, Phyllis Schlafly frequently claimed that the ERA would require unisex public toilets and combat duty for women, but the Supreme Court would have found the first requirement an infringement of the right to privacy and the second would have run afoul of the war powers clause of the Constitution, which gives military commanders the freedom to decide how best to use their forces. Yet despite the fact that the immediate impact of the passage of the ERA would have been largely symbolic, neither proponents nor opponents sufficiently recognized this or, if they did, were not willing to surrender their exaggerated claims about the effects the amendment would have. Leaders on both sides of this debate may have feared the difficulty of motivating their followers if these exaggerated claims were abandoned.

Alternative Views

Yet regardless of what people believed the ERA would or would not have accomplished, is a commitment to equal rights justified? In the first selection (pp. 219–226), Elizabeth Wolgast argues that it is not. Wolgast claims that biological asymmetry with respect to fixing responsibility for parenthood undercuts the idea that men and women have equal basic rights. Wolgast shows that John Stuart Mill's defense of equal rights is compromised by his view that a woman who marries should make managing her household and raising her family her first duties and renounce all other occupations that are inconsistent with those duties. Wolgast also argues against Richard Wasserstrom's view that biological differences between men and women are not enough to nullify a claim to equal rights. Wolgast claims that in a good society, the biological asymmetry with respect to fixing responsibility for parenthood should be taken into account in determining the rights of men and women.

But why should this biological asymmetry with respect to fixing responsibility for parenthood (i.e., that we can more easily determine a child's mother than its father) be sufficient grounds for assigning unequal rights to men and women? When the child's father is known (the case in most instances), why shouldn't both parents share equal responsibility? And in those cases where the father isn't known, why shouldn't he still have the same rights and responsibilities as the child's mother? The

child's father may not be exercising those rights or assuming those responsibilities, but why should we claim he doesn't have them?

The next selection is by Gloria Steinem, the founder and editor of *Ms.* magazine. Steinem is usually taken to be a liberal feminist, that is, one who believes that equality between the sexes can be achieved by legal reform within a capitalist society. When Steinem wrote this piece for the *Time* essay of 1970, she was attempting to sketch the outlines of a liberal feminist utopia. Today, however, many of her goals seem as utopian as ever. Among those goals still to be reached are: (1) free access to the good jobs and decent pay for the bad ones; (2) equalization of parental responsibility; and (3) flexible work schedules.

Although Steinem is careful not to remove the option of being a full-time housewife, one of the consequences of women increasingly joining the work force is their devaluation of the role of housewife.[3] This devaluation seems to be proportionate to education. Between 1957 and 1976, the percentage of college-educated women who said they enjoyed housework fell from 67 to 38 percent. The percentage fell from 66 to 54 percent among women with a high school education, but didn't change at all among women with only a grade school education (76 percent in both 1957 and 1976). The same pattern occurs vis-a-vis career aspirations. Among college-educated homemakers, 60 percent of respondents in 1976 said they had at some point wanted a career, up from 48 percent in 1957. The percentage rose only slightly among homemakers with a high school education, from 37 to 40 percent. In homemakers with a grade school education, however, the percentage actually fell from 30 to 15 percent.

In the next selection (pp. 229–236), Evelyn Reed defends the Marxist feminist position that equality between the sexes can only be achieved by replacing capitalism with socialism. The inferior status of women, Reed claims, can be traced to the appearance of class-divided societies with their institutions of the patriarchal family, private property, and state power. On this account, Reed contends that the complete liberation of women can only come about as part of a social revolution that liberates the entire working class.

However, inequality between the sexes obviously predates capitalist and feudal societies, and although it may not predate the appearance of class-divided societies altogether (which takes us back to the beginnings of recorded history), it does seem to be a distinct problem from economic exploitation. After all, men from all economic classes have joined in the exploitation of women.

But given that the exploitation of women is a distinct problem from the exploitation of workers, aren't both problems equally fundamental? Not according to radical feminists such as Schulamith Firestone (pp. 236–242). Firestone argues that exploitation of women is the more fundamental problem because it is rooted in human biology and can only be changed by changing that biology. That change, she claims, would require us to introduce at least the option of artificial reproduction.

However, socialist feminists, such as Alison M. Jaggar (pp. 243–252), have criticized the radical feminist view for giving simply an ahistorical, biological explanation of the exploitation of women. Socialist feminists believe that the exploitation of women is rooted in both economic exploitation and human biology. Thus, according to socialist feminists, equality between the sexes can only be achieved by replacing capitalism with socialism *and* changing human biology. Radical feminists like Firestone also recognize the need to replace capitalism with socialism, but for them it is simply a means to the end of changing human biology. By contrast, socialist feminists regard replacing capitalism with socialism and changing human biology as equally important goals for achieving women's liberation. Socialist feminists also recognize an interaction between biology and economy not generally appreciated by radical feminists (i.e., that human biology is both the tool and the product of labor).

Jaggar also claims that the socialist feminist ideal can be described as an ideal of androgyny, but so understood, she hastens to add, it must involve a transformation of both physical and psychological capacities. Such a transformation might even include the capacities for insemination, lactation, and gestation so that, for instance, one woman could in-seminate another, men and non-child-bearing women could lactate, and fertilized ova could be transplanted into men's or women's bodies. Thus, given Jaggar's understanding of the view, socialist feminism would retain most of the commitments of radical feminism and simply integrate them with those of Marxist feminism.

Practical Applications

Turning to practical applications, we can see that, at least in the statement of the National Organization for Women (NOW) Bill of Rights (pp. 252–253), there was never any confusion that the ERA would achieve all the goals of the organization. In this Bill of Rights, the ERA is one of eight goals to be achieved.

Recently, maternity leave rights in employment, another of NOW's goals, was at stake in California Federal Savings and Loan vs. the Department of Fair Employment and Housing (pp. 253–256). Here the issue before the Supreme Court was whether Title VII of the Civil Rights Act of 1964 as amended by the Pregnancy Discrimination Act of 1978 (PDA) nullifies a California law that requires employers to provide leave and reinstatement to employees disabled by pregnancy. The majority of the court ruled that it did not nullify the law for two reasons. First, in passing PDA, Congress simply wanted to prohibit discrimination against pregnant women; there was no discussion of preferential treatment for pregnant women. In addition, by allowing both men and women to have families without losing their jobs, the California law did share with Title VII and PDA the goal of equal opportunity. Second, even if PDA did prohibit preferential treatment for pregnant women, an employer could avoid violating both PDA and the California statute by giving comparable benefits to all similarly disabled employees.

What is interesting is that NOW opposed the Court's decision in this case. Apparently, NOW's leaders were concerned that such preferential treatment might lead to a resurgence of nineteenth century protective legislation that encouraged sexual stereotypes and restrained women from taking their rightful place in the workplace. Although this is a legitimate concern, it can be addressed by determining whether each particular piece of relevant legislation advances the goal of equal opportunity. If it does, as the California law seems to do, there shouldn't be any objection to it, at least from a welfare liberal, socialist, or communitarian point of view.

Notes

1. Jane J. Mansbridge, *Why We Lost the ERA* (Chicago: University of Chicago Press, 1986), Chapter 3.
2. *Ibid.*, Chapter 5–7.
3. *Ibid.*, pp. 106–107.

Women Are Different

Elizabeth Wolgast

Opposing a number of arguments for equal rights for men and women, Elizabeth Wolgast argues that a biological asymmetry with respect to fixing responsibility for parenthood undercuts the idea that men and women have exactly the same rights.

Equality is the key to arguments for many kinds of rights and against many kinds of injustices—against slavery, despotism, economic exploitation, the subjection of women, racial oppression. It is not surprising then that arguments for women's rights turn on the notion of equality. But it is wonderful that one idea can serve so many causes. Does it always work the same, for instance, in regard to race and sex? And particularly, what does equality mean when applied to men and women?

I

If people were all alike there would be no question about their equality. Thus the claim of human equality is often linked with the assertion of human similarity. The philosopher John Locke, for instance, said that there is "nothing more evident than that creatures of the same species and rank, promiscuously born to all the same advantages of nature and the use of the same faculties, should also be equal one amongst another without subordination or subjection."[1] Insofar as they are similar in birth and faculties they should be equal in society.

From the equality of men it is natural to infer the equality of their principal rights. "Equals must be equal in rights," one scholar expressed it.[2] If men are equal, then none is privileged by nature, and their rights, like the men themselves, should be similar.

These ways of reasoning are very familiar in discussions of racial equality. Differences of race such as skin color and hair texture are superficial, it is argued; in the important respects the races are similar and therefore equal. To distinguish between the rights of one group and the rights of another when the only differences are these unimportant ones seems patently unjust. So an argument for racial equality based on similarity is tantamount to an argument for equal rights regardless of race.

Women's rights are commonly argued on the same lines. The first step is the assertion of their similarity with men, and the last step is the claim that they should have equal rights. The nineteenth-century philosopher John Stuart Mill argued in this way, long before most philosophers addressed the problem. "There is no natural inequality between the sexes," he claimed, "except perhaps in bodily strength." Women can be thought of as weak men. Now strength by itself is not a good ground for distinguishing among people's rights. Mill infers, "If nature has not made men and women unequal, still less ought the law to make them so." As in the case of race, similarity dictates similar treatment. "Men and women ought to be perfectly coequal," and "a woman ought not to be dependent on a man, more than a man on a woman, except so far as their affections make them so."[3]

If women are like men except perhaps for strength, the argument for sexual equality would be even more powerful than that for racial equality; for with race the differences are several and determined by heredity, while women and men may have the same genetic components and transmit the same ones. If strength alone differentiated women from men, sex equality would be perfectly apparent.

But of course women are not weak men, and Mill is not deceived. Women are talented like men and have imagination, determination, drive, and other capacities the same as men; but they are different in ways other than strength. Sometimes Mill acknowledges differences, even stresses their importance. He thinks that, while a woman should be able to support herself, "in the natural course of events she will *not,*" but her husband will support them both. "It will be for the happiness of both that her occupation should rather be to adorn and beautify" their lives.[4] At the same time her commitment to the home is a large one.

> Like a man when he chooses a profession, so, when a woman marries, it may in general be understood that she makes choice of the management of a household and the bringing up of a family, as the first call upon her exertions, during as many years of her life as may be required for the purpose; and that she renounces . . . all [other occupations] which are not consistent with the requirements of this.[5]

Women should conform to an inflexible set of demands by household and family. Their role does not stem from their weakness—that wouldn't make sense. The real reason for women having this role is that they are the "opposite" sex and the ones to have children. That "coequality" Mill advocates turns out to be a "natural arrangement" with man and wife "each being absolute in the executive branch of their own department."[6] What happened to the equality nature provided? It was not so clear after all.

Mill is more convincing when he speaks of the particular virtues in which the sexes differ. Women have their distinctive contribution to make, he says: they bring depth to issues where men bring breadth; they are practical where men are theoretical; they introduce sentiment where it is needed and would otherwise be lacking; and of course women are especially apt in the care and training of children.[7] To extol these characteristics of women, Mill must put aside that similarity which first supported equality of rights; but here his respect for women is unequivocal and plain.

In sum, Mill is ambivalent about the similarity of the sexes. On the one hand he argues as if women were weak men, on the other, that they have their distinctive and important virtues. On the one hand he espouses legal equality; on the other he endorses a conventional dependent role for married women.

If Mill's claim for sexual equality rested entirely on similarity, it would seem that that equality is in jeopardy. But he has another defense ready. There is, he says, "an *a priori* assumption . . . in favour of freedom and impartiality . . .[and] the law should be no respecter of persons, but should treat all alike, save where dissimilarity of treatment is required by positive reasons."[8] Similar treatment is right by presumption, and dissimilar treatment will always need positive justification. The argument from similarity was unnecessary then. But what kind of reason would justify differences of treatment? Mill doesn't say.

An argument for sex equality deriving from similarity is one that stresses the ways in which men and women are alike. But of course they are not exactly alike or there would not be a problem in the first place. It becomes necessary to make some such statement as: they are alike in all *important* respects, just as people of different races are importantly alike and only trivially different. But now it is necessary to consider whether differences of sex really are trivial.

In the case of race it seems clear that skin color and hair and features are unimportant, being superficial. They are mere physical marks. Can one say the same about the differences of sex? That is not so clear.

There is also a danger in using the argument from similarity, namely that, while it is meant to justify treating people alike, it implies that if people were importantly different they might need to be treated differently. So by implication it allows differences between individuals to justify *unequal* rights. This feature shows the importance for this kind of reasoning of maintaining that differences of sex are really trivial, for if they are not shown to be so, the argument can work against equality of rights. . . .

How can it be argued that sex is an unimportant difference? We can see the issue more clearly through a form of sex egalitarianism more sophisticated and modern than Mill's. Richard Wasserstrom, a philosopher and lawyer, argues that the good society would give no more recognition to sex or racial differences than we presently give to eye color. "Eye color is an irrelevant category" he argues, "nobody cares what color people's eyes are; it is not an important cultural fact; nothing turns on what eye color you have."[9] No laws or institutions distinguish between persons by eye color, nor do even personal decisions turn on it. The same would hold, in the good society, of racial and sexual differences. The good society would be "assimilationist" with respect to race and sex just as our society is with respect to eye color.

Race and sex and eye color would all be viewed in the same way if our society were just. All three kinds of difference are biological, natural; but among them sex is "deeper," he concedes, and seems to have greater social implications:

What opponents of assimilationism seize upon is that sexual difference appears to be a naturally occurring category of obvious and inevitable social relevance in a way, or to a degree, which race is not. . . . An analysis of the social realities reveals that it is the socially created sexual differences which tend in fact to matter the most. It is sex-role differentiation, not gender per se, that makes men and women as different as they are from each other.[10]

It is the way we recognize sex differences in socially created sex roles that gives them their great importance. If we stopped such artificial forms of recognition, we would see that the underlying difference of sex, like that of race, is trivial. Even though it is a naturally occurring difference, that in itself does not justify a social distinction, a distinction in roles. The principal difference of sex is social, not biological. And so sex is analogous to race: the difference allows for assimilation, given a change in laws, in institutions, and in social mores. Although there will still *be* a sexual difference, it will not make a difference.

To compare sex and race in this way implies that reproductive differences and reproduction itself should not much affect our social arrangements: "There appear to be very few, if any, respects in which the ineradicable, naturally occurring differences between males and females *must* be taken into account," Wasserstrom says.[11] The differences can just be ignored. But how do we ignore the reproductive differences? They are not many or very important, he argues, given the present state of medical knowledge:

Sexual intercourse is not necessary, for artificial insemination is available. Neither marriage nor the family is required for conception or child rearing. Given the present state of medical knowledge and the natural realities of female pregnancy, it is difficult to see why any important institutional or interpersonal arrangements must take the existing gender difference of *in utero* pregnancy into account.[12]

When you consider how many differences can be compensated for by medical innovations, there is only the nine months of *in utero* pregnancy left. And why should that make very much difference? Wasserstrom thinks it shouldn't. The sexes should be treated the same. . . .

In the good society there is sex equality: that is a primary consideration. For treating similar people the same would seem inherently just. If therefore it is within our means to make people more similar, through science and medicine, that course has much to recommend it; for with equality the goodness of society is assured. "Even though there are biological differences between men and women by nature, this fact does not determine the question of what the good society can and should make of these differences," Wasserstrom writes.[13] We don't need to be guided by nature; we can use our intelligence to control, adjust, and compensate for the differences nature produces.

Wasserstrom is not, like Mill, guided by existing similarities but is committed to create similarities wherever possible. Equality of the sexes is an ideal, an ideal of justice, and it requires similarities to exist. The good society, then, will create the similarities to go with its ideal, and that means it will create conditions under which its citizens will be, in all important ways, sexually similar.

I will not stop to consider whether this ideal is a pleasant or attractive one, for I want to ask the question: Is it true that merely biological differences of sex should not influence a good society?

II

Part of the egalitarian view expressed most commonly is the idea that biological differences of sex can be separated from social roles. Then the question is raised whether different sex roles, which are social artifacts, are desirable. Put this way, it is difficult to see why the roles should be very different. But it is not clear that the biological differences and the social ones *are* so distinct and separate.

Take the one fact, mentioned by Wasserstrom as unalterable at present, that women bear children after a period of pregnancy. From this one fact of *in utero* pregnancy one consequence directly follows: a woman does not normally have occasion to wonder whether the baby she bears is hers. She does not wonder if she or someone else is the mother. The father stands in a different relation to his child at the outset; his position is logically more distant, depending on inferences a mother need not make. And it is possible that he may doubt and, doubting, even fail to acknowledge a child that is in fact his, while it is difficult to imagine a mother in just that position—to imagine her bearing a child and then wondering whose it can be.

It is easy to imagine confusion about babies in the context of a modern hospital nursery, of course, but what I call attention to is a deeper and inherent asymmetry in parenthood, one that does not stem from institutions but from reproduction itself. As parents mothers have a primary place, one that cannot be occupied by a father.

This fact in turn has consequences. From the fact that mothers are primary parents it is clear that in general a mother is the more easily identifiable of a child's parents. This is important because a child is a very dependent creature and dependent for a very long time. Someone must have responsibility for it, and most generally that responsibility is given to parents. So now, in assigning responsibility for a child, it is simpler and less equivocal to assign the responsibility to a mother than to a father. This is so because doubts can be raised about his parenthood that have no analogue for hers.

From the mere fact of the way children are born, then, there are consequences important to society. Society, in its need to recognize someone as responsible for a child, rightly makes use of this fact of reproduction, the *in utero* pregnancy, so it can identify one parent with reasonable certainty.

I am assuming that parents are responsible for their children. However, this need not be part of the morality of a society, though it is part of the morality of most, and certainly part of ours. If this assumption is not made, the consequences would be different, depending on how society construes the relation of parent and child and places responsibility for the young. But it seems plausible that there will be some connection between parenthood and responsibility, and this connection will reflect the fact that mothers are primary parents.

That mothers are primary parents affects

not only laws and institutions but also the way women look at their lives. The potential of pregnancy and motherhood are present from the time girls reach adolescence, and are part of a young female's life and thought in a way they cannot be for a male. She needs to consider parenthood's connection with her behavior, and this influences her options. It would be surprising if it did not also affect her relations with males, sharpening her sense of their polarity, arousing concern about the durability and stability of her relationships with them. In such ways the merely biological fact of *in utero* pregnancy comes to give different coloring to the sexual identity of males and females, laying the groundwork for some sex roles.

Nor is this all. In a society where paternal responsibility is recognized and valued, there is a need to identify males as fathers. Thus an institution that makes formal identification of fathers, such as marriage, becomes important. As a child has two biological parents, so it comes to have two parents in society, within a social structure. And it would be surprising if some mores involving chastity and fidelity did not arise as well. In this way the merely biological facts of reproduction will tend to influence both the form of society and its customs, even though the details of that influence will vary. Societies are not all formed alike; other influences are at work as well. My point is that the fact of *in utero* pregnancy will have some consequences connected with the asymmetry of parenthood. Wasserstrom complains that society "mistakenly leads many persons to the view that women are both naturally and necessarily better suited than men to be assigned the primary responsibilities of child rearing."[14] If he had said "better situated," the observation he attributes to society would be profoundly right. The maternal role *is* more closely connected to parental responsibility than the paternal one, and neither talents nor conditioning nor tastes enter into it.

Suppose a society chooses not to acknowledge the asymmetry of parenthood. How would it do this? Would it assign equal responsibility to both parents? But what about the cases in which the father of an infant is unknown? It has a father, unless he is since deceased; but knowing this is no help. And what of the cases in which a mother refuses to acknowledge any father; is the child not then

exclusively hers? In Hawthorne's *The Scarlet Letter*, Hester Prynne's Pearl is *hers*, although both she and the Reverend Dimmesdale know he is the father. How would the good society make that parenting equal?

I do not mean at all that fathers are less tender, less devoted, or less responsible than mothers, that parental solicitude and devotion are women's prerogatives. *That* kind of "sex role" is not implied by the primary parenthood of mothers. What is meant is that asymmetries of parenthood are neither small nor trivial. And because of this they will have asymmetrical effects on other aspects of a person's life, some only indirectly related to parenthood. In this sense of "sex role," it is difficult to understand how sex roles could be abolished or made alike. Would one have to ignore the asymmetries of reproduction? But that would be a pretense.

Since the parental roles are asymmetrical, a natural consequence is some asymmetry in the attitudes of young men and young women regarding both reproduction and sex. The same behavior, sexual intercourse for instance, will have different significance for each. A society that gives structure to these differences, that provides a context into which both genders are expected to fit, will thereby provide for differences in sex roles. A great deal may be embroidered here in the way of stereotypes, rituals, myths, and mores. But what I shall mean by sex roles is a minimal set of differences, differences in attitude and behavior and in life outlook, stemming from the asymmetries of reproduction and framed by a social context.

The answer to Wasserstrom then evolves: The biological differences of men and women do not determine what a good society should make of them, but a good society should take them into account, and probably must do so. In order to justify ignoring the asymmetries that characterize human reproduction, that form of reproduction would have to be drastically changed.

So long as babies develop *in utero* and not, for example, in bottles, parenthood will be an asymmetrical business. A good society will no more ignore it than it will ignore the fact that humans start out as babies and do not live forever.

Wasserstrom's next step may be the proposal that reproduction be changed so as to be more symmetrical, for example, by developing fetuses in the laboratory and delivering them at term to two symmetrically related parents. In this situation a child would have no primary parent; on both sides recognition of parenthood would depend on a similar inference. It is difficult to see that from either the child's point of view or society's this loss of a primary parent would be an improvement. . . .

In Wasserstrom's ideal, people will regard one another, even in personal matters, without distinguishing the sexes. We don't distinguish between people on the basis of eye color: "so the normal, typical adult in this kind of nonsexist society would be indifferent to the sexual, physiological differences of other persons for all interpersonal relationships. Bisexuality, not heterosexuality or homosexuality, would be the norm."[15] In order for the sexes to be really equal, he reasons, we need to treat them alike even in personal and private ways. For if there are sex distinctions regularly made in private, they will be echoed somehow in the public sphere, and this means there will be a sex-differentiated form of society. This cure for sexual injustice is extreme: what is required here is a society of individuals who behave and are treated as if they were sexually alike. It requires an androgynous society.

III

Sex equality based on the similarity of the sexes, as advocated by Wasserstrom, will lead to an assimilationist form of society, for insofar as people are similar, similar treatment of them will be justified, and the assimilationist society treats everyone alike. It ignores sex differences just as it ignores racial ones, and for the same reason—because they are unimportant. By this reasoning a nonassimilationist form of society will necessarily be unjust. Wasserstrom writes:

Any . . . nonassimilationist society will make one's sexual identity an important characteristic, so that there are substantial psychological, role, and status differences between persons who are males and those who are females. . . .[But] sex roles, and all that accompany them, necessarily impose limits—restrictions on what one can do, be or become. As such, they are, I think, at least prima facie wrong.[16]

In restricting us sex roles are wrong. Through them "involuntarily assumed restraints have been imposed on the most central factors concerning the way one will shape and live one's life."[17] But sex roles in the narrow sense I mean them are reflections of restrictions; they do not create restrictions or impose them. Rather the restrictions come from the way human reproduction works and the kinds of responsibilities it entails in the framework of a real human society. It is hard to speak of the restrictions being imposed, just as it is hard to think of the character of human vision imposing restrictions on us. We cannot see what is behind our heads at any given moment; that is frustrating and certainly limits our freedom, restricting what we can do, be, or become. But one wouldn't for that reason call the visual system "wrong." Living in a society involves restrictions too, and so does being born to particular parents, in a particular place, in this century. These things too affect "the most central factors concerning the way one will shape and live one's life." But from what point of view can we term them "wrong"? We do not have an abstract viewpoint from which to measure the "wrongness" of such accidents.

Our difficulty with the assimilationist ideal has two sides: on the one, it seems to be based on human similarity, on the triviality of sex differences. But, as I argue, there is much reason to reject this and much justification for recognizing some form of sex roles. On the other hand, the assimilationist ideal seems to commit one to *creating* similarities, through medical and social measures, as if the ideal did not rest on anything, but were self-evident. If all sex roles are wrong, then only a unisex form of society will be just. But we are not unisex creatures; we are not androgynous or hermaphroditic. So assimilationism seems an inappropriate ideal, at least for human beings.

Having sex roles is natural to us and not the creation of society. As Midgley says, maternal instinct is not reducible to "cultural conditioning by the women's magazines."[18] If equality were adopted as an ideal, a massive effort at conditioning would be necessary to make us think like androgynous creatures with similar sex roles and sexual natures and so to fit that form of society. It is the androgynous role that is artificial, the product of a fictitious view of human nature. Instead of encouraging freedom and autonomy, the assimilationist society would thus restrict us to an androgynous form of life. It is a kind of Procrustean bed.

IV

Sex is a deeper phenomenon than race, Wasserstrom concedes. Its differences are more pervasive, more securely built into our institutions and practices. Nevertheless, he believes sex can be treated along the same lines as race, without qualitative adjustments. Lumping race and sex together is also common where there is talk of "group discrimination" and programs to combat it. But the cases are not alike.

One way to see the difference is to consider the way "assimilation" applies in the two cases. It is conceivable that, with less strictness in our mores, the races would come eventually to be assimilated to one. Differences in color and physiognomy would be so muted as to count only as individual ones, on a par with eye color. There is the possibility of real, genetic assimilation in the case of race. But with sex this is obviously not possible, and even if it were, we would have to think hard whether we wanted it. To allow equality to determine the character of our species seems to show a wrong order of things.

Equality based on similarity is connected to the Aristotelian dictum that we should treat likes alike and unlikes differently. But which cases are alike and which different? The answer is not simple. In the matter of race we generally say the cases are alike; in the case of sex this is not at all obvious. The difference of sex is genetically nonassimilable and besides it is difficult to ignore. Perhaps Aristotle's rule should lead us to conclude that with sex the cases require different treatment.

Where similarity is a consideration, racial arguments and sexual ones need to be separated. A person's racial characteristics are not usually correlated with special concerns differentiating racial groups, while many of women's most important concerns, for instance those connected with pregnancy, are distinctive to women as a group. The fair treatment of the two sexes cannot be assumed to consist in the "assimilation" of their rights.

Less compelling is the fact that sex differences have a lot to do with our enjoyment of human relationships. *Could* we treat the sexes alike as Wasserstrom proposes? We normally respond differently to members of the opposite sex than to members of our own. Even putting sexual attraction aside, we still have different relations to members of different sexes. With members of our sex, we have and anticipate having, a good deal in common. To a child we say, "When I was a little girl . . ." (if we are women) with the implication that we lack the same identification with boys. While with members of the opposite sex we perceive contrasts and divergent points of view, for some areas of common experience are lacking. Understanding those other perspectives is often a tenuous matter, ignorance and mystery being the conditions it must work against; but it is also one that fascinates, challenges, delights, and amuses us.

Wasserstrom could respond that these differences are mostly the creation of society, and that the position I suggest amounts to an endorsement of present sex roles and stereotypes. This is not intended. What I propose is rather that biology differentiates us in ways that will have some implications for differentiated sex roles. It is not a "solution" to such differentiation to suggest that everyone have the same roles or pretend to have them. The feminist social critic Dorothy Dinnerstein argues in *The Mermaid and the Minotaur* that "gender symbiosis" is a neurotic condition that needs correcting.[19] Although I agree with many of her observations about sex roles in our society and the need for changes, I am arguing that asymmetry will persist in some form or other, that the implications of biology are pervasive. The idea that, under propitious conditions, sex differences can be flattened out or "nullified" does not seem either necessary or attractive.[20] Nor is it clearly possible. It may be no more possible for us to treat people of different sexes alike than it is for us to treat a baby as an adult, or an elderly man as a youth. Some differences cannot be discounted. . . .

Notes

1. John Locke, *Second Treatise on Civil Government*, Bk. I, ch. ii, para. 4. Locke added "unless the Lord and Master of them all should . . . set one above another, and confer on him . . . right to dominion and sovereignty." Americans in framing the Constitution used only the first part of Locke's principle.

2. Henry Alonzo Myers, *Are Men Equal?* (Ithaca: Cornell University Press, 1945), 136. The connection between human equality and equality of rights in American political thought is carefully traced by J. R. Pole in *The Pursuit of Equality in American History* (Berkeley: University of California Press, 1978); see ch. 6 in particular.

3. J. S. Mill and Harriet Taylor Mill, *Essays on Sex Equality* (Chicago: University of Chicago Press, 1970), 73–74.

4. *Ibid.,* 74–75.

5. *The Subjection of Women* (Cambridge, Mass.: M.I.T. Press, 1970), 48.

6. *Ibid.,* 40.

7. *Ibid.,* 59–63.

8. *Ibid.,* 4.

9. Wasserstrom, "Racism, Sexism and Preferential Treatment: An Approach to the Topics," *U.C.L.A. Law Review,* 24 (July 1977), 586.

10. *Ibid.,* 609–610.

11. *Ibid.,* 611.

12. *Ibid.,* 611–612.

13. *Ibid.,* 610.

14. *Ibid.,* 611.

15. Wasserstrom, 606.

16. *Ibid.,* 615.

17. *Ibid.,* 615–616.

18. Midgley, 326.

19. New York: Harper, 1976.

20. "Nullifying sex differences" is used in Wasserstrom's book, *Philosophy and Social Issues: Five Studies* (Notre Dame: University of Notre Dame Press, 1980).

What It Would Be Like if Women Win

Gloria Steinem

When Gloria Steinem wrote this piece for the *Time* essay of 1970, she was sketching the outlines of a liberal feminist utopia. Among her utopian goals still to be reached are (1) free access to the good jobs and decent pay for the bad ones; (2) equalization of parental responsibility; and (3) flexible work schedules.

Any change is fearful, especially one affecting both politics and sex roles, so let me begin these utopian speculations with a fact. To break the ice.

Women don't want to exchange places with men. Male chauvinists, science-fiction writers and comedians may favor that idea for its

Abridged from *Time* (August 31, 1970), pp. 22–23. Reprinted by permission of Gloria Steinem.

shock value, but psychologists say it is a fantasy based on ruling-class ego and guilt. Men assume that women want to imitate them, which is just what white people assumed about blacks. An assumption so strong that it may convince the second-class group of the need to imitate, but for both women and blacks that stage has passed. Guilt produces the question: What if they could treat us as we have treated them?

That is not our goal. But we do want to change the economic system to one more based on merit. In Women's Lib Utopia, there will be free access to good jobs—and decent pay for the bad ones women have been performing all along, including housework. Increased skilled labor might lead to a four-hour workday, and higher wages would encourage further mechanization of repetitive jobs now kept alive by cheap labor.

With women as half the country's elected representatives, and a woman President once in a while, the country's *machismo* problems would be greatly reduced. . . . I'm not saying that women leaders would eliminate violence. We are not more moral than men; we are only uncorrupted by power so far. When we do acquire power, we might turn out to have an equal impulse toward aggression. Even now, Margaret Mead believes that women fight less often but more fiercely than men, because women are not taught the rules of the war game and fight only when cornered. But for the next 50 years or so, women in politics will be very valuable by tempering the idea of manhood into something less aggressive and better suited to this crowded, post-atomic planet. Consumer protection and children's rights, for instance, might get more legislative attention.

Men will have to give up ruling-class privileges, but in return they will no longer be the only ones to support the family, get drafted, bear the strain of power and responsibility. Freud to the contrary, anatomy is not destiny, at least not for more than nine months at a time. In Israel, women are drafted, and some have gone to war. In England, more men type and run switchboards. In India and Israel, a woman rules. In Sweden, both parents take care of the children. In this country, come Utopia, men and women won't reverse roles; they will be free to choose according to individual talents and preferences.

If role reform sounds sexually unsettling, think how it will change the sexual hypocrisy we have now. No more sex arranged on the barter system, with women pretending interest, and men never sure whether they are loved for themselves or for the security few women can get any other way. (Married or not, for sexual reasons or social ones, most women still find it second nature to [act ser-

vile].) No more men who are encouraged to spend a lifetime living with inferiors; with housekeepers, or dependent creatures who are still children. No more domineering wives, emasculating women, and "Jewish mothers," all of whom are simply human beings with all their normal ambition and drive confined to the home. No more unequal partnerships that eventually doom love and sex.

In order to produce that kind of confidence and individuality, child rearing will train according to talent. Little girls will no longer be surrounded by air-tight, self-fulfilling prophecies of natural passivity, lack of ambition and objectivity, inability to exercise power, and dexterity (so long as special aptitude for jobs requiring patience and dexterity is confined to poorly paid jobs; brain surgery is for males).

Schools and universities will help to break down traditional sex roles, even when parents will not. Half the teachers will be men, a rarity now at preschool and elementary levels; girls will not necessarily serve cookies or boys hoist up the flag. Athletic teams will be picked only by strength and skill. Sexually segregated courses like auto mechanics and home economics will be taken by boys and girls together. New courses in sexual politics will explore female subjugation as the model for political oppression, and women's history will be an academic staple, along with black history, at least until the white-male-oriented textbooks are integrated and rewritten.

As for the American child's classic problem—too much mother, too little father—that would be cured by an equalization of parental responsibility. Free nurseries, school lunches, family cafeterias built into every housing complex, service companies that will do household cleaning chores in a regular, businesslike way, and more responsibility by the entire community for the children: all these will make it possible for both mother and father to work, and to have equal leisure time with the children at home. For parents of very young children, however, a special job category, created by Government and unions, would allow such parents a shorter work day.

The revolution would not take away the option of being a housewife. A woman who prefers to be her husband's housekeeper and/

or hostess would receive a percentage of his pay determined by the domestic relations courts. If divorced, she might be eligible for a pension fund, and for a job-training allowance. Or a divorce could be treated the same way that the dissolution of a business partnership is now.

If these proposals seem farfetched, consider Sweden, where most of them are already in effect. Sweden is not yet a working Women's Lib model; most of the role-reform programs began less than a decade ago, and are just beginning to take hold. But that country is so far ahead of us in recognizing the problem that Swedish statements on sex and equality sound like bulletins from the moon. . . .

What will exist is a variety of alternative life-styles. Since the population explosion dictates that childbearing be kept to a minimum, parents-and-children will be only one of many "families": couples, age groups, working groups, mixed communes, blood-related clans, class groups, creative groups. Single women will have the right to stay single without ridicule, without the attitudes now betrayed by "spinster" and "bachelor." Lesbians or homosexuals will no longer be denied legally binding marriages, complete with mutual-support agreements and inheritance rights. Paradoxically, the number of homosexuals may get smaller. With fewer overpossessive mothers and fewer fathers who hold up an impossibly cruel or perfectionist idea of manhood, boys will be less likely to be denied or reject their identity as males.

Changes that now seem small may get bigger:

Men's Lib

Men now suffer from more disease due to stress, heart attacks, ulcers, a higher suicide rate, greater difficulty living alone, less adaptability to change and, in general, a shorter life span than women. There is some scientific evidence that what produces physical problems is not work itself, but the inability to choose which work, and how much. With women bearing half the financial responsibility, and with the idea of "masculine" jobs gone, men might well feel freer and live longer.

Religion

Protestant women are already becoming ordained ministers; radical nuns are carrying out liturgical functions that were once the exclusive property of priests; Jewish women are rewriting prayers—particularly those that Orthodox Jews recite every morning thanking God they are not female. In the future, the church will become an area of equal participation by women. This means, of course, that organized religion will have to give up one of its great historical weapons: sexual repression. In most structured faiths, from Hinduism through Roman Catholicism, the status of women went down as the position of priests ascended. Male clergy implied, if they did not teach, that women were unclean, unworthy and sources of ungodly temptation, in order to remove them as rivals for the emotional forces of men. Full participation of women in ecclesiastical life might involve certain changes in theology, such as, for instance, a radical redefinition of sin.

Literary Problems

Revised sex roles will outdate more children's books than civil rights ever did. Only a few children had the problem of a *Little Black Sambo*, but most have the male-female stereotypes of "Dick and Jane." A boomlet of children's books about mothers who work has already begun, and liberated parents and editors are beginning to pressure for change in the textbook industry. Fiction writing will change more gradually, but romantic novels with wilting heroines and swashbuckling heroes will be reduced to historical value. Or perhaps to the sado-masochist trade. (*Marjorie Morningstar*, a romantic novel that took the '50s by storm, has already begun to seem as unreal as its '20s predecessor, *The Sheik*.) As for the literary plots that turn on forced marriages or horrific abortions, they will seem as dated as Prohibition stories. Free legal abortions and free birth control will force writers to give up pregnancy as the *deus ex machina*.

Manners and Fashion

Dress will be more androgynous, with class symbols becoming more important than sexual ones. Pro- or anti-Establishment styles may already be more vital than who is wearing them. Hardhats are just as likely to rough up antiwar girls as antiwar men in the street, and police understand that women are just as likely to be pushers or bombers. Dances haven't required that one partner lead the other for years, anyway. Chivalry will transfer itself to those who need it, or deserve respect: old people, admired people, anyone with an armload of packages. Women with normal work identities will be less likely to attach their whole sense of self to youth and appearance; thus there will be fewer nervous breakdowns when the first wrinkles appear. Lighting cigarettes and other treasured niceties will become gestures of mutual affection. "I like to be helped on with my coat," says one Women's Lib worker, "but not if it costs me $2,000 a year in salary."

For those with nostalgia for a simpler past, here is a word of comfort. Anthropologist Geoffrey Gorer studied the few peaceful human tribes and discovered one common characteristic: sex roles were not polarized. Differences of dress and occupation were at a minimum. Society, in other words, was not using sexual blackmail as a way of getting women to do cheap labor, or men to be aggressive.

Thus Women's Lib may achieve a more peaceful society on the way toward its other goals. That is why the Swedish government considers reform to bring about greater equality in the sex roles one of its most important concerns. As Prime Minister Olof Palme explained in a widely ignored speech delivered in Washington this spring: "It is *human beings* we shall emancipate. In Sweden today, if a politician should declare that the woman ought to have a different role from man's, he would be regarded as something from the Stone Age." In other words, the most radical goal of the movement is egalitarianism.

If Women's Lib wins, perhaps we all do.

Women: Caste, Class or Oppressed Sex?

Evelyn Reed

Evelyn Reed argues that the inferior status of women did not result from any biological deficiency as a sex. Rather, its origins can be traced to the appearance of class-divided societies with their institutions of the patriarchal family, private property, and state power. Against those who claim that the oppression of women derives from their belonging to a separate caste or class, Reed points out that women have always belonged to both superior and inferior castes and classes. Reed concludes that the complete liberation of women can only come as part of a social revolution that liberates the entire working class.

The new stage in the struggle for women's liberation already stands on a higher ideological level than did the feminist movement of the last century. Many of the participants today respect the Marxist analysis of capitalism and subscribe to Engels's classic explanation of

From "Women: Caste, Class or Oppressed Sex?" in *Problems of Women's Liberation* (1970), pp. 64–76. © 1970 by International Socialist Review. Reprinted by permission of Pathfinder Press, Inc.

the origins of women's oppression. It came about through the development of class society, founded upon the family, private property, and the state.

But there still remain considerable misunderstandings and misinterpretations of Marxist positions, which have led some women who consider themselves radicals or socialists to go off course and become theoretically disoriented. Influenced by the myth that women have always been handicapped by their childbearing functions, they tend to attribute the roots of women's oppression, at least in part, to biological sexual differences. In actuality its causes are exclusively historical and social in character.

Some of these theorists maintain that women constitute a special class or caste. Such definitions are not only alien to the views of Marxism but lead to the false conclusion that it is not the capitalist system but men who are the prime enemy of women. I propose to challenge this contention.

The findings of the Marxist method, which have laid the groundwork for explaining the genesis of woman's degradation, can be summed up in the following propositions:

First, women were not always the oppressed or "second" sex. Anthropology, or the study of prehistory, tells us the contrary. Throughout primitive society, which was the epoch of tribal collectivism, women were the equals of men and recognized by man as such.

Second, the downfall of women coincided with the breakup of the matriarchal clan commune and its replacement by class-divided society with its institutions of the patriarchal family, private property and state power.

The key factors which brought about this reversal in woman's social status came out of the transition from a hunting and food-gathering economy to a far higher mode of production based upon agriculture, stock raising and urban crafts. The primitive division of labor between the sexes was replaced by a more complex social division of labor. The greater efficiency of labor gave rise to a sizable surplus product, which led first to differentiations and then to deepgoing divisions among the various segments of society.

By virtue of the directing roles played by men in large-scale agriculture, irrigation and construction projects, as well as in stock raising, this surplus wealth was gradually appropriated by a hierarchy of men as their private property. This, in turn, required the institution of marriage and the family to fix the legal ownership and inheritance of a man's property. Through monogamous marriage the wife was brought under the complete control of her husband who was thereby assured of legitimate sons to inherit his wealth.

As men took over most of the activities of social production, and with the rise of the family institution, women became relegated to the home to serve their husbands and families. The state apparatus came into existence to fortify and legalize the institutions of private property, male dominion and the father-family, which later were sanctified by religion.

This, briefly, is the Marxist approach to the origins of woman's oppression. Her subordination did not come about through any biological deficiency as a sex. It was the result of the revolutionary social changes which destroyed the equalitarian society of the matriarchal gens or clan and replaced it with a patriarchal class society which, from its birth, was stamped with discriminations and inequalities of many kinds, including the inequality of the sexes. The growth of this inherently oppressive type of socioeconomic organization was responsible for the historic downfall of women.

But the downfall of women cannot be fully understood, nor can a correct social and political solution be worked out for their liberation, without seeing what happened at the same time to men. It is too often overlooked that the patriarchal class system which crushed the matriarchy and its communal social relations also shattered its male counterpart, the fratriarchy—or tribal brotherhood of men. Woman's overthrow went hand in hand with the subjugation of the mass of toiling men to the master class of men.

The import of these developments can be more clearly seen if we examine the basic character of the tribal structure which Morgan, Engels and others described as a system of "primitive communism." The clan commune was both a sisterhood of women and a brotherhood of men. The sisterhood of women, which was the essence of the matriarchy, denoted its collectivist character. The women worked together as a community of sisters: their social labors largely sustained the whole community. They also raised their children in common. An individual mother did not draw distinctions between her own and her clan sisters' progeny, and the children in turn regarded all the older sisters as their mutual mothers. In other words, communal production and communal possessions were accompanied by communal child-raising.

The male counterpart of this sisterhood was the brotherhood, which was molded in the same communal pattern as the sisterhood. Each clan or phratry of clans comprising the tribe was regarded as a "brotherhood" from the male standpoint just as it was viewed as a "sisterhood" or "motherhood" from the female standpoint. In this matriarchal-brotherhood the adults of both sexes not only produced the necessities of life together but also provided for and protected the children of the community. These features made the sisterhood and brotherhood a system of "primitive communism."

Thus, before the family that had the individual father standing at its head came into existence, the functions of fatherhood were a *social*, not a *family* function of men. More than this, the earliest men who performed the services of fatherhood were not the mates or "husbands" of the clan sisters but rather their clan brothers. This was not simply because the processes of physiological paternity were unknown in ancient society. More decisively, this fact was irrelevant in a society founded upon collectivist relations of production and communal child-raising.

However odd it may seem to people today, who are so accustomed to the family form of child-raising, it was perfectly natural in the primitive commune for the clan brothers, or "mothers' brothers," to perform the paternal functions for their sisters' children that were later taken over by the individual father for his wife's children.

The first change in this sister-brother clan system came with the growing tendency for pairing couples, or "pairing families" as Morgan and Engels called them, to live together in the same community and household. However, this simple cohabitation did not substantially alter the former collectivist relations or the productive role of the women in the community. The sexual division of labor which had formerly been allotted between clan sisters and brothers became gradually transformed into a sexual division of labor between husbands and wives.

But so long as collectivist relations prevailed and women continued to participate in social production, the original equality between the sexes more or less persisted. The whole community continued to sustain the pairing units, just as each individual member of these units made his and her contribution to the labor activities.

Consequently, the pairing family, which appeared at the dawn of the family system, differed radically from the nuclear family of our times. In our ruthless competitive capitalist system every tiny family must sink or swim through its own efforts—it cannot count on assistance from outside sources. The wife is dependent upon the husband while the children must look to the parents for their subsistence, even if the wage earners who support them are stricken by unemployment, sickness or death. In the period of the pairing family, however, there was no such system of dependency upon "family economics," since the whole community took care of each individual's basic needs from the cradle to the grave.

This was the material basis for the absence, in the primitive commune, of those social oppressions and family antagonisms with which we are so familiar.

It is sometimes said or implied that male domination has always existed and that women have always been brutally treated by men. Contrariwise, it is also widely believed that the relations between the sexes in matriarchal society were merely the reverse of our own—with women dominating men. Neither of these propositions is borne out by the anthropological evidence.

It is not my intention to glorify the epoch of savagery nor advocate a romantic return to some past "golden age." An economy founded upon hunting and food-gathering is the lowliest stage in human development, and its living conditions were rude, crude and harsh. Nevertheless, we must recognize that male and female relations in that kind of society were fundamentally different from ours.

Under the clan system of the sisterhood of women and the brotherhood of men there was no more possibility for one sex to dominate the other than there was for one class to exploit another. Women occupied the most eminent position because they were the chief producers of the necessities of life as well as the procreators of new life. But this did not make them the oppressors of men. Their communal society excluded class, racial or sexual tyranny.

As Engels pointed out, with the rise of private property, monogamous marriage and the patriarchal family, new social forces came into play in both society at large and the family setup which destroyed the rights exercised by earliest womankind. From simple cohabitation of pairing couples there arose the rigidly fixed, legal system of monogamous marriage. This brought the wife and children under the complete control of the husband and father who gave the family his name and determined their conditions of life and destiny.

Women, who had once lived and worked together as a community of sisters and raised their children in common, now became dispersed as wives of individual men serving their lords and masters in individual households. The former equalitarian sexual division of labor between the men and women of the commune gave way to a family division of labor in which the woman was more and more removed from social production to serve as a household drudge for husband, home and family. Thus women, once "governesses" of society, were degraded under the class formations to become the governesses of a man's children and his chief housemaid.

This abasement of women has been a permanent feature of all three stages of class society, from slavery through feudalism to capitalism. So long as women led or participated in the productive work of the whole community, they commanded respect and esteem. But once they were dismembered into separate family units and occupied a servile position in home and family, they lost their prestige along with their influence and power.

Is it any wonder that such social changes should bring about intense and long-enduring antagonism between the sexes? As Engels says:

Monogamy then does by no means enter history as a reconciliation of man and wife, and still less as the highest form of marriage. On the contrary, it enters as the subjugation of one sex by the other, as the proclamation of an antagonism between the sexes unknown in all preceding

history. . . . The first class antagonism appearing in history coincides with the development of the antagonism of man and wife in monogamy, and the first class oppression with that of the female by the male sex (Origin of the Family, Private Property, and the State).

Here it is necessary to note a distinction between two degrees of women's oppression in monogamous family life under the system of private property. In the productive farm family of the preindustrial age, women held a higher status and were accorded more respect than they receive in the consumer family of our own city life, the nuclear family.

So long as agriculture and craft industry remained dominant in the economy, the farm family, which was a large or "extended" family, remained a viable productive unit. All its members had vital functions to perform according to sex and age. The women in the family helped cultivate the ground and engaged in home industries as well as bearing children, while the children and older folks produced their share according to ability.

This changed with the rise of industrial and monopoly capitalism and the nuclear family. Once masses of men were dispossessed from the land and small businesses to become wage earners in factories, they had nothing but their labor power to sell to the capitalist bosses for their means of subsistence. The wives of these wage earners, ousted from their former productive farm and homecraft labors, became utterly dependent upon their husbands for the support of themselves and their children. As men became dependent upon their bosses, the wives became more dependent upon their husbands.

By degrees, therefore, as women were stripped of their economic self-dependence, they fell ever lower in social esteem. At the beginning of class society they had been removed from *social* production and social leadership to become farm-family producers, working through their husbands for home and family. But with the displacement of the productive farm family by the nuclear family of industrial city life, they were driven from their last foothold on solid ground.

Women were then given two dismal alternatives. They could either seek a husband as provider and be penned up thereafter as housewives in city tenements or apartments to raise the next generation of wage slaves. Or the poorest and most unfortunate could go as marginal workers into the mills and factories (along with the children) and be sweated as the most downtrodden and underpaid section of the labor force.

Over the past generations women wage workers have conducted their own labor struggles or fought along with men for improvements in their wages and working conditions. But women as dependent housewives have had no such means of social struggle. They could only resort to complaints or wrangles with husband and children over the miseries of their lives. The friction between the sexes became deeper and sharper with the abject dependency of women and their subservience to men.

Despite the hypocritical homage paid to womankind as the "sacred mother" and devoted homemaker, the *worth* of women sank to its lowest point under capitalism. Since housewives do not produce commodities for the market nor create any surplus value for the profiteers, they are not central to the operations of capitalism. Only three justifications for their existence remain under this system: as breeders, as household janitors, and as buyers of consumer goods for the family.

While wealthy women can hire servants to do the dull chores for them, poor women are riveted to an endless grind for their whole lives. Their condition of servitude is compounded when they are obliged to take an outside job to help sustain the family. Shouldering two responsibilities instead of one, they are the "doubly oppressed."

Even middle-class housewives in the Western world, despite their economic advantages, are victimized by capitalism. The isolated, monotonous, trivial circumstances of their lives lead them to "living through" their children—a relationship which fosters many of the neuroses that afflict family life today. Seeking to allay their boredom, they can be played upon by the profiteers in the consumer goods fields. This exploitation of women as consumers is part and parcel of a system that grew up in the first place for the exploitation of men as producers.

The capitalists have ample reason for glorifying the nuclear family. Its petty household is a goldmine for all sorts of hucksters from real estate agents to the manufacturers of detergents and cosmetics. Just as automobiles are produced for individual use instead of developing adequate mass transportation, so the big corporations can make more money by selling small homes on private lots to be equipped with individual washing machines, refrigerators, and other such items. They find this more profitable than building large-scale housing at low rentals or developing community services and child-care centers.

In the second place, the isolation of women, each enclosed in a private home and tied to the same kitchen and nursery chores, hinders them from banding together and becoming a strong social force or a serious political threat to the Establishment.

What is the most instructive lesson to be drawn from this highly condensed survey of the long imprisonment of womankind in the home and family of class society—which stands in such marked contrast to their stronger, more independent position in preclass society? It shows that the inferior status of the female sex is not the result of their biological makeup or the fact that they are the childbearers. Childbearing was no handicap in the primitive commune; it *became* a handicap, above all, in the nuclear family of our times. Poor women are torn apart by the conflicting obligations of taking care of their children at home while at the same time working outside to help sustain the family. Women, then, have been condemned to their oppressed status by the same social forces and relations which have brought about the oppression of one class by another, one race by another, and one nation by another. It is the capitalist system—the ultimate stage in the development of class society—which is the fundamental source of the degradation and oppression of women.

Some women in the liberation movement dispute these fundamental theses of Marxism. They say that the female sex represents a separate caste or class. Ti-Grace Atkinson, for example, takes the position that women are a separate *class:* Roxanne Dunbar says that they comprise a separate *caste*. Let us examine these two theoretical positions and the conclusions that flow from them.

First, are women a caste? The caste hierarchy came first in history and was the prototype and predecessor of the class system. It arose after the breakup of the tribal commune with the emergence of the first marked differentiations of segments of society according to the new divisions of labor and social functions. Membership in a superior or inferior station was established by being born into that caste.

It is important to note, however, that the caste system was also inherently and at birth a class system. Furthermore, while the caste system reached its fullest development only in certain regions of the world, such as India, the class system evolved far beyond it to become a world system, which engulfed the caste system.

This can be clearly seen in India itself, where each of the four chief castes—the Brahmans or priests, the soldiers, the farmers and merchants, and the laborers, along with the "out-castes" or pariahs—had their appropriate places in an exploitative society. In India today, where the ancient caste system survives in decadent forms, capitalist relations and power prevail over all the inherited precapitalist institutions, including the caste relics.

However, those regions of the world which advanced fastest and farthest on the road to civilization bypassed or overleaped the caste system altogether. Western civilization, which started with ancient Greece and Rome, developed from slavery through feudalism to the maturest stage of class society, capitalism.

Neither in the caste system nor the class system—nor in their combinations—have women comprised a separate caste or class. Women themselves have been separated into the various castes and classes which made up these social formations.

The fact that women occupy an inferior status as a sex does not *ipso facto* make women either an inferior caste or class. Even in ancient India women belonged to different castes, just as they belong to different classes in contemporary capitalist society. In the one case their social status was determined by birth into a caste; in the other it is determined by their own or their husband's wealth. But the two can be fused—for women as for men. Both sexes can belong to a superior caste and possess superior wealth, power and status. . . .

Turning to the other position, it is even more incorrect to characterize women as a special "class." In Marxist sociology a class is defined in two interrelated ways: by the role it plays in the processes of production and by the stake it has in the ownership of property. Thus the capitalists are the major power in our society because they own the means of production and thereby control the state and direct the economy. The wage workers who create the wealth own nothing but their labor power, which they have to sell to the bosses to stay alive.

Where do women stand in relation to these polar class forces? They belong to all strata of the social pyramid. The few at the top are part of the plutocratic class: more among us belong to the middle class, most of us belong to the proletarian layers of the population. There is an enormous spread from the few wealthy women of the Rockefeller, Morgan and Ford families to the millions of poor women who subsist on welfare dole. *In short, women, like men, are a multiclass sex.*

This is not an attempt to divide women from one another but simply to recognize the actual divisions that exist. The notion that all women as a sex have more in common than do members of the same class with one another is false. Upper-class women are not simply bedmates of their wealthy husbands. As a rule they have more compelling ties which bind them together. They are economic, social and political bedmates, united in defense of private property, profiteering, militarism, racism—and the exploitation of other women.

To be sure, there can be individual exceptions to this rule, especially among young women today. We remember that Mrs. Frank Leslie, for example, left a $2 million bequest to further the cause of women's suffrage, and other upper-class women have devoted their means to secure civil rights for our sex. But it is quite another matter to expect any large number of wealthy women to endorse or support a revolutionary struggle which threatens their capitalist interests and privileges. Most of them scorn the liberation movement, saying openly or implicitly, "What do we need to be liberated from?". . .

It is true that all forms of class society have been male-dominated and that men are trained from the cradle on to be chauvinistic. But it is not true that men as such represent the main enemy of women. This crosses out the multitudes of downtrodden, exploited men who are themselves oppressed by the main enemy of women, which is the capitalist system. These men likewise have a stake in the liberation struggle of the women: they can and will become our allies.

Although the struggle against male chauvinism is an essential part of the tasks that women must carry out through their liberation movement, it is incorrect to make that the central issue. This tends to conceal or overlook the role of the ruling powers who not only breed and benefit from all forms of discrimination and oppression but are also responsible for breeding and sustaining male chauvinism. Let us remember that male supremacy did not exist in the primitive commune, founded upon sisterhood and brotherhood. Sexism, like racism, has its roots in the private property system.

A false theoretical position easily leads to a false strategy in the struggle for women's liberation. Such is the case with a segment of the Redstockings who state in their *Manifesto* that "women are an oppressed *class.*" If all women compose a class then all men must form a counterclass—the oppressor class. What conclusion flows from this premise? That there are no men in the oppressed class? Where does this leave the millions of oppressed white working men who, like the oppressed blacks, Chicanos and other minorities, are exploited by the monopolists? Don't they have a central place in the struggle for social revolution? At what point and under what banner do these oppressed peoples of all races and both sexes join together for common action against their common enemy? To oppose women as a class against men as a class can only result in a diversion of the real class struggle.

Isn't there a suggestion of this same line in Roxanne Dunbar's assertion that female liberation is the basis for social revolution? This is far from Marxist strategy since it turns the real situation on its head. Marxists say that social revolution is the basis for full female liberation—just as it is the basis for the liberation of the whole working class. In the last analysis the real allies of women's liberation are all those forces which are impelled for their own reasons to struggle against and throw off the shackles of the imperialist masters.

The underlying source of women's oppression, which is capitalism, cannot be abolished by women alone, nor by a coalition of women drawn from all classes. It will require a worldwide struggle for socialism by the working masses, female and male alike, together with every other section of the oppressed, to overthrow the power of capitalism, which is centered today in the United States.

In conclusion, we must ask, what are the connections between the struggle for women's liberation and the struggle for socialism?

First, even though the full goal of women's liberation cannot be achieved short of the socialist revolution, this does not mean that the struggle to secure reforms must be postponed until then. It is imperative for Marxist women to fight shoulder to shoulder with all our embattled sisters in organized actions for specific objectives from now on. This has been our policy ever since the new phase of the women's liberation movement surfaced a year or so ago, and even before.

The women's movement begins, like other movements for liberation, by putting forward elementary demands. These are: equal opportunities with men in education and jobs; equal pay for equal work; free abortions on demand; and child-care centers financed by the government but controlled by the community. Mobilizing women behind these issues not only gives us the possibility of securing some improvements but also exposes, curbs and modifies the worst aspects of our subordination in this society.

Second, why do women have to lead their own struggles for liberation, even though in the end the combined anticapitalist offensive of the whole working class will be required for the victory of the socialist revolution? The reason is that no segment of society which has been subjected to oppression, whether it consists of Third World people or of women, can delegate the leadership and promotion of their fight for freedom to other forces—even though other forces can act as their allies. We reject the attitude of some political tendencies that say they are Marxists but refuse to acknowledge that women have to lead and organize their own independent struggle for emancipation, just as they cannot understand why blacks must do the same.

The maxim of the Irish revolutionists— "who would be free themselves must strike the blow"—fully applies to the cause of women's liberation. Women must themselves strike the blows to gain their freedom. And this holds true after the anticapitalist revolution triumphs as well as before.

In the course of our struggle, and as part of it, we will reeducate men who have been brainwashed into believing that women are naturally the inferior sex due to some flaws in their biological makeup. Men will have to learn that, in the hierarchy of oppressions created by capitalism, their chauvinism and dominance is another weapon in the hands of the master class for maintaining its rule. The exploited worker, confronted by the even worse plight of his dependent housewife, cannot be complacent about it—he must be made to see the source of the oppressive power that has degraded them both.

Finally, to say that women form a separate caste or class must logically lead to extremely pessimistic conclusions with regard to the antagonism between the sexes in contrast with the revolutionary optimism of the Marxists. For unless the two sexes are to be totally separated, or the men liquidated, it would seem that they will have to remain forever at war with each other.

As Marxists we have a more realistic and hopeful message. We deny that women's inferiority was predestined by her biological makeup or has always existed. Far from being eternal, woman's subjugation and the bitter hostility between the sexes are no more than a few thousand years old. They were produced by the drastic social changes which brought the family, private property and the state into existence.

This view of history points up the necessity for a no less thoroughgoing revolution in socioeconomic relations to uproot the causes of inequality and achieve full emancipation for our sex. This is the purpose and promise of the socialist program, and this is what we are fighting for.

The Dialectic of Sex

Shulamith Firestone

According to Shulamith Firestone, the oppression of women is the most fundamental problem society faces. It is more fundamental than even economic oppression because human biology must be changed before it can be resolved. In particular, the biological family must be changed, and, Firestone claims, this change must include at least the option of artificial reproduction.

Sex class is so deep as to be invisible. Or it may appear as a superficial inequality, one that can be solved by merely a few reforms, or perhaps

Abridged from pp. 1–5, 8–11, 205–9 in *The Dialectic of Sex* by Shulamith Firestone. Copyright © 1970 by Shulamith Firestone. Abridged by permission of William Morrow & Company.

by the full integration of women into the labor force. But the reaction of the common man, woman, and child—"*That?* Why you can't change *that!* You must be out of your mind!"— is the closest to the truth. We are talking about something every bit as deep as that. This gut reaction—the assumption that, even when they don't know it, feminists are talking about changing a fundamental biological condition—is an honest one. That so profound a change cannot be easily fit into traditional categories of thought, e.g., "political," is not because these categories do not apply but because they are not big enough: radical feminism bursts through them. If there were another word more all-embracing than *revolution* we would use it.

Until a certain level of evolution had been reached and technology had achieved its present sophistication, to question fundamental biological conditions was insanity. Why should a woman give up her precious seat in the cattle car for a bloody struggle she could not hope to win? But, for the first time in some countries, the preconditions for feminist revolution exist—indeed, the situation is beginning to *demand* such a revolution.

The first women are fleeing the massacre, and, shaking and tottering, are beginning to find each other. Their first move is a careful joint observation, to resensitize a fractured consciousness. This is painful: No matter how many levels of consciousness one reaches, the problem always goes deeper. It is everywhere. The division yin and yang pervades all culture, history, economics, nature itself; modern Western versions of sex discrimination are only the most recent layer. To so heighten one's sensitivity to sexism presents problems far worse than the black militant's new awareness of racism: Feminists have to question, not just all of *Western* culture, but the organization of culture itself, and further, even the very organization of nature. Many women give up in despair: if *that's* how deep it goes they don't want to know. Others continue strengthening and enlarging the movement, their painful sensitivity to female oppression existing for a purpose: eventually to eliminate it.

Before we can act to change a situation, however, we must know how it has arisen and evolved, and through what institutions it now operates. Engels: "[We must] examine the historic succession of events from which the antagonism has sprung in order to discover in the conditions thus created the means of ending the conflict." For feminist revolution we shall need an analysis of the dynamics of sex war as comprehensive as the Marx-Engels analysis of class antagonism was for the economic revolution. More comprehensive. For

we are dealing with a larger problem, with an oppression that goes back beyond recorded history to the animal kingdom itself.

In creating such an analysis we can learn a lot from Marx and Engels: Not their literal opinions about women—about the condition of women as an oppressed class they know next to nothing, recognizing it only where it overlaps with economics—but rather their analytic *method*.

Marx and Engels outdid their socialist forerunners in that they developed a method of analysis which was both *dialectical* and *materialist*. The first in centuries to view history dialectically, they saw the world as process, a natural flux of action and reaction, of opposites yet inseparable and interpenetrating. Because they were able to perceive history as movie rather than as snapshot, they attempted to avoid falling into the stagnant "metaphysical" view that had trapped so many other great minds. . . . They combined this view of the dynamic interplay of historical forces with a materialist one, that is, they attempted for the first time to put historical and cultural change on a real basis, to trace the development of economic classes to organic causes. By understanding thoroughly the mechanics of history, they hoped to show men how to master it.

Socialist thinkers prior to Marx and Engels, such as Fourier, Owen, and Bebel, had been able to do no more than moralize about existing social inequalities, positing an ideal world where class privilege and exploitation should not exist—in the same way that early feminist thinkers posited a world where male privilege and exploitation ought not exist—by mere virtue of good will. In both cases, because the early thinkers did not really understand how the social injustice had evolved, maintained itself, or could be eliminated, their ideas existed in a cultural vacuum, utopian. Marx and Engels, on the other hand, attempted a scientific approach to history. They traced the class conflict to its real economic origins, projecting an economic solution based on objective economic preconditions already present: the seizure by the proletariat of the means of production would lead to a communism in which government had withered away, no longer needed to repress the lower class for the sake of the higher. In the classless society the interests of every individual would be synonymous with those of the larger society.

But the doctrine of historical materialism, much as it was a brilliant advance over previous historical analysis, was not the complete answer, as later events bore out. For though Marx and Engels grounded their theory in reality, it was only a *partial* reality. Here is Engels' strictly economic definition of historical materialism from *Socialism: Utopian or Scientific:*

> Historical materialism is that view of the course of history which seeks the *ultimate* cause and the great moving power of all historical events in the economic development of society, in the changes of the modes of production and exchange, in the consequent division of society into distinct classes, and in the struggles of these classes against one another. (Italics mine)

Further, he claims:

> . . . that all past history with the exception of the primitive stages was the history of class struggles; that these warring classes of society are always the products of the modes of production and exchange—in a word, of the economic conditions of their time; that the *economic* structure of society always furnishes the real basis, starting from which we can alone work out the *ultimate* explanation of the whole superstructure of juridical and political institutions as well as of the religious, philosophical, and other ideas of a given historical period. (Italics mine)

It would be a mistake to attempt to explain the oppression of women according to this strictly economic interpretation. The class analysis is a beautiful piece of work, but limited: although correct in a linear sense, it does not go deep enough. There is a whole sexual substratum of the historical dialectic that Engels at times dimly perceives, but because he can see sexuality only through an economic filter, reducing everything to that, he is unable to evaluate in its own right.

Engels did observe that the original division of labor was between man and woman for the purposes of childbreeding; that within the family the husband was the owner, the wife the means of production, the children the labor; and that reproduction of the human species was an important economic system distinct from the means of production. . . .

But Engels has been given too much credit for these scattered recognitions of the oppression of women as a class. In fact he acknowledged the sexual class system only where it overlapped and illuminated his economic construct. Engels didn't do so well even in this respect. But Marx was worse: There is a growing recognition of Marx's bias against women (a cultural bias shared by Freud as well as all men of culture), dangerous if one attempts to squeeze feminism into an orthodox Marxist framework—freezing what were only incidental insights of Marx and Engels about sex class into dogma. Instead, we must enlarge historical materialism to *include* the strictly Marxian, in the same way that the physics of relativity did not invalidate Newtonian physics so much as it drew a circle around it, limiting its application—but only through comparison—to a smaller sphere. For an economic diagnosis traced to ownership of the means of production, even of the means of *re*production, does not explain everything. There is a level of reality that does not stem directly from economics.

The assumption that, beneath economics, reality is psychosexual is often rejected as ahistorical by those who accept a dialectical materialist view of history because it seems to land us back where Marx began: groping through a fog of utopian hypotheses, philosophical systems that might be right, that might be wrong (there is no way to tell), systems that explain concrete historical developments by *a priori* categories of thought; historical materialism, however, attempted to explain "knowing" by "being" and not vice versa.

But there is still an untried third alternative: We can attempt to develop a materialist view of history based on sex itself. . . .

Let us try to develop an analysis in which biology itself—procreation—is at the origin of the dualism. The immediate assumption of the layman that the unequal division of the sexes is "natural" may be well-founded. We need not immediately look beyond this. Unlike economic class, sex class sprang directly from a biological reality: men and women were created different, and not equally privileged. Although, as De Beauvoir points out, this difference of itself did not necessitate the development of a class system—the domination of one group by another—the reproductive *functions* of these differences did. The biological family is an inherently unequal power distribution. The need for power leading to the development of classes arises from the psychosexual formation of each individual according to this basic imbalance, rather than, as Freud, Norman O. Brown, and others have, once again overshooting their mark, postulated, some irreducible conflict of Life against Death, Eros vs. Thanatos.

The *biological family*—the basic reproductive unit of male/female/infant, in whatever form of social organization—is characterized by these fundamental—if not immutable—facts:

1. That women throughout history before the advent of birth control were at the continual mercy of their biology—menstruation, menopause, and "female ills," constant painful childbirth, wetnursing and care of infants, all of which made them dependent on males (whether brother, father, husband, lover, or clan, government, community-at-large) for physical survival.

2. That human infants take an even longer time to grow up than animals, and thus are helpless and, for some short period at least, dependent on adults for physical survival.

3. That a basic mother/child interdependency has existed in some form in every society, past or present, and thus has shaped the psychology of every mature female and every infant.

4. That the natural reproductive difference between the sexes led directly to the first division of labor at the origins of class, as well as furnishing the paradigm of caste (discrimination based on biological characteristics).

These biological contingencies of the human family cannot be covered over with anthropological sophistries. Anyone observing animals mating, reproducing, and caring for their young will have a hard time accepting the "cultural relativity" line. For no matter how many tribes in Oceania you can find where the connection of the father to fertility is not known, no matter how many matrilineages, no matter how many cases of sex-role reversal, male housewifery, or even empathic labor pains, these facts prove only one thing: the amazing *flexibility* of human nature. But human nature is adaptable *to* something, it is, yes, determined by its environmental conditions. And the biological family that we have described has existed everywhere throughout time. Even in matriarchies where woman's fertility is worshipped, and the father's role is unknown or unimportant, if perhaps not on the genetic father, there is still some dependence of the female and the infant on the male. And though it is true that the nuclear family is only a recent development, one which, as I shall attempt to show, only intensifies the psychological penalties of the biological family, though it is true that throughout history there have been many variations on this biological family, the contingencies I have described existed in all of them, causing specific psychosexual distortions in the human personality.

But to grant that the sexual imbalance of power is biologically based is not to lose our case. We are no longer just animals. And the Kingdom of Nature does not reign absolute. . . .

The "natural" is not necessarily a "human" value. Humanity has begun to outgrow nature: we can no longer justify the maintenance of a discriminatory sex class system on grounds of its origins in Nature. Indeed, for pragmatic reasons alone it is beginning to look as if we *must* get rid of it.

The problem becomes political, demanding more than a comprehensive historical analysis, when one realizes that, though man is increasingly capable of freeing himself from the biological conditions that created his tyranny over women and children, he has little reason to want to give this tyranny up. As Engels said, in the context of economic revolution:

> It is the law of division of labor that lies at the basis of the division into classes

[Note that this division itself grew out of a fundamental biological division]. But this does not prevent the ruling class, once having the upper hand, from consolidating its power at the expense of the working class, from turning its social leadership into an intensified exploitation of the masses.

Though the sex class system may have originated in fundamental biological conditions, this does not guarantee once the biological basis of their oppression has been swept away that women and children will be freed. On the contrary, the new technology, especially fertility control, may be used against them to reinforce the entrenched system of exploitation.

So that just as to assure elimination of economic classes requires the revolt of the underclass (the proletariat) and, in a temporary dictatorship, their seizure of the means of *production,* so to assure the elimination of sexual classes requires the revolt of the underclass (women) and the seizure of control of *reproduction:* not only the full restoration to women of ownership of their own bodies, but also their (temporary) seizure of control of human fertility—the new population biology as well as all the social institutions of childbearing and childrearing. And just as the end goal of socialist revolution was not only the elimination of the economic class *privilege* but of the economic class *distinction* itself, so the end goal of feminist revolution must be, unlike that of the first feminist movement, not just the elimination of male *privilege* but of the sex *distinction* itself: genital differences between human beings would no longer matter culturally. (A reversion to an unobstructed *pansexuality*—Freud's "polymorphous perversity" —would probably supersede hetero/homo/bisexuality.) The reproduction of the species by one sex for the benefit of both would be replaced by (at least the option of) artificial reproduction: children would be born to both sexes equally, or independently of either, however one chooses to look at it; the dependence of the child on the mother (and vice versa) would give way to a greatly shortened dependence on a small group of others in general, and any remaining inferiority to adults in physical strength would be compensated for culturally. The division of labor would be ended by the elimination of labor altogether (cybernation). The tyranny of the biological family would be broken. . . .

Structural Imperatives

Before we talk about revolutionary alternatives, let's summarize—to determine the specifics that must be carefully excluded from any new structures. Then we can go on to "utopian speculation" directed by at least negative guidelines.

We have seen how women, biologically distinguished from men, are culturally distinguished from "human." Nature produced the fundamental inequality—half the human race must bear and rear the children of all of them—which was later consolidated, institutionalized, in the interests of men. Reproduction of the species cost women dearly, not only emotionally, psychologically, culturally but even in strictly material (physical) terms: before recent methods of contraception, continuous childbirth led to constant "female trouble," early aging, and death. Women were the slave class that maintained the species in order to free the other half for the business of the world—admittedly often its drudge aspects, but certainly all its creative aspects as well.

This natural division of labor was continued only at great cultural sacrifice: men and women developed only half of themselves, at the expense of the other half. The division of the psyche into male and female to better reinforce the reproductive division was tragic: the hypertrophy in men of rationalism, aggressive drive, the atrophy of their emotional sensitivity was a physical (war) as well as a cultural disaster. The emotionalism and passivity of women increased their suffering (we cannot speak of them in a symmetrical way, since they were victimized as a class by the division). Sexually men and women were channeled into a highly ordered—time, place, procedure, even dialogue—heterosexuality restricted to the genitals, rather than diffused over the entire physical being.

I submit, then, that the first demand for any alternative system must be:

1 *The freeing of women from the tyranny of their reproductive biology by every means available, and the diffusion of the childbearing and childrearing role to the society as a whole, men as well as women.* There are many degrees of this. Already we have a (hard-won) acceptance of "family planning," if not contraception for its own sake. Proposals are imminent for day-care centers, perhaps even twenty-four-hour child-care centers staffed by men as well as women. But this, in my opinion, is timid if not entirely worthless as a transition. We're talking about *radical* change. And though indeed it cannot come all at once, radical goals must be kept in sight at all times. Day-care centers buy women off. They ease the immediate pressure without asking why that pressure is on *women*.

At the other extreme there are the more distant solutions based on the potentials of modern embryology, that is, artificial reproduction, possibilities still so frightening that they are seldom discussed seriously. We have seen that the fear is to some extent justified: in the hands of our current society and under the direction of current scientists (few of whom are female or even feminist), any attempted use of technology to "free" anybody is suspect. But we are speculating about post-revolutionary systems, and for the purposes of our discussion we shall assume flexibility and good intentions in those working out the change.

To thus free women from their biology would be to threaten the *social* unit that is organized around biological reproduction and the subjection of women to their biological destiny, the family. Our second demand will come also as a basic contradiction to the family, this time the family as an *economic* unit:

2 *The full self-determination, including economic independence, of both women and children.* To achieve this goal would require fundamental changes in our social and economic structure. This is why we must talk about a feminist socialism: in the immediate future, under capitalism, there could be at best a token integration of women into the labor force. For women have been found exceedingly useful and cheap as a transient, often highly skilled labor supply,[1] not to mention the economic value of their traditional function, the reproduction and rearing of the next generation of children, a job for which they are now patronized (literally and thus figuratively) rather than paid. But whether or not officially recognized, these are essential economic functions. Women, in this present capacity, are the very foundation of the economic superstructure, vital to its existence.[2] The paeans to self-sacrificing motherhood have a basis in reality: Mom *is* vital to the American way of life, considerably more than apple pie. She is an institution without which the system really *would* fall apart. In official capitalist terms, the bill for her economic services[3] might run as high as one-fifth of the gross national product. But payment is not the answer. To pay her, as is often discussed seriously in Sweden, is a reform that does not challenge the basic division of labor and thus could never eradicate the disastrous psychological and cultural consequences of that division of labor.

As for the economic independence of children, that is really a pipe dream, realized as yet nowhere in the world. And, in the case of children too, we are talking about more than a fair integration into the labor force; we are talking about the abolition of the labor force itself under a cybernetic socialism, the radical restructuring of the economy to make "work," i.e., wage labor, no longer necessary. In our post-revolutionary society adults as well as children would be provided for—irrespective of their social contributions—in the first equal distribution of wealth in history.

We have now attacked the family on a double front, challenging that around which it is organized: reproduction of the species by females and its outgrowth, the physical dependence of women and children. To eliminate these would be enough to destroy the family, which breeds the power psychology. However, we will break it down still further.

3 *The total integration of women and children into all aspects of the larger society.* All institutions that segregate the sexes, or bar children from adult society, e.g., the elementary school, must be destroyed. *Down with school!*

These three demands predicate a feminist revolution based on advanced technology. And if the male/female and the adult/child cultural distinctions are destroyed, we will no longer need the sexual repression that maintains these unequal classes, allowing for the first time a "natural" sexual freedom. Thus we arrive at:

4 *The freedom of all women and children to do whatever they wish to do sexually.* There will no longer be any reason *not* to. (Past reasons: Full sexuality threatened the continuous reproduction necessary for human survival, and thus, through religion and other cultural institutions, sexuality had to be restricted to reproductive purposes, all nonreproductive sex pleasure considered deviation or worse; The sexual freedom of women would call into question the fatherhood of the child, thus threatening patrimony; Child sexuality had to be repressed because it was a threat to the precarious internal balance of the family. These sexual repressions increased proportionately to the degree of cultural exaggeration of the biological family.) In our new society, humanity could finally revert to its natural polymorphous sexuality—all forms of sexuality would be allowed and indulged. The fully sexuate mind, realized in the past in only a few individuals (survivors), would become universal. Artificial cultural achievement would no longer be the only avenue to sexuate self-realization: one could now realize oneself fully, simply in the process of being and acting. . . .

Notes

1. Most bosses would fail badly had they to take over their secretaries' job, or do without them. I know several secretaries who sign without a thought their bosses' names to their own (often brilliant) solutions. The skills of college women especially would cost a fortune reckoned in material terms of male labor.

2. Margaret Benston ("The Political Economy of Women's Liberation," *Monthly Review,* September 1969), in attempting to show that women's oppression is indeed economic—though previous economic analysis has been incorrect—distinguishes between the male superstructure economy based on *commodity* production (capitalist ownership of the means of production, and wage labor), and the pre-industrial reduplicative economy of the family, production for immediate *use*. Because the latter is not part of the *official* contemporary economy, its function at the basis of that economy is often overlooked. Talk of drafting women into the superstructure commodity economy fails to deal with the tremendous amount of necessary production of the traditional kind now performed by women without pay: Who will do it?

3. The Chase Manhattan Bank estimates a woman's over-all domestic work week at 99.6 hours. Margaret Benston gives her minimal estimate for a *childless* married woman at 16 hours, close to half of a regular work week; a *mother* must spend at least six or seven days a week working close to 12 hours.

Socialist Feminism and Human Nature

Alison M. Jaggar

According to Alison M. Jaggar, socialist feminism is best understood by distinguishing it from both Marxist feminism and radical feminism. On the one hand, socialist feminism shares with Marxist feminism a commitment to a historical materialist method but then denies that women's liberation can be achieved simply by replacing capitalism with socialism. On the other hand, socialist feminism shares with radical feminism a commitment to change human biology but then views such a change as only part of what is needed to bring about women's liberation.

. . . Like radical feminism, socialist feminism is a daughter of the contemporary women's liberation movement. It is a slightly younger daughter, born in the 1970s and, like most younger daughters, impressed by its elder sister, while wanting at the same time to avoid her mistakes. The central project of socialist feminism is the development of a political theory and practice that will synthesize the best insights of radical feminism and of the Marxist tradition and that simultaneously will escape the problems associated with each. So far, socialist feminism has made only limited progress toward this goal: "It is a commitment to the *development* of an analysis and political practice, rather than to one which already exists."[1] In spite of the programmatic nature of its achievement so far, I believe that socialist feminism constitutes a distinctive approach to political life, one that offers the most convincing promise of constructing an adequate theory and practice for women's liberation.

Any attempt to define socialist feminism faces the same problems as attempts to define liberal feminism, radical feminism or Marxism. Feminist theorists and activists do not always wear labels and, even if they do, they are not always agreed on who should wear which label. Moreover, there are differences even between those wearing the same label and, in addition, dialogue between feminists of different tendencies has led to modifications in all their views. Most Marxists, for instance, now

Abridged from *Feminist Politics and Human Nature* (1983), pp. 123–132. Reprinted by permission of Rowman and Allanheld. Notes renumbered.

take the oppression of women much more seriously than they did prior to the emergence of the women's liberation movement, while radical feminists are paying increasing attention to class, ethnic and national differences between women. As a result, the line between socialist feminism and other feminist theories is increasingly blurred, at least on the surface. For all these reasons, it is inevitable that my account of socialist feminism, like my account of the other feminist theories, will be stipulative as well as reportive. As in defining the other theories, I shall identify socialist feminism primarily by reference to its distinctive, underlying conception of human nature.

The easiest way to provide a preliminary outline of socialist feminism is in terms of its similarities and contrasts with the other feminist theories, especially with Marxism and radical feminism to which it is most closely linked. In a very general sense, all feminists address the same problem: what constitutes the oppression of women and how can that oppression be ended? Both liberal feminists and traditional Marxists believe that this question can be answered in terms of the categories and principles that were formulated originally to deal with other problems. For them, the oppression of women is just one among a number of essentially similar types of problems. Socialist feminism shares with radical feminism the belief that older established political theories are incapable, in principle, of giving an adequate account of women's oppression and that, in order to do so, it is necessary to develop new political and economic categories.

Like radical feminists, socialist feminists believe that these new categories must reconceptualize not only the so-called public sphere, but also the hitherto private sphere of human life. They must give us a way of understanding sexuality, childbearing, childrearing and personal maintenance in political and economic terms. Unlike many American radical feminists, however, socialist feminists attempt to conceptualize these activities in a deliberately historical, rather than a universal and sometimes biologistic, way. A defining feature of socialist feminism is that it attempts to interpret the historical materialist method of traditional Marxism so that it applies to the issues made visible by radical feminists. To revise Juliet Mitchell's comment, it uses a feminist version of the Marxist method to provide feminist answers to feminist questions.[2]

Ever since its inception in the mid-1960s, the women's liberation movement has been split by a chronic dispute over the relation between feminism and Marxism. This dispute has taken a number of forms, but one of the most common ways of interpreting it has been in terms of political priorities. The political analysis of traditional Marxism has led to the position that the struggle for feminism should be subordinated to the class struggle, whereas a radical feminist analysis has implied that the struggle for women's liberation should take priority over the struggle for all other forms of liberation. Socialist feminism rejects this dilemma. Not only does it refuse to compromise socialism for the sake of feminism or feminism for the sake of socialism; it argues that either of these compromises ultimately would be self-defeating. On the socialist feminist analysis, capitalism, male dominance, racism and imperialism are intertwined so inextricably that they are inseparable; consequently the abolition of any of these systems of domination requires the end of all of them. Socialist feminists claim that a full understanding of the capitalist system requires a recognition of the way in which it is structured by male dominance and, conversely, that a full understanding of contemporary male dominance requires a recognition of the way it is organized by the capitalist division of labor. Socialist feminists believe that an adequate account of "capitalist patriarchy" requires the use of the historical materialist method developed originally by Marx and Engels. They argue, however, that the conceptual tools of Marxism are blunt and biased until they are ground into precision on the sharp edge of feminist consciousness.

One question that arises from this preliminary characterization is whether socialist feminism is or is not a variety of Marxism. Obviously, the answer to this question depends both on one's understanding of socialist feminism and on one's interpretation of Marxism. Political motivations are also involved. Some Marxists do not want the honorific title of Marxism to be granted to what they see as heresy,[3] others want to appropriate for Marxism at least those aspects of socialist feminism that they perceive as correct. Similarly, some socialist feminists want to define themselves as Marxists in opposition to other types of socialists; others see no reason to give Marx credit for a theory and a practice that reveals a social reality ignored and obscured by traditional Marxism. My own view is that socialist feminism is unmistakably Marxist, at least insofar as it utilizes the method of historical materialism. I shall argue that socialist feminism is in fact the most consistent application of Marxist method and therefore the most "orthodox" form of Marxism. . . .

The Socialist Feminist Conception of Human Nature

Socialist feminism is commited to the basic Marxist conception of human nature as creaated historically through the dialectical interrelation between human biology, human society and the physical environment. This interrelation is mediated by human labor or praxis. The specific form of praxis dominant within a given society creates the distinctive physical and psychological human types characteristic of that society.

Traditional political theory has given theoretical recognition only to a very limited number of human types. It is true that liberals acknowledge individual human variation; indeed, this acknowledgment is a necessary part of their arguments for a firm limitation on the extent of state power. As we have seen, Locke and Mill explain the reasons for at least some of this variation in terms of the social opportunities available to different classes, and liberal feminists explain psychological differences between the sexes in terms of sex-role socialization. Ultimately, however, liberals view the differences between people as relatively superficial, and they assume that underlying these superficial differences is a certain fixed human nature which is modified but not fundamentally created by social circumstances. Marxists, by contrast, view human nature as necessarily constituted in society: they believe that specific historical conditions create distinctive human types. Within contemporary capitalism, they give theoretical recognition to two such types, the capitalist and the proletariat. However, the traditional Marxist conception of human nature is flawed by its failure to recognize explicitly that all human beings in contemporary society belong not only to a specific class; they also have a specific sex and they are at a specific stage in the life cycle from infancy to death. In addition, although this point was not emphasized earlier because it is not a specifically feminist point, all humans in modern industrial society have specific racial, ethnic and national backgrounds. Contemporary society thus consists of groups of individuals, defined simultaneously by age, sex, class, nationality and by racial and ethnic origin, and these groups differ markedly from each other, both physically and psychologically. Liberal political theory has tended to ignore or minimize all these differences. Marxist political theory has tended to recognize only differences of class. The political theory of radical feminism has tended to recognize only differences of age and sex, to understand these in universal terms, and often to view them as determined biologically. By contrast, socialist feminism recognizes all these differences as constituent parts of contemporary human nature and seeks a way of understanding them that is not only materialist but also historical. In particular, it has insisted on the need for a more adequate theoretical understanding of the differences between women and men. Given that its methodological commitment is basically Marxist, it seeks this understanding through an examination of what it calls the sexual division of labor.[4] In other words, it focuses on the different types of praxis undertaken by women and men in order to develop a fully historical materialist account of the social construction of sex and gender.

The differences between women and men are both physical and psychological. Socialist feminists have begun to look at both these aspects of human nature. Some theorists, for instance, have studied variations in menstruation and menopause and have discovered that often these variations are socially determined.[5] Marian Lowe has begun to investigate the ways in which society influences women's sporting achievements, as well as their menstrual patterns.[6] Iris Young has explored some of the socially determined ways in which men and women move differently from each other and experience space, objects, and even their own bodies differently.[7] She has observed that women in sexist society are "physically handicapped." Interesting work has also been done on women's body language.[8] In undertaking these sorts of investigations, socialist feminists focus on the dialectical relationship between sex and society as it emerges through activity organized by gender norms. The methodological approach of socialist feminists makes it obvious that they have abandoned an ahistorical conception of human biology. Instead, they view human biology as being, in part, socially constructed. Biology is "gendered" as well as sexed.

In spite of their interest in the physical differences between women and men, contemporary feminists have been far more concerned with psychological differences, and socialist feminist theory has reflected that priority. Its main focus has been on the social construction not of masculine and feminine physical types, but rather of masculine and feminine character types. Among the many socialist feminist theorists who have worked on this project are Juliet Mitchell, Jane Flax, Gayle Rubin, Nancy Chodorow and, perhaps, Dorothy Dinnerstein.[9] All these theorists have been impressed by how early in life masculine and feminine character structures are established and by the relative rigidity of these structures, once established. To explain the mechanism by which psychological masculinity and femininity are imposed on infants and young children, all utilize some version of psychoanalysis. This is because they view psychoanalytic theory as providing the most plausible and systematic account of how the individual psyche is structured by gender. But unlike Freud, the father of psychoanalysis, socialist feminist theorists do not view psychological masculinity and femininity as the child's inevitable response to a fixed and universal biological endowment. Instead, they view the acquisition of gendered character types as the result of specific social practices, particularly procreative practices, that are not determined by biology and that in principle, therefore, are alterable. They want to de-biologize Freud and to reinterpret him in historical materialist terms. As Gayle Rubin puts it: "Psychoanalysis provides a description of the mechanisms by which the sexes are divided and deformed, of how bisexual, androgynous infants are transformed into boys and girls." . . .[10]

The distinctive aspect of the socialist feminist approach to human psychology is the way in which it synthesizes insights drawn from a variety of sources. Socialist feminism claims all of the following: that our "inner" lives, as well as our bodies and behavior, are structured by gender; that this gender-structuring is not innate but is socially imposed; that the specific characteristics that are imposed are related systematically to the historically prevailing system of organizing social production; that the gender-structuring of our "inner" lives occurs when we are very young and is reinforced throughout our lives in a variety of different spheres; and that these relatively rigid masculine and feminine character structures are a very important element in maintaining male dominance. Given this conception of human psychology, one of the major theoretical tasks that socialist feminism sets itself is to provide a historical materialist account of the relationship between our "inner" lives and our social praxis. It seeks to connect masculine and feminine psychology with the sexual division of labor. . . .

It is generally accepted, by non-feminists and feminists alike, that the most obvious manifestation of the sexual division of labor, in contemporary society if not in all societies, is

marked by the division between the so-called public and private spheres of human life. The line between these two spheres has varied historically: in the political theory of ancient Greece, for instance, "the economy" fell within the private sphere, whereas in contemporary political theory, both liberal and Marxist, "the economy" is considered—in different ways—to be part of the public realm. Wherever the distinction has existed, the private realm has always included sexuality and procreation, has always been viewed as more "natural" and therefore less "human" than the public realm, and has always been viewed as the realm of women.[11] Although women have always done many kinds of work, they have been defined primarily by their sexual and procreative labor; throughout history, women have been defined as "sex objects" and as mothers.

Partly because of this definition of women's work and partly because of their conviction that an individual's gender identity is established very early in life, much socialist feminist theory has focused on the area of sexuality and procreation. Yet the theory has been committed to conceptualizing this area in terms that are historical, rather than biological, and specific, rather than universal. Socialist feminism has accepted the radical feminist insight that sexual activity, childbearing, and childrearing are social practices that embody power relations and are therefore appropriate subjects for political analysis. Because of its rejection of biological determinism, however, socialist feminism denies the radical feminist assumption that these practices are fundamentally invariant. On the contrary, socialist feminists have stressed historical variation both in the practices and in the categories by which they are understood. Zillah Eisenstein writes:

> None of the processes in which a woman engages can be understood separate from the relations of the society which she embodies and which are reflected in the ideology of society. For instance, the act of giving birth to a child is only termed an act of motherhood if it reflects the relations of marriage and the family. Otherwise the very same act can be termed adultery and the child is "illegiti-

mate" or a "bastard." The term "mother" may have a significantly different meaning when different relations are involved—as in "unwed mother." It depends on what relations are embodied in the act.[12]

In the same spirit, Ann Foreman writes that "fatherhood is a social invention . . . located in a series of functions rather than in biology."[13] Rayna Rapp writes that even "being a child is a highly variable social relation."[14] Using the same historical approach, Ann Ferguson has argued that the emergence of lesbianism, as a distinct sexual identity, is a recent rather than a universal phenomenon insofar as it presupposes an urban society with the possibility of economic independence for women.[15] More generally, "It was only with the development of capitalist societies that 'sexuality' and 'the economy' became separable from other spheres of society and could be counter-posed to one another as realities of different sorts."[16]

Other authors have claimed that there is no transhistorical definition of marriage in terms of which the marital institutions of different cultures can be compared usefully.[17] Even within a single society, divisions of class mean that the working-class family unit is defined very differently from the upper-class family unit, and that it performs very different social functions.[18] One author denies that the family is a "bounded universe" and suggests that "we should extend to the study of 'family' [a] thoroughgoing agnosticism."[19] In general, socialist feminist theory has viewed human nature as constructed in part through the historically specific ways in which people have organized their sexual, childbearing and childrearing activities. The organization of these activities both affects and is affected by class and ethnic differences, but it is seen as particularly important in creating the masculine and feminine physiques and character structures that are considered appropriate in a given society.

The beginnings of this conception of human nature are already evident, to some extent, in the work of Marx and Engels. Engels' famous definition of the materialist conception of history in his introduction to *The Origin of the Family, Private Property and the State* states clearly:

The social organization under which the people of a particular historical epoch and a particular country live is determined by both kinds of production: by the state of development of labor on the one hand and of the family on the other.[20]

Moreover, Marx and Engels warn explicitly against conceptualizing procreation in an ahistorical way. In *The German Ideology*, they mock an ahistorical approach to "the concept of the family,"[21] and Engels' own work in *Origin* is designed precisely to demonstrate historical change in the social rules governing the eligibility of an individual's sexual partners. However, Marx and Engels view changes in the social organization of procreation as ultimately determined themselves by changes in the so-called mode of production, at least in postprimitive societies. Consequently, they see procreation as being now only of secondary importance in shaping human nature and society. One reason for this view may be that Marx and Engels still retain certain assumptions about the "natural," presumably biological, determination of much procreative activity. Thus, they do not give a symmetrical treatment to the human needs for food, shelter, and clothing, on the one hand, and to sexual, childbearing and childrearing needs, on the other. They view the former as changing historically, giving rise to new possibilities of social organization, but they regard human procreative needs as more "natural" and less open to historical transformation. Socialist feminists, by contrast, emphasize the social determination of sexual, childbearing and childrearing needs. They understand that these needs have developed historically in dialectical relation with changing procreative practices. Consequently, they are prepared to subject sexual and procreative practices to sustained political analysis and to reflect systematically on how changes in these practices could transform human nature.

Although socialist feminist theory stresses the importance of the so-called private sphere of procreation in constructing the historically appropriate types of masculinity and femininity, it does not ignore the so-called public sphere. It recognizes that women have always worked outside procreation, providing goods and services not only for their families but for the larger society as well. Socialist feminism claims that the conception of women as primarily sexual beings and/or as mothers is an ideological mystification that obscures the facts, for instance, that more than half the world's farmers are women,[22] and that, in the United States, women now make up almost half the paid labor force. Indeed, the Department of Labor projects that women will constitute 51.4 percent of the U.S. paid labor force by 1990.[23]

For socialist feminism, women, just as much as men, are beings whose labor transforms the non-human world. Socialist feminists view the slogan "A women's place is everywhere" as more than a call for change: for them, it is already a partial description of existing reality.

Only a partial description, however. Although socialist feminism recognizes the extent of women's productive work, it recognizes also that this work has rarely, if ever, been the same as men's. Even in contemporary market society, socialist feminism recognizes that the paid labor force is almost completely segregated by sex; at every level, there are "women's specialities." Within the contemporary labor force, moreover, women's work is invariably less prestigious, lower paid, and defined as being less skilled than men's, even when it involves such socially valuable and complex skills as dealing with children or sick people. Socialist feminism sees, therefore, that the sexual division of labor is not just a division *between* procreation and "production": it is also a division *within* procreation and *within* "production." Consequently, socialist feminism does not view contemporary masculinity and femininity as constructed entirely through the social organization of procreation; these constructs are elaborated and reinforced in non-procreative labor as well. . . .

We can now summarize the socialist feminist view of human nature in general and of women's nature in particular. Unlike liberalism and some aspects of traditional Marxism, socialist feminism does not view humans as "abstract, genderless" (and ageless and colorless) individuals,[24] with women essentially indistinguishable from men. Neither does it view women as irreducibly different from men, the

same yesterday, today and forever. Instead, it views women as constituted essentially by the social relations they inhabit. "(T)he social relations of society define the particular activity a woman engages in at a given moment. Outside these relations, 'woman' becomes an abstraction."[25]

Gayle Rubin paraphrases Marx thus:

> What is a domesticated woman? A female of the species. The one explanation is as good as the other. A woman is a woman. She only becomes a domestic, a wife, a chattel, a playboy bunny, a prostitute, or a human dictaphone in certain relations. Torn from these relationships, she is no more the helpmate of a man than gold in itself is money.[26]

To change these relationships is to change women's and so human nature.

Since history is never static, continuing changes in human nature are inevitable. As Marx himself remarked, "All history is nothing but a continuous transformation of human nature."[27] Socialist feminists want women to participate fully in taking conscious social control of these changes. They deny that there is anything especially natural about women's relationships with each other, with children or with men. Instead, they seek to reconstitute those relationships in such a way as to liberate the full power of women's (and human) creative potential.

No contemporary feminist would deny this goal, stated in the abstract. Just as at one time everyone was against sin, so now everyone is in favor of liberating human potential. Just as people used to disagree over how to identify sin, however, so now there is disagreement over what are human potentialities, which ones should be developed and how this development should be undertaken. Every conception of human nature implies an answer to these questions, and socialist feminism has its own distinctive answer. Unlike liberalism, the socialist feminist ideal of human fulfilment is not individual autonomy; for reasons that will be explained more fully later, socialist feminism views the ideal of autonomy as characteristically masculine as well as characteristically capitalist. The socialist feminist conception of human fulfilment is closer to the Marxist ideal of the full development of human potentialities through free productive labor, but socialist feminism construes productive labor more broadly than does traditional Marxism. Consequently, the socialist feminist ideal of human well-being and fulfilment includes the full development of human potentialities for free sexual expression, for freely bearing children and for freely rearing them.

To many Marxists, the theory of alienation expresses Marx's conception of human nature in capitalist society. As the theory is traditionally interpreted, alienation characterizes primarily workers' relation to wage labor; however, Marx saw that the way workers experience wage labor also affects the way they experience the rest of their lives. Because their wage labor is coerced, their activity outside wage labor seems free by contrast.

> We arrive at the result that man (the worker) feels himself to be freely active only in his animal functions—eating, drinking and procreating, or at most also in his dwelling and in personal adornment—while in his human functions he is reduced to an animal. The animal becomes human and the human becomes animal.[28]

To socialist feminists, this conception of alienation is clearly male-biased. Men may feel free when eating, drinking, and procreating, but women do not. As the popular saying has it, "A woman's work is never done." An Englishman's home may be his castle, but it is his wife's prison. Women are compelled to do housework, to bear and raise children and to define themselves sexually in terms of men's wishes. The pressures on women to do this work are almost overwhelming:

> When I say that women are subject to a form of compulsive labor, I mean that they may only resist with great difficulty, and that the majority succumb. The same may be said of non-owners when it comes to wage work. In both cases, it is not compulsive in the sense that one is driven to it with whips and chains (though that

happens, too!), but in the sense that no real alternative is generally available to women, and that everything in society conspires to ensure that women do this work. While a nonowner may attempt small independent production, or simply refuse to work and live off begging or state welfare, that is not proof of his freedom. The same is true of women. While a woman may with great difficulty resist doing reproductive work, that is no proof that she is "free" not to do it.[29]

One way in which socialist feminists are attempting to conceptualize contemporary women's lack of freedom is by extending the traditional Marxist theory of alienation. . . . Iris Young's reflections on "the struggle for our bodies," cited earlier in this chapter, suggest that women suffer a special form of alienation from their bodies. Similarly, Sandra Bartky claims that women are alienated in cultural production, as mothers and sexual beings. She believes that feminine narcissism is the paradigm of a specifically feminine form of sexual alienation.[30] Ann Foreman argues that femininity as such is an alienated condition: "While alienation reduces the man to an instrument of labour within industry, it reduces the woman to an instrument for his sexual pleasure within the family."[31] One may define the goal of socialist feminism as being to overcome all forms of alienation but especially those that are specific to women.

If it is difficult to envision what nonalienated industry would be like, it seems almost impossible to foresee the form of nonalienated sexuality or parenthood. Because of the ideological dogma that these are determined biologically, it is even harder to envision alternatives to prevailing sexual and procreative practices than it is to the capitalist mode of production. Alternative ways of organizing procreation tend to be viewed as science fiction; indeed, they are considered more often in fiction than in political theory. A number of socialist feminists are experimenting with alternatives in procreation, but the extent and validity of those experiments is limited, of course, by their context in a society that is emphatically neither socialist nor feminist.

The one solid basis of agreement among socialist feminists is that to overcome women's alienation, the sexual division of labor must be eliminated in every area of life. Just as sexual segregation in nonprocreative work must be eliminated, so men must participate fully in childrearing and, so far as possible, in childbearing.[32] Normative heterosexuality must be replaced by a situation in which the sex of one's lovers is a matter of social indifference, so that the dualist categories of heterosexual, homosexual and bisexual may be abandoned. Some authors describe the ideal as androgyny,[33] but even this term is implicitly dualistic. If it is retained for the present, we must remember that the ultimate transformation of human nature at which socialist feminists aim goes beyond the liberal conception of psychological androgyny to a possible transformation of "physical" human capacities, some of which, until now, have been seen as biologically limited to one sex. This transformation might even include the capacities for insemination, for lactation and for gestation so that, for instance, one woman could inseminate another, so that men and nonparturitive women could lactate and so that fertilized ova could be transplanted into women's or even into men's bodies. These developments may seem farfetched, but in fact they are already on the technological horizon,[34] however, what is needed much more immediately than technological development is a substantial reduction in the social domination of women by men. Only such a reduction can ensure that these or alternative technological possibilities are used to increase women's control over their bodies and thus over their lives, rather than being used as an additional means for women's subjugation. Gayle Rubin writes: "We are not only oppressed *as* women, we are oppressed by having to *be* women or men as the case may be."[35] The goal of socialist feminism is to abolish the social relations that constitute humans not only as workers and capitalists but also as women and men. Whereas one version of radical feminism takes the human ideal to be a woman, the ideal of socialist feminism is that women (and men) will disappear as socially constituted categories.

Notes

1. Margaret Page, "Socialist Feminism—a political alternative?", *m/f* 2 (1978):41.

2. Juliet Mitchell, a pioneering author whose work broke the ground for socialist feminism but whose basic orientation is ultimately Marxist, writes, "We should ask the feminist questions, but try to come up with Marxist answers." *Women's Estate* (New York: Pantheon Books, 1971), p. 99.

3. Pun intended. There is in fact an exciting journal named *Heresies: A Feminist Publication on Art & Politics*.

4. A clear statement of this methodological approach is given by Iris Young, "Socialist Feminism and the Limits of Dual Systems Theory," *Socialist Review* 50–51, pp. 169–88. Cf. also Iris Young "Beyond the Unhappy Marriage: A Critique of the Dual Systems Theory," in Lydia Sargent, ed., *Women and Revolution* (Boston: South End Press, 1981), pp. 43–69. Young in fact uses the term "gender division of labor", but I prefer to follow Nancy Hartsock in using the more familiar "sexual division of labor." Hartsock justifies her use of the latter term in part because of her belief that the division of labor between women and men is not yet entirely a social affair (women and not men still bear children), in part because she wishes to keep a firm hold of "the bodily aspect of existence." Nancy Hartsock, "The Feminist Standpoint: Developing the Ground for a Specifically Feminist Historical Materialism," in Sandra Harding and Merrill Hintikka, eds., *Discovering Reality: Feminist Perspectives on Epistemology, Metaphysics, Methodology and the Philosophy of Science* (Dordrecht: Reidel Publishing Co.), 1983.

5. Janice Delaney, Mary Jane Lupton, and Emily Toth, *The Curse: A Cultural History of Menstruation* (New York: E. P. Dutton, 1976).

6. Marian Lowe, "The Biology of Exploitation and the Exploitation of Biology," paper read to the National Women's Studies Association Second National Conference, Indiana University, Bloomington, May 16–20, 1980.

7. Iris Marion Young, "Is There a Woman's World?—Some Reflections on the Struggle for

our Bodies," proceedings of *The Second Sex—Thirty Years Later: A Commemorative Conference on Feminist Theory* (New York: The New York Institute for the Humanities, 1979). See also Young's "Throwing Like a Girl: A Phenomenology of Feminine Body Comportment, Motility and Sexuality," *Human Studies* 3 (1980):137–56.

8. For example, see Nancy M. Henley, *Body Politics: Sex, Power and Non-Verbal Communication* (Englewood Cliffs, N.J.: Prentice-Hall, 1977).

9. Juliet Mitchell, *Psychoanalysis and Feminism* (New York: Vintage Books, 1975); Gayle Rubin, "The Traffic in Women: Notes on the 'Political Economy' of Sex," in Rayna R. Reiter, ed., *Toward an Anthropology of Women* (New York: Monthly Review Press, 1975), pp. 157–210; Nancy Chodorow, *Mothering: Psychoanalysis and the Sociology of Gender* (Berkeley and Los Angeles: University of California Press, 1978); Dorothy Dinnerstein, *The Mermaid and the Minotaur: Sexual Arrangements and Human Malaise* (New York: Harper & Row, 1977). Dinnerstein's work is idiosyncratic and consequently difficult to categorize. Many of her assumptions, however, are identical with the assumptions of the other theorists mentioned here.

10. Rubin, "Traffic," p. 185.

11. The significance of this distinction for feminist theory will be discussed later in this chapter and also elsewhere in the book. Other theorists who have examined the distinction include Jean Bethke Elshtain, "Moral Woman and Immoral Man: A Consideration of the Public-Private Split and its Political Ramifications," *Politics and Society,* 1974; Jean Bethke Elshtain, *Public Man, Private Woman: Women in Social and Political Thought* (Princeton: Princeton University Press, 1981); and Linda Nicholson, *Feminism as Political Philosophy* (in progress). Cf. also M. Z. Rosaldo, "The Use and Abuse of Anthropology: Reflections on Feminism and Cross-Cultural Understanding," *Signs: Journal of Women in Culture & Society* 5, no. 3 (1980): esp. pp. 396–401.

12. Zillah Eisenstein, "Some Notes on the Relations of Capitalist Patriarchy," in Zillah Eisenstein, ed., *Capitalist Patriarchy and the Case for Socialist Feminism* (New York: Monthly Review Press, 1979), p. 47.

13. Ann Foreman, *Femininity as Alienation: Women and the Family in Marxism and Psychoanalysis* (London: Pluto Press, 1977), pp. 20 and 21.

14. Rayna Rapp, "Examining Family History," *Feminist Studies* 5, no 1 (Spring 1979):177.

15. Ann Ferguson, "Patriarchy, Sexual Identity and the Sexual Revolution," paper read at University of Cincinnati's Seventeenth Annual Philosophy Colloquium on "Philosophical Issues in Feminist Theory," November 13–16, 1980. This paper was later published in *Signs: Journal of Women in Culture and Society* 7, no. 1 (1981):158–72.

16. Robert A. Padgug, "Sexual Matters: On Conceptualising Sexuality in History," *Radical History Review* 20 (Spring/Summer 1979):16.

17. Kathleen Gough, "The Nayars and the Definition of Marriage," in P. B. Hammond, ed., *Cultural and Social Anthropology* (London, New York: Collier-Macmillan, 1964).

18. Rayna Rapp, "Family & Class in Contemporary America: Notes Toward an Understanding of Ideology," *Science and Society* 52, no. 3 (Fall 1978).

19. Ellen Ross, "Rethinking 'the Family'," *Radical History Review* 20 (Spring/Summer 1979):83.

20. Frederick Engels, *The Origin of the Family, Private Property and the State* (New York: International Publishers, 1972), pp. 71–72.

21. Karl Marx and Frederick Engels, *The German Ideology* (New York: International Publishers, 1970), p. 49.

22. *Isis Bulletin 11,* Geneva, Switzerland.

23. U.S. Bureau of the Census, *A Statistical Portrait of Women in the U.S.* (Washington, D.C.: Department of Commerce, Bureau of the Census, 1977); Current Population Reports, Special Studies Series, P-23, no. 58, pp. 28, 30, 31.

24. Rubin, "Traffic," p. 171.

25. Eisenstein, "Capitalist Patriarchy," p. 47.

26. Rubin, "Traffic," p. 158.

27. Karl Marx, *The Poverty of Philosophy* (New York: International Publishers, 1963), p. 147.

28. Karl Marx, *Early Writings,* translated and edited by T. B. Bottomore (New York: McGraw-Hill, 1963), p. 125.

29. Lynda Lange, "Reproduction in Democratic Theory," in W. Shea and J. King-Farlow, eds., *Contemporary Issues in Political Philosophy,* vol. 2

(New York: Science History Publications, 1976), pp. 140–41.

30. Sandra L. Bartky, "Narcissism, Femininity and Alienation," *Social Theory and Practice* 8, no. 2 (Summer 1982):127–43.

31. Ann Foreman, *Femininity as Alienation*, p. 151.

32. Some feminists are beginning to speculate on whether advanced technology will ultimately make it possible for men to be equally involved with women in bearing children. Two authors who consider this question are Shulamith Firestone, *The Dialectic of Sex: The Case for Feminist Revolution* (New York: W. W. Morrow, 1970), and Marge Piercy, *Woman on the Edge of Time* (New York: Fawcett Books, 1977).

33. Ann Ferguson, "Androgyny as an Ideal for Human Development," in Mary Vetterling-Braggin, Frederick A. Elliston, and Jane English, eds., *Feminism and Philosophy* (Totowa, N.J.: Littlefield, Adams, 1977).

34. Barbara Katz Rothman, "How Science is Redefining Parenthood," *Ms*, August 1982, pp. 154–58.

35. Rubin, "Traffic," p. 204.

National Organization for Women (NOW) Bill of Rights

 I **Equal Rights Constitutional Amendment**

 II **Enforce Law Banning Sex Discrimination in Employment**

 III **Maternity Leave Rights in Employment and in Social Security Benefits**

 IV **Tax Deduction for Home and Child Care Expenses for Working Parents**

 V **Child Care Centers**

 VI **Equal and Unsegregated Education**

 VII **Equal Job Training Opportunities and Allowances for Women in Poverty**

 VIII **The Right of Women to Control Their Reproductive Lives**

We Demand:

I That the United States Congress immediately pass the Equal Rights Amendment to the Constitution to provide that "Equality of rights under the law shall not be denied or abridged by the United States or by any State on account of sex," and that such then be immediately ratified by the several States.

II That equal employment opportunity be guaranteed to all women, as well as men, by insisting that the Equal Employment Opportunity Commission enforces the prohibitions against sex discrimination in employment under Title VII of the Civil Rights Act of 1964 with the same vigor as it enforces the prohibitions against racial discrimination.

III That women be protected by law to ensure their rights to return to their jobs within a reasonable time after childbirth without loss of seniority or other accrued benefits, and be paid maternity leave as a form of social security and/or employee benefit.

IV Immediate revision of tax laws to permit the deduction of home and child care expenses for working parents.

V That child care facilities be established by law on the same basis as parks, libraries, and public schools, adequate to the needs of children from the pre-school years through adolescence, as a community resource to be used by all citizens from all income levels.

VI That the right of women to be educated to their full potential equally with men be secured by Federal and State Legislation, eliminating all discrimination and segregation by sex, written and unwritten, at all levels of education, including colleges, graduate and professional schools, loans and fellowships, and Federal and State training programs such as the Job Corps.

VII The right of women in poverty to secure job training, housing, and family allowances on equal terms with men, but without prejudice to a parent's right to remain at home to care for his or her children; revision of welfare legislation and poverty programs which deny women dignity, privacy and self-respect.

VIII The right of women to control their own reproductive lives by removing from penal codes laws limiting access to contraceptive information and devices and laws governing abortion.

California Federal Savings and Loan v. Department of Fair Employment and Housing

United States Supreme Court

The issue before the Supreme Court was whether Title VII of the Civil Rights Act of 1964 as amended by the Pregnancy Discrimination Act of 1978 (PDA) nullified a California law requiring employers to provide leave and reinstatement to employees disabled by pregnancy. The majority of the Court ruled that it did not for two reasons. First, in passing PDA, Congress was concerned with prohibiting discrimination against pregnancy; preferential treatment, as found in the California law, was not discussed. Second, even if PDA did prohibit preferential treatment of pregnancy, an employer could avoid violating PDA and the California law by giving comparable benefits to all similarly disabled employees. In dissent, Justices White, Berger, and Powell argued that even though Congress did not explicitly consider the possibility of preferential treatment of pregnancy, the language of PDA ruled it out. In addition, they argued that if such preferential treatment were ruled out, those who wrote the California law could not have intended requiring comparable benefits for all similarly disabled employees.

Justice Marshall delivered the opinion of the Court.

The question presented is whether Title VII of the Civil Rights Act of 1964, as amended by the Pregnancy Discrimination Act of 1978, pre-empts a state statute that requires employers to provide leave and reinstatement to employees disabled by pregnancy.

California's Fair Employment and Housing Act (FEHA), Cal. Gov't Code Ann. § 12900 *et seq.* . . . is a comprehensive statute that prohibits discrimination in employment and housing. In September 1978, California amended the FEHA to proscribe certain forms of employment discrimination on the basis of pregnancy. . . . Subdivision (b)(2)—the provision at issue here—is the only portion of the statute that applies to employers subject to Title VII. . . . It requires these employers to provide female employees an unpaid pregnancy disability leave of up to four months. Respondent Fair Employment and Housing Commission, the state agency authorized to interpret the FEHA, has construed § 12945(b)(2) to require California employers to reinstate an employee returning from such pregnancy leave to the job she previously held, unless it is no longer available due to business necessity. In the latter case, the employer must make a reasonable, good faith effort to place the employee in a substantially similar job. The statute does not compel employers to provide *paid* leave to pregnant employees. Accordingly, the only benefit pregnant workers actually derive from § 12945(b)(2) is a qualified right to reinstatement.

Title VII of the Civil Rights Act of 1964 . . . also prohibits various forms of employment discrimination, including discrimination on the basis of sex. However, in *General Electric Co.* v. *Gilbert,* . . . this Court ruled that discrimination on the basis of pregnancy was not sex discrimination under Title VII. In response to the *Gilbert* decision, Congress passed the Pregnancy Discrimination Act of 1978 (PDA). . . . The PDA specifies that sex discrimination includes discrimination on the basis of pregnancy.

Petitioner California Federal Savings and Loan Association (Cal Fed) is a federally chartered savings and loan association based in Los Angeles; it is an employer covered by both Title VII and § 12945(b)(2). Cal Fed has a facially neutral leave policy that permits employees who have completed three months of service to take unpaid leaves of absence for a variety of reasons, including disability and pregnancy. Although it is Cal Fed's policy to try to provide an employee taking unpaid leave with a similar position upon returning, Cal Fed expressly reserves the right to terminate an employee who has taken a leave of absence if a similar position is not available.

Lillian Garland was employed by Cal Fed as a receptionist for several years. In January 1982, she took a pregnancy disability leave. When she was able to return to work in April of that year, Garland notified Cal Fed, but was informed that her job had been filled and that there were no receptionist or similar positions available. Garland filed a complaint with respondent Department of Fair Employment and Housing, which issued an administrative accusation against Cal Fed on her behalf. Respondent charged Cal Fed with violating § 12945(b)(2) of the FEHA. Prior to the scheduled hearing before respondent Fair Housing and Employment Commission, Cal Fed, joined by petitioners . . ., brought this action in the United States District Court for the Central District of California. They sought a declaration that § 12945(b)(2) is inconsistent with and pre-empted by Title VII and an injunction against enforcement of the section. . . .

. . . In order to decide whether the California statute requires or permits employers to violate Title VII, as amended by the PDA, or is inconsistent with the purposes of the statute, we must determine whether the PDA prohibits the States from requiring employers to provide reinstatement to pregnant workers, regardless of their policy for disabled workers generally. . . .

Petitioners argue that the language of the federal statute itself unambiguously rejects California's "special treatment" approach to pregnancy discrimination, thus rendering any resort to the legislative history unnecessary. They contend that the second clause of the PDA forbids an employer to treat pregnant employees any differently than other disabled employees. . . .

The context in which Congress considered the issue of pregnancy discrimination supports this view of the PDA. Congress had before it extensive evidence of discrimination *against* pregnancy, particularly in disability and health insurance programs like those challenged in *Gilbert* and *Nashville Gas Co.* v. *Satty.* . . . . The reports, debates, and hearings make abundantly clear that Congress intended the PDA to provide relief for working women and to end discrimination against pregnant workers. In contrast to the thorough account of discrimination against pregnant workers, the legislative history is devoid of any discussion of preferential treatment of pregnancy, beyond acknowledgments of the existence of state statutes providing for such preferential treatment. . . .

In support of their argument that the PDA prohibits employment practices that favor pregnant women, petitioners and several *amici* cite statements in the legislative history to the effect that the PDA does not *require* employers to extend any benefits to pregnant women that they do not already provide to other disabled employees. For example, the House Report explained that the proposed legislation "does not require employers to treat pregnant employees in any particular manner. . . . We do not interpret these references to support petitioners' construction of the statute. On the contrary, if Congress had intended to *prohibit* preferential treatment, it would have been the height of understatement to say only that the legislation would not *require* such conduct. It is hardly conceivable that Congress would have extensively discussed only its intent not to require preferential treatment if in fact it had intended to prohibit such treatment.

We also find it significant that Congress was aware of state laws similar to California's but apparently did not consider them inconsistent with the PDA. In the debates and reports on the bill, Congress repeatedly acknowledged the existence of state antidiscrimination laws that prohibit sex discrimination on the basis of pregnancy. Two of the States mentioned then required employers to provide reasonable leave to pregnant workers. After citing these state laws, Congress failed to evince the requisite "clear and manifest purpose" to supersede them. . . . To the contrary, both the House and Senate Reports suggest that these laws would continue to have effect under the PDA.

Title VII, as amended by the PDA, and California's pregnancy disability leave statute share a common goal. The purpose of Title VII is "to achieve equality of employment opportunities and remove barriers that have operated in the past to favor an identifiable group of . . . employees over other employees." . . . Rather than limiting existing Title VII principles and objectives, the PDA extends them to cover pregnancy. As Senator Williams, a sponsor of the Act, stated: "The entire thrust . . . behind this legislation is to guarantee women the basic right to participate fully and equally in the workforce, without denying them the fundamental right to full participation in family life." . . .

Section 12945(b)(2) also promotes equal employment opportunity. By requiring employers to reinstate women after a reasonable pregnancy disability leave, § 12945(b)(2) ensures that they will not lose their jobs on account of pregnancy disability. . . . By "taking pregnancy into account," California's pregnancy disability leave statute allows women, as well as men, to have families without losing their jobs.

We emphasize the limited nature of the benefits § 12945(b)(2) provides. The statute is narrowly drawn to cover only the period of *actual physical disability* on account of pregnancy, childbirth, or related medical conditions. Accordingly, unlike the protective labor legislation prevalent earlier in this century, § 12945(b)(2) does not reflect archaic or stereotypical notions about pregnancy and the abilities of pregnant workers. A statute based on such stereotypical assumptions would, of course, be inconsistent with Title VII's goal of equal employment opportunity. . . .

Moreover, even if we agreed with petitioners'

construction of the PDA, we would nonetheless reject their argument that the California statute requires employers to violate Title VII. . . . Section 12945(b)(2) does not compel California employers to treat pregnant workers *better* than other disabled employees; it merely establishes benefits that employers must, at a minimum, provide to pregnant workers. Employers are free to give comparable benefits to other disabled employees, thereby treating "women affected by pregnancy" no better than "other persons not so affected but similar in their ability or inability to work." Indeed, at oral argument, petitioners conceded that compliance with both statutes "is theoretically possible." . . .

Thus, petitioners' facial challenge to § 12945(b)(2) fails. The statute is not pre-empted by Title VII, as amended by the PDA, because it is not inconsistent with the purposes of the federal statute, nor does it require the doing of an act which is unlawful under Title VII.

The judgment of the Court of Appeals is

Affirmed

. . . Justice White, with whom The Chief Justice and Justice Powell join, dissenting.

I disagree with the Court that Cal. Gov't Code Ann. § 12945(b)(2) . . . is not pre-empted by the Pregnancy Discrimination Act of 1978 (PDA). . . . Section 703(a) of Title VII . . . forbids discrimination in the terms of employment on the basis of race, color, religion, sex, or national origin. The PDA gave added meaning to discrimination on the basis of sex:

"The terms 'because of sex' or 'on the basis of sex' [in section 703(a) of this title] include, but are not limited to, because of or on the basis of pregnancy, childbirth or related medical conditions; and women affected by pregnancy, childbirth, or related medical conditions shall be treated the same for all employment-related purposes, including receipt of benefits under fringe benefit programs, as other persons not so affected but similar in their ability or inability to work. . . ."

The second clause quoted above could not

be clearer: it mandates that pregnant employees "shall be treated the same for all employment-related purposes" as nonpregnant employees similarly situated with respect to their ability or inability to work. . . .

Contrary to the mandate of the PDA, California law requires every employer to have a disability leave policy for pregnancy even if it has none for any other disability. An employer complies with California law if it has a leave policy for pregnancy but denies it for every other disability. On its face, § 12945(b)(2) is in square conflict with the PDA and is therefore pre-empted. . . .

The majority nevertheless would save the California law on two grounds. First, it holds that the PDA does not require disability from pregnancy to be treated the same as other disabilities; instead, it forbids less favorable, but permits more favorable, benefits for pregnancy disability. . . .

. . . Given the evidence before Congress of the wide-spread discrimination against pregnant workers, it is probable that most Congresspersons did not seriously consider the possibility that someone would want to afford preferential treatment to pregnant workers. The parties and their *amici* argued vigorously to this Court the policy implications of preferential treatment of pregnant workers. In favor of preferential treatment it was urged with conviction that preferential treatment merely enables women, like men, to have children without losing their jobs. In opposition to preferential treatment it was urged with equal conviction that preferential treatment represents a resurgence of the 19th century protective legislation which perpetuated sex-role stereotypes and which impeded women in their efforts to take their rightful place in the workplace. . . . It is not the place of this Court, however, to resolve this policy dispute. . . .

Congress' acknowledgment of state antidiscrimination laws does not support a contrary inference. The most extensive discussion of state laws governing pregnancy discrimination is found in the House Report. . . . The Report did not in any way set apart the Connecticut and Montana statutes, on which the majority relies, from the other state statutes. The House Report gave no indication that these statutes required anything more than equal treatment. . . .

The Court's second, and equally strange, ground is that even if the PDA does prohibit special benefits for pregnant women, an employer may still comply with both the California law and the PDA: it can adopt the specified leave policies for pregnancy and at the same time afford similar benefits for all other disabilities. This is untenable. California surely had no intent to require employers to provide general disability leave benefits. It intended to prefer pregnancy and went no farther. . . .

In sum, preferential treatment of pregnant workers is prohibited by Title VII, as amended by the PDA. Section 12945(b)(2) of the California Gov't Code, which extends preferential benefits for pregnancy, is therefore pre-empted. . . .

Suggestions for Further Reading

Anthologies

Bishop, Sharon, and Weinzweig, Marjorie. *Philosophy and Women.* Belmont: Wadsworth Publishing Co., 1979.

Freeman, Jo. *Women: A Feminist Perspective.* Palo Alto: Mayfield Publishing Co., 1975.

Gould, Carol C., and Wartofsky, Marx W. *Women and Philosophy.* New York: G. P. Putnam & Sons, 1976.

Jaggar, Alison, and Struhl, Paula Rothenberg. *Feminist Frameworks.* New York: McGraw-Hill Co., 1981.

Vetterling-Braggin, Mary; Elliston, Frederick; and English, Jane. *Feminism and Philosophy.* Totowa: Littlefield, Adams, 1977.

Basic Concepts

Jaggar, Alison M. *Feminist Politics and Human Nature.* Totowa: Rowman & Allanheld, 1983.

Alternative Views

DeCrow, Karen. *Sexist Justice.* New York: Vintage, 1975.

Eisenstein, Zellah. *Feminism and Sexual Equality.* New York: Monthly Review, 1984.

Friedan, Betty. *The Feminine Mystique.* New York: W. W. Norton & Co., 1963.

Frye, Marilyn. *The Politics of Reality.* New York: The Crossing Press, 1983.

Koedt, Anne, Levine, Ellen, and Rapone, Anita. *Radical Feminism.* New York: Quadrangle Press, 1973.

Millet, Kate. *Sexist Politics.* Garden City: Doubleday & Co., 1970.

Sowell, Thomas. *Black Education: Myths and Tragedies.* New York: McKay, 1972.

Practical Applications

Irving, John. *The World According to Garp.* New York: Dutton, 1978.

United States Commission on Civil Rights. *Statement on the Equal Rights Amendment.* Washington D.C.: U. S. Government Printing Office, 1978.

Compensation for Past Wrongs

Basic Concepts

Solutions to the problem of discrimination and prejudice tend to be either backward-looking or forward-looking. Backward-looking solutions seek to rectify and compensate for past injustices caused by discrimination or prejudice. Forward-looking solutions seek to realize an ideal of a society free from discrimination and prejudice. To justify a backward-looking solution to the problem of discrimination and prejudice, it is necessary to determine (1) who has committed or benefited from a wrongful act of discrimination or prejudice and (2) who deserves compensation for that act. To justify a forward-looking solution to the problem, it is necessary to determine (1) what a society free from discrimination and prejudice would be like and (2) how such a society might be realized. Solutions of both types have been proposed to deal with racism and sexism, the dominant forms of discrimination and prejudice in our times.

One useful way of approaching the topic of discrimination and prejudice is to note what particular solutions to the problem are favored by the political ideals of libertarianism, welfare liberalism, socialism, and communitarianism (see Section I).

Libertarians, for whom liberty is the ultimate political ideal, are not likely to recognize any need to rectify acts of discrimination and prejudice. Bad as these acts may be, they usually do not—according to libertarians—violate anyone's rights, and hence do not demand rectification. In particular, because no one can demand a right to equal basic educational opportunities (a person's educational opportunities being simply a function of the property he or she controls), no one can justify affirmative action or preferential treatment on the basis that such a right was previously denied.

Socialists and communitarians, for whom equality and the common good, respectively, are the ultimate political ideals, recognize a need to correct for discrimination and prejudice. However, the corrective measures they favor are not limited to affirmative action or preferential treatment; socialists ultimately want to socialize the means of production and do away with private property, and communitarians ultimately want to establish and maintain the forms of community that are necessary for the common good.

Finally, affirmative action or preferential treatment is a central requirement of the political program of welfare liberals, whose ultimate political ideal is contractual fairness.

Proposed solutions to the problem of discrimination and prejudice usually involve favoring or compensating certain qualified individuals when there has been a denial of equal basic opportunities in the past. This practice is called "affirmative action" and "preferential treatment" (basically forward-looking terminology, usually employed by those who favor the practice), but is also described as "reverse discrimination" (basically backward-looking terminology, usually employed by those who do not favor the practice). Such proposed solutions to the problem of discrimination and prejudice usually presuppose a right of equal opportunity or a standard of hiring by competence.

Alternative Views

On pages 263–271, Alan H. Goldman takes up two central objections to the standard of hiring by competence. The first is the libertarian objection that employers have a right to hire whomever they please; the second is the egalitarian objection that hiring by competence rewards undeserved advantages and purely native talents.

Goldman's initial response to the libertarian objection is that the right of equal opportunity supports the standard of hiring by competence. Goldman admits that libertarians have rarely recognized such a right. Nevertheless, he argues that if libertarians wish to be understood as taking a moral stance, they must endorse such a right because morality requires that practices "operate to the good of all."

Now libertarians might agree that morality requires practices that "operate to the good of all," but they would deny that this necessitates a right to equal opportunity. They might, for example, claim that this requirement can be met simply by respecting each person's rights to life and property (rights libertarians take to be grounded in an ideal of liberty).

Anticipating this line of defense, Goldman argues that hiring by competence is also supported by considerations of social utility that specifically involve certain fundamental liberties. Unfortunately, it's not clear from Goldman's discussion whether the liberties in question are of the sort that would require libertarians to pay them heed. Liberties can be of two sorts, negative and positive. Both negative and positive liberties are states in which one is unconstrained by other persons from doing what one wants; the two kinds of liberty differ as to what counts as a constraint. In the definition of negative liberties, the constraints that would prevent people from doing what they want to do are always acts of commission. When speaking of positive liberties, on the other hand, the constraints envisioned are acts of either commission or omission.

It seems clear enough that an ideal of positive liberty does indeed support a right to equal opportunity because lack of opportunity will frequently be due to the failure of others to provide it (an act of omission). But libertarians interpret their ideal to be one of negative liberty (prohibiting only constraints that are acts of commission). Hence, a quite different defense is needed to show that the libertarian ideal supports a right of equal opportunity. And it is not clear that Goldman has provided such a defense.[1]

A different problem arises when Goldman attempts to answer the egalitarian objection to a standard of hiring by competence. Goldman argues that the alternative suggested by egalitarians, a random allocation of the desirable positions in society, is "the worst of all possible worlds." But while Goldman may be right about the merits of this suggested alternative, he is wrong in thinking that it is an alternative egalitarians usually endorse. For example, egalitarians who follow Marx favor a two-stage approach to realizing their ideal.[2] In the first stage, the principle of distribution is from each according to his or her ability and to each according to his or her contribution. In the second stage, when a society has become sufficiently productive and jobs have been redesigned so as to be generally enjoyable in themselves, the principle of distribution is from each according to his or her ability and to each according to his or her need. At both stages, however, a standard of hiring by competence rather than a system of random allocation seems to be the appropriate method for assigning positions. If people are to be rewarded on the basis of their contributions, as they are at the first stage, it makes sense to hire them on the basis of their competence. Even at the second stage, hiring by competence still seems to be appropriate, especially since at this stage the egalitarian objection that hiring by competence rewards undeserved advantages and native talent no longer applies. Accordingly, egalitarians who follow Marx would have little reason to reject a standard of hiring by competence, although they would, of course, want to link such a standard with a program of restructuring jobs and socializing the means of production.

Acknowledging that gross violations of the standard of hiring by competence as well as the right of equal opportunity have occurred in the past, many have argued that affirmative action is required either to remedy these past violations or to help realize a society free from the evils of racism and sexism. Opponents have argued that affirmative action embodies injustices of its own.

In the next selection, Bernard R. Boxill examines this opposition to affirmative action (see pp. 272–281). Some have contended that affirmative action benefits only those from among the groups that have suffered discrimination who do not deserve compensation. Against this, Boxill argues that even if those who benefit from affirmative action are less deserving of compensation than others, they do still deserve the compensation of affirmative action. Boxill's defense, however, seems to assume that we can compensate virtually all those who are deserving of compensation for past injustices. But this is not always possible because of limited resources or limited political power. Under such circumstances, might it not be more appropriate to use our resources and power to benefit those most deserving of compensation? This might lead us to fund remedial educational programs or job training programs rather than affirmative action programs. It may not be possible, of course, to institute the programs that would effectively compensate for the most serious injustices of the past. In that case, affirmative action programs may be the best alternative. But even when that is the case, it is still important to distinguish what we should do under ideal circumstances from the best we can do given the nonideal circumstances in which we live.

In opposition to affirmative action programs, Charles Murray (pp. 281–288) argues that affirmative action for blacks has actually worked against their interests by encouraging a new form of racism. The old racism openly held that blacks are permanently less competent than whites. The new racism holds that blacks are temporarily less competent than whites. The main problem with the new racism, according to Murray, is that it tends to perpetuate the racial inequalities it purports to remedy. However, the examples of this new racism that Murray discusses are all composites drawn from personal observations and, hence, as even he seems to realize, do not by themselves support any generalizations. At the same time, Murray wants to conclude from his discussion that there is no such thing as good racial discrimination.

In the next selection, Herman Schwartz (pp. 288–296) begins by surveying the law on affirmative action from Bakke to Stotts, noting certain ambiguities in recent Supreme Court decisions and then goes on to analyze the underlying moral issues involved in affirmative action. First, Schwartz charges that people who condemn affirmative action are hypocritical because they also use separate lists when making political appointments. Second, Schwartz argues that there is nothing inherently wrong with taking group identity into account as long as the people selected are qualified. In fact, in some cases, this might be necessary to achieve some legitimate goal, such as ethnic diversity for a university community or community cooperation with a police force. Third, Schwartz argues that it is an egregious

mistake to equate affirmative action with the various forms of discrimination suffered by blacks. Fourth, to those who charge that affirmative action is unfair to white males, Schwartz stresses how few slots are actually allotted to affirmative action and how economically disadvantaged most blacks are in the United States today. What Schwartz seems to be saying is that while affirmative action is unfair to white males, it is nonetheless morally justified. In this respect, Schwartz's argument differs from Boxill's because Boxill contends that white males have no right to the positions and opportunities allotted by affirmative action and, hence, are not treated unfairly when they are denied them for good reason.

Practical Applications

Assuming that we accept the need for affirmative action programs to compensate for past injustices, there remains the question of what form such programs should take. In a recent decision, Sheet Metal Workers vs. The Equal Opportunity Commission, the majority of the U.S. Supreme Court ruled that in appropriate circumstances it was legitimate to order affirmative action that would benefit individuals who are not the actual victims of past discrimination. In this decision, the majority of the court attempted to eliminate the confusion and uncertainty caused by its ruling in Firefighters vs. Stotts, where the court seemed to hold that remedies could be ordered only to people who had been the actual victims of illegal discrimination. In the Sheet Metal Workers case, the majority of the court ruled against this interpretation, claiming that when discrimination has been persistent and egregious, it is appropriate to employ remedies that benefit members of the relevant group even when they are not the identified victims of the past discrimination.

But is such an application justified? It seems to accord with a welfare liberal ideal. Consequently, socialists and communitarians would probably also find it acceptable, although they would think that further corrective measures were required. Libertarians, of course, would strongly object to this application on the grounds that people lack a right to the relevant equal opportunity needed to justify any affirmative action program. Hence, our evaluation of the Supreme Court's decision depends on our evaluations of these alternative political ideals.

Notes

1. For an account of what such a defense might look like, see James P. Sterba, "A Libertarian Justification for a Welfare State," *Social Theory and Practice* Vol. 11 No. 31 (1985).

2. Karl Marx, *Critique of the Gotha Program*, edited by C. P. Dutt (New York: International Publishers, 1966).

Justice and Hiring by Competence

Alan H. Goldman

Alan H. Goldman defends the standard of hiring by competence against the libertarian objection that employers have no obligation to hire the most competent, as well as the egalitarian objection that hiring the most competent rewards undeserved advantages and purely native talents. Against the libertarian objection, Goldman argues that the standard of hiring by competence is supported by considerations of equality of opportunity and social utility. Against the egalitarian objection, Goldman argues that justice and morality support the standard of hiring by competence over a random allocation of the desirable positions in society.

The issue to be settled in this paper regards a general rule for hiring or awarding scarce desirable positions in society. In recent political debates on the subject of reverse discrimination or preferential hiring, the principle of hiring by competence has seemed to remain sacrosanct, at least if one can judge by the lip-service paid to it by all sides of the discussion. Proponents of affirmative action go to great lengths to distinguish minority "goals" from quotas. While strict quotas for raising percentages of blacks and women employed by a fixed date, which would result in strong reverse discrimination, are acknowledged to be incompatible with the maintenance of strict competence standards, percentage goals for minorities toward which good faith efforts are

From "Justice and Hiring by Competence," *American Philosophical Quarterly* (1977), pp. 17–26. Reprinted by permission of the *American Philosophical Quarterly*.

made are held to encourage minority hiring while maintaining existing standards. Opponents of the policy on the other hand seem to feel that by demonstrating how academic standards of excellence suffer and most qualified individuals fail to get positions through pressure for reverse discrimination, they thereby show affirmative action programs in universities to be unjust.

But despite apparent unanimity regarding the principle in the context of this public debate, it has recently come under attack in more sophisticated philosophical circles from both the left and the right. Libertarians argue or imply that corporations or organizations with positions to fill can give them to whomever they choose, that society has no right to interfere in this free process. Corporations like individuals have the right to control their legitimately acquired assets and to disburse them to whom they choose, and the right to freely hire is part of this more general right. Egalitarians on the other hand hold the principle of hiring by competence unjust in rewarding initial undeserved advantages and purely native talents. Individuals do not deserve those initial advantages for which they can claim no responsibility, and hiring by competence alone often rewards just such chance talents and advantageous initial social positions. I will argue here against these attacks. I will be concerned with two central questions: (1) Does society have the right to impose and enforce any rule of hiring against corporations with positions to fill? (2) If the answer to (1) is affirmative, which principle of hiring ought to be adopted from the point of view of justice? I will argue against libertarians in this area that society does have the right and duty to enforce a principle, and against egalitarians that hiring by competence is just, that with several qualifications it is as just as human nature allows, and that even without them it is more just than seemingly equalitarian alternatives.

I. The Libertarian Position

The first question to be faced here is why one system of hiring can be judged more just than another at all, i.e. why the award of jobs by private corporations as opposed to the award of other benefits by private individuals involves considerations of justice rather than simply questions of right and wrong. There are situations in which individuals or corporations can make wrong, even overall morally wrong decisions, without treating anyone unjustly or unfairly. To say that principles of hiring are a matter of distributive social justice is to imply that certain individuals acquire distributive *rights* to certain positions, and that to refuse them these positions is to refuse to grant them what is legitimately due them. The libertarian denies that any such rights exist. He argues that just as Mary has the right to marry whom she pleases, so a private corporation with benefits in the form of jobs to award has the right to hire whom it pleases without interference.

No one acquires a right to marry Mary, and

similarly, argues the libertarian, no one acquires a right to a benefit from a private corporation which it has not contracted away. It will be useful in criticizing this position to see how far this analogy can be pressed. The difference between the case of Mary and that of the corporation cannot lie in the fact that a person's vital interests are affected by the job he works at, since his vital interests appear equally affected by his spouse, and yet as we said no one acquires a right to marry Mary—she can choose as capriciously as she wants. Thus we cannot argue simply from the fact that it makes a great deal of difference to people what jobs they get to the conclusion that society has a right to enforce a certain rule of hiring against private corporations. Nor does the converse seem to create a distinction, for if Mary's right to choose derives from the fact that her vital interests are involved as well, the same holds true of the corporation's vital interests in its personnel. Since a corporation's welfare and even continued existence depends upon who occupies its various positions, it can be argued that these choices should be left to it. It seems then that just as Mary has the right to choose a husband who will make her unhappy in the long run, i.e. she treats no one unjustly in doing so even if some other suitor would make a perfect spouse, so a corporation has the right to hire total incompetents if it chooses to act so unwisely. Nor can we argue simply that a corporation has no right to hire whom it pleases since the consequences of such freedom are bad (given present biases against minorities). For we perhaps can think of more scientific (or traditional?) ways to match spouses in comparison to which free choice has bad long range consequences for happiness, yet we would not want to deny Mary that right, nor contract it away ourselves. Even gains to her own interest or happiness do not justify interference with Mary's free choice, so that her right to choose derives from more than calculation of interests in particular cases. So in the case of a corporation, while it is difficult to see how hiring the most competent could damage its long range interests, perhaps it has a right to ignore those interests if it so chooses.

Are the cases then really totally analogous in relevant ways? First, although interests seem parallel as seen above, are the basic rights involved indeed similar? In Mary's case the general rights underlying her particular freedom in this case include a right over her own body and the freedom to control her life as she sees fit. That these rights, especially the first, have wide scope and absolute priority within their domains is in the interest of all to recognize. In the case of the corporation, the rights presumably involved are at most weaker versions or narrower cases of these: namely the right to property and that of free association. A corporation may be said to have a property right in the positions it chooses to fill in virtue of having legitimately acquired the assets with which to fund the positions. A corporation like an individual has a right to control those goods or assets which it has legitimately acquired. And the right to control its own assets is empty unless it is free to disburse them as or to whom it chooses. Since present members of the corporation must associate with new appointees, the freedom to associate with whom one pleases may also be cited in support of the libertarian position here. An enforced rule for hiring may force present members to work closely with others against their will, making their work unpleasant for them. And the friction created by this forced close association may be detrimental to the continued smooth operation of the company or organization.

Clearly the right over one's body, which applies in the case of Mary's marriage, is more basic than the right to external property, which applies in the hiring case . . . and the freedom to control one's life broader and more precious in total than that of free association. It can nevertheless be argued that just as the former rights constitute the paramount considerations in Mary's case, so do the latter in the case of the corporation. The corporation's property rights to control the disbursement of its assets and the right of free association of its members can be held to imply a specific right to hire whom it pleases without interference from society. In relation to the analogy with Mary's specific right to choose a spouse following from her rights over her own body and to control her life plan, the central questions here are first, whether Mary's rights always entail that she cannot treat others un-

justly in choosing a spouse (i.e. whether these rights are absolute in this sphere), and second, whether there might be other rights involved in the case of the corporation, but not in Mary's case, which limit or override those to which it can appeal in support of free choice. To the extent that Mary's specific right to marry whom she pleases is not absolute, and to the extent that the two cases are disanalogous regarding the rights and interests involved, we cannot argue from Mary's case to an absolute right to hire freely of the corporation.

It should first be noticed regarding the question of the scope of Mary's right that she can treat Dick unfairly or unjustly despite her right to choose, if she has led him on and then rejected him in favor of another at the altar. There are situations in which someone might acquire a legitimate expectation to marry Mary and be treated unjustly or unfairly by her subsequently. This might lead us to suspect that injustice in hiring as well has to do with thwarting legitimate expectations arising from previous efforts. But what could render expectations of individuals to jobs legitimate, given the corporation members' rights of property and free association? It might be held that the only parallel would be a corporation's refusing a job to an individual promised that position, but there are contract laws to prevent that from occurring, and the libertarian acknowledges the state's duty to enforce contracts freely made. (At least the rights in question, as in Mary's case, are already shown to be somewhat limited in scope.)

But there is a difference from the average case of whom one chooses to marry in that whether corporations have competent people or not affects the goods they produce for the rest of society, while whom one marries affects basically only oneself. If Mary happened to be a seventeenth century queen of England and her marriage affected how the country was ruled, she would lose her right to choose whom she pleased, and her subjects could complain of a choice being unfair to them. Similarly it seems society can complain if it fails to get necessary goods and services because of incompetents in positions of responsibility. If one corporation hires incompetents or relative incompetents because of discriminatory practices, it will soon be driven out of business in a competitive situation, but if there is such a practice generally in a whole sector of the economy, the public can complain for the price it pays for such lack of efficiency. To assume that competition will root out all such practices is to oversimplify motives and knowledge of both producers and consumers, and this assumption has proved empirically false.

It may be asked, however, how a social interest in more material goods and services can override recognized rights of individuals or private corporations within the society, like the rights of property and free association here. To determine a social interest is not necessarily to demonstrate the right of society or the state to further that interest, especially when individual or private corporation rights are apparently ignored in the process. For one principal purpose of recognizing individual rights within a system of social justice is to protect individuals from losses whenever utilitarian calculations run against them in particular cases. The recognition of the right to property, for example, means that a person will not be dispossessed whenever another is in greater need, although such forced transfer would raise total or average utility in particular cases. Therefore the rights to property and free association, it could be argued by analogy, should not be overridden here by the social interest in maximizing goods and services. A private corporation with assets to disburse for jobs should be free to hire whom it pleases, even when this results in lower efficiency in its production of goods and services. Efficiency cannot be permitted to override recognized rights, or our rights and freedoms would be fragile indeed. Thus while it may be in the interest of all, even of those in power in corporations, to have the most competent hired, there may exist rights to ignore the maximization of interest satisfaction, as in the case of marriage choices.

While I accept the above account of rights as far as it goes, it presents an oversimplified picture when used only in conjunction with appeal to property and free association rights in the context of this libertarian argument for freedom in hiring. What is ignored is the fact that recognition of particular rights, like that of property, is established in the first place in

relation to a set of varied social values including welfare, and that such rights are therefore rarely (never?) unlimited in scope, but include exception clauses recognizing rights established in relation to other values. My right to dispose of my property as I please does not include a right to dispose of my knife in an editor's chest; my right to use my property according to my own wishes does not include a right to play my stereo at deafening volumes; and my right to spend my assets as I like does not allow me to buy nerve gas, even if I keep it sealed in my basement vault. The above examples represent restrictions of freedom to prevent harm, annoyance or potential harm, but these are not the only possible cases. In the initial formulation of rules and rights the value of freedom may be weighed against those of equality or equity, and welfare, for example. This is compatible with the fact that welfare or utility considerations are no longer applied once the rights have been established and their scopes defined. Thus while it may be in the interest of all to recognize a right to personal property, this right may include an exception clause regarding filling jobs by corporations, again in the interest of all. This does not mean that property rights are to be overridden in specific cases for net gains in social welfare—property would be too precarious in that case—but general exception clauses of narrower scope (than any net gain in welfare) are compatible with the existence and protection of specific rights like that of property.

We have not yet won the argument with the libertarian, however. For his position is precisely that freedoms, including those of disbursing property and associating with those of one's choice, may only be limited to prevent harm. And a defender of this position would undoubtedly want to press the distinction here between the interests of individuals in maximizing available goods and services and any potential harm to them from the exercise of these freedoms on the part of corporations in hiring. I am not sure, however, that the distinction between harm and utility can be drawn at all in relation to many positions of responsibility in society, such as pilots, surgeons, police and even automobile, home or toy manufacturers. Relative incompetents in these positions represent not only losses in efficiency, but serious potential harm. Thus the harm principle itself, if it allows prevention of unnecessary risk or potential harm, which it must to be at all plausible, may require enforcement of a rule for hiring the most competent in many positions. On a deeper level it may be questioned whether considerations of freedom can be so sharply differentiated from considerations of equality and welfare when designing basic institutions or establishing rules and recognizing rights. To approach this question in this present context, we must first examine how considerations of equality or equity figure in the issue of hiring by competence, for this is somewhat less obvious than the relevance of social welfare or utility.

There is in fact another right involved in this issue which libertarians ignore—what is generally recognized as the right to equality of opportunity. To allow jobs to be awarded capriciously, especially given deep-seated prejudices known to exist in our society, is to deny equal opportunity for goods in a most blatant fashion. An equal opportunity for jobs is the necessary condition for an equal chance to all other basic goods. Thus the right of equal opportunity, if recognized at all, must also be acknowledged to figure more prominently in the issue of a social rule for hiring than the right to property or free association. The reason for this unequal weight is that the right to property as well as that of free association continue to exist although limited by exception clauses regarding corporations' doling out jobs, as they continue to exist with clauses involving limited redistributive taxation or open housing in the name of equality. But equal opportunity for social goods does not exist at all without equal opportunity for jobs. While redistributive taxation, open housing, and integrated schools are advocated in the name of this right, they amount to little when jobs can be denied to those who have managed to acquire superior qualifications with their help. The enforcement of some rule for hiring stipulating criteria not based purely upon inborn or initial chance factors is the first prerequisite for equality of opportunity, since decent jobs are not only of highest value in themselves, but means to most other valuable things.

This admittedly may not bother the thoroughgoing libertarian. For he will most likely recognize no such right as that to equal opportunity, nor give it any weight at all against the maximization of individual freedoms in regard to property and association. He holds that people have a right (short of harm) to what they have freely and legitimately acquired, and that no general right like that of equal opportunity should be recognized which involves repeated violations of individuals' rights to their acquired property. Have we then finally reached in regard to this issue an impasse in moral argument, uncovered an ultimate clash in moral attitude? Rather than admit this we can plausibly continue the argument by accusing the libertarian first of failing to assume a moral attitude on this issue at all, and second of inconsistency in his appeal to the absolute value of freedom over equality.

We can first point out then that part of what it means to assume a moral attitude is to recognize the moral equality of others (implied in a recognition of their subjectivity, i.e. feelings, points of view, etc.)—to accept rules which could be willed from their positions in the social context, or at least by neutral agents. If this recognition of moral equality or moral community within a system of social rules is to be given content as well as form, it means that the rules must not only apply to all, but as far as possible operate to the good of all. It also means that there is a presumption of equality not only in worth but in material conditions, which must be weighed against other values such as that of freedom in the formulation of more specific moral rules. A minimal moral outcome of this balancing (too minimal for egalitarians) is to formulate rules which result not in equality of goods, but in something approaching an equal chance to acquire goods through effort. Hence the recognition and protection of this right in social rules, such as a rule for hiring, seem a minimal condition for a moral social system. To bring this argument down to the specific issue at hand, its upshot is that rules protecting equality of opportunity, and specifically the recognition that society has the right to enforce some fair rule for hiring against private corporations, are necessary if distributions of property and other goods are to be just.

I have been speaking thus far as if freedom here is to be balanced against equality and welfare, but also indicated above that absolute liberty with respect to property and association may not result in the overall maximization of freedom desired by the libertarian. For poverty and the lack of satisfaction of basic needs which poverty entails constitute an impediment to freedom as well, to the basic freedom to formulate and pursue a meaningful life plan and control one's life as one desires. This is perhaps the most essential liberty of all, and if it is denied through the operation of a social or economic system which leaves some in need so that others may totally control their property, we can view this as an unwarranted conventional constraint upon liberty (property is only protected in the first place by the social system). It follows that any rule of hiring which results in more goods and services, as long as some of these trickle down to those whose freedom is compromised by want, can be adopted not only in the name of welfare or utility, but to increase freedom as well. This does not mean in general that every increase in welfare is to be counted as an increase in freedom as well, or that despotic states with higher GNP's are to be preferred, but only that no social system can be justified in the name of freedom which leaves those at the bottom constrained within the circle of dire poverty. A society with severe racial biases and no rule for hiring results in that situation. Thus we again arrive at the conclusion that society has the right to impose some rule for hiring against private corporations, this time in the name of freedom. Restrictions upon the freedom of corporations to choose capriciously or invidiously in hiring are necessary to protect or create freedom for those for whom equality of opportunity is its necessary condition.

If rules for hiring are then justified through considerations of utility or welfare and equality of opportunity, why not equal opportunity to marry Mary, or the adoption of mating rules which can be shown to maximize happiness or compatibility in the long run? Do the above arguments apply equally to this case, and if so mustn't they be dismissed in light of our intuitions against social rules for marriage choices? In answer to the first part of the first question, equal opportunity to marry Mary would amount only to an equal opportunity to win her favor, for that is the only relevant qualification we can presently think of for marrying her (we have no independent reliable criteria for what will make her happy in the long run). We might say that equality of opportunity for passing this purely subjective test exists already (Mary's favor might be won by one who could not have been predicted in terms of knowledge of her prior preferences), or given that Mary has certain relatively fixed prejudices, we might deny the possibility of enforcing any rule (except education against such biases) to create equal opportunity for passing this purely subjective test. In answer to the second part of the question, even if we had independent criteria for happiness in marriage as we do for successful job performance, since whom Mary marries affects herself far more than others, others having at most a peripheral interest, we can leave the choice and its consequences to her. Regarding the consideration of social welfare, the welfare of others is not involved in the average marriage cases as it is in who occupies various productive positions. Regarding the consideration of equal opportunity for those applying for jobs versus marriage consents, equality of opportunity in the latter case is not a necessary condition for equal chances at other goods, hence not a necessary condition for basic freedoms or a just social system overall, as it is in the case of jobs. For all these reasons none of my above arguments imply by analogy that society has the right to enforce a rule for mating against Mary.

These last points of difference apply as well to the more important and difficult cases of an individual hiring someone for temporary help, or the small businessman who gives a job to his son. Must we to be consistent apply our rule to all such cases and deny these freedoms as well? The first distinction between the case of the small business or private individual and the large corporation is the interest of the public in their products and services. If a small business is the only source of a vital service or product in a given area, it may be reasonable to demand competents in positions of responsibility. Otherwise it may be unreasonable to demand the proprietor to take the time and bear the cost to advertise the position, etc. (this is especially clear in the case of my hiring someone to unload my rented truck, or similar cases). The right of free association is also more central in the case of a small business, and this was part of the reasoning of Congress in applying nondiscriminatory regulations only to businesses with more than twenty-five employees. Since these differences are real, and since equality of opportunity and social welfare do not require that literally every position in society be open to all, but only a certain proportion of them, we may in applying these rationales establish a rule for hiring only for corporations over a certain size, recognizing that the drawing of a precise line will be somewhat arbitrary.

Thus my argument to the effect that certain individuals acquire rights to certain jobs and that corporations treat them unjustly if they are denied those positions involves two steps; first, society has the right in the name of social utility and equality of opportunity to establish a rule for hiring and enforce it against private as well as public corporations and organizations; second, by satisfying this social rule through effort an individual comes to deserve the position in question. The second step is dependent upon the first, which has been established in this section (the second step will be more prominent in the next). I have now provided criteria for the acceptability of a rule for hiring, i.e. social utility and protection of equal opportunity, without having completely shown how a single rule could meet both. In demonstrating that hiring by competence is the correct rule, we must consider the counterarguments of the egalitarian.

II. The Egalitarian Position

If the argument of the last section is correct, that is if a rule for hiring is to be justified in terms of social utility and equality of opportunity, it seems easy to show that hiring by competence qualifies as a just distributive principle. Many major theories of distributive justice, especially liberal theories, agree that practices are to be preferred which result in Pareto improvements, i.e. in benefits to some without loss to others. In regard to social utility, it can be argued that hiring by competence results not only in improvements over alternatives of this sort, but in the production of more goods for everyone in society (strong Pareto improvements). Hiring the most competent analytically entails increased goods and services, for competence is defined in terms of the ability to perform in a job by satisfying social demand. (I assume here the ability to judge competence according to qualifications, a difficulty which does not in any case affect the argument that we should *aim at* competence.)

The egalitarian attempts to refute the above justification by arguing that those abilities relevant to awarding jobs on the basis of efficiency, which is the basis for hiring in a pure market economy with only profit motives operating, are irrelevant from the point of view of justice; that in rewarding native talent, intelligence and social position (which even if acquired required an ability for acquisition for which the agent can claim no responsibility), the practice of hiring by competence involves rewards which are arbitrary from a moral point of view. Individuals deserve only those benefits which they have earned. They do not deserve their native advantages and so do not deserve those benefits, including good jobs, which flow from them throughout their lives. A child born rich and intelligent stands a far better chance than do other children of acquiring competence qualifications for desirable positions later in life, yet he cannot be said to deserve that better chance from the point of view of justice, nor thus the job which he eventually gets. Thus increments to social welfare from hiring by competence are a matter of social utility from which questions of justice must be separated. The egalitarian appears to have uncovered a conflict between the two criteria for a just rule advanced in the first section, i.e. maximization of utility through hiring by competence seems inconsistent with equality of opportunity in the present social context, and he claims the moral predominance of considerations of equality over those of social utility.

I do not think that any such radical separation of analyses of justice and efficiency could accord with our intuitions regarding the former, as these are aroused by specific examples. Although we may not all be Utilitarians, it seems we must grant that welfare does at least count as a positive consideration, and certainly at the extreme involved in this issue. Following Nicholas Rescher, I would argue that a practice or rule which generates a sum total of goods of 15 units to be distributed in a hypothetical society of 4 individuals in shares of 4, 4, 4, 3 is preferable from the point of view of justice to one which generates 8 units to be distributed in shares of 2, 2, 2, 2, despite its greater inequality. In other words, those who could have received 4 units under the first plan could legitimately claim injustice at being reduced so as to equal the lowest share under the second, other things being equal. If a claim of injustice or unfairness at being so reduced in moving from the first socio-economic plan to the second is justified, then aggregate utility in itself must be a consideration of distributive justice, and plans must be prima facie preferable which result in larger aggregates. To deny this is perhaps to grant too large a moral force to the feelings of envy and pride. For even the person with the lowest share in our hypothetical case is better off under the first plan than the second, except for the fact that he sees others around him with more. There may seem to be a complication here in that those with less relative income (even though more absolute) may be in a worse position to bid for scarce goods. But these alternatives in relation to choices between hiring by competence or other rules for hiring may be taken to refer to goods available, and not simply income. The argument is that more goods will be available to all if competents occupy productive positions, and this is what the egalitarian wrongly claims to be irrelevant to the choice of a just rule for hiring.

Even if we continue to insist upon a radical separation of justice (in a narrow sense) from efficiency, it seems we must admit that the latter can override the former from a moral point of view when it comes to hiring or filling positions of responsibility. It may be, for example, that those best qualified to be brain surgeons do not most deserve the benefits of those positions from a radically egalitarian view of justice, but surely egalitarians would want them to have the jobs anyway (even if they are not the ones on the operating tables). We pointed out in the last section other jobs as well in which incompetents represent not only losses in goods and services, but potential harm of a serious sort. When we think of all the cases of severe harm such as bodily injury or death which occur from defective products or incompetents conducting vital services, it is clear that lowering ranges of competence further would be something to avoid even if at the expense of equality or fairness in the narrowest of senses to job applicants. Since jobs carry responsibilities as well as benefits, society can legitimately complain if its welfare is sacrificed by a policy which leaves those responsibilities unfulfilled. And victims of avoidable irresponsibility (avoidable through a different system of distributive justice or alternative rule for hiring) can complain not only of incompetence or inconvenience, but of injustice. Another way of expressing this is to say, as we said in the last section, that the public has a right to be spared such avoidable harm. . . .

That the egalitarian argument fails becomes more clear if we seriously consider its alternative to hiring by competence, for the central question in this section is whether randomization is more just as claimed, given the present educational system and pay scales. Is a job lottery, which equalizes chances for desirable positions, the ideal of distributive justice in this area, given present inequalities as frozen into education and pay scales? The general principle, . . . which does seem sound in general, is that when shares are unalterably unequal, it is fair, other things being equal, to equalize chances for unequal shares; but of course the crucial issue here, which is generally the case in debates on equality, is whether other things are equal, here regarding job applicants. The central problem for establishing any rule of hiring is the stipulation of criteria regarding which characteristics of individuals are to be considered relevant in awarding the positions. Is winning a lottery to be the only relevant characteristic? It seems at first glance (but I believe at first glance only) the most truly egalitarian.

The central complaint against hiring by

competence without sufficient compensatory mechanisms in the educational system was that it tended to reward initial differences for which the agents could claim no responsibility. But certainly a process of random selection in the job market, aside from losses in efficiency, comes out worse on this score. It can be admitted that differences in competence for various positions constitute reasonable barometers of prior efforts to acquire competence only where the educational system has attempted to correct for initial inequalities. But even when such remedial efforts are lacking, the acquisition of competence still represents the expenditure of some effort in a socially desirable way, although the effort is not strictly proportional to the degree of competence acquired. The question is whether it is more just to ignore socially productive effort altogether and make all reward a matter of pure chance, which seems implausible or inconsistent if the only complaint against hiring by competence was that it rewarded chance factors to some degree. The effect of a lottery at any level is to negate differences in previous efforts, and if the cost of negating initial social differences (which can be equalized otherwise) is to render all effort meaningless as a measure of desert as well, it hardly seems worth it from the point of view of distributive justice.

The argument in favor of randomization now becomes that although it awards jobs on the basis of pure chance, at least it equalizes the chances—if benefits are to be doled out according to rolls of the dice, at least the dice should not be loaded. While the dice are loaded at present in favor of the rich, the talented and the intelligent, randomizing the process of hiring restores the balance which should have been restored by the neglectful educational and economic systems. In reply it could be argued first that in the original Book of Life all had equal chances at intelligence, etc., which is just a colourful way of saying that how intelligent you are or who your parents happen to be is a matter of chance from your point of view: it is simply a matter of chance

operating further in the past. It makes a difference whether the chance factor operated in the past or in the present in the form of a job lottery, however, since in the interim have occurred the efforts of those who have attained requisite skills. Second, there is an important difference ignored in the above argument between correcting for inequalities in the educational or tax systems and annihilating them at the final bell in the hiring process. For there is a limit to the justifiable neglect of those with superior talents, motivation and monetary assets, and their efforts should be ignored no more than those less fortunate once reasonable attempts have been made to motivate the latter and make their success possible.

The real contrast still reduces to that between rewarding chance versus rewarding effort and past and potential social contribution, and it still seems that a random lottery for hiring is the worst of all possible worlds by these criteria. Where there is no ulterior social purpose in the reward of some benefit than the distribution of some windfall good, and where furthermore no previous actions of the individuals in question can be seen to create differential rights or deserts to the goods, a random process of choosing is fairest. This follows from the presumption of equality of persons deduced in the first section. But when positions are assigned for socially productive purposes, and when individuals are therefore encouraged to direct their efforts towards fulfilling these purposes, past and potential productivity achieved through these efforts cannot be justly ignored. The same points apply to a lesser extent to randomization for those above a certain minimal level of competence, and in any case the egalitarian's reasoning must lead him to suggest this only for reasons of efficiency and not justice, which he takes to be distinct. Total randomization functions as the ideal of egalitarian justice in this area (given that jobs and their rewards must be unequal), and it is therefore relevant to argue as I have that it is a misconceived ideal. . . .

The Morality of Preferential Hiring

Bernard R. Boxill

Bernard R. Boxill seeks to rebut two objections to preferential hiring. The first is that preferential hiring benefits just those from among the groups that have suffered discrimination who do not deserve compensation. The second objection is that preferential hiring is unfair to young white men. Against the first objection, Boxill argues that even if those who benefit from preferential hiring are less deserving of compensation than others, they still do deserve to receive the compensation of preferential hiring. Against the second objection, Boxill argues that even if white males have not individually wronged blacks and women, they have unfairly benefited from such wrongs. Accordingly, it is not unfair to require white males to compensate blacks and women to the degree that they have unfairly benefited.

Many philosophers have held that preferential hiring is morally objectionable. They do not object to the compensation of those who have suffered from various forms of discrimination, but hold, rather, that preferential hiring is not, for a number of reasons, an appropriate method of compensation.[1] In this essay I rebut two of the principal arguments raised against preferential hiring, namely (1) that preferential hiring benefits just those from among the groups that have suffered discrimination who do not deserve compensation, and (2) that preferential hiring is unfair to young white men.

1

The most common version of the first argument, always dragged out with an air of having played a trump, is that since those of discriminated groups who benefit from preferential hiring must be minimally qualified, they are not those of the group who deserve compensation. Alan Goldman, for example,

From "The Morality of Preferential Hiring," *Philosophy and Public Affairs* vol. 7, no. 3 (Sporing 1978). Copyright © 1978 by Princeton University Press. Excerpts, pp. 246–257, 261–268, reprinted by permission of Princeton University Press.

argues this way: "Since hiring within the preferred group still depends upon relative qualifications and hence upon past opportunities for acquiring qualifications, there is in fact a reverse ratio established between past discriminations and present benefits, so that those who most benefit from the program, those who actually get jobs, are those who least deserve to." But surely to argue from the above to the conclusion that preferential hiring is unjustified is a non sequitur. Let us grant, that qualified blacks, for example, are less deserving of compensation than unqualified blacks, that those who most deserve compensation should be compensated first, and finally that preferential hiring is a form of compensation. How does it follow that preferential hiring of qualified blacks is unjustified? Surely, the assumption that unqualified blacks are more deserving of compensation than qualified blacks does not require us to conclude that qualified blacks deserve no compensation. Because I have lost only one leg, I may be less deserving of compensation than another who has lost two legs, but it does not follow that I deserve no compensation at all.

Much the same can be said of Simon's somewhat less contentious argument that "preferential hiring policies award compensation to . . . those who have the ability and qualifications to be seriously considered for the jobs available. Surely it is far more plausible to think that collective compensation ought to be equally available to all group members." But again, from the fact that preferential hiring does not award compensation to "all group members" how does it follow that preferential hiring is unjustified compensation to those of the group who "have the ability and qualifications"? It is easy to turn Simon's argument against him. If "all group members" should be compensated, then why insinuate that the qualified ones should be left out? And, if they should not be left out, why not compensate them in the manner best suited to their situation and aspirations—with good jobs—and compensate the unqualified in the manner best suited to their situation—cash settlements, remedial training, and so on.

The premise which would make the above argument less objectionable and which these critics of preferential hiring have not appeared to notice is that compensation can be made to only one section of the group—either the qualified or the unqualified, but not both. Given that the unqualified are most deserving of compensation, then a case should be mounted for claiming that, in the circumstances, preferential hiring should not be instituted because it takes from those who are most deserving of compensation (the unqualified) to give to those who are less deserving (the qualified). But it should be noted that even with the above premise, the argument does not quite yield what the critics want. For they want to show that preferential hiring of qualified minorities is unjustified *tout court*. And that is much more than showing that it is impracticable.

Now suppose the critics say that they meant that qualified blacks, for example, are not simply less deserving of compensation than unqualified blacks but that they deserve no compensation at all, just because they are qualified. The previous argument was that the ground for compensation is wrongful injury, so that if qualified blacks are generally less wronged they are therefore less deserving of compensation than unqualified blacks. The present argument is that the ground for compensation is not wrongful injury but, rather, lack of qualifications. In other words, though qualified blacks are discriminated against or suffer wrongful injury, their qualifications ex-

clude them from consideration for compensation. Thus, James W. Nickel, who is one of the very few to have noticed the complication that discriminated persons can overcome the handicap of discrimination, adopts this last view. Allowing that it is perhaps only the least "problematic approach," he determines that "the ones who have a right to compensation are those who have personally been injured by discrimination and who have not been able to overcome this injury."

But why should this be so? I am not questioning that on practical grounds we may be unable to compensate the qualified members of a generally discriminated group. I am questioning that just because a person has overcome his injury, he no longer has a right to compensation. Nickel himself gives no argument, but it may be that he mistakenly narrows the grounds for compensation.

Certainly the unqualified person is hurt and probably harmed. He is hurt in the sense that he will lose out to the qualified in the competition for jobs. And he is harmed too, if his lack of qualification involves a stunting of his intellectual and moral development. But though these are grounds for saying that he deserves compensation, they are not the only ones. For, as I have argued in an earlier essay, there are at least two very different grounds for compensation or reparation. One ground looks forward; it evaluates present harms and, disregarding whether or not they are due to wrong, seeks to remedy them to secure some future good. The other looks backward; it seeks to rectify past injustices and can ignore whether or not the victims are *now* in a sorry state. Thus, I do not dispute that the unqualified have a claim to compensation—whether or not they have been wronged. What I do dispute is that just because they have overcome their injuries the qualified have no claim to compensation. For if they have overcome their injuries, they have borne the costs of compensation that should be borne by those who inflicted the injuries. If I am swindled and by time and effort retrieve my money, shouldn't I be compensated for my time and effort? Or if I have plenty of money and hire a good lawyer, shouldn't I also claim from my swindlers the money I paid the lawyer?

The costs, in time and effort, of overcoming

an injury have results other than overcoming the injury. A person who has worked hard and long to overcome an injury is not what he would have been had he never been injured. He may be better, or he may be worse. Adversity can strengthen or it can merely harden. Thus middle-class blacks are alternately praised for their toughness and deprecated for their insensitivity. But these side-effects of the cost of overcoming wrongful injury are not the main issue. In particular, though I may be a better person for prevailing over unfair obstacles, this does not absolve my injurers from the obligation to compensate me.

Consequently, being harmed is not the only ground for deserving compensation. There is also the ground of simply having been wronged. Goldman, for example, has overlooked this. Repeatedly he stresses that qualified blacks are the least harmed of blacks, while ignoring that this does not entail they have not been wronged. "Do we want a policy which inverts the ratio of past harm to present benefit . . .?" he asks, pointing to the "inconsistency of compensating past harm with benefits to those harmed least . . ." and to the fact that "the beneficiaries of affirmative action, with the exception of certain blue collar workers, are generally not economically depressed." But this view overlooks that being unqualified and economically depressed are not the only grounds for compensation.

This does not affect the proposition that unqualified blacks are more deserving of compensation than qualified blacks. Irving Thalberg, for example, asks us to consider two groups of persons K' and K". K' consists of persons who, despite "dreadful persecution," now manage to hold their own in the larger society, and K" consists of persons who, though "never oppressed," now are at the "bottom of the socioeconomic-political pecking order." Which of these groups, he asks us, "most deserve special treatment?" It is clear that, though they are admittedly not at all the victims of injustice, he is himself inclined to choose K". But though Thalberg takes this position, he does not at all commit himself to the claim that K' deserves nothing. On the contrary, by stressing that "our resources are enough for one group only" he clearly implies that he would allow that K' has a claim too,

though K" has a stronger claim. Now as it happens, I agree with Thalberg, though the case I have in mind is easier than his. My case is that when we have one group, say K, whose members are equally oppressed because they are K's, those K's who nevertheless manage to qualify themselves are less deserving of compensation than those K's who fail to qualify themselves. This case is easier than Thalberg's because the people to whom he would give preference are not victims but only unqualified, while the people to whom I would give preference are both victims and unqualified.

So far I have agreed that qualified blacks are less deserving of compensation than unqualified blacks. And I have agreed that this is because they may be less harmed and perhaps less wronged than unqualified blacks. What I reject is the facile assumption that this in any way implies or suggests that preferential hiring is unjustified. My premise—which at first seemed to be allowed by critics of preferential hiring—is that qualified blacks, though perhaps less harmed or wronged than unqualified blacks, are still harmed and wronged or, at least, still wronged. But it is just this premise that now seems to be denied. Thus Goldman first makes the claim (which I can allow) that in the preferential hiring of qualified minority candidates, there is "an inverse ratio established between past discrimination and present benefits." But then, on the next page, he makes the very much stronger claim—which does not at all follow from the first—that preferential hiring "singles out for benefits within a generally unjustly treated minority just that minority that has not been unjustly treated."

This confusion between being the *least* wronged and harmed of a group and being only *slightly*, or not at all, harmed or wronged is essential to the present objection to preferential hiring. Thus, since preferential hiring has been proposed as giving the edge to persons characterized by some group quality—for example, being black—the question has been raised about how high the correlation is between being black and being harmed or wronged. We may agree, I trust, that it must be very high. Goldman, for example, does not deny this. It is only perfect correlation, that "every member of the group has suffered from unjust denial of a job or of a decent education" that he labels a "drastic claim." But if so, then the serious objection to preferential hiring as a practice cannot be that a tiny fraction of qualified blacks will get breaks they do not deserve. Surely, if this is the only practical way to help a group, the vast majority of which fully deserves compensation, that objection would be only grudging. But I contend that it is not the serious objection. The serious objection is that no qualified blacks deserve compensation. And that, I submit, can seem plausible only if we confuse being less harmed and wronged than others of their group with being only slightly, or not at all, harmed and wronged.

Suppose, however, that there is not a high correlation between being harmed or wronged and being black. This is an important possibility for, if true, it undoes the argument in the preceding paragraph. Blackstone, for example, after noting the unexceptional proposition that there is "no invariable connection between a person's being black or female and suffering from past invidious discrimination," leaps to the conclusion that there are lots of blacks who have suffered from no invidious discrimination. Thus, he writes, "there are many blacks . . . who are highly advantaged, who are the sons and daughters of well educated and affluent lawyers, doctors and industrialists. A policy of reverse discrimination would mean that such highly advantaged individuals would receive preferential treatment over the sons and daughters of disadvantaged whites . . . I submit that such a situation is not social justice." Now this may seem like a commendable effort to define the groups deserving compensation in socioeconomic, rather than racial, terms. But it raises troubling questions. Why does Blackstone assume so easily, for example, that "reverse discrimination" would mean that the "highly advantaged" blacks he speaks of would be getting preferred treatment over disadvantaged whites? I would have thought that being so advantaged they would likely be vying with their peers—the highly advantaged sons and daughters of white doctors, lawyers, and industrialists—leaving the sons and daughters of disadvantaged blacks to get preferential treatment

over the children of disadvantaged whites. If, with all their advantages, the black people Blackstone describes are still reduced to competing against disadvantaged whites then all the more would it seem that they have been harmed most deeply and grievously.

Taken at its best, Blackstone's objection may be that preferential hiring gives an unfair edge to advantaged blacks who have lost out in the competition for jobs and places. Unquestionably, preferential hiring gives such blacks an edge over disadvantaged blacks. Since, however, this is the edge the middle-class has over the lower class, to make his objection stick, Blackstone should recommend sweeping changes in the class structure. But Blackstone makes no such recommendation. Preferential hiring would give an unfair edge to advantaged blacks over disadvantaged whites, if the positions and places it serves them would otherwise go to disadvantaged whites. But this would be so only if the competition they have "lost out" in were fair. Since the small number of blacks gaining desirable positions and places shows the competition is not fair, the edge advantaged blacks gain is over advantaged whites.

In arriving at the above claim, I have left several assumptions unstated. The most obvious is that the black and white groups are roughly equal in native talent and intelligence. If they are not, then unless differences in native ability between the groups are remediable and justice requires that they be removed, it is not at all clear that the lower qualifications of blacks are any indication that they had been wronged. Fortunately, this difficulty can be avoided. The weight of informed opinion is against Jensen, but even if it is ultimately shown to have some merit, his theory that as a group blacks have less native intellectual talent than whites is, for now, extremely controversial. Jensen himself, though regrettably not chary enough in proposing policies based on this theory, is tentative enough in stating it. Consequently, given its present uncertainty and the great injustice that would be wreaked on a people if it proved false and educational policies were based on it, I submit that we are not warranted now in basing any policies on it.

A more serious attempt to explain the group differences in qualifications between blacks and whites is to attribute them to cultural differences. This is a complex issue. Though controversial, it cannot be swept aside in the manner of the last objection. For it has several different versions which must be considered separately. The first, with which we are all by now familiar, is that the tests administered for admission to colleges and professional schools are culturally biased, giving an unfair advantage to white applicants. This version is irrelevant. It explains, perhaps, why blacks are underrepresented in positions of responsibility and wealth, but it does not purport to show that underrepresentation is just. The second version, more to the point, is that blacks simply are not as interested as whites in society's positions of affluence and prestige. Barry Gross suggests this line in his argument that underrepresentation is no clear indication of discrimination: "The members of a group might simply lack interest in certain jobs (for example, Italians in the public school system are in short supply)." But this analogy fails, though Gross does not appear to notice it, when applied to the case of blacks. For it isn't as if blacks are underrepresented in the public school system or in law or in banking or in the professions. It is that they are underrepresented in all of these. Consequently, though Gross may be right that "sociologically, groups are simply not represented in various jobs and at various levels in percentages closely approximating their percentage of the population," he fails to see that the case of blacks presents a matter of an altogether different order. Lack of interest in this or in that area—presumably culturally determined—may explain away underrepresentation of a cultural group in this or in that area. Unless, however, we assume that some cultures have no interest in any of the traditional areas, we cannot explain a group's general underrepresentation in all desirable positions in society by citing cultural differences.

The more common version of the argument that cultural differences explain black underrepresentation in desirable positions is not that blacks lack an interest in these positions but that they lack the discipline for them. This argument is a non sequitur. Even if the traits which inhibit the success of blacks are

cultural traits—supposedly a lack of appropriate work habits and discipline—it does not follow that they are not wrongful injuries. In order to survive and retain their sanity and equilibrium in impossibly unjust situations, people may have to resort to patterns of behavior and consequently may develop habits or cultural traits which are debilitating and unproductive in a more humane environment. I see no reason why these cultural traits—which may be deeply ingrained and extremely difficult to eradicate—should not be classed as unjust injuries. It is admittedly unusual to think of cultural traits as injuries because we think of cultures as, in an important sense, self-imposed. This is true of most cultures in the traditional sense of national and ethnic cultures. Such cultures come with built-in philosophical self-justifications. In the sense that participants in them necessarily have elaborate resources with which to justify themselves, they may be viewed as self-imposed. Consequently, though such cultures may encourage development of traits which inhibit advancement in modern society, it would be hazardous to call the traits injuries. At most, they would be self-imposed injuries. But not all cultures are, in that important sense, self-imposed. Certain cultures contain none of the elaborate philosophical self-justification of ordinary cultures. Thus, in describing what he called the "culture of poverty" for example, Oscar Lewis notes that though it is a genuine culture in the traditional anthropological sense, in that it provides human beings with a "design for living" it "does not provide much support . . . poverty of culture is one of the crucial traits of the culture of poverty."

But the idea that blacks form a cultural group is not notably advantageous for the critics of preferential hiring. For it can be argued that since blacks have been discriminated against as a group, they deserve compensation as a group. Further, individual blacks—in particular qualified ones—should not have to prove specific cases of discrimination against them in order to qualify for preferential treatment. But the critics claim that blacks do not comprise a group in the sense required by the argument. Goldman, for example, objects to treating blacks as a legitimate group eligible for compensatory treatment because they "do not qualify as genuine groups or social organizations in the sense in which sociologists generally use these terms." He goes on to point out that in genuine groups there is "actual interaction among members, each of whom occupies a certain position or plays a certain role in the group reciprocal to other roles, roles being reciprocal when their performances are mutually dependent." But I submit, on that very account, that cultural groups do qualify as genuine groups. There is, for example, "actual interaction" among the members of a cultural group. That interaction is, of course, not specifically economic or political. Members of a cultural group do not, for example, necessarily buy from each other or employ each other or rule each other. Still they *do* interact and that interaction is just as important as the activities already mentioned.

Members of a cultural group share basic values and ideals—that is what we mean by calling them members of the same cultural group—and they interact intellectually by exchanging ideas about these values and ideals, by clarifying, criticizing, and extending them and by severing and drawing connections between them. In this way they come better to understand themselves. All prosperous and progressive peoples engage in this bustling process of self-clarification. Some call it the cause of all progress, others the reward of progress. In either case, it is a great good. If then it is objected that blacks are underrepresented in positions of wealth and prestige because of cultural differences, then if they have been wronged as a group, preferential hiring of qualified blacks is justified as a way of compensating the group. For it needs no argument to show that the intellectually most active and advanced of a cultural group play a crucial role in the above-mentioned process of self-clarification. If then, as seems likely, they will be among those qualified, and preferential hiring will give them the opportunity to play their crucial role in the group, then it is a way of compensating the group. And it will not do to object that if blacks form a cultural group, then the qualified among them should seek employment within that group. Though cultural groups may have originally been economic

units, this is no longer the case in today's world of mass migrations. There is no reason why distinct cultural groups cannot be economically integrated.

But even if blacks do not form a cultural group, then preferential hiring is still justified. For if blacks have the same basic goals, aspirations, dreams, and hopes as whites and would, if given real opportunities, work assiduously to realize them, then—given the unjustness of assuming at this stage that blacks as a group have less native intelligence than whites and given the existence of independent evidence of widespread and pervasive discrimination against blacks—it is a reasonable assumption that the lesser merit of qualified blacks relative to qualified whites is due to injustice. . . .

II

Even if the force of all the preceding arguments is acknowledged, however, the case for preferential hiring is still not established at this point. For, while I have shown that the qualified members of groups which have been generally discriminated against deserve some compensation, I have not shown that the compensation they deserve is preferential hiring.

This issue raises two different questions. First, given that qualified minorities do deserve some compensation, why is preferential hiring the best form of compensation for them? Second, even if preferential hiring of qualified minorities is best for them, is it best or even justifiable overall? What, for example, about the costs to general productivity? Or to excellence? Most of all, perhaps, what about the costs to the young white males who will be displaced in favor of minorities? Why should the burden of compensation be placed on their shoulders alone?

Professor Thomson has already given, I think, the main answer to the first difficulty. She argues persuasively that "what blacks and women were denied was full membership in the community; and nothing can more appropriately make amends for that wrong than precisely what will make them feel they now finally have it. And that means jobs. Financial compensation . . . slips through the fingers having a job, and discovering you do it well, yield—perhaps better than anything else— that very self-respect which blacks and women have had to do without." It is only necessary to add perhaps that particularly in the case of the qualified is it appropriate that their compensation be jobs. For by the very fact that they have taken the trouble to become qualified they show that what they want is jobs, or at least, that they are fully prepared and anxious to get jobs. Though it may be generally true that jobs will make those previously excluded finally feel that they are "part of it," it need not be generally true, that all those previously excluded will want jobs. Some may prefer "financial compensation."

But, even though it may be admitted that getting and keeping a job is an excellent thing for the self-respect and self-esteem of qualified members of minority groups—for having a job helps a person to feel he is contributing his "fair share" and, if he discovers that he does it well, also helps him to recognize and appreciate his powers—the question has been raised whether getting and keeping a job *because of preferential hiring* may not undermine self-respect. Thus Barry Gross writes that the beneficiary of preferential hiring "may come to feel himself inferior." Thomas Nagel warns that preferential hiring "cannot do much for the self-esteem of those who know they have benefited from it, and it may threaten the self-esteem of those in the favored group who would in fact have gained their positions even in the absence of the discriminatory policy, but who cannot be sure that they are not among its beneficiaries." Thomas Sowell cautions that though "here and there, this program has undoubtedly caused some individuals to be hired who would otherwise not have been hired . . . even that is a doubtful gain in the larger context of attaining self-respect and the respect of others."

Though evidently closely related, these objections are not all quite the same. Gross' objection, for example, seems to be that a person preferentially hired for a job for which he is incompetent or who is out-classed by his colleagues will come to feel inferior. This is true but irrelevant, for preferential hiring

does not require that incompetents be hired or that a candidate be hired who will be outclassed by his colleagues. The points made by Nagel and Sowell overlap but raise two distinct difficulties. On the one hand, the difficulty may be that the beneficiary of preferential hiring may lose self-respect because he may fear that he is getting what he does not deserve. I admit that a person who accepts what he knows he does not deserve (or have a right to) and knows he is taking away from someone more deserving acts in opposition to his self-respect and in trying to rationalize his act, may come to compromise and lose his self-respect. But I deny that this is relevant here. For the major conclusion of all the preceding arguments is that though the preferred candidate may be less excellently qualified than another candidate, he must still overall be the most deserving. Given this, the present difficulty does not arise. On the other hand, the difficulty may be that though the preferred candidate knows that he is overall the most deserving, he may still feel uneasy and compromised because he knows he is not the most qualified or, at least, he does not know that he is the most qualified. This difficulty is quite different from the previous one. Here, the preferred candidate knows his deserts and that he is the most deserving. What he would like to be reassured about are his qualifications. This does not, however, argue against preferential hiring. For suppose preferential hiring is not instituted and that as a result more qualified but perhaps less deserving candidates are routinely hired. What about their self-respect and self-esteem? Shouldn't *they* feel their self-respect jeopardized for filling jobs others deserve more? Since this is evidently a more serious worry than the more deserving person's worry, on this point too, preferential hiring is not unjustified.

Having shown that there is every reason to believe that preferential hiring is the best form of compensatory treatment for qualified minorities and that they would suffer no severe penalties to self-respect and self-esteem from it, I turn to the question whether it is best or justifiable overall. But I shall not spend much time on the question of its costs to efficiency or excellence. I shall concentrate instead on the objection that preferential hiring is unjustified because it puts all the burden of compensation on the white male applicant.

Here again I think that Professor Thomson has proceeded in the right way. She admits first that there is no reason why the young white male applicants should bear the major costs of compensating, but then argues that though few of these have "themselves individually, done any wrongs to blacks and women . . .," because "they have profited from the wrongs the community did" there is reason why they should bear some of the costs of compensation. In opposing the second part of her argument, Simon objects to her "assumption that if someone gains from an unjust practice for which he is not responsible and even opposes, the gain is not his and can be taken from him without injustice." What he fails to notice, however, is that if his objection stands, it just may turn out that no one should have to bear the costs of compensation and thus no compensation should be given. For though it is probably not true of actual societies, it is quite possible to conceive of a society some of whose members have gained at the expense of others because of earlier unjust practices, but none of whose members now have any responsibility for these practices. In such a society all of the beneficiaries of injustice would be analogous to the young white male applicants, and if Simon is right, those who have suffered losses because of the earlier injustice have no claim to compensation. It is important therefore to consider carefully the claim that the innocent beneficiaries of injustice owe no obligation of compensation to those from whose unfair losses they have profited.

Few of its proponents, however, have offered a sustained argument for it. Blackstone, for example, says simply that the fact that the white male applicant has profited from past injustice is "inadequate" ground to exact compensation from him, and Simon seems to argue mainly for the minor point that if the white male applicant has himself suffered from some unjust social practice then it is "questionable" whether he owes anyone compensation. Fullinwider, however, has attempted a more thorough treatment. Conceding first what he calls the compensation principle—"he who wrongs another shall pay for the wrong"—he accuses Professor Thomson of confusing it with the "suspect" principle—"he who benefits from a wrong shall pay for the wrong." To clinch the point, Fullinwider asks us to consider the following ingenious example. A neighbor pays a construction company to pave his driveway, but someone maliciously directs the workmen to pave Fullinwider's driveway instead. Fullinwider admits that his neighbor has been "wronged and damaged" and that he himself has "benefited from the wrong." However, since he is not responsible for the wrong, he denies that he is "morally required to compensate" his neighbor by "paying" him for it.

This example makes us see that not all cases where compensation may be due are straightforward, though one kind of case clearly is. If John steals Jeff's bicycle and "gives" it to me, however innocent I may be, I have no right to it and must return it to Jeff as soon as I discover the theft. Given that this kind of example is unproblematic, in what way does it differ from Fullinwider's, which is problematic?

One difference is that whereas I can simply hand over Jeff's bicycle to him, Fullinwider cannot simply hand over the pavement in his driveway. It will be objected that the proposal was not that Fullinwider should hand over the pavement, but that he should pay his neighbor for it. But now the case has been changed. I did not say that I had a duty to pay Jeff the cost of his bicycle. I said that I had a duty to return the bicycle to Jeff. If Jeff told me to keep the bicycle but pay him for it, I do not admit that I would have a duty to do so. I could fairly object that when I accepted the bicycle I did not believe that I would have to pay for it, and if I had thought that I would have to, I might not have accepted it. Paying for the bicycle now would impose a cost on me because I might have preferred to spend my money in a different way and, being innocent of any wrongdoing, I see no reason why I should be penalized. The point is that though the beneficiary of an injustice has no right to his advantage, if he is innocent of the injustice, he does not deserve to be penalized. Thus, where compensation is concerned, the obligations of the innocent beneficiary of injustice and of the person responsible for the injustice are quite different. Though the former has no right to his benefits, the obligation of compensation cannot impose any losses on him over and above the loss of his unfair benefits. If compensation is impossible without such loss, it is unjustified. On the other hand, in the case of the person responsible for injustice, even if compensation requires him to give up more than he has unfairly gained, it is still justified.

But though Fullinwider's example is cogent as far as it goes, it is irrelevant as an argument against preferential hiring. It is cogent as far as it goes because, as the above analysis shows, requiring young white males to pay women and minorities all the unfair advantages they enjoyed would indeed be unfair. The advantages cannot simply be transferred from their hands into those of the preferred group as in my example of the bicycle. Compensation of this form would impose on young white males costs in time and effort over and above the costs of the unfair advantages they are required to return. They could with justice protest that they are being penalized because they might not have accepted the advantages had they known what it would cost them—now they are "out" both the advantages plus their time and effort. But though cogent, this argument is irrelevant to preferential hiring. Preferential hiring does not require young white males to pay over, at additional costs to themselves, the price of their advantages. It proposes instead to compensate the injured with goods no one yet has established a right to and in a way, therefore, which imposes no unfair losses on anyone. And these goods are, of course, jobs.

To that it may be objected that although a white male applicant may not have established a right to this or that job, he has a right to a fair competition for it, and preferential hiring violates that right. But on the contrary, by refusing to allow him to get the job because of an unfair advantage, preferential hiring makes the competition fairer. The white male applicant can still complain, of course, that had he known that preferential hiring would be instituted, he would not have accepted his advantages in the first place. Since, if he knew that preferential hiring would be instituted,

he would necessarily also have known that his advantages were unfair, his complaint amounts to his saying that had he known his advantages were unfair, he would not have accepted them. But then, if he is so concerned with fairness, and if preferential hiring makes the competition fairer, he should have no objections to it. Or somewhat less contentiously, preferential hiring imposes no unfair losses on him.

Thus, a fairer application of Fullinwider's example of the driveway to preferential hiring would go as follows: Suppose an "improve your neighborhood group" offered a valuable prize for the best driveway on the block. Would Fullinwider, though he is totally innocent of his unfair advantage, be justified in insisting that he deserves to get the prize over his neighbor who has, at further cost to himself, built another somewhat inferior driveway? If someone objects that jobs are not analogous to prizes, suppose a visitor wants to rent a driveway on the block to park his car, would Fullinwider be justified in insisting that he most *deserves* to have his driveway chosen? Of course, Fullinwider can still truly point out that his driveway is the best, and perhaps if efficiency alone were the consideration, it ought to be chosen. But laying aside efficiency as I have, it is clear that it is the neighbor who most deserves that his driveway be chosen.

III

In Part I, I considered one set of objections to preferential hiring: that it compensates those who do not deserve it. At bottom these objections failed, because those who proposed them focused their attentions too exclusively on how much more fortunately placed the black middle class is than the black lower class. This made it seem as if members of the black middle class were absolutely advantaged. From being least harmed of blacks, it came to seem as if they were not appreciably harmed or not harmed at all. For balance, why not compare the black middle class with the white middle class?

Why shouldn't the black community have a

vigorous and prosperous middle class as does the white community? Certainly it is a great tradition in western political philosophy that the stability and progress of a community depends on its having such a class. On the other hand, it may be, of course, as another tradition in western political philosophy has it, that there should be no classes at all. But that is another debate.

In Part II, I took up the objections against preferential hiring as a form of compensation, the most troubling of which was that young white men are compelled to bear the major costs of compensation. I admitted this point but argued that preferential hiring does not require it. What preferential hiring requires is that young white males bear some of the costs of compensation. Here I showed that though they may be innocent of wrongdoing against women and blacks, because they have had the advantage of such wrongdoing, it is not unjustified that they bear some of the costs. I conclude that no telling argument has been raised against preferential hiring.

Affirmative Racism

Charles Murray

Charles Murray argues that preferential treatment for blacks has actually worked against their interest by encouraging a new form of racism that tacitly accepts the view that blacks are temporarily less competent than whites. The problem with this new form of racism, Murray claims, is that it perpetuates the race-based inequality it seeks to eliminate.

A few years ago, I got into an argument with a lawyer friend who is a partner in a New York firm. I was being the conservative, arguing that preferential treatment of blacks was immoral; he was being the liberal, urging that it was the only way to bring blacks to full equality. In the middle of all this he abruptly said, "But you know, let's face it. We must have hired at least ten blacks in the last few years, and none of them has really worked out." He then returned to his case for still stronger affirmative action, while I wondered what it had been like for those ten blacks. And if he could make a remark like that so casually, what remarks would he be able to make some years down the road, if by that time it had been fifty blacks who hadn't "really worked out"?

My friend's comment was an outcropping of a new racism that is emerging to take its place alongside the old. It grows out of preferential treatment for blacks, and it is not just the much-publicized reactions, for example, of the white policemen or firemen who are passed over for promotion because of an affirmative action court order. The new racism that is potentially most damaging is located among the white elites—educated, affluent, and occupying the positions in education, business, and government from which this country is run. It currently focuses on blacks; whether it will eventually extend to include Hispanics and other minorities remains to be seen.

The new racists do not think blacks are inferior. They are typically longtime supporters of civil rights. But they exhibit the classic behavioral symptom of racism: they treat blacks differently from whites, because of their race. The results can be as concretely bad and unjust as any that the old racism produces. Sometimes the effect is that blacks are refused an education they otherwise could have gotten. Sometimes blacks are shunted into dead-end jobs. Always, blacks are denied the right to compete as equals.

The new racists also exhibit another char-

From *The New Republic* (December 31, 1984). Reprinted by permission of *The New Republic* © 1984, The New Republic, Inc.

acteristic of racism: they *think* about blacks differently from the way they think about whites. Their global view of blacks and civil rights is impeccable. Blacks must be enabled to achieve full equality. They are still unequal, through no fault of their own (it is the fault of racism, it is the fault of inadequate opportunity, it is the legacy of history). But the new racists' local view is that the blacks they run across professionally are not, on the average, up to the white standard. Among the new racists, lawyers have gotten used to the idea that the brief a black colleague turns in will be a little less well-rehearsed and argued than the one they would have done. Businessmen expect that a black colleague will not read a balance sheet as subtly as they do. Teachers expect black students to wind up toward the bottom of the class.

The new racists also tend to think of blacks as a commodity. The office must have a sufficient supply of blacks, who must be treated with special delicacy. The personnel problems this creates are more difficult than most because whites barely admit to themselves what's going on.

What follows is a foray into very poorly mapped territory. I will present a few numbers that explain much about how the process gets started. But the ways that the numbers get translated into behavior are even more important. The cases I present are composites constructed from my own observations and taken from firsthand accounts. All are based on real events and real people, stripped of their particularities. But the individual cases are not intended as evidence, because I cannot tell you how often they happen. They have not been the kind of thing that social scientists or journalists have wanted to count. I am writing this because so many people, both white and black, to whom I tell such stories know immediately what I am talking about. It is apparent that a problem exists. How significant is it? What follows is as much an attempt to elicit evidence as to present it.

As in so many of the crusades of the 1960s, the nation began with a good idea. It was called "affirmative action," initiated by Lyndon Johnson through Executive Order 11246 in September 1965. It was an attractive label and a natural corrective to past racism: actively seek out black candidates for jobs, college, or promotions, without treating them differently in the actual decision to hire, admit, or promote. The term originally evoked both the letter and the spirit of the order.

Then, gradually, affirmative action came to mean something quite different. In 1970 a federal court established the legitimacy of quotas as a means of implementing Johnson's executive order. In 1971 the Supreme Court ruled that an employer could not use minimum credentials as a prerequisite for hiring if the credentials acted as a "built-in headwind" for minority groups—even when there was no discriminatory intent and even when the hiring procedures were "fair in form." In 1972 the Equal Employment Opportunity Commission acquired broad, independent enforcement powers.

Thus by the early 1970s it had become generally recognized that a good-faith effort to recruit qualified blacks was not enough—especially if one's school depended on federal grants or one's business depended on federal contracts. Even for businesses and schools not directly dependent on the government, the simplest way to withstand an accusation of violating Title VII of the Civil Rights Act of 1964 was to make sure not that they had not just interviewed enough minority candidates, but that they had actually hired or admitted enough of them. Employers and admissions committees arrived at a rule of thumb: if the blacks who are available happen to be the best candidates, fine; if not, the best available black candidates will be given some sort of edge in the selection process. Sometimes the edge will be small; sometimes it will be predetermined that a black candidate is essential, and the edge will be very large.

Perhaps the first crucial place where the edge applies is in admission to college. Consider the cases of the following three students: John, William, and Carol, 17 years old and applying to college, are all equal on paper. Each has a score of 520 in the mathematics section of the Scholastic Aptitude Test, which puts them in the top third—at the 67th percentile—of all students who took the test. (Figures are based on 1983 data.)

John is white. A score of 520 gets him into the state university. Against the advice of his high school counselor, he applies to a prestigious school, Ivy U. where his application is rejected in the first cut—its average white applicant has math scores in the high 600s.

William is black, from a middle-class family who sent him to good schools. His score of 520 puts him at the 95th percentile of all blacks who took the test. William's high school counselor points out that he could probably get into Ivy U. William applies and is admitted—Ivy U. uses separate standards for admission of whites and blacks, and William is among the top blacks who applied.

Carol is black, educated at an inner-city school, and her score of 520 represents an extraordinary achievement in the face of terrible schooling. An alumnus of Ivy U. who regularly looks for promising inner-city candidates finds her, recruits her, and sends her off with a full scholarship to Ivy U.

When American universities embarked on policies of preferential admissions by race, they had the Carols in mind. They had good reason to be optimistic that preferential treatment would work—for many years, the best universities had been weighting the test scores of applicants from small-town public schools when they were compared against those of applicants from the top private schools, and had been giving special breaks to students from distant states to ensure geographic distribution. The differences in preparation tended to even out after the first year or so. Blacks were being brought into a longstanding and successful tradition of preferential treatment.

In the case of blacks, however, preferential treatment ran up against a large black-white gap in academic performance combined with ambitious goals for proportional representation. This gap has been the hardest for whites to confront. But though it is not necessary or even plausible to believe that such differences are innate, it is necessary to recognize openly that the differences exist. By pretending they don't, we begin the process whereby both the real differences and the racial factor are exaggerated.

The black-white gap that applies most directly to this discussion is the one that separates blacks and whites who go to college. In 1983, for example, the mean Scholastic Aptitude Test score for all blacks who took the examination was more than 100 points below the white score on both the verbal and the math sections. Statistically, it is an extremely wide gap. To convert the gap into more concrete terms, think of it this way: in 1983, the same Scholastic Aptitude Test math score that put a black at the 50th percentile of all blacks who took the test put him at the 16th percentile of all whites who took the test.

These results clearly mean we ought to be making an all-out effort to improve elementary and secondary education for blacks. But that doesn't help much now, when an academic discrepancy of this magnitude is fed into a preferential admissions process. As universities scramble to make sure they are admitting enough blacks, the results feed the new racism. Here's how it works:

In 1983, only 66 black students nationwide scored above 700 in the verbal section of the Scholastic Aptitude Test, and only 205 scored above 700 in the mathematics section. This handful of students cannot begin to meet the demand for blacks with such scores. For example, Harvard, Yale, and Princeton have in recent years been bringing an aggregate of about 270 blacks into each entering class. If the black students entering these schools had the same distribution of scores as that of the freshman class as a whole, then every black student in the nation with a verbal score in the 700s, and roughly 70 percent of the ones with a math score in the 700s, would be in their freshman classes.

The main problem is not that a few schools monopolize the very top black applicants, but that these same schools have much larger implicit quotas than they can fill with those applicants. They fill out the rest with the next students in line—students who would not have gotten into these schools if they were not black, who otherwise would have been showing up in the classrooms of the nation's less glamorous colleges and universities. But the size of the black pool does not expand appreciably at the next levels. The number of blacks scoring in the 600s on the math section in 1983, for example, was 1,531. Meanwhile, 31,704 nonblack students in 1983 scored in the 700s on the math section and 121,640 scored in the 600s. The prestige schools cannot begin to absorb these numbers of other highly qualified freshmen, and they are perforce spread widely throughout the system.

At schools that draw most broadly from the student population, such as the large state universities, the effects of this skimming produce a situation that confirms the old racists in everything they want most to believe. There are plenty of outstanding students in such student bodies (at the University of Colorado, for example, 6 percent of the freshmen in 1981 had math scores in the 700s and 28 percent had scores in the 600s), but the skimming process combined with the very small raw numbers means that almost none of them are black. What students and instructors see in their day-to-day experience in the classroom is a disproportionate number of blacks who are below the white average, relatively few blacks who are at the first rank. The image that the white student carries away is that blacks are less able than whites.

I am not exalting the SAT as an infallible measure of academic ability, or pointing to test scores to try to convince anyone that blacks are performing below the level of whites. I am simply using them to explain what instructors and students already notice, and talk about, among themselves.

They do not talk openly about such matters. One characteristic of the new racism is that whites deny in public but acknowledge in private that there are significant differences in black and white academic performance. Another is that they dismiss the importance of tests when black scores are at issue, blaming cultural bias and saying that test scores are not good predictors of college performance. At the same time, they watch anxiously over their own children's test scores.

The differences in academic performance do not disappear by the end of college. Far from narrowing, the gap separating black and white academic achievement appears to get larger. Various studies, most recently at Harvard, have found that during the 1970s blacks did worse in college (as measured by grade point average) than their test scores would have predicted. Moreover, the black-white gap in the Graduate Record Examination is larger than the gap in the Scholastic Aptitude Test. The gap between black and white freshmen is a bit less than one standard deviation (the technical measure for comparing scores). Black and white seniors who take the Graduate Record Examination reveal a gap of about one and a quarter standard deviations.

Why should the gap grow wider? Perhaps it is an illusion—for example, perhaps a disproportionate number of the best black students never take the examination. But there are also reasons for suspecting that in fact blacks get a worse education in college than whites do. Here are a few of the hypotheses that deserve full exploration.

Take the situation of William—a slightly above-average student who, because he is black, gets into a highly competitive school. William studies very hard during the first year. He nonetheless gets mediocre grades. He has a choice. He can continue to study hard and continue to get mediocre grades, and be seen by his classmates as a black who cannot do very well. Or he can explicitly refuse to engage in the academic game. He decides to opt out, and his performance gets worse as time goes on. He emerges from college with a poor education and is further behind the whites than he was as a freshman.

If large numbers of other black students at the institution are in the same situation as William, the result can be group pressure not to compete academically. (At Harvard, it is said, the current term among black students for a black who studies like a white is "incognegro.") The response is not hard to understand. If one subpopulation of students is conspicuously behind another population and is visibly identifiable, then the population that is behind must come up with a good excuse for doing poorly. "Not wanting to do better" is as good as any.

But there is another crucial reason why blacks might not close the gap with whites during college: they are not taught as well as whites are. Racist teachers impeding the progress of students? Perhaps, but most college faculty members I know tend to bend over backward to be "fair" to black students—and that may be the problem. I suggest that inferior instruction is more likely to be a manifestation of the new racism than the old.

Consider the case of Carol, with outstanding abilities but deprived of decent prior schooling: she struggles the first year, but she gets by. Her academic skills still show the aftereffects of her inferior preparation. Her instructors diplomatically point out the more flagrant mistakes, but they ignore minor lapses, and never push her in the aggressive way they push white students who have her intellectual capacity. Some of them are being patronizing (she is doing quite well, considering). Others are being prudent: teachers who criticize black students can find themselves being called racists in the classroom, in the campus newspaper, or in complaints to the administration.

The same process continues in graduate school. Indeed, because there are even fewer blacks in graduate schools than in undergraduate schools, the pressure to get black students through to the degree, no matter what, can be still greater. But apart from differences in preparation and ability that have accumulated by the end of schooling, the process whereby we foster the appearance of black inferiority continues. Let's assume that William did not give up during college. He goes to business school, where he gets his Masters degree. He signs up for interviews with the corporate recruiters. There are 100 persons in his class, and William is ranked near the middle. But of the 5 blacks in his class, he ranks first (remember that he was at the 95th percentile of blacks taking the Scholastic Aptitude Test). He is hired on his first interview by his first-choice company, which also attracted the very best of the white students. He is hired alongside 5 of the top-ranking white members of the class.

William's situation as one of 5 blacks in a class of 100 illustrates the proportions that prevail in business schools, and business schools are by no means one of the more extreme examples. The pool of black candidates for any given profession is a small fraction of the white pool. This works out to a 20-to-1 edge in business; it is even greater in most of the other professions. The result, when many hiring institutions are competing, is that a major gap between the abilities of new black and white employees in any given workplace is highly likely. Everyone needs to hire a few blacks, and the edge that "being black" confers in the hiring decision warps the sequence of

hiring in such a way that a scarce resource (the blacks with a given set of qualifications) is exhausted at an artificially high rate, producing a widening gap in comparison with the remaining whites from which an employer can choose.

The more aggressively affirmative action is enforced, the greater the imbalance. In general, the first companies to hire can pursue strategies that minimize or even eliminate the difference in ability between the new black and white employees. IBM and Park Avenue law firms can do very well, just as Harvard does quite well in attracting the top black students. But the more effectively they pursue these strategies, the more quickly they strip the population of the best black candidates.

To this point I have been discussing problems that are more or less driven by realities we have very little hope of manipulating in the short term except by discarding the laws regarding preferential treatment. People do differ in acquiring abilities. Currently, acquired abilities in the white and black populations are distributed differently. Schools and firms do form a rough hierarchy when they draw from these distributions. The results follow ineluctably. The dangers they represent are not a matter of statistical probabilities, but of day-to-day human reactions we see around us.

The damage caused by these mechanistic forces should be much less in the world of work than in the schools, however. Schools deal in a relatively narrow domain of skills, and "talent" tends to be assigned specific meanings and specific measures. Workplaces deal in highly complex sets of skills, and "talent" consists of all sorts of combinations of qualities. A successful career depends in large part upon finding jobs that elicit and develop one's strengths.

At this point the young black professional must sidestep a new series of traps laid by whites who need to be ostentatiously nonracist. Let's say that William goes to work for the XYZ Corporation, where he is assigned with another management trainee (white) to a department where much of the time is spent preparing proposals for government contracts. The white trainee is assigned a variety of scut work—proofreading drafts, calculating the costs of minor items in the bid, making photocopies, taking notes at conferences. William gets more dignified work. He is assigned portions of the draft to write (which are later rewritten by more experienced staff), sits in on planning sessions, and even goes to Washington as a highly visible part of the team to present the bid. As time goes on, the white trainee learns a great deal about how the company operates, and is seen as a go-getting young member of the team. William is perceived to be a bright enough fellow, but not much of a detail man and not really much of a self-starter.

Even if a black is hired under terms that put him on a par with his white peers, the subtler forms of differential treatment work against him. Particularly for any corporation that does business with the government, the new employee has a specific, immediate value purely because he is black. There are a variety of requirements to be met and rituals to be observed for which a black face is helpful. These have very little to do with the long-term career interests of the new employee; on the contrary, they often lead to a dead end as head of the minority-relations section of the personnel department.

Added to this is another problem that has nothing to do with the government. When the old racism was at fault (as it often still is), the newly hired black employee was excluded from the socialization process because the whites did not want him to become part of the group. When the new racism is at fault, it is because many whites are embarrassed to treat black employees as badly as they are willing to treat whites. Hence another reason that whites get on-the-job training that blacks do not: much of the early training of an employee is intertwined with menial assignments and mild hazing. Blacks who are put through these routines often see themselves as racially abused (and when a black is involved, old-racist responses may well have crept in). But even if the black is not unhappy about the process, the whites are afraid that he is, and so protect him from it. There are many variations, all having the same effect: the black is denied an apprenticeship that the white has no way of escaping. Without serving the ap-

prenticeship, there is no way of becoming part of the team.

Carol suffers a slightly different fate. She and a white woman are hired as reporters by a major newspaper. They both work hard, but after a few months there is no denying it: neither one of them can write. The white woman is let go. Carol is kept on, because the paper cannot afford to have any fewer blacks than it already has. She is kept busy with reportorial work, even though they have to work around the writing problem. She is told not to worry—there's lots more to being a journalist than writing.

It is the mascot syndrome. A white performing at a comparable level would be fired. The black is kept on, perhaps to avoid complications with the Equal Employment Opportunity Commission (it can be very expensive to fire a black), perhaps out of a more diffuse wish not to appear discriminatory. Everybody pretends that nothing is wrong—but the black's career is at a dead end. The irony, of course, is that the white who gets fired and has to try something else has been forced into accepting a chance of making a success in some other line of work whereas the black is seduced into *not* taking the same chance.

Sometimes differential treatment takes an even more pernicious form: the conspiracy to promote a problem out of existence. As part of keeping Carol busy, the newspaper gives her some administrative responsibilities. They do not amount to much. But she has an impressive title on a prominent newspaper and she is black—a potent combination. She gets an offer from a lesser paper in another part of the country to take a senior editorial post. Her current employer is happy to be rid of an awkward situation and sends along glowing references. She gets a job that she is unequipped to handle—only this time, she is in a highly visible position, and within a few weeks the deficiencies that were covered up at the old job have become the subject of jokes all over the office. Most of the jokes are openly racist.

It is important to pause and remember who Carol is: an extremely bright young woman, not (in other circumstances) a likely object of condescension. But being bright is no protection. Whites can usually count on the market to help us recognize egregious career mistakes and to prevent us from being promoted too far from a career line that fits our strengths, and too far above our level of readiness. One of the most prevalent characteristics of white differential treatment of blacks has been to exempt blacks from these market considerations, substituting for them a market premium attached to race.

The most obvious consequence of preferential treatment is that every black professional, no matter how able, is tainted. Every black who is hired by a white-run organization that hires blacks preferentially has to put up with the knowledge that many of his coworkers believe he was hired because of his race; and he has to put up with the suspicion in his own mind that they might be right.

Whites are curiously reluctant to consider this a real problem—it is an abstraction, I am told, much less important than the problem that blacks face in getting a job in the first place. But black professionals talk about it, and they tell stories of mental breakdowns; of people who had to leave the job altogether; of long-term professional paralysis. What white would want to be put in such a situation? Of course it would be a constant humiliation to be resented by some of your coworkers and condescended to by others. Of course it would affect your perceptions of yourself and your self-confidence. No system that produces such side effects—as preferential treatment *must* do—can be defended unless it is producing some extremely important benefits.

And that brings us to the decisive question. If the alternative were no job at all, as it was for so many blacks for so long, the resentment and condescension are part of the price of getting blacks into the positions they deserve. But is that the alternative today? If the institutions of this country were left to their own devices now, to what extent would they refuse to admit, hire, and promote people because they were black? To what extent are American institutions kept from being racist by the government's intervention?

It is another one of those questions that are seldom investigated aggressively, and I have no evidence. Let me suggest a hypothesis that bears looking into: that the signal event in the struggle for black equality during the last thirty years, the one with real impact, was not the Civil Rights Act of 1964 or Executive Order 11246 or any other governmental act. It was the civil rights movement itself. It raised to a pitch of acute and lasting discomfort the racial consciousness of the generations of white Americans who are now running the country. I will not argue that the old racism is dead at any level of society. I will argue, however, that in the typical corporation or in the typical admissions office, there is an abiding desire to be not-racist. This need not be construed as brotherly love. Guilt will do as well. But the civil rights movement did its job. I suggest that the laws and the court decisions and the continuing intellectual respectability behind preferential treatment are not holding many doors open to qualified blacks that would otherwise be closed.

Suppose for a moment that I am right. Suppose that, for practical purposes, racism would not get in the way of blacks if preferential treatment were abandoned. How, in my most optimistic view, would the world look different?

There would be fewer blacks at Harvard and Yale; but they would all be fully competitive with the whites who were there. White students at the state university would encounter a cross-section of blacks who span the full range of ability, including the top levels, just as whites do. College remedial courses would no longer be disproportionately black. Whites rejected by the school they wanted would quit assuming they were kept out because a less-qualified black was admitted in their place. Blacks in big corporations would no longer be shunted off to personnel-relations positions, but would be left on the mainline tracks toward becoming comptrollers and sales managers and chief executive officers. Whites would quit assuming that black colleagues had been hired because they were black. Blacks would quit worrying that they had been hired because they were black.

Would blacks still lag behind? As a population, yes, for a time, and the nation should be mounting a far more effective program to improve elementary and secondary education for blacks than it has mounted in the last few decades. But in years past virtually every ethnic group in America has at one time or another lagged behind as a population, and has eventually caught up. In the process of catching up, the ones who breached the barriers were evidence of the success of that group. Now blacks who breach the barriers tend to be seen as evidence of the inferiority of that group.

And that is the evil of preferential treatment. It perpetuates an impression of inferiority. The system segments whites and blacks who come in contact with each other so as to maximize the likelihood that whites have the advantage in experience and ability. The system then encourages both whites and blacks to behave in ways that create self-fulfilling prophecies even when no real differences exist.

It is here that the new racism links up with the old. The old racism has always openly held that blacks are permanently less competent than whites. The new racism tacitly accepts that, in the course of overcoming the legacy of the old racism, blacks are temporarily less competent than whites. It is an extremely fine distinction. As time goes on, fine distinctions tend to be lost. Preferential treatment is providing persuasive evidence for the old racists, and we can already hear it *sotto voce:* "We gave you your chance, we let you educate them and push them into jobs they couldn't have gotten on their own and coddle them every way you could. And see: they still aren't as good as whites, and you are beginning to admit it yourselves." Sooner or later this message is going to be heard by a white elite that needs to excuse its failure to achieve black equality.

The only happy aspect of the new racism is that the corrective—to get rid of the policies encouraging preferential treatment—is so natural. Deliberate preferential treatment by race has sat as uneasily with America's equal-opportunity ideal during the post-1965 period as it did during the days of legalized segregation. We had to construct tortuous rationalizations when we permitted blacks to be kept on the back of the bus—and the rationalizations to justify sending blacks to the head of the line have been just as tortuous. Both kinds of rationalization say that sometimes it is all right to treat people of different races in different ways. For years, we have instinctively sensed this was wrong in principle but intellectualized our support for it as an expedient. I submit that our instincts were right. There is no such thing as good racial discrimination.

Affirmative Action

Herman Schwartz

Using a multifaceted argument for affirmative action, Herman Schwartz contends that there is nothing wrong with taking group identity into account so long as the persons selected are adequately qualified. While admitting that affirmative action may be unfair to white males, Schwartz argues that it is nonetheless morally justified.

The American civil rights struggle has moved beyond simply banning discrimination against blacks, women and others. It is now clear that centuries of discrimination cannot be undone

From *The Israeli Yearbook on Human Rights*, v. 14 (1984), pp. 120–133 by permission of the publisher. Copyright © 1984 Faculty of Law, Tel Aviv University, Israel. (Original title "Affirmative Action: The American Experience.")

by merely stopping bad practices. Some kind of affirmative action is necessary to provide members of the disadvantaged groups with equal opportunities to share in the good things society has to offer.

The question of what kind of affirmative action is appropriate has generated intense controversy in the United States. One view is that it is necessary to provide actual preferences to members of disadvantaged groups in hiring, educational opportunities, government benefits and programmes, and the like, often in arrangements calling for specific minimum goals and timetables or quotas to achieve certain proportions of jobs, or other benefits.

In the famous *Bakke* case, Justice Harry Blackmun wrote:

> I suspect that it would be impossible to arrange an affirmative action program in a racially neutral way and have it successful. To ask that this be so is to demand the impossible. In order to get beyond racism, we must first take account of race. There is no other way. And in order to treat some persons equally, we must treat them differently. We cannot—we dare not—let the Equal Protection Clause perpetuate racial supremacy.[1]

And Justice Thurgood Marshall emphasized that "It is because of a legacy of unequal treatment that we now must permit the institutions of this society to give consideration to race in making decisions about who will hold the positions of influence, affluence and prestige in America."[2]

Others, including certain American Jewish organizations, find this kind of race or gender preference immoral and illegal, preferring instead to rely on finding and training disadvantaged group members for the desired opportunities. Thus, United States Civil Rights Commission Vice Chairman Morris Abram declared:

> I do not need any further study of a principle that comes from the basic bedrock of the Constitution, in which the words say that every person in the land shall be entitled to the equal protection of the law. Equal means equal. Equal does not mean you have separate lists of blacks and whites for promotion, any more than you have separate accommodations for blacks and whites for eating. Nothing will ultimately divide a society more than this kind of preference and this kind of reverse discrimination.[3]

Supreme Court Justice John Paul Stevens, who frequently votes with the liberal members of the Court, was so offended by a congressional enactment setting aside ten percent of public works contracts for minority contractors, that he compared it to the Nuremberg laws for its reliance on racial and ethnic identity.[4]

The Legal Issues

The constitutionality of governmental (constitutional limitations do not generally apply to private actions) affirmative action programmes involving race and gender-conscious goals and timetables or quotas seems quite firmly established. Voluntary private affirmative action plans also seem quite legal under the governing statutes. Language in the recent Memphis Fire Department case casts some doubt on whether federal statutory law permits a federal court to order such plans as a remedy for discrimination, but this latter situation seems to be the only situation in which such plans may be barred, and even that is uncertain for reasons to be discussed below.

There are four significant decisions.

1. The decision in *Regents of the University of California v. Bakke* represents a brilliant exercise in judicial statesmanship, engineered primarily by Justice Lewis F. Powell. In that case, the University of California Medical School at Davis had set aside sixteen places out of 100 for minority students. Allan Bakke, a white student, was denied admission because he did not qualify for one of the remaining 84 places; his grades and scores were higher than the average of the sixteen special admittees. He charged the University with racial discrimination against him.

    Four Justices found the programme illegal under a federal statute and never reached the constitutional issue. Four other Justices—Brennan, Marshall, Blackmun and White—ruled that the normally strict scrutiny applicable to governmental classifications by race—characterized frequently in other contexts as " 'strict' in theory and fatal in fact"[5]—was inapplicable when the classification was designed to benefit groups suffering from societal discrimination. These four suggested that the "middle level" test—which requires only that the classification bear a substantial relation to an important governmental purpose[6]—was properly applicable, and for these Justices, the sixteen-seat set-aside met the standard.

Justice Powell walked a middle line. He first insisted that all racial classifications—even those favouring minorities—must meet the exacting strict scrutiny standard. He then declared that eradicating the general "societal" discrimination relied on by Justices Brennan *et al.* was an unacceptable goal and that fixed quotas were an unacceptable means. He found, however, that for a university, ethnic and racial diversity *was* an acceptable objective and that a flexible, individualized programme *taking race into account* was an acceptable means. Thus, Allan Bakke was admitted because the Davis plan was struck down, but race consciousness in university admission was also allowed.

While statesmanship in any setting can always be criticized for shortcomings in logic, accuracy, candor, and the like (and Justice Powell's opinion can be, and has been, on all of these grounds), the judgment was truly Solomonic: while criticizing "rigid quotas" and allowing Allan Bakke to enter, the decision also permitted state universities to continue affirmative action plans if they wanted to. A survey one year later found that the decision had not discouraged any affirmative action by schools and colleges. Moreover, in the course of his opinion, Justice Powell also approved various other preferential plans where prior discrimination had actually been found by an appropriate governmental body.

2. *Fullilove v. Klutznick* (1980). The significance of this latter point came out two years later in the minority set-aside case. During debate in 1977 on a public works bill, an amendment was attached requiring ten percent of the contracts to be given to minority business enterprises; such programmes have also become common on the state and local level. The minority set-aside was promptly challenged as discriminatory

against white contractors, but six members of the Court, in opinions by Chief Justice Burger for three, and by Justices Powell and Marshall, had no difficulty upholding the programme as justified by the long history of discrimination in the construction industry. Justice Powell found that what might be called a "rigid" ten percent was still "reasonably necessary" enough to meet even his conception of the strict scrutiny test.[7] The plan also survived criticisms from Justice Stevens in dissent that the beneficiaries were not themselves necessarily victims of the discrimination—this was a future-oriented plan where, as in most such programmes, the beneficiaries of the remedy may not be the same as the victims of the discrimination.

3. *United Steelworkers, Inc. v. Weber* (1979).[8] In the private sphere, a 5–2 majority of the Court has upheld a voluntarily adopted craft training programme which allocated half the trainee slots to blacks. No constitutional issue was at stake because all the parties were private entities, but the Court has subsequently declined opportunities to distinguish or overturn such voluntary employment plans when adopted by city agencies, which, like the University of California Regents in *Bakke,* are subject to constitutional restraints.

4. *Firefighters Local Union No. 1784 v. Stotts* (1984).[9] Finally, in the *Stotts* case in June 1984, the Court ruled that when it is necessary to lay off workers in a setting where a court had already ordered hiring goals and timetables, if there is an applicable seniority provision, seniority must be followed in the layoffs, even if that eliminates the gains for minorities achieved by the hiring plan.

This result, though deplored by many civil rights activists, was not unexpected. Although not always sacrosanct, seniority is nevertheless a hard-won goal for many workers, and is often indispensable to countering employer arbitrariness with respect to promotions, assignments and other employee benefits. For these reasons, the Supreme Court has frequently upheld seniority rights, particularly in the civil rights context.[10]

What shocked many, however, was a quite gratuitous two and a half page discussion of the general remedial powers of federal courts, which seems to announce that Title VII forbids federal courts from ordering goals and timetable hiring programmes even after a finding of discrimination: "[T]he policy behind § 706 (g) of Title VII, which affects the remedies available in Title VII litigation . . . is to provide make-whole relief only to those who have been actual victims of illegal discrimination",[11] is the way Justice White put it.

Until *Stotts*, the federal Courts of Appeal had unanimously ruled that in employment discrimination cases brought under Title VII of the Civil Rights Act of 1964, federal courts could order certain percentages of minority or female hiring or promotion.[12] Justice White's pronouncement, which was quite unnecessary to the result, as Justice Stevens emphasized, put a cloud on hundreds of orders going back to 1969, arguably affirmed by Congress in 1972 when it expanded Title VII, and never even questioned by the Supreme Court despite numerous opportunities over the last fifteen years to do so.

The Court's pronouncement on this issue is not a square holding, and it could be receded from in the next case without much difficulty. Even if that does happen, however, the opinion has created much confusion and uncertainty. It has removed pressure on employers and unions to hire and promote minorities and women, or to settle employment discrimination litigation. It has also encouraged the Justice Department to try to open up many of the scores of decrees entered during the last fifteen years ordering such relief.

Mr. Abram's constitutional opposition to such plans is thus in no way justified by the Supreme Court's view of "the basic bedrock of the Constitution." Nor is the history cited by Assistant Attorney General Reynolds any better. In January 1984, he told an audience of pre-law students that the Fourteenth Amendment was intended to bar taking race into account for any purpose at all—"we fought the Civil War" over that, he told *The New York Times*. If so, he knows something that the members of the 1865–66 Congress, who adopted that amendment and fought the war, did not: less than a month after Congress approved the Fourteenth Amendment in 1866, the very same Congress enacted eight laws exclusively for the freedmen, granting preferential benefits regarding land, education, banking facilities, hospitals, and more.[13] No comparable programmes existed or were established for whites. And that Congress did not act unthinkingly—the racial preferences involved in those programmes were vigorously debated with a vocal minority led by President Andrew Johnson, who argued that the preferences wrongly discriminated against whites.[14]

The Moral Issues

But law is not always the same as justice. If the case for affirmative action is morally flawed, then sooner or later, the law must change. What then is the moral case against preferences for disadvantaged groups in the allocation of opportunities and benefits?

The arguments are basically two-fold: (1) hiring and other distributional decisions should be made solely on the basis of "individual merit"; and (2) racial preferences are always evil and will take us back to *Plessy v. Ferguson*[15] and worse. Quoting Dr. Martin Luther King, Jr., Thurgood Marshall, and Roy Wilkins to support the claim that anything other than total race neutrality is "discriminatory", Assistant Attorney General Reynolds warns that race consciousness has "creat[ed] . . . a racial spoils system in America", "stifles the creative spirit", erects artificial barriers, and divides the society. It is, he says, unconstitutional, unlawful, and immoral. Ms. Midge Decter, writing in the *Wall Street Journal* a few years ago, sympathized with black and female beneficiaries of affirmative action programmes for the "self-doubts" and loss of "self-regard" that she is sure they suffer, "spiritually speaking", for their "unearned special privileges". Whenever we take race into account to hand out benefits, declares Linda Chavez, the Executive Director of the Reagan Civil Rights Commission, we "discriminate", "destroy[ing] the sense of self".

All of this represents the rankest form of

hypocrisy. Despite Mr. Abram's condemnation of "separate lists", the Administration for which these people speak uses "separate lists" for blacks, Hispanics, women, Republicans, Democrats and any other group, whenever it finds that politically or otherwise useful. For example, does anyone believe that blacks like Civil Rights Commission Chairman Clarence Pendleton or Equal Employment Opportunities Commission Chairman Clarence Thomas were picked because of the color of their *eyes*? Or that Linda Chavez Gersten was made the new Executive Director of the Civil Rights Commission for reasons having nothing to do with the fact that her maiden and professional surname is Chavez?

Perhaps the most prominent recent example of affirmative action is President Reagan's selection of Sandra Day O'Connor for the Supreme Court. Obviously, she was on a "separate list", because on any unitary list this obscure lower-court state judge, with no federal experience and no national reputation, would never have come to mind as a plausible choice for the Nation's highest court. (Incidentally, despite Ms. Decter's. Mr. Reynolds', and Ms. Chavez's concern about the loss of "self-regard" suffered by beneficiaries of such preferences, "spiritually speaking" Justice O'Connor seems to be bearing her loss and "spiritual" pain quite easily.) And, like so many other beneficiaries of affirmative action given an opportunity that would otherwise be unavailable, she may indeed perform well. Mr. Reagan's fickleness on this issue has become so transparent that he was chastized for it by one of his own true believers, Civil Rights Commission Chairman Pendleton.

In fact, there is really nothing inherently wrong with taking group identity into account, so long as the person selected is qualified, a prerequisite that is an essential element of all affirmative action programmes. We do it all the time, with hardly a murmur of protest from anyone. We take group identity into account when we put together political slates, when a university gives preference to applicants from a certain part of the country or to the children of alumni, when Brandeis University restricts itself to Jews in choosing a president (as it did when it chose Morris Abram) or Notre Dame to Roman Catholics or

Howard University to blacks, when this Administration finds jobs in government for children of cabinet members. Some of these examples are less laudable than others. But surely none of these seldom-criticized practices can be valued above the purpose of undoing the effects of past and present discrimination. In choosing a qualified applicant because of a race preference we merely acknowledge, as Morton Horwitz has pointed out, "the burdens, stigmas, and scars produced by history . . . the injustices heaped on his ancestors and, through them, on him. The history and culture of oppression, transmitted through legally anonymous generations, is made antiseptic when each individual is treated as a separate being, disconnected from history."[16]

In some cases, moreover, group-oriented choices are necessary for effective performance of the job. Justice Powell in the *Bakke* case stressed the importance of ethnic and other diversity for a university, as a justification for taking race into account as one factor in university admissions. Such considerations are particularly important in police work, where police-community cooperation is indispensable, and the absence of a fair proportion of minority police in cities like Detroit and New York has not only hindered law enforcement, but has produced violent police-minority confrontations.

For these reasons, it is hard to take at face value this zeal for "individual merit", when it is group identity that determines so many choices on all our parts. As Justice Powell noted in *Bakke*, America is indeed "a Nation of minorities, . . . a 'majority' composed of various minority groups."[17] But as Burke Marshall has observed,

The Constitution generally, and the Fourteenth Amendment specifically . . . do not mean that racial, cultural, ethnic, national, or even religious identification must be excluded from the considerations that lead to actions by government officials, or legislatures, reflecting the pluralism of American society. They cannot mean, for example, that decisions on judicial appointments, political candidates, cabinet officials at all levels, or even bureaucrats in the instrumentalities of the state can never reflect racial, ethnic, cultural, or religious constituencies. If these considerations are valid for the political apparatus of government, they must also be valid, so far as the constitutional command is concerned, for other state decisions with regard to who is, and who is not, included in the discretionary allocation of benefits and power.[18]

Is it not discriminatory against whites or males, however, to deny them something they might otherwise have gotten but for the color of their skin or their gender? Is it true, as Brian Weber's lawyer argued before the Supreme Court, that "you can't avoid discrimination by discriminating"? Will racially influenced hiring take us back to *Plessy v. Ferguson*, as Pendleton and Reynolds assert? Were Martin Luther King, Jr., Thurgood Marshall, Roy Wilkins, and other black leaders really against it?

Hardly. Indeed, it is hard to contain one's outrage at this perversion of what Dr. King, Justice Marshall, and others have said, at this manipulation of their often sorrow-laden eloquence, in order to deny a handful of jobs, school admissions, and other necessities for a decent life to a few disadvantaged blacks out of the many who still suffer from discrimination and would have few opportunities otherwise.

Can anyone honestly equate a remedial preference for a disadvantaged (and qualified) minority member with the brutality inflicted on blacks and other minorities by racist laws and practices? The preference may take away some benefits from some white men, but none of them is being beaten, lynched, denied the right to use a bathroom, a place to sleep or eat, being forced to take the dirtiest jobs or denied any work at all, forced to attend dilapidated and mind-killing schools, subjected to brutally unequal justice, or stigmatized as an inferior being. Setting aside, after proof of discrimination, a few places a year for qualified minorities out of hundreds and perhaps thousands of employees, as in the Kaiser plant in the *Weber* case, or sixteen medical school places out of 100 as in *Bakke*, or ten percent of all federal public work contracts as in *Fullilove*, or

even 50 percent of new hires, cannot be mentioned in the same breath with the brutalities that racism and sexism inflicted on helpless minorities and women. It is nothing short of a shameful insult to the memory of the tragic victims of such oppression to equate the two.

Indeed, the real issue in all matters of equality and fairness is not reflected in the tautological "equal means equal" proclaimed by Mr. Abram. Rather, as H.L.A. Hart and so many others have pointed out, although the "leading precept" of justice "is often formulated as 'Treat like cases alike' . . . we need to add to the latter 'and treat different cases differently.' "[19] When some have been handicapped severely and unfairly by an accidental fact of birth, to treat such "different cases" no differently from others without that handicap is to treat them unjustly. It is not only on the golf course that it is necessary to consider handicaps.

But even if it is not discriminatory, is affirmative action unfair to innocent whites or males? Should a white policeman or fire fighter with ten years in the department be laid off when a black or a woman with less seniority is kept because an affirmative action decree is in force? Aren't those denied a job or opportunity because of an affirmative action programme often innocent of any wrong against the preferred group and just as much in need of the opportunities?

The last question is the most troubling. Brian Weber was not a rich man and he had to support a family on a modest salary, just like any black worker. A craft job would have been a significant step up in money, status, and working conditions. And *he* hadn't discriminated against anyone. Why should he pay for Kaiser's wrongs?

A closer look at the *Weber* case brings some other factors to light, however. Even if there had been no separate list for blacks, Weber would not have gotten the position, for there were too many other whites ahead of him anyway. Moreover, but for the affirmative action plan, there would not have been any craft training programme at the plant at all, for *any* whites. The white workers had been unsuccessfully demanding a craft-training programme for years, but they finally got it only when Kaiser felt it necessary to adopt the affirmative action plan.

Furthermore, even with the separate list, the number of whites adversely affected was really very small. The Kaiser plan contemplated hiring only three to four minority members a year, out of a craft work force of 275–300 and a total work force of thousands. In the first year of its operation, Kaiser still selected only a handful of blacks, because it also brought in 22 outside craftsmen, of whom only one was black. In the 1980 *Fullilove* case, upholding the ten percent set-aside of federal public works projects for minority contractors, only 0.25 percent of the total annual expenditure for construction in the United States was involved. In *Bakke*, only sixteen places out of 100 at one medical school were set aside for minorities. A new Boston University special admissions programme for black medical students will start with three a year, with the hope of rising to ten, increasing the minority enrollment at the school by two percent.

The *Weber* case discloses another interesting aspect of affirmative action plans. Because such plans can adversely affect majority white males, creative ingenuity is often expended to prevent this from happening. In *Weber*, a new craft programme benefiting both whites and blacks was set up; in the lay-off cases, time sharing and other ways of avoiding the dismissals—including raising more money—can be devised. So much for Mr. Reynold's worries about "stifling" creativity.

Strains can and do result, especially if deliberately stirred up. But strain is not inevitable: broad-ranging goals and timetable programmes for women and blacks were instituted in the Bell Telephone Company with no such troubles. The same holds true elsewhere, especially when, as in *Weber*, the programme creates new, previously unavailable opportunities for whites. Conversely, even if, as the Reagan Administration urges, the remedies are limited to specific identifiable victims of discriminatory practices, some whites may be upset. If a black applicant can prove that an employer wrongly discriminated against him personally, he would be entitled to the seniority and other benefits that he would have had but for the discrimination—with the Adminis-

tration's blessing—and this would give him competitive seniority over some white employees, regardless of those employees' innocence. The same thing happens constantly with veterans and other preferences, and few opponents of affirmative action seem to be upset by that.

Among some Jews, affirmative action brings up bitter memories of ceiling quotas, which kept them out of schools and jobs that could on merit have been theirs. This has produced a serious and nasty split within the American civil rights movement. But affirmative action goals and timetables are really quite different. Whereas quotas against Jews, Catholics, and others were ceilings to limit and keep these groups *out* of schools and jobs, today's "benign preferences" are designed to be floors that let minorities *into* a few places they would not ordinarily enter, and with relatively little impact on others. This distinction between inclusive and exclusionary practices is central.[20]

There is also a major confusion, exploited by opponents, resulting from the fact that we are almost all ethnic or religious minorities. Of course we are. And if it were shown that any minority is being victimized by intentional discrimination and that the only way to get more of that minority into a relatively representative portion of the work force or school is through an affirmative action plan, then these people would be entitled to such a remedy.

Group thinking is of course at odds with an individualistic strain that runs deep in American society. But individualism is only one strain among many. And what civil rights is all about, as many have emphasized, is an effort to undo a certain vicious strain of group thinking that established discriminatory *systems*. From *Brown v. Board of Education* on, civil rights decrees have been aimed at dismantling racist systems against groups. Obviously, these racist systems hurt individual group members, and individuals bring the law suits, but even in *Brown*, the "all deliberate speed" remedy gradually dismantling the segregated school systems was future-oriented, with the particular plaintiffs not necessarily the actual beneficiaries: in many cases, only future classes of black children would be allowed in a school to be gradually integrated, not the particular plaintiffs. The same logic applies to systems of allocating jobs and other benefits that systematically discriminated against and excluded people because they were members of minority groups.[21]

For the fact is that the centuries of injustice have created deeply imbedded abuses, and the plight of black Americans not only remains grave, but in many respects, it is getting worse. The black unemployment rate—21 percent in early 1983—is consistently double that for whites and the spread is not shrinking. For black males, the rate—an awful 30 percent—is almost triple that for whites; for black teenagers the rate approaches 50 percent. More than half of all black children under three years of age live in homes below the poverty line. The gap between black and white family income, which prior to the '70s had narrowed a bit, has steadily edged wider, so that black family income is now only 55 percent that of whites. Only three percent of the nation's lawyers and doctors are black and only four percent of its managers, but over 50 percent of its maids and garbage collectors. Black life expectancy is about six years less than that of whites; the black infant mortality rate is nearly double.[22]

Although the situation for women, of all races, is not as bad, women generally still earned only 60–65 percent as much as their male counterparts, and in recent years black women have earned only 84 percent of the white females' incomes. The economic condition of black women, who now head 41 percent of the 6.4 million black families, is particularly bad. A recent Wellesley College study found that black women are not only suffering in the labour market, but they receive substantially less public assistance and child support than white women. The condition of female household heads of any race is troubling: 90 percent of the 8.4 million single parent homes are headed by women, and more than half are below the poverty line.

Affirmative action helps. For example, from 1974 to 1980 minority employment with employers subject to federal affirmative action requirements rose twenty percent, almost twice the increase elsewhere. The employment of women by covered contractors rose fifteen percent, but only two percent among others.[23] The number of black police officers nation-

wide rose from 24,000 in 1970 to 43,500 in 1980; that kind of increase in Detroit produced a sharp decline in citizen hostility toward the police and a concomitant increase in police efficiency. There were also large jumps in minority and female employment among fire fighters, and sheet metal and electrical workers.

Few other remedies work as well or as quickly. As the New York City Corporation Counsel told the Supreme Court about the construction industry in the *Fullilove* case, "less drastic means of attempting to eradicate and remedy discrimination have been repeatedly and continuously made over the past decade and a half. They have all failed." Where affirmative action is ended, progress often stops.[24]

An example from a state like Alabama illustrates the value of affirmative action quotas. Alabama, led by such arch-segregationists as George C. Wallace, had always excluded blacks from any but the most menial state jobs. In the late 1960s, a federal court found that only 27 of 3,000 clerical and managerial employees were black. Federal Judge Frank Johnson ordered extensive recruiting of blacks, as well as the hiring of the few specific identified individual blacks who could prove they were the victims of discrimination; these are, of course, the remedies currently urged by the Justice Department.

Nothing happened. Another suit was filed, this time just against the state police, and this time a 50 percent hiring quota was imposed, until blacks reached 25 percent of the force. Today, Alabama has the most thoroughly integrated state police force in the country, with 20–25 percent of the force black. A threat of such quotas in other agencies has also produced substantial improvements.[25]

Reasonable people will continue to differ about the appropriateness of affirmative action. Color blindness and neutrality are obviously the ultimate goal, and it was one of Martin Luther King, Jr.'s dreams. But it still remains only a dream, and until it comes closer to reality, affirmative action plans are necessary and appropriate. One cannot undo centuries of discrimination by simply saying "stop"—one has to take into account the harm that those centuries have brought, and try to make up for it. Otherwise, we in the United States will remain like Disraeli's "Two Nations".

Notes

1. University of California Regents v. Bakke, 438 *U.S.* 265, 407 (1978).

2. *Id.*, at 401 (Marshall, J., concurring).

3. *New York Times*, 18 January 1984, p. 1, col. 1.

4. Fullilove v. Klutznick, 448 *U.S.* 448, 534 n. 5 (Stevens, J., dissenting).

5. G. Gunther, "Foreword: In Search of Evolving Doctrine on a Changing Court: A Model for a Newer Equal Protection." 86 *Harv. L. Rev.* 1 (1972).

6. Craig v. Boren, 429 *U.S.* 190 (1976).

7. 448 *U.S.*, at 496–97 (Powell, J., concurring).

8. 443 *U.S.* 193 (1979).

9. 52 *U.S.L.W.* 4767 (12 June 1984).

10. International Brhd. of Teamsters v. U.S. 431 *U.S.* 324 (1977).

11. 52 *U.S.L.W.*, at 4772.

12. *See* cases cited by Justice Blackmun, *id.*, at 4781. n. 10.

13. *See, e.g.*, Act of 16 July 1866, 14 *Stat.* 173 (Freedmen's Bureau).

14. *See* the discussion in Justice Marshall's opinion in Bakke, 438 *U.S.*, at 396–98.

15. 163 *U.S.* 537 (1896).

16. M. J. Horwitz, "The Jurisprudence of *Brown* and the Dilemmas of Liberalism", 14 *Harv. Civ. Rts.-Civ. Libs. L. Rev.* 599, 610 (1979).

17. 438 *U.S.*, at 292.

18. B. Marshall, "A Comment on the Nondiscrimination Principle in a '*Nation of Minorities*'," 93 *Yale L.J.* 1006, 1011 (1984).

19. H. L. A. Hart, *The Concept of Law* 155 (1961).

20. Marshall, *supra* note 18, at 1011–1012.

21. *Id.*, at 1007–1008.

22. These statistics are drawn from various sources, but the primary source is the Urban League's annual, *The State of Black America.*

23. *Washington Post*, 20 June 1983, p. A3.

24. *Wall St. J.*, 10 August 1984. p. 31 (decline in minority government contracts upon termination of set-asides).

25. Huron, "But Government *Can* Help", *Washington Post*, 12 August 1984, p. B1.

Sheet Metal Workers
v. Equal Employment Opportunity Commission

United States Supreme Court

The issue before the Supreme Court was whether Section 706 (g) of Title VII of the Civil Rights Act of 1964 prohibited a court from ordering in appropriate circumstances race-conscious relief as a remedy for past discrimination. The majority of the court concluded that 706 (g) does not prohibit such action. In addition, when past discrimination has been persistent and egregious, the majority ruled that the affirmative action program can aim to benefit individuals who are not the actual victims of the past discrimination. In dissent, Justices Rehnquist joined by Justice Berger argued that 706 (g) only provides relief to individuals who have been the actual victims of a particular discriminatory practice.

Justice Brennan announced the judgment of the Court and delivered the opinion of the Court. . . .

In 1975, petitioners were found guilty of engaging in a pattern and practice of discrimination against black and Hispanic in dividuals (nonwhites) in violation of Title VII of the Civil Rights Act of 1964 . . . and ordered to end their discriminatory practices, and to admit a certain percentage of nonwhites to union membership by July 1982. In 1982 and again in 1983, petitioners were found guilty of civil contempt for disobeying the District Court's earlier orders. They now challenge the District Court's contempt finding, and also the remedies the court ordered both for the Title VII violation and for contempt. Principally, the issue presented is whether the remedial provision of Title VII . . . empowers a district court to order race-conscious relief that may benefit individuals who are not identified victims of unlawful discrimination.

Petitioner Local 28 of the Sheet Metal Workers' International Association (Local 28) represents sheet metal workers employed by contractors in the New York City metropolitan area. Petitioner Local 28 Joint Apprenticeship Committee (JAC) is a management-labor committee which operates a 4-year apprenticeship training program designed to teach sheet metal skills. Apprentices enrolled in the program receive training both from classes and from on the job work experience. Upon completing the program, apprentices become journeyman members of Local 28. Successful completion of the program is the principal means of attaining union membership.[1]

In 1964, the New York State Commission for Human Rights determined that petitioners had excluded blacks from the union and the apprenticeship program in violation of state law. The State Commission found, among other things, that Local 28 had never had any black members or apprentices, and that "admission to apprenticeship is conducted largely on a nepot[is]tic basis involving sponsorship by incumbent union members," . . . creating an impenetrable barrier for nonwhite applicants. Petitioners were ordered to "cease and desist" their racially discriminatory practices. The New York State Supreme Court affirmed the State Commission's findings, and directed petitioners to implement objective standards for selecting apprentices. . . .

When the court's orders proved ineffective, the State Commission commenced other state-court proceedings in an effort to end petitioners' discriminatory practices. . . .

Following a trial in 1975, the District Court concluded that petitioners had violated both Title VII and New York law by discriminating against nonwhite workers in recruitment, selection, training, and admission to the union. . . . Noting that as of July 1, 1974, only 3.19% of the union's total membership, including apprentices and journeymen, was nonwhite, the court found that petitioners had denied qualified nonwhites access to union membership through a variety of discriminatory practices. First, the court found that petitioners had adopted discriminatory procedures and standards for admission into the apprenticeship program. The court examined some of the factors used to select apprentices, including the entrance examination and highschool diploma requirement, and determined that these criteria had an adverse discriminatory impact on nonwhites, and were not related to job performance. The court also observed that petitioners had used union funds to subsidize special training sessions for friends and relatives of union members taking the apprenticeship examination.

Second, the court determined that Local 28 had restricted the size of its membership in order to deny access to nonwhites. The court found that Local 28 had refused to administer yearly journeymen's examinations despite a growing demand for members' services. Rather, to meet this increase in demand, Local 28 recalled pensioners who obtained doctors' certificates that they were able to work, and issued hundreds of temporary work permits to nonmembers: only one of these permits was issued to a nonwhite. Moreover, the court found that "despite the fact that Local 28 saw fit to request [temporary workers] from sister locals all across the country, as well as from allied New York construction unions such as plumbers, carpenters, and iron workers, it never once sought them from Sheet Metal Local 400," a New York City union comprised almost entirely of nonwhites. . . . The court concluded that by using the temporary permit system rather than continuing to administer journeymen's tests, Local 28 successfully restricted the size of its membership with the "illegal effect, if not the intention, of denying non-whites access to employment opportunities in the industry." . . .

Third, the District Court determined that Local 28 had selectively organized nonunion sheet metal shops with few, if any, minority employees, and admitted to membership only white employees from those shops. The court found that "[p]rior to 1973 no non-white ever became a member of Local 28 through the organization of a non-union shop." . . . The court also found that, despite insistent pressure from both the International Union and local contractors, Local 28 had stubbornly refused to organize sheet metal workers in the local blowpipe industry because a large percentage of such workers were nonwhite.

Finally, the court found that Local 28 had discriminated in favor of white applicants seeking to transfer from sister locals. The court noted that from 1967 through 1972, Local 28 had accepted 57 transfers from sister locals, all of them white, and that it was only after this litigation had commenced that Local 28 accepted its first nonwhite transfers, two journeymen from Local 400. The court also found that on one occasion, the union's president had incorrectly told nonwhite Local 400 members that they were not eligible for transfer.

The District Court entered an order and judgment (O & J) enjoining petitioners from discriminating against nonwhites, and enjoining the specific practices the court had found to be discriminatory. Recognizing that "the record in both state and federal court against these defendants is replete with instances of . . . bad faith attempts to prevent or delay affirmative action,". . . the court concluded that "the imposition of a remedial racial goal in conjunction with an admission preference in favor of non-whites is essential to place the defendants in a position of compliance with [Title VII].". . . The court established a 29% nonwhite membership goal, based on the percentage of nonwhites in the relevant labor pool in New York City, for the union to achieve by July 1, 1981. The parties were ordered to devise and to implement recruitment and admission procedures designed to achieve this goal under the supervision of a court-appointed administrator. . . .

The Court of Appeals for the Second Circuit affirmed the District Court's determination of liability, finding that petitioners had "consistently and egregiously violated Title VII." . . . The court upheld the 29% nonwhite membership goal as a temporary remedy, justified by a "long and persistent pattern of discrimination.". . .

On remand, the District Court adopted a Revised Affirmative Action Program and Order (RAAPO) to incorporate the Court of Appeals' mandate. RAAPO also modified the original Affirmative Action Program to accommodate petitioners' claim that economic problems facing the construction industry had made it difficult for them to comply with the court's orders. Petitioners were given an additional year to meet the 29% membership goal. . . . A divided panel of the Court of Appeals affirmed RAAPO in its entirety, including the 29% nonwhite membership goal. . . .

In April 1982, the City and State moved in the District Court for an order holding petitioners in contempt. They alleged that petitioners had not achieved RAAPO's 29% nonwhite membership goal, and that this failure was due to petitioners' numerous violations of the O & J, RAAPO, and orders of the administrator. The District Court, after receiving detailed evidence of how the O & J and RAAPO had operated over the previous six years, held petitioners in civil contempt. The court did not rest its contempt finding on petitioners' failure to meet the 29% membership goal, although nonwhite membership in Local 28 was only 10.8% at the time of the hearing. Instead, the court found that petitioners had failed to comply with RAAPO . . . almost from its date of entry.". . . Specifically, the court determined that petitioners had (1) adopted a policy of underutilizing the apprenticeship program in order to limit nonwhite membership and employment opportunities; (2) refused to conduct the general publicity campaign required by the O & J and RAAPO to inform nonwhites of membership opportunities; (3) added a job protection provision to the union's collective-bargaining agreement that favored older workers and discriminated against nonwhites (older workers provision); (4) issued unauthorized work permits to white workers from sister locals; and (5) failed to maintain and submit records and reports required by RAAPO, the O & J, and the administrator, thus making it difficult to monitor petitioners' compliance with the court's orders.

To remedy petitioners' contempt, the court imposed a $150,000 fine to be placed in a fund designed to increase nonwhite membership in the apprenticeship program and the union. The administrator was directed to propose a plan for utilizing the fund. . . .

In 1983, the City brought a second contempt proceeding before the administrator, charging petitioners with additional violations of the O & J, RAAPO, and various administrative orders. . . .

The District Court adopted the administrator's findings and once against adjudicated petitioners guilty of civil contempt. . . .

A divided panel of the Court of Appeals affirmed the District Court's contempt findings. . . . The court also affirmed the District Court's contempt remedies, including the Fund order, and affirmed AAAPO [Amended Affirmative Action Plan and Order] with two modifications. . . .

Local 28 and the JAC filed a petition for a writ of certiorari. They present several claims for review. . . . Principally, however, petitioners, supported by the Solicitor General, maintain that the membership goal and Fund exceed the scope of remedies available under Title VII because they extend race-conscious preferences to individuals who are not the identified victims of petitioners' unlawful discrimination. . . .

Petitioners, joined by the Solicitor General, argue that the membership goal, the Fund order, and other orders which require petitioners to grant membership preferences to nonwhites are expressly prohibited by §706(g), . . . which defines the remedies available under Title VII. Petitioners and the Solicitor General maintain that §706(g) authorizes a district court to award preferential relief only to the actual victims of unlawful discrimination. They maintain that the membership goal and the Fund violate this provision, since they require petitioners to admit to membership, and otherwise to extend benefits to black and Hispanic individuals who are not the identified victims of unlawful discrimination. We reject this argument, and hold that §706(g) does not prohibit a court from ordering, in appropriate circumstances, affirmative race-conscious relief as a remedy for past discrimination. Specifically, we hold that such relief may be appropriate where an employer or a labor union has engaged in persistent or egregious discrimination, or where necessary to dissipate the lingering effects of pervasive discrimination. . . .

Section 706(g) states:

"If the court finds that the respondent has intentionally engaged in or is intentionally engaging in an unlawful employment practice . . . , the court may enjoin the respondent from engaging in such unlawful employment practice, and order such affirmative action as may be appropriate, which may include, but is not limited to, reinstatement or hiring of employees, with or without back pay . . . , or any other equitable relief as the court deems appropriate. . . . No order of the court shall require the admission or reinstatement of an individual as a member of a union, or the hiring, reinstatement, or promotion of an individual as an employee, or the payment to him of any back pay, if such individual was refused admission, suspended, or expelled, or was refused employment or advancement or was suspended or discharged for any reason other than discrimination on account of race, color, religion, sex, or national origin in violation of . . . this title." . . .

The language of §706(g) plainly expresses Congress's intent to vest district courts with broad discretion to award "appropriate" equitable relief to remedy unlawful discrimination. . . . Nevertheless, petitioners and the Solicitor General argue that the last sentence of §706(g) prohibits a court from ordering an employer or labor union to take affirmative steps to eliminate discrimination which might incidentally benefit individuals who are not the actual victims of discrimination. This reading twists the plain language of the statute.

The last sentence of §706(g) prohibits a court from ordering a union to admit an individual who was "refused admission . . . for any reason other than discrimination." It does not, as petitioners and the Solicitor General suggest, say that a court may order relief only for the actual victims of past discrimination. The sentence on its face addresses only the situation where a plaintiff demonstrates that a union (or an employer) has engaged in unlawful discrimination, but the union can show that a particular individual would have been refused admission even in the absence of discrimination, for example because that individual was unqualified. In these circumstances, §706(g) confirms that a court could not order the union to admit the unqualified individual. . . . In this case, neither the membership goal nor the Fund order required petitioners to admit to membership individuals who had been refused admission for reasons unrelated to discrimination. Thus, we do not read §706(g) to prohibit a court from ordering the kind of affirmative relief the District Court awarded in this case.

The availability of race-conscious affirmative relief under §706(g) as a remedy for a violation of Title VII also furthers the broad purposes underlying the statute. Congress enacted Title VII based on its determination that racial minorities were subject to pervasive and systematic discrimination in employment. . . . In order to foster equal employment opportunities, Congress gave the lower courts broad power under §706(g) to fashion "the most complete relief possible" to remedy past discrimination. . . .

In most cases, the court need only order the employer or union to cease engaging in discriminatory practices, and award make-whole relief to the individuals victimized by those practices. In some instances, however, it may be necessary to require the employer or union to take affirmative steps to end discrimination effectively to enforce Title VII. Where an employer or union has engaged in particularly longstanding or egregious discrimination, an injunction simply reiterating Title VII's prohibition against discrimination will often prove useless and will only result in endless enforcement litigation. In such cases, requiring recalcitrant employers or unions to hire and to admit qualified minorities roughly in proportion to the number of qualified minorities in the work force may be the only effective way to ensure the full enjoyment of the rights protected by Title VII. . . .

Further, even where the employer or union formally ceases to engage in discrimination, informal mechanisms may obstruct equal employment opportunities. An employer's reputation for discrimination may discourage minorities from seeking available employment. . . . In these circumstances, affirmative race-conscious relief may be the only means available "to assure equality of employment opportunities and to eliminate those discriminatory practices and devices which have fostered racially stratified job environments to the disadvantage of minority citizens.". . .

Finally, a district court may find it necessary to order interim hiring or promotional goals pending the development of nondiscriminatory hiring or promotion procedures. In these cases, the use of numerical goals provides a compromise between two unacceptable alternatives: an outright ban on hiring or promotions, or continued use of a discriminatory selection procedure.

We have previously suggested that courts may utilize certain kinds of racial preferences to remedy past discrimination under Title VII. . . . The Courts of Appeals have unanimously agreed that racial preferences may be used, in appropriate cases, to remedy past discrimination under Title VII.

. . . Our examination of the legislative history of Title VII convinces us that, when examined in context, the statements relied upon by petitioners and the Solicitor General do not indicate that Congress intended to limit relief under §706(g) to that which benefits only the actual victims of unlawful discrimination. Rather, these statements were intended largely to reassure opponents of the bill that it would not require employers or labor unions to use racial quotas or to grant preferential treatment to racial minorities in order to avoid being charged with unlawful discrimination. . . .

Our reading of the scope of the district court's remedial powers under §706(g) is confirmed by the contemporaneous interpretations of the EEOC and the Justice Department. . . .

Finally, our interpretation of §706(g) is confirmed by the legislative history of the Equal Employment Opportunity Act of 1972, . . . which amended Title VII in several respects. . . .

Petitioners claim to find their strongest support in *Firefighters* v. *Stotts.* . . . In *Stotts*, the city of Memphis, Tennessee had entered into a consent decree requiring affirmative steps to increase the proportion of minority employees in its Fire Department. Budgetary cuts subsequently forced the city to lay off employees; under the city's last-hired, first-fired seniority system, many of the black employees who had been hired pursuant to the consent decree would have been laid off first. These employees sought relief, and the District Court, concluding that the proposed layoffs would have a racially discriminatory effect, enjoined the city from applying its seniority policy "insofar as it will decrease the percentage of black[s] that are presently employed." . . . We held that the District Court exceeded its authority.

. . . We decline petitioners' invitation to read *Stotts* to prohibit a court from ordering any kind of race-conscious affirmative relief that might benefit nonvictims. This reading would distort the language of §706(g), and would deprive the courts of an important means of enforcing Title VII's guarantee of equal employment opportunity. . . .

Although we conclude that §706(g) does not foreclose a district court from instituting some sorts of racial preferences where necessary to remedy past discrimination, we do not mean to suggest that such relief is always proper. While the fashioning of "appropriate" remedies for a particular Title VII violation invokes the "equitable discretion of the district courts," . . . we emphasize that a court's judgment should be guided by sound legal principles. In particular, the court should exercise its discretion with an eye towards Congress' concern that race-conscious affirmative measures not be invoked simply to create a racially balanced work force. In the majority of Title VII cases, the court will not have to impose affirmative action as a remedy for past discrimination, but need only order the employer or union to cease engaging in discriminatory practices and award make-whole relief to the individuals victimized by those practices. However, in some cases, affirmative action may be necessary in order effectively to enforce Title VII. As we noted before, a court may have to resort to race-conscious affirmative action when confronted with an employer

or labor union that has engaged in persistent or egregious discrimination. Or, such relief may be necessary to dissipate the lingering effects of pervasive discrimination. Whether there might be other circumstances that justify the use of court-ordered affirmative action is a matter that we need not decide here. We note only that a court should consider whether affirmative action is necessary to remedy past discrimination in a particular case before imposing such measures, and that the court should also take care to tailor its orders to fit the nature of the violation it seeks to correct. . . .

In this case, there is no problem, as there was in *Wygant*, with a proper showing of prior discrimination that would justify the use of remedial racial classifications. Both the District Court and Court of Appeals have repeatedly found petitioners guilty of egregious violations of Title VII, and have determined that affirmative measures were necessary to remedy their racially discriminatory practices. More importantly, the District Court's orders were properly tailored to accomplish this objective. First, the District Court considered the efficacy of alternative remedies, and concluded that, in light of petitioners' long record of resistance to official efforts to end their discriminatory practices, stronger measures were necessary. . . . The court devised the temporary membership goal and the Fund as tools for remedying past discrimination. More importantly, the District Court's orders will have only a marginal impact on the interests of white workers. . . . Again, petitioners concede that the District Court's orders did not disadvantage *existing* union members. While white applicants for union membership may be denied certain benefits available to their nonwhite counterparts, the court's orders do not stand as an absolute bar to the admission of such individuals; again, a majority of those entering the union after entry of the court's orders have been white. We therefore conclude that the District Court's orders do not violate the equal protection safeguards of the Constitution. . . .

To summarize our holding today, six members of the Court agree that a district court may, in appropriate circumstances, order preferential relief benefitting individuals who are not the actual victims of discrimination as a remedy for violations of Title VII. . . . Five members of the Court agree that in this case, the District Court did not err in evaluating petitioners' utilization of the apprenticeship program, . . . and that the membership goal and the Fund order are not violative of either Title VII or the Constitution. . . . The judgment of the Court of Appeals is hereby *Affirmed.*

. . . Justice Rehnquist, with whom The Chief Justice joins, dissenting.

Today, in *Local Number 93 v. City of Cleveland,* . . . (REHNQUIST, J., dissenting), I express my belief that §706(g) forbids a court from ordering racial preferences that effectively displace non-minorities except to minority individuals who have been the actual victims of a particular employer's racial dis-

crimination. Although the pervasiveness of the racial discrimination practiced by a particular union or employer is likely to increase the number of victims who are entitled to a remedy under the Act, §706(g) does not allow us to go further than that and sanction the granting of relief to those who were not victims at the expense of innocent nonminority workers injured by racial preferences. I explain that both the language and the legislative history of §706(g) clearly support this reading of §706(g), and that this Court stated as much just two Terms ago in *Firefighters* v. *Stotts.* . . . Because of this, I would not reach the equal protection question, . . . but would rely solely on §706(g) to reverse the Court of Appeals' judgment approving the order of class-based relief for petitioners' past discrimination.

Suggestions for Further Reading

Anthologies

Blackstone, W., and Heslep, R. *Social Justice and Preferential Treatment.* Athens, GA: University of Georgia Press, 1977.

Cohen, M., Nagel, T., and Scanlon, T. *Equality and Preferential Treatment.* Princeton, NJ: Princeton University Press, 1977.

Gould, C. C., and Wartofsky, M. W. *Women and Philosophy.* New York: G. P. Putnam & Sons, 1976.

Gross, B. *Reverse Discrimination.* Buffalo, NY: Prometheus, 1976.

Remick, H. *Comparable Worth and Wage Discrimination.* Philadelphia: Temple University Press, 1985.

Alternative Views

Bittker, B. *The Case for Black Reparations.* New York: Random House, 1973.

Fullinwider, R. *The Reverse Discrimination Controversy.* Ottowa: Rowman and Littlefield, 1980.

Goldman, A. *Justice and Reverse Discrimination.* Princeton, NJ: Princeton University Press, 1979.

Gross, B. *Discrimination in Reverse.* New York: New York University Press, 1979.

Jencks, C., et al. *Inequality: A Reassessment of the Effect of Family and Schooling in America.* New York: Basic Books, 1972.

Livingston, J. *Fair Game.* San Francisco: W. H. Freeman & Co., 1979.

Sowell, T. *Markets and Minorities.* New York: Basic Books, 1981.

Practical Applications

Sindles, A. P. *Bakke, De Funio and Minority Admissions.* New York: Youngman, 1978.

United States Commission on Civil Rights. *Toward an Understanding of Bakke.* Washington, D.C.: U.S. Government Printing Office, 1979.

Animal Rights

Basic Concepts

The problem of animal rights has only recently attracted widespread public attention. Beginning with the 1973 publication of Peter Singer's article, "Animal Liberation," in the *New York Review of Books,* followed by the publication two years later of his book of the same title, people have become increasingly concerned with the problem of animal rights, especially two of the most serious forms of animal exploitation: animal experimentation and factory farming.

Animal experimentation is a big business, involving 60–100 million animals a year. Two experiments alone—the rabbit-blinding Draize eye test and the LD50 toxicity test designed to find the lethal dose for 50 percent of a sample of animals—cause the deaths of more than 5 million animals per year in the United States alone. In factory farming, millions of animals are raised in such a way that their short lives are dominated by pain and suffering. Veal calves are put in narrow stalls and tethered with a chain so that they cannot turn around, lie down comfortably, or groom themselves. They are fed a totally liquid diet to promote rapid weight gain, and they are given no water because thirsty animals eat more than those who drink water.

The problem of animal rights raises the question of what should be our policy for the treatment of nonhuman animals, or, alternatively, what is the moral status of nonhuman animals. One possible answer is that animals have no independent moral status at all but that their moral status depends completely on the impact they have on human welfare. Another possible answer is that animals have an independent moral status such that their welfare has to be weighed against, and at least sometimes outweighs, considerations of human welfare.

Obviously, supporters of animal liberation favor some version of this latter answer, but they disagree as to the grounds for this independent moral status. Some claim that animals have independent moral status because taking their welfare into account would maximize overall utility. Others claim that the in-dependent moral status of animals rests on a nonutilitarian foundation.

This conflict among supporters of animal liberation over the grounds for animal rights reflects a general conflict among utilitarians and nonutilitarians with respect to a wide range of practical problems (see the General Introduction to this anthology). However, with respect to this particular problem, supporters of animal liberation cannot rely on some form of social contract theory to reach an acceptable resolution because most animals are incapable of forming either an actual or hypothetical contract with human beings for the purpose of securing their common welfare. Social contract theory, however, is only a means to a goal, which is to achieve a fair resolution of morally relevant interests. Consequently, if animals do have morally relevant interests, then to achieve that goal some means other than social contract theory will have to be employed.

This is not to say that social contract theory is not useful for achieving a fair resolution of conflicts when only human interests pertain. In fact, it would seem that a fair resolution of conflicts among human and nonhuman interests would mirror a fair resolution of conflicts among purely human interests. For example, if a utilitarian (or a nonutilitarian) resolution were fair when only human interests are taken into account, a utilitarian (or a nonutilitarian) resolution would seem to be fair when both human and animal interests are considered.

In brief, to resolve the problem of animal rights, we must determine whether animals have an independent moral status, and, if they do, whether a utilitarian or nonutilitarian justification best accounts for that status.

Alternative Views

In the first selection (pp. 307–318), Peter Singer argues for the independent moral status of animals by comparing the bias against animals, which he calls "speciesism," with biases against blacks and women. According to Singer, the grounds we have for opposing racism and sexism are also grounds for opposing speciesism because all forms of discrimination run counter to the principle of equal consideration. Racists violate this principle by giving greater weight to the interests of members of their own race in cases of conflict; sexists violate this principle by favoring the interests of their own specific sex; and speciesists violate this principle by allowing the interests of their own species to override the greater interests of other species.

Animals have interests, Singer maintains, because they have a capacity for suffering and enjoyment. According to the principle of equal consideration, there is no justification for regarding the pain animals feel as less important than the same amount of pain (or pleasure) humans feel. As for the practical requirements of this view, Singer contends that we cannot go astray if we give the same respect to the lives of animals that we give to the lives of humans at a similar mental level. In the end, Singer thinks, this requires a utilitarian weighing of both human and animal interests.

One difficulty with Singer's view concerns whether when calculating what maximizes overall utility, qualitative differences between human and animal interests might not always lead us to favor human over animal interests. If this were the case, then, although in theory nonhuman animals would have independent moral status, in practice, their interests would always be outweighed by human interests.

To avoid this difficulty, Tom Regan, in the next selection (pp. 319–326), adopts a different approach to defending animal rights. According to Regan, what is fundamentally wrong with our treatment of nonhuman animals is that it implies that they are simply resources for our use. Regan begins by considering how the moral status of animals has been understood by people who deny that animals have rights.

Regan first considers the view that all of our duties toward animals are indirect, ultimately grounded in duties to other human beings. This view holds that animals have no independent moral status. Regan argues that this view cannot be supported on the grounds that animals feel no pain or that only human pain matters. Nor can this view be supported,

Regan argues, on the basis of contractarianism because contractarianism is inadequate even in accounting for the moral status of human beings.

Regan next considers the view that we do have direct duties toward animals but that these duties do not support animal rights. According to this view, animals do have an independent moral status, but that status falls short of having rights. In one interpretation of this view, we have direct duties to be kind and not cruel to animals but nothing more. Regan argues, however, that this interpretation does not suffice for an account of right action. In another interpretation of this view, our duties toward animals are simply a consequence of what maximizes overall utility. But, as noted previously, Regan believes that the aggregative requirement of utilitarianism will lead us to act unjustly and at least sometimes ignore animal rights. The correct grounding for our duties to animals and their rights against us, Regan argues, is their inherent value, which they possess, equally with ourselves as experiencing subjects of life. To those who might concede that animals have inherent value but to a lesser degree than humans, Regan argues that this view would only be defensible if similarly deficient humans were also seen as having less inherent value—a stance Regan feels his opponents are not willing to take.

One obvious difficulty with Regan's view is its absolutist character. According to Regan, it is always wrong to sacrifice a few animals, or even just one animal, to save the lives of countless others, even if this were the only way to develop a general cure for cancer, for example. However, it is difficult to see why such absolutism is needed to ground animal rights, for surely it is possible to have a nonutilitarian theory that is not absolutist (see the General Introduction).

Jan Narveson (pp. 327–334) raises yet another objection to Regan's defense of animal rights. According to Narveson, the most defensible account of morality is a contractarian view that grounds all rights in a self-interested agreement made by individuals capable of keeping that agreement. But clearly this account of morality leaves animals outside of its scope.

Narveson examines two other accounts of

morality—the libertarian account and the utilitarian account—but concludes that neither clearly favors animal rights to any significant degree. Besides, unlike the contractarian account, which grounds morality in long-term self-interest, Narveson argues that neither the libertarian nor the utilitarian account provides an acceptable justification for being moral. The General Introduction to this text, however, argued that a standard of reasonable conduct acceptable to rational egoism justifies a morality that is certainly more other-regarding than the self-interest-based contractarianism that Narveson defends. If this argument can be sustained, such a morality may provide a foundation for animal rights that is superior to Narveson's self-interest-based morality.

In the next selection (pp. 335–344), R. G. Frey develops in great detail one line of argument against Singer's utilitarian defense of animal rights that Narveson touches on. Frey argues that utilitarianism does not ultimately support a strong case for animal rights for several reasons. First of all, by Singer's own omission, it is permissible to eat farm animals, typically cattle and sheep, that are reared and killed without suffering. Second, Singer's objection to the suffering inflicted on animals in factory farms can be overcome by reforming the practices used on such farms rather than by requiring that we become vegetarians. Third, a radical turn to vegetarianism would probably result in the elimination of most farm animals as we know them because they certainly cannot survive in the wild. This would seriously disrupt and/or eliminate many industries and social practices, resulting in significant disutility.

Responding to these criticisms in a recent article in the *New York Review of Books*, Singer makes two points. He first claims that adopting vegetarianism would improve people's general health, eliminate Third World poverty, and create new and beneficial industries and social practices. Second, Singer claims that in political campaigning, opposition to the current techniques of factory farming is not taken seriously unless one is also a committed vegetarian. According to Singer, only vegetarians can silence that invariable objection to reforming our treatment of animals: But don't you eat them?

Nevertheless, Singer's response turns on the political effectiveness of being a vegetarian and the effects vegetarianism would have on human welfare rather than its effects on animal welfare. However, it is in terms of animal welfare that the case for animal rights must ultimately be made.

Practical Applications

The next two selections (p. 345) come from the only federal law in the United States pertaining to the treatment of animals. The provisions of the Animal Welfare Act of 1970 pertain only to the transportation of animals and the treatment of animals for research and experimentation. The act does not mention the treatment of animals in factory farms. The act also simply requires research facilities to report on their appropriate use of anesthetics and analgesics but does not define appropriate use. Similarly, although the Animal Welfare Act of 1976 takes a step in the direction of animal rights by prohibiting animal fights, it does so only in the case of live birds when state law also prohibits such fights. Although these federal laws are limited in scope, it seems clear that any solution to the problem of animal rights that gives substantial rights to animals will, if implemented, have a significant impact on the way we live and work and, accordingly, on the solutions we will be able to give to the other practical problems discussed in this anthology.

All Animals Are Equal

Peter Singer

Peter Singer begins his defense of animal liberation by comparing the bias against animals with biases against blacks and women. According to Singer, all of these forms of discrimination violate the principle of equal consideration. According to this principle, there is no justification for regarding the pain that animals feel as less important than the same amount of pain (or pleasure) felt by humans.

"Animal Liberation" may sound more like a parody of other liberation movements than a serious objective. The idea of "The Rights of Animals" actually was once used to parody the case for women's rights. When Mary Wollstonecraft, a forerunner of today's feminists, published her *Vindication of the Rights of Women* in 1792, her views were widely regarded as absurd, and before long an anonymous publication appeared entitled *A Vindication of the Rights of Brutes*. The author of this satirical work (now known to have been Thomas Taylor, a distinguished Cambridge philosopher) tried to refute Mary Wollstonecraft's arguments by showing that they could be carried one stage further. If the argument for equality was sound when applied to women, why should it not be applied to dogs, cats, and horses? The reasoning seemed to hold for these "brutes" too; yet to hold that brutes had rights was manifestly absurd; therefore the reasoning by which this conclusion had been reached must be unsound, and if unsound when applied to brutes, it must also be unsound when applied to women, since the very same arguments had been used in each case.

In order to explain the basis of the case for the equality of animals, it will be helpful to start with an examination of the case for the equality of women. Let us assume that we wish to defend the case for women's rights against the attack by Thomas Taylor. How should we reply?

From *Animal Liberation* (New York: New York Review, 1975), pp. 1–22. Reprinted by permission of Peter Singer.

One way in which we might reply is by saying that the case for equality between men and women cannot validly be extended to nonhuman animals. Women have a right to vote, for instance, because they are just as capable of making rational decisions about the future as men are; dogs, on the other hand, are incapable of understanding the significance of voting, so they cannot have the right to vote. There are many other obvious ways in which men and women resemble each other closely, while humans and animals differ greatly. So, it might be said, men and women are similar beings and should have similar rights, while humans and nonhumans are different and should not have equal rights.

The reasoning behind this reply to Taylor's analogy is correct up to a point, but it does not go far enough. There *are* important differences between humans and other animals, and these differences must give rise to *some* differences in the rights that each have. Recognizing this obvious fact, however, is no barrier to the case for extending the basic principle of equality to nonhuman animals. The differences that exist between men and women are equally undeniable, and the supporters of Women's Liberation are aware that these differences may give rise to different rights. Many feminists hold that women have the right to an abortion on request. It does not follow that since these same feminists are campaigning for equality between men and women they must support the right of men to have abortions too. Since a man cannot have an abortion, it is meaningless to talk of his right to have one. Since a dog can't vote, it is meaningless to talk of its right to vote. There is no reason why either Women's Liberation or Animal Liberation should get involved in such nonsense. The extension of the basic principle of equality from one group to another does not imply that we must treat both groups in exactly the same way, or grant exactly the same rights to both groups. Whether we should do so will depend on the nature of the members of the two groups. The basic principle of equality does not require equal or identical *treatment;* it requires equal *consideration.* Equal consideration for different beings may lead to different treatment and different rights.

So there is a different way of replying to Taylor's attempt to parody the case for women's rights, a way that does not deny the obvious differences between humans and nonhumans but goes more deeply into the question of equality and concludes by finding nothing absurd in the idea that the basic principle of equality applies to so-called "brutes." At this point such a conclusion may appear odd; but if we examine more deeply the basis on which our opposition to discrimination on grounds of race or sex ultimately rests, we will see that we would be on shaky ground if we were to demand equality for blacks, women, and other groups of oppressed humans while denying equal consideration to nonhumans. To make this clear we need to see, first, exactly why racism and sexism are wrong.

When we say that all human beings, whatever their race, creed, or sex, are equal, what is it that we are asserting? Those who wish to defend hierarchical, inegalitarian societies have often pointed out that by whatever test we choose it simply is not true that all humans are equal. Like it or not we must face the fact that humans come in different shapes and sizes; they come with different moral capacities, different intellectual abilities, different amounts of benevolent feeling and sensitivity to the needs of others, different abilities to communicate effectively, and different capacities to experience pleasure and pain. In short, if the demand for equality were based on the actual equality of all human beings, we would have to stop demanding equality.

Still, one might cling to the view that the demand for equality among human beings is based on the actual equality of the different races and sexes. Although, it may be said, humans differ as individuals there are no differences between the races and sexes *as such.* From the mere fact that a person is black or a woman we cannot infer anything about that person's intellectual or moral capacities. This, it may be said, is why racism and sexism are wrong. The white racist claims that whites are superior to blacks, but this is false—although there are differences among individuals, some blacks are superior to some whites in all of the capacities and abilities that could conceivably be relevant. The opponent of sexism would say the same: a person's sex is no guide to his or her abilities, and this is why it is unjustifiable to discriminate on the basis of sex.

The existence of individual variations that cut across the lines of race or sex, however, provides us with no defense at all against a more sophisticated opponent of equality, one who proposes that, say, the interests of all those with IQ scores below 100 be given less consideration than the interests of those with ratings over 100. Perhaps those scoring below the mark would, in this society, be made the slaves of those scoring higher. Would a hierarchical society of this sort really be so much better than one based on race or sex? I think not. But if we tie the moral principle of equality to the factual equality of the different races or sexes, taken as a whole, our opposition to racism and sexism does not provide us with any basis for objecting to this kind of inegalitarianism.

There is a second important reason why we ought not to base our opposition to racism and sexism on any kind of actual equality, even the limited kind that asserts that variations in capacities and abilities are spread evenly between the different races and sexes: we can have no absolute guarantee that these capacities and abilities really are distributed evenly, without regard to race or sex, among human beings. So far as actual abilities are concerned there do seem to be certain measurable differences between both races and sexes. These differences do not, of course, appear in each case, but only when averages are taken. More important still, we do not yet know how much of these differences is really due to the different genetic endowments of the different races and sexes, and how much is due to poor schools, poor housing, and other factors that are the result of past and continuing discrimination. Perhaps all of the important differences will eventually prove to be environmental rather than genetic. Anyone opposed to racism and sexism will certainly hope that this will be so, for it will make the task of ending discrimination a lot easier; nevertheless it would be dangerous to rest the case against racism and sexism on the belief that all significant differences are environmental in origin. The opponent of, say, racism who takes this line will be unable to avoid conceding that *if* differences in ability do after all prove to have some genetic connection with race, racism would in some way be defensible.

Fortunately there is no need to pin the case for equality to one particular outcome of a scientific investigation. The appropriate response to those who claim to have found evidence of genetically based differences in ability between the races or sexes is not to stick to the belief that the genetic explanation must be wrong, whatever evidence to the contrary may turn up: instead we should make it quite clear that the claim to equality does not depend on intelligence, moral capacity, physical strength, or similar matters of fact. Equality is a moral idea, not an assertion of fact. There is no logically compelling reason for assuming that a factual difference in ability between two people justifies any difference in the amount of consideration we give to their needs and interests. *The principle of the equality of human beings is not a description of an alleged actual equality among humans: it is a prescription of how we should treat humans.*

Jeremy Bentham, the founder of the reforming utilitarian school of moral philosophy, incorporated the essential basis of moral equality into his system of ethics by means of the formula: "Each to count for one and none for more than one." In other words, the interests of every being affected by an action are to be taken into account and given the same weight as the like interests of any other being. A later utilitarian, Henry Sidgwick, put the point in this way: "The good of any one individual is of no more importance, from the point of view (if I may say so) of the Universe, than the good of any other." More recently the leading figures in contemporary moral philosophy have shown a great deal of agreement in specifying as a fundamental presupposition of their moral theories some similar requirement which operates so as to give everyone's interests equal consideration—although these writers generally cannot agree on how this requirement is best formulated.[1]

It is an implication of this principle of equality that our concern for others and our readiness to consider their interests ought not to depend on what they are like or on what abilities they may possess. Precisely what this concern or consideration requires us to do may vary according to the characteristics of those affected by what we do: concern for the well-being of a child growing up in America would require that we teach him to read; concern for the well-being of a pig may require no more than that we leave him alone with other pigs in a place where there is adequate food and room to run freely. But the basic element—the taking into account of the interests of the being, whatever those interests may be —must, according to the principle of equality, be extended to all beings, black or white, masculine or feminine, human or nonhuman.

Thomas Jefferson, who was responsible for writing the principle of the equality of men into the American Declaration of Independence, saw this point. It led him to oppose slavery even though he was unable to free himself fully from his slaveholding background. He wrote in a letter to the author of a book that emphasized the notable intellectual achievements of Negroes in order to refute the then common view that they had limited intellectual capacities:

> Be assured that no person living wishes more sincerely than I do, to see a complete refutation of the doubts I have myself entertained and expressed on the grade of understanding allotted to them by nature, and to find that they are on a par with ourselves . . . but whatever be their degree of talent it is no measure of their rights. Because Sir Isaac Newton was superior to others in understanding, he was not therefore lord of the property or person of others.[2]

Similarly when in the 1850s the call for women's rights was raised in the United States a remarkable black feminist named Sojourner Truth made the same point in more robust terms at a feminist convention:

> . . . they talk about this thing in the head; what do they call it? ["Intellect," whispered someone near by.] That's it. What's that got to do with women's rights or Negroes' rights? If my cup won't hold but a pint and yours holds a quart, wouldn't you be mean not to let me have my little half-measure full?[3]

It is on this basis that the case against racism and the case against sexism must both ultimately rest; and it is in accordance with this principle that the attitude that we may call "speciesism," by analogy with racism, must also be condemned. Speciesism—the word is not an attractive one, but I can think of no better term—is a prejudice or attitude of bias toward the interests of members of one's own species and against those of members of other species. It should be obvious that the fundamental objections to racism and sexism made by Thomas Jefferson and Sojourner Truth apply equally to speciesism. If possessing a higher degree of intelligence does not entitle one human to use another for his own ends, how can it entitle humans to exploit nonhumans for the same purpose?[4]

Many philosophers and other writers have proposed the principle of equal consideration of interests, in some form or other, as a basic moral principle; but not many of them have recognized that this principle applies to members of other species as well as to our own. Jeremy Bentham was one of the few who did realize this. In a forward-looking passage written at a time when black slaves had been freed by the French but in the British dominions were still being treated in the way we now treat animals, Bentham wrote:

> The day *may* come when the rest of the animal creation may acquire those rights which never could have been withholden from them but by the hand of tyranny. The French have already discovered that

the blackness of the skin is no reason why a human being should be abandoned without redress to the caprice of a tormentor. It may one day come to be recognized that the number of the legs, the villosity of the skin, or the termination of the *os sacrum* are reasons equally insufficient for abandoning a sensitive being to the same fate. What else is it that should trace the insuperable line? Is it the faculty of reason, or perhaps the faculty of discourse? But a full-grown horse or dog is beyond comparison a more rational, as well as a more conversable animal, than an infant of a day or a week or even a month, old. But suppose they were otherwise, what would it avail? The question is not, Can they *reason?* nor Can they *talk?* but, *Can they suffer?*[5]

In this passage Bentham points to the capacity for suffering as the vital characteristic that gives a being the right to equal consideration. The capacity for suffering—or more strictly, for suffering and/or enjoyment or happiness—is not just another characteristic like the capacity for language or higher mathematics. Bentham is not saying that those who try to mark "the insuperable line" that determines whether the interests of a being should be considered happen to have chosen the wrong characteristic. By saying that we must consider the interests of all beings with the capacity for suffering or enjoyment Bentham does not arbitrarily exclude from consideration any interests at all—as those who draw the line with reference to the possession of reason or language do. The capacity for suffering and enjoyment is *a prerequisite for having interests at all,* a condition that must be satisfied before we can speak of interests in a meaningful way. It would be nonsense to say that it was not in the interests of a stone to be kicked along the road by a schoolboy. A stone does not have interests because it cannot suffer. Nothing that we can do to it could possibly make any difference to its welfare. A mouse, on the other hand, does have an interest in not being kicked along the road, because it will suffer if it is.

If a being suffers there can be no moral justification for refusing to take that suffering into consideration. No matter what the nature of the being, the principle of equality requires that its suffering be counted equally with the like suffering—in so far as rough comparisons can be made—of any other being. If a being is not capable of suffering, or of experiencing enjoyment or happiness, there is nothing to be taken into account. So the limit of sentience (using the term as a convenient if not strictly accurate shorthand for the capacity to suffer and/or experience enjoyment) is the only defensible boundary of concern for the interests of others. To mark this boundary by some other characteristic like intelligence or rationality would be to mark it in an arbitrary manner. Why not choose some other characteristic, like skin color?

The racist violates the principle of equality by giving greater weight to the interests of members of his own race when there is a clash between their interests and the interests of those of another race. The sexist violates the principle of equality by favoring the interests of his own sex. Similarly the speciesist allows the interests of his own species to override the greater interests of members of other species. The pattern is identical in each case.

Most human beings are speciesists. The following chapters show that ordinary human beings—not a few exceptionally cruel or heartless humans, but the overwhelming majority of humans—take an active part in, acquiesce in, and allow their taxes to pay for practices that require the sacrifice of the most important interests of members of other species in order to promote the most trivial interests of our own species.

There is, however, one general defense of the practices to be described in the next two chapters that needs to be disposed of before we discuss the practices themselves. It is a defense which, if true, would allow us to do anything at all to nonhumans for the slightest reason, or for no reason at all, without incurring any justifiable reproach. This defense claims that we are never guilty of neglecting the interests of other animals for one breathtakingly simple reason: they have no interests. Nonhuman animals have no interests, according to this view, because they are not capable of suffering. By this is not meant merely that they are not capable of suffering in all the ways that humans are—for instance, that a calf is not capable of suffering from the knowledge that it will be killed in six months time. That modest claim is, no doubt, true; but it does not clear humans of the charge of speciesism, since it allows that animals may suffer in other ways—for instance, by being given electric shocks, or being kept in small, cramped cages. The defense I am about to discuss is the much more sweeping, although correspondingly less plausible, claim that animals are incapable of suffering in any way at all; that they are, in fact, unconscious automata, possessing neither thoughts nor feelings nor a mental life of any kind.

Although, as we shall see in a later chapter, the view that animals are automata was proposed by the seventeenth-century French philosopher René Descartes, to most people, then and now, it is obvious that if, for example, we stick a sharp knife into the stomach of an unanesthetized dog, the dog will feel pain. That this is so is assumed by the laws in most civilized countries which prohibit wanton cruelty to animals. Readers whose common sense tells them that animals do suffer may prefer to skip the remainder of this section, moving straight on to page 312, since the pages in between do nothing but refute a position which they do not hold. Implausible as it is, though, for the sake of completeness this skeptical position must be discussed.

Do animals other than humans feel pain? How do we know? Well, how do we know if anyone, human or nonhuman, feels pain? We know that we ourselves can feel pain. We know this from the direct experiences of pain that we have when, for instance, somebody presses a lighted cigarette against the back of our hand. But how do we know that anyone else feels pain? We cannot directly experience anyone else's pain, whether that "anyone" is our best friend or a stray dog. Pain is a state of consciousness, a "mental event," and as such it can never be observed. Behavior like writhing, screaming, or drawing one's hand away from the lighted cigarette is not pain itself; nor are the recordings a neurologist might make of activity within the brain observations of pain itself. Pain is something that we feel, and we can only infer that others are feeling it from various external indications.

In theory, we *could* always be mistaken when we assume that other human beings feel pain. It is conceivable that our best friend is really a very cleverly constructed robot, controlled by a brilliant scientist so as to give all the signs of feeling pain, but really no more sensitive than any other machine. We can never know, with absolute certainty, that this is not the case. But while this might present a puzzle for philosophers, none of us has the slightest real doubt that our best friends feel pain just as we do. This is an inference, but a perfectly reasonable one, based on observations of their behavior in situations in which we would feel pain, and on the fact that we have every reason to assume that our friends are beings like us, with nervous systems like ours that can be assumed to function as ours do, and to produce similar feelings in similar circumstances.

If it is justifiable to assume that other humans feel pain as we do, is there any reason why a similar inference should be unjustifiable in the case of other animals?

Nearly all the external signs which lead us to infer pain in other humans can be seen in other species, especially the species most closely related to us—other species of mammals, and birds. Behavioral signs—writhing, facial contortions, moaning, yelping or other forms of calling, attempts to avoid the source of pain, appearance of fear at the prospect of its repetition, and so on—are present. In addition, we know that these animals have nervous systems very like ours, which respond physiologically as ours do when the animal is in circumstances in which we would feel pain: an initial rise of blood pressure, dilated pupils, perspiration, an increased pulse rate, and, if the stimulus continues, a fall in blood pressure. Although humans have a more developed cerebral cortex than other animals, this part of the brain is concerned with thinking functions rather than with basic impulses, emotions, and feelings. These impulses, emotions, and feelings are located in the diencephalon, which is well developed in many other species of animals, especially mammals and birds.[6]

We also know that the nervous systems of other animals were not artificially constructed to mimic the pain behavior of humans, as a robot might be artificially constructed. The nervous systems of animals evolved as our own did, and in fact the evolutionary history of humans and other animals, especially mammals, did not diverge until the central features of our nervous systems were already in existence. A capacity to feel pain obviously enhances a species' prospects of survival, since it causes members of the species to avoid sources of injury. It is surely unreasonable to suppose that nervous systems which are virtually identical physiologically, have a common origin and a common evolutionary function, and result in similar forms of behavior in similar circumstances should actually operate in an entirely different manner on the level of subjective feelings.

It has long been accepted as sound policy in science to search for the simplest possible explanation of whatever it is we are trying to explain. Occasionally it has been claimed that it is for this reason "unscientific" to explain the behavior of animals by theories that refer to the animal's conscious feelings, desires, and so on—the idea being that if the behavior in question can be explained without invoking consciousness or feelings, that will be the simpler theory. Yet we can now see that such explanations, when placed in the over-all context of the behavior of both human and nonhuman animals, are actually far more complex than their rivals. For we know from our own experience that explanations of our own behavior that did not refer to consciousness and the feeling of pain would be incomplete; and it is simpler to assume that the similar behavior of animals with similar nervous systems is to be explained in the same way than to try to invent some other explanation for the behavior of nonhuman animals as well as an explanation for the divergence between humans and nonhumans in this respect.

The overwhelming majority of scientists who have addressed themselves to this question agree. Lord Brain, one of the most eminent neurologists of our time, has said:

> I personally can see no reason for conceding mind to my fellow men and denying it to animals. . . . I at least cannot doubt that the interests and activities of animals are correlated with awareness and feeling in the same way as my own,

and which may be, for aught I know, just as vivid.[7]

While the author of a recent book on pain writes:

Every particle of factual evidence supports the contention that the higher mammalian vertebrates experience pain sensations at least as acute as our own. To say that they feel less because they are lower animals is an absurdity; it can easily be shown that many of their senses are far more acute than ours—visual acuity in certain birds, hearing in most wild animals, and touch in others; these animals depend more than we do today on the sharpest possible awareness of a hostile environment. Apart from the complexity of the cerebral cortex (which does not directly perceive pain) their nervous systems are almost identical to ours and their reactions to pain remarkably similar, though lacking (so far as we know) the philosophical and moral overtones. The emotional element is all too evident, mainly in the form of fear and anger.[8]

In Britain, three separate expert government committees on matters relating to animals have accepted the conclusion that animals feel pain. After noting the obvious behavioral evidence for this view, the Committee on Cruelty to Wild Animals said:

. . . we believe that the physiological, and more particularly the anatomical, evidence fully justifies and reinforces the commonsense belief that animals feel pain.

And after discussing the evolutionary value of pain they concluded that pain is "of clear-cut biological usefulness" and this is "a third type of evidence that animals feel pain." They then went on to consider forms of suffering other than mere physical pain, and added that they were "satisfied that animals do suffer from acute fear and terror." In 1965, reports by British government committees on experiments on animals, and on the welfare of animals under intensive farming methods, agreed with this view, concluding that animals are capable of suffering both from straightforward physical injuries and from fear, anxiety, stress, and so on.[9]

That might well be thought enough to settle the matter; but there is one more objection that needs to be considered. There is, after all, one behavioral sign that humans have when in pain which nonhumans do not have. This is a developed language. Other animals may communicate with each other, but not, it seems, in the complicated way we do. Some philosophers, including Descartes, have thought it important that while humans can tell each other about their experience of pain in great detail, other animals cannot. (Interestingly, this once neat dividing line between humans and other species has now been threatened by the discovery that chimpanzees can be taught a language.)[10] But as Bentham pointed out long ago, the ability to use language is not relevant to the question of how a being ought to be treated—unless that ability can be linked to the capacity to suffer, so that the absence of a language casts doubt on the existence of this capacity.

This link may be attempted in two ways. First, there is a hazy line of philosophical thought, stemming perhaps from some doctrines associated with the influential philosopher Ludwig Wittgenstein, which maintains that we cannot meaningfully attribute states of consciousness to beings without language. This position seems to me very implausible. Language may be necessary for abstract thought, at some level anyway; but states like pain are more primitive, and have nothing to do with language.

The second and more easily understood way of linking language and the existence of pain is to say that the best evidence that we can have that another creature is in pain is when he tells us that he is. This is a distinct line of argument, for it is not being denied that a non-language-user conceivably *could* suffer, but only that we could ever have sufficient reason to *believe* that he is suffering. Still, this line of argument fails too. As Jane Goodall has pointed out in her study of chimpanzees, *In the Shadow of Man*, when it comes to the expressions of feelings and emotions language is less important than in other areas. We tend to fall back on nonlinguistic modes of communication such as a cheering pat on the back, an exuberant embrace, a clasp of the hands, and so on. The basic signals we use to convey pain, fear, anger, love, joy, surprise, sexual arousal, and many other emotional states are not specific to our own species.[11]

Charles Darwin made an extensive study of this subject, and the book he wrote about it, *The Expression of the Emotions in Man and Animals*, notes countless nonlinguistic modes of expression. The statement "I am in pain" may be one piece of evidence for the conclusion that the speaker is in pain, but it is not the only possible evidence, and since people sometimes tell lies, not even the best possible evidence.

Even if there were stronger grounds for refusing to attribute pain to those who do not have a language, the consequences of this refusal might lead us to reject the conclusion. Human infants and young children are unable to use language. Are we to deny that a year-old child can suffer? If not, language cannot be crucial. Of course, most parents understand the responses of their children better than they understand the responses of other animals; but this is just a fact about the relatively greater knowledge that we have of our own species, and the greater contact we have with infants, as compared to animals. Those who have studied the behavior of other animals, and those who have pet animals, soon learn to understand their responses as well as we understand those of an infant, and sometimes better. Jane Goodall's account of the chimpanzees she watched is one instance of this, but the same can be said of those who have observed species less closely related to our own. Two among many possible examples are Konrad Lorenz's observations of geese and jackdaws, and N. Tinbergen's extensive studies of herring gulls.[12] Just as we can understand infant human behavior in the light of adult human behavior, so we can understand the behavior of other species in the light of our own behavior—and sometimes we can understand our own behavior better in the light of the behavior of other species.

So to conclude: there are no good reasons, scientific or philosophical, for denying that animals feel pain. If we do not doubt that other humans feel pain we should not doubt that other animals do so too.

Animals can feel pain. As we saw earlier, there can be no moral justification for regarding the pain (or pleasure) that animals feel as less important than the same amount of pain (or pleasure) felt by humans. But what exactly does this mean, in practical terms? To prevent misunderstanding I shall spell out what I mean a little more fully.

If I give a horse a hard slap across its rump with my open hand, the horse may start, but it presumably feels little pain. Its skin is thick enough to protect it against a mere slap. If I slap a baby in the same way, however, the baby will cry and presumably does feel pain, for its skin is more sensitive. So it is worse to slap a baby than a horse, if both slaps are administered with equal force. But there must be some kind of blow—I don't know exactly what it would be, but perhaps a blow with a heavy stick—that would cause the horse as much pain as we cause a baby by slapping it with our hand. That is what I mean by "the same amount of pain" and if we consider it wrong to inflict that much pain on a baby for no good reason then we must, unless we are speciesists, consider it equally wrong to inflict the same amount of pain on a horse for no good reason.

There are other differences between humans and animals that cause other complications. Normal adult human beings have mental capacities which will, in certain circumstances, lead them to suffer more than animals would in the same circumstances. If, for instance, we decided to perform extremely painful or lethal scientific experiments on normal adult humans, kidnaped at random from public parks for this purpose, every adult who entered a park would become fearful that he would be kidnaped. The resultant terror would be a form of suffering additional to the pain of the experiment. The same experiments performed on nonhuman animals would cause less suffering since the animals would not have the anticipatory dread of being kidnaped and experimented upon. This does not mean, of course, that it would be right to perform the experiment on animals, but only that there is a reason, which is *not* speciesist, for preferring to use animals rather than normal adult humans, if the experiment is to be done at all. It should be noted, however, that this same argument gives us a reason for preferring to use human infants—orphans perhaps—or retarded humans for experiments, rather than adults, since infants and retarded humans would also have no idea of what was going to happen to them. So far as this argument is concerned nonhuman animals and infants and retarded humans are in the same category; and if we use this argument to justify experiments on nonhuman animals we have to ask ourselves whether we are also prepared to allow experiments on human infants and retarded adults; and if we make a distinction between animals and these humans, on what basis can we do it, other than a barefaced—and morally indefensible —preference for members of our own species?

There are many areas in which the superior mental powers of normal adult humans make a difference: anticipation, more detailed memory, greater knowledge of what is happening, and so on. Yet these differences do not all point to greater suffering on the part of the normal human being. Sometimes an animal may suffer more because of his more limited understanding. If, for instance, we are taking prisoners in wartime we can explain to them that while they must submit to capture, search, and confinement they will not otherwise be harmed and will be set free at the conclusion of hostilities. If we capture a wild animal, however, we cannot explain that we are not threatening its life. A wild animal cannot distinguish an attempt to overpower and confine from an attempt to kill; the one causes as much terror as the other.

It may be objected that comparisons of the sufferings of different species are impossible to make, and that for this reason when the interests of animals and humans clash the principle of equality gives no guidance. It is probably true that comparisons of suffering between members of different species cannot be made precisely, but precision is not essential. Even if we were to prevent the infliction of suffering on animals only when it is quite certain that the interests of humans will not be affected to anything like the extent that animals are affected, we would be forced to make radical changes in our treatment of an-

imals that would involve our diet, the farming methods we use, experimental procedures in many fields of science, our approach to wildlife and to hunting, trapping and the wearing of furs, and areas of entertainment like circuses, rodeos, and zoos. As a result, a vast amount of suffering would be avoided.

So far I have said a lot about the infliction of suffering on animals, but nothing about killing them. This omission has been deliberate. The application of the principle of equality to the infliction of suffering is, in theory at least, fairly straightforward. Pain and suffering are bad and should be prevented or minimized, irrespective of the race, sex, or species of the being that suffers. How bad a pain is depends on how intense it is and how long it lasts, but pains of the same intensity and duration are equally bad, whether felt by humans or animals.

The wrongness of killing a being is more complicated. I have kept, and shall continue to keep, the question of killing in the background because in the present state of human tyranny over other species the more simple, straightforward principle of equal consideration of pain or pleasure is a sufficient basis for identifying and protesting against all the major abuses of animals that humans practice. Nevertheless, it is necessary to say something about killing.

Just as most humans are speciesists in their readiness to cause pain to animals when they would not cause a similar pain to humans for the same reason, so most humans are speciesists in their readiness to kill other animals when they would not kill humans. We need to proceed more cautiously here, however, because people hold widely differing views about when it is legitimate to kill humans, as the continuing debates over abortion and euthanasia attest. Nor have moral philosophers been able to agree on exactly what it is that makes it wrong to kill humans, and under what circumstances killing a human being may be justifiable.

Let us consider first the view that it is always wrong to take an innocent human life. We may call this the "sanctity of life" view. People who take this view oppose abortion and euthanasia. They do not usually, however, oppose the killing of nonhumans—so perhaps it would be more accurate to describe this view as the "sanctity of *human* life" view.

The belief that human life, and only human life, is sacrosanct is a form of speciesism. To see this, consider the following example.

Assume that, as sometimes happens, an infant has been born with massive and irreparable brain damage. The damage is so severe that the infant can never be any more than a "human vegetable," unable to talk, recognize other people, act independently of others, or develop a sense of self-awareness. The parents of the infant, realizing that they cannot hope for any improvement in their child's condition and being in any case unwilling to spend, or ask the state to spend, the thousands of dollars that would be needed annually for proper care of the infant, ask the doctor to kill the infant painlessly.

Should the doctor do what the parents ask? Legally, he should not, and in this respect the law reflects the sanctity of life view. The life of every human being is sacred. Yet people who would say this about the infant do not object to the killing of nonhuman animals. How can they justify their different judgments? Adult chimpanzees, dogs, pigs, and many other species far surpass the brain-damaged infant in their ability to relate to others, act independently, be self-aware, and any other capacity that could reasonably be said to give value to life. With the most intensive care possible, there are retarded infants who can never achieve the intelligence level of a dog. Nor can we appeal to the concern of the infant's parents, since they themselves, in this imaginary example (and in some actual cases), do not want the infant kept alive.

The only thing that distinguishes the infant from the animal, in the eyes of those who claim it has a "right to life," is that it is, biologically, a member of the species Homo sapiens, whereas chimpanzees, dogs, and pigs are not. But to use *this* difference as the basis for granting a right to life to the infant and not to the other animals is, of course, pure speciesism.*

It is exactly the kind of arbitrary difference that the most crude and overt kind of racist uses in attempting to justify racial discrimination.

This does not mean that to avoid speciesism we must hold that it is as wrong to kill a dog as it is to kill a normal human being. The only position that is irredeemably speciesist is the one that tries to make the boundary of the right to life run exactly parallel to the boundary of our own species. Those who hold the sanctity of life view do this because while distinguishing sharply between humans and other animals they allow no distinctions to be made within our own species, objecting to the killing of the severely retarded and the hopelessly senile as strongly as they object to the killing of normal adults.

To avoid speciesism we must allow that beings which are similar in all relevant respects have a similar right to life—and mere membership in our own biological species cannot be a morally relevant criterion for this right. Within these limits we could still hold that, for instance, it is worse to kill a normal adult human, with a capacity for self-awareness, and the ability to plan for the future and have meaningful relations with others, than it is to kill a mouse, which presumably does not share all of these characteristics; or we might appeal to the close family and other personal ties which humans have but mice do not have to the same degree; or we might think that it is the consequences for other humans, who will be put in fear of their own lives, that makes the crucial difference; or we might think it is some combination of these factors, or other factors altogether.

Whatever criteria we choose, however, we will have to admit that they do not follow precisely the boundary of our own species. We may legitimately hold that there are some fea-

*I am here putting aside religious views, for example the doctrine that all and only humans have immortal souls, or are made in the image of God. Historically these views have been very important, and no doubt are partly responsible for the idea that human life has a special sanctity. Logically, however, these religious views are unsatisfactory, since a reasoned explanation of why it should be that all humans and no nonhumans have immortal souls is not offered. This belief too, therefore, comes under suspicion as a form of speciesism. In any case, defenders of the "sanctity of life" view are generally reluctant to base their position on purely religious doctrines, since these doctrines are no longer as widely accepted as they once were.

tures of certain beings which make their lives more valuable than those of other beings; but there will surely be some nonhuman animals whose lives, by any standards, are more valuable than the lives of some humans. A chimpanzee, dog, or pig, for instance, will have a higher degree of self-awareness and a greater capacity for meaningful relations with others than a severely retarded infant or someone in a state of advanced senility. So if we base the right to life on these characteristics we must grant these animals a right to life as good as, or better than, such retarded or senile humans.

Now this argument cuts both ways. It could be taken as showing that chimpanzees, dogs, and pigs, along with some other species, have a right to life and we commit a grave moral offense whenever we kill them, even when they are old and suffering and our intention is to put them out of their misery. Alternatively one could take the argument as showing that the severely retarded and hopelessly senile have no right to life and may be killed for quite trivial reasons, as we now kill animals.

Since the focus of this book is on ethical questions concerning animals and not on the morality of euthanasia I shall not attempt to settle this issue finally. I think it is reasonably clear, though, that while both of the positions just described avoid speciesism, neither is entirely satisfactory. What we need is some middle position which would avoid speciesism but would not make the lives of the retarded and senile as cheap as the lives of pigs and dogs now are, nor make the lives of pigs and dogs so sacrosanct that we think it wrong to put them out of hopeless misery. What we must do is bring nonhuman animals within our sphere of moral concern and cease to treat their lives as expendable for whatever trivial purposes we may have. At the same time, once we realize that the fact that a being is a member of our own species is not in itself enough to make it always wrong to kill that being, we may come to reconsider our policy of preserving human lives at all costs, even when there is no prospect of a meaningful life or of existence without terrible pain.

I conclude, then, that a rejection of speciesism does not imply that all lives are of equal worth. While self-awareness, intelligence, the capacity for meaningful relations with others, and so on are not relevant to the question of inflicting pain—since pain is pain, whatever other capacities, beyond the capacity to feel pain, the being may have—these capacities may be relevant to the question of taking life. It is not arbitrary to hold that the life of a self-aware being, capable of abstract thought, of planning for the future, of complex acts of communication, and so on, is more valuable than the life of a being without these capacities. To see the difference between the issues of inflicting pain and taking life, consider how we would choose within our own species. If we had to choose to save the life of a normal human or a mentally defective human, we would probably choose to save the life of the normal human; but if we had to choose between preventing pain in the normal human or the mental defective—imagine that both have received painful but superficial injuries, and we only have enough painkiller for one of them—it is not nearly so clear how we ought to choose. The same is true when we consider other species. The evil of pain is, in itself, unaffected by the other characteristics of the being that feels the pain; the value of life is affected by these other characteristics.

Normally this will mean that if we have to choose between the life of a human being and the life of another animal we should choose to save the life of the human; but there may be special cases in which the reverse holds true, because the human being in question does not have the capacities of a normal human being. So this view is not speciesist, although it may appear to be at first glance. The preference, in normal cases, for saving a human life over the life of an animal when a choice *has* to be made is a preference based on the characteristics that normal humans have, and not on the mere fact that they are members of our own species. This is why when we consider members of our own species who lack the characteristics of normal humans we can no longer say that their lives are always to be preferred to those of other animals. This issue comes up in a practical way in the following chapter. In general, though, the question of when it is wrong to kill (painlessly) an animal is one to which we need give no precise answer. As long as we remember that we should give the same respect to the lives of animals as we give to the lives of those humans at a similar mental level, we shall not go far wrong.

Notes

1. For Bentham's moral philosophy, see his *Introduction to the Principles of Morals and Legislation*, and for Sidgwick's see *The Methods of Ethics* (the passage quoted is from the seventh edition, p. 382). As examples of leading contemporary moral philosophers who incorporate a requirement of equal consideration of interests, see R. M. Hare, *Freedom and Reason* (New York: Oxford University Press, 1963) and John Rawls, *A Theory of Justice* (Cambridge: Harvard University Press, Belknap Press, 1972). For a brief account of the essential agreement on this issue between these and other positions, see R. M. Hare, "Rules of War and Moral Reasoning," *Philosophy and Public Affairs*, vol. 1, no. 2 (1972).

2. Letter to Henri Gregoire, February 25, 1809.

3. Reminiscences by Francis D. Gage, from Susan B. Anthony, *The History of Woman Suffrage*, vol. 1; the passage is to be found in the extract in Leslie Tanner, ed., *Voices from Women's Liberation* (New York: Signet, 1970).

4. I owe the term "speciesism" to Richard Ryder.

5. *Introduction to the Principles of Morals and Legislation*, chapter 17.

6. Lord Brain, "Presidential Address" in C. A. Keele and R. Smith, eds., *The Assessment of Pain in Men and Animals* (London: Universities Federation for Animal Welfare, 1962).

7. Ibid., p. 11.

8. Richard Serjeant, *The Spectrum of Pain* (London: Hart-Davis, 1969), p. 72.

9. See the reports of the Committee on Cruelty to Wild Animals (Command Paper 8268, 1951), paragraphs 36–42; the Departmental Committee on Experiments on Animals (Command Paper 2641, 1965), paragraphs 179–182; and the Technical Committee to Enquire into the Welfare of Animals Kept under Intensive Livestock Husbandry Systems (Command Paper 2836, 1965), paragraphs 26–28 (London: Her Majesty's Stationery Office).

10. One chimpanzee, Washoe, has been taught the sign language used by deaf people, and acquired a vocabulary of 350 signs. Another, Lana, communicates in structured sentences by pushing buttons on a special machine. For a brief account of Washoe's abilities, see Jane van Lawick-Goodall, *In the Shadow of Man* (Boston: Houghton Mifflin, 1971), pp. 252–254; and for Lana, see *Newsweek*, 7 January 1974, and *New York Times*, 4 December 1974.

11. *In the Shadow of Man*, p. 225; Michael Peters makes a similar point in "Nature and Culture," in Stanley and Roslind Godlovitch and John Harris, eds., *Animals, Men and Morals* (New York: Taplinger Publishing Co., 1972).

12. Konrad Lorenz, *King Solomon's Ring* (New York: T. Y. Crowell, 1952); N. Tinbergen, *The Herring Gull's World*, rev. ed. (New York: Basic Books, 1974).

The Case for Animal Rights

Tom Regan

Tom Regan believes that what is fundamentally wrong with our treatment of nonhuman animals is that it implies that they are simply resources for our use. Regan rejects the various grounds that have been proposed to support the view that all of our duties toward animals are indirect, ultimately based on duties to other human beings. He also rejects grounds proposed for the view that we do have direct duties toward animals but that these duties do not support animal rights. The correct grounding for our duties toward animals and their rights against us, Regan argues, is the inherent value they possess, equally with ourselves, as experiencing subjects of life.

I regard myself as an advocate of animal rights—as a part of the animal rights movement. That movement, as I conceive it, is committed to a number of goals, including:

- the total abolition of the use of animals in science;
- the total dissolution of commercial animal agriculture;
- the total elimination of commercial and sport hunting and trapping.

There are, I know, people who profess to believe in animal rights but do not avow these goals. Factory farming, they say, is wrong—it violates animals' rights—but traditional animal agriculture is all right. Toxicity tests of cosmetics on animals violates their rights, but important medical research—cancer research, for example—does not. The clubbing of baby seals is abhorrent, but not the harvesting of adult seals. I used to think I understood this reasoning. Not any more. You don't change unjust institutions by tidying them up.

What's wrong—fundamentally wrong—with the way animals are treated isn't the details that vary from case to case. It's the whole system. The forlornness of the veal calf is pathetic, heart wrenching; the pulsing pain of the chimp with electrodes planted deep in her brain is repulsive; the slow, tortuous death of the raccoon caught in the leg-hold trap is agonizing. But what is wrong isn't the pain, isn't the suffering, isn't the deprivation. These compound what's wrong. Sometimes—often—they make it much, much worse. But they are not the fundamental wrong.

The fundamental wrong is the system that allows us to view animals as *our resources*, here for *us*—to be eaten, or surgically manipulated, or exploited for sport or money. Once we accept this view of animals—as our resources—the rest is as predictable as it is regrettable. Why worry about their loneliness, their pain, their death? Since animals exist for us, to benefit us in one way or another, what harms them really doesn't matter—or matters only if it starts to bother us, makes us feel a trifle uneasy when we eat our veal escalope, for example. So, yes, let us get veal calves out of solitary confinement, give them more space, a little straw, a few companions. But let us keep our veal escalope.

But a little straw, more space and a few companions won't eliminate—won't even touch—the basic wrong that attaches to our viewing and treating these animals as our resources. A veal calf killed to be eaten after living in close confinement is viewed and treated in this way: but so, too, is another who is raised (as they say) 'more humanely'. To right the wrong of our treatment of farm animals requires more than making rearing methods 'more humane'; it requires the total dissolution of commercial animal agriculture.

From "The Case for Animal Rights," in *In Defense of Animals* edited by Peter Singer (1985), pp. 13–26. Reprinted by permission of Peter Singer and Tom Regan.

How we do this, whether we do it or, as in the case of animals in science, whether and how we abolish their use—these are to a large extent political questions. People must change their beliefs before they change their habits. Enough people, especially those elected to public office, must believe in change—must want it—before we will have laws that protect the rights of animals. This process of change is very complicated, very demanding, very exhausting, calling for the efforts of many hands in education, publicity, political organization and activity, down to the licking of envelopes and stamps. As a trained and practising philosopher, the sort of contribution I can make is limited but, I like to think, important. The currency of philosophy is ideas—their meaning and rational foundation—not the nuts and bolts of the legislative process, say, or the mechanics of community organization. That's what I have been exploring over the past ten years or so in my essays and talks and, most recently, in my book, *The Case for Animal Rights.* I believe the major conclusions I reach in the book are true because they are supported by the weight of the best arguments. I believe the idea of animal rights has reason, not just emotion, on its side.

In the space I have at my disposal here I can only sketch, in the barest outline, some of the main features of the book. Its main themes—and we should not be surprised by this—involve asking and answering deep, foundational moral questions about what morality is, how it should be understood and what is the best moral theory, all considered. I hope I can convey something of the shape I think this theory takes. The attempt to do this will be (to use a word a friendly critic once used to describe my work) cerebral, perhaps too cerebral. But this is misleading. My feelings about how animals are sometimes treated run just as deep and just as strong as those of my more volatile compatriots. Philosophers do—to use the jargon of the day—have a right side to their brains. If it's the left side we contribute (or mainly should), that's because what talents we have reside there.

How to proceed? We begin by asking how the moral status of animals has been understood by thinkers who deny that animals have rights. Then we test the mettle of their ideas by seeing how well they stand up under the heat of fair criticism. If we start our thinking in this way, we soon find that some people believe that we have no duties directly to animals, that we owe nothing to them, that we can do nothing that wrongs them. Rather, we can do wrong acts that involve animals, and so we have duties regarding them, though none to them. Such views may be called indirect duty views. By way of illustration: suppose your neighbour kicks your dog. Then your neighbour has done something wrong. But not to your dog. The wrong that has been done is a wrong to you. After all, it is wrong to upset people, and your neighbour's kicking your dog upsets you. So you are the one who is wronged, not your dog. Or again: by kicking your dog your neighbour damages your property. And since it is wrong to damage another person's property, your neighbour has done something wrong—to you, of course, not to your dog. Your neighbour no more wrongs your dog than your car would be wronged if the windshield were smashed. Your neighbour's duties involving your dog are indirect duties to you. More generally, all of our duties regarding animals are indirect duties to one another—to humanity.

How could someone try to justify such a view? Someone might say that your dog doesn't feel anything and so isn't hurt by your neighbour's kick, doesn't care about the pain since none is felt, is as unaware of anything as is your windshield. Someone might say this, but no rational person will, since, among other considerations, such a view will commit anyone who holds it to the position that no human being feels pain either—that human beings also don't care about what happens to them. A second possibility is that though both humans and your dog are hurt when kicked, it is only human pain that matters. But, again, no rational person can believe this. Pain is pain wherever it occurs. If your neighbour's causing you pain is wrong because of the pain that is caused, we cannot rationally ignore or dismiss the moral relevance of the pain that your dog feels.

Philosophers who hold indirect duty views—and many still do—have come to understand that they must avoid the two defects just noted: that is, both the view that animals don't feel anything as well as the idea that only human pain can be morally relevant. Among such thinkers the sort of view now favoured is one or other form of what is called *contractarianism*.

Here, very crudely, is the root idea: morality consists of a set of rules that individuals voluntarily agree to abide by, as we do when we sign a contract (hence the name contractarianism). Those who understand and accept the terms of the contract are covered directly; they have rights created and recognized by, and protected in, the contract. And these contractors can also have protection spelled out for others who, though they lack the ability to understand morality and so cannot sign the contract themselves, are loved or cherished by those who can. Thus young children, for example, are unable to sign contracts and lack rights. But they are protected by the contract none the less because of the sentimental interests of others, most notably their parents. So we have, then, duties involving these children, duties regarding them, but no duties to them. Our duties in their case are indirect duties to other human beings, usually their parents.

As for animals, since they cannot understand contracts, they obviously cannot sign; and since they cannot sign, they have no rights. Like children, however, some animals are the objects of the sentimental interest of others. You, for example, love your dog or cat. So those animals that enough people care about (companion animals, whales, baby seals, the American bald eagle), though they lack rights themselves, will be protected because of the sentimental interests of people. I have, then, according to contractarianism, no duty directly to your dog or any other animal, not even the duty not to cause them pain or suffering; my duty not to hurt them is a duty I have to those people who care about what happens to them. As for other animals, where no or little sentimental interest is present—in the case of farm animals, for example, or laboratory rats—what duties we have grow weaker and weaker, perhaps to vanishing point. The pain and death they endure, though real, are not wrong if no one cares about them.

When it comes to the moral status of animals' contractarianism could be a hard view to refute if it were an adequate theoretical approach to the moral status of human beings. It is not adequate in this latter respect, however, which makes the question of its adequacy in the former case, regarding animals, utterly moot. For consider: morality, according to the (crude) contractarian position before us, consists of rules that people agree to abide by. What people? Well, enough to make a difference—enough, that is, *collectively* to have the power to enforce the rules that are drawn up in the contract. That is very well and good for the signatories but not so good for anyone who is not asked to sign. And there is nothing in contractarianism of the sort we are discussing that guarantees or requires that everyone will have a chance to participate equally in framing the rules of morality. The result is that this approach to ethics could sanction the most blatant forms of social, economic, moral and political injustice, ranging from a repressive caste system to systematic racial or sexual discrimination. Might, according to this theory, does make right. Let those who are the victims of injustice suffer as they will. It matters not so long as no one else—no contractor, or too few of them—cares about it. Such a theory takes one's moral breath away . . . as if, for example, there would be nothing wrong with apartheid in South Africa if few white South Africans were upset by it. A theory with so little to recommend it at the level of the ethics of our treatment of our fellow humans cannot have anything more to recommend it when it comes to the ethics of how we treat our fellow animals.

The version of contractarianism just examined is, as I have noted, a crude variety, and in fairness to those of a contractarian persuasion it must be noted that much more refined, subtle and ingenious varieties are possible. For example, John Rawls, in his *A Theory of Justice*, sets forth a version of contractarianism that forces contractors to ignore the accidental features of being a human being—for example, whether one is white or black, male or female, a genius or of modest intellect. Only by ignoring such features, Rawls believes, can we ensure that the principles of justice that contractors would agree upon are not based on bias or prejudice. Despite the improvement a view such as Rawls's represents over the cruder forms of contractarianism, it remains deficient: it systematically denies that we have direct duties to those human beings who do not have a sense of justice—young children, for instance, and many mentally retarded humans. And yet it seems reasonably certain that, were we to torture a young child or a retarded elder, we would be doing something that wronged him or her, not something that would be wrong if (and only if) other humans with a sense of justice were upset. And since this is true in the case of these humans, we cannot rationally deny the same in the case of animals.

Indirect duty views, then, including the best among them, fail to command our rational assent. Whatever ethical theory we should accept rationally, therefore, it must at least recognize that we have some duties directly to animals, just as we have some duties directly to each other. The next two theories I'll sketch attempt to meet this requirement.

The first I call the cruelty-kindness view. Simply stated, this says that we have a direct duty to be kind to animals and a direct duty not to be cruel to them. Despite the familiar, reassuring ring of these ideas, I do not believe that this view offers an adequate theory. To make this clearer, consider kindness. A kind person acts from a certain kind of motive—compassion or concern, for example. And that is a virtue. But there is no guarantee that a kind act is a right act. If I am a generous racist, for example, I will be inclined to act kindly towards members of my own race, favouring their interests above those of others. My kindness would be real and, so far as it goes, good. But I trust it is too obvious to require argument that my kind acts may not be above moral reproach—may, in fact, be positively wrong because rooted in injustice. So kindness, notwithstanding its status as a virtue to be encouraged, simply will not carry the weight of a theory of right action.

Cruelty fares no better. People or their acts are cruel if they display either a lack of sympathy for or, worse, the presence of enjoyment in another's suffering. Cruelty in all its guises is a bad thing, a tragic human failing. But just as a person's being motivated by kindness does not guarantee that he or she does what is right, so the absence of cruelty does not ensure that he or she avoids doing what is wrong. Many people who perform abortions, for example, are not cruel, sadistic people. But that fact alone does not settle the terribly difficult question of the morality of abortion. The case is no different when we examine the ethics of our treatment of animals. So, yes, let us be for kindness and against cruelty. But let us not suppose that being for the one and against the other answers questions about moral right and wrong.

Some people think that the theory we are looking for is utilitarianism. A utilitarian accepts two moral principles. The first is that of equality: everyone's interests count, and similar interests must be counted as having similar weight or importance. White or black, American or Iranian, human or animal—everyone's pain or frustration matters, and matters just as much as the equivalent pain or frustration of anyone else. The second principle a utilitarian accepts is that of utility: do the act that will bring about the best balance between satisfaction and frustration for everyone affected by the outcome.

As a utilitarian, then, here is how I am to approach the task of deciding what I morally ought to do: I must ask who will be affected if I choose to do one thing rather than another, how much each individual will be affected, and where the best results are most likely to lie—which option, in other words, is most likely to bring about the best results, the best balance between satisfaction and frustration. That option, whatever it may be, is the one I ought to choose. That is where my moral duty lies.

The great appeal of utilitarianism rests with its uncompromising *egalitarianism:* everyone's interests count and count as much as the like interests of everyone else. The kind of odious discrimination that some forms of contractarianism can justify—discrimination based on race or sex, for example—seems disallowed in principle by utilitarianism, as is speciesism, systematic discrimination based on species membership.

The equality we find in utilitarianism, however, is not the sort an advocate of animal or human rights should have in mind. Utilitarianism has no room for the equal moral rights of different individuals because it has no room for their equal inherent value or worth. What has value for the utilitarian is the satisfaction of an individual's interests, not the individual whose interests they are. A universe in which you satisfy your desire for water, food and warmth is, other things being equal, better than a universe in which these desires are frustrated. And the same is true in the case of an animal with similar desires. But neither you nor the animal has any value in your own right. Only your feelings do.

Here is an analogy to help make the philosophical point clearer: a cup contains different liquids, sometimes sweet, sometimes bitter, sometimes a mix of the two. What has value are the liquids: the sweeter the better, the bitterer the worse. The cup, the container, has no value. It is what goes into it, not what they go into, that has value. For the utilitarian you and I are like the cup; we have no value as individuals and thus no equal value. What has value is what goes into us, what we serve as receptacles for; our feelings of satisfaction have positive value, our feelings of frustration negative value.

Serious problems arise for utilitarianism when we remind ourselves that it enjoins us to bring about the best consequences. What does this mean? It doesn't mean the best consequences for me alone, or for my family or friends, or any other person taken individually. No, what we must do is, roughly, as follows: we must add up (somehow!) the separate satisfactions and frustrations of everyone likely to be affected by our choice, the satisfactions in one column, the frustrations in the other. We must total each column for each of the options before us. That is what it means to say the theory is aggregative. And then we must choose that option which is most likely to bring about the best balance of totalled satisfactions over totalled frustrations. Whatever act would lead to this outcome is the one we ought morally to perform—it is where our moral duty lies. And that act quite clearly might not be the same one that would bring about the best results for me personally, or for my family or friends, or for a lab animal. The best aggregated consequences for everyone concerned are not necessarily the best for each individual.

That utilitarianism is an aggregative theory—different individuals' satisfactions or frustrations are added, or summed, or totalled—is the key objection to this theory. My Aunt Bea is old, inactive, a cranky, sour person, though not physically ill. She prefers to go on living. She is also rather rich. I could make a fortune if I could get my hands on her money, money she intends to give me in any event, after she dies, but which she refuses to give me now. In order to avoid a huge tax bite, I plan to donate a handsome sum of my profits to a local children's hospital. Many, many children will benefit from my generosity, and much joy will be brought to their parents, relatives and friends. If I don't get the money rather soon, all these ambitions will come to naught. The once-in-a-lifetime opportunity to make a real killing will be gone. Why, then, not kill my Aunt Bea? Of course I *might* get caught. But I'm no fool and, besides, her doctor can be counted on to co-operate (he has an eye for the same investment and I happen to know a good deal about his shady past). The deed can be done . . . professionally, shall we say. There is *very* little chance of getting caught. And as for my conscience being guilt-ridden, I am a resourceful sort of fellow and will take more than sufficient comfort—as I lie on the beach at Acapulco—in contemplating the joy and health I have brought to so many others.

Suppose Aunt Bea is killed and the rest of the story comes out as told. Would I have done anything wrong? Anything immoral? One would have thought that I had. Not according to utilitarianism. Since what I have done has brought about the best balance between totalled satisfaction and frustration for all those affected by the outcome, my action is not wrong. Indeed, in killing Aunt Bea the physician and I did what duty required.

This same kind of argument can be repeated in all sorts of cases, illustrating, time after time, how the utilitarian's position leads to results that impartial people find morally callous. It *is* wrong to kill my Aunt Bea in the name of bringing about the best results for others. A good end does not justify an evil means. Any adequate moral theory will have to explain why this is so. Utilitarianism fails in this respect and so cannot be the theory we seek.

What to do? Where to begin anew? The place to begin, I think, is with the utilitarian's view of the value of the individual—or, rather, lack of value. In its place, suppose we consider that you and I, for example, do have value as individuals—what we'll call *inherent value*. To say we have such value is to say that we are something more than, something different from, mere receptacles. Moreover, to ensure that we do not pave the way for such injustices as slavery or sexual discrimination, we must believe that all who have inherent value have it equally, regardless of their sex, race, religion, birthplace and so on. Similarly to be discarded as irrelevant are one's talents or skills, intelligence and wealth, personality or pathology, whether one is loved and admired or despised and loathed. The genius and the retarded child, the prince and the pauper, the brain surgeon and the fruit vendor, Mother Teresa and the most unscrupulous used-car salesman—all have inherent value, all possess it equally, and all have an equal right to be treated with respect, to be treated in ways that do not reduce them to the status of things, as if they existed as resources for others. My value as an individual is independent of my usefulness to you. Yours is not dependent on your usefulness to me. For either of us to treat the other in ways that fail to show respect for the other's independent value is to act immorally, to violate the individual's rights.

Some of the rational virtues of this view— what I call the rights view—should be evident. Unlike (crude) contractarianism, for example, the rights view *in principle* denies the moral tolerability of any and all forms of racial, sexual or social discrimination; and unlike utilitarianism, this view *in principle* denies that we can justify good results by using evil means that violate an individual's rights—denies, for example, that it could be moral to kill my Aunt Bea to harvest beneficial consequences for others. That would be to sanction the disrespectful treatment of the individual in the name of the social good, something the rights view will not—categorically will not—ever allow.

The rights view, I believe, is rationally the most satisfactory moral theory. It surpasses all other theories in the degree to which it illuminates and explains the foundation of our duties to one another—the domain of human morality. On this score it has the best reasons, the best arguments, on its side. Of course, if it were possible to show that only human beings are included within its scope, then a person like myself, who believes in animal rights, would be obliged to look elsewhere.

But attempts to limit its scope to humans only can be shown to be rationally defective. Animals, it is true, lack many of the abilities humans possess. They can't read, do higher mathematics, build a bookcase or make *baba ghanoush*. Neither can many human beings, however, and yet we don't (and shouldn't) say that they (these humans) therefore have less inherent value, less of a right to be treated with respect, than do others. It is the *similarities* between those human beings who most clearly, most non-controversially have such value (the people reading this, for example), not our differences, that matter most. And the really crucial, the basic similarity is simply this: we are each of us the experiencing subject of a life, a conscious creature having an individual welfare that has importance to us whatever our usefulness to others. We want and prefer things, believe and feel things, recall and expect things. And all these dimensions of our life, including our pleasure and pain, our enjoyment and suffering, our satisfaction and frustration, our continued existence or our untimely death—all make a difference to the quality of our life as lived, as experienced, by us as individuals. As the same is true of those animals that concern us (the ones that are eaten and trapped, for example), they too must be viewed as the experiencing subjects of a life, with inherent value of their own.

Some there are who resist the idea that animals have inherent value. 'Only humans have such value,' they profess. How might this narrow view be defended? Shall we say that only humans have the requisite intelligence, or autonomy, or reason? But there are many, many humans who fail to meet these standards and yet are reasonably viewed as having value above and beyond their usefulness to others. Shall we claim that only humans belong to the right species, the species *Homo sapiens*? But this is blatant speciesism. Will it be said, then, that all—and only—humans have immortal souls? Then our opponents have their work cut out for them. I am myself not ill-disposed to the proposition that there are immortal souls. Personally, I profoundly hope I have one. But I would not want to rest my position on a controversial ethical issue on the even more controversial question about who or what has an immortal soul. That is to dig one's hole deeper, not to climb out. Rationally, it is better to resolve moral issues without making more controversial assumptions than are needed. The question of who has inherent value is such a question, one that is resolved more rationally without the introduction of the idea of immortal souls than by its use.

Well, perhaps some will say that animals have some inherent value, only less than we have. Once again, however, attempts to defend this view can be shown to lack rational justification. What could be the basis of our having more inherent value than animals? Their lack of reason, or autonomy, or intellect? Only if we are willing to make the same judgement in the case of humans who are similarly deficient. But it is not true that such humans—the retarded child, for example, or the mentally deranged—have less inherent value than you or I. Neither, then, can we rationally sustain the view that animals like them in being the experiencing subjects of a life have less inherent value. *All* who have inherent value have it *equally*, whether they be human animals or not.

Inherent value, then, belongs equally to those who are the experiencing subjects of a life. Whether it belongs to others—to rocks and rivers, trees and glaciers, for example—we do not know and may never know. But neither do we need to know, if we are to make the case for animal rights. We do not need to know, for example, how many people are eligible to vote in the next presidential election before we can know whether I am. Similarly, we do not need to know how many individuals have inherent value before we can know that some do. When it comes to the case for animal rights, then, what we need to know is whether the animals that, in our culture, are routinely eaten, hunted and used in our laboratories, for example, are like us in being subjects of a life. And we do know this. We do know that

many—literally, billions and billions—of these animals are the subjects of a life in the sense explained and so have inherent value if we do. And since, in order to arrive at the best theory of our duties to one another, we must recognize our equal inherent value as individuals, reason—not sentiment, not emotion—reason compels us to recognize the equal inherent value of these animals and, with this, their equal right to be treated with respect.

That, *very* roughly, is the shape and feel of the case for animal rights. Most of the details of the supporting argument are missing. They are to be found in the book to which I alluded earlier. Here, the details go begging, and I must, in closing, limit myself to four final points.

The first is how the theory that underlies the case for animal rights shows that the animal rights movement is a part of, not antagonistic to, the human rights movement. The theory that rationally grounds the rights of animals also grounds the rights of humans. Thus those involved in the animal rights movement are partners in the struggle to secure respect for human rights—the rights of women, for example, or minorities, or workers. The animal rights movement is cut from the same moral cloth as these.

Second, having set out the broad outlines of the rights view, I can now say why its implications for farming and science, among other fields, are both clear and uncompromising. In the case of the use of animals in science, the rights view is categorically abolitionist. Lab animals are not our tasters; we are not their kings. Because these animals are treated routinely, systematically as if their value were reducible to their usefulness to others, they are routinely, systematically treated with a lack of respect, and thus are their rights routinely, systematically violated. This is just as true when they are used in trivial, duplicative, unnecessary or unwise research as it is when they are used in studies that hold out real promise of human benefits. We can't justify harming or killing a human being (my Aunt Bea, for example) just for these sorts of reason. Neither can we do so even in the case of so lowly a creature as a laboratory rat. It is not just refinement or reduction that is called for, not just larger, cleaner cages, not just more generous use of anaesthetic or the elimination of multiple surgery, not just tidying up the system. It is complete replacement. The best we can do when it comes to using animals in science is—not to use them. That is where our duty lies, according to the rights view.

As for commercial animal agriculture, the rights view takes a similar abolitionist position. The fundamental moral wrong here is not that animals are kept in stressful close confinement or in isolation, or that their pain and suffering, their needs and preferences are ignored or discounted. All these *are* wrong, of course, but they are not the fundamental wrong. They are symptoms and effects of the deeper, systematic wrong that allows these animals to be viewed and treated as lacking independent value, as resources for us—as, indeed, a renewable resource. Giving farm animals more space, more natural environments, more companions does not right the fundamental wrong, any more than giving lab animals more anaesthesia or bigger, cleaner cages would right the fundamental wrong in their case. Nothing less than the total dissolution of commercial animal agriculture will do this, just as, for similar reasons I won't develop at length here, morality requires nothing less than the total elimination of hunting and trapping for commercial and sporting ends. The rights view's implications, then, as I have said, are clear and uncompromising.

My last two points are about philosophy, my profession. It is, most obviously, no substitute for political action. The words I have written here and in other places by themselves don't change a thing. It is what we do with the thoughts that the words express—our acts, our deeds—that changes things. All that philosophy can do, and all I have attempted, is to offer a vision of what our deeds should aim at. And the why. But not the how.

Finally, I am reminded of my thoughtful critic, the one I mentioned earlier, who chastised me for being too cerebral. Well, cerebral I have been: indirect duty views, utilitarianism, contractarianism—hardly the stuff deep passions are made of. I am also reminded, however, of the image another friend once set before me—the image of the ballerina as expressive of disciplined passion. Long hours of sweat and toil, of loneliness and practice, of doubt and fatigue: those are the discipline of her craft. But the passion is there too, the fierce drive to excel, to speak through her body, to do it right, to pierce our minds. That is the image of philosophy I would leave with you, not 'too cerebral' but *disciplined passion*. Of the discipline enough has been seen. As for the passion: there are times, and these not infrequent, when tears come to my eyes when I see, or read, or hear of the wretched plight of animals in the hands of humans. Their pain, their suffering, their loneliness, their innocence, their death. Anger. Rage. Pity. Sorrow. Disgust. The whole creation groans under the weight of the evil we humans visit upon these mute, powerless creatures. It *is* our hearts, not just our heads, that call for an end to it all, that demand of us that we overcome, for them, the habits and forces behind their systematic oppression. All great movements, it is written, go through three stages: ridicule, discussion, adoption. It is the realization of this third stage, adoption, that requires both our passion and our discipline, our hearts and our heads. The fate of animals is in our hands. God grant we are equal to the task.

Animal Rights Revisited

Jan Narveson

Jan Narveson examines three accounts of morality—the libertarian account, the utilitarian account, and the contractarian account and concludes that the contractarian account, which clearly leaves animals outside of the scope of morality, is the most defensible.

What do we owe to the animals? What, that is to say, do we owe them *qua* animal, rather than in their various possible roles as pets, watchdogs, potential sources of protein, or potential sources of knowledge on various matters of medical interest? Our usual repertoire of moral ideas does not give us a very clear answer to this question, for those ideas have been framed for dealing with our fellow humans, by and large. When we address ourselves to this nonstandard case, then, we must scrutinize those ideas rather closely. Our habit of relying on our "intuitions" will not get us far, for those intuitions, I believe, push us in different directions when we try to extend them, and extension is necessary under the circumstances.

It may be well to begin by trying to assemble the options, though even to do this is assuredly to begin to do moral theory. Here, then, are the main ones as I see it:

(1) The moral status of animals is simply that of things, potentially useful or dangerous in various ways; the proper way to deal with them is simply whatever way is dictated by our interests in such things.

(2) Animals are in the same moral boat as we are: to wit, they have the capacity to suffer or prosper, to be better or worse off, and we ought to attach the same weight to a given degree of well-or ill-being on their part as we do to our own, endeavoring to do the best we can for all concerned.

Abridged from "Animal Rights Revisited," in *Ethics and Animals* edited by Harlan B. Miller and William H. Williams (1983), pp. 45–59. Reprinted by permission of The Humana Press Inc. and the author.

(3) Animals are in the same moral boat as we are, but it is a different boat: to wit, they have the right to lead their lives as they choose, without interference from us—but also, without *help* from us, if we do not wish to give it.

This list of options is not exhaustive of the logical possibilities, obviously. I have come to suspect, however, that it exhausts all the *interesting* possibilities. And curiously enough, those are the same possibilities that obtain with respect to our moral dealings with our fellow humans. In effect, the three views are (1) that morality is based on the interests of the agent only, at bottom; (2) that morality is based on the interests of all parties, taken equally; and (3) that morality is based not on interests as such, but rather on respect for the capacity to lead a life as one chooses. These, as I say, seem to me to be the interesting possibilities, and in the present paper I wish to explore each at some length. Eventually, as will be seen, I will be inclining towards view (1). The plan of this paper will simply be to discuss each one in turn. I will, however, discuss them in reverse order, beginning with what is, in a sense, the most committal view, in the sense of the one that would make our duties to animals the most stringent of the three.

1

View (3) is, of course, Libertarianism. What makes it interesting for our purposes is not so much that it is a plausible view about animals' rights, as that it is an interesting and even plausible view about people's rights that prompts us to think about why it should not apply to animals too, if in fact, it does not.

The essence of libertarianism, I believe, is to be found in this passage from Robert Nozick's much-discussed *Anarchy, State and Utopia:* "A line (or hyper-plane) circumscribes an area in moral space around an individual" (1974, p. 57). Some entirely non-arbitrary method for determining that space is supposed to be in principle available, and once determined, justice consists simply in not crossing that line. Moral beings are not to be damaged, harmed, used exclusively as means to the ends of others, and so on, and the prohibitions on doing so are supposed to be absolute rather than *prima facie*. It is essentially a property view of justice. Within the region enclosed by one's moral boundaries, the individual may do whatever he wishes: his will is there absolute, as absolute as that of the most absolute despot. His freedom of action is limited by the boundaries of others. Often, of course, the relevant boundaries will be literal, physical ones delimiting regions of land or whatever, but the idea is the same whether or not the items in the region are physically "in" it.

I believe that Libertarianism can be sufficiently characterized as the view that people have only *negative rights*, and that those rights are absolute. But since there is some confusion about notions of negative and positive rights, it might be well to pause for a moment to fix this idea. The *normative content* of any statement about rights consists in a correlative statement(s) about the obligations or duties of a specified or specifiable class of others: the right of A to x consists (normatively speaking) in the duty of B to do y, for relevant B. Now, the difference between negative and positive rights is this:

To say that A has a *negative right* that p = B must not intentionally *make it the case that* ∼ p (or: bring it about that ∼ p) whereas to say that A has a *positive right* that p = B must (help, to some relevant degree, to) *bring it about that p.*

Thus, if p is the proposition that A does x, then the negative right of A to do it consists in its being the case that B is obliged not to prevent or interfere with A's doing x. Nothing, however, is said about the case where A is, for lack of power, ability, or requisite means, unable to do x. But if A has the positive right to do x, then the duty of B is to (help) make good the deficiencies of A. Note that this distinction cuts across the distinction between welfare rights and action-rights, which is often confused with it. But whether p consists in A being in some condition or having something, or in A doing something, the distinction between A's negative right and the positive right that p remains: it is the difference between the duty not to hinder and the duty to help.

It has sometimes been supposed that there is a conceptual impossibility in attributing rights to animals. But if this is so, it is at least not because of the sheer normative structure of rights statements. It is easy enough to see what I am being told to do or refrain from doing when I am told that animals have rights. The question is surely not about that, but rather about how they could *come to be eligible* for the status(es) in question. What is there about animals, if anything, that makes it impossible for them to be eligible for it while humans are? To answer this question, of course, is to supply a moral theory, and so far as I can see, there is no reason to doubt that it is the same theory, whatever it is, for animals as for humans: this one theory will tell us what it is that endows whatever has it with rights and makes whatever lacks it lack rights. In the case of libertarianism, unfortunately, this matter remains obscure. Robert Nozick has presented a characterization of what he takes to be the relevant property(ies): rationality, free will, moral agency, and "the ability to regulate and guide its life in accordance with some overall conception it chooses to accept" (1974, p. 49). Unfortunately, it is not clear that we all think that possession of those properties is either necessary or sufficient for having the sort of rights libertarianism proclaims for (at least) us humans. . . .

Meanwhile there is the question of what the implications would be if animals *did* have side-constraint-type rights of the same sort as we supposedly do. Are there circumstances in which we could morally do what we now in fact do, viz., eat them?

One thing that this hard-headed theory does

allow is the acknowledgment that there are circumstances in which we morally *could* eat *people*. For on it, I need only have a valid contract with someone that calls for my eating him/her under certain conditions, and then have those circumstances arise. Someone might find the prospect of living the kind of life I offer prior to his/her tenure expiring so attractive as to be quite prepared to live on those terms. . . . Now, the question arises whether Nozick was not too quick in dismissing the suggestion that animals might find it a good deal from their point of view to be well-fed and otherwise looked after in exchange for allowing us to slaughter them and turn them into hamburger. I rather think he was; but we gain some insight into moral theory by considering the matter, anyway.

Nozick's objection to this is that even if I bring someone into existence for the purpose of violating his rights, that still does not justify my violating them. "An existing person has claims, even against those whose purpose in creating him was to violate those claims" (1974, p. 38). Yes, but those claims are only those involved in negative rights. So the proper procedure is as follows: Bring the newborn individual up until it reaches the age of Libertarian discretion. At that point, you give it its choice. Either stay in the game, which involves being well treated until age such-and-such, and then be eaten, or we turn you out next Tuesday. This seems consistent with Libertarian principles.

Now it seems very likely that human individuals would rarely or never have to accept such a macabre option. For one thing, the neighbors would surely put up a great fuss at the idea that such a deal is even being offered, let alone accepted; but more importantly, the individual will invariably have a better deal if the other option to move out is elected. But this may well not be true with animals. Few have such sympathy with the cow that if someone makes the cow that offer and it elects to move out, someone else will take reasonable care of it. And then we run up against the other snag, which is that the cow is not about to *address* itself to the question of which horn of this bovine dilemma to take. We would have to do its thinking for it. That, of course, is the very reason why cows do not seem eligible for

libertarian constraints anyway: not even the world-class geniuses in that species are very plausibly thought to be busy formulating *weltanschauungen* by the light of which to make their life decisions! . . .

In current circumstances, it is certainly true that there would be very few domestic animals if vegetarianism held sway, and so it is true that from the species point of view, so to speak, The Cow is doing a lot better with slaughter than it would without. But if we reject the "species point of view," as it seems to me we should (*whose* point of view is it, after all?), that is beside the point. What is not beside the point is that the cow would do very badly indeed if turned out into the woods to fend for itself, even if one could find a wood to let it fend in. It may perhaps also be true, though, that given animal utility schedules, the ones that are raised by "methods which as nearly as possible reduce animals to the level of vegetables" (as I put it when first addressing myself to this matter (Narveson, 1977, p. 162) might nevertheless do better on their own. Perhaps from the pig's point of view, it is better to root about half-starved in the forest, dying of frost or at the mouths of hungry wolves, than to be crowded into a penful of fellow pigs and forcefed until one could scarcely move even if there were room to.

It may seem that this is social contract talk rather than libertarian talk. In section 3 below, I will explain why I think that is not so. Meanwhile, my conclusion is that libertarianism either leaves the animals with no rights at all, or with the same rights we have; and if the latter, then it is unclear that vegetarianism issues from it. Humane slaughter, perhaps, and possibly the condemnation of certain particularly unattractive methods of animal husbandry, and quite likely the condemnation of sheer gratuitous torture, but that is about it. Above all, meanwhile, there remains the enormous problem of what sort of foundations might be available for this theory; and even if provided it is problematic at best whether animals get anything out of them. Perhaps if clear foundations are discerned, they will make it excruciatingly clear that animals do not qualify for rights at all. Let us, then, move on to the next theory, utilitarianism.

2

At this stage of the game, it is presumably not necessary to say very much about the general framework of utilitarianism. Its leading principle is statable in two words: maximize utility! Or in five: utility counts; nothing else does. The simplicity ends there, unfortunately. We do not know quite what it means to say that everyone else's utility counts as much as our own, if it is even meaningful at all; nor do we know whether it is possible to act in accordance with that principle. Most unfortunately of all, we do not know *why* we ought to do so, if we ought. Utilitarianism, I think, has the same kind of foundational problem as does libertarianism; perhaps even worse. . . .

What assumptions is it reasonable to make about the utility of animals? It seems very reasonable indeed to suppose that animals can feel pain and pleasure. It seems reasonable to attribute to them some degree of intelligence (but unclear just what we are attributing to them in doing so, nor whether it is a capacity of the same sort we attribute to humans). Does that matter? Mill thought it did. It is tempting to say that he thought that the utility of intelligent beings counts more than the utility of less intelligent ones, but that surely will not do. What we must say instead, and what Mill really does say (I think), is that intelligent beings have a greater capability of utility than less intelligent ones: the satisfaction of a satisfied Socrates (if that is possible) involves a great deal more utility than the satisfaction of a satisfied pig. For that matter, even the satisfactions of a dissatisfied Socrates outweigh those of the pig. One question to worry about is: Is Mill right, or even believable, about that? Another is: What follows if he is? We tend, I believe, to be too fast on the second question, but let us take up the first anyway.

Utility is to be a quantity of something; but what? Classically, it is pleasure; but it is not clear how helpful it is to say that. Another idea (perhaps) is that utility is really just preference. More precisely, it is that x has more utility for A than y if A prefers x to y. This is the view employed in recent decision theory. But recent decision theory does not assume cardinal utility, which classical utilitarianism certainly does. (Cardinal utility is utility of which it makes sense to say not only that x has more utility than y, but also how much.) Or rather, recent decision theory does not employ interpersonally comparable cardinal utility, for there are ways of cardinalizing over preferences, at least in a sizable class of cases. Without interpersonally comparable cardinal utility, the pig would properly be able to criticize Mill for anthropocentricity. Even with it, it is not clear how we are to proceed. Mill's point of reference in this matter is the judgment of those who have experienced both; but how much does this include? How do we go about having the pig's experiences? And if we do not and cannot, then how do we know that getting ourselves into piggish-seeming situations is even relevant, let alone decisive? If *we* were pigs, rather than just philosophers attempting to find out what it is presumably like to be them, perhaps we would enjoy wallowing in the mud ever so much more than we now enjoy reading Plato?

We do, certainly, make judgments of the form "people would in general be happier if . . ." Although there is a good deal of disagreement about such judgments, it may also be admitted that we are not entirely out in left field in making them. The problem is to make judgments of the form, "people *and animals* would be happier if . . .," and that is trickier. It is acutely trickier in just the cases we have to worry about in the present paper—all the cases wherein there is a genuine conflict between the interests of us and the animals: namely, if our main interest in animals is realized, then their interest in *whatever* they may be interested in is thwarted, because they end up on our dinner plates. And that is a loss of utility that, in the case of humans, would certainly not be thought to be outweighed by the gourmet's interest in them, however powerful that interest might be. So we would surely be headed for vegetarianism if there were no reason for downrating the animals' utility quite substantially.

Actually, there are two sorts of "downrating." One way is to claim that the utility of animals, although admittedly quite comparable to ours, simply does not count, or that it counts very little: as if, for instance, we were allowed to multiply the animal's utility score by 0.01. The other way is to claim that animals have very little utility, really, at least by comparison with our own. As we have noted, utilitarianism must surely take the latter tack. It is axiomatic on it, after all, that everyone counts for one and none for more (or less).

What might reasonably (as opposed to just self-interestedly) persuade us that animals *do* have a lesser capacity for utility than we? Many would point to their supposedly lesser intelligence as a justification for treating them as we do. But they may or may not have in mind intelligence as a factor influencing utility. They may instead be thinking of it as an intrinsic good. Can we find a reason for supposing that intellect affects capacity for utility, then?

One thing that has long intrigued me in this connection is the involvement of intelligent beings with their own, or indeed, any futures. We are acutely aware of the future stretching out before us, and of the past in the other direction. We are, indeed, often so involved with time that we might be accused of neglecting our present. And we can at least conjecture that with animals things are different. Perhaps it is still excessively anthropomorphic to think so, but we do seem to think that animal awareness of their own future, indeed of their own identity in general, is rather dim; this despite homing pigeons and whatnot, who certainly seem to have a clear idea where to go next. But we do suppose that they are, as the saying goes, guided by instinct rather than reason. (It is unclear what to think of that. But we will suppose it makes some sense, and is reasonably close to true.)

Still, *why* might this matter? I have suggested that animals might "experience only more or less isolated sensations and uninterpreted feelings. If such beings are killed, all that happens is that a certain series of such feelings which would otherwise have occurred, do not occur . . . When beings having a future are killed, they lose that future; when beings lacking it are killed, they do not. So no interest in continued life is lost in their case" (Narveson, 1977). Well, setting aside the critical question of whether some such thing is true of animals, there remains the question just why it might make the kind of difference I supposed

it did *on utilitarian grounds*. If two beings, one of whom has and one of whom lacks a future, each had a nonutilitarian-type right to its future, then we could agree that if we painlessly killed each of them, we would have violated one creature's rights, but not the other's. Unfortunately, utilitarians are not entitled to nonutilitarian rights. So if this difference is to make a difference, it must be because beings with futures experience more utility than beings without. For otherwise, the two creatures in question might be exactly on all fours *qua* utility sources. The universe might have lost exactly the *same* amount of utility by their deaths, instead of vastly more in the one case than the other.

Can we say "Well, so much the worse for the universe, then: let it go its way, and we will go ours!"? Not easily. If we *care* only about sophisticated beings with futures and the ability to master differential equations or to comprehend the late quartets of Beethoven *and* we admit that these favored beings do not actually experience any more utility than the average cow, then we obviously have abandoned utilitarianism.

What we need to think, therefore, if we are to remain utilitarians *and* we think that normal humans are much greater in their capacity for utility than animals, is that at each typical moment in the sentient life of a human, he or she is chalking up a much higher utility score than a beast at any typical moment for it. And what the basis of this judgment would be is, again, unclear. There is certainly the danger of anthropocentric bias here, if anywhere, one would think. Presumably utilitarianism supposes that utility estimates are not simply value judgments: when we compare the utility of experiencer X with that of experiencer Y, we are *not* supposed to be simply reporting our preference for having X or having Y around. Instead, I take it we are supposed to be reporting on the value *to X* of having X around and the value *to Y* of having Y around (so to speak). There is supposed to be an objective quantity, existing independently of the feelings and interests of observers, that simply is the amount of utility that being enjoys at that time. The basis of our report may still be preferences, but if so, they are its preferences rather than ours. The utilitarian, indeed, is someone who prefers to maximize over the preferences of all and sundry sources of utility, whereas nonutilitarians do not, but in principle the quantities at issue are what they are independently of this difference, or so we suppose. . . .

If that amount of elitism is accepted, what about vegetarianism? It is axiomatic that some beings may, in principle, be sacrificed for others, on the utilitarian view. But may animals be sacrificed merely in order to enable humans to have a wider variety of gustatory pleasures? In order for it to be so, the marginal increment of such pleasure for humans has to exceed the marginal cost to the animals. Consider, then, the case of Kentucky Fried Chicken. Suppose that one chicken feeds three people for one meal. We might suppose that the cost of this is all the utility that the chicken might have experienced had it been allowed to live to a ripe old age. But wrongly. For that is only the cost to *that* chicken. But it is also reasonable to believe that, under the carnivorous regime we are investigating, this chicken will be replaced by another one which would not have existed at all if its predecessor were not eaten. In fact, the plot is thicker than that, for as Derek Parfit points out, its predecessor would most likely not have existed either, were it not for the prospect of *its* being eaten. Given that we in fact raise animals to be eaten, it is not unreasonable to believe that the total utility of the animal population is enormously higher than it would be if we did not eat them, because so comparatively few would exist at all otherwise. And if we count that way, then the marginal cost to any given animal is the wrong thing to weigh against the marginal benefit to us of eating it. Viewed globally, those costs are very handily outweighed by the total utility increase in question.

That, of course, is to assume that we can apply "total" rather than average or some other sort of utilitarianism here. If we do not, and insist that it is the average utility of animals that should be our sole concern, the prospects for animal rights are much better, perhaps. Or are they? For now we also must reckon the cost of upkeep and care for the animals, which is borne by people. Their cost would certainly not be borne, in fact, if the animals were not beneficial to people in this way. Chickens would be raised only to lay eggs,

cows for milk; but most would have little if any use. It might be argued that the loss in utility to people from having to care for useless beasts would exceed the loss to the beasts if they were (painlessly) killed. So even on average principles, it is far from clear that maximization would preclude the eating of animals.

Of course, if we do use total utilitarianism, then we have another small matter to contend with. Animals are, in fact, quite an inefficient source of food. If humans ate only vegetarian diets, it would be possible for there to be a great many more of *them*. And if, as has been imagined above, each human is so much larger a source of utility than any animal, it might seem that the tables are turned again, since the large animal population is keeping the human population smaller, and yet the human population is so much more efficient a source of utility than the animal one. But that, in turn, is to assume that the marginal utility change associated with the addition of each further human is in fact positive, and it can be argued that *that* is not so. Perhaps a world with two billion humans would have more total utility than one with ten billions. If so, we would have a global justification of carnivorousness from the above arguments.

I am sure that no one will think me excessively conservative if I conclude with the observation that the situation regarding the ethics of our treatment of animals is not entirely clear if we opt for utilitarianism. This is not exactly a surprise, but it is of some importance that it should be so. The vegetarians do not have things all their way on that theory; and it is, I think, the theory that offers the best prospects for animal rights among those I am considering.

This brings us to the last one, contractarianism. On that theory, I shall argue, the situation is not unclear at all, at least if what is in question is basic animal rights: they don't have any.

3

The tendency in the past few years has been to take John Rawls' well-known theory of justice as the model of contractualist moral theory. I must therefore begin by explaining why that is a mistake.

On the contract view of morality, morality is a sort of agreement among rational, independent, self-interested persons, persons who have something to gain from entering into such an agreement. It is of the very essence, on such a theory, that the parties to the agreement know who they are and what they want— what they in particular want, and not just what a certain general class of beings of which they are members generally tend to want. Now, Rawls' theory has his parties constrained by agreements that they would have made if they *did not* know who they were. But if we can have that constraint, why should we not go just a little further and specify that one is not only not to know *which* person he or she is, but also whether he or she will be a person *at all:* reason on the assumption that you might turn out to be an owl, say, or a vermin, or a cow. We may imagine that *that* possibility would make quite a difference, especially if one were tempted by maximin! (Some proponents of vegetarianism, I believe, are tempted by it, and do extend the veil of ignorance that far.)

The "agreement" of which morality consists is a voluntary undertaking to limit one's behavior in various respects. In a sense, it consists in a renunciation of action on unconstrained self-interest. It is, however, self-interested overall. The idea is to come out ahead in the long run, by refraining, contingently on others' likewise refraining, from certain actions, the general indulgence in which would be worse for all and therefore for oneself. There are well-known problems generated by this characterization, and I do not claim to have solutions for them. I only claim that this is an important and plausible conception of morality, worth investigating in the present context.

A major feature of this view of morality is that it explains why we have it and who is a party to it. We have it for reasons of long-run self-interest, and parties to it include all and only those who have *both* of the following characteristics: (1) they stand to gain by subscribing to it, at least in the long run, compared with not doing so, and (2) they are *capable* of entering into (and keeping) an agreement. Those

not capable of it obviously cannot be parties to it, and among those capable of it, there is no reason for them to enter into it if there is nothing to gain for them from it, no matter how much the others might benefit.

Given these requirements, it will be clear why animals do not have rights. For there are evident shortcomings on both scores. On the one hand, humans have nothing generally to gain by voluntarily refraining from (for instance) killing animals or "treating them as mere means." And on the other, animals cannot generally make agreements with us anyway, even if we wanted to have them do so. Both points are worth expanding on briefly.

(1) In saying that humans have "nothing generally to gain" from adopting principled restraints against behavior harmful to animals, I am in one respect certainly overstating the case, for it is possible that animal food, for instance, is bad for us, or that something else about animals, which requires such restraint from us, would be for our long-term benefit. Those are issues I mostly leave on one side here, except to note that some people may think that we gain on the score of purity of soul by treating animals better. But if the purity in question is moral purity, then that would be question-begging on the contractarian conception of morality. In any case, those people are, of course, welcome to treat animals as nicely as they like. The question is whether others may be prevented from treating animals badly, e.g., by eating them, and the "purity of soul" factor cannot be appealed to in that context.

A main motive for morality on the contract view is, of course, diffidence. Humans have excellent reason to be fearful about each other. Our fellows, all and sundry, are quite capable of doing damage to us, and not only capable but often quite interested in doing so; and their rational (or at least, calculative) capacities only make things worse. There is compelling need for mutual restraint. Now, animals can, many of them, be harmful to us. But the danger is rather specialized and limited in most cases, and in those cases we can deal with it by such methods as caging the animals in question, or by shooting them, and so on. There is no general need for moral methods, and there is also the question whether they are available. In any case, we have much to gain from eating them, and if one of the main planks in a moral platform is refraining from killing merely for self-interest, then it is quite clear that such a plank, in the case of animals, would not be worth it from the point of view of most of us. Taking our chances in the state of nature would be preferable.

(2) What about the capability of entering into and keeping such agreements? Animals have been pretty badly maligned on this matter in the past, I gather. Really beastly behavior is a phenomenon pretty nearly unique to the human species. But still, when animals refrain from killing other animals or people just for the fun of it, there is no good reason to think that they do so out of moral principle. Rather, it is just that it is not really their idea of fun!

There remains a genuine question about the eligibility of animals for morality on the score of their abilities. A very few individuals among some animal species have been enabled, after years of highly specialized work, to communicate in fairly simple ways with people. That does not augur well for animals' entering quite generally into something as apparently sophisticated as an agreement. But of course agreements can be tacit and unwritten, even unspoken. Should we postulate, at some such inexplicit level, an "agreement" among humans, it is largely tacit there. People do not enter into agreements to refrain from killing each other, except in fairly specialized cases; the rule against killing that we (virtually) all acknowledge is one we adopt out of common sense and antecedent inculcation by our mentors. Still, it is reasonable to say that when one person does kill another one, he or she is (among other things) taking *unfair advantage* of the restraint that one's fellows have exercised with regard toward one over many years. But can any such thing be reasonably said of animals? I would think not.

On the whole, therefore, it seems clear that contractarianism leaves animals out of it, so far as rights are concerned. They are, by and large, to be dealt with in terms of our self-interest, unconstrained by the terms of hypothetical agreements with them. Just exactly what our interest in them is may, of course, be matter for debate; but that those are the terms on which we may deal with them is, on this view of morality, overwhelmingly indicated.

There is an evident problem about the treatment of what I have called "marginal cases" on this view, of course: infants, the feebleminded, and the incapacitated are in varying degrees in the position of the animals in relation to us, are they not? True: but the situation is very different in several ways. For one thing, we generally have very little to gain from treating such people badly, and we often have much to gain from treating them well. For another, marginal humans are invariably members of families, or members of other groupings, which makes them the object of love and interest on the part of other members of those groups. Even if there were an interest in treating a particular marginal person badly, there would be others who have an interest in their being treated well and who are themselves clearly members of the moral community on contractarian premises. Finally, it does have to be pointed out that there is genuine question about the morality of, for instance, euthanasia, and that infanticide has been approved of in various human communities at various times. On the whole, it seems to me not an insurmountable objection to the contractarian account that we grant marginal humans fairly strong rights.

It remains that we may think that suffering is a bad thing, no matter whose. But although we think so, we do not think it is so bad as to require us to become vegetarians. Here by 'we,' of course, I mean most of us. And what most of us think is that, although suffering is too bad and it is unfortunate for animals that they are turned into hamburgers at a tender age, we nevertheless are justified on the whole in eating them. If contractarianism is correct, then these attitudes are not inconsistent. And perhaps it is.

Pain, Amelioration, and the Choice of Tactics

R. G. Frey

R. G. Frey argues that utilitarianism does not provide a strong case for animal rights because (1) some animals are already reared and killed without suffering; (2) factory farming could be reformed; and (3) the widespread practice of vegetarianism would cause great disutility.

The Argument and the Concerned Individual

If the pain food animals undergo and the period over which they undergo it were insignificant, then I suspect many people would not be unduly worried by factory farming, with the result that they might well either see no need for the argument from pain and suffering, or see it as a manifestation of an undue sensitivity. Either way, the chances of the argument serving as the vehicle of widespread dietary change would recede.

The above, however, is certainly not the picture of factory farming which Singer paints, which, whether one considers *Animal Liberation, Practical Ethics,* or (with James Mason) *Animal Factories,*[1] is in the blackest terms. As we saw in the last chapter, he thinks, and would have us think, of factory farming in terms of animals who 'are so crowded together and restricted in their movements that their lives seem to be more of a burden than a benefit to them'[2] and who 'do not have pleasant lives'.[3] His view is that these animals lead miserable lives, that, in short, the pain inflicted upon them is substantial and its duration prolonged.

The argument itself points the direction in which the meat-eater will try to move: since what is held to be wrong with the particular farming practices objected to is that they are

Abridged from *Rights, Killing and Suffering* (Oxford: Basil Blackwell, 1983), pp. 175–189. Reprinted by permission of R. G. Frey. Notes renumbered.

productive of pain, the meat-eater will, among other things, try to make improvements in and to find alternatives to these practices. It is by no means obvious that such improvements and alternatives are not to be had, so that the only remaining course is to abolish intensive farming. Nothing whatever in, say, *Animal Liberation* rules out such improvements and alternatives; thus, any conclusion to the effect that the only way to mitigate, reduce, or eliminate the pains of food animals is to abolish factory farming is simply not licensed by that book.

If we do think of factory farming as Singer would have us, then . . . vast numbers of intensively farmed food animals, such as cattle, cows, sheep, a great many hogs, some pigs, elude the argument from pain and suffering. For vast numbers of commercially-farmed animals lead lives which are not, on balance, miserable, nor are those methods of rearing which are held to produce misery in the cases of laying hens and veal calves used on all food animals. Singer concedes the point: he remarks that, for example, 'as long as sheep and cattle graze outdoors . . . arguments directed against factory farming do not imply that we should cease eating meat altogether.'[4]

Two things follow. First, even if the argument from pain and suffering were successful, it would demand only that we abstain from the flesh of those creatures leading miserable lives; and even if we did so, large-scale, technology-intensive, commercial farming would by no means disappear, since there are numerous food animals so farmed who do not lead miserable lives.

Second, the amelioration argument becomes applicable. The more animals that can be brought to lead pleasant lives, the more animals that escape the argument from pain and suffering and so may be eaten. A concerned individual, therefore, can perfectly consistently strive, not for the abolition of factory farming, but for improvements and alternative methods on factory farms, in order that the animals no longer lead, on balance, miserable lives. With this the case, factory farming could continue, consistently with the application of the argument to it.

In short, if the argument demands that we abstain from the flesh of creatures whose lives are a burden to them, then a perfectly consistent response from the concerned individual, besides pointing to the huge numbers of commercially-farmed as well as traditionally-farmed animals which escape the argument, is to do his best to reduce the misery incurred on factory farms. Thus, when Singer has us think of factory farms in terms of the quality of life being lived upon them (and remarks such as 'our society tolerates methods of meat production that confine sentient animals in cramped, unsuitable conditions for the entire duration of their lives'[5] leave little doubt that, at least for those animals covered by his argument, he regards the quality of their lives as very low), the task of the concerned individual is to improve the quality of the lives being lived on those farms. It is just not true, however, that the only way to do this, the only tactic available, is to abolish large-scale, commercial farming.

One can always insist, of course, that the quality of life of the commercially farmed animals in question (remember, vast numbers of such animals are not in question) will never rise high enough; but this sort of issue cannot be decided *a priori*. Precisely how high a quality of life must be reached before animals may be said to be leading pleasant lives is, as we have seen, a contentious and complex issue; but we may at least use as a benchmark the situation at present. As improvements in and alternatives to the particular farming practices objected to arise, we can reasonably regard the pain associated with these practices as diminishing, if the improvements and alternatives are of the sort our concerned individual is seeking.

We have here, then, two parties, the Singer vegetarian and the concerned individual, both of whom are concerned to reduce the pain and suffering involved in factory farming. The Singer vegetarian's way is to adopt vegetarianism; the concerned individual's way is, among other things, to seek improvements in and alternatives to those practices held to be the source of the pain and suffering in question.

Suffering: Miserable Life and Single Experience Views

Singer's remarks on suffering in farming are not always of the sort depicted in the previous section. In both *Animal Liberation* and *Practical Ethics,* he occasionally writes as if any amount of suffering whatever sufficed, in terms of his argument, to condemn some method of rearing animals for food. For instance, he remarks that his 'case against using animals for food is at its strongest when animals are made to lead miserable lives . . .',[6] with the implication that his argument applies even when food animals suffer on a few or even a single occasion. Again, of traditional livestock farming, he maintains that it involves suffering, even if one has on occasion to go to such things as the breaking up of herds in order to find it, and he remarks in *Animal Liberation,* of these and other aspects of traditional farming, that 'it is difficult to imagine how animals could be raised for food without suffering in any of these ways.'[7]

Passages such as these suggest that Singer believes his argument condemns any method of rearing animals for food which causes them any suffering, however transient, however low-level, indeed, which causes them even a single, isolated painful experience. When he speaks of the permissibility of eating only 'the flesh of animals reared and killed without suffering',[8] therefore, he might be taken to mean by 'without suffering', not suffering of an amount and duration short of that required to make a life miserable, but any suffering whatever, so that the permissibility claim extends only to animals who have not had a single painful experience, a single trace of suffering in being bred and killed for food. But if this is what he means, how can he allow, as we have seen that he does, that sheep and cattle (these he cites as examples only,[9] so there may well, even in his eyes, be others) escape his argument? For it seems extremely unlikely that sheep and cattle are reared for food without a single painful experience. So either he is inconsistent to allow these exceptions, because he is operating with something like the single experience view of suffering, or he consistently allows them, but only because he is operating with something like the miserable life view of suffering.

These two views of suffering plainly do not come to the same thing. In order to lead, on balance, a pleasant life, pain, even significant pain, need not be absent from that life; indeed, it can recur on a daily basis, provided it falls short of that quantity over that duration required to tip the balance in the direction of a miserable life. Certainly, isolated, painful experiences or, for that matter, painful interludes, cannot, without further argument, be said to produce a miserable life.

Singer's whole position is affected by this ambiguity, if not inconsistency, over suffering. For instance, one of the most important points he wants to make concerns the possibility of rearing animals painlessly:

> Whatever the theoretical possibilities of rearing animals without suffering may be, the fact is that the meat available from butchers and supermarkets comes from animals who did suffer while being reared. So we must ask ourselves, not: is it *ever* right to eat meat? but: is it right to eat *this* meat?[10]

In *Practical Ethics,* he says that the question is not 'whether animal flesh *could* be produced without suffering, but whether the flesh we are considering buying *was* produced without suffering.'[11] But he has already allowed that vegetarianism is not demanded of us with respect to sheep and beef cattle, precisely because they do not lead miserable lives; so how can he say of all meats that it is a fact 'that the meat available from butchers and supermarkets comes from animals who did suffer while

being reared'? Again, there is a question of consistency. The problem can be favourably resolved, of course, if Singer shifts from the miserable life view of suffering to something like the single experience view; for he can be reasonably certain that the meat on display in supermarkets, including that from sheep and beef cattle, has come from animals who have had at least one painful experience, in being reared for food.

Without this shift, Singer has difficulty in discouraging you from buying the meat in question. If you are standing before the meats from sheep and beef cattle in your supermarket, if you have read Singer's book, and if you put to yourself the question of whether the meats before you have come from animals who have suffered in the course of being reared for food, then, on the miserable life view of suffering, you may cite Singer's own works to justify your purchase of the meats. You have every reason to believe that sheep and beef cattle do not lead miserable lives and so escape his argument; you have no reason whatever to believe, of course, that commercially- and traditionally-farmed food animals of any sort have not suffered at least once at human hands.

We have here, then, two views of suffering and, accordingly, two views on the argument from pain and suffering of what counts as a morally unacceptable method of rearing animals for food. On one, a method is unacceptable if it so affects an animal's quality of life as to make it miserable. This is why Singer so often stresses confinement in cramped conditions: this has the effect, which isolated painful experiences or interludes do not, of converting a life from a benefit to a burden. This view of suffering is compatible, however, with farm animals experiencing pain. On the second view, a method of rearing is unacceptable if it produces any pain or suffering whatever, whether or not the animal's general quality of life is affected thereby.

This division over unacceptable methods has several obvious implications here. First, to see one's task as reducing suffering in commercial farming is on one view of suffering, at least in many cases, not really to the point. Since the reduction of suffering is nevertheless compatible with the presence of suffering, only if the method of reduction eliminates all suffering in rearing may reduction, on something like the single experience view, really be to the point. On the miserable life view, however, any reduction in suffering is *prima facie* to the point, since that view is concerned with the quality of life of animals. That is, though it is tempting to think one method of rearing more acceptable than another if it involves considerably less suffering, this is only true on the miserable life view, at least if the method which causes less suffering causes any suffering; for reduction in suffering is very likely to affect animals' quality of life. This is true of any attempt to reduce suffering in farming, whether it succeeds partially or wholly, since, extraordinary circumstances aside, any decrease in suffering represents an increase or a contributory factor to an increase in quality of life.

Second, a meat-eater will not respond to both views of suffering in the same way; in the case of the miserable life view, his response will be much more varied. Broadly speaking, there are the methods of rearing themselves and the animals, and the meat-eater will, for example, seek ever gradual reduction in suffering through, for example, ever better improvements in and alternatives to (very) painful methods and the development of new pain-preventing and pain-killing drugs. He will seek development on these fronts simultaneously. In the case of something like the single experience view, however, since it is unlikely that any improvements in or alternatives to present methods would not involve even a single painful experience, a single trace of suffering, there may seem little point in seeking continuous evolution in rearing methods, beyond, say, those initial measures which substantially improve on the methods under attack. Accordingly, the meat-eater will be forced to rely primarily on pain-preventing and pain-killing drugs, an area in which he will seek continuous technological advances.

There is also the further possibility of genetic engineering to consider, to which both John Rodman[12] and Michael Martin[13] have drawn attention. So far as something like the single experience view is concerned, genetic engineering would have to take the form of the development of food animals which lacked the ability to feel pain. Precisely how feasible that is, I do not know; but given the incredible advances in genetic engineering during the past 30 years, it would be rash to dismiss the idea out of hand. On the miserable life view, however, nothing so dramatic is required; here, the development of animals who felt pain less intensively or who felt it only in some minimal sense or who felt it only above a certain threshold would, especially given evolution in rearing methods and pain-preventing and pain-killing drugs, suffice to ensure the animals did not have miserable lives.

Finally, though the single experience view may strike some readers as reflecting an undue sensitivity, I shall not pursue this claim; rather, I want to draw attention to a rather curious upshot of the view. If the only acceptable method of rearing animals for food is one free of even a single painful experience or trace of suffering, then it is hard to see why the same should not be said of pets. It is extremely unlikely, however, that any method of rearing and keeping pets could be entirely without pain and suffering; so if we must give up farming animals because there are no morally acceptable ways of doing so, then it would appear that we must give up rearing and keeping pets on the same ground. But if the only acceptable method of rearing animals, whether for food or companionship, is one free of all pain and suffering, then it is hard to see why the same should not be said of our own children. It is extremely unlikely, however, that any method of rearing children could be entirely without pain or suffering; so if we must give up farming animals because there are no morally acceptable methods of doing so, then it would appear that we must give up having children on the same ground.

On the other hand, if it is acceptable to rear children by painful methods, why is it unacceptable to rear food animals by painful methods? Nothing is gained by saying that the pain we inflict upon children is in order to benefit them (this, I think, is questionable anyway, a good portion of the time), whereas the pain we inflict upon food animals is in order to benefit ourselves, i.e., in order to eat them; for, so far, it has not been shown that it is wrong to benefit ourselves in this way, that the end of eating meat is immoral. Indeed, it was the infliction of pain that was to have shown this. Nor is anything gained by saying that, in the case of children, we at least seek, or, probably more accurately, ought to seek to rear them by methods as painless as we can devise, since the concerned individual I have been describing is quite prepared to consent to this in the case of animals. Nor will it do to say that the level of pain and suffering in food animals cannot be brought to a level commensurate with their leading pleasant lives; not only is one not entitled to legislate in this way on what is not a conceptual matter but it is also not at all obvious, if the concerned individual pursues evolution in rearing methods, drugs, and genetic engineering, that this claim is true.

It is tempting to say that the suffering of children is necessary whereas that of food animals is unnecessary, but it is not at all clear that this is the case. If there is no method of rearing children which is free of all suffering, and if there is no method of rearing animals for food or as pets which is free of all suffering, then the suffering in each case is necessary. If there were a way to rear children or to turn them into responsible, upright citizens without suffering, then it would be incumbent upon us to adopt it; and if there were a way of turning animals into food without suffering, it would be equally incumbent upon us to take it. Certainly, my concerned individual concurs in this; so, on this score, if the suffering in the one case is necessary, then so is it in the other. If we shift the terms of the argument to a different level, so that suffering is necessary *only if* it is inflicted in order for us to live, then the suffering in both cases is unnecessary. Just as I can live without meat, so I can live without children; they are as superfluous to my existence, to my carrying on living, as cars, houses, rose bushes, and pets. In this sense, then, if the only way to avoid unnecessary suffering in pets and food animals is to give them up entirely and cease breeding them, then it seems that we should give up having children for the same reason.

Now I am not suggesting that one cannot draw any differences among these cases; that would be silly. On something like the single experience view of suffering, however, the criterion of acceptability in rearing methods is pitched so high that we appear barred from

rearing any feeling creature, including our own children. Readers may well believe, therefore, that we must cast our sights lower. To do so, however, is to settle for a criterion of acceptability which permits some suffering. Precisely how much will be a matter of dispute; but a strong contender for the criterion, in both man and beast, will be the miserable life view. This in turn makes the varied course advocated by the concerned individual into an option on all fours with Singer's option of vegetarianism.

The Concerned Individual's Tactic as a Response to the Argument

The concerned individual's tactic is a direct response to Singer's argument: it addresses itself precisely to what the argument from pain and suffering objects to in factory farming. Indeed, it arises directly out of the terms of that argument. This fact enables us to appreciate several further points about the two tactics before us.

First, someone who took *Animal Liberation* and Singer's argument seriously might maintain that what Singer has shown is not that it is wrong to eat meat but that it is wrong to rear and kill animals by (very) painful methods; and this same reader might very well go on to conclude, not that we must all become vegetarians, but rather that we must (a) strive to improve conditions on factory farms, to eradicate some of the devices and practices upon them, and to replace these devices and practices with more humane ones, (b) divert resources into the development of new and relatively painless methods of breeding, feeding, and killing animals, of new pain-preventing and pain-killing drugs, of new types of tranquillizers and sedatives, etc., and (c) seek further appropriate breakthroughs in genetic engineering. After all, as we have seen, if we could be practically certain that the meat before us did not come from an animal bred and/or killed by (very) painful methods, and if we ate the meat, then Singer's argument would provide no ground for complaint against us. Accordingly, why not seek to obtain that practical certainty? The problem would then be how to go about this, and the concerned individual's tactic arises as an option.

Once we see that the concerned individual's tactic arises out of the terms of Singer's argument, we are in a position to appreciate that, even if we take that argument in its own terms and take it seriously, vegetarianism is not the obvious conclusion to draw from it. The course advocated by the concerned individual could equally well be the conclusion drawn. One needs some further reason for picking the one tactic as opposed to the other.

Second, as the meat-eater's option flourishes, Singer's case for vegetarianism is progressively undercut. That case loses its applicability, as the amount and intensity of pain produced on factory farms diminish. In other words, his case for vegetarianism hinges upon the actual state of evolution in rearing methods, drugs, and genetic engineering: each development in these areas which reduces pain in farming undercuts Singer's position still further.

If it is true that pain in farming has been drastically reduced or eliminated, however, why should the erosion of his position bother Singer? Whether or not it bothers Singer, it certainly is going to bother countless other vegetarians. For the concerned individual's tactic envisages the continuation of meat-eating and, with (some) changed methods, intensive farming; and the whole point is that, under the conditions set out, the argument from pain and suffering is compatible with, and places no further barrier in the way of, these things.

Third, the meat-eater's option must be faced by all readers of *Animal Liberation* who feel the force of the argument from pain and suffering; *per se*, there is nothing about Singer's position which enables them to avoid a choice between the two tactics I have described. A concerned reader of *Animal Liberation* may well feel impelled by what he reads there about factory farming to take up the cudgels and seek among people at large for a commitment to evolution in rearing methods, drugs, and genetic engineering. Could he not thereby be said to be following the book's lesson, that what is seriously wrong is not eating meat but raising and killing animals by painful methods? Certainly, this individual, who seeks the elimination of (very) painful devices and practices on factory farms and their replacement with more humane ones, who seeks technological advances on all fronts likely to be relevant to the diminution of pain in farming, and who actively tries to stir people up to commit themselves to these ends, is responding directly to Singer's message.

Accordingly, anyone convinced by Singer's argument, anyone convinced that we must reduce, if not eliminate, pain in farming faces a choice between the concerned individual's tactic and vegetarianism as the way to go about this. Neither tactic is *per se* more favoured than the other.

Attempts to Prejudice the Choice between Tactics

Finally, before turning to Singer's reasons for choosing vegetarianism as one's tactic for combating the pains of food animals, I want to consider two ways in which one might try at the outset to prejudice this choice in tactics between Singer and the concerned individual.

A Life Proper to Their Species

One way of trying to compromise the concerned individual's tactic involves a quite specific use of a very broad sense of pain or suffering.[14] It might be suggested, that is, that to deprive animals of the sort of life proper to their species is a form of pain or suffering in some broad sense, even if the means involved in carrying out this deprivation are, as the result of the concerned individual's option flourishing, so far as new rearing methods and new advances in technology are concerned, free of all pain or suffering in the narrow sense. Thus, even if the concerned individual's tactic was entirely successful in its aims, so long as some intensive methods of rearing were held to deprive some food animals of the sort of life proper to their species, it might be suggested that these animals would continue to have pain or suffering inflicted upon them.

Singer's argument from pain and suffering takes these terms, in the light of the above distinction, in the narrow sense; and I myself do not find much value in inflating their extension, in the way the broad sense envisages.

So far as the concerned individual's tactic is concerned, one must not focus upon his concern with technology to the exclusion of his concern with improvements in and alternatives to some present rearing methods. Take confinement in cruelly narrow spaces, which is by far the most commonly cited reason not only for food animals' miserable lives but also, so it is claimed, for their not leading lives proper to their species: this is a cardinal instance where the concerned individual will seek improvements and alternatives. Already there is some movement in the right direction. For example, in perhaps the most widely cited case of abuse, veal calves, Quantock Veal, which dominates the British veal market, has introduced a new method of rearing these calves.[15] They are not kept alone but in groups of 30; they are not kept in narrow stalls with slatted bottoms but in straw-filled pens in which they can move around freely; they are not kept in darkness but in light; they are not fed an iron-deficient diet but can obtain iron-laced milk from automatic feeders at any time. In this particular case, too, Quantock Veal maintains that this method of rearing veal calves, particularly given the availability of the European Community's dairy surplus, is cheaper than the objectionable method. Plainly, a development of this sort is likely to have a profound, positive effect on the quality of veal calves' lives; as well, it moves to meet the claim that, under present conditions, veal calves are not allowed to lead lives proper to their species.

Or consider the other, major case of abuse commonly cited, laying hens: one development in this area has been the Aviary method. It does not confine hens in cages but allows them to roam freely in poultry sheds, as a result of which they can scratch, flap about, and exercise; they lay in nest boxes or shelves above the ground. So far as I know, debeaking forms no part of the method. This development is not the end of evolution in rearing laying hens, but it seems a beginning.

I give these two examples as instances of the sorts of developments the concerned individual will favour, but I do not pretend either that they are the end of the process of evolution or that they are representative of recent developments as a whole in intensive farming. Rather, they are but two sorts of developments for which the concerned individual must lobby and work, examples of the kinds of evolution in rearing methods for which he must press.

It may be objected, however, that while the concerned individual is pressing for such developments and for advances in technology, food animals are still suffering. But so they are on the other tactic, vegetarianism.

If you face up to the choice of tactics I have been delineating, and you opt for vegetarianism, you would be wrong to think the suffering of food animals is going to come to a halt. In fact, of course, you are going to be left waiting for a sufficient number of others to make a similar choice, in order to give your act any efficacy whatever on the rearing of food animals. And, clearly, you are in for a long wait: even as the number of vegetarians in the United States has grown, the amount of meat consumed there has reached even more colossal heights. It was estimated in December, 1979, that meat consumption in the United States would amoun to 214.4 pounds per person during 1980.[16] For a more homely example, a single hamburger establishment in Oxford reported in mid-1981 that it had, since it had opened only six or seven years previously, sold more than 5½ million hamburgers. That is a single establishment, in a single, relatively small city, with a host of fast-food and other restaurants. In facing up to the decision before you, you know beyond doubt that, if you decide in favour of vegetarianism, food animals are going to continue to suffer.[17] On this score, you have no real basis for choosing one tactic over the other.

In sum, evolution in rearing methods seems likely to meet the objection that some methods do not permit some food animals to lead lives proper to their species, if only because improvements in and alternatives to these methods can be sought specifically on this basis. And this moves to meet another objection: it might be charged that the concerned individual's tactic is uncharitable to food animals because it only tries to relieve and not abolish their pains; but this is not true. While the concerned individual does want to relieve animal pain, his response to that pain is varied and includes, through his stress on evolution in rearing methods, the search for improvements in and alternatives to precisely those rearing methods held to be the primary source of the pain in question.

I am also unhappy with this first attempt to prejudice the choice between tactics on another count as well. This has to do with the expression 'the sort of life proper to their species'.

The contemporary *penchant* for studying animals in the wild, in order to find out what they are really like, and, therefore, what sort of life is proper to their respective species, cannot be indulged here, since virtually none of our food animals are found in the wild. Beef, ham, pork, chicken, lamb, mutton, and veal all come from animals who are completely our own productions, bred by us in ways we select to ends we desire. Indeed, the gene pools of these creatures of ours have been manipulated by us to a point today where we can in a great many respects produce the type and strain of creature we want,[18] and the amount of research presently going on in this area is enormous. My point is this: it is a mistake to use expressions like 'the sort of life proper to their species' as if this sort of life were itself immune to technological advance; for by manipulating the gene pools of food animals, by varying our drugs and breeding practices, and by having funded research for progressive advances in all these areas, we already breed these animals to a sort of life which to their bred species—there is no other—is proper.

For example, chickens have been bred with weak leg and wing muscles and with shorter necks, both to reduce their mobility and so to help fatten them and to reduce the sheer amount of each chicken which cannot be turned into food. Even a variation in the size of their bones can now be bred into them. In a word, the descendants of these bred chickens have had bred out of them many of the traits which food producers have wanted eliminated, and they are characterized by reduced mobility, a larger appetite, increased lethargy,

significantly increased (or decreased) size, etc. We have manipulated them to this end, and we are carrying on research in this area, funded by major food interests, government organizations, international bodies, and universities, at an accelerated pace. Thus, one very recent development has been a featherless chicken, for use in warm climates. In the southern United States, for example, plumed birds succumb to the heat at a sufficient rate to be a significant cost to farmers, and the featherless bird has in part been developed to meet this problem.[19] (Developments to meet specific problems are increasingly commonplace. For example, cows have a slightly longer gestation period than women, which has meant that they can have only one calf a year; farmers have long wanted more. A procedure has now been developed, which involves the use of multiple ovulation hormones, artificial insemination, and the non-surgical implantation of fertilized eggs in other cows, to solve this problem.)

What sort of life is proper to these chickens? One cannot appeal to chickens in the wild or 'non-developed' chickens for an answer, since there are none; chickens are, to repeat, developments or productions of our own, produced in order to satisfy the fast-food chains and the demands of our Sunday lunches and school picnics. But if one asks what sort of life is proper to 'developed' chickens, we get the above answer. Or are we to turn back the clock and say that the sort of life proper to chickens is the sort they enjoyed when, say, they were first introduced into the United States, long before the first of the developmental farms and any thought of mass-producing them arose? Unless we artificially select some time as that time which reveals to us what chickens are really like, to ask 'What is it in the nature of chickens to be like?' is to ask a question the answer to which must be framed in the light of 'developed' chickens and of technological change.

Now the manipulation of animal gene pools to the extent that we have long since affected the very species of animal in question may well be repugnant to many, and I can easily imagine it being condemned as tampering with nature (and, through nature, with our kith and kin) or with God's handiwork. But I do not really see how it can be condemned on the grounds of inflicting pain and suffering, unless the extension of these terms is simply bloated, not merely beyond anything Singer envisages, but beyond any reasonable degree. There does not seem to be much difference, in fact, between the animal and human cases in this regard: much of the genetic research being conducted with respect to human beings, including experiments involving determination of sex and number of children, test-tube breeding, cloning, and eliminating an extra Y chromosome in males, is widely condemned; but no one condemns it on the ground of inflicting pain and suffering. . . .

Valuing Suffering but Not Life

A second way of trying to compromise the concerned individual's tactic is, in a quite specific way, to try to reduce it to absurdity. The concerned individual seeks to relieve, minimize, and eliminate the pains of food animals but continues to eat meat; it is tempting to portray him, therefore, as valuing animal suffering but not valuing animal life, and then, on the basis of this portrayal, to force him to draw the unpalatable conclusion that, since every animal is going to suffer at some time in its life, he ought now to exterminate all animals painlessly.[20]

I do not myself think well of this argument, which I believe Michael Martin has shown how to answer;[21] but, I contend, if it works against anyone, it works against Singer.

The difficulty with the argument, apart from the very obvious fact that the concerned individual is in no way whatever committed to giving animal life a value of zero, is that, in typically simplistic fashion, it makes it appear that minimizing animal suffering is the only factor applicable to the situation. This is obviously false. For example, to destroy all animals now would result in financial collapse of the meat markets, in financial ruin for food producers and those in related and support industries, in massive unemployment in these industries as well as among farmers, in financial loss to rail and road haulage firms, in a substantial loss in television, newspaper, and magazine advertising revenues, with consequent effect upon the media's viability and

profitability, and so on. Here, in quite mercenary terms, is one good reason why the concerned individual will not exterminate all animals. It is the effects upon human beings and their interests, financial and otherwise, which are here held to outweigh minimizing animal suffering through total extermination or are held at least to be applicable to the situation. Other factors come to mind with equal facility. To kill all animals now would mean the collapse of all experimentation upon animals for human benefit, would depopulate our zoos, which so many children and adults enjoy visiting, and would deprive countless lonely people of their companions. Here, it is human well-being and enjoyment which are held to outweigh minimizing animal suffering through total extermination, or are held at least to be applicable to the situation.

I must stress again, however, that the concerned individual is not compelled to give animal life *no value whatever;* all he has to do is to give human interests, human well-being, and human enjoyment the same or a higher value than minimizing animal suffering through complete extermination.

I do not, then, think much of this argument. But what is little recognized, is that, if the argument applies to anyone, it applies to Singer. His case for vegetarianism, as we have seen, turns exclusively upon minimizing animal pain and suffering, and not in the least upon the value of animal life, which, for the purposes of his case, he is prepared to allow to be anything you like, including zero. Again, he openly endorses the view that a genuine concern for the pains of animals demands that we become vegetarians, without in the least endorsing a view about the value of animal life demanding that we become vegetarians. Pain alone is the basis of his case, and its diminution, minimization, and elimination is his goal. Surely, if anyone must now envisage the complete extermination of animals, because of a concern with the minimization of their suffering, if anyone is forced to conclude that all animals should now be painlessly eliminated, it is Singer?

I am not concerned here to go into possible ways in which Singer might resist this conclusion, except to emphasize that, if they begin even partially to include or make reference to those already sketched, he will be using human interests, well-being, and enjoyment to justify restraint in slaughtering animals, a surprising result in his case.

Notes

1. Peter Singer and James Mason, *Animal Factories*, New York, Crown Publishers Inc., 1980.

2. Peter Singer, 'Killing humans and killing animals', p. 149.

3. Peter Singer, *Practical Ethics*, p. 105.

4. Ibid., p. 56.

5. Ibid., p. 55.

6. Ibid.

7. Peter Singer, *Animal Liberation*, p. 165.

8. Ibid.

9. 'These arguments do not take us all the way to a vegetarian diet, since some animals, for instance sheep and beef cattle, still graze freely outdoors' (Peter Singer, *Practical Ethics*, p. 56).

10. Peter Singer, *Animal Liberation*, p. 165 (italics in original).

11. Peter Singer, *Practical Ethics*, pp. 56–7 (italics in original).

12. John Rodman, 'The liberation of nature?', *Inquiry*, vol. 20, 1977, pp. 90 ff, 103 ff, 112 ff.

13. Michael Martin, 'A critique of moral vegetarianism', *Reason Papers No. 3*, Fall 1976, pp. 16, 18, 20.

14. See, e.g., John Benson, 'Duty and the beast', *Philosophy*, vol. 53, 1978, p. 532.

15. See Hugh Clayton, 'Veal farmers aim to erase the stigma of cruelty', *The Times*, 8 May 1980; Ena Kendall, ' "Welfare" for veal calves', *Observer*, 4 May 1980.

16. See Sue Shellenbarger, 'Pork Gains on Beef as Meat Choice in U.S.', *International Herald Tribune*, December 23, 1979.

17. In the next chapter, I take up Singer's recent statement that he envisages (his argument working over) a considerable period of time in bringing a halt to the meat industry. Had this statement appeared in *Animal Liberation* alongside the picture of the effects of becoming vegetarians sketched there, I think readers might have found it at odds with that picture.

18. See Rodman, 'The liberation of nature', pp. 90–1; Martin, 'A critique of moral vegetarianism', pp. 18, 20; Benson, 'Duty and the beast', p. 531.

19. See, for example, 'Plucky US poultry experts breed featherless fowl for better eating', *International Herald Tribune*, 28 December 1979.

20. See A. Linzey, *Animal Rights* (London, SCM Press, 1976), pp. 29 ff; and R. Godlovitch, 'Animals and morals', in S. and R. Godlovitch, J. Harris, (eds), *Animals, Men and Morals* (London, Gollancz, 1971), pp. 167 ff.

21. Michael Martin, 'A critique of moral vegetarianism', pp. 31–2.

From the Animal Welfare Act of 1970

"Sec. 13. The Secretary shall promulgate standards to govern the humane handling, care, treatment, and transportation of animals by dealers, research facilities, and exhibitors. Such standards shall include minimum requirements with respect to handling, housing, feeding, watering, sanitation, ventilation, shelter from extremes of weather and temperatures, adequate veterinary care, including the appropriate use of anesthetic, analgesic or tranquilizing drugs, when such use would be proper in the opinion of the attending veterinarian of such research facilities, and separation by species when the Secretary finds such separation necessary for the humane handling, care, or treatment of animals. In promulgating and enforcing standards established pursuant to this section, the Secretary is authorized and directed to consult experts, including outside consultants where indicated. Nothing in this Act shall be construed as authorizing the Secretary to promulgate rules, regulations, or orders with regard to design, outlines, guidelines, or performance of actual research or experimentation by a research facility as determined by such research facility: *Provided* That the Secretary shall require, at least annually, every research facility to show that professionally acceptable standards governing the care, treatment, and use of animals, including appropriate use of anesthetic, analgesic, and tranquilizing drugs, during experimentation are being followed by the research facility during actual research or experimentation."

From the Animal Welfare Act of 1976

"Sec. 26. (a) It shall be unlawful for any person to knowingly sponsor or exhibit an animal in any animal fighting venture in which any animal was moved in interstate or foreign commerce.

"(b) It shall be unlawful for any person to knowingly buy, transport, or deliver to another person or receive from another person for purposes of transportation, in interstate or foreign commerce any dog or other animal for purposes of having the dog or other animal participate in an animal fighting venture.

"(c) It shall be unlawful for any person to knowingly use the mail service of the United States Postal Service or any interstate instrumentality for purposes of promoting or in any other manner furthering an animal fighting venture except as performed outside the limits of the States of the United States.

"(d) Notwithstanding the provisions of subsections (a), (b), or (c) of this section, the activities prohibited by such subsections shall be unlawful with respect to fighting ventures involving violations only if the fight is to take place in a State where it would be in violation of the laws thereof.

"(e) Any person who violates subsection (a), (b), or (c) shall be fined not more than $5,000 or imprisoned for not more than 1 year, or both, for each such violation.

Suggestions for Further Reading

Anthologies

Miller, H., and Williams, W. (eds.). *Ethics and Animals*. Clifton, NJ: Humana Press, 1983.

Regan, T., and Singer, P. (eds.). *Animal Rights and Human Obligation*. Englewood Cliffs, NJ: Prentice-Hall, 1976.

Basic Concepts

Nelson, J. "Recent Studies in Animal Ethics." *American Philosophical Quarterly* Vol. 22, No. 1 (1985) pp. 13–24.

Regan, T. *The Case for Animal Rights.* Berkeley: University of California Press, 1984.

Singer, P. *Animal Liberation.* New York: New York Review, 1975.

Alternative Views

Clark, S. *The Moral Status of Animals.* Oxford, England: Clarendon Press, 1977.

Dombrowski, D. *The Philosophy of Vegetarianism.* Amherst, MA: The University of Massachusetts Press, 1984.

Frey, R. G. *Rights, Killing and Suffering.* Oxford, England: Basil Blackwell, 1983.

Francis, L., and Norman, R. "Some Animals are More Equal than Others." *Philosophy* (1978) pp. 507–527.

Practical Applications

Akers, K. *A Vegetarian Sourcebook.* New York: G. P. Putnam and Sons, 1983.

Boas, M., and Chain, S. *Big Mac: The Unauthorized Story of McDonald's.* New York: New American Library, 1976.

Swanson, W., and Schultz, G. *Prime Rip.* Englewood Cliffs, NJ: Prentice-Hall, 1982.

Punishment and Responsibility

Basic Concepts

The problem of punishment and responsibility is the problem of who should be punished and in what their punishment should consist. It is a problem of punishment *and* responsibility because determining who should be punished and in what their punishment should consist involves an assessment of responsibility. However, before discussing alternative justifications for assigning punishment, it is important to first clarify the concepts of punishment and responsibility.

Let us begin with the concept of punishment. Consider the following definition:

  (a) Punishment is hardship inflicted on an offender by someone entitled to do so.

This definition certainly seems adequate to many standard cases of punishment. For example, suppose you pursue and capture a young man who has just robbed a drug store. The police then arrive and arrest the fellow. He is tried, convicted, and sentenced to two years in prison. Surely it would seem that a sentence of two years in prison in this case would constitute punishment, and obviously the sentence meets the conditions of (a).

But suppose we vary the example a bit. Suppose that, as before, you pursue the robber, but this time he gets away and in the process drops the money he took from the drug store, which you then retrieve. Suppose further that two eyewitnesses identify you as the robber, and you are arrested by the police, tried, and sentenced to two years in prison. Surely we would like to say that in this example it is you who are being punished, albeit unjustly; however, according to (a), this is not the case. For according to this definition, punishment can only be inflicted on offenders, and you are not an offender. But this simply shows that (a) is too narrow a definition of punishment. There clearly are cases, like our modified example, in which we can truly say that nonoffenders, i.e., innocent people, are being punished. Accordingly, an accept-able definition of punishment should allow for such cases.

Let us consider, then, the following definition of punishment, which does allow for the possibility that nonoffenders can be punished:

  (b) Punishment is hardship inflicted on a person by someone entitled to do so.

Although (b) clearly represents an advance over (a) in that it allows for the possibility that innocent people can be punished, serious difficulties remain. For according to (b), paying taxes is punishment, as is civil commitment of mentally ill persons who have not committed any offense. And even though we may have good reasons for opposing taxation and even good reasons for opposing civil commitment it is usually not because we regard such impositions as punishments. Clearly, then, a definition of punishment that includes paying taxes and civil commitment as punishments is simply too broad; what is needed is a definition that is narrower than (b) but broader than (a).

Consider the following possibility:

  (c) Punishment is hardship inflicted on a person who is found guilty of an offense by someone entitled to do so.

This definition, like (b), allows that innocent people can be punished, since it is possible that a person can be found guilty by some procedure or other without really being guilty. Yet (c), unlike (b), does not allow that just any hardship imposed by someone entitled to do so is punishment. Rather, only a hardship imposed *for an offense* can be a punishment.

But is this definition adequate? It would seem it is not. For, according to (c), paying a $5 parking ticket or suffering a 15 yard penalty in a football game are both punishments. Yet in both cases, the hardship imposed lacks the moral condemnation and denunciation that is characteristic of punishment. This suggests the following definition:

  (d) Punishment is hardship involving moral condemnation and denunciation inflicted on a person who is found guilty of an offense by someone entitled to do so.

Examples like the $5 parking ticket and the 15 yard penalty indicate that we need to distinguish between punishments proper, which satisfy the conditions of (*d*), and mere penalties, which only satisfy the conditions of (*c*). When we impose mere penalties, we are claiming that a person has done something wrong, perhaps even something morally wrong, but, because of the insignificant nature of the offense, we don't attempt to determine whether the person is morally blameworthy for so acting. Since we don't make this determination, we don't go on to morally condemn and denounce those we penalize. By contrast, when we impose punishments, proper we do make such a determination and, as a consequence, we do condemn and denounce those we penalize.

Turning to the concept of responsibility, we find that this concept is employed in a variety of different but related ways. For example, in everyday usage, we say that people are responsible for their actions if they could have acted otherwise than they did. In making this claim, we usually assume that people could have acted otherwise than they did in two respects. First, we assume that they could have acted otherwise if they had the ability to do so; for example, as presumably most varsity athletes have even when they play badly. Second, we assume that people could have acted otherwise if they had the opportunity to do so; for example, as you or I might have, even if we lacked the relevant ability, when, by chance, we were substituted in some varsity game and performed miserably. Thus, we can say that people are responsible for their actions if they had the ability and opportunity to act otherwise than they did.

Lawyers, however, usually approach the concept of responsibility differently. They are typically concerned with determining whether people have "mens rea," which translated means "a guilty mind." When people are said to have mens rea, they are held responsible for their actions.

Mens rea is said to involve three conditions:

1. Knowledge of circumstances
2. Foresight of consequences
3. Voluntariness

The first condition of mens rea is said to be absent when, for example, you didn't know the gun was loaded, or you didn't know the person you shot breaking into your home was a plainclothes police officer operating on a false lead. In such a case, lawyers would say you lacked mens rea because you lacked the knowledge of the relevant circumstances. The second condition of mens rea is said to be absent when, for example, you had no reason to suspect the person you shot would be wandering behind your target in a fenced-off range. In such a case, lawyers would say you lacked mens rea because you lacked foresight of the relevant consequences. The third condition of mens rea is said to be absent when, for example, you are having an epileptic fit or being attacked by a swarm of bees. This third condition is the least understood of the three conditions of mens rea.

But actually this weakness of the lawyer's mens rea notion of responsibility with respect to its third condition seems to be the strength of the everyday notion. This is because the everyday notion of responsibility is an unpacking of what it is for an action to be voluntary. Consequently, if we put the two notions together, we arrive at the following more adequate analysis:

People are responsible for their action if they have:

1. Knowledge of circumstances
2. Foresight of consequences
3. The ability and opportunity to act otherwise than they did.

Armed with a clearer understanding of the notions of punishment and responsibility, we should be in a better position to examine alternative justifications for assigning punishment in society.

Forward-Looking and Backward-Looking Views

There are basically two kinds of justifications for punishment: forward-looking and backward-looking. Forward-looking justifications maintain that punishment is justified because of its relationship to what *will occur*. Backward-looking justifications maintain that punishment is justified because of its relationship to what *has occurred*. An example of a forward-looking justification would be the claim that punishment is justified because it deters or reforms persons from crime. An example of a backward-looking justification would be the claim that punishment is justified because it fits or is proportionate to a crime or because it is applied to a person who is responsible for a crime. Those who adopt forward-looking justifications for punishment view punishment from the point of view of a social engineer seeking to produce certain good consequences in society. By contrast, those who adopt backward-looking justifications view punishment from the point of view of a stern balancer seeking to achieve a moral balance between punishment and the crime.

Karl Menninger provides us with a forceful example of a forward-looking justification for punishment—one that is directed at the reform of the offender (pp. 352–359). Menninger criticizes the existing criminal justice system as ineffective at preventing crime, grounded as it is on a theory of human motivation that fails to recognize the similarities between the motives of offenders and nonoffenders. In its place, Menninger advocates a therapeutic treatment program that would detain offenders, and possibly potential offenders, until they are reformed. Thus, Menninger would replace vengeful punishment—which he regards as itself a crime—with humanitarian reform.

One prerequisite for the justification of Menninger's system of humanitarian reform that is not generally recognized is that the opportunities open to offenders for leading a good life must be reasonably adequate, or at least arguably just and fair. If this is not the case, there would be little justification for asking criminal offenders to live their lives within the bounds of the legal system. Nor for that matter could we expect any attempt at implementing a system of reform like Menninger's to be generally effective in a society characterized by basic social and economic injustices. For in such a society, criminal offenders who perceive these injustices will have a strong moral reason to resist any attempt to turn them into law-abiding citizens.

Richard B. Brandt (pp. 360–365), however, argues that a system of punishment similar to the actual systems found in the United States and Great Britain can be justified on utilitarian or forward-looking grounds. Such a system would be justified, Brandt claims, because it would secure the good consequences of both reform and deterrence. Yet, C. S. Lewis (pp. 365–369) claims that the goals of both reform and deterrence are opposed to a fundamental requirement of justice—giving people what they deserve. Obviously, if Lewis's critique is sound, it presents a serious difficulty for both Menninger's and Brandt's views, as well as for any other forward-looking view.

Needless to say, raising difficulties for forward-looking justifications for punishment is not the same as directly defending backward-looking justifications. Hence the importance of the attempt by Edmund L. Pincoffs (pp. 369–379) to provide us with such a defense. Pincoffs begins by setting out the following three principles, which, he claims, are characteristic of a traditional backward-looking justification for punishment:

1. The only acceptable reason for punishing a person is that he or she has committed a crime.

2. The only acceptable reason for punishing a person in a given manner and degree is that the punishment is equal to the crime.

3. Whoever commits a crime must be punished in accordance with his or her desert.

Pincoffs claims that the underlying rationale for these principles can be expressed as follows:

(a) A proper justification for punishment is one that justifies it to the criminal.

(b) Punishment is justified because the criminal has willed the punishment he or she now suffers.

But how can criminals be said to will their own punishment if they do not like or want to be punished? One possible answer, which seems consistent with Pincoffs's analysis, is that criminals, by deliberately violating the rights of others (e.g., by harming others in some way), imply that they think it is reasonable for them to do so. But if this were the case, it would be reasonable for anyone else in similar circumstances to do the same. As a result, criminals would be implicitly conceding that it is all right for others to violate their rights by punishing them, and in this sense they could be said to will their own punishment.

In response to such a defense of a backward-looking justification for punishment, supporters of the forward-looking view might claim that the above principles and their underlying rationale are only proximate answers to the question of why punishment is justified, the ultimate answer to which is still given by the forward-looking view. Since Pincoffs's principles and their underlying rationale do not seem to be compatible with Menninger's system of humanitarian reform, such a response does imply that the ultimate forward-looking justification for punishment is to be found more in general deterrence, as in Brandt's system, than in humanitarian reform. But even if this were the case, the ultimate justification for punishment would still be forward-looking.

To meet this response, supporters of a backward-looking view need to show why Pincoffs's principles and their underlying rationale cannot be subsumed under a forward-looking justification. This might be done by showing that Pincoffs's principles and their underlying rationale can be grounded in a social contract theory of corrective justice analogous to the social contract theory of distributive justice discussed in Section I. Because many philosophers believe that a social contract theory of distributive justice conflicts with forward-looking goals, it should be possible to argue that a social contract theory of corrective justice does the same.[1]

Practical Application

Obviously, a crucial area for the application of forward-looking and backward-looking views

is that of capital punishment. Ernest van den Haag and Louis Schwartz state briefly some of the main arguments for and against capital punishment (pp. 379–382). Sometimes van den Haag and Schwartz present their arguments simply by way of example, in which case we must ask ourselves about the generality of the examples they give.

In 1976 the Supreme Court of the United States (pp. 382–388) examined the question of whether capital punishment violates the Eighth Amendment prohibition of cruel and unusual punishment. The majority of the Court held that it does not violate that prohibition. In support of its ruling, the majority of the Court maintained that capital punishment does not offend against contemporary standards of decency as shown by recent legislation in this area. But with regard to the harder question of whether capital punishment is contrary to human dignity and so lacks either a forward-looking or a backward-looking justification, the Court simply deferred to state legislatures. That left the Court with the easier task of deciding whether the procedures for imposing capital punishment, as provided by the Georgia statute that was under review, were capricious and arbitrary. On this score the Court found no reason to fault the Georgia statute.

In more recent cases, however, the Court has gone beyond this purely procedural issue and ruled that the imposition of capital punishment for rape (*Coker* v. *Georgia*) and the imposition of capital punishment on anyone who did not fire the fatal shot or intend the death of the victim (*Locket* v. *Ohio*) would be unconstitutional. Given that the Court has not seen fit to defer to the judgment of state legislatures in these matters, it is not clear why the Court should continue to defer to their judgment with regard to the question of whether capital punishment can be supported by an adequate forward-looking or backward-looking justification.

In any case, once you have faced that question yourself and worked out a theory of corrective justice, you will still not know exactly how to apply that theory unless you also know how just the distribution of goods and resources is in your society. This is because regardless of whether you adopt an essentially forward-looking or backward-looking theory of corrective justice, you will need to know what economic crimes—that is, crimes against property—should be punished according to your theory; and in order to know that, you will need to know what demands are placed on the available goods and resources by solutions to the other moral problems discussed in this anthology. Of course, some crimes (e.g., many cases of murder and rape) are crimes against people rather than property. And presumably these crimes would be proscribed by your theory of corrective justice independent of the solutions to other contemporary moral problems. Nevertheless, because most crimes are crimes against property, the primary application of your theory will still depend on solu-tions to the other moral problems discussed in this anthology. In particular, you will need to know to what extent goods and resources can legitimately be expended for military de-fense—which just happens to be the moral problem taken up next in the next section of this anthology.

Note

1. James P. Sterba, "Retributive Justice," *Political Theory* (1977); "Social Contract Theory and Ordinary Justice," *Political Theory* (1981); "Is There a Rationale for Punishment?" *American Journal of Jurisprudence* (1984).

The Crime of Punishment

Karl Menninger

Karl Menninger argues that the reason crime is so difficult to eradicate is that it serves the needs of offenders and nonoffenders alike. In fact, according to Menninger, the motives of offenders and nonoffenders are quite similar; what distinguishes serious offenders is simply a greater sense of helplessness and hopelessness in the pursuit of their goals. Menninger concludes that we must find better ways to enable people to realize their goals. Menninger also argues that punishment as a vengeful response to crime does not work because crime is an illness requiring treatment by psychiatrists and psychologists. Thus, Menning-er finds vengeful punishment itself to be a crime.

Few words in our language arrest our atten-tion as do "crime," "violence," "revenge," and "injustice." We abhor crime; we adore justice; we boast that we live by the rule of law. Vio-lence and vengefulness we repudiate as un-worthy of our civilization, and we assume this sentiment to be unanimous among all human beings.

Yet crime continues to be a national dis-grace and a world-wide problem. It is threat-ening, alarming, wasteful, expensive, abun-

dant, and apparently increasing! In actuality it is decreasing in frequency of occurrence, but it is certainly increasing in visibility and the reac-tions of the public to it.

Our system for controlling crime is in-effective, unjust, expensive. Prisons seem to operate with revolving doors—the same peo-ple going in and out and in and out. *Who cares?*

Our city jails and inhuman reformatories and wretched prisons are jammed. They are known to be unhealthy, dangerous, immoral, indecent, crime-breeding dens of iniquity. Not everyone has smelled them, as some of us have. Not many have heard the groans and the curses. Not everyone has seen the hate and despair in a thousand blank, hollow faces. But, in a way, we all know how miserable prisons are. *We want them to be that way.* And they are. *Who cares?*

Professional and big-time criminals prosper as never before. Gambling syndicates flourish. White-collar crime may even exceed all others, but goes undetected in the majority of cases. We are all being robbed and we know who the robbers are. They live nearby. *Who cares?*

The public filches millions of dollars worth of food and clothing from stores, towels and sheets from hotels, jewelry and knick-knacks from shops. The public steals, and the same public pays it back in higher prices. *Who cares?*

Time and time again somebody shouts about this state of affairs, just as I am shouting now. The magazines shout. The newspapers shout. The television and radio commentators shout (or at least they "deplore"). Psychologists, sociologists, leading jurists, wardens, and intelligent police chiefs join the chorus. Governors and mayors and Congressmen are sometimes heard. They shout that the situation is bad, bad, bad, and getting worse. Some suggest that we immediately replace obsolete procedures with scientific methods. A few shout contrary sentiments. Do the clear indications derived from scientific discovery for appropriate changes continue to fall on deaf ears? Why is the public so long-suffering, so apathetic and thereby so continuingly self-destructive? How many Presidents (and other citizens) do we have to lose before we do something?

The public behaves as a sick patient does when a dreaded treatment is proposed for his ailment. We all know how the aching tooth may suddenly quiet down in the dentist's office, or the abdominal pain disappear in the surgeon's examining room. Why should a sufferer seek relief and shun it? Is it merely the fear of pain of the treatment? Is it the fear of unknown complications? Is it distrust of the doctor's ability? All of these, no doubt.

But, as Freud made so incontestably clear, the sufferer is always somewhat deterred by a kind of subversive, internal opposition to the work of cure. He suffers on the one hand from the pains of his affliction and yearns to get well. But he suffers at the same time from traitorous impulses that fight against the ac-

complishment of any change in himself, even recovery! Like Hamlet, he wonders whether it may be better after all to suffer the familiar pains and aches associated with the old method than to face the complications of a new and strange, even though possibly better way of handling things.

The inescapable conclusion is that society secretly *wants* crime, *needs* crime, and gains definite satisfactions from the present mishandling of it! We condemn crime; we punish offenders for it; but we need it. The crime and punishment ritual is a part of our lives. We need crimes to wonder at, to enjoy vicariously, to discuss and speculate about, and to publicly deplore. We need criminals to identify ourselves with, to envy secretly, and to punish stoutly. They do for us the forbidden, illegal things we *wish* to do and, like scapegoats of old, they bear the burdens of our displaced guilt and punishment—"the iniquities of us all."

We have to confess that there is something fascinating for us all about violence. That most crime is not violent we know but we forget, because crime is a breaking, a rupturing, a tearing—even when it is quietly done. To all of us crime seems like violence.

The very word "violence" has a disturbing, menacing quality. . . . In meaning it implies something dreaded, powerful, destructive, or eruptive. It is something we abhor—or do we? Its first effect is to startle, frighten—even to horrify us. But we do not always run away from it. For violence also intrigues us. It is exciting. It is dramatic. Observing it and sometimes even participating in it gives us acute pleasure.

The newspapers constantly supply us with tidbits of violence going on in the world. They exploit its dramatic essence often to the neglect of conservative reporting of more extensive but less violent damage—the flood disaster in Florence, Italy, for example. Such words as crash, explosion, wreck, assault, raid, murder, avalanche, rape, and seizure evoke pictures of eruptive devastation from which we cannot turn away. The headlines often impute violence metaphorically even to peaceful activities. Relations are "ruptured," a tie is "broken," arbitration "collapses," a proposal is "killed."

Meanwhile on the television and movie screens there constantly appear for our amusement scenes of fighting, slugging, beating, torturing, clubbing, shooting, and the like which surpass in effect anything that the newspapers can describe. Much of this violence is portrayed dishonestly; the scenes are only semirealistic; they are "faked" and romanticized.

Pain cannot be photographed; grimaces indicate but do not convey its intensity. And wounds—unlike violence—are rarely shown. This phony quality of television violence in its mentally unhealthy aspect encourages irrationality by giving the impression to the observer that being beaten, kicked, cut, and stomped, while very unpleasant, are not very painful or serious. For after being slugged and beaten the hero rolls over, opens his eyes, hops up, rubs his cheek, grins, and staggers on. The *suffering* of violence is a part both the TV and movie producers *and* their audience tend to repress.

Although most of us *say* we deplore cruelty and destructiveness, we are partially deceiving ourselves. We disown violence, ascribing the love of it to other people. But the facts speak for themselves. We do love violence, all of us, and we all feel secretly guilty for it, which is another clue to public resistance to crime-control reform.

The great sin by which we all are tempted is the wish to hurt others, and this sin must be avoided if we are to live and let live. If our destructive energies can be mastered, directed, and sublimated, we can survive. If we can love, we can live. Our destructive energies, if they cannot be controlled, may destroy our best friends, as in the case of Alexander the Great, or they may destroy supposed "enemies" or innocent strangers. Worst of all—from the standpoint of the individual—they may destroy us.

Over the centuries of man's existence, many devices have been employed in the effort to control these innate suicidal and criminal propensities. The earliest of these undoubtedly depended upon fear—fear of the unknown, fear of magical retribution, fear of social retaliation. These external devices were replaced gradually with the law and all its machinery, religion and its rituals, and the conventions of the social order.

The routine of life formerly required every individual to direct much of his aggressive energy against the environment. There were trees to cut down, wild animals to fend off, heavy obstacles to remove, great burdens to lift. But the machine has gradually changed all of this. Today, the routine of life, for most people, requires no violence, no fighting, no killing, no life-risking, no sudden supreme exertion: occasionally, perhaps, a hard pull or a strong push, but no tearing, crushing, breaking, forcing.

And because violence no longer has legitimate and useful vents or purposes, it must *all* be controlled today. In earlier times its expression was often a virtue, today its control is the virtue. The control involves symbolic, vicarious expressions of our violence—violence modified; "sublimated," as Freud called it; "neutralized," as Hartmann described it. Civilized substitutes for direct violence are the objects of daily search by all of us. The common law and the Ten Commandments, traffic signals and property deeds, fences and front doors, sermons and concerts, Christmas trees and jazz bands—these and a thousand other things exist today to help in the control of violence.

My colleague, Bruno Bettelheim, thinks we do not properly educate our youth to deal with their violent urges. He reminds us that nothing fascinated our forefathers more. The *Iliad* is a poem of violence. Much of the Bible is a record of violence. One penal system and many methods of child-rearing express violence—"violence to suppress violence." And, he concludes [in the article "Violence: A Neglected Mode of Behavior"]: "We shall not be able to deal intelligently with violence unless we are first ready to see it as a part of human nature, and then we shall come to realize the chances of discharging violent tendencies are now so severely curtailed that their regular and safe draining-off is not possible anymore."

Why aren't we all criminals? We all have the impulses; we all have the provocations. But becoming civilized, which is repeated ontologically in the process of social education, teaches us what we may do with impunity. What then evokes or permits the breakthrough? Why is it necessary for some to bribe their consciences and do what they do not approve of doing? Why does all sublimation sometimes fail and overt breakdown occur in the controlling and managing machinery of the personality? Why do we sometimes lose self-control? Why do we "go to pieces"? Why do we explode?

These questions point up a central problem in psychiatry. Why do some people do things they do not want to do? Or things we do not want them to do? Sometimes crimes are motivated by a desperate need to act, to do *something* to break out of a state of passivity, frustration, and helplessness too long endured, like a child who shoots a parent or a teacher after some apparently reasonable act. Granting the universal presence of violence within us all, controlled by will power, conscience, fear of punishment, and other devices, granting the tensions and the temptations that are also common to us all, why do the mechanisms of self-control fail so completely in some individuals? Is there not some pre-existing defect, some moral or cerebral weakness, some gross deficiency of common sense that lets some people tumble or kick or strike or explode, while the rest of us just stagger or sway?

When a psychiatrist examines many prisoners, writes [Seymour] Halleck [in *Psychiatry and the Dilemmas of Crime*], he soon discovers how important in the genesis of the criminal outbreak is the offender's previous *sense of helplessness or hopelessness*. All of us suffer more or less from infringement of our personal freedom. We fuss about it all the time; we strive to correct it, extend it, and free ourselves from various oppressive or retentive forces. We do not want others to push us around, to control us, to dominate us. We realize this is bound to happen to some extent in an interlocking, interrelated society such as ours. No one truly has complete freedom. But restriction irks us.

The offender feels this way, too. He does not want to be pushed around, controlled, or dominated. And because he often feels that he is thus oppressed (and actually is) and because he does lack facility in improving his situation without violence, he suffers more intensely from feelings of helplessness.

Violence and crime are often attempts to escape from madness; and there can be no doubt that some mental illness is a flight from the wish to do the violence or commit the act. Is it hard for the reader to believe that suicides are sometimes committed to forestall the committing of murder? There is no doubt of it. Nor is there any doubt that murder is sometimes committed to avert suicide.

Strange as it may sound, many murderers do not realize whom they are killing, or, to put it another way, that they are killing the wrong people. To be sure, killing anybody is reprehensible enough, but the worst of it is that the person who the killer thinks should die (and he has reasons) is not the person he attacks. Sometimes the victim himself is partly responsible for the crime that is committed against him. It is this unconscious (perhaps sometimes conscious) participation in the crime by the victim that has long held up the very humanitarian and progressive-sounding program of giving compensation to victims. The public often judges the victim as well as the attacker.

Rape and other sexual offenses are acts of violence so repulsive to our sense of decency and order that it is easy to think of rapists in general as raging, oversexed, ruthless brutes (unless they are conquering heroes). Some rapists are. But most sex crimes are committed by undersexed rather than oversexed individuals, often undersized rather than oversized, and impelled less by lust than by a need for reassurance regarding an impaired masculinity. The unconscious fear of women goads some men with a compulsive urge to conquer, humiliate, hurt, or render powerless some available sample of womanhood. Men who are violently afraid of their repressed but nearly emergent homosexual desires, and men who are afraid of the humiliation of impotence, often try to overcome these fears by violent demonstrations.

The need to deny something in oneself is frequently an underlying motive for certain odd behavior—even up to and including crime. Bravado crimes, often done with particular brutality and ruthlessness, seem to prove *to the doer* that "I am no weakling! I am no sissy! I am no coward. I am no homosexual! I am a tough man who fears nothing." The Nazi storm troopers, many of them mere boys, were systematically trained to stifle all tender emotions and force themselves to be heartlessly brutal.

Man perennially seeks to recover the magic of his childhood days—the control of the mighty by the meek. The flick of an electric light switch, the response of an automobile throttle, the click of a camera, the touch of a match to a skyrocket—these are keys to a sudden and magical display of great power induced by the merest gesture. Is anyone already so blasé that he is no longer thrilled at the opening of a door specially for him by a magic-eye signal? Yet for a few pennies one can purchase a far more deadly piece of magic—a stored explosive and missile encased within a shell which can be ejected from a machine at the touch of a finger so swiftly that no eye can follow. A thousand yards away something falls dead—a rabbit, a deer, a beautiful mountain sheep, a sleeping child, or the President of the United States. Magic! Magnified, projected power. "Look what I can do. I am the greatest!"

It must have come to every thoughtful person, at one time or another, in looking at the revolvers on the policemen's hips, or the guns soldiers and hunters carry so proudly, that these are instruments made for the express purpose of delivering death to someone. The easy availability of these engines of destruction, even to children, mentally disturbed people, professional criminals, gangsters, and even high school girls is something to give one pause. The National Rifle Association and its allies have been able to kill scores of bills that have been introduced into Congress and state legislatures for corrective gun control since the death of President Kennedy. Americans still spend about $2 billion on guns each year.

Fifty years ago, Winston Churchill declared that the mood and temper of the public in regard to crime and criminals is one of the unfailing tests of the civilization of any country. Judged by this standard, how civilized are we?

The chairman of the President's National Crime Commission, Nicholas de B. Katzenbach, declared . . . that organized crime flourishes in America because enough of the public wants its services, and most citizens are apathetic about its impact. It will continue uncurbed as long as Americans accept it as inevitable and, in some instances, desirable.

Are there steps that we can take which will reduce the aggressive stabs and self-destructive lurches of our less well-managing fellow men? Are there ways to prevent and control

the grosser violations, other than the clumsy traditional maneuvers which we have inherited? These depend basically upon intimidation and slow-motion torture. We call it punishment, and justify it with our "feeling." We know it doesn't work.

Yes, there *are* better ways. There are steps that could be taken; some *are* taken. But we move too slowly. Much better use, it seems to me, could be made of the members of my profession and other behavioral scientists than having them deliver courtroom pronunciamentos. The consistent use of a diagnostic clinic would enable trained workers to lay what they can learn about an offender before the judge who would know best how to implement the recommendation.

This would no doubt lead to a transformation of prisons, if not to their total disappearance in their present form and function. Temporary and permanent detention will perhaps always be necessary for a few, especially the professionals, but this could be more effectively and economically performed with new types of "facility" (that strange, awkward word for institution).

I assume it to be a matter of common and general agreement that our object in all this is to protect the community from a repetition of the offense by the most economical method consonant with our other purposes. Our "other purposes" include the desire to prevent these offenses from occurring, to reclaim offenders for social usefulness, if possible, and to detain them in protective custody, if reclamation is *not* possible. But how?

The treatment of human failure or dereliction by the infliction of pain is still used and believed in by many nonmedical people. "Spare the rod and spoil the child" is still considered wise counsel by many.

Whipping is still used by many secondary schoolmasters in England, I am informed, to stimulate study, attention, and the love of learning. Whipping was long a traditional treatment for the "crime" of disobedience on the part of children, pupils, servants, apprentices, employees. And slaves were treated for centuries by flogging for such offenses as weariness, confusion, stupidity, exhaustion, fear, grief, and even overcheerfulness. It was assumed and stoutly defended that these "treatments" cured conditions for which they were administered.

Meanwhile, scientific medicine was acquiring many new healing methods and devices. Doctors can now transplant organs and limbs; they can remove brain tumors and cure incipient cancers; they can halt pneumonia, meningitis, and other infections; they can correct deformities and repair breaks and tears and scars. But these wonderful achievements are accomplished on *willing* subjects, people who voluntarily ask for help by even heroic measures. And the reader will be wondering, no doubt, whether doctors can do anything with or for people who *do not want* to be treated at all, in any way! Can doctors cure willful aberrant behavior? Are we to believe that crime is a *disease* that can be reached by scientific measures? Isn't it merely "natural meanness" that makes all of us do wrong things at times even when we "know better"? And are not self-control, moral stamina, and will power the things needed? Surely there is no medical treatment for the lack of those!

Let me answer this carefully, for much misunderstanding accumulates here. I would say that according to the prevalent understanding of the words, crime is *not* a disease. Neither is it an illness, although I think it *should* be! It *should* be treated, and it could be; but it mostly isn't.

These enigmatic statements are simply explained. Diseases are undesired states of being which have been described and defined by doctors, usually given Greek or Latin appellations, and treated by long-established physical and pharmacological formulae. Illness, on the other hand, is best defined as a state of impaired functioning of such a nature that the public expects the sufferer to repair to the physician for help. The illness may prove to be a disease; more often it is only vague and nameless misery; but something which doctors, not lawyers, teachers, or preachers, are supposed to be able and willing to help.

When the community begins to look upon the expression of aggressive violence as the symptom of an illness or as indicative of illness, it will be because it believes doctors can do something to correct such a condition. At present, some better-informed individuals do believe and expect this. However angry at

or sorry for the offender, they want him "treated" in an effective way so that he will cease to be a danger to them. And they know that the traditional punishment, "treatment-punishment," will not effect this.

What *will*? What effective treatment is there for such violence? It will surely have to begin with motivating or stimulating or arousing in a cornered individual the wish and hope and intention to change his methods of dealing with the realities of life. Can this be done by education, medication, counseling, training? I would answer *yes*. It can be done successfully in a majority of cases, if undertaken in time.

The present penal system and the existing legal philosophy do not stimulate or even expect such a change to take place in the criminal. Yet change is what medical science always aims for. The prisoner, like the doctor's other patients, should emerge from his treatment experience a different person, differently equipped, differently functioning, and headed in a different direction than when he began the treatment.

It is natural for the public to doubt that this can be accomplished with criminals. But remember that the public *used* to doubt that change could be effected in the mentally ill. No one a hundred years ago believed mental illness to be curable. Today *all* people know (or should know) that *mental illness is curable* in the great majority of instances and that the prospects and rapidity of cure are directly related to the availability and intensity of proper treatment.

The forms and techniques of psychiatric treatment used today number in the hundreds. No one patient requires or receives all forms, but each patient is studied with respect to his particular needs, his basic assets, his interests, and his special difficulties. A therapeutic team may embrace a dozen workers—as in a hospital setting—or it may narrow down to the doctor and the spouse. Clergymen, teachers, relatives, friends, and even fellow patients often participate informally but helpfully in the process of readaptation.

All of the participants in this effort to bring about a favorable change in the patient—i.e., in his vital balance and life program—are imbued with what we may call a *therapeutic attitude*. This is one in direct antithesis to attitudes of avoidance, ridicule, scorn, or punitiveness. Hostile feelings toward the subject, however justified by his unpleasant and even destructive behavior, are not in the curriculum of therapy or in the therapist. This does not mean that therapists approve of the offensive and obnoxious behavior of the patient; they distinctly disapprove of it. But they recognize it as symptomatic of continued imbalance and disorganization, which is what they are seeking to change. They distinguish between disapproval, penalty, price, and punishment.

Doctors charge fees; they impose certain "penalties" or prices, but they have long since put aside primitive attitudes of retaliation toward offensive patients. A patient may cough in the doctor's face or may vomit on the office rug; a patient may curse or scream or even struggle in the extremity of his pain. But these acts are not "punished." Doctors and nurses have no time or thought for inflicting unnecessary pain even upon patients who may be difficult, disagreeable, provocative, and even dangerous. It is their duty to care for them, to try to make them well, and to prevent them from doing themselves or others harm. This requires love, not hate. This is the deepest meaning of the therapeutic attitude. Every doctor knows this; every worker in a hospital or clinic knows it (or should).

There is another element in the therapeutic attitude. It is the quality of hopefulness. If no one believes that the patient can get well, if no one—not even the doctor—has any hope, there probably won't be any recovery. Hope is just as important as love in the therapeutic attitude.

"But you were talking about the mentally ill," readers may interject, "those poor, confused, bereft, frightened individuals who yearn for help from you doctors and nurses. Do you mean to imply that willfully perverse individuals, our criminals, can be similarly reached and rehabilitated? Do you really believe that effective treatment of the sort you visualize can be applied to people *who do not want any help*, who are so willfully vicious, so well aware of the wrongs they are doing, so lacking in penitence or even common decency that punishment seems to be the only thing left?"

Do I believe there is effective treatment for offenders, and that they *can* be changed? *Most certainly and definitely I do.* Not all cases, to be sure; there are also some physical afflictions which we cannot cure at the moment. Some provision has to be made for incurables—pending new knowledge—and these will include some offenders. But I believe the majority of them would prove to be curable. The willfulness and the viciousness of offenders are part of the thing for which they have to be treated. These must not thwart the therapeutic attitude.

It is simply not true that most of them are "fully aware" of what they are doing, nor is it true that they want no help from anyone, although some of them say so. Prisoners are individuals: some want treatment, some do not. Some don't know what treatment is. Many are utterly despairing and hopeless. Where treatment is made available in institutions, many prisoners seek it even with the full knowledge that doing so will not lessen their sentences. In some prisons, seeking treatment by prisoners is frowned upon by the officials.

Various forms of treatment are even now being tried in some progressive courts and prisons over the country—educational, social, industrial, religious, recreational, and psychological treatments. Socially acceptable behavior, new work-play opportunities, new identity and companion patterns all help toward community reacceptance. Some parole officers and some wardens have been extremely ingenious in developing these modalities of rehabilitation and reconstruction—more than I could list here even if I knew them all. But some are trying. The secret of success in all programs, however, is the replacement of the punitive attitude with a therapeutic attitude.

Offenders with propensities for impulsive and predatory aggression should not be permitted to live among us unrestrained by some kind of social control. *But the great majority of offenders, even "criminals," should never become prisoners if we want to "cure" them.*

There are now throughout the country many citizens' action groups and programs for the prevention and control of crime and delinquency. With such attitudes of inquiry and concern, the public could acquire information (and incentive) leading to a change of feeling about crime and criminals. It will discover how unjust is much so-called "justice," how baffled and frustrated many judges are by the ossified rigidity of old-fashioned, obsolete laws and state constitutions which effectively prevent the introduction of sensible procedures to replace useless, harmful ones.

I want to proclaim to the public that things are not what it wishes them to be, and will only become so if it will take an interest in the matter and assume some responsibility for its own self-protection.

Will the public listen?

If the public does become interested, it will realize that we must have more facts, more trial projects, more checked results. It will share the dismay of the President's Commission in finding that no one knows much about even the incidence of crime with any definiteness or statistical accuracy.

The average citizen finds it difficult to see how any research would in any way change his mind about a man who brutally murders his children. But just such inconceivably awful acts most dramatically point up the need for research. Why should—how can—a man become so dreadful as that in our culture? How is such a man made? Is it comprehensible that he can be born to become so depraved?

There are thousands of questions regarding crime and public protection which deserve scientific study. What makes some individuals maintain their interior equilibrium by one kind of disturbance of the social structure rather than by another kind, one that would have landed him in a hospital? Why do some individuals specialize in certain types of crime? Why do so many young people reared in areas of delinquency and poverty and bad example never become habitual delinquents? (Perhaps this is a more important question than why some of them do.)

The public has a fascination for violence, and clings tenaciously to its yen for vengeance, blind and deaf to the expense, futility, and dangerousness of the resulting penal system. But we are bound to hope that this will yield in time to the persistent, penetrating light of intelligence and accumulating scientific knowledge. The public will grow increasingly ashamed of its cry for retaliation, its persistent demand to punish. This is its crime, *our* crime against criminals—and, incidentally, our crime against ourselves. For before we can diminish our sufferings from the ill-controlled aggressive assaults of fellow citizens, we must renounce the philosophy of punishment, the obsolete, vengeful penal attitude. In its place we would seek a comprehensive constructive social attitude—therapeutic in some instances, restraining in some instances, but preventive in its total social impact.

In the last analysis this becomes a question of personal morals and values. No matter how glorified or how piously disguised, vengeance as a human motive must be personally repudiated by each and every one of us. This is the message of old religions and new psychiatries. Unless this message is heard, unless we, the people—the man on the street, the housewife in the home—can give up our delicious satisfactions in opportunities for vengeful retaliation on scapegoats, we cannot expect to preserve our peace, our public safety, or our mental health.

A Utilitarian Theory of Punishment

Richard B. Brandt

Richard B. Brandt argues that a system of punishment similar to that found in the United States and Great Britain can be justified on utilitarian or forward-looking grounds. He rejects the view that a utilitarian theory cannot approve of any excuses for criminal liability. He also denies that a utilitarian theory must approve of occasionally punishing the innocent provided the theory is understood in an extended sense to require a principle of equal distribution.

The ethical foundations of the institution and principles of criminal justice require examination just as do the ethical foundations of systems of economic distribution. In fact, the two problems are so similar that it is helpful to view either one in the light of conclusions reached about the other. It is no accident that the two are spoken of as problems of "justice," for the institution of criminal justice is essentially a mode of allocating welfare (or "illfare," if we prefer). Also, just as an economic return can be regarded as a reward for past services, the punishment of criminals can be regarded as punishment for past disservices. Moreover, just as a major reason for differences in economic reward is to provide motivation for promoting the public welfare by industrious effort, so a major reason for a system of punishment for criminals is to give motivation for not harming the public by crime. The two topics, then, are very similar; but they are also sufficiently different to require separate discussion. . . .

The broad questions to be kept in the forefront of discussion are the following: (1) What justifies anyone in inflicting pain or loss on an individual on account of his past acts? (2) Is there a valid general principle about the punishments proper for various acts? (Possibly there should be no close connection between offense and penalty; perhaps punishment should be suited to the individual needs of the criminal, and not to his crime.) (3) What kinds

Abridged from *Ethical Theory* (1959), pp. 480, 489–495, 503–505. Reprinted by permission of Richard B. Brandt. Notes renumbered.

of defense should excuse from punishment? An answer to these questions would comprise prescriptions for the broad outlines of an ideal system of criminal justice. . . .

The Utilitarian Theory of Criminal Justice

. . . It is convenient to begin with the utilitarian theory. Since we have tentatively concluded that an "extended" rule-utilitarianism is the most tenable form of theory, we shall have this particular type of theory in mind. For present purposes, however, it would make no difference, except at two or three points where we shall make note of the fact, if we confined our attention to a straight rule-utilitarian principle. There is no harm in thinking of the matter in this way. . . .

The essence of the rule-utilitarian theory, we recall, is that our actions, whether legislative or otherwise, should be guided by a set of prescriptions, the conscientious following of which by all would have maximum net expectable utility. As a result, the utilitarian is not, just as such, committed to any particular view about how anti-social behavior should be treated by society—or even to the view that society should do anything at all about immoral conduct. It is only the utilitarian principle *combined* with statements about the kind of laws and practices which will maximize expectable utility that has such consequences. Therefore, utilitarians are free to differ from one another about the character of an ideal system of criminal justice; some utilitarians think that the system prevalent in Great Britain and the United States essentially corresponds to the ideal, but others think that the only system that can be justified is markedly different from the actual systems in these Western countries. We shall concentrate our discussion, however, on the more traditional line of utilitarian thought which holds that roughly the actual system of criminal law, say in the United States, is morally justifiable, and we shall follow roughly the classic exposition of the reasoning given by Jeremy Bentham[1]—but modifying this freely when we feel amendment is called for. At the end of the chapter we shall look briefly at a different view.

Traditional utilitarian thinking about criminal justice has found the rationale of the practice, in the United States, for example, in three main facts. (Those who disagree think the first two of these "facts" happen not to be the case.) (1) People who are tempted to misbehave, to trample on the rights of others, to sacrifice public welfare for personal gain, can usually be deterred from misconduct by fear of punishment, such as death, imprisonment, or fine. (2) Imprisonment or fine will teach malefactors a lesson; their characters may be improved, and at any rate a personal experience of punishment will make them less likely to misbehave again. (3) Imprisonment will certainly have the result of physically preventing past malefactors from misbehaving, during the period of their incarceration.

In view of these suppositions, traditional utilitarian thinking has concluded that having laws forbidding certain kinds of behavior on pain of punishment, and having machinery for the fair enforcement of these laws, is justified by the fact that it maximizes expectable utility. Misconduct is not to be punished just for its own sake; malefactors must be punished for their past acts, according to law, as a way of maximizing expectable utility.

The utilitarian principle, of course, has implications for decisions about the severity of punishment to be administered. Punishment is itself an evil, and hence should be avoided where this is consistent with the public good. Punishment should have precisely such a degree of severity (not more or less) that the probable disutility of greater severity just balances the probable gain in utility (less crime because of the more serious threat). The cost, in other words, should be counted along with the value of what is bought; and we should buy protection up to the point where the cost is greater than the protection is worth. How severe will such punishment be? Jeremy Bentham had many sensible things to say about this. Punishment, he said, must be severe enough so that it is to no one's advantage to commit an offense even if he receives the punishment; a fine of $10 for bank robbery would give no security at all. Further, since many criminals will be undetected, we must make the penalty heavy enough in comparison with the prospective gain from crime, that a prospective criminal will consider the risk hardly worth it, even considering that it is not certain he will be punished at all. Again, the more serious offenses should carry the heavier penalties, not only because the greater disutility justifies the use of heavier penalties in order to prevent them, but also because criminals should be motivated to commit a less serious rather than a more serious offense. Bentham thought the prescribed penalties should allow for some variation at the discretion of the judge, so that the actual suffering caused should roughly be the same in all cases; thus, a heavier fine will be imposed on a rich man than on a poor man.

Bentham also argued that the goal of maximum utility requires that certain facts should *excuse* from culpability, for the reason that punishment in such cases "must be inefficacious." He listed as such (1) the fact that the relevant law was passed only after the act of the accused, (2) that the law had not been made public, (3) that the criminal was an infant, insane, or was intoxicated, (4) that the crime was done under physical compulsion, (5) that the agent was ignorant of the probable consequences of his act or was acting on the basis of an innocent misapprehension of the facts, such that the act the agent thought he was performing was a lawful one, and (6) that the motivation to commit the offense was so strong that no threat of law could prevent the crime. Bentham also thought that punishment should be remitted if the crime was a collective one and the number of the guilty so large that great suffering would be caused by its imposition, or if the offender held an important post and his services were important for the public, or if the public or foreign powers would be offended by the punishment; but we shall ignore this part of his view.

Bentham's account of the logic of legal "defenses" needs amendment. What he should have argued is that *not* punishing in certain types of cases (cases where such defenses as those just indicated can be offered) reduces the amount of suffering imposed by law and the insecurity of everybody, and that failure to impose punishment in these types of case will cause only a negligible increase in the incidence of crime.

How satisfactory is this theory of criminal justice? Does it have any implications that are far from being acceptable when compared with concrete justified convictions about what practices are morally right?[2]

Many criminologists, as we shall see at the end of this chapter, would argue that Bentham was mistaken in his facts: The deterrence value of [the] threat of punishment, they say, is much less than he imagined, and criminals are seldom reformed by spending time in prison. If these contentions are correct, then the ideal rules for society's treatment of malefactors are very different from what Bentham thought, and from what actual practice is today in the United States. To say all this, however, is not to show that the utilitarian *principle* is incorrect, for in view of these facts presumably the attitudes of a "qualified" person would not be favorable to criminal justice as practiced today. Utilitarian theory might still be correct, but its implications would be different from what Bentham thought—and they might coincide with justified ethical judgments. We shall return to this.

The whole utilitarian approach, however, has been criticized on the ground that it ought not in consistency to approve of *any* excuses from criminal liability.[3] Or at least, it should do so only after careful empirical inquiries. It is not obvious, it is argued, that we increase net expectable utility by permitting such defenses. At the least, the utilitarian is committed to defend the concept of "strict liability." Why? Because we could get a more strongly deterrent effect if everyone knew that *all behavior* of a certain sort would be punished, irrespective of mistaken supposals of fact, compulsion, and so on. The critics admit that knowledge that all behavior of a certain sort will be punished will hardly deter from crime the insane, persons acting under compulsion, persons acting under erroneous beliefs about facts, and others, but, as Professor Hart points out, it does not follow from this that general knowledge that certain acts will always be punished will not be salutary.

The utilitarian, however, has a solid defense against charges of this sort. We must bear in mind (as the critics do not) that the utilitarian principle, *taken by itself, implies nothing whatever* about whether a system of law should excuse persons on the basis of certain defenses. What the utilitarian does say is that, when we *combine* the principle of utilitarianism with *true* propositions about a certain thing or situation, then we shall come out with true statements about obligations. The utilitarian is certainly not committed to saying that one will derive true propositions about obligations if one starts with *false* propositions about fact or about what will maximize welfare, or with *no* such propositions at all. Therefore the criticism sometimes made (for example, by Hart), that utilitarian theory does not render it "obviously" or "necessarily" the case that the recognized excuses from criminal liability should be accepted as excusing from punishment, is beside the point. Moreover, in fact the utilitarian can properly claim that we do have excellent reason for believing that the general public would be no better motivated to avoid criminal offenses than it now is, if the insane and others were also punished along with intentional wrong-doers. Indeed, he may reasonably claim that the example of punishment of these individuals could only have a hardening effect—like public executions. Furthermore, the utilitarian can point out that abolition of the standard exculpating excuses would lead to serious insecurity. Imagine the pleasure of driving an automobile if one knew one could be executed for running down a child whom it was absolutely impossible to avoid striking! One certainly does not maximize expectable utility by eliminating the traditional excuses. In general, then, the utilitarian theory is not threatened by its implications about exculpating excuses.

It might also be objected against utilitarianism that it cannot recognize the validity of *mitigating* excuses (which presumably have the support of "qualified" attitudes). Would not consequences be better if the distinction between premeditated and impulsive acts were abolished? The utilitarian can reply that people who commit impulsive crimes, in the heat of anger, do not give thought to legal penalties; they would not be deterred by a stricter law. Moreover, such a person is unlikely to repeat his crime, so that a mild sentence saves an essentially good man for society.[4] Something can also be said in support of the practice of judges in giving a milder sentence when a person's temptation is severe: at least the *extended* rule-utilitarian can say, in defense of the practice of punishing less severely the crime of a man who has had few opportunities in life, that a judge ought to do what he can to repair inequalities in life, and that a mild sentence to a man who has had few opportunities is one way of doing this. There are, then, utilitarian supports for recognizing the mitigating excuses. . . .

Another popular objection to the utilitarian theory is that the utilitarian must approve of prosecutors or judges occasionally withholding evidence known to them, for the sake of convicting an innocent man, if the public welfare really is served by so doing. Critics of the theory would not deny that there *can* be circumstances where the dangers are so severe that such action is called for; they only say that utilitarianism calls for it all too frequently. Is this criticism justified? Clearly, the utilitarian is not committed to advocating that a provision should be written into the *law* so as to permit punishment of persons for crimes they did not commit if to do so would serve the public good. Any such provision would be a shattering blow to public confidence and security. The question is only whether there should be an informal moral rule to the same effect, for the guidance of judges and prosecutors. Will the rule-utilitarian necessarily be committed to far too sweeping a moral rule on this point? We must recall that he is not in the position of the act-utilitarian, who must say that an innocent man must be punished if in *his particular*

case the public welfare would be served by his punishment. The rule-utilitarian rather asserts only that an innocent man should be punished if he falls within a class of cases such that net expectable utility is maximized if *all* members of the class are punished, taking into account the possible disastrous effects on public confidence if it is generally known that judges and prosecutors are guided by such a rule. Moreover, the "extended" rule-utilitarian has a further reason for not punishing an innocent man unless he has had more than his equal share of the good things of life already; namely, that there is an obligation to promote equality of welfare, whereas severe punishment is heaping "illfare" on one individual person. When we take these considerations into account, it is *not* obvious that the rule-utilitarian (or the "extended" rule-utilitarian) is committed to action that we are justifiably convinced is immoral.[5] . . .

Utilitarianism and Reform

Some thinkers today believe that criminal justice in Great Britain and the United States is in need of substantial revision. If we agree with their proposals, we have even less reason for favoring the retributive principle; but we must also question the traditional utilitarian emphasis on deterrence as the primary function of the institution of criminal justice.

Their proposal, roughly, is that we should extend, to all criminal justice, the practices of juvenile courts and institutions for the reform of juvenile offenders. Here, retributive concepts have been largely discarded at least in theory, and psychiatric treatment and programs for the prevention of crime by means of slum clearance, the organization of boys' clubs, and so forth, have replaced even deterrence as guiding ideas for social action.

The extension of these practices to criminal justice as a whole would work somewhat as follows: First, the present court procedure would be used to determine whether an offense has actually been committed. Such procedure would necessarily include ordinary rules about the admission of evidence, trial by jury, and the exculpating justifications and excuses for offenses (such as wrong suppositions about the facts). Second, if an accused were adjudged guilty, decisions about his treatment would then be in the hands of the experts, who would determine what treatment was called for and when the individual was ready for return to normal social living. The trial court might, of course, set some maximum period during which such experts would have a right to control the treatment of the criminal. What the experts would do would be decided by the criminal's condition; it would be criminal-centered treatment, not crime-centered treatment.

One might object to this proposal that it overlooks the necessity of disagreeable penalties for crime, in order to deter prospective criminals effectively. But it is doubtful whether threats of punishment have as much deterrent value as is often supposed. Threats of punishment will have little effect on morons, or on persons to whom normal living offers few prospects of an interesting existence.[6] Moreover, persons from better economic or social circumstances will be deterred sufficiently by the prospect of conviction in a public trial and being at the disposal of a board for a period of years.

Such proposals have their difficulties. For instance, would the police be as safe as they are, if criminals knew that killing a policeman would be no more serious in its consequences than the crime for which the policeman was trying to arrest them? However, there is much factual evidence for answering such questions, since systems of criminal justice along such lines are already in operation in some parts of the world, in particular among the Scandinavian countries. In fact, in some states the actual practice is closer to the projected system than one might expect from books on legal theory.

Another objection that many would raise is that psychiatry and criminology have not yet advanced far enough for such weighty decisions about the treatment of criminals to be placed in their hands. The treatment of criminals might vary drastically depending on the particular theoretical predilections of a given theorist, or on his personal likes and dislikes. One can probably say as much, or more,

however, about the differences between judges, in their policies for picking a particular sentence within the range permitted by law.

An institution of criminal justice operating on such basic principles would come closer to our views about how parents should treat their children, or teachers their students, than the more traditional practices of criminal justice today.

We should repeat that this view about the ideal form for an institution of criminal justice is not in conflict with utilitarianism; in fact it is utilitarian in outlook. The motivation behind advocating it is the thought that such a system would do more good. It differs from the kind of institution traditionally advocated by utilitarians like Bentham only in making different factual assumptions, primarily about the deterrence value of threat of imprisonment, and the actual effect of imprisonment on the attitudes of the criminal.

Notes

1. In *Principles of Morals and Legislation.*

2. Act-utilitarians face some special problems. For instance, if I am an act-utilitarian and serve on a jury, I shall work to get a verdict that will do the most good, irrespective of the charges of the judge, and of any oath I may have taken to give a reasonable answer to certain questions on the basis of the evidence presented—unless I think my doing so will have indirect effects on the institution of the jury, public confidence in it, and so on. This is certainly not what we think a juror should do. Of course, neither a juror nor a judge can escape his prima facie obligation to do what good he can; this obligation is present in some form in every theory. The act-utilitarian, however, makes this the whole of one's responsibility.

3. See H. L. A. Hart, "Legal Responsibility and Excuses," in Sidney Hook (ed.), *Determinism and Freedom* (New York: New York University Press, 1958), pp. 81–104; and David Braybrooke, "Professor Stevenson, Voltaire, and the Case of Admiral Byng," *Journal of Philosophy*, LIII (1956), 787–96.

4. The utilitarian must admit that the same thing is true for many deliberate murders; and probably he should also admit that some people who commit a crime in the heat of anger would have found time to think had they known that a grave penalty awaited them.

5. In any case, a tenable theory of punishment must approve of punishing persons who are *morally* blameless. Suppose someone commits treason for moral reasons. We may have to say that his deed is not reprehensible at all, and might even (considering the risk he took for his principles) be morally admirable. Yet we think such persons must be punished no matter what their motives; people cannot be permitted to take the law into their own hands.

6. It is said that picking pockets was once a capital offense in England, and hangings were public, in order to get the maximum deterrent effect. But hangings in public had to be abolished, because such crimes as picking pockets were so frequent during the spectacle! See N. F. Cantor, *Crime, Criminals, and Criminal Justice* (New York: Henry Holt & Company, Inc., 1932).

A Critique of the Humanitarian Theory of Punishment

C. S. Lewis

C. S. Lewis argues that the humanitarian theory of punishment is not in the interests of the criminal. According to Lewis, this is because the humanitarian theory is concerned with the goals of reform and deterrence and not the requirements of justice. Hence, the theory permits the violation of the criminal's rights as a way of promoting these goals. Moreover, Lewis claims, deciding what promotes reform and deterrence, unlike deciding what is required by justice, seems best left to experts. Yet these experts, Lewis argues, even with the best of intentions, may act "as cruelly and unjustly as the greatest tryants."

In England we have lately had a controversy about Capital Punishment. I do not know whether a murderer is more likely to repent and make a good end on the gallows a few weeks after his trial or in the prison infirmary thirty years later. I do not know whether the fear of death is an indispensable deterrent. I need not, for the purpose of this article, decide whether it is a morally permissible deterrent. Those are questions which I propose to leave untouched. My subject is not Capital Punishment in particular, but that theory of punishment in general which the controversy showed to be almost universal among my fellow-countrymen. It may be called the Humanitarian theory. Those who hold it think that it is mild and merciful. In this I believe that they are seriously mistaken. I believe that the "Humanity" which it claims is a dangerous illusion and disguises the possibility of cruelty and injustice without end. I urge a return to the traditional or Retributive theory not solely, not even primarily, in the interests of society, but in the interests of the criminal.

According to the Humanitarian theory, to punish a man because he deserves it, and as much as he deserves, is mere revenge, and, therefore, barbarous and immoral. It is maintained that the only legitimate motives for punishing are the desire to deter others by example or to mend the criminal. When this theory is combined, as frequently happens, with the belief that all crime is more or less pathological, the idea of mending tails off into that of healing or curing and punishment be-

From "The Humanitarian Theory of Punishment," *Res Judicatae* (1953) pp. 224–230. Reprinted by permission of the *Melbourne University Law Review* and the Trustee for the C. S. Lewis Estate.

comes therapeutic. Thus it appears at first sight that we have passed from the harsh and self-righteous notion of giving the wicked their deserts to the charitable and enlightened one of tending the psychologically sick. What could be more amiable? One little point which is taken for granted in this theory needs, however, to be made explicit. The things done to the criminal, even if they are called cures, will be just as compulsory as they were in the old days when we called them punishments. If a tendency to steal can be cured by psychotherapy, the thief will no doubt be forced to undergo the treatment. Otherwise, society cannot continue.

My contention is that this doctrine, merciful though it appears, really means that each one of us, from the moment he breaks the law, is deprived of the rights of a human being.

The reason is this. The Humanitarian theory removes from Punishment the concept of Desert. But the concept of Desert is the only connecting link between punishment and justice. It is only as deserved or undeserved that a sentence can be just or unjust. I do not here contend that the question "Is it deserved?" is the only one we can reasonably ask about a punishment. We may very properly ask whether it is likely to deter others and to reform the criminal. But neither of these two last questions is a question about justice. There is no sense in talking about a "just deterrent" or a "just cure". We demand of a deterrent not whether it is just but whether it will deter. We demand of a cure not whether it is just but whether it succeeds. Thus when we cease to consider what the criminal deserves and consider only what will cure him or deter others, we have tacitly removed him from the sphere of justice altogether; instead of a person, a subject of rights, we now have a mere object, a patient, a "case".

The distinction will become clearer if we ask who will be qualified to determine sentences when sentences are no longer held to derive their propriety from the criminal's deservings. On the old view the problem of fixing the right sentence was a moral problem. Accordingly, the judge who did it was a person trained in jurisprudence: trained, that is, in a science which deals with rights and duties, and which, in origin at least, was consciously accepting guidance from the Law of Nature, and from Scripture. We must admit that in the actual penal code of most countries at most times these high originals were so much modified by local custom, class interests, and utilitarian concessions, as to be very imperfectly recognizable. But the code was never in principle, and not always in fact, beyond the control of the conscience of the society. And when (say, in eighteenth-century England) actual punishments conflicted too violently with the moral sense of the community, juries refused to convict and reform was finally brought about. This was possible because, so long as we are thinking in terms of Desert, the propriety of the penal code, being a moral question, is a question on which every man has the right to an opinion, not because he follows this or that profession, but because he is simply a man, a rational animal enjoying the Natural Light. But all this is changed when we drop the concept of Desert. The only two questions we may now ask about a punishment are whether it deters and whether it cures. But these are not questions on which anyone is entitled to have an opinion simply because he is a man. He is not entitled to an opinion even if, in addition to being a man, he should happen also to be a jurist, a Christian, and a moral theologian. For they are not questions about principle but about matter of fact; and for such *cuiquam in sua arte credendum*. Only the expert "penologist" (let barbarous things have barbarous names), in the light of previous experiment, can tell us what is likely to deter: only the psychotherapist can tell us what is likely to cure. It will be in vain for the rest of us, speaking simply as men, to say, "but this punishment is hideously unjust, hideously disproportionate to the criminal's deserts". The experts with perfect logic will reply, "but nobody was talking about deserts. No one was talking about *punishment* in your archaic vindictive sense of the word. Here are the statistics proving that this treatment deters. Here are the statistics proving that this other treatment cures. What is your trouble?"

The Humanitarian theory, then, removes sentences from the hands of jurists whom the public conscience is entitled to criticize and places them in the hands of technical experts whose special sciences do not even employ such categories as rights or justice. It might be argued that since this transference results from an abandonment of the old idea of punishment, and, therefore, of all vindictive motives, it will be safe to leave our criminals in such hands. I will not pause to comment on the simple-minded view of fallen human nature which such a belief implies. Let us rather remember that the "cure" of criminals is to be compulsory; and let us then watch how the theory actually works in the mind of the Humanitarian. The immediate starting point of this article was a letter I read in one of our Leftist weeklies. The author was pleading that a certain sin, now treated by our laws as a crime, should henceforward be treated as a disease. And he complained that under the present system the offender, after a term in gaol, was simply let out to return to his original environment where he would probably relapse. What he complained of was not the shutting up but the letting out. On his remedial view of punishment the offender should, of course, be detained until he was cured. And of course the official straighteners are the only people who can say when that is. The first result of the Humanitarian theory is, therefore, to substitute for a definite sentence (reflecting to some extent the community's moral judgment on the degree of ill-desert involved) an indefinite sentence terminable only by the word of those experts—and they are not experts in moral theology nor even in the Law of Nature—who inflict it. Which of us, if he stood in the dock, would not prefer to be tried by the old system?

It may be said that by the continued use of the word punishment and the use of the verb "inflict" I am misrepresenting Humanitarians. They are not punishing, not inflicting, only healing. But do not let us be deceived by a name. To be taken without consent from my home and friends; to lose my liberty; to undergo all those assaults on my personality which modern psychotherapy knows how to deliver; to be re-made after some pattern of "normality" hatched in a Viennese laboratory to which I never professed allegiance; to know that this process will never end until either my captors have succeeded or I grown wise enough to cheat them with apparent success— who cares whether this is called Punishment or

not? That it includes most of the elements for which any punishment is feared—shame, exile, bondage, and years eaten by the locust—is obvious. Only enormous ill-desert could justify it; but ill-desert is the very conception which the Humanitarian theory has thrown overboard.

If we turn from the curative to the deterrent justification of punishment we shall find the new theory even more alarming. When you punish a man *in terrorem*, make of him an "example" to others, you are admittedly using him as a means to an end; someone else's end. This, in itself, would be a very wicked thing to do. On the classical theory of Punishment it was of course justified on the ground that the man deserved it. That was assumed to be established before any question of "making him an example" arose. You then, as the saying is, killed two birds with one stone; in the process of giving him what he deserved you set an example to others. But take away desert and the whole morality of the punishment disappears. Why, in Heaven's name, am I to be sacrificed to the good of society in this way?—unless, of course, I deserve it.

But that is not the worst. If the justification of exemplary punishment is not to be based on desert but solely on its efficacy as a deterrent, it is not absolutely necessary that the man we punish should even have committed the crime. The deterrent effect demands that the public should draw the moral, "If we do such an act we shall suffer like that man." The punishment of a man actually guilty whom the public think innocent will not have the desired effect; the punishment of a man actually innocent will, provided the public think him guilty. But every modern State has powers which make it easy to fake a trial. When a victim is urgently needed for exemplary purposes and a guilty victim cannot be found, all the purposes of deterrence will be equally served by the punishment (call it "cure" if you prefer) of an innocent victim, provided that the public can be cheated into thinking him guilty. It is no use to ask me why I assume that our rulers will be so wicked. The punishment of an innocent, that is, an undeserving, man is wicked only if we grant the traditional view that righteous punishment means deserved punishment. Once we have abandoned that criterion, all punishments have to be justified, if at all, on other grounds that have nothing to do with desert. Where the punishment of the innocent can be justified on those grounds (and it could in some cases be justified as a deterrent) it will be no less moral than any other punishment. Any distaste for it on the part of a Humanitarian will be merely a hang-over from the Retributive theory.

It is, indeed, important to notice that my argument so far supposes no evil intentions on the part of the Humanitarian and considers only what is involved in the logic of his position. My contention is that good men (not bad men) consistently acting upon that position would act as cruelly and unjustly as the greatest tyrants. They might in some respects act even worse. Of all tyrannies a tyranny sincerely exercised for the good of its victims may be the most oppressive. It may be better to live under robber barons than under omnipotent moral busybodies. The robber baron's cruelty may sometimes sleep, his cupidity may at some point be satiated; but those who torment us for our own good will torment us without end for they do so with the approval of their own conscience. They may be more likely to go to Heaven yet at the same time likelier to make a Hell of earth. Their very kindness stings with intolerable insult. To be "cured" against one's will and cured of states which we may not regard as disease is to be put on a level with those who have not yet reached the age of reason or those who never will; to be classed with infants, imbeciles, and domestic animals. But to be punished, however severely; because we have deserved it, because we "ought to have known better", is to be treated as a human person made in God's image.

In reality, however, we must face the possibility of bad rulers armed with a Humanitarian theory of punishment. A great many popular blue prints for a Christian society are merely what the Elizabethans called "eggs in moonshine" because they assume that the whole society is Christian or that the Christians are in control. This is not so in most contemporary States. Even if it were, our rulers would still be fallen men, and, therefore, neither very wise nor very good. As it is, they will usually be unbelievers. And since wisdom and virtue are not the only or the commonest qualifications for a place in the government, they will not often be even the best unbelievers. The practical problem of Christian politics is not that of drawing up schemes for a Christian society, but that of living as innocently as we can with unbelieving fellow-subjects under unbelieving rulers who will never be perfectly wise and good and who will sometimes be very wicked and very foolish. And when they are wicked the Humanitarian theory of punishment will put in their hands a finer instrument of tyranny than wickedness ever had before. For if crime and disease are to be regarded as the same thing, it follows that any state of mind which our masters choose to call "disease" can be treated as crime; and compulsorily cured. It will be vain to plead that states of mind which displease government need not always involve moral turpitude and do not therefore always deserve forfeiture of liberty. For our masters will not be using the concepts of Desert and Punishment but those of disease and cure. We know that one school of psychology already regards religion as a neurosis. When this particular neurosis becomes inconvenient to government, what is to hinder government from proceeding to "cure" it? Such "cure" will, of course, be compulsory; but under the Humanitarian theory it will not be called by the shocking name of Persecution. No one will blame us for being Christian, no one will hate us, no one will revile us. The new Nero will approach us with the silky manners of a doctor, and though all will be in fact as compulsory as the *tunica molesta* or Smithfield or Tyburn, all will go on within the unemotional therapeutic sphere where words like "right" and "wrong" or "freedom" and "slavery" are never heard. And thus when the command is given, every prominent Christian in the land may vanish overnight into Institutions for the Treatment of the Ideologically Unsound, and it will rest with the expert gaolers to say when (if ever) they are to reemerge. But it will not be persecution. Even if the treatment is painful, even if it is life-long, even if it is fatal, that will be only a regrettable accident; the intention was purely therapeutic. Even in ordinary medicine there were painful operations and fatal operations; so in this. But because they are "treatment", not punishment, they can be criticized only by fellow-experts and on technical grounds, never by men as men and on grounds of justice.

This is why I think it essential to oppose the Humanitarian theory of punishment, root and branch, wherever we encounter it. It carries on its front a semblance of mercy which is wholly false. That is how it can deceive men of good will. The error began, perhaps, with Shelley's statement that the distinction between mercy and justice was invented in the courts of tyrants. It sounds noble, and was indeed the error of a noble mind. But the distinction is essential. The older view was that mercy "tempered" justice, or (on the highest level of all) that mercy and justice had met and kissed. The essential act of mercy was to pardon; and pardon in its very essence involves the recognition of guilt, and ill-desert in the recipient. If crime is only a disease which needs cure, not sin which deserves punishment, it cannot be pardoned. How can you pardon a man for having a gumboil or a club foot? But the Humanitarian theory wants simply to abolish Justice and substitute Mercy for it. This means that you start being "kind" to people before you have considered their rights, and then force upon them supposed kindnesses which they in fact had a right to refuse, and finally kindnesses which no one but you will recognize as kindnesses and which the recipient will feel as abominable cruelties.

You have overshot the mark. Mercy, detached from Justice, grows unmerciful. That is the important paradox. As there are plants which will flourish only in mountain soil, so it appears that Mercy will flower only when it grows in the crannies of the rock of Justice: transplanted to the marshlands of mere Humanitarianism, it becomes a man-eating weed, all the more dangerous because it is still called by the same name as the mountain variety. But we ought long ago to have learned our lesson. We should be too old now to be deceived by those humane pretensions which have served to usher in every cruelty of the revolutionary period in which we live. These are the "precious balms" which will "break our heads."

There is a fine sentence in Bunyan: "It came burning hot into my mind, whatever he said, and however he flattered, when he got me home to his house, he would sell me for a slave." There is a fine couplet, too, in John Ball:

Be ware ere ye be woe
Know your friend from your foe.

One last word. You may ask why I sent this to an Australian periodical. The reason is simple and perhaps worth recording: I can get no hearing for it in England.

Classical Retributivism

Edmund L. Pincoffs

Edmund L. Pincoffs begins by setting out three principles that, he holds, express the essence of a Kantian retributive theory of punishment. He then claims that the underlying rationale for these principles is to provide a justification of the punishment to the criminal on the grounds that she has willed the punishment she now suffers. Pincoffs concludes by noting two difficulties for the retributive theory of punishment which he has not addressed: how to make punishment equal to the crime and how to distinguish punishment from revenge.

From *The Rationale of Legal Punishment* (1966) pp. 2–16. Reprinted by permission of Humanities Press, Inc., Atlantic Highlands, N.J., 07716.

I

The classification of Kant as a retributivist[1] is usually accompanied by a reference to some part of the following passage from the *Rechtslehre*, which is worth quoting at length.

Juridical punishment can never be administered merely as a means for promoting another good either with regard to the criminal himself or to civil society, but must in all cases be imposed only because the individual on whom it is inflicted *has committed a crime.* For one man ought never to be dealt with merely as a means subservient to the purpose of another, nor be mixed up with the subjects of real right. Against such treatment his inborn personality has a right to protect him, even though he may be condemned to lose his civil personality. He must first be found guilty and *punishable* before there can be any thought of drawing from his punishment any benefit for himself or his fellow-citizens. The penal law is a categorical imperative; and woe to him who creeps through the serpent-windings of utilitarianism to discover some advantage that may discharge him from the justice of punishment, or even from the due measure of it, according to the Pharisaic maxim: "It is better that *one* man should die than the whole people should perish." For if justice and righteousness perish, human life would no longer have any value in the world.

. . .

But what is the mode and measure of punishment which public justice takes as its principle and standard? It is just the principle of equality, by which the pointer of the scale of justice is made to incline no more to the one side than the other. It may be rendered by saying that the undeserved evil which any one commits on another, is to be regarded as perpetrated on himself. Hence it may be said: "If you slander another, you slander yourself; if you steal from another, you steal from yourself; if you strike another, you strike yourself; if you kill another, you kill yourself." This is the Right of RETALIATION (*jus talionis*); and properly understood, it is the only principle which in regulating a public court, as distinguished from mere private judgment, can definitely assign both the quality and the quantity of a just penalty. All other standards are wavering and uncertain; and on account of other considerations involved in them, they contain no principle conformable to the sentence of pure and strict justice.[2]

Obviously we could mull over this passage for a long time. What, exactly, is the distinction between the Inborn and the Civil Personality? How is the Penal Law a Categorical Imperative: by derivation from one of the five formulations in the *Grundlegung*, or as a separate formulation? But we are on the trail of the traditional retributive theory of punishment and do not want to lose ourselves in niceties. There are two main points in this passage to which we should give particular attention:

i. The only acceptable reason for punishing a man is that he has committed a crime.

ii. The only acceptable reason for punishing a man in a given manner and degree is that the punishment is "equal" to the crime for which he is punished.

These propositions, I think it will be agreed, express the main points of the first and second paragraphs respectively. Before stopping over these points, let us go on to a third. It is brought out in the following passage from the *Rechtslehre*, which is also often referred to by writers on retributivism.

Even if a civil society resolved to dissolve itself with the consent of all its members—as might be supposed in the case of a people inhabiting an island resolving to separate and scatter themselves throughout the whole world—the last murderer lying in prison ought to be executed before the resolution was carried out. This ought to be done in order that every one may realize the desert of his deeds, and that bloodguiltiness may not remain upon the people; for otherwise they will all be regarded as participators in the murder as a public violation of justice.[3]

It is apparent from this passage that, so far anyway as the punishment of death for murder is concerned, the punishment awarded not only may but must be carried out. If it must be carried out "so that everyone may realize the desert of his deeds," then punishment for deeds other than murder must be carried out too. We will take it, then, that Kant holds that:

iii. Whoever commits a crime must be punished in accordance with his desert.

Whereas (i) tells us what kind of reason we must have *if* we punish, (iii) now tells us that we must punish *whenever* there is desert of punishment. Punishment, Kant tells us elsewhere, is "The *juridical* effect or consequence of a culpable act of Demerit."[4] Any crime is a culpable act of demerit, in that it is an "*intentional* transgression—that is, an act accompanied with the consciousness that it is a transgression."[5] This is an unusually narrow definition of crime, since crime is not ordinarily limited to intentional acts of transgression but may also include unintentional ones, such as acts done in ignorance of the law, and criminally negligent acts. However, Kant apparently leaves room for "culpable acts of demerit" outside of the category of crime. These he calls "faults," which are unintentional transgressions of duty, but "are nevertheless imputable to a person."[6] I can only suppose, though it is a difficulty in the interpretation of the *Rechtslehre*, that when Kant says that punishment must be inflicted "only because he has committed a crime," he is not including in "crime" what he would call a fault. Crime would, then, refer to any *intentional* imputable transgressions of duty; and these are what must be punished as involving ill desert. The difficulties involved in the definition of crime as the transgression of duty, as opposed to the mere violation of a legal prohibition, will be taken up later.

Taking the three propositions we have iso-

lated as expressing the essence of the Kantian retributivistic position, we must now ask a direct and obvious question. What makes Kant hold this position? Why does he think it apparent that consequences should have *nothing to do* with the decision whether, and how, and how much to punish? There are two directions an answer to this question might follow. One would lead us into an extensive excursus on the philosophical position of Kant, the relation of this to his ethical theory, and the relation of his general theory of ethics to his philosophy of law. It would, in short, take our question as one about the consistency of Kant's position concerning the justification of punishment with the whole of Kantian philosophy. This would involve discussion of Kant's reasons for believing that moral laws must be universal and categorical in virtue of their form alone, and divorced from any empirical content; of his attempt to make out a moral decision-procedure based upon an "empty" categorical imperative; and, above all, of the concept of freedom as a postulate of practical reason, and as the central concept of the philosophy of law. This kind of answer, however, we must forego here; for while it would have considerable interest in its own right, it would lead us astray from our purpose, which is to understand as well as we can the retributivist position, not as a part of this or that philosophical system but for its own sake. It is a position taken by philosophers with diverse philosophical systems; we want to take another direction, then, in our answer. Is there any *general* (nonspecial, nonsystematic) reason why Kant rejects consequences in the justification of punishment?

Kant believes that consequences have nothing to do with the justification of punishment partly because of his assumptions about the *direction* of justification; and these assumptions are, I believe, also to be found underlying the thought of Hegel and Bradley. Justification is not only *of* something, it is also *to* someone: it has an addressee. Now there are important confusions in Kant's and other traditional justifications of punishment turning on the question what the "punishment" *is* which is being justified. . . . But if we are to feel the force of the retributivist position, we can no longer put off the question of the addressee of justification.

To whom is the Kantian justification of punishment directed? The question may seem a difficult one to answer, since Kant does not consider it himself as a separate issue. Indeed, it is not the kind of question likely to occur to a philosopher of Kant's formalistic leanings. A Kantian justification or rationale stands, so to speak, on its own. It is a structure which can be examined, tested, probed by any rational being. Even to speak of the addressee of justification has an uncomfortably relativistic sound, as if only persuasion of A or B or C is possible, and proof impossible. Yet, in practice, Kant does not address his proffered justification of punishment so much to any rational being (which, to put it otherwise, is to address it not at all), as to the being most affected: the criminal himself.

It is the criminal who is cautioned not to creep through the serpent-windings of utilitarianism. It is the criminal's rights which are in question in the debate with Beccaria over capital punishment. It is the criminal we are warned not to mix up with property or things: the "subjects of Real Right." In the *Kritik der Praktischen Vernunst*, the intended direction of justification becomes especially clear.

Now the notion of punishment, as such, cannot be united with that of becoming a partaker of happiness; for although he who inflicts the punishment may at the same time have the benevolent purpose of directing this punishment to this end, yet it must be justified in itself as punishment, that is, as mere harm, so that if it stopped there, and the person punished could get no glimpse of kindness hidden behind this harshness, he must yet admit that justice was done him, and that his reward was perfectly suitable to his conduct. In every punishment, as such, there must first be justice, and this constitutes the essence of the notion. Benevolence may, indeed, be united with it, but the man who has deserved punishment has not the least reason to reckon upon this.[7]

Since this matter of the direction of justification is central in our understanding of traditional retributivism, and not generally appreciated, it will be worth our while to pause over this paragraph. Kant holds here, as he later holds in the *Rechtslehre*, that once it has been decided that a given "mode and measure" of punishment is justified, then "he who inflicts punishment" may do so in such a way as to increase the long-term happiness of the criminal. This could be accomplished, for example, by using a prison term as an opportunity for reforming the criminal. But Kant's point is that reforming the criminal has nothing to do with justifying the infliction of punishment. It is not inflicted because it will give an opportunity for reform, but because it is merited. The passage does not need my gloss; it is transparently clear. Kant wants the justification of punishment to be such that the criminal "who could get no glimpse of kindness behind this harshness" would have to admit that punishment is warranted.

Suppose we tell the criminal, "We are punishing you for your own good." This is wrong, because it is then open to him to raise the question whether he deserves punishment, and what you consider good to be. If he does not deserve punishment, we have no right to inflict it, especially in the name of some good of which the criminal may not approve. So long as we are to treat him as rational—a being with dignity—we cannot force our judgments of good upon him. This is what makes the appeal to supposedly good consequences "wavering and uncertain." They waver because the criminal has as much right as anyone to question them. They concern ends which he may reject, and means which he might rightly regard as unsuited to the ends.

In the "Supplementary Explanations of the Principles of Right" of the *Rechtslehre*, Kant distinguishes between "punitive justice (*justitia punitiva*), in which the ground of the penalty is moral (*quia peccatum est*)," and "punitive *expediency*, the foundation of which is merely pragmatic (*ne peccetur*) as being grounded upon the experience of what operates most effectively to prevent crime." Punitive justice, says Kant, has an "entirely distinct place (*locus justi*) in the topical arrangement of the juridical conceptions." It does not seem reasonable to suppose that Kant makes this distinction merely to discard punitive expediency entirely, that he has no concern at all for the *ne peccetur*. But he does hold that there is no place for it in the justification of punishment proper: for this can only be to show the criminal that the punishment is just.

How is this to be done? The difficulty is that on the one hand the criminal must be treated as a rational being, an end in himself; but on the other hand the justification we offer him cannot be allowed to appear as the opening move in a rational discussion. It cannot turn on the criminal's acceptance of some premise which, as rational being, he has a perfect right to question. If the end in question is the well-being of society, we are assuming that the criminal will not have a different view of what that well-being consists in, and we are telling him that he should sacrifice himself *to* that end. As a rational being, he can question whether any end we propose is a good end. And we have no right to demand that he sacrifice himself to the public well-being, even supposing he agrees with us on what that consists in. No man has a duty, on Kant's view, to be benevolent.[8]

The way out of the quandary is to show the criminal that we are not inflicting the punishment on him for some questionable purpose of our own choice, but that he, as a free agent, has exercised *his* choice in such a way as to make the punishment a necessary consequence. "His own evil deed draws the punishment upon himself."[9] "The undeserved evil which anyone commits on another, is to be regarded as perpetuated on himself."[10] But may not the criminal rationally question this asserted connection between crime and punishment? Suppose he wishes to regard the punishment *not* as "drawn upon himself" by his own "evil deed?" Suppose he argues that no good purpose will be served by punishing him? But this line of thought leads into the "serpent-windings of utilitarianism," for if it is good consequences that govern, then justice goes by the board. What may not be done to him in the name of good consequences? What proportion would remain between what he has done and what he suffers?[11]

But punishment is *inflicted*. To tell the criminal that he "draws it upon himself" is all very well, only how do we justify *to ourselves* the infliction of it? Kant's answer is found early in the *Rechtslehre*.[12] There he relates punishment to crime *via* freedom. Crime consists in compulsion or constraint of some kind: a hindrance of freedom.[13] If it is wrong that freedom should be hindered, it is right to block this hindrance. But to block the constraint of freedom it is necessary to apply constraint. Punishment is a "hindering of a hindrance of freedom." Compulsion of the criminal is, then, justified only to the extent that it hinders his compulsion of another.

But how are we to understand Kant here? Punishment comes after the crime. How can it hinder the crime? The reference cannot be to the hindrance of future crime, or Kant's doctrine reduces to a variety of utilitarianism. The picture of compulsion *vs.* compulsion is clear enough, but how are we to apply it? Our answer must be somewhat speculative, since there is no direct answer to be found in the *Rechtslehre*. The answer must begin from yet another extension of the concept of a crime. For the crime cannot consist merely in an act. What is criminal is acting in accordance with a wrong maxim: a maxim which would, if made universal, destroy freedom. The adoption of the maxim is criminal. Should we regard punishment, then, as the hindrance of a wrong maxim? But how do we hinder a maxim? We show, exhibit, its wrongness by taking it at face value. If the criminal has adopted it, he is claiming that it can be universalized. But if it is universalized it warrants the same treatment of the criminal as he has accorded to his victim. So if he murders he must be executed; if he steals we must "steal from" him.[14] What we do to him he willed, in willing to adopt his maxim as universalizable. To justify the punishment to the criminal is to show him that the compulsion we use on him proceeds according to the same rule by which he acts. This is how he "draws the punishment upon himself." In punishing, we are not adopting his maxim but demonstrating its logical consequences if universalized: We show the criminal *what* he has willed. This is the positive side of the Kantian rationale of punishment.

II

Hegel's version of this rationale has attracted more attention, and disagreement, in recent literature. It is the Hegelian metaphysical terminology which is in part responsible for the disagreement, and which has stood in the way of an understanding of the retributivist position. The difficulty turns around the notions of "annulment of crime," and of punishment as the "right" of the criminal. Let us consider "annulment" first.

In the *Philosophie des Rechts*[15] Hegel tells us that

> Abstract right is a right to coerce, because the wrong which transgresses it is an exercise of force against the existence of my freedom in an external thing. The maintenance of this existent against the exercise of force therefore itself takes the form of an external act and an exercise of force annulling the force originally brought against it.[16]

Holmes complains that by the use of his logical apparatus, involving the negation of negations (or annulment), Hegel professes to establish what is only a mystic (though generally felt) bond between wrong and punishment.[17] Hastings Rashdall asks how any rational connection can be shown between the evil of the pain of punishment, and the twin evils of the suffering of the victim and the moral evil which "pollutes the offender's soul," unless appeal is made to the probable good consequences of punishment. The notion that the "guilt" of the offense must be, in some mysterious way, wiped out by the suffering of the offender does not seem to provide it.[18] Crime, which is an evil, is apparently to be "annulled" by the addition to it of punishment, which is another evil. How can two evils yield a good?[19]

But in fact Hegel is following the *Rechtslehre* quite closely here, and his doctrine is very near to Kant's. In the notes taken at Hegel's lectures,[20] we find Hegel quoted as follows:

> If crime and its annulment . . . are treated as if they were unqualified evils, it must, of course, seem quite unreasonable to will an evil merely because "another evil is there already." . . . But it is not merely a question of an evil or of this, that, or the other good; the precise point at issue is wrong, and the righting of it. . . . The various considerations which are relevant to punishment as a phenomenon and to the bearing it has on the particular consciousness, and which concern its effects (deterrent, reformative, etcetera) on the imagination, are an essential topic for examination in their place, especially in connection with modes of punishment, but all these considerations presuppose as their foundation the fact that punishment is inherently and actually just. In discussing this matter the only important things are, first, that crime is to be annulled, not because it is the producing of an evil, but because it is the infringing of the right as right, and secondly, the question of what that positive existence is which crime possesses and which must be annulled; it is this existence which is the real evil to be removed, and the essential point is the question of where it lies. So long as the concepts here at issue are not clearly apprehended, confusion must continue to reign in the theory of punishment.[21]

While this passage is not likely to dethrone confusion, it does bring us closer to the basically Kantian heart of Hegel's theory. To "annul crime" should be read "right wrong." Crime is a wrong which consists in an "infringement of the right as right."[22] It would be unjust, says Hegel, to allow crime, which is the invasion of a right, to go unrequited. For to allow this is to admit that the crime is "valid": that is, that it is not in conflict with justice. But this is what we do want to admit, and the only way of showing this is to pay back the deed to the agent: coerce the coercer. For by intentionally violating his victim's rights, the criminal in effect claims that the rights of others are not binding on him; and this is to attack *das Recht* itself: the system of justice in which there are rights which must be respected. Punishment not only keeps the system in balance, it vindicates the system itself.

Besides talking about punishment's "annulment" of crime, Hegel has argued that it is the "right of the criminal." The obvious reaction to this is that it is a strange justification of punishment which makes it someone's right, for it is at best a strange kind of right which no one would ever want to claim! McTaggart's explanation of this facet of Hegel's theory is epitomized in the following quotation:

What, then, is Hegel's theory? It is, I think, briefly this: In sin, man rejects and defies the moral law. Punishment is pain inflicted on him because he has done this, and in order that he may, by the fact of his punishment, be forced into recognizing as valid the law which he rejected in sinning, and so repent of his sin—really repent, and not merely be frightened out of doing it again.[23]

If McTaggart is right, then we are obviously not going to find in Hegel anything relevant to the justification of legal punishment, where the notions of sin and repentance are out of place. And this is the conclusion McTaggart of course reaches. "Hegel's view of punishment," he insists, "cannot properly be applied in jurisprudence, and . . . his chief mistake regarding it lay in supposing that it could."[24]

But though McTaggart may be right in emphasizing the theological aspect of Hegel's doctrine of punishment, he is wrong in denying it a jurisprudential aspect. In fact, Hegel is only saying what Kant emphasized: that to justify punishment to the criminal is to show him that *he* has chosen to be treated as he is being treated.

The injury (the penalty) which falls on the criminal is not merely *implicitly* just—as just, it is *eo ipso* his implicit will, an embodiment of his freedom, his right; on the contrary, it is also a right *established* within the criminal himself, that is, in his objectively embodied will, in his action. The reason for this is that his action is the action of a rational being and this implies that it is something universal and that by doing it the criminal has laid down a law which he has explicitly recognized in his action and under which in consequence he should be brought as under his right.[25]

To accept the retributivist position, then, is to accept a thesis about the burden of proof in the justification of punishment. Provided we make the punishment "equal" to the crime it is not up to us to justify it to the criminal, beyond pointing out to him that it is what he willed. It is not that he initiated a chain of events likely to result in his punishment, but that in willing the crime he willed that he himself should suffer in the same degree as his victim. But what if the criminal simply wanted to commit his crime and get away with it (break the window and run, take the funds and retire to Brazil, kill but live?) Suppose we explain to the criminal that *really* in willing to kill he willed to lose his life; and, unimpressed, he replies that *really* he wished to kill and save his skin. The retributivist answer is that to the extent that the criminal understands freedom and justice he will understand that his punishment was made inevitable by his own choice. No moral theory can hope to provide a justification of punishment which will seem such to the criminal merely as a nexus of passions and desires. The retributivist addresses him as a rational being, aware of the significance of his action. The burden of proof, the retributivist would argue, is on the theorist who would not start from this assumption. For to assume from the beginning that the criminal is not rational is to treat him, from the beginning, as merely a "harmful animal."

What is involved in the action of the criminal is not only the concept of crime, the rational aspect present in crime as such whether the individual wills it or not, the aspect which the state has to vindicate, but also the abstract rationality of the individual's *volition*. Since that is so, punishment is regarded as containing the criminal's right and hence by being punished he is honored as a rational being. He does not receive this due of honor unless the concept and measure of his punishment are derived from his own act. Still less does he receive it if he is treated as a harmful animal who has to be made harmless, or with a view to deterring and reforming him.[26]

To address the criminal as a rational being aware of the significance of his action is to address him as a person who knows that he has not committed a "bare" act; to commit an act is to commit oneself to the universalization of the rule by which one acted. For a man to complain about the death sentence for murder is as absurd as for a man to complain that when he pushed down one tray of the scales, the other tray goes up; whereas the action, rightly considered, is of pushing down *and* up. "The criminal gives his consent already by his very act."[27] "The Eumenides sleep, but crime awakens them, and hence it is the very act of crime which vindicates itself."[28]

F. H. Bradley's contribution to the retributive theory of punishment adds heat but not much light. The central, and best-known, passage is the following:

> If there is any opinion to which the man of uncultivated morals is attached, it is the belief in the necessary connection of Punishment and guilt. Punishment is punishment, only where it is deserved. We pay the penalty because we owe it, and for no other reason; and if punishment is inflicted for any other reason whatever than because it is merited by wrong, it is a gross immorality, a crying injustice, an abominable crime, and not what it pretends to be. We may have regard for whatever considerations we please—our own convenience, the good of society, the benefit of the offender; we are fools, and worse, if we fail to do so. Having once the right to punish, we may modify the punishment according to the useful and the pleasant; but these are external to the matter, they cannot give us a right to punish, and nothing can do that but criminal desert. This is not a subject to waste words over; if the fact of the vulgar view is not palpable to the reader, we have no hope, and no wish, to make it so.[29]

Bradley's sympathy with the "vulgar view" should be apparent. And there is at least a seeming variation between the position he expresses here and that we have attributed to Kant and Hegel. For Bradley can be read here as leaving an open field for utilitarian reasoning, when the question is how and how much to punish. Ewing interprets Bradley this way, and argues at some length that Bradley is involved in an inconsistency.[30] However, it is quite possible that Bradley did not mean to allow kind and quantity of punishment to be determined by utilitarian considerations. He could mean, as Kant meant, that once punishment is awarded, then "it" (what the criminal must suffer: time in jail, for example) may be made use of for utilitarian purposes. But, it should by this time go without saying, the retributivist would then wish to insist that we not argue backward from the likelihood of attaining these good purposes to the rightness of inflicting the punishment.

Bradley's language is beyond question loose when he speaks, in the passage quoted, of our "modifying" the punishment, "having once the right to punish." But when he says that "we pay the penalty because we owe it, and for no other reason," Bradley must surely be credited with the insight that we may owe more or less according to the gravity of the crime. The popular view, he says, is "that punishment is justice; that justice implies the giving what is due."[31] And, "punishment is the complement of criminal desert; is justifiable only so far as deserved."[32] If Bradley accepts this popular view, then Ewing must be wrong in attributing to him the position that kind and degree of punishment may be determined by utilitarian considerations.[33]

III

Let us sum up traditional retributivism, as we have found it expressed in the paradigmatic passage we have examined. We have found no reason in Hegel or Bradley, to take back or qualify importantly the *three propositions* we found central in Kant's retributivism:

i. The only acceptable reason for punishing a man is that he has committed a crime.

ii. The only acceptable reason for punishing a man in a given manner and degree is that the punishment is "equal" to the crime.

iii. Whoever commits a crime must be punished in accordance with his desert.

To these propositions should be added *two underlying assumptions:*

i. An assumption about the direction of justification: to the criminal.

ii. An assumption about the nature of justification: to show the criminal that it is he who has willed what he now suffers.

Though it may have been stated in forbidding metaphysical terms, traditional retributivism cannot be dismissed as unintelligible, or absurd, or implausible.[34] There is no obvious contradiction in it; and there are no important disagreements among the philosophers we have studied over what it contends. Yet in spite of the importance of the theory, no one has yet done much more than sketch it in broad strokes. If, as I have surmised, it turns mainly on an assumption concerning the direction of justification, then this assumption should be explained and defended.

And the key concept of "desert" is intolerably vague. What does it mean to say that punishment must be proportionate to what a man *deserves?* This seems to imply, in the theory of the traditional retributivists, that there is some way of measuring desert, or at least of balancing punishment against it. How this measuring or balancing is supposed to be done, we will discuss later. What we must recognize here is that there are alternative criteria of "desert," and that it is not always clear which of these the traditional retributivist means to imply.

When we say of a man that he "deserves severe punishment" how, if at all, may we support our position by arguments? What kind of considerations tend to show what a man does or does not deserve? There are at least two general sorts: those which tend to show that what he has done is a member of a class of action which is especially heinous; and those which tend to show that his doing of this action was, in (or because of) the circumstances, par-

ticularly wicked. The argument that a man deserves punishment may rest on the first kind of appeal alone, or on both kinds. Retributivists who rely on the first sort of consideration alone would say that anyone who would do a certain sort of thing, no matter what the circumstances may have been, deserves punishment. Whether there are such retributivists I do not know. Kant, because of his insistence on *intention* as a necessary condition of committing a crime, clearly wishes to bring in considerations of the second sort as well. It is not, on his view, merely *what* was done, but the intention of the agent which must be taken into account. No matter what the intention, a man cannot commit a crime deserving punishment if his deed is not a transgression. But if he does commit a transgression, he must do so intentionally to commit a crime; and all crime is deserving of punishment. The desert of the crime is a factor both of the seriousness of the transgression, considered by itself, and the degree to which the intention to transgress was present. If, for Kant, the essence of morality consists in knowingly acting from duty, the essence of immorality consists in knowingly acting against duty.

The retributivist can perhaps avoid the question of how we decide that one crime is morally more heinous than another by hewing to his position that no such decision is necessary so long as we make the punishment "equal" to the crime. To accomplish this, he might argue, it is not necessary to argue to the *relative* wickedness of crimes. But at best this leaves us with the problem how we *do* make punishments equal to crimes, a problem which will not stop plaguing retributivists. And there is the problem *which* transgressions, intentionally committed, the retributivist is to regard as crimes. Surely not every morally wrong action!

And how is the retributivist to fit in appeals to punitive expediency? None of our authors denies that such appeals may be made, but where and how do they tie into punitive justice? It will not do simply to say that justifying punishment to the criminal is one thing, and justifying it to society is another. Suppose we must justify in both directions at once? And who are "we" anyway—the players of which roles, at what stage of the game? And has the retributivist cleared himself of the charge, sure to arise, that the theory is but a cover for a much less commendable motive than respect for justice: elegant draping for naked revenge?

Notes

1. . . . since in our own time there are few defenders of retributivism, the position is most often referred to by writers who are opposed to it. This does not make for clarity. In the past few years, however, there has been an upsurge of interest, and some good articles have been written. Cf. esp. J. D. Mabbott, "Punishment," *Mind*, XLVIII (1939), pp. 152–67; C. S. Lewis, "The Humanitarian Theory of Punishment," *20th Century* (Australian), March, 1949; C. W. K. Mundle, "Punishment and Desert," *The Philosophical Quarterly*, IV (1954), pp. 216–228; A. S. Kaufman, "Anthony Quinton on Punishment," *Analysis*, October, 1959; and K. G. Armstrong, "The Retributivist Hits Back," LXX (1961), pp. 471–90.

2. *Rechtslehre*. Part Second, 49, E. Hastie translation, Edinburgh, 1887, pp. 195–7.

3. *Ibid.*, p. 198. Cf. also the passage on p. 196 beginning "What, then, is to be said of such a proposal as to keep a Criminal alive who has been condemned to death . . ."

4. *Ibid.*, Prolegomena, General Divisions of the Metaphysic of Morals, IV. (Hastie, p. 38).

5. *Ibid.*, p. 32.

6. *Ibid.*, p. 32.

7. Book I, Ch. I, Sect. VIII, Theorem IV, Remark II (T. K. Abbott translation, 5th ed., revised, London, 1898, p. 127).

8. *Rechtslehre*.

9. "Supplementary Explanation of The Principles of Right," V.

10. Cf. long quote from the *Rechtslehre*, above.

11. How can the retributivist allow utilitarian considerations even in the administration of the sentence? Are we not then opportunistically imposing our conception of good on the convicted man? How did we come by this right, which we did not have when he stood before the bar awaiting sentence? Kant would refer to the loss of his "Civil Personality;" but what rights remain with the "Inborn Personality," which is not lost? How is human dignity modified by conviction of crime?

12. Introduction to The Science of Right, General Definitions and Divisions, D. Right is Joined with the Title to Compel. (Hastie, p. 47).

13. This extends the definition of crime Kant has given earlier by specifying the nature of an imputable transgression of duty.

14. There are serious difficulties in the application of the "Principle of Equality" to the "mode and measure" of punishment. This will be considered . . .

15. I shall use this short title for the work with the formidable double title of *Naturrecht und Stattswissenschaft in Grundrisse; Grundlinien der Philosophie des Rechts (Natural Law and Political Science in Outline: Elements of The Philosophy of Right.)* References will be to the T. M. Knox translation (*Hegel's Philosophy of Right*, Oxford, 1942).

16. *Philosophie des Rechts*, Sect. 93 (Knox, p. 67).

17. O. W. Holmes, Jr., *The Common Law*, Boston, 1881, p. 42.

18. Hastings Rashdall, *The Theory of Good and Evil*, 2nd. Edn., Oxford, 1924, vol. 1, pp. 285–6.

19. G. E. Moore holds that, consistently with his doctrine of organic wholes, they might; or at least they might yield that which is less evil than the sum of the constituent evils. This indicates for him a possible vindication of the Retributive theory of punishment. (*Principia Ethica*, Cambridge, 1903, pp. 213–214).

20. Included in the Knox translation.

21. Knox translation, pp. 69–70.

22. There is an unfortunate ambiguity in the German word *Recht*, here translated as "right." The word can mean either that which is a right or that which is in accordance with the law. So when Hegel speaks of "infringing the right as right" it is not certain whether he means a right as such or the law as such, or whether, in fact, he is aware of the ambiguity. But to say that the crime infringes the law is analytic, so we will take it that Hegel uses *Recht* here to refer to that which is right. But what the criminal does is not merely to infringe a right, but "the right *(das recht)* as right," that is, to challenge by his action the whole system of rights. (On *"Recht,"* Cf. J. Austin, *The Province of Jurisprudence Determined*, London, Library of Ideas Edition, 1954), Note 26, pp. 285–288 esp. pp. 287–8).

23. J. M. E. McTaggart, *Studies in The Hegelian Cosmology*, Cambridge, 1901, Ch. V, p. 133.

24. *Ibid.*, p. 145.

25. *Op Cit.*, Sect. 100 (Hastie, p. 70.)

26. *Ibid.*, Lecture-notes on Sect. 100, Hastie, p. 71.

27. *Ibid.*, Addition to Sect. 100, Hastie, p. 246.

28. *Ibid.*, Addition to Sect. 101, Hastie, p. 247. There is something ineradicably *curious* about retributivism. We keep coming back to the metaphor of the balance scale. Why is the metaphor powerful and the same time strange? Why do we agree so readily that "the assassination" cannot "trammel up the consequence," that "even-handed justice commends the ingredients of our poisoned chalice to our own lips?"

29. F. H. Bradley, *Ethical Studies*, Oxford, 1952, pp. 26–7.

30. A. C. Ewing, *The Morality of Punishment*, London, 1929, pp. 41–42.

31. *Op. Cit.*, p. 29.

32. *Ibid.*, p. 30.

33. *Op. Cit.*, p. 41.

34. Or, more ingeniously, "merely logical," the "elucidation of the use of a word;" answering the question, "When (logically) *can* we punish?" as opposed to the question answered by the utilitarians, "When (morally) *may* or *ought* we to punish?" (Cf. A. M. Quinton, "On Punishment," *Analysis*, June, 1954, pp. 133–142)

The Death Penalty: For and Against

Ernest van den Haag and Louis Schwartz

Ernest van den Haag favors the death penalty because (1) it is the indispensable deterrent for certain crimes, (2) some evidence seems to support its deterrent value, (3) imposing the death penalty is the least risky alternative, and (4) it is a requirement of justice.

Louis B. Schwartz opposes the death penalty because (1) mistakes occur in our trial system, (2) having the death penalty makes it difficult to get convictions, (3) some evidence seems to indicate that the death penalty does not deter, (4) having the death penalty can in certain cases stimulate a criminal to kill, and (5) the process of choosing those to be executed is inevitably arbitrary.

Q Professor van den Haag, why do you favor the use of the death penalty?

A For certain kinds of crimes it is indispensable.

Thus: The federal prisons now have custody of a man sentenced to life imprisonment who, since he has been in prison, has committed three more murders on three separate occasions—both of prison guards and inmates. There is no further punishment that he can receive. In effect, he has a license to murder.

Take another case: When a man is threatened with life imprisonment for a crime he has already committed, what reason has he

not to kill the arresting officer in an attempt to escape? His punishment would be the same.

In short, there are many cases where the death penalty is the only penalty available that could possibly deter.

I'll go a step further. I hold life sacred. Because I hold it sacred, I feel that anyone who takes someone else's life should know that thereby he forsakes his own and does not just suffer an inconvenience about being put into prison for some time.

Q Could the same effect be achieved by putting the criminal in prison for life?

A At present, "life imprisonment" means anything from six months—after which the parole board in Florida can release the man—to 12 years in some States. But even if it were real life imprisonment, its deterrent effect will never be as great as that of the death penalty. The death penalty is the only actually irrevocable penalty. Because of that, it is the one that people fear most. And because it is feared most, it is the one that is most likely to deter.

Q Authorities seem to differ as to whether the death sentence really does deter crime—

A Usually the statistics quoted were compiled more than 10 years ago and seem to indicate that the absence or presence of the death penalty made no difference in murder rates.

However, in the last 10 years there have been additional investigations. The results indicate, according to Isaac Ehrlich's recent article in the *American Economic Review:* Over the period 1933 to 1969, "an additional execution per year . . . may have resulted on the average in seven or eight fewer murders."

In New York in the last six years, the murder rate went up by 60 per cent. Previous to the abolition of the death penalty, about 80 percent of all murders committed in New York were so-called crimes of passion, defined as crimes in which the victim and the murderer were in some way involved with each other. Right now, only 50 per cent of all murders in New York are crimes of passion.

Q How do you interpret those figures?

A As long as the death penalty existed, largely only people in the grip of passion could not be deterred by the threat of the death penalty. Now that there's no death penalty, people who previously were deterred—who are not in the grip of passion—are no longer deterred from committing murder for the sake of gain. Murder is no longer an irrational act, least of all for juveniles for whom it means at most a few months of inconvenience.

Even if you assume the evidence for the deterrent effect of the death penalty is not clear—I make this point in my book "Punishing Criminals"—you have two risks. Risk 1: If you impose the death penalty and it doesn't have an additional deterrent effect, you have possibly lost the life of a convicted murderer without adding to deterrence and thereby sparing future victims. Risk 2: If you fail to execute the convicted murderer and execution would have had an additional deterrent effect, you have failed to spare the lives of a number of future victims.

Between the two risks, I'd much rather execute the convicted murderer than risk the lives of innocent people who could have been saved.

Q You noted that the death penalty is irrevocable once it is imposed. Does this make death such a different penalty that it should not be used?

A It makes it a different penalty. This is why it should be used when the crime is different—so heinous and socially dangerous to call for this extreme measure. When you kill a man with premeditation, you do something very different from stealing from him. I think the punishment should be appropriate. I favor the death penalty as a matter of justice and human dignity even apart from deterrence. The penalty must be appropriate to the seriousness of the crime.

Q Can you elaborate on your statement that the penalty should match the seriousness of the crime?

A Our system of punishment is based not just on deterrence but also on what is called "justice"—namely, that we feel a man who has committed a crime must be punished in proportion to the seriousness of the crime. Since the crime that takes a life is irrevocable, so must be the punishment.

All religions that I'm aware of feel that human life is sacred and that its sacredness must be enforced by depriving of life anyone who deprives another person of life. Once we make it clear to a person that if he deprives someone else of life he will suffer only minor inconvenience, we have cheapened human life. We are at that point today.

Q Some argue that capital punishment tends to brutalize and degrade society. Do you agree?

A Many of the same people also argue that the death penalty is legalized murder because it inflicts on the criminal the same situation that he inflicted on his victim. Yet most punishments inflict on the criminal what he inflicted on the victim. The difference between the punishment and the crime is that one is a legal measure and the other is not.

As for brutalizing, I think that people are more brutalized by their daily TV fare. At any rate, people are not so much brutalized by punishment as they are brutalized by our failure to seriously punish brutal acts.

Q Professor Schwartz, why do you oppose the death penalty?

A For a number of reasons. In the first place, mistakes do occur in our trial system. And, if the victim of a mistake has been executed, that mistake is irremediable.

For example: I myself once represented a man who had been frightened into confessing a murder. He was afraid he'd get the electric chair if he stood trial. So he pleaded guilty and got life imprisonment. Twelve years later I was able to prove he was innocent. That would have been too late if he had been executed.

In the second place—and, for me, very important—the death penalty, rarely administered as it is, distorts the whole penal system. It makes the criminal procedure so complex that it turns the public off.

Q How does it do that?

A People are so reluctant to administer the death penalty until every last doubt is eliminated that the procedural law gets encumbered with a lot of technical rules of evidence. You not only get this in the trial, but you get habeas corpus proceedings after the trial.

This highly technical procedure is applied not only to capital cases but to other criminal cases as well. So it makes it hard to convict anybody.

I believe the death penalty actually does more harm to security in this country than it does good. Without it, we would be safer from criminals than with it.

Q Do you think the death penalty is a deterrent to crime?

A The evidence is inconclusive about that.

The best studies I know, done by Thorsten Sellin, Marvin Wolfgang and their students at the University of Pennsylvania, would indicate that there is no deterrent effect. This study compared States using the death penalty with next-door States that did not use it. They also compared the homicide rates in the same State during periods when it used the death penalty and when it did not. And they found no statistical differences in homicide rates—with or without the death penalty.

I agree that there may be cases where a robber will not shoot because he doesn't want to risk "the hot seat." But, in my opinion, there are also situations where the death penalty stimulates a criminal to kill. I'm talking about cases, for instance, where a kidnaper decides

to kill the only witness who could identify him, or where witnesses or informers get wiped out because the criminal says: "If I'm convicted, I'm going to get the chair anyway, and I'm safer if I kill him."

So if the death penalty is not demonstrably helpful in saving innocent lives, I don't think we ought to use it—especially considering the risk of mistakes.

Q Are there no criminals who commit crimes so heinous that they ought to be executed for society's safety?

A My view is that society is not well enough organized to make a list of those people who ought to be executed. Sometimes I think if I were permitted to make up the list of those to be executed I wouldn't mind eliminating some people. But the list that society or the Government might make would probably not be the same as my list. Who is to decide who should live and who should die?

Now we're getting to the essential basis of what the Supreme Court must decide. This is whether the processes for choosing the ones to be killed are inevitably irrational, arbitrary and capricious.

Q Do you think this element of arbitrariness or capriciousness can ever be eliminated—even by making the death penalty mandatory for certain crimes, as many States have?

A No, I don't. No society has ever been able to make the death-penalty system operate fairly, even by making it mandatory. Look at the British system, which operated for a century with mandatory death penalties. They found juries just wouldn't convict in many cases where the conviction meant execution. And even if the death penalty was imposed, the Home Office eventually decided who would actually be killed by granting or withholding clemency.

Taking human nature as it is, I know of no way of administering a death penalty which would be fair. Not every problem has a solution, you know—and I think this is one of those insoluble problems.

Q Have we given the death penalty a chance to prove its deterrent effect? It hasn't been applied in this country in recent years—

A Not just in recent years. Use of the death penalty has been declining for decades. In 1933, there were something like 233 people executed in the United States. Since then, the figures have been going down steadily. And, of course, there haven't been any executions since 1967 because of the litigation over the death penalty's legality. But even before that, the American public was turning against the death penalty.

If you take a poll, you find people overwhelmingly in favor of the death penalty. But when you ask a person to sit on a jury and vote to execute a defendant, you find a great reluctance—increasingly so in the modern era.

Q It has been suggested that jurors and judges who impose a death penalty be required to push the buttons that would carry out the execution—

A Of course, society would reject that at once. You couldn't get 12 or 13 people who would do it. They may be willing to vote for it to be done, but they don't want to be a part of it. If you really want to make execution a deterrent, make it public—put it on TV—so people can see what it can be like if they kill someone. But, of course, we won't do that. We keep it hidden away from ourselves.

Q Do you regard it as immoral to execute a criminal?

A I steer away from that question because I know people's views on the morality of it are varied—and almost unchangeable. I'm a pragmatist. I just don't think it can be made fair or workable.

Gregg *v.* Georgia

United States Supreme Court

The issue before the Supreme Court of the United States was whether capital punishment violates the Eighth Amendment prohibition of cruel and unusual punishment. The majority of the Court held that it does not violate this prohibition because (1) capital punishment accords with contemporary standards of decency, (2) capital punishment may serve some deterrent or retributive purpose that is not degrading to human dignity, and (3) in the case of the Georgia law under review, capital punishment is no longer arbitrarily applied. Dissenting Justice Brennan argued that (1) through (3) do not suffice to show that capital punishment is constitutional; it would further have to be shown that capital punishment is not degrading to human dignity. Dissenting Justice Marshall objected to the majority's decision on the grounds that capital punishment is not necessary for deterrence, and that a retributive purpose for capital punishment is not consistent with human dignity. He also contended that contemporary standards of decency with respect to capital punishment are not based on informed opinion.

We address initially the basic contention that the punishment of death for the crime of murder is, under all circumstances, "cruel and unusual" in violation of the Eighth and Fourteenth Amendments of the Constitution. . . .

The Court on a number of occasions has both assumed and asserted the constitutionality of capital punishment. In several cases that assumption provided a necessary foundation for the decision, as the Court was asked to decide whether a particular method of carrying out a capital sentence would be allowed to stand under the Eighth Amendment. But until *Furman* v. *Georgia*, (1972), the Court never confronted squarely the fundamental claim that the punishment of death always, regardless of the enormity of the offense or the procedure followed in imposing the sentence, is cruel and unusual punishment in violation of the Constitution. Although this issue was presented and addressed in *Furman*, it was not resolved by the Court. Four Justices would have held that capital punishment is not unconstitutional *per se;* two Justices would have reached the opposite conclusion; and three Justices, while agreeing that the statutes then before the Court were invalid as applied, left open the question whether such punishment may ever be imposed. We now hold that the punishment of death does not invariably violate the Constitution. . . .

It is clear from the foregoing precedents that the Eighth Amendment has not been regarded as a static concept. As Mr. Chief Justice Warren said, in an oft-quoted phrase, "[t]he Amendment must draw its meaning from the evolving standards of decency that mark the progress of a maturing society." . . . Thus, an assessment of contemporary values concerning the infliction of a challenged sanction is relevant to the application of the Eighth Amendment. As we develop below more fully, this assessment does not call for a subjective judgment. It requires, rather, that we look to objective indicia that reflect the public attitude toward a given sanction.

But our cases also make clear that public perceptions of standards of decency with respect to criminal sanctions are not conclusive. A penalty also must accord with "the dignity of man," which is the "basic concept underlying the Eighth Amendment." This means, at least, that the punishment not be "excessive." When a form of punishment in the abstract (in this case, whether capital punishment may ever be imposed as a sanction for murder) rather than in the particular (the propriety of death as a penalty to be applied to a specific defendant for a specific crime) is under consideration, the inquiry into "excessiveness" has two aspects. First, the punishment must not involve the unnecessary and wanton infliction of pain. Second, the punishment must not be grossly out of proportion to the severity of the crime.

Of course, the requirements of the Eighth Amendment must be applied with an awareness of the limited role to be played by the courts. This does not mean that judges have no role to play, for the Eighth Amendment is a restraint upon the exercise of legislative power. . . .

But, while we have an obligation to insure that constitutional bounds are not overreached, we may not act as judges as we might as legislators.

"Courts are not representative bodies. They are not designed to be a good re-

flex of a democratic society. Their judgment is best informed, and therefore most dependable, within narrow limits. Their essential quality is detachment, founded on independence. History teaches that the independence of the judiciary is jeopardized when courts become embroiled in the passions of the day and assume primary responsibility in choosing between competing political, economic and social pressures." Dennis v. United States (1951)

Therefore, in assessing a punishment selected by a democratically elected legislature against the constitutional measure, we presume its validity. We may not require the legislature to select the least severe penalty possible so long as the penalty selected is not cruelly inhumane or disproportionate to the crime involved. And a heavy burden rests on those who would attack the judgment of the representatives of the people.

This is true in part because the constitutional test is intertwined with an assessment of contemporary standards and the legislative judgment weighs heavily in ascertaining such standards. "[I]n a democratic society legislatures, not courts, are constituted to respond to the will and consequently the moral values of the people." Furman v. Georgia. The deference we owe to the decisions of the state legislatures under our federal system, is enhanced where the specification of punishments is concerned, for "these are peculiarly questions of legislative policy." Gore v. United States. . . . A decision that a given punishment is impermissible under the Eighth Amendment cannot be reversed short of a constitutional amendment. The ability of the people to express their preference through the normal democratic processes, as well as through ballot referenda, is shut off. Revisions cannot be made in the light of further experience.

. . . We now consider specifically whether the sentence of death for the crime of murder is a per se violation of the Eighth and Fourteenth Amendments to the Constitution. We note first that history and precedent strongly support a negative answer to this question.

The imposition of the death penalty for the crime of murder has a long history of acceptance both in the United States and in England. The common-law rule imposed a mandatory death sentence on all convicted murderers. And the penalty continued to be used into the 20th century by most American States, although the breadth of the common-law rule was diminished, initially by narrowing the class of murders to be punished by death and subsequently by widespread adoption of laws expressly granting juries the discretion to recommend mercy.

It is apparent from the text of the Constitution itself that the existence of capital punishment was accepted by the Framers. At the time the Eighth Amendment was ratified, capital punishment was a common sanction in every State. Indeed, the First Congress of the United States enacted legislation providing death as the penalty for specified crimes. . . .

For nearly two centuries, this Court, repeatedly and often expressly, has recognized that capital punishment is not invalid *per se*. . . .

Four years ago, the petitioners in *Furman* and its companion cases predicated their argument primarily upon the asserted proposition that standards of decency had evolved to the point where capital punishment no longer could be tolerated. The petitioners in those cases said, in effect, that the evolutionary process had come to an end, and that standards of decency required that the Eighth Amendment be construed finally as prohibiting capital punishment for any crime regardless of its depravity and impact on society. This view was accepted by two Justices. Three other Justices were unwilling to go so far; focusing on the procedures by which convicted defendants were selected for the death penalty rather than on the actual punishment inflicted, they joined in the conclusion that the statutes before the Court were constitutionally invalid.

The petitioners in the capital cases before the Court today renew the "standards of decency" argument, but developments during the four years since *Furman* have undercut substantially the assumptions upon which their argument rested. Despite the continuing debate, dating back to the 19th century, over the morality and utility of capital punishment, it is now evident that a large proportion of American society continues to regard it as an appropriate and necessary criminal sanction.

The most marked indication of society's endorsement of the death penalty for murder is the legislative response to *Furman*. The legislatures of at least 35 States have enacted new statutes that provide for the death penalty for at least some crimes that result in the death of another person. And the Congress of the United States, in 1974, enacted a statute providing the death penalty for aircraft piracy that results in death. These recently adopted statutes have attempted to address the concerns expressed by the Court in *Furman* primarily (i) by specifying the factors to be weighed and the procedures to be followed in deciding when to impose a capital sentence, or (ii) by making the death penalty mandatory for specified crimes. But all of the post-*Furman* statutes make clear that capital punishment itself has not been rejected by the elected representatives of the people. . . .

As we have seen, however, the Eighth Amendment demands more than that a challenged punishment be acceptable to contemporary society. The Court also must ask whether it comports with the basic concept of human dignity at the core of the Amendment. Although we cannot "invalidate a category of penalties because we deem less severe penalties adequate to serve the ends of penology," the sanction imposed cannot be so totally without penological justification that it results in the gratuitous infliction of suffering.

The death penalty is said to serve two principal social purposes: retribution and deterrence of capital crimes by prospective offenders.

In part, capital punishment is an expression of society's moral outrage at particularly offensive conduct. This function may be unappealing to many, but it is essential in an ordered society that asks its citizens to rely on legal processes rather than self-help to vindicate their wrongs.

"The instinct for retribution is part of the nature of man, and channeling that instinct in the administration of criminal justice serves an important purpose in promoting the stability of a society governed by law. When people begin to believe that organized society is unwilling or unable to impose upon criminal offenders the punishment they 'deserve,'" then there are sown the seeds of anarchy—of self-help, vigilante justice, and lynch law."
Furman *v.* Georgia.

"Retribution is no longer the dominant objective of the criminal law," but neither is it a forbidden objective nor one inconsistent with our respect for the dignity of men. Indeed, the decision that capital punishment may be the appropriate sanction in extreme cases is an expression of the community's belief that certain crimes are themselves so grievous an affront to humanity that the only adequate response may be the penalty of death.

Statistical attempts to evaluate the worth of the death penalty as a deterrent to crimes by potential offenders have occasioned a great deal of debate. The results simply have been inconclusive. As one opponent of capital punishment has said:

"[A]fter all possible inquiry, including the probing of all possible methods of inquiry, we do not know; and for systematic and easily visible reasons cannot know; what the truth about this 'deterrent' effect may be. . . .

"The inescapable flaw is . . . that social conditions in any state are not constant through time, and that social conditions are not the same in any two states. If an effect were observed (and the observed effects, one way or another, are not large) then one could not at all tell whether any of this effect is attributable to the presence or absence of capital punishment. A 'scientific'—that is to say, a soundly based—conclusion is simply impossible, and no methodological path out of this tangle suggests itself." C. Black, Capital Punishment: The Inevitability of Caprice and Mistake 25–26 (1974).

Although some of the studies suggest that the death penalty may not function as a significantly greater deterrent than lesser penalties, there is no convincing empirical evidence either supporting or refuting this view. We may nevertheless assume safely that there are murderers, such as those who act in passion, for whom the threat of death has little or no deterrent effect. But for many others, the death penalty undoubtedly is a significant deterrent. There are carefully contemplated murders, such as murder for hire, where the possible penalty of death may well enter into

the cold calculus that precedes the decision to act. And there are some categories of murder, such as murder by a life prisoner, where other sanctions may not be adequate.

The value of capital punishment as a deterrent of crime is a complex factual issue the resolution of which properly rests with the legislatures, which can evaluate the results of statistical studies in terms of their own local conditions and with a flexibility of approach that is not available to the courts. . . .

In sum, we cannot say that the judgment of the Georgia Legislature that capital punishment may be necessary in some cases is clearly wrong. Considerations of federalism, as well as respect for the ability of a legislature to evaluate, in terms of its particular State, the moral consensus concerning the death penalty and its social utility as a sanction, require us to conclude, in the absence of more convincing evidence, that the infliction of death as a punishment for murder is not without justification and thus is not unconstitutionally severe.

Finally, we must consider whether the punishment of death is disproportionate in relation to the crime for which it is imposed. There is no question that death as a punishment is unique in its severity and irrevocability. When a defendant's life is at stake, the Court has been particularly sensitive to insure that every safeguard is observed. But we are concerned here only with the imposition of capital punishment for the crime of murder, and when a life has been taken deliberately by the offender, we cannot say that the punishment is invariably disproportionate to the crime. It is an extreme sanction, suitable to the most extreme of crimes.

We hold that the death penalty is not a form of punishment that may never be imposed, regardless of the circumstances of the offense, regardless of the character of the offender, and regardless of the procedure followed in reaching the decision to impose it.

We now consider whether Georgia may impose the death penalty on the petitioner in this case. . . .

The basic concern of *Furman* centered on those defendants who were being condemned to death capriciously and arbitrarily. Under the procedures before the Court in that case, sentencing authorities were not directed to give attention to the nature or circumstances of the crime committed or to the character or record of the defendant. Left unguided, juries imposed the death sentence in a way that could only be called freakish. The new Georgia sentencing procedures, by contrast, focus the jury's attention on the particularized nature of the crime and the particularized characteristics of the individual defendant. While the jury is permitted to consider any aggravating or mitigating circumstances, it must find and identify at least one statutory aggravating factor before it may impose a penalty of death. In this way the jury's discretion is channeled. No longer can a jury wantonly and freakishly impose the death sentence; it is always circumscribed by the legislative guidelines. In addition, the review function of the Supreme Court of Georgia affords additional assurance that the concerns that prompted our decision in *Furman* are not present to any significant degree in the Georgia procedure applied here.

For the reasons expressed in this opinion, we hold that the statutory system under which Gregg was sentenced to death does not violate the Constitution. Accordingly, the judgment of the Georgia Supreme Court is affirmed. . . .

Mr. Justice Brennan, dissenting.*

The Cruel and Unusual Punishments Clause "must draw its meaning from the evolving standards of decency that mark the progress of a maturing society." The opinions of Mr. Justice Stewart, Mr. Justice Powell, and Mr. Justice Stevens today hold that "evolving standards of decency" require focus not on the essence of the death penalty itself but primarily upon the procedures employed by the State to single out persons to suffer the penalty of death. Those opinions hold further that, so viewed, the Clause invalidates the mandatory infliction of the death penalty but not its infliction under sentencing procedures that Mr. Justice Stewart, Mr. Justice Powell, and Mr. Justice Stevens conclude adequately safeguard against the risk that the death penalty was imposed in an arbitrary and capricious manner.

In *Furman* v. *Georgia,* I read "evolving standards of decency" as requiring focus upon the essence of the death penalty itself and not

primarily or solely upon the procedures under which the determination to inflict the penalty upon a particular person was made. . . .

This Court inescapably has the duty, as the ultimate arbiter of the meaning of our Constitution, to say whether, when individuals condemned to death stand before our Bar, "moral concepts" require us to hold that the law has progressed to the point where we should declare that the punishment of death, like punishments on the rack, the screw, and the wheel, is no longer morally tolerable in our civilized society. My opinion in *Furman* v. *Georgia* concluded that our civilization and the law had progressed to this point and that therefore the punishment of death, for whatever crime and under all circumstances, is "cruel and unusual" in violation of the Eighth and Fourteenth Amendments of the Constitution. I shall not again canvass the reasons that led to that conclusion. I emphasize only that foremost among the "moral concepts" recognized in our cases and inherent in the Clause is the primary moral principle that the State, even as it punishes, must treat its citizens in a manner consistent with their intrinsic worth as human beings—a punishment must not be so severe as to be degrading to human dignity. A judicial determination whether the punishment of death comports with human dignity is therefore not only permitted but compelled by the Clause.

. . . Death for whatever crime and under all circumstances "is truly an awesome punishment. The calculated killing of a human being by the State involves, by its very nature, a denial of the executed person's humanity. . . . An executed person has indeed 'lost the right to have rights.' " Death is not only an unusually severe punishment, unusual in its pain, in its finality, and in its enormity, but it serves no penal purpose more effectively than a less severe punishment; therefore the principle inherent in the Clause that prohibits pointless infliction of excessive punishment when less severe punishment can adequately achieve the same purposes invalidates the punishment. . . .

Mr. Justice Marshall, dissenting.

. . . My sole purposes here are to consider the suggestion that my conclusion in *Furman* has been undercut by developments since then, and briefly to evaluate the basis for my

*[This opinion applies also to No. 75-5706, *Proffitt* v. *Florida, post,* p. 242, and No. 75-5394, *Jurek* v. *Texas, post,* p. 262.]

Brethren's holding that the extinction of life is a permissible form of punishment under the Cruel and Unusual Punishments Clause.

In *Furman* I concluded that the death penalty is constitutionally invalid for two reasons. First, the death penalty is excessive. And second, the American people, fully informed as to the purposes of the death penalty and its liabilities, would in my view reject it as morally unacceptable.

Since the decision in *Furman*, the legislatures of 35 States have enacted new statutes authorizing the imposition of the death sentence for certain crimes, and Congress has enacted a law providing the death penalty for air piracy resulting in death. I would be less than candid if I did not acknowledge that these developments have a significant bearing on a realistic assessment of the moral acceptability of the death penalty to the American people. But if the constitutionality of the death penalty turns, as I have urged, on the opinion of an *informed* citizenry, then even the enactment of new death statutes cannot be viewed as conclusive. In *Furman*, I observed that the American people are largely unaware of the information critical to a judgment on the morality of the death penalty, and concluded that if they were better informed they would consider it shocking, unjust, and unacceptable. A recent study, conducted after the enactment of the post-*Furman* statutes, has confirmed that the American people know little about the death penalty, and that the opinions of an informed public would differ significantly from those of a public unaware of the consequences and effects of the death penalty.

Even assuming, however, that the post-*Furman* enactment of statutes authorizing the death penalty renders the prediction of the views of an informed citizenry an uncertain basis for a constitutional decision, the enactment of those statutes has no bearing whatsoever on the conclusion that the death penalty is unconstitutional because it is excessive. An excessive penalty is invalid under the Cruel and Unusual Punishments Clause "even though popular sentiment may favor" it. The inquiry here, then, is simply whether the death penalty is necessary to accomplish the legitimate legislative purposes in punishment, or

whether a less severe penalty—life imprisonment—would do as well.

The two purposes that sustain the death penalty as nonexcessive in the Court's view are general deterrence and retribution. In *Furman*, I canvassed the relevant data on the deterrent effect of capital punishment. The state of knowledge at that point, after literally centuries of debate, was summarized as follows by a United Nations Committee:

"It is generally agreed between the retentionists and abolitionists, whatever their opinions about the validity of comparative studies of deterrence, that the data which now exist show no correlation between the existence of capital punishment and lower rates of capital crime."

The available evidence, I concluded in *Furman*, was convincing that "capital punishment is not necessary as a deterrent to crime in our society."

The Solicitor General in his *amicus* brief in these cases relies heavily on a study by Isaac Ehrlich, reported a year after *Furman*, to support the contention that the death penalty does not deter murder. . . .

. . . Ehrlich found a negative correlation between changes in the homicide rate and changes in execution risk. His tentative conclusion was that for the period from 1933 to 1967 each additional execution in the United States might have saved eight lives.

The methods and conclusions of the Ehrlich study have been severely criticized on a number of grounds. . . .

. . . Analysis of Ehrlich's data reveals that all empirical support for the deterrent effect of capital punishment disappears when the five most recent years are removed from his time series—that is to say, whether a decrease in the execution risk corresponds to an increase or a decrease in the murder rate depends on the ending point of the sample period. This finding has cast severe doubts on the reliability of Ehrlich's tentative conclusions. . . .

The Ehrlich study, in short, is of little, if any, assistance in assessing the deterrent impact of the death penalty. The evidence I reviewed in *Furman* remains convincing, in my view, that "capital punishment is not necessary as a deterrent to crime in our society." The justification for the death penalty must be found elsewhere.

The other principal purpose said to be served by the death penalty is retribution. The notion that retribution can serve as a moral justification for the sanction of death finds credence in the opinion of my Brothers Stewart, Powell, and Stevens, and that of my Brother White in *Roberts* v. *Louisiana.* It is this notion that I find to be the most disturbing aspect of today's unfortunate decisions.

The concept of retribution is a multifaceted one, and any discussion of its role in the criminal law must be undertaken with caution. On one level, it can be said that the notion of retribution or reprobation is the basis of our insistence that only those who have broken the law be punished, and in this sense the notion is quite obviously central to a just system of criminal sanctions. But our recognition that retribution plays a crucial role in determining who may be punished by no means requires approval of retribution as a general justification for punishment. It is the question whether retribution can provide a moral justification for punishment—in particular, capital punishment—that we must consider. . . .

The . . . contentions—that society's expression of moral outrage through the imposition of the death penalty pre-empts the citizenry from taking the law into its own hands and reinforces moral values—are not retributive in the purest sense. They are essentially utilitarian in that they portray the death penalty as valuable because of its beneficial results. These justifications for the death penalty are inadequate because the penalty is, quite clearly I think, not necessary to the accomplishment of those results.

There remains for consideration, however, what might be termed the purely retributive justification for the death penalty—that the death penalty is appropriate, not because of its beneficial effect on society, but because the taking of the murderer's life is itself morally good. . . .

The mere fact that the community demands the murderer's life in return for the evil he has done cannot sustain the death penalty, for . . . "The Eighth Amendment demands more than that a challenged punishment be acceptable to contemporary society." To be sustained under the Eighth Amendment, the death penalty must "compor[t] with the basic concept of human dignity at the core of the Amendment"; the objective in imposing it must be "[consistent] with our respect for the dignity of [other] men." Under these standards, the taking of life "because the wrongdoer deserves it" surely must fall, for such a punishment has as its very basis the total denial of the wrongdoer's dignity and worth.

The death penalty, unnecessary to promote the goal of deterrence or to further any legitimate notion of retribution, is an excessive penalty forbidden by the Eighth and Fourteenth Amendments. I respectfully dissent from the Court's judgment upholding the sentences of death imposed upon the petitioners in these cases.

Suggestions for Further Reading

Anthologies

Acton, H. B. *The Philosophy of Punishment.* London: Macmillan & Co., 1969.

Cains, Huntington. *Legal Philosophy from Plato to Hegel.* Baltimore: Johns Hopkins Press, 1967.

Ezorsky, Gertrude. *Philosophical Perspectives on Punishment.* Albany: State University of New York Press, 1972.

Feinberg, Joel, and Gross, Hyman. *Philosophy of Law.* Belmont: Wadsworth Publishing Co., 1980.

Gerber, Rudolph J., and McAnany, Patrick D. *Contemporary Punishment.* Notre Dame: University of Notre Dame Press, 1972.

Murphy, Jeffrie G. *Punishment and Rehabilitation.* Belmont: Wadsworth Publishing Co., 1984.

Basic Concepts

Golding, Martin P. *Philosophy of Law.* Englewood Cliffs: Prentice-Hall, 1975.

Richards, David A. J. *The Moral Criticism of Law.* Belmont: Dickenson Publishing Co., 1977.

The Forward-Looking and Backward-Looking Views

Andenaes, Johannes. *Punishment and Deterrence.* Ann Arbor: The University of Michigan Press, 1974.

Menninger, Karl. *The Crime of Punishment.* New York: The Viking Press, 1968.

Gross, Hyman. *A Theory of Criminal Justice.* New York: Oxford University Press, 1979.

Murphy, Jeffrie G. *Retribution, Justice and Therapy.* Boston: D. Reidel Publishing Co., 1979.

Packer, Herbert. *The Limits of the Criminal Sanction.* Stanford: Stanford University Press, 1968.

Von Hirsh, Andrew. *Doing Justice.* New York: Hill and Wang, 1976.

Practical Application

Black, Charles L., Jr. *Capital Punishment.* New York: W.W. Norton & Co., 1974.

———. "Reflections on Opposing the Penalty of Death." *St. Mary's Law Journal* (1978), pp. 1–12.

Bedau, Hugo. *The Death Penalty in America.* New York: Oxford University Press, 1982.

Van den Haag, Ernest. *Punishing Criminals.* New York: Basic Books, 1975.

Terrorism

Basic Concepts

The problem of terrorism is usually framed in terms of what would be the proper response to terrorist actions. The idea that terrorism itself might be morally justified is rarely entertained. But whether this presumption is justified or not depends on what we understand terrorism to be.

Consider the following definition:

(a) Terrorism is the random murder of innocent people.

This definition does seem to adequately apply to many standard cases of terrorism. For example, in the wave of terrorist bombing that occurred in the heart of Paris during September, 1986, eight innocent people were randomly killed. And according to the U. S. State Department, 5,700 people worldwide have lost their lives to terrorist attacks since 1972.[1] Nevertheless, there are at least two difficulties with this definition. First, the random murder of innocent people can be the work of persons who are simply mentally ill, such as the Son of Sam killer in New York City or the Hillside Strangler in Los Angeles. Terrorists, however, are different in that they are motivated at least in part by political objectives. For example, the Palestinian Liberation Organization (PLO) wants to establish a Palestinian state, and the Irish Republican Army (IRA) wants to unite Northern Ireland with the Republic of Ireland. Second, terrorists do not always engage in murder; sometimes lesser forms of violence, such as breaking people's kneecaps, or simply the threat of violence are used.

Consider then the following definition, which attempts to remedy both of these difficulties:

(b) Terrorism is the unlawful use or threat of violence against innocent people to further some political objective.

This definition is clearly an improvement over the previous one, but it does introduce a diffi-culty of its own. Definition (a) allowed that terrorism might be engaged in by states, as well as by groups or organizations. But the second definition, by limiting terrorism to "unlawful" acts, excludes state terrorism directed either at the state's own population or at other nations. Unfortunately, governments usually have little difficulty passing laws that direct violence against innocent people. Apartheid, for example, is required by South African law.

Suppose, then, we simply eliminate the restriction "unlawful," giving us the following definition:

(c) Terrorism is the use or threat of violence against innocent people to further some political objective.

Is this definition adequate? We certainly can say more about terrorism than is captured by this definition. For example, terrorists do not need a defined territorial base nor a specific organizational structure. Their goals do not need to be related to any one country, and they do not need nor necessarily seek a popular base of support. These additional features, however, simply alert us to the variety of forms terrorism can take; they do not undercut the usefulness of (c) as a general definition.

Assuming, then, that (c) is a reasonably adequate general definition of terrorism, we are now in a position to ask whether terrorism can ever be morally justified. Obviously, our first inclination is an emphatic no. Before taking this position, however, we should first reflect a bit more on what such a stance would entail. As noted previously, definition (c) allows that states, as well as groups or organizations, can practice terrorism, and it also allows that terrorism can be practiced by directing violence or the threat of violence at innocent people. Accordingly, it would follow that not only are the actions of the IRA, the PLO, the Italian Red Brigades, the Baader-Meinhof of Germany, and the Armed Forces of Puerto Rican National Liberation (FALN) terrorist actions, but also the threats of massive nuclear retaliation made by the United States, the Soviet Union, and the other nuclear powers would be terrorist actions as well. This is because such threats are at least implicitly directed against the civilian populations of other nations that by just war criteria are usually taken to be innocent (see Section IX). It would seem, therefore, that if any of the nuclear powers, especially the United States, is going to consistently stand against terrorism, it must renounce its commitment to massive nuclear retaliation.

Could it be, however, that terrorism might be justified when practiced by states but not when practiced by groups or organizations because more might be gained from state terrorism? But if terrorism is going to be justified at all, it would seem to be more likely to be justified when practiced on the small scale because fewer innocent people would actually be jeopardized by small-scale terrorism than by large-scale terrorism. In fact, it has been estimated that the death toll of state-sponsored terrorism as compared with non–state-sponsored terrorism is already half a million to one.[2]

There must, therefore, be a certain ambivalence in our moral evaluation of terrorism. We want to condemn all acts of terrorism, but to do so would also involve condemning the massive nuclear retaliation policies of the nuclear powers. Nor could we claim these policies to be morally justified without also allowing that particular terrorist actions by groups or organizations might also be morally justified. This ambivalence is also reflected to some degree in the readings of this section, which tend to focus on understanding the causes of group terrorism and determining what our responses to it should be.

Alternate Views

In the first selection, Robert L. Phillips (pp. 395–398) contends that the intellectual roots of terrorism can be found in three peculiarly Western ideas: popular sovereignty, self-determination, and ethical consequentialism. Phillips claims that popular sovereignty lends

support to terrorism because it defuses political responsibility over the entire population, making civilians accountable for national policy. Self-determination is said to support terrorism because it is often the terrorist's own objective. Finally, ethical consequentialism is said to lend support to terrorism because it rejects the protection to innocents provided by absolute human rights.

Yet after linking these three ideas to terrorism, Phillips evaluates them differently. Despite their common connections with terrorism, Phillips only rejects ethical consequentialism as an utterly pernicious idea. To follow ethical consequentialism and abandon absolute rights, Phillips argues, is self-destructive.

But is this the case? Certainly, Plato's tyrant, who abandons human rights altogether, may destroy himself or herself, but whether such self-destruction is likely to occur in other cases depends on the extent to which there is a departure from absolute human rights. For example, if one allows that human rights can be overridden only when the bad consequences are trivial, easily reparable, or sufficiently outweighed by the good consequences of an action, it is difficult to see how so acting would be immoral or lead to self-destruction. Nor would such a stance involve commitment to ethical consequentialism either, if the good consequences had to be many times greater than the bad before the action would be regarded as morally justified (see the General Introduction). Such a limited abandoning of absolute human rights would no more open the door to terrorist action than would the ideas of popular sovereignty and self-determination.

Yet despite the fact that popular sovereignty, self-determination, and a limited abandoning of absolute human rights do lend some support to terrorism, the case for the moral defensibility of any particular terrorist action would still be difficult to establish. To justify a terrorist action, one would at least need to show that it is the most effective means of achieving a morally defensible political objective—not an easy thing to do.

In the next selection, Moorhead Kennedy (pp. 399–405) argues that there are a number of distinct causes of terrorism, the most important of which for understanding Middle Eastern terrorism are resistance to post-colonial rule and religious ideology. Viewed in these terms, terrorist actions are often a response to grievances, as in the case of the Palestinians, or an assertion of identity, as in the case of the Iranians, who are saying, "We exist, take us and our values seriously." Kennedy points out that frequently our responses to terrorist actions are seen as hypocritical because we approve of or engage in policies that have similar effects. In responding to terrorism, Kennedy suggests that we use covert means like the Russians rather than overt air strikes, as in the case of our attack on Libya. He also suggests that we need to reopen the Camp David peace process and pursue more vigorously a homeland for the Palestinian people.

In contrast with Phillips, who focused on the general intellectual roots of terrorism, Kennedy seems to have pinpointed the particular causes of Middle Eastern terrorism. His suggestion, however, that we use covert means like the Russians to fight terrorism is really a suggestion that we use terrorism to fight terrorism. But if we do this, can we still morally condemn terrorism?

Unlike Moorhead Kennedy, who shows a certain ambivalence in his evaluation of terrorism, Paul Johnson (pp. 405–409) views terrorism as intrinsically evil, necessarily evil, and wholly evil. He claims there are seven demonstrable reasons for this, which he calls "the seven deadly sins of terrorism." These reasons are: (1) terrorism is the deliberate and cold-blooded exaltation of violence over all forms of political activity; (2) it is the deliberate suppression of the moral instincts of men and women; (3) it is the rejection of politics as the normal means by which communities resolve conflicts; (4) it actively, systematically, and necessarily assists the spread of the totalitarian state; (5) it can destroy a democracy; (6) it exploits and endangers the apparatus of freedom in liberal societies; and (7) it saps the will of civilized society to defend itself and thereby induces society to commit suicide.

Johnson supports each of these reasons with bits of evidence. For example, (1) is supported by references to the writings of Sartre

and Fanon. But evidence against at least some of these reasons can be found. For example, with respect to (1) and (3), the Irgun zvai Luumi (National Military Organization) headed by Menachem Begin in 1946 was willing to accept politics as a means of resolving conflicts after the formation of the State of Israel, and conceivably the PLO would be willing to do the same after the formation of a Palestinian state.

Offering yet another contrasting view, Conor Cruise O'Brien (pp. 410–414) contends that terrorism is subject to two misleading stereotypes: a sentimental stereotype and a hysterical stereotype. According to the sentimental stereotype, the terrorist is a misguided idealist or an unsublimated social reformer. According to the hysterical stereotype, the terrorist is either a nut (i.e., "a disgruntled abnormal" given to "mindless violence"), a thug engaged in criminal activity, or an agent or a dupe of the other superpower. On the one hand, O'Brien claims that those who believe the sentimental stereotype fail to see that being a terrorist has its own rewards that are not easy to give up, even when the terrorist's political objective is attainable. On the other hand, O'Brien claims that those who believe the hysterical stereotype fail to see that making the elimination of terrorism the highest priority and using unilateral military actions against terrorists are both counterproductive. The only approach that is likely to be effective, O'Brien argues, is one that involves the cooperation of all the major powers, and, consequently, would require that the United States cease to support the terrorist activities of the contras in Nicaragua.

One difficulty with O'Brien's approach to dealing with terrorism is that it is basically a military approach involving cooperative rather than unilateral military action. In effect, O'Brien thinks that terrorism today can be handled the way the Barbary pirates were handled in the nineteenth century by a unified military response of the major powers. But this approach ignores the political dimension of terrorist activities, and it is difficult to see how any approach to terrorism can be effective that does not take this dimension into account.

Practical Applications

The practical applications for this section are a political statement of purpose by the IRA and a representative selection from the legal code enacted to deal with the actions of the IRA. The first is considered to be a terrorist program of action; the second a reaction to that program. Here we need to evaluate the morality of particular actions of the IRA. If those actions are morally justified, the proper response to such actions would have to be primarily political rather than military. But if those actions are not morally justified, the proper response would be primarily military rather than political. Obviously, a society's answers to these questions will have considerable impact on its own welfare and defense policies as well as those of other nations. Thus, a solution to the problem of terrorism will affect the solutions to the other practical problems discussed in this anthology as well.

Notes

1. *Defense and Disarmament* (July–August, 1986), p. 1.
2. Eqbal, Ahmed, "Comprehending Terror," *Middle East Report* (June, 1986). Notice the discrepancy between this estimate and the estimate by the U.S. State Department. Apparently, the State Department did not include deaths from state terrorism in their total.

The Roots of Terrorism

Robert L. Phillips

Robert L. Phillips contends that the intellectual roots of terrorism can be found in three peculiarly Western ideas: (1) popular sovereignty, which makes civilians responsible for national policy; (2) self-determination, which is the objective of many terrorist groups; and (3) ethical consequentialism, which denies to the innocent the protection of absolute human rights.

When nations find themselves in trouble, their difficulties have usually been a long time in the making. In the case of the terrorism that now afflicts the nations of the West, there is a long intellectual history behind it—one which is rather unflattering to those who see themselves as the main victims of terrorism. The intellectual roots of terrorism lie in three philosophical ideas which, ironically, are peculiarly Western: popular sovereignty, self-determination and ethical consequentialism. The diffusion of political responsibility that results from popular sovereignty, the belief that every group has a right to its own

From "The Roots of Terrorism," *The Christian Century* (April 9, 1986), pp. 355–357. © 1986 Christian Century Foundation. Reprinted by permission.

state, and the decline in the belief in absolute human rights have together fostered a hospitable intellectual climate for terrorism. Even opponents of terrorism may feel a certain moral ambivalence when faced with acts of terror.

One reason academics, journalists and politicians have had difficulty in responding to terrorism is that it is hard to define terrorism in such a way that it refers only to one's opponents' activities and not also one's own. As a result, condemnations of terrorism are often seen by neutral observers as hypocritical. This does not mean that moral denunciations of terrorism are not appropriate and mandatory. Terrorist acts are profoundly immoral. In addition, they are not as politically effective as their practitioners claim. One has only to look at the areas of the world where terror has held sway to see that the violence there is typically prolonged by terrorism, sometimes indefinitely, as the opposing sides come to perceive each other as "criminal" and thus as beyond the pale of civilized negotiation.

But while it is correct for the Reagan administration, for example, to condemn terrorism as a means of effecting political and social change, such a denunciation makes sense only in the context of a moral stance that (1) rigidly distinguishes between combatants and non-combatants and (2) rigidly adheres to the principle that innocent people have an absolute right not to be murdered for any reason whatever. Both of these tenets have been steadily eroding since 1940, in the West as much as elsewhere. Despite repeated commitments to a plethora of declarations of human rights, few if any governments are scrupulous in their military policies regarding such rights. In what follows, I shall try to show how we got ourselves into this predicament.

Popular sovereignty. The doctrine of popular sovereignty developed as the profoundly moral idea that human beings are born free and equal and, as such, have a right to an equal share of political power. The slogan "one man, one vote" perfectly expresses the idea that democracy is the fairest of all political systems because it correctly reflects the natural human condition of freedom and equality. However, it has long been observed that popular sovereignty tends to diffuse responsibility for political acts, particularly acts of war. Everything from conscription to the saturation bombing of cities can find a rationale in popular sovereignty. If the people are the state, then is it not their responsibility both to defend it and to bear the burden of attacks upon it? This question has never been satisfactorily answered.

Despite efforts in international law to distinguish between degrees of culpability with regard to politicians, generals and ordinary citizens, policies of direct attacks upon civilians continue to find a rationale in the identification of the citizen with the state—even if the ordinary citizen is both ignorant of and indifferent to affairs of state. Thus, the principle of popular sovereignty has provided modern states with the moral leverage to nationalize

the lives of their citizens in a way that puts them at risk. Terrorists of all stripes use this principle for their own purposes, and they capitalize on the moral ambivalence reflected in the remark: "One man's terrorist is another man's freedom fighter."

Self-determination. Self-determination is one of those 19th-century liberal ideas which has worked its way into the primary documents of 20th-century international law, including the United Nations Charter. The principle claims that "a people" has the right to determine its destiny and the disposition of the land upon which it lives without the intervention of outside parties. The principle of self-determination came to the fore after 1945 as a rubric for decolonization.

Gradually, self-determination became synonymous with the right of every religious and ethnic group to have its own state. Despite the fact that demographics make such a world unfeasible, terrorist groups continue to fly the banner of self-determination. They are able to get away with this because the principle is fatally vague. Consider the case of Northern Ireland. Protestant loyalists there have steadfastly appealed to the principle of self-determination, saying that as "a people" they have a right to shape their own future, which means, for them, continued membership in the United Kingdom. But Catholic nationalists appeal to the same principle with equal sincerity. For them, self-determination means what "the people" of the whole island of Ireland want. Thus, crucial to making self-determination work is the ability to specify which sample of a given population is to be considered "the people." Unfortunately, the principle of self-determination is silent on this point. The terrorist is not really playing fast and loose when he appeals to the principle of self-determination; it is the principle itself which is fast and loose. The idea of self-determination will continue to complicate efforts to deal with terrorism.

Ethical consequentialism. The moral tradition that shaped the West is an amalgam of classical and Christian sources. This ethical confluence has been possible despite considerable differences between the two sources because both agree that the good life involves strict adherence to categorical moral principles.

Both Plato and Aristotle insisted that injustice was not permitted as a means of producing good consequences. In the *Republic,* Plato makes this point in many diverse and intellectually subtle ways. He argued (as did Aristotle) that there are certain basic human values which are simply worth having for their own sake, and that the ultimate consequence of immoral behavior is self-destruction. Plato, in one of the most powerful passages in Western philosophy, describes the decline of the unjust man into the tyrant, the most unhappy of all men.

The main thrust of these classical arguments, then, is that the man of good character is also the only truly happy man. Maintaining such a character will involve avoiding injustice and, in particular, the pitfall of thinking one can do evil in order that good may come of it. Plato understood that such a life is difficult to achieve, and he was extremely pessimistic about the possibility of the masses ever becoming just. The best they could hope for would be to live in a society governed by a just ruler. Nevertheless, he insisted that there are objectively discernible goods, the participation in which constitutes the good life, and that such a life is irretrievably damaged by acts of injustice, even if undertaken for the "best" of reasons.

Plato and Aristotle initiated what was later to be called the natural-law tradition. Central to natural-law thinking is the Platonic insight that it is possible to define objectively what it means to be good at being a person. Just as there are standards of excellence for being a doctor and a teacher, so there are knowable standards of excellence for being human. The good society is one in which people are allowed to conform to these standards.

The Judeo-Christian idea of a transcendent source of all value is consonant with these classical insights. The commandments that govern the life of the Jew and the Christian are strictly categorical in nature, as indeed are most ethical codes based on theistic sources. Friendship with God is closely linked to walking the path of justice; it is understood that to damage any basic human value is to attack the very source of value and being. What Plato understood to be the consequence of injustice—self-destruction—the Judeo-Christian

tradition understands as the cutting off of oneself from the very source of being.

The absolutist conception of justice was reflected in the medieval theory of the just war. The notion that in war noncombatants must never be made the object of direct attacks is but one instance of the application of the categorical prohibition of murder to the realm of war. As provisions of the just-war theory passed into the developing corpus of international law in the 17th century, they retained their categorical or absolutist character. And, needless to say, the Christian churches continued to promulgate a similar view of justice.

Starting in the 16th century, however, this mainstream tradition in ethics was subject to a challenge, which culminated in the 19th century with the development and popularization of a full-blown consequentialism. Machiavelli is a key figure in this development. He argued that while the prince should adhere to the good, there will arise situations when state necessity requires the prince to damage a known good in order to "save the state." The ends, that is, may justify evil means.

Machiavelli does not make it entirely clear why the preservation of the political order outweighs any other known good, but we may understand his thinking as a response to the rise of the modern, centralized state. In a world of absolute sovereign states, no structure exists to which appeal can be made over the heads of the princes. The state, therefore, becomes the only hope for the survival of any conception of the good life. A transitional figure, Machiavelli reflected the tension between the old and the new ways of thinking about justice. On the one hand, he recognized the good in the traditional sense—that there are certain qualities of character that are worth having for their own sake, and goods that are self-evident in the sense that no argument or further justification is necessary for them. On the other hand, he believed that necessities of state require the sacrifice of some of these principles (in particular, the prohibition against murder) for a greater good.

In Machiavelli's account of the prince, we begin to see the outline of a certain type of modern human who rejects the classical warning that acting against the good will irretrievably damage one's own character, eventually causing one to lose a knowledge of the good altogether. The prince, according to Machiavelli, is a technician in statecraft and, to that extent, beyond good and evil in the conventional sense. Furthermore, the prince rejects the Christian notion of divine providence. The prince must make his own future, even when this involves doing evil; the prince must play God in order to secure the desired outcome. All of this, of course, is "tragically necessary."

Machiavelli's thought was brought to completion in the 19th century by philosophers like Jeremy Bentham and John Stuart Mill whose work faced up to the pure consequentialism of much modern politics. In its mature 19th-century formulations, consequentialism was a theory devised, in part, to deal with the perceived disappearance of generally agreed-upon moral standards. The skepticism brought on in some quarters by the rise of empiricism, Darwinism and various forms of atheism led to the search for some standard that would unite radically heterogeneous values. Mill and others fixed upon certain subjective ends, styled variously as "happiness" or "pleasure." As the aforementioned belief in divine providence continued to decline, the terrible burden of completely securing the future seemed to fall entirely upon human shoulders. In principle, no possible course of action could be ruled out as wrong or impermissible in itself and no sacrifice of known goods could be regarded as too great if it would secure greater happiness in the fu-

ture. Thus, in the search for a means of maximizing the good, moral rules lost their categorical force.

Given the pervasiveness of this moral theory and its impact upon the common person, it is no accident that our own century is replete with political movements that require or threaten the destruction of known values in order to create a future of unlimited happiness. The belief in the mutability of moral obligations is one of the main arguments for terrorism. If there are no absolute human rights, the innocent are in danger. "Calculations" about whether or not to kill an innocent person become no more than arguments of advocacy based on hypothetical scenarios of the future. But can we really be reasonably expected to deal with other people on the basis of deciding whether they live or die by trying to project their life prospects for an indeterminate time period?

Terrorists the world over have appropriated concepts and military strategies (consider the nuclear bombing of Hiroshima and the fire bombing of Dresden) that originated in the West. This fact should not, however, in any way debilitate us in our fight against terrorism. No government, no matter what its own past transgressions, should fail to protect its own citizens. If anything positive can be said about this grim and ironic situation, it is that as victims of terrorism we may be forced to rethink our own policies on the use of force (including nuclear force) in order to bring them into line with our moral denunciations of terrorism.

The Root Causes of Terrorism

Moorhead Kennedy

Moorhead Kennedy argues that there are a number of distant causes of terrorism but that the most important for understanding Middle Eastern terrorism are resistance to postcolonial rule and religious ideology.

It is particularly true for humanists that ethical questions raised by terrorism are among the most important questions we have to consider. It is not that all that large a number of people get killed in terrorist attacks—at least, not so far—but that the damage that terrorism can do is very deep. It is moral damage because it produces fear. And fear produces the most ignominious reactions.

The U.S. government is chiding the European governments for not taking stronger stands against terrorism, but somehow the great, courageous, macho, Rambo-minded American people prefer Glacier National Park or Yosemite to Mt. Blanc, and I think this is a very direct effect of terrorism. It *does* work. It *does* have this effect. It certainly brought about the withdrawal of our marines and the Israeli army from Lebanon. It had a lot to do with the creation of Israel and the withdrawal of Britain from that country's then Palestine Mandate. It can be very, very effective.

But worse than the political consequences, perhaps, might be the civil rights disturbances that terrorism can bring about. It is perfectly true, for example, that there is no terrorism in Israel. The Israelis have managed to seal off their borders. But it takes about four or five hours to get on an El Al plane. And I want to suggest to you that, if terrorism spreads to the United States—as well it might—would you look forward to being strip-searched every time you board the Boston shuttle?

But more important than the inconvenience is the suspicion that terrorism can cause. A friend of mine, Abdul Aziz Said, a Bedouin from the Syrian desert who is now a most

From "The Root Causes of Terrorism," *The Humanist* (September/October 1986), pp. 5–9, 30. Reprinted by permission.

distinguished professor at American University in Washington, D.C., told me once that his son who is ten said to him, "Dad, when you come for me at school, please don't come inside." And when Said asked, "Why, son?" he replied, "Just wait in the car, Dad. You look like an Arab."

And this kind of suspicion and hate can cut the other way just as easily. In lecturing throughout the United States, the question I find increasingly being asked is: "If we did not support Israel, would we have to put up with Arab terrorism?" It's very easy to turn that question around. The anti-Semites in this country who are still around use this as a weapon against our own Jewish community and to encourage the spread in this country of the vilest, most noxious and hateful of all ethnic prejudices.

We must look very hard at terrorism. We cannot defeat it militarily or by covert means. It exists in the Middle East despite everything Israel has done to combat it, and Israel's efforts have been very extensive. But in spite of Israel's efforts, terrorism continues to spread. Therefore, if we are going to get to the bottom of the terrorism problem, we are going to have to examine its root causes.

And so, to introduce the subject, I'd like to ask you to come back with me in time, back to February 1980, when three of us hostages were in a small basement room in the chancery of the office building of the U.S. embassy in Teheran. We had been held there since the previous November. The three of us were getting ready for bed when suddenly the door burst open and in came the group of our student guards dressed in their captured marine fatigues. But this time their faces were covered.

They had masks on and they were shouting, "*SAVAK, SAVAK,*" which was the name of the secret police of the Shah whom they had helped displace the previous January. They were reenacting, in this bursting into our room, the kind of raids that SAVAK used to pull on them when they were young revolutionaries. They hauled us out into the freezing corridor and made us strip down to our underdrawers and brace ourselves against the wall in the frisk position. I remember them snapping at the elastic of my underdrawers. They chambered their weapons beside our ears. They poked the muzzles of their weapons into the napes of our necks.

I stood up against the wall, freezing cold because the unheated corridor in Teheran in February could be bitterly cold, and began to shake. I said to myself, "Now, Kennedy, you're not afraid. This is just the cold." And I remembered that King Charles I, facing his execution in January 1649 on a bitterly cold day, wore an extra shirt so that he would not tremble, or be seen to tremble, from the cold, lest people think he was afraid to die. So, I stood up against the wall, thinking about all of the interesting and not-so-interesting things I could remember about King Charles I. Incidentally, I have used this illustration in colleges and schools all over the country to demonstrate, beyond question of a doubt, the usefulness of a liberal arts education.

We were then told to dress and were herded back into our room where we found the room absolutely ransacked. My belt was missing, my razor was missing, and my green polka-dot tie with which I entered captivity was missing. There had been another suicide attempt among the hostages, and, of course, they were doing an oldfashioned shakedown. We were left alone to speak, which was unusual because "donna speak" was the rule. They always had a guard with us to be sure we couldn't communicate. But this time, we obviously were supposed to exchange impressions. When the first guard appeared, we decided that we would tell him that we were very impressed with the security measures which they had just taken.

The guard who came in was Hassan, a most important one—he took us to the showers in another building once every ten days. With three persons confined in a small room, the visits of Hassan were very important. Hassan asked us what had happened, and we told him, and he said, "Yes, there is a group of students who perform these inspections. We don't know them very well. They do this from time to time." The only problem with Hassan's explanation, although we obviously were careful not to let on, was that from his body language, his voice, and his unusual height, it was very clear that one of the guards who had burst into our room had been Hassan.

And the question in my mind, now and then, is "Why?" Why did they feel that they had to conceal their identities? Why the sudden subterfuge? And why did some of the students apologize to us afterward for that episode, for the mock execution?

This is really what I want to discuss: the mixed feelings of a lot of these terrorists. What caused their mixed feelings about themselves, about the United States, and about how they relate to us and to our society? These are the questions which are not very often discussed but which form a vital part of the whole terrorist picture.

I think the first question, then, is: "Who are the terrorists?" You read a great deal in the newspapers and from authors such as Claire Sterling and from much of what comes out of official Washington about the "terror network." And often, wherever possible, it is attributed to the Soviet Union. It is supposed to be Soviet inspired. The problem with this alleged Soviet relationship is that it ignores a certain reality: some of my captors had volunteered to fight the Soviets in Afghanistan. The Middle East is generally anti-Soviet, even though they use the equipment the Soviets are only too willing to give them.

Now, there is coordination among terrorist groups in the area of procurement, communications, sanctuary, and, particularly, of course, training. There is one good way to hijack a plane: you dominate the flight deck and then you terrorize the passengers, make them look down, and keep them quiet. It's the only way you can dominate. You have to establish your ascendancy. And you are taught how to do this in schools in South Yemen as well as in Libya.

But, there is an obvious difference between

the students who attend these institutions—differences between, say, the IRA and the Baader Meinhof gang, between Breton and Corsican terrorists and those from the Middle East. The motivations are different. And why are they putting their lives at risk? For a number of different reasons.

I say there are five general categories of which the first is resistance to colonial rule; this is the simplest one, the basic one. It was the motivation of the Irgun zvai Leumi, headed by Menachem Begin in 1946. It's the same motivation behind the resistance that is part of our own history. You may remember a tea party in the city of Boston which was wanton destruction of property for political ends or the privateering that was the foundation of a number of New England fortunes which was licensed piracy. Resistance to colonial rule requires that you equalize your weaker military power with that of the stronger colonizing power. One leader who did this effectively was Jomo Kenyatta of Kenya. All of these examples are of the first category.

The second category is ethnic separation. A good example of this category is the Puerto Rican FALN which had the bomb factory in Queens and created episodes in this country that would inspire a desire to grant Puerto Rico its independence.

A third category of terrorists is motivated by internal political factors. These are people who don't make it in the polls and who take to the streets, who don't make it in the streets and so they take to terror. The Symbionese Liberation Army with Patricia Hearst is a very good example. A fourth category of terrorists shows its support for external factors, such as the Viet Cong supporting the invasion from North Vietnam. There is a fifth category, ideological belief, of which the anarchist who killed President McKinley is a prime example.

Of all of these different motivations, we are dealing with Middle Eastern terrorism, which is a combination of categories one and five—a combination of colonial rule and ideological motivation, in this case religious ideology. You could call it *Middle Eastern post-colonial religious and national terrorism.*

You may wonder why I define it as *post-colonial* when there is no longer a Western political presence in the Middle East and the days of the colonies and the mandates are finished. But the United States, the West, still penetrates the Middle East. We do so commercially. We do so culturally. We do so psychologically. Middle Eastern terrorism is a response to a great many of these factors, some of which we can discuss.

It is a reaction against Western penetration; it's an effort to drive us out, to resist us culturally. It's a reaction of anger and disappointment. It's a product of frustrations, unemployment chief among them. It's an effort to make us aware of some deeply felt political grievances, most notable being the Palestinians'.

Perhaps we can take a look at some of these factors. I think the most important of all of them is that terrorism is a statement of identity—a cry of "We *exist*. We Middle Easterners, we Arabs, we Lebanese Shiites, we Iranians. We, our people, our values, our institutions have to be taken seriously by the West, by the United States."

I was particularly reminded of this in November of 1984, the fifth anniversary of the embassy takeover. Ted Koppel of "Nightline," whom, you may remember, owes the beginning of his career to the hostage crisis, had the grace to invite some of us hostages back for a reunion. There was my wife coming in on the satellite from Harrisburg, I was in New York with Barry Rosen, Koppel was in Washington, and, coming in from Teheran by the magic of satellite transmission was Hossein Sheikoleslam, who was the leader and spokesman for our captors.

Today he is deputy foreign minister of Iran and coordinator of terrorism. In career terms, he has done better than any of us. I remember my first meeting with him in that same basement room that I described earlier. He warned us that, unless the United States met the students' terms, all the hostages would be put on trial and some would be executed. Being trained for the law, I knew when to shut up and not say anything that could be used against me. Hossein Sheikoleslam said that he noticed an atmosphere of constraint. But he said that perhaps we might meet afterward in Paris or some neutral ground and discuss things more freely. Fine, I thought.

So there I had him on the satellite and

asked him the question that I had always wanted to ask him: "Why did you take over the American Embassy in Teheran?" His reply was, "When I was a student in the United States" (he had been at the University of California at Berkeley), "none of my classmates knew where Iran was. But now, every American knows where Iran is." But he meant more than a mere geography lesson. He was saying, "We exist. We're real." He went on to amplify his point: "Americans now know what Iran says, what Iran stands for. We're Eastern. We're not Western." In other words, "You in the West have your values, and we in Iran have ours. We're rejecting your values."

I recalled an earlier conversation, as he was speaking on "Nightline," and how I had said to him at the time, "You are holding us contrary to international law." He had replied to me very contemptuously, "What is international law? They are your rules by which you—the rich, industrialized countries—justify what you do to poor, developing countries like Iran. Besides," he added, "you don't observe them yourself." He was referring, alas, to the Belgian and West German passports taken in the Embassy which had in them pictures of our embassy officers. They captured the CIA station intact along with forged Iranian entry stamps. This was a detail; I told him so.

But you know, I wish I could have talked to him during the TWA hostage crisis. You remember the outcry, a quite legitimate one, against the Lebanese Shiites holding thirty-nine Americans illegally. But when, in defiance of the Fourth Geneva Protocol, Israel had brought across a national boundary non-uniformed Lebanese civilians and interned them as virtual hostages until the safe withdrawal of the Israeli army from Lebanon, nobody said very much. There's sort of a double standard here, and you see this again and again in our dealings with the Middle East.

One of the Shiite gunmen who hijacked the TWA flight 847 in June 1985 went up and down the aisle of the plane saying, "New Jersey, New Jersey." One of the terrified passengers, apparently hoping to establish common ground, said, "Hey, I'm from Jersey." Not much came of that; the gunman went to the back of the plane, and before long he shot a U.S. navy diver. He was about to shoot

a second one when, upon the intervention of a stewardess, the diver said, "I have a wife and daughter." The Shiite gunman said, "Yes, so did I. They were killed in the shelling of our village in Lebanon by the U.S.S. *New Jersey*."

It's as if we have two standards here. One standard is for national states which, in pursuit of their own national interests, can take innocent lives. It is regrettable, nobody applauds it, but it is morally tolerable. Secretary Schultz said so. The other standard applies to the subnational groupings, for example, the Palestinians or the Shiites. At least for the Palestinians, this is a Catch-22 because they want nothing more than a national state of their own. It is often hard to realize how seriously our Declaration of Independence, our great American message, is taken by the Third World. We have advocated self-determination and majority rule for all peoples but not for the Palestinians.

So, for a number of different reasons quite unrelated to Arab-Israeli relations or Palestine, the Middle East views us as hypocrites and the Middle East is very hard on hypocrites. It is written in the Scriptures, "Woe unto ye scribes and Pharisees, hypocrites." Jimmy Carter was the first American president to make explicit in foreign policy declarations the United States' commitment to human rights. But when, in September 1978, the Shah's household troops, the Imperial Guard, gunned down students kneeling, practicing Gandhi-type nonresistance in Jaleh Square in Teheran, Mr. Carter reiterated his support for the Shah—something the students, our captors, never ceased to remind us of.

What is most disappointing is that there is a relationship that continues to exist between us and the young people of the Third World that results in very, very mixed feelings about the United States. I remember Hamid, one of our senior guards, saying, "The sad thing about what we are doing is that some of us may never be able to visit the United States again."

I had another exchange with Hamid in the television room where we were taken at all hours of the day and night to watch "Fantasy Island" and things of that nature. On the wall were posters, one of which was, of course, of the Chicago Democratic Convention of 1968 showing the police beating on students. On another wall was a slogan, "America, get out of our country, get out of our region." So, I asked Hamid, "What are you going to do if the Soviets do to Iran what they are now doing to Afghanistan?" He replied, without hesitation, "Well, you will have to come to our defense. We're too important to you."

Now, there's a lot of irony there. It's pathetic, because what he is really saying is not just "We Iranians are too important to you" but really "You are too important to us." And there is such love-hatred in these feelings which these young Iranians have about the United States and which are replicated by people all over the Third World. Our guards used to say, "We like Americans. It's the United States that we hate." They were making a distinction for partly political purposes. They were hoping that this episode would divide the American people from their government as Vietnam had divided the American people. (Some of them had been students in the United States then.) They didn't realize how the crisis would pull the American people together. But more important, they were coping with mixed feelings by dividing the object of those feelings.

This is a well-known psychological device that we use when we admire people who make us feel inferior. If certain people are superior to us and we have low or diminished self-esteem, we resent them and we tend to try to cut them down to size. For example, we might say, "I like this about John, I admire that about Mary, but I do wish . . ." and then there is some slightly denigrating remark to bring them down to your perceived level. I challenge anyone to tell me that he or she has never had these feelings. We have all had such feelings. The takeover and destruction of embassies and much of terrorism is simply a retaliation, a hitting back at those who are more successful, a way of playing out feelings of inferiority.

There is a curious mixture in terrorists of violence and gentleness, and every hostage and a lot of people who have been hijacked pay tribute to this same baffling mixture of real concern mingled with real abuse. I remember Ahmad, a guard who could be very cruel, saying to me, "Mr. Kennedy, your toothbrush looks a little wide at the top. Perhaps I can get you a new one." Again, they've got very mixed feelings about what they are doing.

Terrorists are idealists. And I say *terrorists* meaning the great majority of them, and I exclude, let me say quickly, the Abu Nidals or some of the truly fanatic terrorists who'd be doing what they do no matter what the political circumstances. The great mass of young Shiites, young Palestinians, and young Iranians are idealists willing to give up their lives for a cause and an acute sense of justice. Yet, they are aware that, in hostage taking, they are denying justice to others. Thus, the need of those who handled the mock executions to conceal their faces and to apologize afterward.

There is also among these young people, particularly among the Islamic fundamentalists, a very strong reaction against Western culture. They admire us, they admire our success, but they want to expel our culture because it threatens their own sense of identity. I remember talking to another guard once and making the point I referred to earlier about Afghanistan. I asked, "Why are you taking such chances antagonizing the United States when the Soviets are right on your border?" And he said, "The Soviets are an enemy, but *you* are the worst enemy." Soviet culture is pretty boring, let's face it. It doesn't offer anything compared to this tremendously seductive society which we have built and which the rest of the world simultaneously resists and emulates.

The Shah, remember, was the great westernizer. He forced the pace of westernization, disorienting the people and forcing them to think in categories that were not theirs. He made them feel humiliated by their inadequacies as they tried to be westerners and found themselves unable to do so. They were disinclined to be second-class Americans, to be in our kind of cultural Appalachia. In looking for their own sense of identity, they found something in fundamentalist religion. When they expelled us from Iran, they were expelling the agent of their disorientation.

In Lebanon today, who are the hostages being held? Consider their occupations. Peter Kilbourne, recently executed, was librarian of the American University. (The press said, "A librarian. Librarians are nice people." Nonsense. Librarians are very dangerous people if they are the custodians of the ideas that deeply threaten your own.) The dean of the agricultural faculty of the American University of Beirut is still being held. The administrator of the hospital at the American University of Beirut is still being held, as are the local bureau chief of the Associated Press and a Roman Catholic missionary. Those no longer hostage are: Benjamin Weir, a Presbyterian missionary, released; Jeremy Levin, bureau chief of Cable News Network, escaped (the bureau chief of AP was kidnapped to take his place); David Dodge, formerly acting president of the American University of Beirut, whose family founded the institution, kidnapped and held for a year and then released; and Malcolm Kerr, with whom I studied Arabic, president of the American University of Beirut, shot and killed outside his office. Don't you hear this theme, the same theme, repeated? "American University of Beirut. American University of Beirut." These are people on the cutting edge of Western penetration.

Now what are we going to do? How are we going to react? I think that our most basic problem is to redefine some of our moral criteria in dealing with terrorism. What we call retaliation for *terrorism*, they call retaliation against *them*. We've got to learn to avoid being hostage to our own anger, hostage to some notion that "we've got to nail these guys."

We frequently hear about the raid against Libya. People say, "Mr. Reagan had no choice; he was forced to do something. The American people insisted upon doing something." This may be true. But what do you *do* about it? Reagan singled out Khadafy, who was gaining a lot of credit for the terrorism of others. But Khadafy was not the terrorist. We shaped our view of terrorism to make it fit the familiar pattern of a bad state, such as Libya, and a bad ruler, such as Khadafy. But by "nailing" Khadafy you don't do very much about terrorism.

And the worst aspect of the U.S. raid is that we were hostage to our own technology. I asked a senior State Department official recently why we used carrier-based aircraft and bombs that could take innocent civilian lives and create martyrs, including Khadafy's own daughter. He said, "We didn't have anything else."

Surely, there are covert means. When the Soviets had four diplomats taken, did they bomb? Did they make these moralistic noises, which would have sounded a little funny coming out of Moscow, anyway? No. Their solution was perfectly simple. They went to Walid Jumblatt, the head of the Druzes and put the problem into his hands in a manner a little bit redolent of the Mafia. Representatives of every group that might have been involved in the Soviet kidnapping were themselves kidnapped by Walid, parts of their anatomy, I am told, were sent back, and, within twenty-four hours, all the remaining Soviets (one of them had been killed) were released. *We have to play that game.* We have to do it covertly. When possible, we should do so deniably, to avoid giving excuses for retaliation. Action that cannot be traced is far more threatening.

But we've got to break away from the kind of scenario invented by the Italian general Douhet in the 1920s: if you bomb a civilian population long enough and hard enough, you break their will to resist and then they give up. And you know very well that the Germans tried this against England, and, of course, Mr. Churchill yielded immediately. England is now a German protectorate. We used the Douhet theory very effectively against Hanoi, and that's why we won the war in Southeast Asia.

There is room in this fight against terrorism for retaliation, and Mr. Carter understood this very well. He sent a message to our captors saying that if one hair on the hostages' heads were touched there would be military retaliation. He never had to use it, you see. What he did, I strongly believe, was strengthen the stance and the arguments of the more moderate. He kept us alive. But the worst stance to take is one which says, "Unless you do what we want, we're going to nail you," because then the onus for action is on *you* instead of on *them*. You are in the morally wrong position. If you do something, you look like a villain, and, if you don't do something, you look like a fool.

Our goal ought to be to divide the terrorists from the moderates, to reduce rather than increase moderate support for the terrorists in the Middle East. We can certainly begin nowhere better than by reopening the peace process and the agenda that was never completed at Camp David. It is one, you may recall, that promised a homeland to the Palestinian people. This is not to say that a homeland for the Palestinian people will end the problem of world terror. It won't. However, we've got to begin somewhere, and there are many reasons why this is so much in both Israel's and our best interest.

But the most basic tool against terrorism is to show, as we Americans have shown in the past, that we are open-minded, that we are willing to listen, and that we may not always agree but at least we will address grievances when they are presented to us. We must give, once again, to these young people in the Third World the hope that they don't have to resort to these terrible attention-getting devices in order to enlist our attention. They must believe that we are prepared to listen, prepared, once again, to exercise true leadership—not because we have more guns or bigger economies but because we articulate the highest aspirations of the people we want to lead.

The Seven Deadly Sins of Terrorism

Paul Johnson

Paul Johnson argues that terrorism is intrinsically evil, necessarily evil, and entirely evil for seven reasons: (1) it exalts violence; (2) it suppresses moral instincts; (3) it rejects politics; (4) it spreads totalitarianism; (5) it is the enemy of democracy; (6) it exploits freedom; and (7) it induces civilization to commit suicide.

Before identifying the correct approach to the terrorist problem, let us look at the wrong one. The wrong approach is to see terrorism as one of many symptoms of a deep-seated malaise in our society, part of a pattern of violence which includes juvenile delinquency, rising crime rates, student riots, vandalism and football hooliganism, and which is to be attributed to the shadow of the H-bomb, rising divorce rates, inadequate welfare services and poverty. This analysis usually ends in the meaningless and defeatist conclusion that society itself is to blame: "We are all guilty."

The truth is, international terrorism is not part of a generalised human problem. It is a specific and identifiable problem on its own; and because it is specific and identifiable, because it can be isolated from the context which breeds it, it is a remediable problem. That is the first point to get clear.

But to say it is remediable is not to un-

From "The Seven Deadly Sins of Terrorism," *NATO Review* (October 1980), pp. 28–33. Reprinted by permission of the publisher.

derestimate the size and danger of the problem. On the contrary: it is almost impossible to exaggerate the threat which terrorism holds for our civilisation because, unlike many other current threats, it is not being contained. Quite the reverse, it is increasing steadily, and one reason is that very few people in the civilised world—governments, parliaments, journalists and the public generally—take terrorism seriously enough.

Most people, lacking an adequate knowledge of history, tend to underestimate the fragility of a civilisation. They do not appreciate that civilisations fall as well as rise, that they can be and have been, destroyed by malign forces. In our recoverable history, there have been at least three Dark Ages. One occurred in the third millennium B.C., and smashed the civilisation of the Egyptian Old Kingdom—the culture which built the pyramids. Another occurred towards the end of the second millennium B.C., and destroyed Mycenaean Greece, Minoan Crete, the Hittite Empire, and much else. We are more familiar with the third, which destroyed the Roman Empire in the

West in the fifth century A.D.: it took Europe 800 years to recover, in terms of organisation, technical skills and living standards. The great catastrophes had varying causes, but there was a common factor in all of them. They occurred when the spread of metals technology, and the availability of raw materials, enabled the forces of barbarism to equal or surpass the civilised powers in the quality and quantity of their weapons, for in the last resort, civilisations stand or fall, not by covenants, but by the sword.

Enemies of Society

Edward Gibbon, at the end of his great book, *The Decline and Fall of the Roman Empire*, wrote: "The savage nations of the globe are the common enemies of civilised society, and we may well inquire with anxious curiosity whether Europe is still threatened with a repetition of those calamities which formerly oppressed the arms and institutions of Rome." Writing in the 1780s, on the threshold of the Industrial Revolution, Gibbon thought he could answer his own question with a reasonably confident negative. He rightly estimated the strength of the civilised world to be increasing, and he believed the scientific and rational principles on which that strength was based were becoming more firmly established with every year that passed.

Now nearly 200 years later, we cannot be so sure. The principles of objective science and human reason, the notion of the rule of law, the paramountcy of politics over force, are everywhere under growing and purposeful challenge; and the forces of savagery and violence, which constitute this challenge, are becoming bolder, more numerous and, above all, better armed. The arms available to terrorists, the skills with which they use them and, not least, the organisational techniques with which these weapons and skills are deployed, are all improving at a fast and accelerating rate—a rate much faster than the countermeasures available to civilised society.

Take one example—Northern Ireland. In August last year members of the Provisional IRA killed Lord Mountbatten and other members of his party, and, in another attack that same day, killed 18 British soldiers. They suffered no casualties themselves, a pattern of success which is all too familiar. There are two reasons for this. The first is the replacement of the old amateurish IRA structure by what the BBC Defence Correspondent has called, "a modern clandestine force, well-organised and well-equipped, with a classic cellular structure which is strong and almost impossible to penetrate or break." During a single night, for instance, they were able to plant 49 bombs in 22 towns throughout Northern Ireland which, again according to the BBC, "must have meant staff work of a very high standard." The second is that the range and quality of weapons now used by Irish terrorists are becoming very formidable.

These menacing improvements in weaponry and organisation have been brought about by the international availability of terrorist support, supply and training services. Terrorism is no longer a purely national phenomenon, which can be destroyed at national level. It is an international offensive—an open and declared war against civilisation itself—which can only be defeated by an international alliance of the civilised powers.

To the argument that terrorists are not enemies of civilisation in that they are often idealists pursuing worthy ultimate aims, I would answer that the terrorist can never be an idealist, and that the objects sought can never justify terrorism. For what is terrorism? It is the deliberate, systemic murder, maiming and menacing of the innocent to inspire fear in order to gain political ends. By this definition, the impact of terrorism, not merely on individuals, not merely on single nations, but on humanity as a whole is intrinsically evil, necessarily evil and wholly evil. It is so for a number of demonstrable reasons—what I call the Seven Deadly Sins of Terrorism.

Exaltation of Violence

First, terrorism is the deliberate and cold-blooded exaltation of violence over all forms of political activity. The modern terrorist does not employ violence as a necessary evil but as a desirable form of action. There is a definite intellectual background to the present wave of terrorism. It springs not only from the Leninist and Trotskyist justification of violence, but from the post-war philosophy of violence derived from Nietzsche through Heidegger, and widely popularised by Sartre, his colleague and disciple. No one since 1945 has influenced young people more than Sartre and no one has done more to legitimise violence on the Left. It was Sartre who adapted the linguistic technique, common in German philosophy, of identifying certain political frameworks as the equivalent of "violence," thus justifying violent correctives or responses. In 1962 he said: "For me, the essential problem is to reject the theory according to which the Left ought not to answer with violence." Note his words: not "a problem," but "the essential problem."

Some of those influenced by Sartre went much further—notably Franz Fanon. His most influential work, *Les Damnés de la Terre*, which has a preface by Sartre, has probably played a bigger part in spreading terrorism in the Third World than any other tract. Violence is presented as liberation, a fundamental Sartrean theme. For a black man, writes Sartre in his preface, "to shoot down a European is to kill two birds with one stone, to destroy an oppressor and the man he oppresses at the same time." By killing, the terrorist is born again—free. Fanon preached that violence is a necessary form of social and moral regeneration for the oppressed. "Violence alone," he writes, "violence committed by the people, violence organised and educated by its leaders, makes it possible for the masses to understand social truths and gives the key to them." The notion of "organised and educated violence," conducted by elites is, of course, the formula for terrorism. Fanon goes further: "At the level of individuals, violence is a cleansing force. It frees [the oppressed] from his inferiority complex and from his despair and inaction."

It is precisely this line of thought, that violence is positive and creative, which enables the terrorists to perform the horrifying acts for which they are responsible. Of course the same argument—almost word for word—was used by Hitler, who repeated endlessly, "Virtue lies in shedding blood." Hence the first deadly sin of terrorism is the moral justification of murder not merely as a means to an end but for its own sake.

Moral Instincts Suppressed

The second is the deliberate suppression of the moral instincts in man. Terrorist organisers have found that it is not enough to give their recruits intellectual justifications for murder: the instinctive humanity in us all has to be systematically blunted, or else it rejects such sophistry. In the Russia of the 1870s and 1880s, the Neznavhalie terror group favoured what it called "motiveless terror" and regarded any murder as a "progressive action." Once indiscriminate terror is adopted, the group rapidly suffers moral disintegration—indeed the abandonment of any system of moral criteria becomes an essential element in its training. The point is brilliantly made in Dostoevsky's great anti-terrorist novel, *The Possessed,* by one of the gangsters, who argues that the terror-group can be united only by fear and moral depravity: "Persuade four members of the circle to murder a fifth," he says, "on the excuse that he is an informer, and you will at once tie them all up in one knot by the blood you have shed. They will be your slaves." This technique is undoubtedly used by some terror groups today, on the assumption that neither man nor woman can be an effective terrorist so long as he or she retains the moral elements of a human personality. One might say, then, that the second deadly sin of terrorism is a threat not merely to civilisation but to humanity as such.

Rejection of Politics

The third, following directly from the first two, is the rejection of politics as the normal means by which communities resolve conflicts. To terrorists, violence is not a political weapon, to be used *in extremis;* it is a substitute for the entire political process. Middle East terrorist groups, the IRA, the Bader-Meinhoff gang, Red Armies or Brigades in Japan, Italy and elsewhere, have never shown any desire to engage in the democratic political process. The notion that violence is a technique of last resort, to be adopted only if all other attempts to obtain justice have failed, is rejected by them. In doing so, they reject the mainstream of civilised thought, based, like so much of our political grammar, on the social-contract theorists of the 17th century. Hobbes and Locke rightly treated violence as the antithesis of politics, a form of action characteristic of the archaic realm of the state of nature. They saw politics as an attempt to create a tool to avoid barbarism and make civilisation possible: politics makes violence not only unnecessary but unnatural to civilised man. Politics is an essential part of the basic machinery of civilisation, and in rejecting politics, terrorism seeks to make civilisation unworkable.

Spreads Totalitarianism

Terrorism, however, is not neutral in the political battle. It does not, in the long run, tend towards anarchy: it tends towards despotism. The fourth deadly sin of terrorism is that it actively, systematically and necessarily assists the spread of the totalitarian state. The countries which finance and maintain the international infrastructure of terrorism—which give terrorists refuge and havens, training-camps and bases, money, arms and diplomatic support as a matter of deliberate state policy—are, without exception, totalitarian states. The governments of all these states rule by military and police force. The notion that terrorism is opposed to the "repressive forces" in society is false—indeed, it is the reverse of the truth. International terrorism, and the various terrorist movements it serves, are entirely dependent on the continuing good will and active support of police states. The terrorist is sustained by the totalitarian paraphernalia of tanks, torture, and the secret police. The terrorist is the direct beneficiary of the Gulag Archipelago and everything it stands for.

Enemy of Democracy

Which brings us to the fifth deadly sin. International terrorism poses no threat to the totalitarian state. That kind of state can always defend itself by judicial murder, preventative arrest, torture of prisoners and suspects, and complete censorship of terrorist activities. It does not have to abide by the rule of law or any other consideration of humanity or morals. Hence, the fifth deadly sin is that terrorism can destroy a democracy, as it destroyed the Lebanon, but it cannot destroy a totalitarian state. All it can do is to transform a nation struggling towards progress and legality into a nightmare of oppression and violence.

Exploits Freedom

This leads us to another significant generalisation about terrorism. Its ultimate base is in the totalitarian worlds—that is where its money, training, arms and protection come from. But at the same time, it can only operate effectively in the freedom of a liberal civilisation. Terrorists are the advance scouts of the totalitarian armies. The sixth deadly sin of terrorism is that it exploits the apparatus of freedom in liberal societies, and thereby endangers it.

In meeting the threat of terrorism, a free society must arm itself. But that very process of arming itself against the danger within threatens the freedoms, decencies and standards which make it civilised. Terrorism then—and it is this we must get across to intelligent young people who may be tempted to sympathise with it—is a direct and continuous threat to all the protective devices of a free society. It is a threat to the freedom of the press and television to report without restraints. It is a threat to the rule of law, necessarily damaged by emergency legislation and special powers. It is a threat to *habeas corpus,* to the continuous process of humanising the legal code and civilising our prisons. It is a threat to any system designed to curb excesses by the police or prison authorities or any other restraining force in society.

Inducement to Suicide

Yet the seventh deadly sin of terrorism operates, paradoxically, in the reverse direction—and is yet more destructive. A free society which reacts to terrorism by invoking authoritarian methods of repression necessarily damages itself. But an even graver danger—and a much more common one today—is of free societies, in their anxiety to avoid authoritarian excesses, *failing* to arm themselves against the terrorist threat, and so abdicating their responsibility to uphold the law. The terrorists succeed when they provoke oppression: but they triumph when they are met with appeasement.

The seventh and deadliest sin of terrorism therefore is that it saps the will of a civilised society to defend itself. We have seen it happen. We find governments negotiating with terrorists—negotiations aimed not at destroying or disarming them, for such negotiations may sometimes be necessary—but negotiations whose natural and inevitable result is to concede part of the terrorists' demands. We find governments providing ransom money to terrorists—or permitting private individuals to do so, even assisting the process whereby such funds reach terrorist hands. We find governments releasing convicted criminals in response to terrorist demands, according terrorists the status, rights and advantages, and above all, the legitimacy, of negotiating partners. We find governments conceding to terrorist convicts the official and privileged status of political prisoners. We find governments yielding to demands—an invariable and well-organised part of terrorist strategy—for official enquiries, or international investigations, into alleged ill-treatment of terrorist suspects or convicts. We find newspapers and television networks—often, indeed, state networks—placing democratic governments and the terrorists on a level of moral equality. We find governments failing, time and again, in their duty to persuade the public—that terrorists are not misguided politicians: they are criminals; extraordinary criminals indeed, in that they are exceptionally dangerous to us all and pose a unique threat not merely to the individuals they murder without compunction but to the whole fabric of society—but criminals just the same.

In short, the seventh and deadliest sin of terrorism is its attempt to induce civilisation to commit suicide.

These seven mortal dangers must be seen in the light of the fact that terrorism is not a static threat but a dynamic one. Not only is the international infrastructure of terrorism becoming better organised and more efficient, but the terrorists' own sights are being raised by their successes. We must expect and prepare for yet further improvements in the types of weapons which they deploy. We cannot rule out the possibility that terrorists will obtain access to nuclear devices or even to their production process.

Terrorism, in short, is no longer a marginal problem, something to be contained and lived with, a nuisance. It is a real, important and growing threat to the peace and stability of all legitimate states—that is, all those states which live under the rule of law. It is an international threat—therein lies its power. That power can only be destroyed or emasculated when there is international recognition of its gravity and international action by the united forces of civilisation to bring it under control.

Thinking About Terrorism

Conor Cruise O'Brien

Conor Cruise O'Brien argues that terrorism is either subject to a sentimental stereotype, according to which the terrorist is a misguided idealist, or subject to a hysterical stereotype, according to which the terrorist is either a nut, a thug, or a dupe. Rejecting both these stereotypes, O'Brien claims that the only effective approach to terrorism is one that involves the cooperation of all the major powers and, consequently, would require that the United States give up its support for the terrorist activities of the contras in Nicaragua.

Terrorism is disturbing not just emotionally and morally but intellectually, as well. On terrorism, more than on other subjects, commentary seems liable to be swayed by wishful thinking, to base itself on unwarranted or flawed assumptions, and to draw from these assumptions irrational inferences, muzzily expressed.

Let me offer one example, typical of many more. The following is the conclusion to a recent *Washington Post* editorial, "Nervous Mideast Moment":

> The United States, however, cannot afford to let its struggle against terrorism be overwhelmed by its differences with Libya. That gives the Qaddafis of the world too much importance and draws attention from the requirement to go to the political sources of terrorism. A principal source, unquestionably, is the unresolved Palestinian question. The State Department's man for the Middle East, Richard Murphy, has been on the road again, cautiously exploring whether it is possible in coming months to bring Israel and Jordan closer to a negotiation. This quest would be essential even if terrorism were not the concern it is. It marks the leading way that American policy must go.

From "Thinking About Terrorism," *The Atlantic Monthly* (June, 1986), pp. 62–66. Reprinted by permission of the author.

The clear implication is that negotiation between Israel and Jordan can dry up "a principal source of terrorism." Now, nobody who has studied that political context at all, and is not blinded by wishful thinking, could possibly believe that. For the Arab terrorists—and most other Arabs—"the unresolved Palestinian question" and the existence of the State of Israel are one and the same thing. The terrorists could not possibly be appeased, or made to desist, by Jordan's King Hussein's getting back a slice of the West Bank, which is the very most that could come out of a negotiation between Jordan and Israel. The terrorists and their backers would denounce such a deal as treachery and seek to step up their attacks, directing these against Jordan as well as Israel.

That *Washington Post* editorial, like many others to the same tune, exemplifies a dovish, or sentimental, variety of wishful thinking on the subject of terrorism. There is also a hawkish, or hysterical, variety. Each has its own misleading stereotype (or stereotypes) of the terrorist. Let us look at the stereotypes:

Sentimental stereotype. According to this stereotype, the terrorist is a misguided idealist, an unsublimated social reformer. He has been driven to violence by political or social injustice or both. What is needed is to identify the measures of reform that will cause him to desist. Once these can be identified and undertaken, the terrorist, having ceased to be driven, stops.

Hysterical stereotype. Less stable than the sentimental variety, this can be divided into subvarieties:

(a) The terrorist is some kind of a nut—a "disgruntled abnormal" given to "mindless violence." ("Mindless violence" may be applicable to the deeds of isolated, maverick assassins. As applied to the planned activities of armed conspiracies, it is itself a mindless expression.)

(b) The terrorist is nothing more than a thug, a goon, a gangster. His "political" demands are simply a cover for criminal activity.

(c) The terrorist is an agent, or dupe, or cat's-paw of the other superpower. (He might, of course, be a nut or a goon as well as a dupe.)

These stereotypes serve mainly to confuse debate on the subject. There is no point in arbitrarily attributing motives, nice or nasty, to the terrorist. It might be more useful to look at the situations in which terrorists find themselves and at how they act, and may be expected to act, given their situations.

In what follows I shall bear in mind mainly (though not exclusively) the members of the most durable terrorist organizations of the twentieth century: the IRA (including its splinter groups) and the PLO (including its splinter groups).

Terrorists have a grievance, which they share with members of a wider community: the division of Ireland, the division of Palestine, the inroads of secularism into Islam, or whatever. But they also have, from the moment they become terrorists, significant amounts of power, prestige, and access to wealth, and these constitute vested interests in the present, irrespective of the attainment or non-attainment of their declared long-term political objectives.

The sentimentalist thinks of the terrorist as driven to violence by grievance or oppression. It would be more realistic to think of the terrorist as hauling himself up, by means of the grievance or oppression and the violence it legitimizes, to relative power, prestige, and privilege in the community to which he belongs. For an unemployed young man in a slum in Sidon or Strabane, for example, the most promising channel of upward social mobility is his neighborhood branch of the national terrorist organization. There are risks

to be run, certainly, but for the adventurous, aggressive characters among the unemployed or the otherwise frustrated, the immediate rewards outweigh the risks. In this situation the terrorist option is a rational one: you don't have to be a nut, a dupe, or an idealist.

I don't mean that the terrorist is necessarily, or even probably, insincere about the national (or religious or other collective) grievance or in his hatred toward those seen as responsible for the grievance. On the contrary, hatred is one of the things that keep him going, and the gratification of hatred is among the rewards of the terrorist. The terrorist is not just a goon, out for the loot. His political motivation is genuine. But there are other rewards in his way of life as well as the hazy reward of progress toward the political objective. The possession of a known capacity and willingness to kill confers authority and glamour in the here and now, even on rank-and-file members in the urban ghetto or in the village. On the leaders it confers national and even international authority and glamour, and independence from financial worries.

If we accept that the terrorist's way of life procures him immediate rewards of that nature, and that he is probably not insensible to at least some of the rewards in question, it seems to follow that he will probably be reluctant to relinquish those rewards by voluntarily putting himself out of business.

The situation thus outlined has a bearing of a negative nature on the notion that there are "negotiated solutions" to the "problems" that "cause" terrorism.

First of all, a negotiated solution—being by definition an outcome that offers some satisfaction to both parties—will be inherently distasteful to terrorists and their admirers, accustomed as these are to regarding *one* of the parties (Britain, Israel, or another) as evil incarnate.

Second, to exploit that genuine distaste will be in the interests of the terrorists, in relation to the reward system discussed above. So pride and profit converge into a violent rejection of the "negotiated solution"—which therefore is not a solution to terrorism.

This is most obvious where the solution is to be negotiated between people who are not spokesmen for the terrorists. When Garret

FitzGerald and Margaret Thatcher negotiated the Hillsborough Agreement over Northern Ireland, last November, that neither caused the IRA to give up nor deprived it of its hard-core popular support (though there was a drop of about 10 percent in electoral support for the IRA's political front, Sinn Fein).[1] Similarly, if King Hussein and Shimon Peres were to reach agreement, it would not be likely to cause any of the Arab terrorist groups to go out of business or forfeit their hard-core support.

Suppose a terrorist (or putatively *ex*-terrorist) organization joined in the deal. That would presumably earn a cessation, or at least a suspension, of terrorist activity by the negotiating group and its immediate following. But the deal would be repudiated by other organizations, who would see no reason to go out of business; and since these intransigents would be demonstrably in line with the absolutist policies previously proclaimed by the whole movement, they would have high credibility and widespread support.

So the prospects for ending terrorism through a negotiated settlement are not bright, whether or not the terrorists are involved in the negotiations. But the insistence that negotiated solution *can* end terrorism actually helps the terrorists. It does so because it places the responsibility for continuing terrorism equally on the terrorists and those they seek to terrorize. The enhanced respectability with which the terrorist is thereby invested gives him a foretaste of success and an encouragement to persevere. This is the opposite of what the dovish advisers desire, but it is the main result of their ill-advised endeavors.

Not only do doves sometimes help terrorists but some hawkish advisers also give inadvertent aid and comfort to the forces they abhor. The combating of terrorism is not helped by bombastic speeches at high levels, stressing what a monstrous evil terrorism is and that its elimination is to be given the highest priority. I'm afraid that the most likely terrorist reaction to such a speech, whether it comes from a President, a Secretary of State, or other important official, is: "You see, they *have* to pay attention to us now. We are hurting them. Let's give them more of the same." And

it all helps with recruitment. A movement that is denounced by a President is in the big time. And some kind of big time is what is most wanted by the aggressive and frustrated, who constitute the pool on which terrorist movements can draw.

What applies to speeches applies *a fortiori* to unilateral military action against countries harboring terrorists. Whatever short-term advantages may be derived from such attacks, a price will be paid—in increased international sympathy for the "cause" of the terrorists in question, and so in enhanced glamour and elbow room for them, all tending to legitimize and so facilitate future "counterattacks."

Nor does it help to suggest that terrorism is about to be extirpated—because it almost certainly isn't. Today's world—especially the free, or capitalist, world—provides highly favorable conditions for terrorist recruitment and activity. The numbers of the frustrated are constantly on the increase, and so is their awareness of the life-style of the better-off and the vulnerability of the better-off. Among the better-off themselves are bored young people looking for the kicks that violence can provide, and thus for causes that legitimize violence, of which there are no shortage. A wide variety of people feel starved for attention, and one surefire way of attracting instantaneous worldwide attention through television is to slaughter a considerable number of human beings, in a spectacular fashion, in the name of a cause.

Although the causes themselves hardly constitute the sole motivation of the terrorists—as terrorists claim they do—they are not irrelevant, either. The cause legitimizes the act of terror in the terrorist's own eyes and in those of others belonging to his nation, faith, or culture. Certain cultures and subcultures, homes of frustrated causes, are destined breeding grounds for terrorism. The Islamic culture is the most notable example. That culture's view of its own rightful position in the world is profoundly at variance with the actual order of the contemporary world. It is God's will that the House of Islam should triumph over the House of War (the non-Moslem world), and not just by spiritual means. "Islam Means Victory" is a slogan of the Iranian fundamentalists in the Gulf War. To strike a blow against the House of War is meritorious; consequently, there is widespread support for activities condemned in the West as terrorist. Israel is one main target for these activities, but the activities would not be likely to cease even if Israel came to an end. The Great Satan in the eyes of Ayatollah Khomeini—and of the millions for whom he speaks—is not Israel but the United States. The defeat of Israel would, in those eyes, be no more than a portent of the impending defeat of the Great Satan. What the West calls terrorism should then be multiplied rather than abandoned.

The wellsprings of terrorism are widespread and deep. The interaction between modern communications systems and archaic fanaticism (and other sources of resentment and ambition) is likely to continue to stimulate terrorist activity. In these conditions, talk about extirpating terrorism—and unilateral exploits backing such talk—are likely to be counterproductive. They present terrorists with a "victory," merely by the fact of being able to continue their activity. Similarly, solemn promises never to negotiate with terrorists can play into the hands of terrorists. Terrorists holding hostages can force a democratic government to negotiate, as happened in the case of the hijacked TWA airliner last June. If the democratic government then pretends that no negotiation took place, this helps the credibility of the terrorists, not that of the democratic government.

It is not possible to extirpate terrorism from the face of the globe, but it should be possible to reduce the incidence and effectiveness of terrorism, through coordinated international action. The Reagan Administration's efforts to get better cooperation in this matter from the European allies are justified in principle but flawed in practice. They are justified because the performance of several European countries in relation to international terrorism has often amounted to turning a blind eye, for commercial reasons. The British government, for example, tolerated the conversion of the Libyan Embassy in London into a "Revolutionary People's Bureau," and ignored all reports that the bureau was a center of terrorist activity, until the point was reached at which the revolutionary diplomatists actually opened fire from the embassy windows into St. James's Square, killing a British policewoman. Even after that the policy of playing ball with Qaddafi, as long as there was money to be made out of it, did not altogether disappear, either in Britain or elsewhere in Europe. (Mrs. Thatcher's support for the recent U.S. air strikes against Libyan targets seems to stem from a wish to be seen as the most dependable ally of the United States, rather than from any spontaneous change of heart about the proper way in which to deal with Libya.)

So President Reagan had good reasons for urging the European allies to adopt less complaisant attitudes toward international terrorism. But, unfortunately, the President's remonstrances lack the moral leverage they need to have. They lack such leverage because a very wide international public sees the Reagan Administration itself as engaged in supporting terrorism in Central America, in its backing for the contras in Nicaragua. Public cynicism about American anti-terrorist rhetoric is increased by the strong component of Cold War ideology that the Reagan Administration has been putting into its anti-terrorism, implying that almost all terrorism has its ultimate roots in the Soviet Union. Most of the interested public outside the superpowers tends to see each superpower as calling the terrorists whom it favors "freedom fighters" while reserving the term "terrorists" for the "freedom fighters" favored by the other side. That view of the matter is debatable, but the point, in the present context, is that it is shared by so many people that it inhibits effective international cooperation against international terrorism.

Such cooperation is unlikely to have a strong impact unless both superpowers are prepared to participate in it. Bringing about such cooperation will be difficult but is not inconceivable. Limited superpower consensus has emerged, in the second half of the twentieth century, on at least three occasions: in 1956, against the Anglo-French-Israeli invasion of Egypt; in 1963, against the continued existence of the secessionist "state" of Katanga; and in 1977, against the supply of arms to South Africa.

Can limited superpower consensus be attained for coordinated action against terrorism? I think it can, especially if international terrorist activity grows to the degree that it begins to pose a clear threat to international peace and stability—not just as these are perceived by one superpower but as perceived by both. There is a historical precedent, flawed—like all such precedents—but suggestive. This is the case of the Barbary pirates, who used to operate in the Mediterranean, out of North African ports. In the seventeenth and eighteenth centuries, rivalries between the European powers provided the Barbary pirates with conditions propitious to their activities, much as global rivalries tend to protect state terrorism today. The Barbary pirates were a general nuisance, but they were a worse nuisance to some powers than to others, and so the enemies of the powers for whom the pirates were making the most trouble were apt to give the pirates a helping hand from time to time. In the first half of the nineteenth century, however, the powers decided, in effect, that the pirates should be treated as a common enemy: the enemy of the human race, *hostes humani generis*. With that change in international approach piracy was brought under control in the Mediterranean.

International terrorism has yet to reach the stage that Mediterranean piracy reached in the nineteenth century. Terrorism is a worse nuisance to one superpower—the United States—than it is to the other. Democratic societies, committed to freedom of information and having governments necessarily sensitive to changing public moods, are far more vulnerable to terrorist blackmail, and offer a far more stimulating environment for terrorist activity, than closed societies like the Soviet Union. (We are often told that there is no terrorist activity in the Soviet Union; in reality we don't know whether there is terrorism or not. But the fact that we don't know and that the Soviet public doesn't know would certainly be advantageous to the Soviet authorities in coping with any terrorists that they may have.)

So the Soviets have no clear and present incentive to join in international activity against terrorism. On the contrary, they have given cautious aid and encouragement to some forms of terrorism (less than right-wing propagandists suggest, but more than the left admits). But it would be wrong to conclude, as

most right-wing analysts do, that the Soviets are operating under a doctrinal imperative to destabilize the West. The Soviet authorities—despite their ideological bravado—know well that a destabilized West could be extremely dangerous, and specifically dangerous to the Soviet Union. The superpowers do have an elemental common interest—in survival. That is why limited superpower consensus has been possible in the past, and that is why it remains a possibility for the future with regard to terrorism. Such consensus could take the form of a joint warning that any country harboring terrorists would no longer be allowed to invoke its sovereignty as a protection against international intervention. Once superpower agreement had been reached, that warning could be embodied in a mandatory resolution of the Security Council.

We are very far indeed from that point, though here as elsewhere thought should not treat present actuality as if it were eternal. In the meantime, it appears that the United States has two main alternatives for anti-terrorist policy.

The first alternative, which seems likely to be followed for the remainder of the Reagan Administration, is to go on backing the contras and simultaneously calling for an end to terrorism, with occasional armed spectaculars to lend conviction to such calls. As already indicated, I think this policy is internationally incredible and hopeless, and unnecessarily dangerous, whatever its merits may be in terms of domestic electoral politics.

The second alternative is to provide clear and consistent political and moral leadership in this matter to U.S. allies and the rest of what is called the free world. That would require the United States both to abandon completely its support for the contras in Nicaragua and to accept, without the present reservations, the authority of the World Court. I believe that a President of the United States who had taken these steps would be in a far stronger position than is now the case to give the world a lead in combined action against terrorism and to prepare the way for eventual superpower consensus on this matter. And I think that a President who took such a stand would be bringing new hope on other matters, also, to many people in the world.

Note

1. The Hillsborough Agreement gave the Dublin Government simply an advisory role in the affairs of Northern Ireland (editor).

Freedom Struggle by the Provisional IRA

Quite frankly it suited IRA strategy to carry out selective bombings in Belfast, Derry, and other towns in Occupied Ulster. They see these actions as a legitimate part of war, the targets chosen being military and police barracks, outposts, customs offices, administrative and government buildings, electricity transformers and pylons, certain cinemas, hotels, clubs, dance halls, pubs, all of which provide relaxation and personal comforts for the British forces; also business targets e.g., factories, firms, stores (sometimes under the guise of CO-OPs) owned in whole or part by British financiers or companies, or who in any way are a contributory factor to the well-being of Her Majesty's invading forces, and in certain instances residences of people known to harbor or be in league with espionage personnel or *agents provocateurs* namely the S.A.S., MRF, and S.I.B. In many ways this campaign is reminiscent of that carried out by the underground Resistance in France during World War II.

In all cases IRA bomb squads give adequate warning though these warnings are sometimes withheld or delayed deliberately by the British army as a counter-tactic, with view to making optimum publicity out of the injured and the dead in their propaganda war on the IRA. In no instance has the "warning rule" been violated by the guerrilla forces in sharp contrast with the "no warning" methods used by the Unionist gangs and British army *agents provocateurs.*

The Abercorn Restaurant, McGurk's Bar, Benny's Bar and more recently McGlades Bar are frightening examples of the latter type of instant bombing. Naturally it presents less risk

to the bombers in terms of personal safety and lessens the chances of being apprehended. As well as giving warnings, the IRA always claims full responsibility for all military action taken even should this redound unfavorably on the Republican Movement's popularity; E.B.N.I. and Donegall Street are classic examples of this. Over the years the press has learned to accept the veracity of Irish Republican Publicity Bureau statements, whereas, with the British army's constant propaganda handouts, various versions of incidents and blatant covering-up of tracks have created for them a gross credibility gap.

The effect of the IRA bombing campaign can be gauged in many different ways. Firstly, they have struck at the very root of enemy morale, confining and tying down large numbers of troops and armored vehicles in center city areas, thus relieving much of the pressure on the much-oppressed nationalist areas. In terms of direct financial loss (structural damage, goods, machinery), also in the crippling of industrial output and perhaps worst of all in the scaring-off of foreign capital investments, IRA bombs have hit Britain where she feels it most—in her pocket.

England always found unfortunate soldiers quite dispensable and to a certain extent replaceable, but she always counted in terms of cost to the Treasury. Any peace through the granting of freedom emanating to rebellious colonies from London came by means of calculation—the cost of occupation. Since 1969 a bill of warfare running to at least a conservative £500,000,000 has not gone unnoticed back home in Britain where recent opinion polls showed that over 54 percent of the ordinary people wanted the troops withdrawn forthwith.

Already some 1,500 troops have left Northern Ireland never to return. In many cases death certificates have been issued as for fatal road accident victims to the unsuspecting next-of-kin of soldiers killed in action in a heartless attempt at cooking records and hiding telling manpower losses. Suddenly Northern Ireland has become England's Vietnam. In the knowledge that the will to overcome of a risen people can never be defeated by brute force or even overwhelming odds more enlightened British politicians have seen the light and are themselves thinking along Tone's famous dictum: "Break the connection!"

Great Britain too, of course, has suffered losses other than bomb damage and loss of personnel. Her prestige and credibility in terms of world opinion and world finance have been severely shaken; her duplicity and selective sense of justice have been seriously exposed; her puerile hankering after "holding the last vestige of the Empire" has marked her as a recidivist nation, psychologically vulnerable, unstable, and mentally immature. These considerations have not been lost on the European Common Market countries, especially France and Monsieur Pompidou. Britain's dilemma in Ireland is of her own making and is now seen as a black mark against her in the new capital—Brussels. Time is running out along the Thames.

Northern Ireland Emergency Provisions Act

Powers of Arrest, Detention, Search and Seizure, Etc.

Arrest and Detention of Terrorists

10.—(1) Any constable may arrest without warrant any person whom he suspects of being a terrorist.

(2) For the purpose of arresting a person under this section a constable may enter and search any premises or other place where that person is or where the constable suspects him of being.

(3) A person arrested under this section shall not be detained in right of the arrest for more than seventy-two hours after his arrest, and section 182 of the Magistrates' Courts Act (Northern Ireland) 1964 and section 50 (8) of the Children and Young Persons Act (Northern Ireland) 1968 (requirement to bring arrested person before a magistrates' court not later than forty-eight hours after his arrest) shall not apply to any such person.

(4) Where a person is arrested under this section, an officer of the Royal Ulster Constabulary not below the rank of chief inspector may order him to be photographed and to have his finger prints and palm prints taken by a constable, and a constable may use such reasonable force as may be necessary for that purpose.

(5) The provisions of Schedule 1 to this Act shall have effect with respect to the detention of terrorists and persons suspected of being terrorists.

Constables' General Power of Arrest and Seizure

11.—(1) Any constable may arrest without warrant any person whom he suspects of committing, having committed or being about to commit a scheduled offence or an offence under this Act which is not a scheduled offence.

(2) For the purposes of arresting a person under this section a constable may enter and search any premises or other place where that person is or where the constable suspects him of being.

(3) A constable may seize anything which he

suspects is being, has been or is intended to be used in the commission of a scheduled offence or an offence under this Act which is not a scheduled offence.

Powers of Arrest of Members of Her Majesty's Forces

12.—(1) A member of Her Majesty's forces on duty may arrest without warrant, and detain for not more than four hours, a person whom he suspects of committing, having committed or being about to commit any offence.

(2) A person effecting an arrest under this section complies with any rule of law requiring him to state the ground of arrest if he states that he is effecting the arrest as a member of Her Majesty's forces.

(3) For the purpose of arresting a person under this section a member of Her Majesty's forces may enter and search any premises or other place where that person is or, if that person is suspected of being a terrorist or of having committed an offence involving the use or possession of an explosive, explosive substance or firearm, where that person is suspected of being.

Power to Search for Munitions

13.—(1) Any member of Her Majesty's forces on duty or any constable may enter any premises or other place other than a dwelling-house for the purpose of ascertaining whether there are any munitions unlawfully at that place and may search the place for any munitions with a view to exercising the powers conferred by subsection (4) below.

(2) Any member of Her Majesty's forces on duty authorised by a commissioned officer of those forces or any constable authorised by an officer of the Royal Ulster Constabulary not below the rank of chief inspector may enter any dwelling-house in which it is suspected that there are unlawfully any munitions and may search it for any munitions with a view to exercising the said powers.

(3) Any member of Her Majesty's forces on duty or any constable may—

(a) stop any person in any public place and with a view to exercising the said powers search him for the purpose of ascertaining whether he has any munitions unlawfully with him; and

(b) with a view to exercising the said powers search any person not in a public place whom he suspects of having any munitions unlawfully with him.

(4) A member of Her Majesty's forces or a constable authorised to search any premises or other place or any person under this Act may seize any munitions found in the course of the search unless it appear to the person so authorised that the munitions are being, have been and will be used only for a lawful purpose and may retain and, if necessary, destroy them.

(5) In this section "munitions" means—

(a) explosives, explosive substances, firearms and ammunition and

(b) anything used or capable of being used in the manufacture of any explosive, explosive substance, firearm or ammunition.

Powers of Explosives Inspectors

14.—(1) An inspector appointed under section 58 of the Explosives Act 1875 may, for the purpose of ascertaining whether there is unlawfully in any premises or other place other than a dwelling-house any explosive or explosive substance, enter that place and search it with a view to exercising the powers conferred by subsection (3) below.

(2) Any such inspector may stop any person in a public place and search him for the purpose of ascertaining whether he has any explosive or explosive substance unlawfully with him with a view to exercising the said powers.

(3) Any such inspector may seize any explosive or explosive substance found in the course of a search under this section unless it appears to him that it is being, has been and will be used only for a lawful purpose and may retain and, if necessary, destroy it.

Entry to Search for Persons Unlawfully Detained

15. Where any person is believed to be unlawfully detained in such circumstances that his life is in danger, any member of Her

Majesty's forces on duty or any constable may enter any premises or other place for the purpose of ascertaining whether that person is so detained there, but a dwelling-house may be entered in pursuance of this section by a member of Her Majesty's forces only when authorised to do so by a commissioned officer of those forces and may be so entered by a constable only when authorised to do so by an officer of the Royal Ulster Constabulary not below the rank of chief inspector.

Power to Stop and Question

16.—(1) Any member of Her Majesty's forces on duty or any constable may stop and question any person for the purpose of ascertaining that person's identity and movements and what he knows concerning any recent explosion or any other incident endangering life or concerning any person killed or injured in any such explosion or incident.

(2) Any person who fails to stop when required to do so under this section, or who refuses to answer or fails to answer to the best of his knowledge and ability, any question addressed to him under this section, shall be liable on summary conviction to imprisonment for a term not exceeding six months or to a fine not exceeding £400, or both.

General Powers of Entry and Interference with Rights of Property and with Highways

17.—(1) Any member of Her Majesty's forces on duty or any constable may enter any premises or other place—

(a) if he considers it necessary to do so in the course of operations for the preservation of the peace or the maintenance of order; or

(b) if authorised to do so by or on behalf of the Secretary of State.

(2) Any member of Her Majesty's forces on duty, any constable or any person specifically authorised to do so by or on behalf of the Secretary of State may, if authorised to do so by or on behalf of the Secretary of State—

(a) take possession of any land or other property;

(b) take steps to place buildings or other structures in a state of defence;

(c) detain any property or cause it to be destroyed or moved;

(d) do any other act interfering with any public right or with any private rights of property, including carrying out any works on any land of which possession has been taken under this subsection.

(3) Any member of Her Majesty's forces on duty, any constable or any person specifically authorised to do so by or on behalf of the Secretary of State may, so far as he considers it immediately necessary for the preservation of the peace or the maintenance or order, wholly or partly close a highway or divert or otherwise interfere with a highway or the use of a highway, or prohibit or restrict the exercise of any right of way or the use of any waterway.

(4) Any person who, without lawful authority or reasonable excuse (the proof of which lies on him), interferes with works executed, or any apparatus, equipment or any other thing used, in or in connection with the exercise of powers conferred by this section shall be liable on summary conviction to imprisonment for a term not exceeding six months or to a fine not exceeding £400, or both.

(5) Any authorisation to exercise any powers under any provision of this section may authorise the exercise of all those powers, or powers of any class or a particular power so specified, either by all persons by whom they are capable of being exercised or by persons of any class or a particular person so specified.

Supplementary Provisions

18.—(1) Any power conferred by this Part of this Act—

(a) to enter premises or other place includes power to enter any vessel, aircraft or vehicle;

(b) to search any premises or other place includes power to stop and search any vehicle or vessel or any aircraft which is not airborne and search any container;

and in this Part of this Act references to any premises or place shall be construed accordingly and references to a dwelling-house shall include references to a vessel or vehicle which is habitually stationary and used as a dwelling.

(2) Any power so conferred to enter any place, vessel, aircraft or vehicle shall be exercisable, if need be, by force.

(3) Any power conferred by virtue of this section to search a vehicle or vessel shall, in the case of a vehicle or vessel which cannot be conveniently or thoroughly searched at the place where it is, include power to take it or cause it to be taken to any place for the purpose of carrying out the search.

(4) Any power conferred by virtue of this section to search any vessel, aircraft, vehicle or container includes power to examine it.

(5) Any power conferred by this Part of this Act to stop any person includes power to stop a vessel or vehicle or an aircraft which is not airborne.

(6) Any person who, when required by virtue of this section to stop a vessel or vehicle or any aircraft which is not airborne, fails to do so shall be liable on summary conviction to imprisonment to a term not exceeding six months or to a fine not exceeding £400, or both.

(7) A member of Her Majesty's Forces exercising any power conferred by this Part of this Act when he is not in uniform shall, if so requested by any person at or about the time of exercising that power, produce to that person documentary evidence that he is such a member.

(8) The Documentary Evidence Act 1868 shall apply to any authorisation given in writing under this Part of this Act by or on behalf of the Secretary of State as it applies to any order made by him.

Suggestions for Further Reading

Anthologies

Crenshaw, Martha, *Terrorism, Legitimacy and Power,* Middletown: Wesleyan University Press, 1983

Freedman, Lawrence and Yonah, Alexander, *Perspectives on Terrorism,* Wilmington: Scholarly Resources, 1983

Laquer, Walter, *The Terrorism Reader,* New York: New American Library, 1978

Netanyahu, Benjamin, *International Terrorism: Challenge and Response,* New Brunswick: Transaction Books, 1981

Basic Concepts

Burtchael, James, "Moral Responses to Terrorism" in *Fighting Back,* edited by Livingston and Arnold, Lexington Books, 1985

Leiser, Burton, "Defining Terrorism" in his *Liberty Justice and Morals,* New York: Macmillan Publishing Co. 1979

Alternative Views

Beres, Louis Rene, *Terrorism and Global Security,* Bolder: Westview Press, 1979

Dobson, Christopher and Ronald Payne, *The Terrorists: Their Weapons, Leaders, and Tactics,* New York: Facts on File, 1982

Raynor, Thomas *Terrorism: Past, Present and Future,* New York: Franklin Watts, 1982

Sterling, Clair, *The Time of Assassins,* New York: Holt, Rinehart and Winston, 1984

Wardlaw, Grant, *Political Terrorism: Theory, Tactics and Countermeasures,* Cambridge: Cambridge University Press, 1982

Practical Applications

Muravchik, Joshua, "Reagan's Carter Policy on Handling Terrorism," *New York Times,* January 15, 1986

Quainton, Anthony, "Moral and Ethical Considerations in Defining a Counter-Terrorist Policy in the *Rationalization of Terrorism* edited by Rapoport and Alexander, University Press of America, 1982

Nuclear Deterrence and Strategic Defense

Basic Concepts

The problem of nuclear deterrence and strategic defense is simply the contemporary version of the problem of determining the moral limits of military defense, which has been with us since the dawn of human history. *Just war theories* attempt to specify what these moral limits are. Such theories have two components: a set of criteria that establish a right to go to war *(jus ad bellum),* and a set of criteria that determine legitimate conduct in war *(jus in bello).* The first set of criteria can be grouped under the label "just cause," the second under "just means."

Consider the following specification of just cause:

> There must be substantial aggression, and nonbelligerent correctives must be hopeless or too costly.

This specification of just cause implicitly contains a number of criteria, for example, last resort, formal declaration, and reasonable hope of success. It does, however, exclude the criterion of legitimate authority, which has had a prominent place in just war theories. That criterion is excluded because it has the character of a second-order requirement: it is a requirement that must be satisfied whenever there is a question of group action with respect to any moral problem whatsoever. For example, with respect to the problem of the distribution of goods and resources in a society, we can certainly ask who has the (morally legitimate) authority to distribute or redistribute goods and resources in a society; and with respect to the problem of punishment and responsibility, we can ask who has the (morally legitimate) authority to punish offenders in a society. But before we ask such questions with respect to particular moral problems, it is important to first understand what are the morally defensible solutions to these problems because a standard way of identifying morally legitimate authorities is by their endorsement of such solutions. With respect to the problem of nuclear deterrence and strategic defense,

we first need to determine the nature and existence of just causes before we try to identify morally legitimate authorities by their endorsement of such causes.

Regardless of whether we define just cause independently of legitimate authority, pacifists will simply deny that there are any just causes that ought to be recognized. Pacifists hold that it is never morally too costly to use nonbelligerent correctives against aggression. According to pacifists, people should never defend themselves against aggression by intentionally killing other human beings.

But military actions can be condemned for failing to satisfy the criteria of just means as well as the criteria of just cause. Consider the following specification of just means:

1. The harm inflicted on the aggressor must not be disproportionate to the aggression.
2. Harm to innocents should not be directly intended as an end or a means.
3. Harm to innocents must be minimized by accepting risks (costs) to oneself that would not doom the military venture.

The first criterion is a widely accepted requirement of just means. The second criterion is also widely accepted and contains the main requirement of the doctrine of double effect (see the introduction to Section III). Many philosophers seem willing to endorse the application of the doctrine in this context given that those to whom the doctrine applies are generally recognized to be persons with full moral status.

The doctrine of double effect, however, does not require (3), which incorporates an even stronger safeguard against harming innocents in warfare than (2).

To evaluate these requirements of just war theory, we need to determine to what degree they can be supported by the moral approaches to practical problems presented in the General Introduction. Of course, one or more of these approaches may ultimately favor the pacifist position, but assuming that these approaches favored some version of a just war theory, which version would that be?

Obviously, the utilitarian approach would have little difficulty accepting the requirement of just cause and requirement (1) on just means because these requirements can be interpreted as having a utilitarian backing. However, this approach would only accept requirements (2) and (3) on just means conditionally because occasions would surely arise when violations of these requirements would maximize net utility.

Unlike the Utilitarian Approach, the Human Nature Approach is relatively indeterminate in its requirements. All that is certain, as I have interpreted the approach, is that it would be absolutely committed to requirement (2) on just means. Of course, the other requirements on just cause and just means would be required by particular versions of this approach.

The Social Contract Approach is distinctive in that it seeks to combine and compromise both the concern of the Utilitarian Approach for maximal net utility and the concern of the Human Nature Approach for the proper development of each individual. In its hypothetical choice situation, persons would clearly favor the requirement of just cause and requirement (1) on just means, although they would not interpret them in a strictly utilitarian fashion.

Yet what about the requirements (2) and (3) on just means? Because persons behind a veil of ignorance would not be committed simply to whatever maximizes net utility, they would want to put a stricter limit on the harm that could be inflicted on innocents in defense of a just cause than could be justified on utilitarian grounds alone. This is because persons behind a veil of ignorance would be concerned not only with what maximizes net utility but also with the distribution of utility to particular individuals. Persons imagining themselves to be ignorant of what position they are in would be particularly concerned that they might turn out to be in the position of those who are innocent, and, consequently, they would want strong safeguards against harming those who are innocent, such as requirements (2) and (3) on just means.

Yet even though persons behind a veil of ignorance would favor a differential restriction on harm to innocents, they would not favor an absolute restriction on intentional harm to innocents. They would recognize as

exceptions to such a restriction cases where intentional harm to innocents is either:

1. Trivial (e.g., stepping on someone's foot to get out of a crowded subway).
2. Easily reparable (e.g., lying to a temporarily depressed friend to keep her from committing suicide).
3. Sufficiently outweighed by the consequences of the action (e.g., shooting one of two hundred civilian hostages to prevent in the only way possible the execution of all two hundred).

Accordingly, while persons behind a veil of ignorance would favor requirement (2) on just means, their commitment to this requirement would also have to incorporate the above exceptions. Even so, these exceptions are far more limited than those that would be tolerated by the Utilitarian Approach.

In sum, the Social Contract Approach would strongly endorse the requirement of just cause and requirements (1), (2), and (3) on just means. Yet its commitment to requirement (2) on just means would fall short of the absolute commitment that is characteristic of the Human Nature Approach to practical problems.

It is clear, therefore, that our three moral approaches to practical problems differ significantly with respect to their requirements for a just war theory. The Utilitarian Approach strongly endorses the requirement of just cause and requirement (1) on just means but only conditionally endorses requirements (2) and (3) on just means. The Human Nature Approach endorses requirement (2) on just means as an absolute requirement but is indeterminate with respect to the other requirements of just war theory. Only the Social Contract Approach strongly endorses all of the basic requirements of a traditional just war theory, although it does not regard requirement (2) on just means as an absolute requirement. Fortunately for traditional just war theory, there are good reasons for favoring the Social Contract Approach over each of the other two moral approaches to practical problems.

One reason for favoring the Social Contract

Approach over the Utilitarian Approach is that its requirements are derived from a veil of ignorance decision-procedure that utilitarians and contractarians alike recognize to be fair. It is not surprising, therefore, to find such utilitarians as John Harsanyi and R. M. Hare simply endorsing this decision-procedure and then trying to show that the resulting requirements would maximize utility.[1] Yet we have just seen how the concern of persons behind a veil of ignorance with the distribution of utility would lead them to impose a stricter limit on the harm that could be inflicted on innocents in defense of a just cause than could be justified on grounds of maximizing utility alone. At least with respect to just war theory, therefore, the Utilitarian Approach and the Social Contract Approach differ significantly in their practical requirements.

Utilitarians who endorse this decision-procedure are faced with a difficult choice: give up their commitment to this decision-procedure or modify their commitment to utilitarian goals. Utilitarians cannot easily choose to give up their commitment to this decision-procedure because the acceptability of utilitarianism as traditionally conceived has always depended on showing that fairness and utility rarely conflict, and that when they do, it is always plausible to think that the requirements of utility are morally overriding. Consequently, when a fair decision-procedure significantly conflicts with utility, which it is not plausible to think can always be morally overridden by the requirements of utility, that procedure exposes the inadequacy of the Utilitarian Approach to practical problems.

These reasons for favoring the Social Contract Approach over the Utilitarian Approach to practical problems are also reasons for favoring the human nature approach because the Human Nature Approach is also concerned with fairness and the distribution of utility to particular individuals. Nevertheless, there are other reasons for favoring the Social Contract Approach over the Human Nature Approach.

One reason is that the Social Contract Approach does not endorse any absolute requirements. In particular, the Social Contract Approach does not endorse an absolute requirement not to intentionally harm inno-

cents. The Social Contract Approach recognizes that if the harm is trivial, easily reparable, or sufficiently outweighed by the consequences, such harm can be morally justified.

Another reason for favoring the Social Contract Approach over the Human Nature Approach is that the Social Contract Approach is determinate in its requirements; it actually leads to a wide range of practical recommendations. By contrast, the Human Nature Approach lacks a deliberative procedure that can produce agreement with respect to practical requirements. This is evident from the fact that supporters of this approach tend to endorse radically different practical requirements. In this regard, the veil of ignorance decision-procedure employed by the Social Contract Approach appears to be just the sort of morally defensible device needed to achieve determinate requirements.

Finally, the particular requirements of just war theory endorsed by the Social Contract Approach are further supported by the presence of analogous requirements for related areas of conduct. Thus, the strong legal prohibitions that exist against punishing the innocent provide support for the strong prohibition against harming innocents expressed by requirements (2) and (3) on just means. This is the type of correspondence we would expect from an adequate moral theory: requirements in one area of conduct would be analogous to those in related areas of conduct.

Alternative Views

In the first selection (pp. 427–438), James P. Sterba attempts to answer a number of challenges that have been directed at just war theory. Against the pacifist challenge to just cause, Sterba argues that killing in self-defense can be morally justified provided either that the killing is the foreseen consequence of an action whose intended consequence is stopping an attempt on one's life or that the killing is not morally evil because those engaging in the attempt on one's life have already forfeited their right to life. Against the conventionalist challenge to just means, Sterba argues that there is a perfectly acceptable convention-independent way of supporting condition (2) of just means. Sterba also argues against the collectivist challenge that not just any contribution to the unjust actions of one's leaders opens one to attack or the threat of attack. Rather, one's contribution must be significant enough to justify such a response. Finally, against the feminist challenge to both components of just war theory, Sterba concedes that the only way of meeting the challenge is to rid society of its sexist and militarist attitudes and practices so as to increase the chances that just war theory will be applied correctly in the future.

In this selection, Sterba then applies the requirements of just war theory to the use and threat to use nuclear weapons and concludes that, under present conditions, the United States and the Soviet Union are only morally justified in simply possessing a survivable nuclear force to be able to quickly threaten or bluff nuclear retaliation should conditions change for the worse. If conditions do worsen, however, Sterba claims that it would be morally justified at some point for the United States or the Soviet Union to threaten a form of limited nuclear retaliation or bluff a form of massive nuclear retaliation.

Sterba even allows that under certain conceivable but unlikely conditions, a limited retaliatory use of nuclear weapons against tactical and strategic targets would be morally justified to restore deterrence. In the next selection (pp. 439–443), Caspar Weinberger argues for a much broader justification for nuclear deterrence. Weinberger rejects a "no first use" policy with respect to nuclear weapons on the grounds that it might imply that the first use of conventional forces was somehow acceptable. Citing figures to indicate a buildup of Soviet nuclear forces in the 1970s, Weinberger argues that the United States must match this buildup while seeking to promote meaningful arms reduction. However, the claim that the Soviet Union outspent the United States in the 1970s is based on an estimate of what it would cost in dollars for the United States to deploy the very same forces by the Soviet Union during the period. However, given that the United States pays its all-volunteer military forces much more than

the Soviet Union pays its conscripted military forces, this approach grossly overestimates Soviet military spending. U.S. military spending would also be grossly overestimated if we were to determine in rubles what it would cost the Soviet Union to build the more technologically sophisticated weapons in the U.S. arsenal. Attempting to avoid both of these errors, the Stockholm International Peace Research Institute placed the U.S. military budget for 1980 at $110 billion, which was slightly higher than the Soviet military budget for that year. Moreover, when the contribution of the United States' NATO partners are taken into account, it turns out that the United States and its allies outspent the Warsaw Pact nations by $207 billion during the 1970s. Even the CIA recently revised downward its estimate of the increase in Soviet spending for 1977–1982 from 3 percent or 4 percent a year to no more than 2 percent, which is lower than the average U.S. increase for that period. In the final analysis, therefore, the proclaimed spending gap between the Soviet Union and the United States is more illusion than reality. In addition, given the huge increase in U.S. military spending in recent years, it seems clear enough that the United States and its allies are also currently outspending the Soviet Union and the Warsaw Pact nations.

In his address to the nation on March 23, 1983, President Reagan advocated that the United States "embark on a program to counter the awesome Soviet missile threat with measures that are defensive." He called on the American scientific community, "those who gave us nuclear weapons, to turn their great talents now to the cause of mankind and world peace, to give us the means of rendering these nuclear weapons impotent and obsolete." To meet these goals, President Reagan has proposed a research and development budget of 30 billion dollars. Initial funding for what has come to be called the Strategic Defense Initiative (SDI) was 1.4 billion in 1984, 2.6 billion in 1986, and 3.2 billion for 1987.

However, Colin Gray (pp. 443–448), a well-known defender of strategic defense, argues for a form of SDI significantly different from Reagan's program. Specifically, the form of SDI defended by Gray does not "promise that society as a whole can for certain be defended directly." Rather, it is primarily "an exploration of ways in which the stability of the existing system of offensive, retaliatory deterrence might be enhanced."

According to Gray, "there is no prudent choice available other than to press on carefully to explore the possibility of strategic defense."

In response to critics who contend that the Soviet Union may choose to take forceful measures to prevent the United States from achieving a military advantage through a defensive deployment, Gray argues that the existing strategic balance between the United States and the Soviet Union should deter any such action. Gray also claims that "if the Soviet leaders believe that U.S. offensive forces will fare considerably better against Soviet defenses than will Soviet offensive forces against U.S. defenses then they should be motivated to agree to negotiated reductions of offensive forces."

In the following selection, Robert M. Bowman (pp. 448–455) discusses four possible objectives for SDI, or what he more appropriately calls a ballistic missile defense (BMD):

1. To replace a policy of deterrence
2. To enhance deterrence
3. To provide a shield for a disarming first-strike capacity
4. To limit the damage should deterrence fail

Bowman argues that BMD will never be effective enough to achieve objectives (1) and (4), and that as a means for achieving objective (2), BMD is both unnecessary and counterproductive. According to Bowman, BMD could only achieve (3), an objective Bowman feels is morally repugnant.

We can see, therefore, that although Gray favors SDI and Bowman opposes it, they agree in a number of respects. First of all, both agree that SDI could not achieve the objective of replacing a policy of nuclear deterrence. Second, both agree that SDI could enhance nuclear deterrence, yet Bowman contends that to do so would be unnecessary and ultimately counterproductive. Third, Gray and Bowman also seem to agree that SDI could provide a shield for a disarming first-strike capacity.

However, Bowman regards this objective as morally indefensible, whereas Gray does not, contending that the Soviet Union would not strike first to prevent the deployment of such a shield and that, in fact, when faced with the prospect of strategic inferiority, the Soviet Union would be receptive to negotiations. Yet Gray fails to explain why the Soviet Union would be interested in negotiating from weakness when the United States has always sought to negotiate only from strength. Nor does he explain why, if the Soviets were sufficiently fearful of the possibility of a disarming first strike once SDI was deployed, they wouldn't be willing to risk a limited military action designed simply to prevent that deployment.

Where Gray and Bowman disagree is over whether SDI would provide protection should deterrence fail. Gray thinks it would, whereas Bowman contends that SDI is not sufficiently leakproof to significantly improve the chances of survival. According to Bowman, if more than 50 warheads were to fall on the United States, we would lose most of our people and probably cease to function as a society. Note, however, that this depends on where those warheads were to fall. If most of them fell on major U.S. cities, Bowman would probably be right, but he would most certainly be wrong if most of them fell on Minuteman missile silos.

Practical Application

The readings in this section have already suggested a variety of practical solutions to the problem of nuclear deterrence and strategic defense, ranging from complete acceptance to complete rejection of nuclear deterrence and from complete acceptance to complete rejection of strategic defense. Yet two of the most prominent practical proposals in this area, in addition to President Reagan's SDI proposal, are the Kennedy/Hatfield Nuclear Freeze Resolution and Mikhail S. Gorbachev's proposal for Nuclear Disarmament by the year 2000. At various times, the freeze resolution has been strongly supported by U.S. public opinion (85%), and Gorbachev's proposal for Nuclear Disarmament by the year 2000 was the basis for the Soviet negotiating stance at the Reykjavik Summit. By drawing on the previous readings in this section, you should be in a better position to assess the moral defensibility of these practical proposals.

Nevertheless, it is important to recognize that a solution to this practical problem cannot stand alone; it requires solutions to the other practical problems discussed in this anthology as well. For example, a solution to the problem of the distribution of income and wealth may show that it is morally illegitimate to increase military security by sacrificing the basic needs of the less advantaged members of a society rather than by sacrificing the nonbasic needs of the more advantaged members of the society. Accordingly, it is impossible to reach a fully adequate solution to this or any other practical problem discussed in this anthology without solving the other practical problems as well.

Notes

---

1. See John Harsanyi, *Rational Behavior and Bargaining Equilibrium in Games and Social Situations* (Cambridge: Cambridge University Press, 1977), and R. M. Hare, "Justice and Equality," in *Justice: Alternative Political Perspectives*, edited by James P. Sterba (Belmont, CA: Wadsworth Publishing Co., 1980).

Just War Theory and Nuclear Strategy

James P. Sterba

This article defends just war theory against pacifist, conventionalist, collectivist, and feminist challenges that have recently been directed against it. Just war theory is then applied to the use of and threat to use nuclear weapons, and the article concludes that under present conditions the possession of, but not the threat to use, nuclear weapons is morally justified.

In traditional just war theory, there are two basic components: a set of criteria which establish a right to go to war (jus ad bellum) and a set of criteria which determine legitimate conduct in war (jus in bello). The first set of criteria can be grouped under the label "just cause," the second under the label "just means." In recent years, the just cause component of just war theory has been subjected to a pacifist challenge, the just means component has been subjected to conventionalist and collectivist challenges and both components have been subject to a feminist challenge. In this paper, I will attempt to respond to each of these challenges in turn and then go on to determine the practical implications of just war theory for nuclear strategy.

From "Just War Theory and Nuclear Strategy," *Analyse & Kritik* (Special Issue) 1987. Reprinted by permission.

The Pacifist Challenge to Just Cause

In traditional just war theory, just cause is usually specified as follows:

Just Cause There must be substantial aggression and nonbelligerent correctives must be hopeless or too costly.

Needless to say, the notion of substantial aggression is a bit fuzzy, but it is generally understood to be the type of aggression that violates people's most fundamental rights. To suggest some specific examples of what is and what is not substantial aggression, usually nationalization of particular firms owned by foreigners is not regarded as substantial aggression while the taking of hostages is so regarded. But even when substantial aggression occurs, frequently nonbelligerent correctives are neither hopeless nor too costly.

However, according to the pacifist challenge to just war theory nonbelligerent correctives, or at least nonlethal correctives, are never hopeless or too costly. Thus, for pacifists there aren't any just causes.

But this pacifist challenge to just war theory is sometimes claimed to be incoherent. In a well-known article, Jan Narveson rejects pacifism as incoherent because it recognizes a right to life yet rules out any use of force in defense of that right.[1] The view is incoherent, Narveson claims, because having a right entails the legitimacy of using force in defense of that right at least on some occasions. But as Cheney Ryan has pointed out Narveson's argument only works against the following extreme form of pacifism:

Pacifism I   Any use of force is morally prohibited.

It doesn't touch the form of pacifism that Ryan thinks is most defensible, which is the following:

Pacifism II   Any lethal use of force is morally prohibited.[2]

This form of pacifism only prohibits the use of lethal force in defense of people's rights.

Ryan goes on to argue that there is a substantial issue between the pacifist and the nonpacifist concerning whether we can or should create the necessary distance between ourselves and other human beings in order to make the act of killing possible. To illustrate, Ryan cites George Orwell's reluctance to shoot at an enemy soldier who jumped out of a trench and ran along the top of a parapet half-dressed and holding up his trousers with both hands. Ryan contends that what kept Orwell from shooting was that he couldn't think of the soldier as a thing rather than a fellow human being.

But do we have to objectify other human beings in order to kill them? If we do, this would seem to tell in favor of the form of pacifism Ryan defends. However, it is not clear that Orwell's encounter supports such a view. For it may be that what kept Orwell from shooting the enemy soldier was not his inability to think of the soldier as a thing rather than a fellow human being but rather his inability to think of the soldier who was holding up his trousers with both hands as a threat or a combatant. Under this interpretation, Orwell's decision not to shoot would accord well with the requirements of just war theory.

Let us suppose, however, that someone is attempting to take your life. Why does that permit you, the pacifist might ask, to kill the person making the attempt? Isn't such killing prohibited by the principle that one should never intentionally do evil that good may come of it? Of course, someone might not want to endorse this principle as an absolute requirement, but surely it cannot be reasonable to regard all cases of justified killing in self-defense as exceptions to this principle.

One response to this pacifist objection is to allow that killing in self-defense can be morally justified provided that the killing is the foreseen consequence of an action whose intended consequence is the stopping of the attempt upon one's life. Another response is to allow that intentional killing in self-defense can be morally justified provided that you are reasonably certain that your attacker is wrongfully engaged in an attempt upon your life. It is claimed that in such a case the intentional killing is not evil, or at least not morally evil, because anyone who is wrongfully engaged in an attempt upon your life has already forfeited her or his right to life by engaging in such aggression.

Taken together, these two responses seem to constitute an adequate reply to the pacifist challenge. The first response is theoretically closer to the pacifist's own position since it rules out all intentional killing, but the second response is also needed when it does not seem possible to stop a threat to one's life without intentionally killing one's attacker.

The Conventionalist Challenge to Just Means

Now the just means component of just war theory, can be specified as follows:

Just Means

1) The harm resulting from the belligerent means employed should not be disproportionate to the military objective to be attained.

2) Harm to innocents should not be directly intended as an end or a means.

3) Harm to innocents should be minimized by accepting risks (costs) to oneself that would not render it impossible to attain the military objective.

Obviously, the notion of what is disproportionate is a bit fuzzy in (1), but the underlying idea is that the harm resulting from the belligerent corrective should not outweigh the benefit to be achieved from attaining the military objective. By contrast, (2) is a relatively precise requirement. Where it was obviously violated was in the antimorale terror bombing of Dresden and Hamburg and in the use of atomic bombs against Hiroshima and Nagasaki in World War II.[3]

Some people think that (1) and (2) capture the essential requirements of just means. Others maintain that something like (3) is also required. Michael Walzer provides an example from Frank Richard's memoir of World War I which shows the attractiveness of (3).

> When bombing dug-outs or cellars, it was always wise to throw the bombs into them first and have a look around after. But we had to be very careful in this village as there were civilians in some of the cellars. We shouted down to them to make sure. Another man and I shouted down one cellar twice and receiving no reply were just about to pull the pins out of our bomb when we heard a woman's voice and a young lady came up the cellar steps. . . . She and the members of her family . . . had not left (the cellar) for some days. They guessed an attack was being made and when we first shouted down had been too frightened to answer. If the young lady had not cried out when she did we would have innocently murdered them all.[4]

Many restrictions on the operation of police forces also seem to derive from a requirement like (3).

As one would expect, these criteria of just means have been incorporated to some degree in the military codes of different nations and adopted as international law. Yet rarely has anyone contended that the criteria ought to be met simply because they have been incorporated into military codes or adopted as international law. Recently, however, George Mavrodes has defended just such a conventionalist view.[5] Mavrodes arrives at this conclusion largely because he finds the standard attempts to specify the convention-independent basis for (2) and (3) to be so totally unsuccessful. All such attempts, Mavrodes claims, are based on an identification of innocents with noncombatants. But by any plausible standard of guilt and innocence that has moral content, Mavrodes contends, noncombatants can be guilty and combatants innocent. For example, noncombatants who are doing everything in their power to financially support an unjust war would be morally guilty, and combatants who were forced into military service and intended never to fire their weapons at anyone would be morally innocent. Consequently, the guilt/innocence distinction will not support the combatant/noncombatant distinction.

Hoping to still support the combatant/noncombatant distinction, Mavrodes suggests that the distinction might be grounded on a convention to observe it. This would mean that our obligation to morally abide by (2) and (3) would be a convention-dependent obligation. Nevertheless, Mavrodes does not deny that we have some convention-independent obligations. Our obligation to refrain from wantonly murdering our neighbors is given as an example of a convention-independent obligation, as is our obligation to reduce the pain and death involved in combat. But to refrain from harming noncombatants when harming them would be the most effective way of pursuing a just cause is not included among our convention-independent obligations.

Yet Mavrodes does not claim that our obligation to refrain from harming noncombatants is *purely* convention-dependent. He allows that, in circumstances in which the convention of refraining from harming noncombatants does not exist, we might still have an obligation to unilaterally refrain from harming noncombatants provided that our action will help give rise to a convention prohibiting such harm with its associated good consequences. According to Mavrodes, our primary obligation is to maximize good consequences, and this obligation requires that we refrain from harming noncombatants when that will help bring about a convention prohibiting such harm. By contrast, someone who held that our obligation to refrain from harming noncombatants was purely convention-dependent, would never recognize an obligation to unilaterally refrain from harming noncombatants. On a purely convention-dependent account, obligations can only be derived from existing conventions; the expected consequences from establishing a particular convention could never ground a purely convention-dependent obligation. But while Mavrodes does not claim that our obligation to refrain from harming noncombatants is purely convention-dependent, he does claim that this obligation generally arises only when there exists a convention prohibiting such harm. According to Mavrodes, the reason for this is that generally only when there exists a convention prohibiting harm to noncombatants will our refraining from harming them, while pursuing a just cause, actually maximize good consequences.

But is there no other way to support our obligation to refrain from harming noncombatants? Mavrodes would deny that there is. Consider, however, Mavrodes's own example of the convention-independent obligation not to wantonly kill our neighbors. There are at least two ways to understand how this obligation is supported. Some would claim that we ought not to wantonly kill our neighbors because this would not maximize good consequences. This appears to be Mavrodes's view. Others would claim that we ought not to wantonly kill our neighbors, even if doing so would maximize good consequences, simply because it is not reasonable to believe that our neighbors are engaged in an attempt upon our lives. Both these ways of understanding how the obligation is supported account for the convention-independent character of the obligation, but the second approach can also be used to show how our obligation to refrain from harming noncombatants is convention-independent. According to this approach

since it is not reasonable to believe that non-combatants are engaged in an attempt upon our lives, we have an obligation to refrain from harming them. So interpreted, our obligation to refrain from harming noncombatants is itself convention-independent, although it will certainly give rise to conventions.

Of course, some may argue that whenever it is not reasonable to believe that persons are engaged in an attempt upon our lives, an obligation to refrain from harming such persons will also be supported by the maximization of good consequences. Yet even if this were true, which seems doubtful, all it would show is that there exists a utilitarian or forward-looking justification for a convention-independent obligation to refrain from harming noncombatants; it would not show that such an obligation is a convention-dependent obligation, as Mavrodes claims.

The Collectivist Challenge to Just Means

Now according to the collectivist challenge to just means, more people should be included under the category of combatants than the standard interpretation of (2) allows. The reason for this is that the standard interpretation of (2) does not assume, as the advocates of the collectivist challenge do, that the members of a society are collectively responsible for the actions of their leaders unless they have taken radical steps to oppose or disassociate themselves from those actions, e.g., by engaging in civil disobedience or emigration. Of course, those who are unable to take such steps, particularly children, would not be responsible in any case, but, for the rest, advocates of the collectivist challenge contend that failure to take the necessary radical steps, when one's leaders are acting aggressively, has the consequence that one is no longer entitled to full protection as a noncombatant. Some of those who press this objection against the just means component of just war theory, like Gregory Kavka, contend that the members of a society can be directly threatened with nuclear attack to secure deterrence but then deny that carrying out such an attack could ever be morally justified.[6] Others, like James Child, contend that the members of a society who fail to take the necessary radical steps can be both indirectly threatened and indirectly attacked with what would otherwise be a disproportionate attack.[7]

In response to this collectivist challenge, the first thing to note is that people are more responsible for disassociating themselves from the unjust acts of their leaders than they are for opposing those same acts. For there is no general obligation to oppose all unjust acts, even all unjust acts of one's leaders. Nevertheless, there is a general obligation to disassociate oneself from unjust acts and to minimize one's contribution to them. Of course, how much one is required to disassociate oneself from the unjust acts of one's leaders depends upon how much one is contributing to those actions. If one's contribution is insignificant, as presumably a farmer's or a teacher's would be, only a minimal effort to disassociate oneself would be required, unless one's action could somehow be reasonably expected, in cooperation with the actions of others, to put a stop to the unjust actions of one's leaders. However, if one's contribution is significant, as presumably a soldier's or a munitions worker's would be, a maximal effort at disassociating oneself would be immediately required, unless by delaying, one could reasonably expect to put a stop to the unjust actions of one's leaders.

In support of the collectivist challenge, James Child offers the following example:

A company is considering engaging in some massively immoral and illegal activity—pouring large quantities of arsenic into the public water supply as a matter of ongoing operations, let us say. A member of the board of directors of the company, when the policy is before the board, votes no but does nothing else. Later, when sued in tort (or charged in crime) with these transgressions of duty, she pleads that she voted no. What would our reaction be? The answer is obvious! We would say, you are responsible as much, or nearly as much, as your fellow board members who voted yes. You

should have blown the whistle, gone public or to regulatory authorities, or at the very least, resigned from the board of so despicable a company. Mere formal dissent in this case does almost nothing to relieve her liability, legal or moral.[8]

But while one might agree with Child that in this case the member of the board of directors has at least the responsibility to disassociate herself from the actions of the board by resigning, this does not show that farmers and teachers are similarly responsible for disassociating themselves from the unjust actions of their leaders either by engaging in civil disobedience or by emigration. This is because neither their contributions to the unjust actions of their leaders nor the effect of their disassociation on those unjust actions would typically be significant enough to require such a response.

This is not to deny that some other response (e.g. political protest or remunerations at the end of the war) would not be morally required. However, to meet the collectivist challenge, it suffices to show that not just any contribution to the unjust actions of one's leaders renders the contributor subject to attack or threat of attack; one's contribution must be significant enough to morally justify such a response.

The Feminist Challenge to Just Cause and Just Means

According to the feminist challenge to both components of just war theory, sexism and militarism are inextricably linked in society. They are linked, according to Betty Reardon, because sexism is essentially a prejudice against all manifestations of the feminine, and militarism is a policy of excessive military preparedness and eagerness to go to war that is rooted in a view of human nature as limited to masculine characteristics.[9] Seen from a militarist perspective, other nations are competitive, aggressive and adverse to cooperation, the same traits that tend to be fostered exclusively in men in a sexist society. By contrast, the traits of openness, cooperativeness and nurturance which promote peaceful solutions to conflicts tend to be fostered exclusively in women who are then effectively excluded from positions of power and decision-making in a sexist society. Consequently, if we are to rid society of militarism, Reardon argues, we need to rid society of sexism as well.

But even granting that sexism and militarism are inextricably linked in society in just the way Reardon maintans, how does this effect the validity of just war theory? Since just war theory expresses the values of proportionality and respect for the rights of innocents, how could it be linked to militarism and sexism? The answer is that the linkage is practical rather than theoretical. It is because the leaders in a militarist/sexist society have been socialized to be competitive, aggressive and adverse to cooperation that they will tend to misapply just war theory when making military decisions. This represents an important practical challenge to just war theory. And, the only way of meeting this challenge, as far as I can tell, is to rid society of its sexist and militarist attitudes and practices so as to increase the chances that just war theory will be correctly applied in the future.

Practical Implications for the Use of Nuclear Weapons

The requirements for just war theory that have been defended so far are directly applicable to the question of the morality of nuclear war. In particular, requirements (2) and (3) on just means would prohibit any counter-city or counter-population use of nuclear weapons. While this prohibition need not be interpreted as absolute, it is simply not foreseeable that any use of nuclear weapons could ever be a morally justified exception to this prohibition.

But what about a counter-force use of nuclear weapons? Consider the massive use of nuclear weapons by the United States or the Soviet Union against industrial and economic centers. Such a strike, involving three to five thousand warheads, could destroy between 70–80% of each nation's industry and result in the immediate death of as many as 165 million

Americans and 100 million Russians respectively, in addition to running a considerable risk of a retaliatory nuclear strike by the opposing superpower.[10] It has also been estimated by Carl Sagan and others that such a strike is very likely to generate firestorms which would cover much of the earth with sooty smoke for months, creating a "nuclear winter" that would threaten the very survival of the human species.[11] Applying requirement (1) on just means, there simply is no foreseeable military objective which could justify such morally horrendous consequences.

The same holds true for a massive use of nuclear weapons against tactical and strategic targets. Such a strike, involving two to three thousand warheads, directed against only ICBMs and submarine and bomber bases could wipe out as many as 20 million Americans and 28 million Russians respectively, in addition to running a considerable risk of a retaliatory nuclear strike by the opposing superpower.[12] Here too there is a considerable risk of a "nuclear winter" occurring. This being the case what military objective might foreseeably justify such a use of nuclear weapons?

Of course, it should be pointed out that the above argument does not rule out a limited use of nuclear weapons at least against tactical and strategic targets. Such a use is still possible. Yet practically it would be quite difficult for either superpower to distinguish between a limited and a massive use of nuclear weapons, especially if a full-scale conventional war is raging. In such circumstances, any use of nuclear weapons is likely to be viewed as part of a massive use of such weapons, thus increasing the risk of a massive nuclear retaliatory strike.[13] In addition, war games have shown that if enough tactical nuclear weapons are employed over time in a limited area, such as Germany, the effect on noncombatants in that area would be much the same as in a massive nuclear attack.[14] As Bundy, Kennan, McNamara and Smith put the point in their recent endorsement of a doctrine of no first use of nuclear weapons:

> Every serious analysis and every military exercise, for over 25 years, has demonstrated that even the most restrained bat-

tlefield use would be enormously destructive to civilian life and property. There is no way for anyone to have any confidence that such a nuclear action will not lead to further and more devastating exchanges. Any use of nuclear weapons in Europe, by the Alliance or against it, carries with it a high and inescapable risk of escalation into the general nuclear war which would bring ruin to all and victory to none.[15]

For these reasons, even a limited use of nuclear weapons generally would not meet requirement (1) on just means.

Nevertheless, there are some circumstances in which a limited use of nuclear weapons would meet all the requirements on just means. For example, suppose that a nation was attacked with a massive nuclear counterforce strike and it was likely that, if the nation did not retaliate with a limited nuclear strike on tactical and strategic targets, a massive attack on its industrial and population centers would follow. Under such circumstances, it can be argued, a limited nuclear retaliatory strike would satisfy all the requirements on just means. Of course, the justification for such a strike would depend on what foreseen effect the strike would have on innocent lives and how likely it was that the strike would succeed in deterring a massive attack on the nation's industrial and population centers. But assuming a limited nuclear retaliatory strike on tactical and strategic targets was the best way of avoiding a significantly greater evil, it would be morally justified according to the requirements on just means.

Practical Implications for the Threat to Use Nuclear Weapons

Yet what about the morality of threatening to use nuclear weapons to achieve nuclear deterrence? Obviously, the basic requirements of just war theory are not directly applicable to threats to use nuclear weapons. Nevertheless, it seems clear that the just war theory would support the following analogous requirements of what we could call "just threat theory."

Just Cause   There must be a substantial threat or the likelihood of such a threat and nonthreatening correctives must be hopeless or too costly.

Just Means

1) The risk of harm resulting from the use of threats (or bluffs) should not be disproportionate to the military objective to be attained.

2) Actions that are prohibited by just war theory cannot be threatened as a end or a means.

3) The risk of harm to innocents from the use of threats (bluffs) should be minimized by accepting risks (costs) to oneself that would not render it impossible to attain the military objective.

Now if we assume that the requirement of just cause is met, the crucial restriction of just threat theory is requirement (2) on just means. This requirement puts a severe restriction on what we can legitimately threaten to do, assuming, that is, that threatening implies an intention to carry out under appropriate conditions what one has threatened to do. In fact, since, as we have seen, only a limited use of nuclear weapons could ever foreseeably be morally justified, it follows from requirement (2) that only such a use can be legitimately threatened. Obviously, this constitutes a severe limit on the use of threats to achieve nuclear deterrence.

Nevertheless, it may be possible to achieve nuclear deterrence by other means, for example, by bluffing. Now there are two ways that one can be bluffing while proclaiming that one will do actions that are prohibited by just war theory. One way is *by not being committed to doing* what one proclaims one will do should deterrence fail. The other is *by being committed not to do* what one proclaims one would do should deterrence fail. Of course, the first form of bluffing is more morally problematic than the second since it is less of a barrier to the subsequent formation of a commitment to do what would be prohibited by just war theory, but since it lacks a present commitment to carry out actions prohibited by just war theory should deterrence fail, it still has the form of a bluff rather than a threat.[16]

The possibility of achieving nuclear deterrence by bluffing, however, has not been sufficiently explored because it is generally not thought to be possible to institutionalize bluffing. But suppose we imagine bluffing to include deploying a survivable nuclear force and preparing that force for possible use in such a way that leaders who are bluffing a morally prohibited form of nuclear retaliation need outwardly distinguish themselves from those who are threatening such retaliation only in their strong moral condemnation of this use of nuclear weapons. Surely this form of bluffing is capable of being institutionalized.

This form of bluffing can also be effective in achieving deterrence because it is subject to at least two interpretations. One interpretation is that the leaders of a nation are actually bluffing because while the leaders do deploy nuclear weapons and do appear to threaten to use them in certain ways, they also morally condemn those uses of nuclear weapons, so they can't really be intending to so use them. The other interpretation is that the leaders are not bluffing but are in fact immoral agents intentionally committed to doing what they regard as a grossly immoral course of action. But since the leaders of other nations can never be reasonably sure which interpretation is correct, a nation's leaders can effectively bluff under these conditions.

Moreover, citizens who think that only a bluffing strategy with respect to certain forms of nuclear retaliation can ever be morally justified would look for leaders who express their own views on this issue in just this ambiguous manner. It is also appropriate for those who are in places of high command within a nation's nuclear forces to express the same ambiguous views; only those low in the command structure of a nation's nuclear forces need not express the same ambiguous views about the course of action they would be carrying out, assuming they can see themselves as carrying out only (part of) a limited nuclear retaliatory strike. This is because, as we noted earlier, such a strike would be morally justified under certain conceivable but unlikely conditions.

Yet even granting that a threat of limited nuclear retaliation and a bluff of massive nuclear retaliation can be justified by the requirements of just means, it would not follow that we are presently justified in so threatening or bluffing unless there presently exists a just cause for threatening or bluffing. Of course, it is generally assumed that such a cause does presently exist. That is, it is generally assumed that both superpowers have a just cause to maintain a state of nuclear deterrence vis-a-vis each other by means of threats and bluffs of nuclear retaliation.

But to determine whether this assumption is correct, let us consider two possible stances a nation's leaders might take with respect to nuclear weapons:

1) A nation's leaders might be willing to carry out a nuclear strike *only* in response to either a nuclear first strike or a massive conventional first strike on itself or its principal allies.

2) A nation's leaders might be willing to carry out a massive conventional strike *only* in response to either a nuclear first strike or a massive conventional first strike on itself or its principal allies.

Now assuming that a nation's leaders were to adopt (1) and (2) then threats or bluffs of nuclear retaliation could not in fact be made against them! For a threat or bluff must render less eligible something an agent might otherwise want to do, and leaders of nations who adopt (1) and (2) have a preference structure that would not be affected by any attempt to threaten or bluff nuclear retaliation. Hence, such threats or bluffs could not be made against them either explicitly or implicitly.

Of course, a nation's leaders could try to threaten or bluff nuclear retaliation against another nation but if the intentions of the leaders of that other nation are purely defensive then although they may succeed in restricting the liberty of the leaders of that other nation by denying them a possible option, they would not have succeeded in threatening them for that would require that they render less eligible something those leaders might otherwise want to do.[17]

Now if we take them at their word, the leaders of both superpowers seem to have adopted (1) and (2). As Casper Weinberger recently characterized U.S. policy:

Our strategy is a defensive one, designed to prevent attack, particularly nuclear attack, against us or our allies.[18]

And a similar statement of Soviet policy can be found in Mikhail Gorbachev's recent appeal for a return to a new era of detente.[19] Moreover, since 1982 Soviet leaders appear to have gone beyond simply endorsing (1) and (2) and have ruled out the use of a nuclear first strike under any circumstances.[20]

Assuming the truth of these statements, it follows that the present leaders of the U.S. and the Soviet Union could not be threatening or bluffing each other with nuclear retaliation despite their apparent attempts to do so. This is because a commitment to (1) and (2) rules out the necessary aggressive intentions that it is the purpose of such threats or bluffs to deter. Leaders of nations whose strategy is a purely defensive one would be immune from threats or bluffs of nuclear retaliation. In fact, leaders of nations who claim their strategy is purely defensive yet persist in attempting to threaten or bluff nuclear retaliation against nations whose proclaimed strategy is also purely defensive eventually throw into doubt their own commitment to a purely defensive strategy. It is for these reasons, that a just cause for threatening or bluffing nuclear retaliation does not exist under present conditions.

Of course, the leaders of a superpower might claim that threatening or bluffing nuclear retaliation would be morally justified under present conditions on the grounds that the proclaimed defensive strategy of the other superpower is not believable. Surely this stance would be reasonable if the other superpower had launched an aggressive attack against the superpower or its principal allies. But neither U.S. intervention in Nicaragua nor Soviet intervention in Afghanistan nor other military actions taken by either superpower are directed against even a principal ally of the other superpower. Consequently, in the absence of an aggressive attack of the appropriate sort and in the absence of an opposing military force that could be used without risking unacceptable losses from retaliatory strikes, each superpower is morally required to provisionally place some trust in the proclaimed defensive strategy of the other superpower.

Nevertheless, it would still be morally legitimate for both superpowers to retain a retaliatory nuclear force so as to be able to threaten or bluff nuclear retaliation in the future should conditions change for the worse. For as long as nations possess nuclear weapons, such a change could occur simply with a change of leadership bringing to power leaders who can only be deterred by a threat or bluff of nuclear retaliation.

For example, suppose a nation possesses a survivable nuclear force capable of inflicting unacceptable damage upon its adversary, yet possession of such a force alone would not suffice to deter an adversary from carrying out a nuclear first strike unless that possession were combined with a threat of limited nuclear retaliation or a bluff of massive nuclear retaliation. (With respect to massive nuclear retaliation, bluffing would be required here since leaders who recognize and respect the above just war constraints on the use of nuclear weapons could not in fact threaten such retaliation.) Under these circumstances, I think the required threat or bluff would be morally justified. But I also think that there is ample evidence today to indicate that neither the leadership of the United States nor that of the Soviet Union requires such a threat or bluff to deter them from carrying out a nuclear first strike.[21] Consequently, under present conditions, such a threat or bluff would not be morally justified.

Nevertheless, under present conditions it would be legitimate for a nation to maintain a survivable nuclear force in order to be able to deal effectively with a change of policy in the future. Moreover, if either superpower does in fact harbor any undetected aggressive intentions against the other, the possession of a survivable nuclear force by the other superpower should suffice to deter a first strike since neither superpower could be sure whether in response to such strike the other superpower would follow its moral principles or its national interest.[22]

Of course, if nuclear forces were only used to retain the capacity for threatening or bluffing in the future should conditions change for the worse then surely at some point this use of nuclear weapons could also be eliminated. But its elimination would require the establishment of extensive political, economic and cultural ties between the superpowers so as to reduce the present uncertainty about the future direction of policy, and obviously the establishment of such ties, even when it is given the highest priority, which it frequently is not, requires time to develop.

In the meantime a nuclear force deployed for the purpose of being capable of threatening or bluffing in the future should conditions change for the worse, should be capable of surviving a first strike and then inflicting either limited or massive nuclear retaliation on an aggressor. During the Kennedy-Johnson years, Robert McNamara estimated that massive nuclear retaliation required a nuclear force capable of destroying one-half of a nation's industrial capacity along with one-quarter of its population, and comparable figures have been suggested by others. Clearly, ensuring a loss in this neighborhood should constitute unacceptable damage from the perspective of any would-be aggressor.

Notice, however, that in order for a nation to maintain a nuclear force capable of inflicting such damage, it is not necessary that components of its land-, its air- and its sea-based strategic forces all be survivable. Accordingly, even if all of the land-based ICBMs in the United States were totally destroyed in a first strike, surviving elements of the U.S. air and submarine forces could easily inflict the required degree of damage and more. In fact, any one of the 37 nuclear submarines maintained by the United States, each with up to 192 warheads, could almost single-handedly inflict the required degree of damage. Consequently, the U.S. submarine force alone should suffice as a force capable of massive nuclear retaliation.

But what about a nuclear force capable of limited nuclear retaliation? At least with respect to U.S. nuclear forces, it would seem that as Trident I missiles replace less accurate Poseidon missiles, and especially when Trident II missiles come on line in the next few years, the U.S. submarine force will have the capacity for both limited and massive nuclear retaliation. However, until this modernization is complete, the U.S. will still have to rely, in part, on survivable elements of its air- and land-based strategic forces for its capacity to inflict limited nuclear retaliation. And it would seem that the Soviet Union is also in a comparable situation.[23]

To sum up, I have argued for the following practical implications of just war theory and just threat theory for nuclear strategy:

1) Under present conditions, it is morally justified to possess a survivable nuclear force in order to be able to quickly threaten or bluff nuclear retaliation should conditions change for the worse.

2) If conditions do change for the worse, it would be morally justified at some point to threaten a form of limited nuclear retaliation.

3) If conditions worsen further so that a massive nuclear first strike can only be deterred by the bluff or threat of a massive nuclear retaliation, it would be morally justified to bluff but not threaten massive nuclear retaliation.

4) Under certain conceivable but unlikely conditions, a limited retaliatory use of nuclear weapons against tactical and strategic targets would be morally justified in order to restore deterrence.

Yet isn't there something better than the practical implications of just war theory and just threat theory that I have just proposed? What about President Reagan's Strategic Defense Initiative or "Star Wars" defense? Admittedly, this strategy is presently only at the research and development stage, but couldn't such a strategy turn out to be morally preferable to the one I have proposed? Not as far as I can tell, for the following reasons.

Strategic Defense Initiative or SDI is sometimes represented as an umbrella defense and sometimes as a point or limited defense. As an umbrella defense, SDI is pure fantasy. Given the variety of countermeasures either superpower might employ, such as shortening the booster phase of their rockets so as to make them less of a target for lasers and dispersing various types of decoys, no defensive system could track and destroy all the land- and sea-based warheads either superpower could use in an all out attack.[24] Estimates by supporters of SDI have put the effectiveness of such a defensive system at 30%.[25] This means that SDI could reduce by 30% the effective nuclear force either superpower might use against the other.

But a similar or greater reduction of nuclear forces could more easily be achieved by bilateral negotiations if a reduction of nuclear forces is what both superpowers want. Moreover, a unilateral attempt to get such a reduction though SDI is not likely to succeed. Either superpower only needs to increase their nuclear forces by 30% to offset the effect of SDI. And this is what either superpower might do if they thought that an SDI program was part of a general defensive and offensive nuclear buildup.

In addition, the cost of SDI is astronomical. President Reagan wants a research and development budget for SDI of over $30 billion for the next five years. For comparison that is more than the total research and development and *production* costs for the B1 bomber or for the MX missile system. And estimates for the total cost of SDI are in the neighborhood of 1 trillion dollars.[26] For comparison the total federal budget for 1985 was only 1.8 trillion dollars. Now what kind of a nation would spend 1 trillion dollars for an SDI that gave it a 30% reduction of the nuclear forces that could be used against it—a reduction that could have been achieved by bilateral negotiations and would most likely be negated in the absence of such negotiations? Certainly not a nation that is known for the wisdom of its leaders or its citizenry. For these and other reasons, I think that SDI is certainly not morally preferable to those practical implications of just war theory and just threat theory for nuclear strategy that I have been defending.

Notes

1. Jan Narveson, "Pacifism: A Philosophical Analysis," *Ethics* Vol. 75 (1965).

2. Cheyney Ryan, "Self-Defense and Pacifism," in *The Ethics of War and Nuclear Deterrence,* edited by James P. Sterba (Belmont, Wadsworth Publishing Co. 1985).

3. Even if these bombings did help shorten World War II, and there is considerable evidence that they did not, they would have still been in violation of requirement (2) on just means.

4. See Michael Walzer, *Just and Unjust Wars* (New York, 1977) p. 152.

5. George Mavrodes, "Conventions and the Morality of War, in *Morality in Practice*, 1st ed., edited by James P. Sterba, (Belmont, 1983) pp. 302–310.

6. Gregory Kavka, "Nuclear Deterrence: Some Moral Perplexities," in *The Ethics of War and Nuclear Deterrence,* edited by James P. Sterba (Belmont, 1985) pp. 127–138.

7. James Child, *Nuclear War: The Moral Dimension,* (Bowling Green, 1986) especially pp. 140–149.

8. Child, p. 142.

9. Betty Reardon, *Sexism and the War System* (New York, 1985) especially Chapter 3.

10. *The Effects of Nuclear War,* Office of Technology Assessment (Washington, D.C., U.S. Government Printing Office 1979), pp. 94, 100; Nigel Calder, *Nuclear Nightmare* (New York, Viking 1979), p. 150; Sidney Lens, *The Day Before Doomsday* (Boston, Beacon Press 1977), p. 102.

11. Carl Sagan, "Nuclear War and Climate Catastrophe: Some Policy Implications," *Foreign Affairs* Vol 62 (1983) pp. 257–292.

12. *The Effects of Nuclear War,* pp. 83, 91; Jerome Kahan, *Security in the Nuclear Age* (Washington, D.C., The Brookings Institution, pp. 202; Lens, pp. 98, 99, 102.

13. Lens, pp. 78–79; Spurgeon Keeny and Wolfgang Panofsky "MAD verse NUTS" *Foreign Affairs* Vol 60 (1981–2), pp. 297–298; Ian Clark, *Limited Nuclear War,* (Princeton, Princeton University Press 1982) p. 242.

14. Lens, p. 73.

15. McGeorge Bundy, George F. Kennan, Robert S. McNamara and Gerald Smith, "Nuclear Weapons and the Atlantic Alliance," *Foreign Affairs* Vol 61 (1982), p. 757. It should be noted that Bundy, Kennan, McNamara and Smith believed that their endorsement of a doctrine of no first use of nuclear weapons *may* involve increased spending for conventional forces in Europe. Others, however, have found NATO's existing conventional strength to be adequate to meet a Soviet attack. See David Barash and Judith Lipton, *Stop Nuclear War* (New York, Gwne Press 1982), pp. 138–140; Harold Brown, *Department of Defense, Annual Report* (1981).

16. For a defense of this second form of bluffing although mistakenly classified as a form of threatening, see Kenneth Kemp, "Nuclear Deterrence and the Morality of Intentions" *The Monist* (1987).

17. On my view to succeed in threatening two conditions must be met:

1) One must have the intention to carry out the action one is purporting to threaten under the stated conditions, that is, one must expect that if the stated conditions do obtain then one will carry out that action.

2) The preference structure of the party that one is trying to threaten must be so affected that something the party might otherwise have wanted to do is rendered less eligible.

18. Caspar Weinberger, "Why We Must Have Nuclear Deterrence," *Defense* (March 1983) p. 3.

19. *The New York Times*, May 9, 1985.

20. See Leonid Brezhnev's message to the U.N. General Assembly on June 2, 1982.

21. See Kahan, *Security in the Nuclear Age*; Lens, *The Day Before Doomsday*; Henry Kendall and others, *Beyond the Freeze* (Boston, Beacon Press (1982); George Kistiakowsky "False Alarm: The Story Behind Salt II," *The New York Review of Books* (April 1, 1979); Les Aspin, "How to Look at the Soviet-American Balance" *Foreign Policy* Vol 22 (1976); Gordon Adams, "The Iron Triangle,"

The Nation (October, 1981), pp. 425, 441–444. Much of this evidence is reviewed in my paper "How to Achieve Nuclear Deterrence Without Threatening Nuclear Destruction," included in *The Ethics* of *War and Nuclear Deterrence*.

22. It might be objected that this proposed policy is hypocritical because it allows a nation following it to benefit from an adversary's uncertainty as to whether that nation would follow its moral principles or its national interest. But it seems odd to deny a nation such a benefit. For we all know that moral people can lose out in so many ways to those who are immoral. Occasionally, however, being immoral does have its liabilities and one such liability is that it is hard for immoral people to believe that others will not act in just the way they themselves do, especially when the benefits from doing so are quite substantial. Why then should not moral people be allowed to extract some benefit from the inability of immoral people to believe that moral people are as good as they say they are. After all, it is not the fault of moral people that immoral people are blinded in their judgment in this regard. Consequently, I see no reason to allow a nation to benefit from its adversary's uncertainty as to whether it will follow the requirements of morality or those of national interest.

23. *Soviet Military Power*, U.S. Department of Defense (Washington, D.C., U.S. Government Printing Office, 1983); David Holloway, *The Soviet Union and the Arms Race* (New Haven, Yale University Press 1983); Andrew Cockburn, *The Threat* (New York, Random House 1983) Chapter 12.

24. U.S. Office of Technology Assessment, *Ballistic Missile Defense Technologies* (Washington D.C., U.S. Government Printing Office 1985); Union of Concerned Scientists "Ballistic Missile Defense: A Dangerous Dream" in *Braking Point* Vol 2 (1984).

25. See Colin Campbell, "At Columbia, 3 Days of Arms Talks," *New York Times*, February 11, 1985 and "Star Wars Chief Takes Aim at Critics," *Science*, August 10, 1984.

26. Union of Concerned Scientists, "Boosting Star Wars," *Nucleus* Vol 6 (1985), pp. 2, 4.

A Rational Approach to Nuclear Disarmament

Caspar W. Weinberger

While characterizing U.S. policy as one of deterrence, Caspar W. Weinberger asserts that the requirements for deterrence have changed over time. He argues that the current requirements for deterrence do not allow the United States to adopt a policy of "no first use." Moreover, contending that the Soviet Union outspent the United States in the 1970s, he stresses the need to build up U.S. forces to ensure deterrence and promote meaningful arms reduction.

I would like to talk about a matter which concerns all of us equally. That is the threat of nuclear war which all of us, to our dismay, have lived with now for some 34 years. This is a most disagreeable and difficult subject, but I am very concerned because some Americans are expressing doubts that our President and his Administration share their abhorrence for war and, in particular, nuclear war.

This is a terrible misconception made even worse by various grim prognoses of the destruction nuclear weapons would wreak and by the pictures we see on television of old nuclear tests.

We have seen enough images of war lately, and indeed many of us have seen far too much of war itself in our lifetimes. I would, therefore, prefer to offer, here, the possibility of peace even though I offer it in an undeniably turbulent world, at a most dangerous period of our history.

In the early part of Homer's *Iliad,* Hector finds his wife, Andromache, with their child, Astyanax, on the walls above Troy. The little boy, frightened by his father's armor and helmet, cries out. Hector removes his helmet, and the two parents laugh as the son recognizes the father. Hector then lifts Astyanax in his arms, jostles him in the air over his head, and the family shares a moment of peace.

This is a picture of life as we want it, not the terrible carnage churning below on the plains of Troy, not even the glory of great soldiers which the *Iliad* also celebrates. The contrast

From "A Rational Approach to Nuclear Disarmament," *Defense* (August 1982).

intended by Homer between these scenes of war and peace is as vivid as the choice which every generation has had to face.

We choose peace, but not because we are Democrats or Republicans. We want peace because we are Americans and a civilized people. We reject war as a deliberate instrument of foreign policy because it is repugnant to our national morality. War prevents people from leading the kinds of lives which this country was fashioned to protect and to enhance. As civilized people, we reject war because it kills and maims soldiers and civilians alike and undermines the fabric of life.

But nuclear war is even more horrible than war in any other form. Its destructive power has been described at length in popular journals recently. The images are sufficiently terrible that the temptation is strong to turn our backs on the whole subject. But, grim as they are, those matters have to be thought about and dealt with. It is part of my task to do that and to know not only what we are faced with, but how we may best prevent such a catastrophe from happening.

Physicians, it seems to me, should adopt a similar attitude to their work. A physician who deals with the sick every day sees many unpleasant things; cancer, heart disease, disorders of the nervous system, the patient's pain and the family's anguish. The response to these manifestly is not to walk away. It is not to throw up one's hands in dismay and respond with sentiment and emotion alone. That will save no one's life. What is required is a mixture of the compassion we all feel for the sick, plus the most objective and informed judgment about a course of action, followed by an equally steady hand in restoring the patient's health and easing his pain.

Those of us who are charged with the responsibility for the health and strength of this nation's defense are in a somewhat parallel position. The prospect of nuclear war is ghastly in the extreme. But we cannot allow the dread with which we look upon it to obscure our judgment on how to prevent it. Obviously, this too would not save lives.

To the extent of our powers we must, using all the judgment and technical skills and latest knowledge available, arrive at an objective, rational policy which will accomplish what we all want. Of course, we take, as our starting point, that which everyone agrees to: that nuclear war is so terrible that it must not be allowed to happen. This, however, is not a policy. It is a national objective which all of us share, very much like the compassion one feels for the sick. The policy question is, how do we achieve our objective?

Our policy to prevent war since the age of nuclear weapons began has been one of deterrence. Our strategic nuclear weapons are only retaliatory. Their purpose is to provide us with a credible retaliatory capability in the event we are struck first. The idea on which this is based is quite simple: it is to make the cost of starting a nuclear war much higher than any possible benefit to an aggressor. This policy has been approved, through the political processes of the democratic nations it protects, since at least 1950. Most important, it works. It has worked in the face of major international tensions involving the great powers, and it has worked in the face of war itself.

But while the idea of deterrence has stood the test of time and usefulness beyond reproach, the things we must do to maintain that deterrence have changed substantially, as the Soviets' quest for nuclear superiority grew to fruition.

In the fifties, the requirements of deterrence were minimal. Our overwhelming nuclear superiority both in weapons and the means of their delivery made moot the question of whether an adversary would be deterred by unacceptable costs, if he attacked first. It also gave us the ability to deter conventional attacks on our allies. By the mid-sixties, however, the Soviets' nuclear force had grown greatly in strength. They had also achieved a major edge in conventional weapons in Europe. To discourage the prospect of conflict there, NATO decided that it would meet and answer force at whatever level it might be initiated, while retaining the option to use even greater force as the most effective preventative against aggression in the first place. It is important to remember here that the retention of this option is absolutely consistent with our nuclear weapons; that is, to deter aggression and to prevent other nuclear weapons being used against us or our allies. In simple language, we do not start fights—in Europe or anywhere.

We see disturbing evidence such as the Soviets' development of a refiring capability and major expenditures for civil defense shelters and air defense which indicates that they do think they can fight and win a nuclear war. We do not share this perception; we know nuclear war is unwinnable.

But we do not feel we can successfully deter attack from an adversary such as the USSR, if we relieve them of the necessity of all defensive planning. To do so would erode our deterrent by announcing that under no circumstances would we ever use our weapons first.

Recently it has been argued that we should adopt such a policy of "no first use" of nuclear force in the defense of Europe. While this sounds plausible enough, it lessens the effectiveness of deterrence. We must remember that NATO has effectively prevented Soviet aggression against Europe. In no small part, this is because our policy makes clear to the Soviets the tremendous risks to them of aggression there. Also, a "no first use" policy might imply that the first use of conventional force is somehow acceptable.

We reject this entirely. And we do so because *our policy is to deter—not to encourage—the first use of force against us.*

The point is that we oppose the use of forces and arms as a means for anyone to secure his objectives. Force of arms is not the way to resolve international disputes.

I wish I could tell you that the Soviets shared this view. Unfortunately, history and all the facts we know stand in the way of such a policy by them.

For the past 21 years, the Soviets have concentrated tremendous efforts and resources on achieving a clear superiority in nuclear forces. The result has been the addition to their arsenal of new weapons systems such as the SS-17, SS-18, and SS-19 ICBMs, the Backfire bomber, the Typhoon submarine, several new types of cruise missiles, and the SS-20 intermediate range missile. These efforts dwarf our own. In fact, since 1970, they have out-vested us by about $400 billion in military armaments.

No less important is the fact that the Soviets do regard their nuclear forces as a means of coercion. Well over two-thirds of their nuclear force sits in land-based ICBM weapons whose speed, destructive power, and above all, accuracy give those who possess them the capability to aim with assurance at the military targets in the United States in a first strike or to aim at targets in Europe or Asia with their SS-20s.

By contrast, our own strategic weapons are apportioned among our submarines, land-based ICBMs, and bombers. The Soviets' clear advantage in land-based ICBMs gives them the ability to destroy segments of our relatively smaller and unfortunately less effective land-based missile force. We do not intend to match them missile for missile in land-based ICBMs. Our system of deterrence requires simply that we must be able to inflict damage so unacceptable that no one would attack us.

This does not mean, however, that we can allow any part of our Triad to become vulnerable. Our ongoing ability to maintain deterrence rests on the continued accuracy, power, communications structure, and survivability of all our nuclear forces. The point is that while the number of weapons is important, it is less so than the combination of capabilities, forces, and their survivability, along with the national resolve and will essential to convince an aggressor that he could not hope to gain from attacking first.

What then has deterrence done? Again, I must stress that it has worked and is working today. There have been 37 years of peace in Europe. Despite the threat of the Soviet Army; despite the threat of the Soviets' nuclear weapons, Western Europe has prospered. Its political freedoms have flourished, and its so-cial institutions have grown stronger. Indeed, there has not been an equal period of uninterrupted peace on the European continent since the Roman Empire fell. At the risk of stating the obvious, the United States and the rest of the world have also avoided the scourge of nuclear fire. Deterrence, thus, is and remains our best immediate hope of keeping peace.

However, it is not enough to assume that deterrence can be maintained simply by doing what we have done in the past. For the unavoidable fact is that even though the world remains at nuclear peace and nuclear threats do not appear on the horizon, still we do not feel safe. Many worry about the sophistication of modern delivery systems. Others fear the results of continuing to compete with the Soviets on this barren plain. Still more are alarmed at the destructive capability within the great powers' arsenals.

We are worried about all these matters too. That is why we are absolutely serious about the arms reductions negotiations currently underway in Geneva, and the President's new strategic arms reductions plans. But again, as with the policy of deterrence, the right approach to this process can only be one based on rational, prudent, and statesman-like determination of ends and means.

The one thing we must not expect from arms reductions negotiations is the kind of world that existed before nuclear weapons were tested. The forbidden fruit has been tasted, and in this case, the fruit is not the weapons, but the knowledge of them. As much as we would like to, we cannot erase that knowledge. Setting our sights on that object would be utterly unrealistic. The proper aim of arms reduction, therefore, should be first to reduce the probability of war. If possible, it should also aim to reduce the costs of maintaining deterrence and should reduce the possibilities of war through misinterpretation or misunderstanding.

The proposal to freeze current levels of nuclear weapons was born partly at least of deeply felt convictions which this Administration shares. A freeze, however, would not reduce the probability of war. It would go against the first and foremost aim of arms control because it would lock the United States and our allies into a position of permanent military disadvantage. And that disadvantage or imbalance, if you will, erodes deterrence which we believe has kept the peace. For if one side improves its forces, either by dint of its own efforts or through the other's inactivity, then the temptation will grow for the stronger to use its superior systems, or, at a minimum, to contemplate achieving domination by the threat of nuclear war—nuclear blackmail it is called. It is an understatement that we must not allow either of these things to happen, under any circumstances.

For similar reasons, *a freeze would chill any hopes we have of convincing the Soviets to agree to any meaningful arms reductions.* If a freeze went into effect now, the advantage the Soviets currently enjoy would be irreversibly sealed and stamped with the official imprimatur of an international agreement. Why, then, would they wish to change—that is to lower their forces together with us? Granting them but a thread of rationality, or even a normal supply, if we froze an imbalance in their favor, I cannot see that the Soviets would have the slightest incentive to achieve the major and bilateral reductions we must have if we are to lessen the danger now existing.

It is exactly those bilateral reductions which President Reagan's arms reduction proposals aim to achieve. In the past few months, our highest priority has been to lay the groundwork for the strategic arms negotiations with the Soviet Union. The President has now proposed major reductions in strategic arms to verifiable, equal, and agreed levels. We are also continuing our negotiations to reduce the intermediate range nuclear weapons that threaten Europe and Asia. In Geneva, we have put forward detailed proposals designed to limit those intermediate range nuclear forces and to eliminate entirely the missiles of greatest concern to each side. This approach, which has won the strong support of our allies, would go far towards lowering the threshold of risk which the Europeans feel so acutely today.

These proposals are not bargaining chips or ploys. Let all who doubt this know that President Reagan's greatest wish is for peace. I have heard him say more times than I can recall that if he could leave no other legacy, it would be that of having improved the pros-

pects for peace. A meaningful reduction in nuclear arms would be a welcome first step in the arms control process and an historic step towards the peace which lowered tensions nurture. No one should doubt that this is what drives our efforts. No one should doubt that this is what we are pledged to—in hope, in word, and in deed.

I wish that I could end by assuring you that our hopes and good faith could accomplish all that we want. But that I cannot do in all good conscience. Instead I must tell you what I see as the truth about our situation and not what I am sure all of us would prefer to hear: that is, there is no easy or royal road to peace, just as there is no easy road to anything really worthwhile. There is no miracle drug which will keep us and our allies safe and free while the nuclear threat is excised.

In the short term, we must remember that as health is not just the absence of sickness, neither is peace just the absence of war. Health requires care to insure that it will continue, that disease will not occur. One needs the right diet, exercise, personal habits, and so on. So it is with peace. It cannot stand by itself. It needs care to ensure its continuance. A nation must conduct its own business, maintain its strength, and aided by alliances be prepared to resist those for whom peace is not the first priority. Peace without these steps will not be peace for long. Thus we dare not permit our abhorrence of war to keep us from the work which our love of peace demands.

We cannot blink in the face of our worst fears. The Soviets are aware that their buildup is frightening. I think it safe to say that one of the chief effects which it was designed to create is the natural horror which all feel who are willing to face that buildup with realism. We cannot, though, and we must not let this apprehension unstring us.

If we fail in the short term to reestablish the balance, the danger will surely increase. "If you make yourself into a sheep, you'll find a wolf nearby," says the Russian proverb. We don't want to be wolves or sheep. We only want to live in peace with freedom, and that means we must be able to deter any attack on us or our allies.

But if our immediate goal is to avoid war, our long-term goal is to reduce its probability. Here, too, in the area of arms control we have seen the frustrating paradox that the road to peace is marked with the preparations for war. But there is no other rational solution. Who, for instance, can believe that the Soviets would ever consent to reduce their forces if they thought that we lacked the national will or resolve to maintain a balance in the first place?

Thus we must draw deeply upon our national patience and fortitude in the future if we are to accomplish what all of us really agree we must do: protecting and strengthening the peace. For negotiations cannot succeed without patience—peace cannot succeed without fortitude.

I began with a story in the *Iliad*. There is, it seems to me, another metaphor in Astyanax's reaction to his helmeted father. And that is that the young and maybe even the not so young sometimes fail to recognize what it is that protects them. We are too old and, I hope, too wise to respond by crying out at the sight of our protectors. And we are too young to surrender our hopes in despair or our principles in fear.

The *Iliad* is the first book of great literature in a long tradition which reaches to us across the ages. It is a book about war, but it questions war and it questions politics and it questions life. This questioning is one of the noblest traits of our civilization and it is one enshrined at Harvard under the rubric of "healthy skepticism." Others call it freedom. We owe it to our ancestors and to "the age that is waiting before" to do all within our power to ensure that this civilization is preserved—and preserved in peace with freedom.

A Case for Strategic Defense

Colin S. Gray

Colin S. Gray defends a form of SDI that does not promise to protect U.S. society as a whole. Rather, the form of SDI Gray defends is primarily an exploration of ways to enhance and transform the existing deterrent system to provide much greater safety for civilians everywhere.

There is need for a forward-looking debate on strategic defence. Unfortunately, the attitude of many people towards this subject was forged fifteen or more years ago, and their minds are not open to new possibilities. For example, there is a widespread tendency to consider the ABM (anti-ballistic missile) Treaty sacrosanct, forgetting what arms control is all about. Arms control, first and above all else, is about reducing the risks of war—that overriding goal may or may not be served by a particular, formal treaty regime. If an arms-

Excerpted from *Survival*, March–April 1985 (London: International Institute for Strategic Studies, 1985). The article is a revised version of a prepared statement delivered before the Subcommittee on Strategic and Theater Nuclear Forces of the Senate Armed Services Committee on April 24, 1984. Reprinted by permission.

control treaty precludes weapons development and deployment that should reduce first-strike incentives, then that treaty does not function as an arms-control measure.

The ABM Treaty of 1972, as amended in 1974, reflected contemporary predictions concerning probable trends in strategic offensive forces that have not been borne out by events. . . .

The SDI: What It Is, and What It Is Not

What is the SDI? It should be (a) an exploration of ways in which the stability of the *existing* system of offensive, retaliatory deterrence might be enhanced: (b) an exploration of ways in which the terms of deterrence might be transformed in favour of much greater safety for civilians everywhere; and it should be recognized as (c) the only remotely feasible path by which nuclear disarmament on a truly massive scale might be secured.

The SDI is *not* (a) yet a weapons programme; (b) a promise that society as a whole can for certain be defended directly; (c) a quest after some ever-elusive, illusory 'ultimate weapon' (such cannot exist); nor is it (d) a promise of political peace.

Lest the point be lost in subsequent discussion, it might be emphasized that Soviet-American rivalry is political in its origins, is fuelled overwhelmingly by political anxieties and ambitions, and can be alleviated or resolved only by political action. Those who, like this author, strongly favour the possibilities inherent in the SDI are under no illusions about the limitations of a 'technological peace.' Even if the SDI should prove to be a magnificent technological success story, which—looking forward 20 or 30 years from now—is certainly possible, strategic defence will not be a panacea for deeply political security problems. The SDI and a defensive transition can change the terms of deterrence, away from retaliatory nuclear threat (which would be no small accomplishment), but, in and of itself, it cannot arrest the arms competition. The 'last move' in that competition must be political, not military-technological. . . . A very major portion of the case for proceeding with the SDI is the virtually self-evident fact that there are no attractive alternative paths to greater security.

Eventually, the Soviet-American rivalry will be resolved, hopefully by formal or tacit political agreement rather than by military decision. However, historically speaking, all security systems break down or are transformed as conditions change. The nuclear deterrence system familiar today, with very dominant offensive capabilities, is adequate all the time that it either functions as we intend or, as generally is the case, all the time that it is not severely tested. The problem, indeed the enduring problem, is that the future rests upon a nuclear deterrence system concerning which even a single serious malfunction cannot be

tolerated. So 40 years into the nuclear age it is uncertain whether the absence of bilateral nuclear war should be attributed more to luck than to sound policy. The question is, for how long should this system of reciprocated nuclear retaliatory threats be expected to work satisfactorily? One may be confident that stability reigns today, but how confident can one be for the next 50 or 100 years?

The SDI and a defensive transition cannot effect a benign transformation in the politics of East-West competition, but it *may*, and only *may*, serve to buy time for the alleviation and resolution of political differences. At the very least, it would be grossly irresponsible and imprudent to refuse the challenge to try to live in greater safety with nuclear weapons that cannot be disinvented.

Before discussing transition issues in some detail, it is important that the range of choice available be appreciated. If one rejects the very idea of strategic defence one is, *ipso facto*, endorsing the seemingly endless competition in offensive nuclear arms. The alternative to the SDI is not a happy world of super-stable, jointly well-managed offensive arsenals; instead it is a world of acute competition and anxiety over net war-fighting prowess that cannot withstand a single breakdown in the extant deterrence system. Not only is strategic defence not an alternative to disarmament, strategic defence is the only way by which nuclear disarmament worthy of the name might be achieved. In the absence of defence, no one knows how to achieve nuclear disarmament on a scale such that civilization, and even the ecosphere itself, would not be at prompt or delayed fatal risk in the event of a failure of deterrence. Even the US 'build-down' proposal[1] in START—which the Soviet Union has rejected in very unflattering terms (describing it in *Pravda* as being 'designed for fools'[2])—would leave the super-powers with truly massive nuclear arsenals.

If one is serious about nuclear disarmament, as one should be, and given that no one knows how to achieve a general political settlement with the Soviet Union that would render issues of competitive nuclear armament politically irrelevant, there is no prudent choice available other than to press on carefully to explore the possibilities of strategic defence.

Only in the presence of multi-layered strategic defences would the super-powers be able to endorse a very radical scale of nuclear disarmament. With such defences, East and West could live with a disarmament treaty that would not be verifiable with absolute confidence. In the absence of homeland defences, the incentive to cheat on a disarmament regime would be matched only by the ease with which the Soviet Union could cheat.

Far distant though nuclear disarmament may be, it is morally and politically essential that the US government should be able to articulate a not-implausible theory of how such disarmament might be effected in ways compatible with US and US-allied security. This theory should be an integral part of the policy story for the SDI, notwithstanding the proximate necessity for having a very prudent and robust appreciation of the difficulties attendant upon proceeding from here to there.

Managing a Defensive Transition

It is always possible that as a consequence of focusing upon the shape of distant woods one may walk into a tree or two in the foreground. One can hardly stress too much the importance of approaching and managing a process of defensive transition with extreme care, while it is essential that the US (and her allies) understands whether it would like to proceed in the long term with strategic defence, there is everything to be said in favour of being cautious lest the price of the journey to a directly defended Western Alliance be an increased risk of war along the way.

Whatever may or may not be possible eventually by way of the active defence of cities, the first necessary steps must be the intermediate capabilities emphasized in the Hoffman Report[3] for the protection of US retaliatory forces and C[3]I assets. These capabilities would comprise necessary underlayers for what might one day become a comprehensive architecture of (multi-) nation-wide defence. But whether or not it proves feasible to destroy ballistic missiles in their 'boost-phase' or 'post-boost-phase' terminal nonnuclear defences could provide a very attractive and effective way of strengthening strategic stability. Such defences would have to promote massive new uncertainties in Soviet attack calculations—calculations that already are beset with major technical, tactical, strategic and political uncertainties. American (and NATO-European) policy-makers in the 1990s should be provided with active defence alternatives, or partial alternatives, to the proliferation of offensive weapons, the proliferation of aim points through mobility, and the adoption of dangerous launch tactics. There is no need to decide today whether the US will exercise such intermediate defensive options, but the case for purchasing the ability to choose in a timely fashion would seem to be overwhelming.

Probably the single most frequent objection that is raised to the nearer-term aspects of the SDI and a defensive transition is that it will 'stimulate the arms race'. This objection is really no more than a truism. Any US strategic-force development which threatens to thwart some aspects of Soviet strategy, to deny some measure of military advantage, may serve as fuel for Soviet competitive behaviour. There are some interesting co-operative possibilities for a defensive transition, but those possibilities can rest only upon effective US competitive performance. The Soviet Union certainly will be motivated to seek to dissuade the US from pursuing the SDI and an effective defensive transition. Dissuasion will take the forms of weapon development optimized for penetration of defences and, very likely, of arms-control blandishments.

The SDI and Arms Control

Should the US decide to move with the SDI from technology exploration into weapon development, formal arms-control negotiations could assume great importance. First, late in the 1980s the US may wish to renegotiate the terms of the ABM Treaty so as to permit development and limited deployment of defences for strategic forces and strategic C[3]I facilities. American policy-makers would confront a choice that relates to the heart of deterrence reasoning. Should they seek an arms-control regime that would assist the pre-launch survivability of nuclear forces, though at the price of impeded access—courtesy of Soviet deployments of ballistic missile defences—to Soviet territory? Or, should the ABM Treaty be retained in its pristine form, at the price of denying US forces and C^3I a potentially valuable measure of prelaunch survivability? In the opinion of this author it would be wise to choose pre-launch survivability rather than unimpeded access.

Second, later in the 1990s, or perhaps early in the next century, the opportunity could arise for a truly radical, benign restructuring of strategic forces through the arms-control process. While the effectiveness of a US defensive transition can never be permitted to hinge upon co-operation with the Soviet Union—for the obvious reason that they seek military advantage, and certainly they seek to deny any military advantage to the US—there is no doubt that a large-scale reduction in the quantity of Soviet offensive forces, not to mention some qualitative restraints upon the forces that remained, would enhance greatly the prospective performance of strategic defenses. So, the problem then, as today, is one of negotiating leverage. President Reagan's vision of a much reduced scale of nuclear threat is more likely to be achievable if the Soviet Union can be brought to believe that nuclear disarmament on a massive scale is in her net security interest. This will not be a matter of strategic theoretical persuasion, of lectures on the new US theory of stability through dominant defences, or of devising ingenious formulae for reciprocal reductions. Stated directly, Soviet leaders and strategic planners will need to look at the actual and the potential of US competitive performance in defensive and offensive weaponry, and decide that they face an important military disadvantage if they choose to let the competition run its course in a legally unregulated fashion.

By way of a contingent prediction, if Soviet leaders believe that US offensive forces will fare considerably better against Soviet defences than will Soviet offensive forces against US defences, then they should be motivated to agree to negotiated reductions in offensive forces. In American perspective, given that the US is far more interested in protecting Americans that she is in threatening Soviet citizens, the US should be prepared to forgo some measure of military advantage conferred by the superior penetrative prowess of her offensive forces, as a price well worth paying for the reduction in the scale and quality of the Soviet offensive threat.

Nuclear Ambush of a Defensive Transition?

Some critics of the SDI have expressed concern that, should the Soviet Union anticipate the US achieving a significant military advantage through defensive deployments, she may elect to take very forceful measures to prevent a US defensive transition, or addition, from maturing. Several responses to this valid concern are appropriate, but the leading one is to the effect that it must be a mission of the strategic offensive forces to guard the defensive transition. . . .

The nightmare scenario of a desperate Soviet Union choosing to fight today rather than live with the consequences of a measure of military inferiority tomorrow, is thoroughly implausible, if not totally ridiculous. Should Soviet leaders anticipate military disadvantage as the defensive transitions (on both sides) mature, the extant US offensive force posture, if properly modernised, would provide them with the most persuasive of reasons for eschewing prompt military adventure. Even if the military balance tomorrow looks likely to be worse than that today, the balance today is most unlikely to offer a good prospect of success. Furthermore, Soviet leaders will have an attractive alternative both to suicide today and to inferiority tomorrow—and that is a defensive competition managed by arms control.

The point should not be missed that the earliest US deployment action during a transition to defences will be systems for the defence of strategic retaliatory forces and C^3I. That deployment must function so as to discourage any Soviet theorizing about a nuclear ambush of a US defensive transition. . . .

The SDI and The Western Alliance

Critics of the SDI are able to point, accurately enough, to some disquiet in NATO-Europe over what US strategic defence developments may imply for East-West relations and for US motives and prospective performance as a security guarantor. Space precludes detailed treatment of this issue here, but the following points are relevant:

- Near-term strategic defence developments, for the enhancement of the pre-launch survivability of US strategic forces, would simply strengthen the familiar terms of nuclear deterrence.
- Near-term, point-defence technology, if deployed in Europe, would greatly strengthen the stability of deterrence. Anti-tactical ballistic missile (ATBM) defence against shorter-range Soviet missiles would deny the Soviet Union an important measure of confidence concerning the prospects for conventional success. ATBM defence of NATO airfields, supply dumps, C^3 facilities, transportation nodes and the like would play a literally vital role in facilitating the defence of NATO-Europe and, *ergo*, in discouraging aggression.
- Far-term defensive technology (probably space-based, or space-deployable) could protect US allies as well as the US herself. Moreover, it we can move into an era wherein the American homeland enjoys a growing measure of direct, physical protection, the willingness of US presidents to run risks on behalf of distant allies logically should be strengthened. Far from being an instrument with 'decoupling' implications, strategic defence would work to enhance solidarity of behaviour in crisis and war.
- Soviet strategic missile defences must work to challenge the credibility of the small national deterrents of France and Britain. . . . To the end of the century, and probably beyond, the French and British national deterrents would retain sufficient potential to 'leak through' Soviet defences that they would not face an immediate crisis of technical relevance. For

the longer term, should both super-powers proceed to deploy heavy, multitiered nation-wide defences, then small nuclear forces, no matter how sophisticated their penetration aids, would indeed lack credibility. Given the benefits of a defensive transition in strategic forces, and the likely very high scale of effectiveness of theatre and tactical missile defences, NATO-European countries should welcome the opportunity to be able to devote their attention wholeheartedly to the problems of local conventional deterrence.

Conclusions

No one can say what the balance of technological and tactical advantage between offence and defence will be in 20 or 30 years. But we do know that the history of military technology records swings of the pendulum of advantage from one to the other; and that strategic offensive technologies today are relatively mature, while strategic defensive technologies are very immature—meaning that for the next several decades at least the advantage in growth in performance potential ought plain to lie with the defence.

Lest there be any misunderstanding, this author is *not* predicting particular weapons, for particular missions, by particular dates, with particular costs. There is no way of knowing whether multi-tiered strategic defences capable of rendering ICBM and SLBM as obsolete as the horse cavalry will be technologically feasible. But, there is a major, indeed an overwhelming, arms-control case for investment in the SDI to explore the possibility that the defence could reassume a position of strategic pre-eminence. . . .

It must be acknowledged that the West faces a sharply growing threat from Soviet air-breathing vehicles. Hence, a defensive transition, to have strategic integrity, must include air as well as missile defences. Also, it would be foolish to ignore the unfortunate fact that the strategic nuclear deterrent does have a range of specific missions of the highest importance for foreign policy. If the political structure of Soviet-American relations remains much as today, then there will be a need to find strategic substitutes for the nuclear threat to the Soviet homeland. Even in the context of a mature defensive transition, the Soviet Union will still need to be deterred from pursuing military solutions to her most pressing political problems.

Notes

1. 'Build-down' would require the dismantling of more than one older strategic warhead for each new warhead deployed. For descriptions of the various 'build-down' concepts, see Alton Frye, "Strategic Build-down: A Context for Restraint', *Foreign Affairs*, Winter 1983/84, vol. 62, no. 2, pp. 293–317; and 'Negotiating a Build-down', *Time*, 17 October 1983, pp. 16–18.

2. 'Bogus Flexibility But Real Deception', *Pravda*, 23 October 1983, as translated by the Federal Broadcast Information Service, *Daily Report: USSR*, 24 October 1983, p. AA6.

3. Fred S. Hoffman (Study Director), *Ballistic Missile Defenses and US National Security*, Summary Report of the Future Security Strategy Study (Washington DC: October 1983).

Ballistic Missile Defense: A Strategic Issue

Robert M. Bowman

Robert M. Bowman considers four possible objectives for a ballistic missile defense: (1) to replace a policy of deterrence; (2) to enhance deterrence; (3) to provide a shield for a first strike; and (4) to limit damage should deterrence fail. He then rejects them all as either ineffective or immoral.

Introduction

The President has challenged the scientific and engineering community with "the development of an intensive effort to define a long-term research and development program aimed at the ultimate goal of eliminating the threat posed by nuclear ballistic missiles." He also held out the hope of rendering nuclear weapons "impotent and obsolete" and asked if it wasn't better to "save lives, rather than avenge them." These statements, along with some of the clarifications issued later, indicate a desire to replace the policy of deterrence

From "Ballistic Missile Defense: A Strategic Issue," in Committee on Appropriations, Subcommittee on the Department of Defense. Hearings on Department of Defense Appropriations for 1985, Part 5, May 9, 1984, pp. 869–880.

through the threat of retaliation with a new policy of pure defense. Indeed, in his "Star Wars" speech, he clearly acknowledged the fact that the systems he was talking about, if combined with offensive systems, would be threatening and destabilizing. Clearly, he was talking about the kind of defensive system that would allow us to (indeed, *require* us to) discard our offensive systems.

The systems requirements and technological demands of such a defensive system are staggering. The allowable leakage rate would be something like 0.01% or less. The system would have to be itself invulnerable, impervious to countermeasures, and absolutely reliable. Moreover, it would have to provide such a defense against not only ballistic missiles, but all other means of delivery (cruise missiles, light aircraft, sailboats, diplomatic pouches, . . .) as well.

So far, numerous study groups both in and out of government have declared such a system an impossibility. Impossible or not, it is a worthy objective and worthy of serious consideration. It was perhaps imprudent to announce such a long shot objective so publicly and give the American people the idea that the technology was available. But it was perfectly proper for the President to ask for the idea to be studied. The problem is that all the groups studying it have quickly concluded that a perfect defense is impossible, but instead of telling the President so, they have waffled. They have spent 99% of their time investigating systems for a different objective (enhancing retaliatory deterrence) or no objective at all. Now there is nothing wrong with enhancing deterrence. But it is wrong to confuse the public about our objectives. It is wrong to ask the public to pay 25 billion dollars or so as the initial step in a program to protect missile silos and let them think they are buying protection for people. It is also wrong to mislead the President. We must insist that his original question be answered. The President deserves the truth—whether or not it's what we think he wants to hear.

As a first step in a rational discussion of BMD—before looking at system requirements and technology challenges—it is necessary to look at the various possible objectives of a BMD program, and the strategic issues associated with each. Then for each of the objectives, the consequent system requirements and technology issues can be analyzed.

BMD Objectives

There are four possible objectives for ballistic missile defense:

(1) to replace a policy of deterrence by the threat of retaliation with a policy of assured survival based on a near-perfect defense against all types of offensive weapons (as proposed by the President in his "Star Wars" speech of March 23, 1983).

(2) to enhance deterrence by reducing the vulnerability of our retaliatory offensive forces,

(3) to complete a disarming first strike ca-

pability by providing a shield against the 5% of enemy missiles surviving our MX, Trident II, and Pershing II attack, and

(4) to limit the damage to our country should deterrence fail, by reducing the number of warheads getting through.

Each of these four objectives results in its own unique set of system requirements and associated technology challenges. Each also presents its own political and diplomatic challenge. The first, in particular, faces the diplomatic problem of managing the transition from the current offense-dominated to a defense-dominated strategy without passing through an unstable situation. Implementing it would have to be done so that at no time did the combination of offensive and defensive capabilities bring about the situation sought for in objective 3, the disarming first strike.

The fourth possible objective for a BMD system (limiting the damage should deterrence fail) is particularly troublesome. Such an objective is legitimate, provided the system implementing it doesn't increase the likelihood of deterrence failing. And since the system requirements are very similar to those for objective 3, the chances of it doing so are very good. Damage-limiting is essentially preparing to fight and win (or at least survive) a nuclear war. There is almost unanimous agreement now that a nuclear war cannot be won and must not be fought. Scientists are arguing over whether even people in the southern hemisphere, thousands of miles from the battle, can survive. Since it is not clear that damage-limiting will do any good, we should not allow it to increase the likelihood of war occurring in the first place.

Having now enumerated the possible objectives of BMD, let us turn to establishing the system requirements, technology requirements, and strategic implications of each.

BMD to Replace Deterrence

The following is quoted from the beginning of a typical position paper on Ballistic Missile Defense:

There can be no perfect defense against nuclear ballistic missiles. Avoidance of nuclear conflict must therefore always be our nation's primary security objective, whether through arms control or deterrence. To deter war we must continue to convince any potential attacker that on balance his losses would be unacceptable.

Having thus disposed of the President's initiative, the rest of the paper was devoted to systems serving other objectives. Rather than take that easy way out, however, let us take an honest look at BMD to replace deterrence and the threat of retaliation with pure defense, and what such a system would require.

First, it would require that the country possessing it get rid of all its offensive strategic weapons. Otherwise, a nation protected behind such a shield could threaten its neighbors in the world community with impunity, even with a small number of nuclear weapons. If a nation attempted to complete such a system while retaining offensive weapons, the other nations would never allow it, but would attempt to destroy the shield before it was complete or even launch a preemptive nuclear attack.

Secondly, once the transition is made and a nation has entrusted its security to the defensive system instead of retaliation, it is then totally dependent on the defensive system. It must therefore be totally reliable, invulnerable to destruction by opposing forces, impervious to countermeasures employed by opposing offensive forces, and essentially perfect in its ability to protect against thousands of nuclear weapons deployed against it in any manner whatsoever. The Soviet Union now has about 8000 strategic warheads (we have 10,000). Thus if one or two warheads getting through is acceptable, we can get by with a leakage rate of 0.01% (*an order of magnitude better than the Fletcher commission was asked to consider*). Of course, by the time a system is deployed, it may be facing 100,000 warheads and ten times as many decoys. (If we abrogate the limitations on defensive systems contained in the ABM portion of the SALT I Treaty, we can hardly expect the Soviet Union to continue to abide by the already-expired limits on offensive

weapons in the same Treaty and watch their retaliatory deterrent made impotent.)

It is commonly accepted that to even approach these low leakage rates a layered system utilizing several different technologies would be required. Moreover, an extremely high percentage of attacking ballistic missiles would have to be destroyed in the boost phase, before they could release large numbers of RV's and decoys.

One of the obvious countermeasures which an attacker would employ would be to shorten the boost phase by using quick-burn rockets. Without much difficulty, the burn phase could be shortened to the point where it would terminate while the missile was still within the atmosphere. Since most of the proposed BMD kill mechanisms are unable to penetrate even the outer fringes of the atmosphere (this is true of particle beams, x-rays, and homing kinetic-energy kill vehicles, for example), this simple measure would make boost-phase interception using such systems impossible. This would leave lasers of relatively long wavelength as the only remaining boost-phase candidate. But such systems have enormous problems of their own, including a host of technical difficulties (such as making the enormous cooled mirrors required), special vulnerabilities (the mirrors, for example, can be rendered useless by a bucket of sand, a balloon full of water, or a thimbleful of oil), and unique susceptibilities to countermeasures (like spinning the ICBM to distribute the laser energy, using ablative coatings, or polishing the missile surface to reflect away the energy). It appears therefore that if a boost-phase interception system is to be found, it will use a kill mechanism not even thought of as yet.

But the kill mechanism (discussed above) is only one of many elements in a BMD system. The Department of Defense has identified at least eight other elements, including the sensors that detect and track the missiles, the battle-management computers that must automatically initiate hostilities and direct thousands of defensive systems against as many targets within seconds, and the pointing and tracking systems which must aim the kill mechanisms to within inches over distances of thousands of miles. UnderSecretary DeLauer has testified that each of these nine elements is individually as complex as the Manhattan Project. The advances in individual technical parameters (such as pointing accuracy, sensor sensitivity, and computation speed) needed to make the system even theoretically possible are typically factors of 10^6 to 10^8, that is, we need to be able to do things a million or so times faster and better than we can now.

Once all these technical problems are overcome, then the whole thing must be made to work together—and it must work flawlessly the very first time, for it can never be tested under realistic conditions. With the difficulty we have had making such relatively simple things as cruise missiles, air defense guns, and tanks work, the thought of such a complex system as this working perfectly boggles the mind—even without enemy countermeasures or attempts to destroy or disrupt the system.

With all this, there is an overwhelming temptation to dismiss such a system as an utter impossibility. Rather than doing so, however, let us merely point out that such defenses are the proper subject of basic research. An appropriate broadly-based research program need not cost a lot of money. One cannot obtain the kind of scientific breakthroughs needed for such a system by simply throwing money at the problem.

The worst mistake we could possibly make would be to let our fascination with the possibility of such a system cause us to neglect the means we have in hand for preventing nuclear war—survivable deterrent forces, arms control to ward off destabilizing changes, and quiet diplomacy.

BMD to Enhance Deterrence

Another legitimate objective of Ballistic Missile Defense is the enhancement of deterrence by reducing the vulnerability of retaliatory offensive forces. The ABM Treaty allows each side to deploy one such system with up to 100 ABM interceptors, providing the system is ground-based and within certain constraints. The constraints are designed to preclude either side being able to shield a broad area containing its populace and industrial base and thereby approach the capability for first strike to be discussed in the next section.

The United States chose to dismantle its one allowed system some time ago, believing the system was not worth its cost of upkeep. The Soviets have chosen to maintain their system, and now have 64 of the allowed 100 interceptors. (They had 100 interceptors at the time the treaty was being negotiated 15 years ago, but have replaced them with a smaller number of more capable systems. It is expected that they will deploy a second layer (also ground-based, but with longer-range interceptors) bringing them back up to the allowed limit. It is interesting to note that the 64 Soviet interceptors compares with 10,000 we expected them to have by 1980 in the absence of treaty constraints. Keep that in mind the next time someone suggests that treaties never do any good.)

With this background in mind, let us examine the system requirements for a BMD system to enhance deterrence. The basic requirement is that enough offensive missiles survive any enemy attempt at a disarming first strike to enable us to retaliate in sufficient strength to cause unacceptable damage to the attacking country.

The first task is thus to determine what constitutes unacceptable damage to the Soviet Union in the minds of their leaders. We can never know this exactly, of course, and the answer undoubtedly depends on the desperateness of their situation. But we should be able to bound the answer in a conservative way. Would they be willing to lose ten of their cities? Who knows? How about 50? Probably not. Certainly the prospect of losing 100 of their cities should be more than deterrence enough. Let us adopt that as the basic requirement.

The next question is: How good a BMD system would we need in order to assure the survival of enough offensive systems to destroy the heart of 100 Soviet cities? The answer for the foreseeable future is . . . none.

It is estimated that if the Soviet Union continues to modernize their ICBM fleet with missiles containing many warheads and ever greater accuracy, by the end of this decade they will be able to destroy about 95% of our land-based CBMs in their silos. This would leave us with about 50 missiles, 45 of which would be Minutemen III with 3 warheads apiece and 5 of which would be MX with 10 warheads apiece. That would give us 185 remaining warheads to retaliate with, which should be more than enough. Even without the MX, we would have 150 warheads.

Of course, that isn't the whole story. We would also have our manned bombers, the second leg of the triad. Whether at the time they are B-52s, B-1s, or Stealth, they will carry a couple of thousand cruise missiles, any one of which can devastate a city. Of course, the Soviets have an air defense system. We saw it in action against the KAL airliner. And they are developing the capability to "look down, shoot down" against low-flying targets like cruise missiles. Perhaps by the 1990s, they will have the capability to shoot down most of our cruise missiles, but under the worst of circumstances we should expect a few hundred to get through. This second leg of the triad should thus provide sufficient deterrence by itself. It is possible, though, that unforeseen air defenses could change the picture and render the manned bomber totally obsolete. This would certainly seem to be an easier task than defending against CBMs. We should therefore not count on this leg of the triad by itself, but should retain the capability within the other legs to attack at least 100 cities.

The third leg of the strategic triad is the nuclear-powered ballistic missile submarine. This leg is by far the most important leg of the triad because it contains the majority of our nuclear warheads and, more importantly, because it is completely invulnerable to a disarming first strike. Most analysts agree that it should remain invulnerable for the foreseeable future, certainly for the next twenty years. This means that well into the next century the sea leg will be able to deliver over 5000 nuclear warheads to their targets. But what if the Soviets pull off a miracle and find a way to overcome our enormous lead in anti-submarine warfare (ASW), so that they are able to locate our submarines in the ocean depths, track them, and destroy them? What if they get an ASW capability so good that they could count on being able to destroy almost all our submarines in a first strike (along with all our land-based missiles and all our bombers

and cruise missiles)? What if they could figure that they might only have to face retaliation from a single submarine? What kind of retaliation could they expect? The answer is that they would face about 240 warheads, more than twice what we would need to gut their 100 largest cities.

The surprising answer from this analysis is that for the foreseeable future, even after absorbing everything the Soviets could throw at us, we would retain sufficient capability in each one of the three legs of the triad to retaliate with devastating results. Then why does deterrence need enhancing? How much deterrence is enough? The answer is that our survival is at stake (as is that of the Soviet Union). That's why neither of us seems to ever have "enough." Rationally, BMD to enhance deterrence is unnecessary. But our land-based leg does face a known and growing threat, and there is something that can be done about it—BMD point defense. It is natural to expect that military leaders, charged with ensuring our survival as they are, would wish to investigate this option.

There doesn't seem to be much that a BMD system could do to enhance the survivability of the other two legs of the triad. But it could do something for land-based ICBMs (assuming we don't decide just to scrap them all to eliminate targets in our homeland). What would it take then, in terms of BMD, to ensure the survival of twice as many ICBM warheads—at least 300, even if we didn't deploy the MX? The answer is that it could be done by redeploying the one ground-based ABM system we are allowed by treaty. There would still be technical problems associated with making the radar system survivable, but this problem is more amenable to solution than it was 15 years ago. While it could certainly be argued that it is unnecessary, such additional protection for our land-based ICBMs could be achieved at relatively low cost and without abrogating the ABM Treaty (and thereby touching off an unconstrained arms race in both offensive and defensive systems). Indeed, the Pentagon has been pursuing research toward such a system continuously since the late 1950s, and considerable progress has been made. One of the effects of the Strategic Defense Initiative (SDI) has been to constrain the funding for this work in favor of the more exotic space-based technologies.

The question arises: Wouldn't "Star Wars" space-based elements contribute to this effort to make our land-based ICBMs more survivable? The answer has to be an unqualified "NO!" As shown above, they are unnecessary. But in addition to that, an attempt to add space-based elements runs into all the problems discussed in connection with the first objective. Even if one is demanding only 10% effectiveness, instead of 99.99%, one has to deal with the enormous technical complexities, the many countermeasures, and the vulnerability of space-based systems. In addition, since such systems involve abrogation of the ABM Treaty and therefore the SALT limits on offensive weapons, one would wind up always losing ground. If we spent half a trillion dollars or so putting up a system capable of stopping 10% of attacking weapons, the Soviets would probably fear that it could stop 50%. They would therefore double the number of offensive weapons in their arsenal (at a fraction of the cost of our defenses). The result would be that in the event of an attack, many more weapons would get through than if we had done nothing.

The simple fact is that if the objective is enhancing deterrence, space-based BMD systems are both unnecessary and counterproductive.

BMD for First Strike

The vast majority of American citizens would say that a disarming first strike against the Soviet Union is unthinkable, and that seeking such a capability is not a legitimate objective of U.S. military preparations. Yet this is one of the military uses of Ballistic Missile Defense and must be analyzed, if only to understand the legitimate fears raised by the "Star Wars" speech in the Soviet Union.

Unfortunately, "Flexible Response" and the many variations of this strategy over the last few years have taken us closer and closer to a military posture which seems to be designed solely and purposefully for first strike.

The original purpose of the MX, for example, was to give us a mobile missile which would be more survivable than our existing Minuteman force. What we have wound up with is a missile no more survivable than its predecessors, but with awesome silo-busting accuracy, and which therefore poses a first-strike threat to Soviet forces. Worse than that, by concentrating ten warheads in each vulnerable silo, we present the Soviets with a very tempting target. Because this system does very little for our retaliatory capability, the obvious conclusion of cautious planners on the other side is that it is intended for exactly what it seems to be designed for—a first strike.

The Pershing II is an even better example. It is an extremely accurate system capable of destroying Soviet hardened command posts and communications nodes, targets which would have to be eliminated quickly in a first strike, with very little warning. Sited in Western Europe, only minutes from the Soviet Union, this system gives us the capability of dealing with these "time-urgent targets".

Finally, the backbone of our retaliatory forces, the Trident submarine, is being given first-strike accuracy in its upgrade to Trident II.

Faced with all this, the Soviets have to go through a similar analysis to what we went through in the last section. They must determine how much deterrence is enough. But their problem is a little different. Whereas only 35% of our warheads are potentially vulnerable (being on land-based ICBMs or submarines in port), 96% of Soviet warheads are potentially vulnerable!

In addition, we have an enormous lead in anti-submarine warfare (ASW), and therefore have the potential for even putting the other 4% of their retaliatory capability at risk. Soviet strategic planners must therefore face the prospect that the "modernization" program now underway could give the United States the capability to destroy up to 95% of their warheads in a first strike. This would leave them with perhaps 70 missiles containing some 400 warheads, clearly enough to wreak unacceptable damage to the United States and therefore enough to deter us from attacking them in the first place. But what if we also had a "Star Wars" system?

The proponents of systems like the "High Frontier", the laser battle stations, and the "Excalibur" nuclear-pumped X-ray laser claim that they could stop a very high percentage of attacking missiles—up to 99.9% with a layered defense. As shown in the discussion of BMD to replace deterrence, such claims are wildly optimistic, particularly if they were attempting to deal with 1000 or so missiles. But if they were faced with only 70, their task would be immensely simpler (though probably still impossible). From the point of view of Soviet reactions, however, it isn't the real capability of the system that counts, but the worst fears of Soviet planners faced with them. If *we* only had 70 missiles and were faced with the Soviet deployment of a "Star Wars" defense, would we still have confidence in the ability of our retaliatory capability to deter a Soviet first strike? Hardly.

Even if we believe that the United States would never initiate a nuclear war, we must acknowledge that Soviet *fears* are real. When faced with such a capability, those fears could cause the Soviets to launch a desperation pre-emptive attack.

For the sake of understanding, therefore, let us compute the kind of system we'd need if we really wanted to be able to disarm the Soviet Union and have a chance of escaping unscathed. Faced with about 400 warheads after a first strike by MX, Pershing II, and Trident II, we would want to give ourselves a decent chance to stop them all. To give ourselves an even chance (about 50/50) of stopping all 400 warheads, we'd need a leakage rate of about 1 in a thousand (0.1%)—exactly what was laid down as a requirement to the Fletcher Commission!

If we compare the system required for this objective (aiding first strike) to that for replacing deterrence with assured survival, we note the following differences:

• The allowable leakage rate is greater by a factor of 20.

• The total amount of energy required to accomplish the mission is reduced by a factor of 20.

• The speed of engagement (which dictates the speed of operation of battle management

computers and the time available for repointing and retargeting, for example) is reduced by a factor of 20.

• The element of surprise is no longer with the attacker (retaliator), but is with the defender (first striker).

These factors make a big difference, of course. But they still leave enormous technological shortfalls, the inherent vulnerability of space systems, and the lack of a good kill mechanism for boost-phase interception. We should conclude that, in addition to being morally repugnant, a BMD system for first strike is probably unobtainable. Hopefully, the Soviets will come to the same conclusion and quit worrying—but I wouldn't bet on it.

The above analysis points up one fact quite clearly. Except for the factors listed above, a BMD system for replacing deterrence looks exactly like a BMD system for first strike. The only difference is in whether or not you discard your offensive weapons—*before you complete the defense*.

BMD for Damage Limiting

It must be reiterated here that *prevention* of nuclear war is and must be our overriding objective. Nothing should be done to compromise that objective. Having said that, let us consider what the system requirements would be on a BMD system for limiting damage to this country should deterrence fail.

If more than 50 warheads were to fall on the United States we would lose most of our people and probably cease to function as a society. It might not take even that many. I think we could agree that unless a BMD system could reduce the number of warheads impacting to this level, it's probably not worth having. So we would be looking for a system that would stop 199 out of every 200 missiles. This is a 99.5% system—not quite as high a requirement as the one to support first strike, but one which has to achieve this rate against 20 times as many attacking missiles. Except for the difference in the leakage rate, this system would have the same set of impossible technical requirements as the system to replace deterrence.

The strategic situation in which this system would operate, however, would be very different, for we would have retained our offensive deterrent forces. Potential adversaries would still fear us. They would see a system in place as capable as one which could shield us from retaliation after we conducted a first strike. They would therefore be under intense pressure to preempt. If they restrained, they would at least be on a hair trigger. Our space-based layered defense would, of necessity, be under computer-automated response. The chances of a software error, a computer malfunction, or a response to a natural event initiating war would be immense.

The net result of attempting to implement such a system would therefore be an enormous increase in the likelihood of war occurring and little if any improvement in our chances of surviving it.

We must conclude therefore that a BMD system for damage limiting makes no sense whatsoever.

Conclusions

We have examined the four possible objectives for BMD systems and have concluded that the last two should be rejected out of hand. To pursue an extremely effective defensive shield while retaining offensive weapons carries an enormous danger of provoking war or causing one by accident, while yielding very little hope of providing sufficient protection to enable the nation to survive.

The first two objectives, on the other hand, are worthy of closer scrutiny.

The first, BMD to replace deterrence, seems to be impossible, but is a legitimate objective of long-range basic research. It would demand a permanently invulnerable system with a leakage rate of better than 0.01% and could only be based on scientific phenomena as yet undiscovered. None of the technologies proposed to date have any chance of meeting these requirements.

The second, BMD to enhance deterrence, does not seem to be required by a rational look at the strategic situation, but could be implemented at a reasonable cost within the constraints of the ABM Treaty and without increasing the danger of war. It does not require any space-based elements beyond existing launch detection and early warning systems, which are required in any event. Such a system would not be impacted by a treaty banning space weapons.

If the United States is going to pursue BMD, it is absolutely essential that the objective of such a program be clearly defined and that the nature of the program is in keeping with its objectives. The American people will enthusiastically support any such clearly-defined program in the security interest of the United States.

The Nuclear Freeze Resolution

Kennedy-Hatfield

Whereas the greatest challenge facing the earth is to prevent the occurrence of nuclear war by accident or design;

Whereas the nuclear arms race is dangerously increasing the risk of a holocaust that would be humanity's final war; and

Whereas a freeze followed by reductions in nuclear warheads, missiles, and other delivery systems is needed to halt the nuclear arms race and to reduce the risk of nuclear war;

Resolved by the Senate and the House of Representatives of the United States of America in Congress assembled,

1. As an immediate strategic arms control objective, the United States and the Soviet Union should:

(a) pursue a complete halt to the nuclear arms race;

(b) decide when and how to achieve a mutual and verifiable freeze on the testing, production, and future deployment of nuclear warheads, missiles, and other delivery systems; and

(c) give special attention to destabilizing weapons whose deployment would make such a freeze more difficult to achieve.

2. Proceeding from this freeze, the United States and the Soviet Union should pursue major, mutual, and verifiable reductions in nuclear warheads, missiles, and other delivery systems, through annual percentages of equally effective means, in a manner that enhances stability.

Nuclear Disarmament by the Year 2000

Mikhail S. Gorbachev

. . . The Soviet Union proposes that a step-by-step, consistent process of ridding the earth of nuclear weapons be implemented and completed within the next 15 years, before the end of this century.

. . . How does the Soviet Union envisage today in practical terms the process of reducing nuclear weapons, both delivery vehicles and warheads, up to their complete elimination? Our proposals on this subject can be summarized as follows.

Stage One. Within the next 5 to 8 years the USSR and the USA will reduce by one half the nuclear weapons that can reach each other's territory. As for the remaining delivery vehicles of this kind, each side will retain no more than 6,000 warheads.

It stands to reason that such a reduction is possible only if both the USSR and the USA renounce the development, testing and deployment of space strike weapons. As the Soviet Union has repeatedly warned, the development of space strike weapons will dash the hopes for a reduction of nuclear armaments on earth.

The first stage will include the adoption and implementation of a decision on the complete elimination of medium-range missiles of the USSR and the USA in the European zone—both ballistic and cruise missiles—as a first step towards ridding the European conflict of nuclear weapons.

At the same time the United States should undertake not to transfer its strategic and medium-range missiles to other countries, while Great Britain and France should pledge not to build up their respective nuclear arsenals.

Reprinted by permission of the Information Department of the USSR Embassy in Washington, D.C.

The USSR and the USA should from the very beginning agree to stop all nuclear explosions and call upon other states to join in such a moratorium as soon as possible.

The reason why the first stage of nuclear disarmament should concern the Soviet Union and the United States is that it is they who should set an example for the other nuclear powers. We said that very frankly to President Reagan of the United States during our meeting in Geneva.

Stage Two. At this stage, which should start no later than 1990 and last for 5 to 7 years, the other nuclear powers will begin to join the process of nuclear disarmament. To start with, they would pledge to freeze all their nuclear arms and not to have them on the territories of other countries.

In this period the USSR and the USA will continue to carry out the reductions agreed upon during the first stage and also implement further measures aimed at eliminating their medium-range nuclear weapons and freezing their tactical nuclear systems.

Following the completion by the USSR and the USA of a 50 percent reduction of their respective armaments at the second stage, another radical step will be taken: All nuclear powers will eliminate their tactical nuclear weapons, i.e., weapons having a range (or radius of action) of up to 1,000 kilometres.

At this stage the Soviet-U.S. accord on the prohibition of space strike weapons would become multilateral, with the mandatory participation in it of major industrial powers.

All nuclear powers would stop nuclear tests.

There would be a ban on the development of nonnuclear weapons based on new physical principles, whose destructive power is close to that of nuclear arms or other weapons of mass destruction.

Stage Three will begin no later than 1995. At this stage the elimination of all remaining nuclear weapons will be completed. By the end of 1999 there will be no nuclear weapons on earth. A universal accord will be drawn up that such weapons should never again come into being.

We envisage that special procedures will be worked out for the destruction of nuclear weapons as well as for the dismantling, re-equipment or scrapping of delivery vehicles. In the process, agreement will be reached on the number of weapons to be scrapped at each stage, the sites of their destruction, and so on.

Verification of the destruction or limitation of arms should be carried out both by national technical means and through on-site inspections. The USSR is ready to reach agreement on any other additional verification measures. . . .

Suggestions for Further Reading

Anthologies

Haley, Edward and Merritt, Jack, *Strategic Defense Initiative*, Boulder: Westview, 1986.

Marrin, Albert, *War and the Christian Conscience.* Chicago: Henry Regnery Co. 1971.

Sterba, James, P. *The Ethics of War and Nuclear Deterrence*, Belmont: Wadsworth, 1985.

Thompson, W. Scott. *From Weakness to Strength.* San Francisco: Institute for Contemporary Studies, 1980.

Wakin, Malham. *War, Morality and the Military Profession.* Boulder: Westview Press, 1979.

Wasserstrom, Richard A. *War and Morality.* Belmont: Wadsworth Publishing Co., 1970.

Basic Concepts

Walters, LeRoy, *Five Classic Just-War Theories.* Ann Arbor: University Microfilms, 1971.

Walzer, Michael. *Just and Unjust Wars.* New York: Basic Books, 1977.

Alternative Views

Allison, Graham T. *Essence of Decision.* Boston: Little, Brown & Co., 1971.

Fallow, James, *National Defense*, New York: Vintage Books, 1981.

Graham, Daniel, *High Frontier.* New York: TOR Books, 1983.

Lens, Sidney. *The Day Before Doomsday.* Boston: Beacon Press, 1977.

Kahan, Jerome H. *Security in the Nuclear Age.* Washington, D.C.: The Brookings Institution, 1975.

Union of Concerned Scientists, *Empty Promise* Boston: Beacon, 1986.

United States Department of Defense, *The President's Strategic Defense Initiative,* Washington, D.C. 1985.

Practical Application

Barton, John H., and Weiler, Lawrence D. *International Arms Control.* Stanford: Stanford University Press, 1976.

Ground Zero, *Nuclear War.* New York: Pocket Books, 1982.

Kennedy, Edward M., and Hatfield, Mark O. *Freeze,* New York: Bantam Books, 1982.